The *Essay* *Connection*

The *Essay Connection*

READINGS FOR WRITERS

Sixth Edition

Lynn Z. Bloom
The University of Connecticut

Houghton Mifflin Company
Boston   New York

Senior Sponsoring Editor: Dean Johnson
Editorial Associate: Bruce Cantley
Senior Project Editor: Kellie Cardone
Senior Production/Design Coordinator: Carol Merrigan
Senior Manufacturing Coordinator: Priscilla Bailey
Senior Marketing Manager: Nancy Lyman

Cover Design: Sarah Melhado Bishins
Cover Image: © Photonica—Brooklyn Bridge Detail

Text Credits appear on pages 775–780, which constitute a continuation
of the copyright page.

Printed in the U.S.A.

Library of Congress Catalog Card Number: 0-130083

ISBN: 0-618-03965-1

23456789-QF-05 04 03 02 01

Contents

❀ *Student writings.*

Part II   Determining Ideas in a Sequence   159

Topical Table of Contents

❀ *Student writings.*

2 People and Portraits

3 Families/Heritage

9 Society and Community

10 Turning Points/Watershed Experiences

11 Language, Literature, and the Arts

12 Humor and Satire

Preface

Like the symbolic bridge on the cover of this book, *The Essay Connection* attempts to span the distance between reading and writing and bring the two activities closer together. To read, to write is to be human, to be empowered. "Writing," observes Toni Morrison, "is discovery; it's talking deep within myself." In *The Essay Connection* the voices in this conversation are many and varied—professionals and students side by side. Their good writing is good reading in itself, provocative, elegant, engaging. This writing is also a stimulus to critical thinking, ethical reflection, social and literary analysis, and humorous commentary—among the many possibilities when students write essays of their own.

What's Familiar, What's New

The sixth edition of *The Essay Connection* incorporates a number of new features and new essays into the format and essays retained from the fifth edition.

Readings

This books includes eighty-two readings, lively, varied, timely, provocative—and of high literary quality. This edition, which includes twenty-eight new essays, has been expanded from fifteen to sixteen chapters; the last chapter is titled *"Death of a Salesman:* Responses to An American Classic." To provide a special tribute in the new millennium to this beloved American classic, now over half a century old, *The Essay Connection* includes material from Arthur Miller's autobiography, *Timebends* (see Chapter 3). Chapter 16, new to this edition, contains John Lahr's "Making Willy Loman," two reviews—fifty years apart—of *Death of a Salesman* by premier *New York Times* drama critics Brooks Atkinson and Ben Brantley, and two critical essays: Brenda Murphy's "Willy Loman, Icon of Business Culture" and student Valerie M. Smith's "Death of a Salesman's Wife." The works in each section are intended not only to serve as commentaries on each other, but to resonate throughout the book.

Fifty-three favorite essays have been retained from the previous edition, by authors such as Joan Didion, Frederick Douglass, Stephen Jay Gould, Linda Hogan, Maxine Hong Kingston, Nancy Mairs, Richard Rodriguez, Scott Russell Sanders, Eudora Welty, E. B. White, and Elie Wiesel. Cathy N. Davidson's "Laughing in English" opens the readings, a happy balance to the concluding discussions of *The Death of a Salesman*—which are themselves affirmations of literature, and of life. Although humorous works by authors such as Mark Twain, Garry Trudeau, and Judy Brady signal the book's up-beat tone, they do not diminish the seriousness of its essential concerns or its underlying ethical stance.

New Authors

Among the authors new to *The Essay Connection* are Natalie Angier, Stewart Brand, Louise Erdrich, Howard Gardner, Lucy Grealy, Thomas Jefferson, Anne Lamott, Eric Liu, Cynthia Ozick, Ntozake Shange, Gary Soto, John Trimbur, Abraham Verghese, and Nancy Willard. The representations of women, cultures, and writers who address issues of class and race have again increased in this edition, as in its predecessor.

Student Authors

Sixteen essays are by students, although a total of twenty-nine pieces of student work appear because thirteen excerpts from student notebooks are combined in one selection. Among the student writings are entries from Anne Frank's diary written when she was thirteen to fourteen. Although all the student works except Frank's were written when the students were enrolled in American universities, these students have come from places throughout the United States and the world, from Pennsylvania to Minnesota to Colorado, from Jamaica to England to the People's Republic of China. These distinguished student writings not only discuss compelling subjects such as coming to terms with oneself; with one's parents—whether known or unknown, living, or dead—with one's ethnic background—African-American, Asian, Indian, Jewish, Malaysian, Mexican, Native American—and with one's social and economic class. The student writings also deal with understanding the endangered—from hospital patients in medical crisis or family farms in economic distress—and with topics provoking irreverence—learning to drive, playing video games, goofing around on the computer. All provide examples of excellent writing that other students should find meaningful as models in form, technique, and substance.

Whole Essays

In order to maintain the integrity of the authors' style and structure as well as their arguments, most of these essays are printed in their entirety, averaging three to six pages; a number are chapters or self-contained sections of books. Footnotes are the authors' own.

Varied Subjects, Varied Disciplines

The essays in this edition are drawn from many sources, mostly engaging and distinguished contemporary writing on varied subjects, as indicated in the Topical Table of Contents, with a leavening of classics by such authors as Swift, Lincoln, and Darwin. In addition to professional writers, the authors include physicians (Lewis Thomas, Abraham Verghese), lawyers (Lani Guinier, Eric Liu), two American presidents (Jefferson and Lincoln), clergy (Martin Luther King, Jr., Jonathan Swift), a psychologist (Howard Gardner), an economist (Robert Reich), a cartoonist (Garry Trudeau), scientists and science writers (Natalie Angier, Isaac Asimov, Thomas Kuhn, Stephen Jay Gould), a naturalist (Terry Tempest Williams), an animal trainer (Vicki Hearne), a futuristic businessman (Stewart

Brand), reviewers (Brooks Atkinson, Ben Brantley), and literary critics (Gilbert Highet, Brenda Murphy).

Writing Processes

It should be noted that whatever is said or implied about writing processes in Chapters 1–4, or in the study questions and suggestions for writing following most selections, may be adapted as the instructor or student chooses to accommodate either individual or collaborative writing. The book's first section concentrates on the writing process, from the start in "Laughing, Speaking, and Reading" (Chapter 1), to "Definition and Reasons for Writing" (Chapter 2), to "Getting Started" (Chapter 3), to "Writing: Re-Vision and Revision" (Chapter 4). Works by professional writers of distinction (Amy Tan, Eudora Welty, Elie Wiesel) are joined by equally memorable student writing. Thus the writer's notebook of Mark Twain joins an excerpt from thirteen-to-fourteen-year-old Anne Frank's diary and notebook entries from eleven other students of diverse ages, ethnic backgrounds, life experience, and sexual preference. The section concludes with ten drafts of student Mary Ruffin's work, culminating in the stunning essay, "Mama's Smoke."

Critical Thinking, Reading, and Writing

Many readings are clustered to encourage dialogue and debate among authors, and among student readers and writers. This thematic arrangement is far more extensive in this edition than in the earlier editions. For example, Chapter 5, "Narration," emphasizes the significance of family and ancestry, race and class. Chapter 6, "Process Analysis," clusters essays on science and mechanics, and two on processes reflecting racial and family heritage—harvesting and potting. Chapter 7, "Cause and Effect," focuses on education as it pertains to both margin and mainstream and on our understanding of how social policies affect individuals and families; Chapter 9, "Division and Classification," extends the subject to totalitarian, democratic, and postcolonial societies. Chapter 8, "Description," concentrates on places, natural and unnatural, and the values and folkways of people who live in these diverse habitats. It is also concerned with self-description, whether the writer sees himself as an insider, as Eric Liu does despite his Asian heritage, or as an outsider as Lucy Grealy does because of the visible ravages of cancer, concealed only at Halloween by a comforting mask. Chapter 11, "Definition," deals with the nature, meaning, and interpretations of two iconic underclass figures, Judy Brady's *wife* in "I Want a Wife" and Gary Soto's representation of the manual laborer, in "Black Hair." In Chapter 12, "Comparison and Contrast," essays by Stephen Jay Gould, on evolution, and Vicki Hearne, on animal rights, refract with Darwin's "Understanding Natural Selection" and Howard Gardner's "Who Owns Intelligence?" in Chapter 11. Chapter 13, "Appealing to Reason," debates civil rights and civil disobedience; and issues of social class and poverty, domestic and world-wide. Chapter 14, "Appealing to Emotion and Ethics," features essays on power and oppression, life and death—of individuals, nations, farms, and families; while Chapter 15, "Critical Argument," provides various perspectives on critical textual analysis, with essays on "The Gettysburg Address" and on "Cinderella," just as the new Chapter 16 provides five perspectives on Arthur Miller's *Death of a Salesman:* its genesis, history, reviews, and criticism from popular culture, business, and feminist points of view.

Conceptual Context of the Book

The Essay Connection is informed conceptually by extensive classroom testing of the essays and writing assignments included here. The book is likewise informed by contemporary scholarship in the dynamic fields of composition, literary and rhetorical theory, autobiography, and the teaching of writing. The language of *The Essay Connection* intentionally remains clear and reader-friendly.

Blended Types

In difficulty the essays range from the easily accessible to the more complicated. They have been chosen to represent the common essay types indicated by the chapter divisions, from narration and definition through argumentation and critical analysis. Nevertheless, because these are real essays by real writers, who use whatever writing techniques suit their purpose, there are very few "pure" types. An essay of illustration and example, such as Nancy Mairs's "On Being a Cripple," for instance, includes definition, comparisons and contrasts, narrative, description. The entire essay, like many others in this book, could in fact be considered an argument for the author's point of view. Consequently, although the introduction to each essay and the study questions following it often encourage the reader to view the work through the lens of its designated category in the Table of Contents, the reader should be aware that the category represents only one segment of a broad spectrum of possible readings.

Apparatus

The essays are placed in a context of materials designed to encourage reading, critical thinking, and good writing. The following materials reinforce *The Essay Connection*'s pervasive emphasis on the process(es) of writing.

- **Tables of Contents.** The main Table of Contents reflects the book's organization, by types of writing. The Topical Table of Contents offers an alternative organization by subject ("Science and Technology," "Society and Community," "Human and Civil Rights," "Turning Points/Watershed Experiences," etc.). This arrangement provides many alternative possibilities for discussion and writing.
- **Chapter introductions.** These have two purposes. They define the particular type of writing in the chapter and identify its purposes (descriptions, process analysis, etc.), uses, and typical forms. They also discuss the rhetorical strategies authors typically use in that type of writing (for instance, how to structure an argument to engage a hostile audience), illustrated with reference to essays in the chapter. For quick reference, these strategies are summarized in a checklist at the end of the introduction.
- **Biographical introductions to each author.** These capsule biographies are intended to transform the writers from names into real people. They focus on how and why the authors write (in general, and in particular) and how and for what audience they wrote the work that appears in *The Essay Connection*.

- **Study questions.** These follow most of the essays, and are intended to encourage thoughtful discussion and writing about Content, rhetorical Strategies/Structures, Language, and larger concerns.
- **Suggestions for Writing.** Each set of study questions ends with suggestions For Writing pertinent to a given work. Most chapters end with a longer list of Additional Topics for Writing that encourage dialogue and debate about essays related in theme, technique, or mode. Often these incorporate strategic suggestions, derived from extensive classroom testing, for writing particular papers and for avoiding potential pitfalls.
- **Glossary.** The Glossary (759–74) defines terms useful in discussing writing (analogy, argument, voice) with illustrations from the essays.

Acknowledgments

The Essay Connection has, in some ways, been in the making for the past forty years, and I am particularly indebted to the candid commentaries of multitudes of writing students over the years whose preferences and perplexities have so significantly influenced both the shape and emphasis of this volume, and the process-oriented style of teaching that it reflects. I am likewise grateful for the thoughtful suggestions of writing teachers throughout the country who have commented on earlier editions of *The Essay Connection:* Susan Ahern, Chris Anderson, Lois Avery, Lynn Dianne Beene, Judith L. Bleicher, Ruth Brown, Larry Carver, Roberta Clipper-Sethi, Pat Coldwell, Sara G. Cutting, Daryl Dance, Kathleen Danker, Charla Dawson, Charles R. Duke, Janet E. Eber, Mark Edelstein, David Fleming, J. Vail Foy, Tahita Fulkerson, Donald Gadow, Edgar Glenn, Howard Hamrick, Sandra Hanson, Joanne M. Haynes, Nan Johnson, Daniel Kasowitz, Robert Keane, Walter Klarner, Geraldine Lash, Kay Litten, Arline March, Jay K. Maurer, John M. McCluskey, Charles C. Nash, Alvin W. Past, Linda H. Peterson, Elaine Roberts, Edna H. Shaw, Charles Smith, Louise Z. Smith, William E. Smith, Jeffrey Smitten,

Bill Stiffler, Barbara Stout, Karen Sylte, Frank Thornton, Barbara Turnwall, Arthur Wagner, Tom Waldrep, Cheryl L. Ware, Rosemary Winslow, Margarett Ann Wolfe, Marie Woolf, Pauline Wheeler, and Richard Yarborough.

I am also indebted to the reviewers who contributed to the development of the sixth edition of *The Essay Connection:* Lou-Ann Crouther, Western Kentucky University; Sydney Darby, Chemeketa Community College, Oregon; Michael J. Emery, Cottey College, Missouri; Julie M. Farrar, Fontbonne College, Missouri; John Faulkner, Ohio University–Lancaster; Marcy Jane Knopf, Miami University, Ohio; Susan Romano, University of Texas–San Antonio; and Rosemary Winslow, The Catholic University of America, District of Columbia.

To Donald M. Murray who contributed an original text on revising, and Margaret Whitt who contributed student essays, I am particularly grateful. I also owe special thanks to the students who contributed to this volume not only their essays but comments on how they wrote them: Rosalind Bradley Coles, Ann Upperco Dolman, Art Greenwood, Jasmine Innerarity, Amy Jo Keifer, Kristin King, Richard Loftus, Leslie S. Moore, Matt Nocton, Mary Ruffin, Stephen E. Ryan, Barbara Schofield, Kelly Shea, Valerie M. Smith, Jenny Spinner, Nate Stulman, Craig Swanson, Asiya S. Tschannerl, Betty J. Walker, Cheryl Watanabe, Tammy Weast, Jill Woolley, Susan Yoritomo, and Ning Yu.

Laird Bloom (yes, he is my son), a graduate of Massachusetts Institute of Technology, read much of the manuscript with uncommonly good critical sense and the parodist's intolerance of the banal and the sentimental—a perspective supplemented by the critical scrutiny of Stephen Albrecht when he was a graduate student at the University of Connecticut. Bard Bloom (yes, he too is my son), also an MIT grad, provided computer expertise. Laura Tharp, a student intern from DePauw University, helped to prepare this edition for publication. My doctoral research assistants at the University of Connecticut have been superb. Ning Yu translated the version of "Cinderella" (701–05) that he read in Chinese to his young son. Combining his knowledge of ancient and contemporary Chinese history and literature with his graduate studies in English, he wrote an incisive critical essay on the two Chinese "Cinderellas," (705–13), in addition to "Red and Black" (405–18).

Valerie M. Smith, like her predecessor Sarah Aguiar, in the manner of James Boswell willingly "ran half over London" to locate obscure information and double-check the facts. Her ever-increasing knowledge as an award-winning critic and teacher made her an ideal contributor of an essay on *Death of a Salesman* and coauthor of the *Instructor's Guide*.

For the first four editions, D. C. Heath was *The Essay Connection*'s publisher and the editorial process was conducted with thoughtful care by Paul Smith, Linda Bieze, and Rosemary Jaffe. At Houghton Mifflin, Dean Johnson, Bruce Cantley, and Kellie Cardone have assumed equivalent responsibilities with comparable good will, good humor, and good sense. Craig Mertens's painstaking attention to permissions deserves special thanks.

When the first edition of *The Essay Connection* was in process, my sons were in high school. Over the intervening twenty years they've earned doctorates (in biology and computer science), have married inspiring women, Sara (a U.S. attorney) and Vicki (a food scientist), and parented joyous children, Paul and Beth. An ever-active participant in the protracted process of making *The Essay Connection* more friendly to readers has been my writer-friendly husband, Martin Bloom, social psychologist, professor, world traveler, and fellow author. He has provided a retentive memory for titles and key words that I've called out from an adjacent lane during our early morning lap swims, homemade apple pies at bedtime, and all the comforts in between. My whole family keeps me cheerful; every day is a gift.

Lynn Z. Bloom

The *Essay Connection*

Part I

On Writing

1 Writers in Process— Laughing, Speaking, and Reading

You will encounter essays in this book that, as E. B. White remarked, philosophize, scold, jest, tell stories, argue, or plead, among the many things they can do. You'll be able to read essays more easily and understand them better if you bear in mind as you read some of the following questions concerning the essay's author, intended audience, type, purposes, and rhetorical strategies, as well as your own responses as a reader.

Who Is the Author?

a. When did the author live? Where? Is the author's ethnic origin, gender, or regional background relevant to understanding this essay?

b. What is the author's educational background? Job experience? Do these or other significant life experiences make him or her an authority on the subject of the essay?

c. Does the author have political, religious, economic, cultural or other biases that affect the essay's treatment of the subject? The author's credibility? The author's choice of language?

What Are the Context and Audience of the Essay?

a. When was the essay first published? Is it dated, or still relevant?

b. Where (in what magazine, professional journal, or book, if at all) was the essay first published?

c. For what audience was the essay originally intended? How much did the author expect the original readers to know about the subject? To what extent did the author expect the original readers to share his point of view? To resist that view?

d. Why would the original audience have read this essay?

e. What similarities and differences exist between the essay's original audience and the student audience now reading it?

f. What am I as a student reader expected to bring to my reading of this essay? My own or others' beliefs, values, past history, personal experience? Other reading? My own writing, previous or in an essay I will write in response to the essay(s) I am reading?

What Are the Purposes of the Essay?

a. Why did the author write the essay? To inform, describe, define, explain, argue, or for some other reason or combination of reasons?

b. Is the purpose explicitly stated anywhere in the essay? If so, where? Is this the thesis of the essay? Or is the thesis different?

c. If the purpose is not stated explicitly, how can I tell what the purpose is? Through examples? Emphasis? Tone? Other means?

d. Does the form of the essay suit the purpose? Would other forms have been more appropriate?

What Are the Strategies of the Essay?

a. What does the author do to make the essay interesting? Is he or she successful?

b. What organizational pattern (and subpatterns, if any) does the author use? How do these patterns fit the subject? The author's purpose?

c. What emphasis do the organization and proportioning provide to reinforce the author's purpose?

d. What evidence, arguments, and illustrations does the author employ to illustrate or demonstrate the thesis?

e. On what level of language (formal, informal, slangy) and in what tone (serious, satiric, sincere, etc.) does the author write?

f. Have I enjoyed the essay, or found it stimulating or otherwise provocative? Why or why not?

g. If I disagree with the author's thesis, or am not convinced by or attached to the author's evidence, illustrations, or use of language, am I nevertheless impelled to continue reading? If so, why? If not, why not?

The ways we read and write, and how we think about the ways we read and write, have been dramatically altered in the past thirty years. The New Critics, whose views dominated the teaching of reading and writing during early and mid-twentieth century, promoted a sense of the text as a static, often enigmatic entity, whose sleeping secrets awaited a master critic or brilliant teacher to arrive, like Prince Charming on a white horse, and awaken their meaning. The numerous courses and textbooks encouraging students to read for experience, information, ideas, understanding, and appreciation, reflect that view.

Yet contemporary literary theory encourages the sense of collaboration between author, text, and readers to make meaning. How we interpret any written material, whether a recipe, computer manual, love letter, or Martin Luther King, Jr.'s "Letter from Birmingham Jail" (596–616) depends, in part, on our prior knowledge of the subject, our opinion of the author, our experience with other works of the genre under consideration (what other recipes, or love letters, have we known?), and the context in which we're reading. We read Dr. King's "Letter" differently today than when he wrote it, jailed in Birmingham in 1963 for civil rights protests; liberals read it differently than conservatives; African-Americans may read it differently than whites, Southern or Northern. Where readers encounter a piece of writing greatly influences their interpretation, as well. Readers might read Dr. King's "Letter" as a document of news, history, social protest, argument, literary style—or some combination of these—depending on whether they encounter it in a newspaper of the time, in a history of the United States or of the civil rights movement, or in *The Essay Connection.*

A variety of critical theories reinforce the view that a work invites multiple readings, claiming that strong readers indeed bring powerful meanings to the texts they read. The selections in *The Essay Connection* open up a world of possibilities in interpreting not only what's on the written page, but also what is not on the page. What's there for the writer, as for the reader, is not just another story but an assemblage of stories, all that has occurred in one's life and thought, waiting to bleed through and into the paper on which these stories, in all their variations, will be told. Readers and writers alike are always in process, always in flux, no matter what their sources of inspiration or places to think.

As we experience and learn more, our understanding changes. Cathy Davidson's "Laughing in English" (6–17) demonstrates how two cultures, American and Japanese, learn to "read" each other and themselves. Students and teachers learn to differentiate the literal from the figurative meanings, to listen to the music (and gestures) as well as the words, to interpret the contexts of their dialogues, and to revise their understanding as they collaborate in making new meanings from words, gestures, and laughter—newly strange, newly familiar.

Throughout the process of maturation our consciousness evolves. Eudora Welty and Richard Wright, who grew up concurrently in Jackson, Mississippi, wrote years afterward to explain the phenomenon of learning to read from dramatically different perspectives. Welty's "In Love with Books" (34–39) explains part of her own background, showing how very young children can learn to love both reading and being read to. Wright's "The Power of Books" (425–35) offers yet a different focus on the relations between writers and readers, showing how an awakened social or racial consciousness can radically affect the reader.

When several (or more) readers share a background, common values, and a common language, they may be considered a *discourse community*. In "Mother Tongue" (17–25), Amy Tan explores how her writing reflects her Chinese-American discourse community. She understands, and uses, "all the Englishes I grew up with" (18)—one for formal writing, another for intimate conversation with Chinese family members, and a combination of public and private languages for storytelling. In "Parables from Danny Weinstein's Magic Book," Nancy Willard endows a menagerie— "an attractive young magpie," "a young parrot who longed to become a chef," "a buzzard running for governor of the forest," two coyote brothers "who made their living chopping wood," as well as a lord, a lady, and two sisters looking for a party—with the ability to speak in breezy, engaging conversational language, precise and to the point.

Thus, all the words, all the languages we speak, all the languages we understand (including the nonverbal communication of body language and social conventions), invariably influence how we write, for ourselves and those strangers who become friends—or antagonists—as they read our writing.

CATHY N. DAVIDSON

Davidson, born in 1949, grew up in Chicago, earned a B.A. from Elmhurst College (1970), and a Ph.D. in English at the State University of New York at Binghamton (1974). Before becoming professor of English at Duke University in 1989, where she is the editor of *American Literature,* Davidson taught English at Michigan State. She has published books on *Mothers and Daughters in Literature* (1980), Ambrose Bierce (1984), American novels (1986), and *Writers and Their Love Letters* (1992).

"Laughing in English" is from *36 Views of Mount Fuji* (1993), Davidson's autobiographical account of "finding myself in Japan" as a teacher of English at Kansai Women's University in Osaka in the 1980s. The book is titled after the series of Hokusai woodblocks depicting Mount Fuji, "the soul of Japan," in the context of multiple glimpses of "different, even contradictory, aspects of Japanese life." Like the Hokusai prints, Davidson's book uses "individual encounters, intimate moments, and small revelations" not only to "make sense of Japan," but to explain the ongoing process of attaining a better understanding of herself. She says, "What I learned almost immediately after I arrived in Japan for the first time, in 1980, was that I was destined to failure. My Japanese language skills were minimal, and I faced a culture that operated on assumptions completely different from my own. But I also learned that the Japanese were willing to tolerate my mistakes so long as I *acknowledged* them as mistakes, rather than as 'the right way' (read: The American Way) to do things. Most of my Japanese friends were willing to meet me more than halfway, also acknowledging those features of their culture that were specifically 'Japanese.' Over and over, I learned that a little laughter goes a long way towards smoothing over the places where cultures clash. I laughed a lot in Japan, and incorporated laughing into my classroom teaching as a way of easing cultural tensions and creating a comfortable environment where my students would feel less self-conscious about speaking English."

"Sometimes it is the person passing through . . . who has the clearest view," she adds. "I was in Japan to see, to experience, to learn, to understand. I wanted to be a good tourist, receptive to new experiences, new sights and sounds. It never occurred to me . . . that I would *become* one of the sights—examined, not just the examiner." In several senses, "Laughing in English" is about how two cultures, American and Japanese, learn to "read" each other and themselves.

Laughing in English

There was only one course in which Professor Sano, my depart-   1
ment head, thought I might have trouble. I was assigned to
teach Oral English for Non-English Majors, the B class, and
Professor Sano made a point of warning me that these students
would be very different from my English majors. Few, if any,
would have had any contact with English except through the traditional Japanese educational system. Intelligent young women,
they still would have learned English the way my young friend
Kenji had—lots of "who" and "whom," virtually nothing resembling practical conversational English. Most never would have
heard a native speaker of English, except in Hollywood movies.
The "English" taught in their Japanese schoolrooms was actually
katakana, the Japanese syllabary for foreign words, a way of trans-
literating all foreign sounds into the forty-six basic Japanese sound
patterns: *r* becomes *l*, *v* becomes *b*, each consonant (except *n*) must
be followed by a vowel. *Rocket* is *rokketo* (pronounced "locketo"),
ventilator is *benchireta*, and, the classic example, *blacklist* is the six-
syllable *burakku-risuto*.

Perhaps because I was struggling so hard to learn even the   2
most rudimentary Japanese, I was eager to teach these students
English. My dislike of the traditional Japanese way of teaching
English also made me feel almost a missionary zeal upon entering
my Oral English course at KWU. I'd never taken any courses in
the field of TOESL, Teaching of English as a Second Language, but
I certainly knew from colleagues that the way English is taught in
the Japanese schools is exactly the *wrong* way to encourage people
to really communicate in a new language.

I tried a different tack, beginning with the conscious demo-   3
lition of *sensei* ["teacher"]. Unlike many language teachers who
refuse to speak anything but the language being taught, I delighted in speaking to the students in my execrable Japanese.
Partly this was selfish; I practiced more Japanese in beginner's
Oral English class than anywhere else. But it was also pedagogical. I figured if they realized that *sensei* wasn't ashamed to make
mistakes, they certainly didn't have a right to be—a way of using
the Japanese proclivity for authoritarianism and punctiliousness

against itself. To show what I expected on the first formal presentation, a requirement in all of the Oral English sections, I initially prepared the same assignments—in Japanese. At first I thought I'd intentionally throw in a few mistakes, but quickly realized my Japanese was quite bad enough on its own without my having to invent errors.

4   I came up with a whopper. It is the kind of mistake often made by native English-speakers, who have a hard time differentiating between repeated consonants. Mine, I found out later, was already a famous mistake; it happened when an American introduced the oldest and most revered woman in the Japanese parliament on national television. The American meant to say that this legislator was not only "very distinguished" but also "very feminine" (*onna-rashii*). She ended up saying the legislator was both distinguished and *onara shi* (which means, roughly, to cut a fart).

5   "That double *n* is hard for foreigners," I said when one of my students started to giggle. "We can't really hear the difference between *onna ra* and *onara*."

6   The students were now all laughing, but in polite Japanese-girl fashion, a hand covering the mouth.

7   "Wait!" I shouted in my sternest voice. "This is Oral English class!"

8   The laughter stopped. They looked ashamed.

9   "No, no. In this class, you must *laugh* in English. Think about it. You've all seen American movies. How do you laugh in English?"

10   I could see a gleam in Miss Shimura's eye, and I called on her: "Would an American woman ever put her hand over her mouth when she laughed, Miss Shimura?"

11   "No, *sensei*—I mean, teacher."

12   "Show me. Laugh like an American movie star."

13   Miss Shimura kept her hands plastered at her side. She threw back her head. She opened her mouth as far as it would go. She made a deep, staccato sound at the back of her throat. *Hanh. Hanh. Hanh.*

14   We all laughed hysterically.

15   "Hands down!" I shouted again. "This is Oral English!"

16   They put their hands at their sides and imitated Miss Shimura's American head-back, open mouth plosive laugh.

17   "What about the body?" I asked.

I parodied a Japanese laugh, pulling my arms in to my sides, 18
bowing my head and shoulders forward, putting a hand coyly to
my mouth.

Again they laughed. This time it was American-style.   19

"Oral English is about bodies too, not just words," I smiled.   20

Miss Kato raised her hand.   21

"Hai?" (Yes?)   22

"Americans also laugh like this." She put her head back, 23
opened her mouth, and rocked her upper body from side to side,
her shoulders heaving and dodging, like Santa Claus.

There were gleeful shouts of "Yes! Yes!" and again a room- 24
ful of American-style laughter. It would start to die down, then
someone would catch her friend doing the funny American
laugh, and she'd break into hysterics again, the hand going to her
mouth, me pointing, her correcting herself with the Santa Claus
laughter. I continued to laugh Japanese-style, which made them
laugh even louder, bouncier. We were off and running, laughing
in each other's languages.

I'm convinced shame kills language learning faster than anything, 25
even more so in Japan, where shame lurks so close to the surface
of every social interaction. The laughing routine was childish
exercise, but then all language learning is childish, inherently in-
fantilizing, a giving up and a giving in, a loss of control. Learning
a language means returning to a state of near-idiocy.

And honesty. Language learning is so consuming, there's no 26
energy left over for invention. Ask someone to tell you their
height and weight in a beginning foreign language class, and
you'll likely get a much more reliable answer than the one on her
driver's license.

This quickly became the case in beginners' Oral English, 27
where I learned aspects of Japanese life that the sophisticated,
cosmopolitan students in the advanced classes at KWU would
not have revealed, under normal circumstances, to a *gaijin*. My
beginners talked in English the way they might talk in Japanese,
among friends. They didn't know enough about Western culture
to anticipate what we might consider strange or exotic, controversial or even reprehensible. Consequently, they spoke without
excessive censoring, something I never experienced later on,
when I taught an Advanced Oral English class.

28   My advanced students often dodged my questions with polite evasions. "The Japanese myth of racial homogeneity is as erroneous as the American myth of the melting pot," offered a student who has spent several years in the States. I had thought my opening question, "What is racism?", would provoke a heated debate that would lead us around, by the end of the class period, to addressing each country's particular brand of racism. Typically, Japanese are happy to discuss American racism but blind to the equivalent prejudice in their own country. The student's pointed answer effectively short-circuited the lesson I had hoped to make that day by anticipating what my own point of view might be. The rest of the class period was filled with platitudes and bored and knowing nods. The students in the advanced class knew exactly where to fudge.

29   After summer break, I require students in beginning Oral English for Non-Majors to give a brief presentation on what they've done over the vacation. It's designed to be simple, to ease them back into the term. They've been in Oral English since April, the beginning of the Japanese school year. They have had six weeks off for the summer, and now must return to classes for three more weeks before the grueling end-of-semester exams in late September.

30   I call on the first student.

31   "I was constipated most of the way to Nikko," a lovely young woman in a Kenzo flower-print jumper begins her talk.

32   I set my face like a Japanese mask, careful to express no emotion, and steal glances around the room. No one seems even remotely surprised at this beginning except me, and I know that it is absolutely mandatory that I act as if this is the most ordinary opening in the world.

33   "I was with the tennis club, and my *sensei* made sure I ate *konnyaku* for my constipation."

34   At this point she gets flustered. She is obviously embarrassed.

35   "It's okay," I jumped in hastily, searching for my most soothing and encouraging Japanese. "You're doing very well. Please go on."

36   "It's just," she stammers, also in Japanese, "I don't know the English for *konnyaku*. Do you know?"

I assure her that there's no American equivalent. *Konnyaku*   37
is a glutinous substance, made from the root of a plant that seems
to grow only in Japan. In America, I tell her, most people eat bran
to cure constipation or we take over-the-counter medicines such
as Ex-Lax.

"Ecks Racks," she repeats solemnly, then breaks into giggles   38
(American-style). So does everyone.

The word sounds so funny. It becomes the class joke for the   39
next few weeks. If anyone forgets a word in English, someone else
inevitably whispers to a friend, loud enough for the rest of us to
hear, "Ecks Racks!"

Three or four other speeches that morning give blow-by-   40
blow reports of near gastro-intestinal crises and how they were
averted, usually by the wise intervention of some *sensei*.

What surprises me most about the morning is how embarrassed   41
I am, although I think I've concealed it pretty well. These students
would wilt with shame if they had any inkling that this is not
something we would talk about in America, and I find myself in
a quandary. They trust me to tell them about Western culture, but
I know that if I tell them it's not considered polite to talk about
one's bowel movements in Western society, it will destroy the
easy camaraderie I've worked so hard to foster this year. But if I
don't tell them, I'm violating a trust.

I decide to resolve this by keeping a list of things they bring   42
up that wouldn't be acceptable in the West. All semester I've been
working to correct certain Japanese misconceptions and stereotypes, especially their idea that English is a completely logical and
direct language, and that Americans always say exactly what they
mean, regardless of social status or power relationships. Often my
students say things that sound very rude because they've been
taught that English lacks the politeness levels of Japanese. These
are topics we discuss all the time, so it will work just fine to devote
the last week of the semester to lecturing, in my comical Japanese,
about misconceptions and cultural differences that I've discovered
during my year in Japan. I can tell them about how surprised I
was the first time I used a public restroom that turned out to be
coed or about bathing Japanese-style with a group of women I
barely knew or having a male colleague slip around a corner on

the way home from a party. I started to follow, then realized he was taking a quick pee. I know I can act out my own surprise, making my Westerner's prudishness about bodily functions seem funny but also relevant. This is as close as I can come to having my pedagogical cake and eating it too.

43   From my beginning non-English majors in Oral English, I learn a great deal about Japan, including the rituals and super-stitions that have not been effaced by the rampant capitalism of modern, urban Japanese life. They tell of phone numbers one can call for horoscopes, fortunes, curses, cures. Rituals for marriages, pregnancies, births, divorces. A kind of Japanese voodoo that takes place in the forest on a certain kind of night. Number symbolism. Lucky and unlucky days, lucky and unlucky years, lucky and un-lucky directions ("Never sleep with your head to the North, the way the dead are buried"). Blood-type match-making. Tengu, the wicked long-nosed trickster goblin. Kappa, the amphibious river imp. Tanuki, the raccoonlike creature with the money bag and enormous testicles, a symbol of plenty. Dragons, supernatural foxes, thunder gods, long-life noodles, boiled eels for stamina on hot summer days, chewy *mochi* rice cakes for strength and en-durance on the New Year, the ashes of a burnt *imori* (salamander) served to someone you want to fall in love with you. They talk seriously about prejudice and injustice toward the *burakumin* (Japan's untouchable caste) the Ainu (the indigenous people, now almost extinct), and Koreans (who must take Japanese names before being allowed citizenship or who are denied citizenship even two or three generations after their family immigrated to Japan and who must carry alien registration papers with their thumbprint, like foreigners). They talk of burial customs, going to the crematorium with the long chopsticks to pick out the vertebra that goes into the urn in the family altar at home.

44   When they talk of *omiai* and arranged marriage, one woman starts to cry. Her friends comfort her. It's the only time I've ever seen someone express personal sorrow in a Japanese classroom. Several students insist that they will never marry an eldest son, because they do not want to be responsible for taking care of his aged parents. Two say they will never have children because they do not want their children to hate them the way they hated their mothers all through school. One young woman says if she marries, it will be to a foreigner because she knows from the

movies that foreign husbands help around the house. Another protests that she wouldn't want to marry a *gaijin*, because she doesn't want a *gokiburi teishu* (a cockroach husband), some man scurrying around underfoot in her kitchen. Funny or serious, they talk with candor. And, mostly, they talk. In English.

"There was so much laughing going on in the next room this semester, I checked the schedule," sniffs one of the part-time teachers. "It's your Oral English class. My students are getting jealous. All we hear from your room is laughter. Is anyone learning anything at all in there?"   45

I've had conversations before with this woman, none of them pleasant. She teaches at one of the more conventional Japanese universities and come to Kansai Women's University only one day a week. I've heard her say more than once that she's been here so long that now "she's more Japanese than the Japanese."   46

We're sitting and talking together over our *bento* boxes, eating our lunch in the faculty room. I tell her, proudly, that my students are learning to speak English very well, and, maybe more importantly, they are learning to speak freely and confidently.   47

"And you think that's a good thing?" she asks rhetorically. "They graduate and get to be OLs [office ladies] for a while. Then they're married off to some jerk of a *sarariiman*. But it's okay, you've taught them how to 'speak freely.'"   48

I am not liking this woman. I am not liking the insinuation in her voice or the smirk on her face. But I can't ignore her comment. I've thought about it myself, many times, especially on the train to and from the university, as I watch the faces of older Japanese women and think about where and how my students will fit in.   49

Most of these KWU students will graduate and they will, indeed, work as OLs for a few years before marriage, smiling politely and serving tea for busy male executives in Japanese firms. The closest they will come to real "business" might be working the Xerox machine or the paper shredder. Since only about a quarter of the population at four-year colleges in Japan is female (compared to well over half in the United States), there are lots of women available to work after the completion of secondary schools. OLs are perpetually replenishable, an eternally young group of women. Most quit—or are fired—once they are married or after they become pregnant.   50

51   The KWU women are the *crème de la crème* of Japanese female students. Some might advance further in corporate life than the OLs. A few might even achieve their dreams. One of my students wants to be a composer. Another wants to be an international news correspondent. Still others want to be doctors, lawyers. The odds are stacked against them, but the very fact that they are here shows that they are good at overcoming odds. "My dream is be a housewife and a mother," one of my Oral English students said in class one day. "But when I am a mother, I will give my children a *choice* of whether or not they want to go to *juku*. I will help to improve Japanese society by allowing my children to be free."

52   *To be free.* It's a phrase I've heard a lot this year, and I suspect some of this is just student grandstanding to please the *gaijin* teacher. Some of it is probably wishful thinking. Many of these smart, polished young women will become thoroughly conventional upper-middle-class housewives and mothers. It's hard for me to understand the point of all their study, all their years of deprivation, all those hours in *juku* cramming for "examination hell," just so one day they, too, can become "education moms," sending their young sons and daughters off under the falling cherry blossoms, the whole cycle beginning again with a new generation.

53   "We are told Japanese workers are better than American," one of my students says in an assignment about the work ethic. "We are told this so that we keep working—hard, harder, and hardest. Even as children, we're told to work hard. We Japanese work ourselves to death."

54   She is as startled as the rest of us by the burning quality of her speech. Her accent isn't perfect and her vocabulary has its limits but her eloquence is unmistakable. We have heard her. She returns to her seat, flushed with attention.

55   When I take the train home to my apartment in Nigawa that afternoon, I can't help noticing that the only men on the train are elderly, retired. The train is filled with mothers coming home from shopping and with schoolchildren in uniform, finished with one more day of regular school and now on their way to *juku*.

56 I find myself asking the big question, the dangerous question. What am I really doing here? My students are having fun, they're learning English, but what is my role here? I have learned a lot

teaching at Kansai Women's University, and I know my students have learned things too. I don't think it's romanticizing to say we've touched one another, shown each other glimpses of one another's culture. Is that enough?

I can tell sometimes, as I look out over the classroom, that 57 something like love is happening in there. It scares me. My students are convinced I look like a Western movie star. If I wear my shoulder-length hair up in a twist on a hot day, I can predict that at least a dozen of them will have their hair in a twist the next week. If I roll my jacket sleeves, they will roll theirs. My Oral English class has fun imitating my American slang, especially my habit of saying "Oh wow!" They have fun telling me their culture's secrets. They have fun making jokes and laughing and speaking English, hair in a twist, jacket sleeves rolled.

Maybe that's my function. Not very consequential but 58 perhaps necessary. "Visiting Foreign Teacher" is the official title on my visa. The students call me *"sensei,"* but I'm not like other *sensei* in the Japanese scheme of things. I am exotic and I am temporary. My embittered colleague might be right. In the sum total of their existence, it doesn't matter greatly that their English has improved. At my most cynical, I think of myself as a diversion, a respite from frenetic Japanese life, the pedagogical equivalent of the *sarariiman's* whiskey.

But I don't think you can be a teacher unless you believe in 59 the possibility of change. When I'm feeling optimistic, I like to think I give my Japanese students the same thing I try to give my American students back home: a space in which to speak and be heard.

Sometimes I look at middle-aged women in Japan and I'm 60 filled with awe. Often they *look* middle-aged—not engaged in the frantic and self-defeating American quest to look forever young— and often they look happy. Their children grown, many become adventurous. For some, it's ballroom dancing or traditional Japanese *koto,* hobbies given up during the busy child-rearing years. For others, it's running for local government or working for school reform or in the peace or environmental movements. KWU recently started accepting "returning women"—older women, including mothers whose children are grown—into its graduate program, and the success rate, both in school and for subsequent employment, has been impressive.

61   That's what I think about when I teach the brilliant young women of Kansai Women's University. I think about their future, and hope that someday, soon or late, they will stop and hear the sound of their voices and remember their young fire.

Content

1. What does Davidson teach her students—explicitly and implicitly—when she teaches them to "laugh in English"?
2. How do we learn what's polite in our own culture and what's not? (In other words, how do we learn to "read" that particular aspect of the culture?) How can a person tell someone else—politely—that they're not being polite (see ¶s 31–42)?
3. "I don't think you can be a teacher unless you believe in the possibility of change," says Davidson (¶ 59). What changes occurred in Davidson's Japanese students during the time she taught them? What changes occurred in her? On what grounds is the rival teacher critical of Davidson's teaching (¶s 45–50)? Is the criticism justified, or is the other teacher simply jealous?

Strategies/Structures

4. Very early in the essay Davidson admits—to her students and her readers—the "whopper" and other mistakes she made in learning Japanese (¶s 3–5). What is the effect of such an admission on her students? On the character she presents to her readers?
5. What is the effect of Davidson's admission "I can tell sometimes, as I look out over the classroom, that something like love is happening in there. It scares me. My students are convinced I look like a Western movie star" [and they imitate me] (¶ 57)?
6. Assuming that Davidson is writing for an American audience, why is it important that her confession of the mistakes she makes as a teacher begin the essay that ends with an acknowledgement of the "love that is happening" in the classroom?

Language

7. Why is laughter, though nonverbal, a type of "language"? What do Davidson and her students immediately communicate through laughter? In what ways does this laughter resonate throughout the remainder of the class sessions? Throughout this essay?

For Writing

8. Can—and should–learning be fun? Write an argument for, or against, laughing in any language as a way of learning to "read" or understand the culture it represents.

9. Write an essay to convince people wanting to learn another language that "to understand a language it is necessary to understand the culture of its native speakers." To illustrate your point, use examples from "Laughing in English" and your own experiences (or the experiences of others you know well) in learning another language and in trying to understand another culture, including making mistakes!

10. Identify a common means of nonverbal communication, such as laughing, smiling, frowning, looking someone straight in the eye, standing, sitting, walking, gesturing. Identify several typical expressions of your chosen means of communication (such as a broad smile, a faint smile, a come-hither smile) in particular contexts, and show how their meaning changes depending on the nature of the occasion, the place, the communicator's intent and skill, and the needs and understanding of the receiver of the message. Since the communication is nonverbal, and often (though not always) subtle, how can the communicator make sure the audience gets the point?

AMY TAN

Tan has always been fascinated with language, as revealed in the essay that follows, and on the relation of speaking to writing and reading. Born in Oakland, California, in 1952, Tan earned a B.A. in English at San Jose State University (1973), from which she also obtained an M.A. in linguistics in 1974. After working as a language development specialist for developmentally disabled children, she made a major career switch at age thirty, becoming a free-lance business writer the week after her former boss told her "that writing was my worst skill." So successful was she at writing speeches for executives that she was soon working ninety hours a week. To relieve her workaholism and find her own voice she switched careers again, writing the first of the stories that ultimately comprised *The Joy Luck Club,* whose publication in 1989 brought her immediate fame, fortune, and critical esteem.

Tan followed this book with the equally successful *The Kitchen God's Wife* (1991), a novel modeled on her mother's traumatic life in China before she emigrated to the United States after World War II, and *The Hundred Secret Senses* (1995). Indeed, as Tan explains in the essay "Mother Tongue," originally published in *Threepenny Review* in 1990, her ideal reader became her mother, "because these were stories about mothers." Tan wrote "in all the Englishes I grew up with"—the "simple" English "I spoke to my mother," the "broken" English "she used with me," my "'watered down' translation of her Chinese," and her "internal language"—"her intent, her passion, her imagery, the rhythms of her speech and the nature of her thoughts." Her mother paid the book the ultimate compliment. "'So easy to read.'" Hearing these multiple languages by reading the essay aloud weds the words and the music.

Mother Tongue

1   I am not a scholar of English or literature. I cannot give you much more than personal opinions on the English language and its variations in this country or others.

2   I am a writer. And by that definition, I am someone who has always loved language. I am fascinated by language in daily life. I spend a great deal of my time thinking about the power of language—the way it can evoke an emotion, a visual image, a complex idea, or a simple truth. Language is the tool of my trade. And I use them all—all the Englishes I grew up with.

3   Recently, I was made keenly aware of the different Englishes I do use. I was giving a talk to a large group of people, the same talk I had already given to half a dozen other groups. The nature of the talk was about my writing, my life, and my book, *The Joy Luck Club*. The talk was going along well enough, until I remembered one major difference that made the whole talk sound wrong. My mother was in the room. And it was perhaps the first time she had heard me give a lengthy speech, using the kind of English I have never used with her. I was saying things like, "The intersection of memory upon imagination" and "There is an aspect of my fiction that relates to thus-and-thus"—a speech filled

with carefully wrought grammatical phrases, burdened, it suddenly seemed to me, with nominalized forms, past perfect tenses, conditional phrases, all the forms of standard English that I had learned in school and through books, the forms of English I did not use at home with my mother.

Just last week, I was walking down the street with my mother, and I again found myself conscious of the English I was using, the English I do use with her. We were talking about the price of new and used furniture and I heard myself saying this: "Not waste money that way." My husband was with us as well, and he didn't notice any switch in my English. And then I realized why. It's because over the twenty years we've been together I've often used that same kind of English with him, and sometimes he even uses it with me. It has become our language of intimacy, a different sort of English that relates to family talk, the language I grew up with.

So you'll have some idea of what this family talk I heard sounds like, I'll quote what my mother said during a recent conversation which I videotaped and then transcribed. During this conversation, my mother was talking about a political gangster in Shanghai who had the same last name as her family's, Du, and how the gangster in his early years wanted to be adopted by her family, which was rich by comparison. Later, the gangster became more powerful, far richer than my mother's family, and one day showed up at my mother's wedding to pay his respects. Here's what she said in part:

"Du Yusong having business like fruit stand. Like off the street kind. He is Du like Du Zong—but not Tsung-ming Island people. The local people call putong, the river east side, he belong to that side local people. That man want to ask Du Zong father take him in like become own family. Du Zong father wasn't look down on him, but didn't take seriously, until that man big like become a mafia. Now important person, very hard to inviting him. Chinese way, came only to show respect, don't stay for dinner. Respect for making big celebration, he shows up. Mean give lots of respect. Chinese custom. Chinese social life that way. If too important won't have to stay too long. He come to my wedding. I didn't see, I heard it. I gone to boy's side, they have YMCA dinner. Chinese age I was nineteen."

7   You should know that my mother's expressive command of English belies how much she actually understands. She reads the *Forbes* report, listens to *Wall Street Week,* converses daily with her stockbroker, reads all of Shirley MacLaine's books with ease—all kinds of things I can't begin to understand. Yet some of my friends tell me they understand 50 percent of what my mother says. Some say they understand 80 to 90 percent. Some say they understand none of it, as if she were speaking pure Chinese. But to me, my mother's English is perfectly clear, perfectly natural. It's my mother tongue. Her language, as I hear it, is vivid, direct, full of observation and imagery. That was the language that helped shape the way I saw things, expressed things, made sense of the world.

8   Lately, I've been giving more thought to the kind of English my mother speaks. Like others, I have described it to people as "broken" or "fractured" English. But I wince when I say that. It has always bothered me that I can think of no way to describe it other than "broken," as if it were damaged and needed to be fixed, as if it lacked a certain wholeness and soundness. I've heard other terms used, "limited English," for example. But they seem just as bad, as if everything is limited, including people's perceptions of the limited English speaker.

9   I know this for a fact, because when I was growing up, my mother's "limited" English limited *my* perception of her. I was ashamed of her English. I believed that her English reflected the quality of what she had to say. That is, because she expressed them imperfectly her thoughts were imperfect. And I had plenty of empirical evidence to support me: the fact that people in department stores, at banks, and at restaurants did not take her seriously, did not give her good service, pretended not to understand her, or even acted as if they did not hear her.

10   My mother has long realized the limitations of her English as well. When I was fifteen, she used to have me call people on the phone to pretend I was she. In this guise, I was forced to ask for information or even to complain and yell at people who had been rude to her. One time it was a call to her stockbroker in New York. She had cashed out her small portfolio and it just happened we were going to go to New York the next week, our very first trip outside California. I had to get on the phone and say in an adolescent voice that was not very convincing, "This is Mrs. Tan."

And my mother was standing in the back whispering 11
loudly, "Why he don't send me check, already two weeks late. So
mad he lie to me, losing me money."

And then I said in perfect English, "Yes, I'm getting rather 12
concerned. You had agreed to send the check two weeks ago, but
it hasn't arrived."

Then she began to talk more loudly. "What he want, I come 13
to New York tell him front of his boss, you cheating me?" And I
was trying to calm her down, make her be quiet, while telling the
stockbroker, "I can't tolerate any more excuses. If I don't receive
the check immediately, I am going to have to speak to your manager when I'm in New York next week." And sure enough, the
following week there we were in front of this astonished stockbroker, and I was sitting there red-faced and quiet, and my
mother, the real Mrs. Tan, was shouting at his boss in her impec-
cable broken English.

We used a similar routine just five days ago, for a situation 14
that was far less humorous. My mother had gone to the hospital
for an appointment, to find out about a benign brain tumor a CAT
scan had revealed a month ago. She said she had spoken very
good English, her best English, no mistakes. Still, she said, the
hospital did not apologize when they said they had lost the CAT
scan and she had come for nothing. She said they did not seem to
have any sympathy when she told them she was anxious to know
the exact diagnosis, since her husband and son had both died of
brain tumors. She said they would not give her any more information until the next time and she would have to make another
appointment for that. So she said she would not leave until the
doctor called her daughter. She wouldn't budge. And when the
doctor finally called her daughter, me, who spoke in perfect
English—lo and behold—we had assurances the CAT scan would
be found, promises that a conference call on Monday would be
held, and apologies for any suffering my mother had gone
through for a most regrettable mistake.

I think my mother's English almost had an effect on limit- 15
ing my possibilities in life as well. Sociologists and linguists
probably will tell you that a person's developing language skills
are more influenced by peers. But I do think that the language
spoken in the family, especially in immigrant families which
are more insular, plays a large role in shaping the language of

the child. And I believe that it affected my results on achievement tests, IQ tests, and the SAT. While my English skills were
never judged as poor, compared to math, English could not be
considered my strong suit. In grade school I did moderately well,
getting perhaps B's, sometimes B-pluses, in English and scoring
perhaps in the sixtieth or seventieth percentile on achievement
tests. But those scores were not good enough to override the
opinion that my true abilities lay in math and science, because in
those areas I achieved A's and scored in the ninetieth percentile
or higher.

16   This was understandable. Math is precise; there is only one
correct answer. Whereas, for me at least, the answers on English
tests were always a judgment call, a matter of opinion and personal experience. Those tests were constructed around items like
fill-in-the-blank sentence completion, such as, "Even though Tom
was _____, Mary thought he was _____." And the correct
answer always seemed to be the most bland combinations of
thoughts, for example "Even though Tom was shy, Mary thought
he was charming," with the grammatical structure "even though"
limiting the correct answer to some sort of semantic opposites, so
you wouldn't get answers like, "Even though Tom was foolish,
Mary thought he was ridiculous." Well, according to my mother,
there were very few limitations as to what Tom could have been
and what Mary might have thought of him. So I never did well on
tests like that.

17   The same was true with word analogies, pairs of words in
which you were supposed to find some sort of logical, semantic
relationship—for example, "*Sunset* is to *nightfall* as _____ is to
_____." And here you would be presented with a list of four
possible pairs, one of which showed the same kind of relation-
ship: *red* is to *spotlight, bus* is to *arrival, chills* is to *fever, yawn* is to
boring. Well, I could never think that way. I knew what the tests
were asking, but I could not block out of my mind the images
already created by the first pair, "*sunset* is to *nightfall*"—and I
would see a burst of colors against a darkening sky, the moon
rising, the lowering of a curtain of stars. And all the other pairs of
words—red, bus, spotlight, boring—just threw up a mass of confusing images, making it impossible for me to sort out something
as logical as saying: "A sunset precedes nightfall" is the same as

"a chill precedes a fever." The only way I would have gotten that answer right would have been to imagine an associative situation, for example, my being disobedient and staying out past sunset, catching a chill at night, which turns into feverish pneumonia as punishment, which indeed did happen to me.

I have been thinking about all this lately, about my mother's   18 English, about achievement tests. Because lately I've been asked as a writer, why there are not more Asian Americans represented in American literature. Why are there few Asian Americans enrolled in creative writing programs? Why do so many Chinese students go into engineering? Well, these are broad sociological questions I can't begin to answer. But I have noticed in surveys— in fact, just last week—that Asian students, as a whole, always do significantly better on math achievement tests than in English. And this makes me think that there are other Asian-American students whose English spoken in the home might also be described as "broken" or "limited." And perhaps they also have teachers who are steering them away from writing and into math and science, which is what happened to me.

Fortunately, I happen to be rebellious in nature and enjoy the   19 challenge of disproving assumptions made about me. I became an English major my first year in college, after being enrolled as premed. I started writing nonfiction as a freelancer the week after I was told by my former boss that writing was my worst skill and I should hone my talents toward account management.

But it wasn't until 1985 that I finally began to write fiction.   20 And at first I wrote using what I thought to be wittily crafted sentences, sentences that would finally prove I had mastery over the English language. Here's an example from the first draft of a story that later made its way into *The Joy Luck Club,* but without this line: "That was my mental quandary in its nascent state." A terrible line, which I can barely pronounce.

Fortunately, for reasons I won't get into today, I later decided   21 I should envision a reader for the stories I would write. And the reader I decided upon was my mother, because these were stories about mothers. So with this reader in mind—and in fact she did read my early drafts—I began to write stories using all the Englishes I grew up with: the English I spoke to my mother, which for lack of a better term might be described as "simple"; the English she used with me, which for lack of a better term might be described as "broken"; my translation of her Chinese, which could certainly be described as "watered down"; and what I imagined to be her translation of her Chinese if she could speak in perfect English, her internal language, and for that I sought to preserve the essence, but neither an English nor a Chinese structure. I wanted to capture what language ability tests can never reveal: her intent, her passion, her imagery, the rhythms of her speech and the nature of her thoughts.

22   Apart from what any critic had to say about my writing, I knew I had succeeded where it counted when my mother finished reading my book and gave me her verdict: "So easy to read."

Content

1. What connections does Tan make throughout the essay between speaking and writing? Why is it necessary for the writer to be "keenly aware of the different Englishes" she uses?
2. What is Tan's relationship with her mother? How can you tell?
3. What problems does Mrs. Tan experience as a result of not speaking standard English? Are her problems typical of other speakers of "limited" English?
4. Do you agree with Tan that "math is precise," but that English is "always a judgment call, a matter of opinion and personal experience" (¶ 16)? Why or why not? If English is so subjective, how is it possible to write anything that is clear, "so easy to read" (¶ 22)?

Strategies/Structures

5. Tan uses illustrative examples: a story told in her mother's speech (¶ 6), her mother's altercation with the stockbroker (¶s 10–13), her mother's encounter with rude and indifferent hospital workers who lost her CAT scan (¶ 14). What is the point of each example? Does Tan have to explain them? Why or why not?

Language

6. In what English has Tan written "Mother Tongue"? Why?
7. How do the "Englishes" that Tan and her mother use convey their characters, personalities, intelligence? In what ways are mother and daughter similar? Different?

For Writing

8. How many Englishes did you grow up with? Explain, either in speaking or in writing, to someone who doesn't know you very well, two of the different languages—whether these are variations of English or another language—that you use and identify the circumstances under which you use each of them—perhaps at home, in conversation with friends, or in writing papers. Consider such features as vocabulary (and amount of slang or specialized words), sentence length, and simplicity or complexity of what you're trying to say. How much can you count on your readers to understand without elaborate explanation on your part? Do you write papers for English classes in a different language than papers for some of your other courses?

9. If you are trying to communicate with someone whose native language or dialect is different from yours, how do you do it? To what extent did this communication depend on words? Other means (such as gestures, tone of voice)? As Tan does, tell the story of such an experience (to a reader who wasn't there) in order to explain the nature of your communication. If there were any misunderstandings, what were they? How did they occur, and how did you resolve (or attempt to resolve) them? What advice would you offer to help others in similar situations to communicate clearly?

10. Present to an audience of college-educated readers an argument for or against the necessity of speaking in standard English. Are there any exceptions to your position?

NANCY WILLARD

Willard was born (1936), raised, and educated in Ann Arbor, Michigan, where she earned a B.A. (1958) and Ph.D. (1963) in English from the University of Michigan, punctuated by an M.A. in creative writing from Stanford (1960). She teaches creative writing at Vassar, and writes poetry, fiction, and children's books, including *Pish, Posh, Said Hieronymous Bosch* (1991), and the Newbery Medal-winning *A Visit to William Blake's Inn: Poems for Innocent and Experienced Travelers* (1981). Her poetry, observes reviewer Stanley Poss, is about "cooking, food, sports headlines, marriages that're doing OK, pregnancy, kids, animals, unwashed feet, plants, flea circuses, but her domestic in not merely cozy, and she's not merely domestic." Poet Donald Hall explains why: "Willard's imagination—in verse or prose, for children or adults—builds castles stranger than any mad King of Bavaria ever built. She imagines with a wonderful concreteness. But also, she takes real language and by literal-mindedness turns it into the structure of dream"

Telling Time: Angels, Ancestors, and Stories: Essays on Writing (Harcourt, 1993) was the first home of "Danny Weinstein's Magic Book," Willard's collection of parables, stories that embed good advice on how to write. The essay begins by explaining her title. Danny Weinstein, a fraternity pledge who rented a room in the Willard house for a semester when Willard was ten, carried around a magic book whose title she thought was *The Artistic Personality* (she discovered later that it was actually *The Autistic Personality*). One day he told her a parable to illustrate why truth is more palatable when embedded in a story than when it is told plain:

"Once upon a time Truth used to walk around town stark naked. Think of it—not a stitch on! People were shocked. Scandalized. They shut the door on him, they avoided him, they wouldn't risk being seen with him. One day, as Truth was wandering through town, outcast, hangdog, alone, who should he happen to meet but Parable. Parable was dressed to the nines. A tuxedo, a cape, a top hat.

" 'Truth, old friend,' said Parable. 'What's the problem?'

"Truth shook his head.

" 'I'm old and ugly, brother Nobody loves me.'

" 'Nonsense!' exclaimed Parable. 'I'm no younger than you are. Listen, brother, you've got to dress better. People don't like you going around all naked. I'll give you some of my clothes, and you'll be the life of the party.'

"Truth put on a white linen suit, a pink shirt, and a black tie, and what do you know? People invited him here, they invited him there, they shook his hand when they met him in the street. Since that time Truth and Parable have been great friends."

Parables from Danny Weinstein's Magic Book

Diamonds for Supper

1   An attractive young magpie was standing in her kitchen, wondering what to cook for dinner. She had been married only three months and had run through the small repertoire of dishes she knew. Though her husband hadn't complained, the magpie

worried about the longterm effects of ninety successive dinners of franks and beans.

She put a pot of water on the stove, hoping a cup of instant 2 coffee would clear her brain, when suddenly the diamond in her engagement ring dropped out and sparkled its way to the bottom of the pot.

"Diamond soup!" she exclaimed, "I'll make diamond soup." 3

Naturally there was no recipe for diamond soup in *The Joy* 4 *of Cooking,* but the magpie thought back to soups she had enjoyed in the past and counted on instinct and memory to instruct her. She thought of garnets and added carrots, she thought of pearls and added onions, she thought of jet and added peppercorns. She longed for emeralds and rubies and added rosemary and tomatoes. Amethysts crossed her mind, and she added purple sage.

When her husband came home, he exclaimed, "Something 5 smells divine! I hope it's dinner."

"Sit down," said the magpie modestly, "and I'll serve the 6 soup."

As she was about to ladle it into two bowls, the diamonds 7 called to her, "Take me out."

"But you're brilliant," said the magpie. "You're beautiful." 8

"This soup by any other name would taste as good," said 9 the diamond. "Take me out. Do you want your husband to break a tooth?"

Moral: The line you love best is the hardest to cut. 10

A Feast for the Ears

There was once a young parrot who longed to become a chef. 11

"Okay," said his father, "you can apprentice yourself to a 12 master chef, or you can go to cooking school."

The parrot enrolled at the Culinary Institute of Birds. Right 13 away everyone could see he would go far. For "Introduction to Feasts 101: A History of Banquets from 1000 A.D. to the Present," he handed in a paper on soup in the Middle Ages that his professor felt was publishable, and she encouraged the parrot to major in feasts, since he showed such a talent for it.

His senior year, in lieu of a thesis, the parrot chose to prepare 14 a banquet for twelve distinguished ravens who were among the most renowned chefs in the country. On the appointed day, the ravens arrived and seated themselves at a table set with the finest china and crystal. The parrot stepped forward and made a little bow.

15   "I have prepared a feast that I believe will prove unlike any you have ever tasted. The only ingredients I have allowed myself are flowers."

16   He said he hoped the ravens would enjoy his daylily soup. He told them he'd risen before sunrise to gather the daylilies and he'd cooked them in a fine French sherry.

17   "Some people," he added, "cook the buds. But I use only the blossoms. And these daylilies are not the common variety."

18   He told them of a clearing in the middle of a forest to the east where the finest lilies grew. He told them it took five hours to reach the place by care and another hour on foot, since neither roads nor trials disturbed the forest.

19   "Some people wouldn't go to so much trouble," he said. "But you have only to compare the wild lily with the garden variety to taste the difference."

20   A raven at the head of the table raised his wing. "It sounds wonderful. We're all famished. Where is the food?"

21   "I . . . I haven't started cooking it yet," stammered the parrot, "but wait till you hear my menu."

22   *Moral:* If you start your story with a clutter of details, you'll never get to the main course.

The Buzzard and Aesop's Fable

23   A buzzard running for governor of the forest was invited one evening to speak to a large gathering of prospective voters, mostly rich owls who were known to be undecided. The polls showed the election would be a close one. The buzzard reminded them of his good political record. He'd voted to save the elms. He'd voted for zoning against termites. He supported medical benefits for all birds, and for rich owls in particular. He pointed out how the incumbent governor, a fox, favored mammals and did nothing to help other forms of life. He spoke of lower taxes, better housing for wrens, cleaner water for swans.

24   The night was hot, and the owls grew drowsy. At this moment Aesop strolled by. Noting the snoozing owls, he tapped the buzzard on the shoulder and said, "You'll never win the election that way."

25   "What else can I do?" asked the buzzard.

Aesop stood up and addressed the crowd, "Once upon a   26
time there was a fox, a buzzard, and an owl. And one day—"

Instantly he had their complete attention.   27

Moral: Show, don't tell. Information touches the mind, story   28
sinks into the heart.

Two Sisters and a House

Two sisters were invited to an open house given by a friend of   29
their deceased father. Neither of them could recall ever having
met the friend, but both remembered what their father had
said about him: "He's traveled all over the world. You can't imagine the adventures he's had. And his house is absolutely fascinating. He designed it himself. It's like a museum full of marvels."

Naturally the sisters could hardly wait to meet the gentle-   30
man and see these marvels. On the evening of the party the
younger woman was so slow in getting dressed that the older one
said, "I'll go on ahead and meet you there, I don't want to miss a
single moment."

And she called a cab and gave the driver the address. When   31
they arrived, he asked her which door she wanted.

"The front door," replied the woman.   32

"And which door is that?" asked the driver.   33

Well might he ask. There were at least twenty-five doors   34
by which the house could be entered. The driver cruised up and
down the street while the woman examined them all. She finally
chose the door closet to the center. It had columns and steps leading to a little round porch and looked more imposing than the
others. She paid the driver and marched up the steps. When she
rang the bell, the door opened and the woman was dismayed to
find herself alone in a large living room. All the furnishings were
beige—from the carpet to the nubby wing chairs hidden under
shiny plastic covers. The room looked like the lobby of a third-
class motel—everything tasteful, everything dull. It was impossible to imagine interesting people living here.

The woman wandered into several adjacent rooms but met   35
no one.

"I must have the wrong time," she said to the air, "and I cer-   36
tainly have the wrong place." She was relieved to find a telephone
on the coffee table, and she called for the cab to take her home.

37   When she got back, her younger sister was gone. The woman clicked on the TV. Only the Weather Channel came through clearly, and she watched till she fell asleep.

38   She was awakened by her younger sister coming in at two A.M., breathless with excitement.

39   "Where were you?" she exclaimed. "I've never met so many remarkable people. And you should have seen the house! The living room had a sycamore tree growing right through the roof. In the crown of the tree there was an aviary with hundreds of birds. You never heard such exquisite singing in all your life."

40   "What are you talking about?" said the older sister. "The living room was nothing but beige junk."

41   "You went in through the front door," said the younger girl. "When I saw that beige room, I figured the real entrance must be somewhere else. So I kept trying different doors until I found the right one."

42   *Moral:* Look for your real beginning a couple of pages into your rough draft.

The River and the Map

43 On the edge of a vast forest lived two coyotes who made their living chopping wood. All day the brothers sawed and chopped and hauled wood, and in the evening they sat around with their coyote buddies in the Racoon Saloon and talked about what lay on the other side of the forest.

44   "Fame and fortune," said the bartender. "That's why nobody ever comes back."

45   One night the younger brother turned to the older brother and said, "Let's cross the forest. What have we got to lose?"

46   "Our lives," said the older brother.

47   "The world is a strange place," said the younger brother, "and nobody gets out of it alive. If you won't come with me, I'll go alone."

48   The older brother wouldn't hear of that, so he asked this animal and that animal for help, and at last he found a beaver who offered to sell him a map for five cords of maple chopped small. The map showed a path winding through the forest. In the right-hand bottom corner were the numbers 1801.

"It's a little out of date," said the beaver. "If it doesn't work   49
as a map, you can use it as a decorative item for your den."

The next morning the brothers set out, and they were de-   50
lighted to find a path that ran beside the river just as the map
promised. Toward evening, however, the path forked, with the
left-hand fork leading away from the river.

"According to the map," said the older brother, "we should   51
go to the left."

"That doesn't feel right," said the younger brother. "I'm for   52
following the river. A river has a beginning, a middle, and an end.
The path could lead to nothing."

"Not this path," said the older brother. "It's on the map."   53

"You follow the map, and I'll follow the river," said the   54
younger brother, "and let's see who arrives first."

They hugged each other good-bye. The older brother set off   55
clutching the map in his paw and was never seen again. The
younger brother had his own troubles. The forest grew so dense
he could not even see the river. But he could hear it—sometimes
close, sometimes distant—and after a long, difficult journey he
stepped out into a glorious garden on the other side.

Moral: Though you may be lost, your story is not. It is wait-   56
ing for you to catch up with it.

The Artist and the Goat

Lord Derby prided himself on the variety of exotic beasts he kept   57
in a private zoo he maintained on his estate in the south of England. He owned panthers and peacocks, zebras, fallow deer, and
Barbary apes. Of all his acquisitions, none pleased him more than
a rare mountain goat that had been sent to him by a veterinarian
from Colorado. She was the only goat scientists had ever seen
who carried a thread of gold and three freshwater pearls twisted
into her tiny black horns.

The goat was very shy and seldom showed herself.   58

"Why don't you have her portrait painted?" suggested Lady   59
Derby. "On the days she doesn't come around, we can look at her
picture."

Lord Derby thought this an excellent idea. He advertised in   60
the newspaper for an artist to paint the portrait of his Colorado

mountain goat and added that if the work was satisfactory he would commission the artist to do a portrait of himself and Lady Derby as well.

61   The newspaper had scarcely hit the stands when an artist knocked at the Derby mansion and presented himself for the job.

62   "Are you familiar with the mountain goats of Colorado?" asked Lord Derby.

63   "Don't worry," replied the artist. "I was born in Colorado."

64   Because the artist was hungry, he did not say that he was born in a small town called Colorado (population three hundred) located in northeast Iowa and that he had never seen a mountain in his life. Lord Derby hired him on the spot, and Lady Derby showed him his room and his studio, gave him a tour of the grounds, and pointed out the mountain goat's favorite haunts.

65   The artist started work that very day. But the mountain goat of Colorado was more elusive than he'd ever dreamed she would be. It took him three months to make his preliminary sketches and another month to finish the picture. Eagerly he summoned Lord and Lady Derby to his studio. They stood and stared at the painting in silence.

66   "Well?" said the artist. "What do you think?"

67   "It's a goat all right," said Lord Derby, "but it's not my goat. My goat's horns are black with a stripe of gold and three fresh-water pearls twisted into them."

68   "Your goat moved so fast I couldn't get a good look at her horns," said the artist. "But that's a small mistake. Do you want me to start work on your portrait tomorrow?"

69   "Certainly not," said Lord Derby. "If you let a small mistake pass into your work, how can I trust you not to make a large one?"

70   *Moral:* The grass of fiction grows on the soil of fact. A single error can infect a whole story.

Content

1. Under what conditions is it preferable to tell the plain truth without adornment? When is it better to embed it in a story?

2. Willard's parables offer advice about writing, particularly about writing stories, true or fictional. Would all or most of the advice apply to all kinds of writing? Readers are expected to be able to make comparisons, analogies between the stories they hear and analogous real-life situations. How will you apply Willard's advice to your own writing?

3. Parables are designed to teach. Must a parable always offer advice, or are there other types of lessons one can learn from them?

Strategies/Structures

4. In what ways has Willard updated an ancient storytelling form? Compare Willard's parables with biblical parables or others you know.

5. If the point of a parable is obvious to the audience—and it is supposed to be apparent—why is it underscored with an explicitly stated "moral"? Is the storyteller afraid the audience will miss the point otherwise? Explain your answer.

6. Many kinds of writing employ narration, storytelling, as a way to help readers remember the subject and the points at hand, as "The Buzzard and Aesop's Fable" reminds us. Find some examples of other pieces in *The Essay Connection* that incorporate stories, and show how these work to reinforce the point.

7. Are there any exceptions to the moral Willard cites, "Show, don't tell. Information touches the mind, story sinks into the heart" (¶ 28)? Is it always true that "A single error can infect a whole story" (¶ 70)?

8. Why are parables always short? Can you think of any exceptions?

9. In some parables, animal characters are typecast by species-specific traits; foxes are crafty, rabbits are timid (but can run fast), and so on. Does Willard expect her readers to have preconceived connotations about her principal characters—"an attractive young magpie" (¶ 1), "a young parrot who longed to become a chef" (¶ 11), the two coyote brothers (¶s 43–56), the two sisters in "Two Sisters and a House"? If so, what are your preconceptions and how do they reinforce the stories in which these characters appear? Would the stories have been any different if different animals or people had been the principal characters in them?

Language

10. Why are readers willing to suspend their disbelief and allow animals to talk in fables? What's the effect of the conversational language Willard uses, even when it's spoken by "an attractive young magpie," "a young parrot who longed to become a chef," two sisters, even "a diamond"?

For Writing

11. With a partner, try writing a conversation in the casual language that people use informally. Bounce the dialogue back and forth out loud until it has the cadence and sounds of actual speech; you can tape it as you talk so you can hear what it sounds like. Then, provide a point to the conversation to give the dialogue focus.

12. Supply a suitable context for the conversation you've just created and see whether you can transform it into a parable. The structure of the story—its skeleton and conspicuous features—should lead to the ultimate point. You should then be able to state this as the moral.

EUDORA WELTY

Welty's editor at the *New Yorker*, William Maxwell, sums up her reputation, "I can't think of any American writer more universally acknowledged to be a great writer. Everybody—every *cat*— knows that Eudora Welty is a great writer." Yet Welty, winner of a Pulitzer Prize for her novel *The Optimist's Daughter* (1972), the Gold Medal award of the National Institute of Arts and Letters, and a Presidential Medal of Freedom, among other honors, retains her lifelong modesty and sense of humor. She still lives, writes, and gardens in the beloved home in Jackson, Mississippi, where she was born in 1909. She left town to attend college, transferring in 1927 from Mississippi State College for Women to the University of Wisconsin, where she earned a B.A. in 1929, followed by a year of graduate work in advertising at the Columbia University Graduate School of Business.

In the mid-1930s Welty traveled through "Depression-worn" Mississippi towns as a junior publicist for the Works Progress Administration. There she took the photographs that became the basis for *One Time, One Place: Mississippi in the Depression* (1971), but her record of small-town Mississippi life lingered in these "revelations of the instant. Like the flash of a camera, the record of a movement or an emotion is what fiction is, really" she says. She explains her career as a writer of short stories and fiction, including *A Curtain of Green* (1941), *The Wide Net* (1943), *Delta Wedding* (1946), *The Ponder Heart* (1952), and *Losing Battles* (1970) with a characteristically honest understatement, "I think I became a writer because I love stories. I never had any idea that I could be a professional writer. I'm now realizing, maybe the reason I first sent stories out to magazines was that I was too shy to show them to anybody I knew."

"In Love with Books" is from Welty's autobiography, *One Writer's Beginnings* (1983), which began as a series of three lectures at Harvard that memorably demonstrated the importance of "Listening," "Learning to See," and "Finding a Voice" in her development as a writer.

In Love with Books

I learned from the age of two or three that any room in our house, at any time of day, was there to read in, or to be read to. My mother read to me. She'd read to me in the big bedroom in the mornings, when we were in her rocker together, which ticked in rhythm as we rocked, as though we had a cricket accompanying the story. She'd read to me in the diningroom on winter afternoons in front of the coal fire, with our cuckoo clock ending the story with "Cuckoo," and at night when I'd got in my own bed. I must have given her no peace. Sometimes she read to me in the kitchen while she sat churning, and the churning sobbed along with *any* story. It was my ambition to have her read to me while *I* churned; once she granted my wish, but she read off my story before I brought her butter. She was an expressive reader. When she was reading "Puss in Boots," for instance, it was impossible not to know that she distrusted *all* cats.

It had been startling and disappointing to me to find out that story books had been written by *people*, that books were not natural wonders, coming up of themselves like grass. Yet regardless of where they came from, I cannot remember a time when I was not in love with them—with the books themselves, cover and binding and the paper they were printed on, with their smell and their weight and with their possession in my arms, captured and carried off to myself. Still illiterate, I was ready for them, committed to all the reading I could give them.

Neither of my parents had come from homes that could afford to buy many books, but though it must have been something of a strain on his salary, as the youngest officer in a young insurance company, my father was all the while carefully selecting and ordering away for what he and Mother thought we children should grow up with. They bought first for the future.

Besides the bookcase in the livingroom, which was always called "the library," there were the encyclopedia tables and dictionary stand under windows in our diningroom. Here to help us grow up arguing around the diningroom table were the Unabridged Webster, the Columbia Encyclopedia, Compton's Pictured Encyclopedia, the Lincoln Library of Information, and later the Book of Knowledge. And the year we moved into our new house, there was room to celebrate it with the new 1925 edition of the Britannica, which my father, his face always deliberately turned toward the future, was of course disposed to think better than any previous edition.

5   In "the library," inside the mission-style bookcase with its three diamond-latticed glass doors, with my father's Morris chair and the glass-shaded lamp on its table beside it, were books I could soon begin on—and I did, reading them all alike and as they came, straight down their rows, top shelf to bottom. There was the set of Stoddard's lectures, in all its late nineteenth-century vocabulary and vignettes of peasant life and quaint beliefs and customs, with matching halftone illustrations: Vesuvius erupting, Venice by moonlight, gypsies glimpsed by their camp-fires. I didn't know then the clue they were to my father's longing to see the rest of the world. I read straight through his other love-from-afar: the Victrola Book of the Opera, with opera after opera in synopsis, with portraits in costume of Melba, Caruso, Galli-Curci, and Geraldine Farrar, some of whose voices we could listen to on our Red Seal records.

6   My mother read secondarily for information; she sank as a hedonist into novels. She read Dickens in the spirit in which she would have eloped with him. The novels of her girlhood that had stayed on in her imagination, besides those of Dickens and Scott and Robert Louis Stevenson, were *Jane Eyre, Trilby, The Woman in White, Green Mansions, King Solomon's Mines.* Marie Corelli's name would crop up but I understood she had gone out of favor with my mother, who had only kept *Ardath* out of loyalty. In time she absorbed herself in Galsworthy, Edith Wharton, above all in Thomas Mann of the *Joseph* volumes.

7   *St. Elmo* was not in our house; I saw it often in other houses. This wildly popular Southern novel is where all the Edna Earles in our population started coming from. They're all named for the heroine, who succeeded in bringing a dissolute, sinning roué and atheist of a lover (St. Elmo) to his knees. My mother was able to forgo it. But she remembered the classic advice given to rose growers on how to water their bushes long enough: "Take a chair and *St. Elmo.*"

8   To both my parents I owe my early acquaintance with a beloved Mark Twain. There was a full set of Mark Twain and a

short set of Ring Lardner in our bookcase, and those were the volumes that in time united us all, parents and children.

Reading everything that stood before me was how I came 9
upon a worn old book without a back that had belonged to my
father as a child. It was called *Sanford and Merton*. Is there anyone
left who recognizes it, I wonder? It is the famous moral tale written
by Thomas Day in the 1780s, but of him no mention is made
on the title page of this book; here it is *Sanford and Merton in Words
of One Syllable* by Mary Godolphin. Here are the rich boy and the
poor boy and Mr. Barlow, their teacher and interlocutor, in long
discourses alternating with dramatic scenes—danger and rescue
allotted to the rich and the poor respectively. It may have only
words of one syllable, but one of them is "quoth." It ends with not
one but two morals, both engraved on rings: "Do what you
ought, come what may," and "If we would be great, we must first
learn to be good."

This book was lacking its front cover, the back held on by 10
strips of pasted paper, now turned golden, in several layers, and
the pages stained, flecked, and tattered around the edges; its
garish illustrations had come unattached but were preserved, laid
in. I had the feeling even in my heedless childhood that this was
the only book my father as a little boy had had of his own. He had
held onto it, and might have gone to sleep on its coverless face: he
had lost his mother when he was seven. My father had never
made any mention to his own children of the book, but he had
brought it along with him from Ohio to our house and shelved it
in our bookcase.

My mother had brought from West Virginia that set of 11
Dickens; those books looked sad, too—they had been through fire
and water before I was born, she told me, and there they were,
lined up—as I later realized, waiting for *me*.

I was presented, from as early as I can remember, with books 12
of my own, which appeared on my birthday and Christmas morning.
Indeed, my parents could not give me books enough. They
must have sacrificed to give me on my sixth or seventh birthday—
it was after I became a reader for myself—the ten-volume set of
Our Wonder World. These were beautifully made, heavy books I
would lie down with on the floor in front of the diningroom
hearth, and more often than the rest volume 5, *Every Child's Story*

Book, was under my eyes. There were the fairy tales—Grimm, Andersen, the English, the French, "Ali Baba and the Forty Thieves"; and there was Aesop and Reynard the Fox; there were the myths and legends, Robin Hood, King Arthur, and St. George and the Dragon, even the history of Joan of Arc; a whack of *Pilgrim's Progress* and a long piece of *Gulliver.* They all carried their classic illustrations. I located myself in these pages and could go straight to the stories and pictures I loved; very often "The Yellow Dwarf" was first choice, with Walter Crane's Yellow Dwarf in full color making his terrifying appearance flanked by turkeys. Now that volume is as worn and backless and hanging apart as my father's poor *Sanford and Merton.* The precious page with Edward Lear's "Jumblies" on it has been in danger of slipping out for all these years. One measure of my love for Our Wonder World was that for a long time I wondered if I would go through fire and water for it as my mother had done for Charles Dickens; and the only comfort was to think I could ask my mother to do it for me.

13   I believe I'm the only child I know of who grew up with this treasure in the house. I used to ask others, "Did you have Our Wonder World?" I'd have to tell them the Book of Knowledge could not hold a candle to it.

14   I live in gratitude to my parents for initiating me—and as early as I begged for it, without keeping me waiting—into knowledge of the word, into reading and spelling, by way of the alphabet. They taught it to me at home in time for me to begin to read before starting to school. I believe the alphabet is no longer considered an essential piece of equipment for traveling through life. In my day it was the keystone to knowledge. You learned the alphabet as you learned to count to ten, as you learned "Now I lay me" and the Lord's Prayer and your father's and mother's name and address and telephone number, all in case you were lost.

15   My love for the alphabet, which endures, grew out of reciting it but, before that, out of seeing the letters on the page. In my own story books, before I could read them for myself, I fell in love with various winding, enchanted-looking initials drawn by Walter Crane at the heads of fairy tales. In "Once up a time," an "O" had a rabbit running it as a treadmill, his feet upon flowers. When the day came, years later, for me to see the Book of Kells, all the wizardry of letter, initial, and word swept over me a thousand times

over, and the illumination, the gold, seemed a part of the world's beauty and holiness that had been there from the start.

Content

1. Most professional writers of quality have been in love with books since childhood. Why?
2. How can parents encourage their children to become avid readers? What are the benefits of this process?
3. What else does Welty's adoration of books as a child reveal about her as a person? What does her discussion of how she came to know and love books reveal about her parents?

Strategies/Structures

4. Throughout the essay Welty describes the context in which she encountered the books she loved; why are these contexts important?
5. Welty refers to several books that people don't read anymore, such as *St. Elmo* and *Sanford and Merton*—perhaps even *Pilgrim's Progress*. How can her readers understand what's she's talking about if they haven't read the books?

Language

6. Comment on Welty's rich, embellished language in the last paragraph. How does it fit the subject?

For Writing

7. If you love to read, write an essay for an audience of television viewers explaining the joys of reading, either in general or with reference to particular kinds of books or other materials. See also Wright, "The Power of Books" (425–35).
8. Describe your ideal collection of books, general or specialized, either as a child or as an adult. Let your readers see, as Welty does, why your favorites are so treasured.
9. See the suggestion for writing (#8) in connection with Kozol's essay, "The Human Cost of an Illiterate Society" (283–94).

2 The Essay, a Vision: Definition and Reasons for Writing

There are two sorts of essays in this book, essays of literary nonfiction (sometimes called *literature of fact,* or *creative nonfiction,* or *belletristic essays*) and articles. In essays of literary nonfiction, the writer's artistry is paramount, illuminated by, as Elizabeth Hardwick says, an "individual intelligence and sparkle. We consent to watch a mind at work, without agreement often, but only for pleasure." Essays of literary nonfiction, which some people claim are the only true essays, are short prose pieces that use many of the same techniques that fiction does. They can present characters in action, in dialogue (even in interior monologue), in context, and in costume. They can play with time, with language, with points of view, and with narrative persona. As professional essayist E. B. White claims in "The Essayist and the Essay" (44–47), an essayist "can pull on any sort of shirt, be any sort of person, according to his mood or his subject matter—philosopher, scold, jester, raconteur, confidant, pundit, devil's advocate, enthusiast."

According to this view, the essay, says Annie Dillard, herself an essayist, "can do everything a poem can do, and everything a short story can do—everything but fake it. The elements in any nonfiction should be true not only artistically, the connections must hold at base and must be veracious," for essayists claim and readers believe that what they're reading is the truth. As Dillard says, "There's a lot of truth out there to work with. The real world arguably exerts a greater fascination on people than any fictional one. . . . The essayist thinks about actual things. He can make sense of them analytically or artistically."

The Essay Connection includes many types of essays of literary nonfiction: *memoir* and *partial autobiography*, such as Scott Russell Sanders's "Under the Influence" (441–56); *character sketches*, among them Leslie S. Moore's "Framing My Father" (301–08); *descriptions of a place*, as in Cynthia Ozick's "A Drugstore Eden" (316–30), or of *an experience*, such as the excerpts from Zitkala-Sa's *The School Days of an Indian Girl* (273–83); *narratives of events*, including Frederick Douglass's account of how he stood up to his cruel overseer ("You have seen how a man was made a slave; you shall see how a slave was made a man.") (164–70); *interpretive reviews* that comment at length on a work or a performance, as in Gilbert Highet's "The Gettysburg Address" (691–98); and *social commentary*, such as Jonathan Kozol's "The Human Cost of an Illiterate Society" (283–94) and Mike Rose's "'I Just Wanna Be Average'" (263–73).

Articles, in contrast, claims critic William Gass, are more concerned with substance than with style, for charm and elegance "will interfere with the impression of seriousness" they wish to maintain. An article, Gass continues, "must appear complete and straightforward and footnoted and useful and certain," for the article "pretends that everything is clear, that its argument is unassailable, that there are no soggy patches, no illicit interferences." Articles, he says, are written by professionals whose personality is unobtrusive in academic prose that "sounds like writing written down" rather than spoken aloud.

Although Gass clearly prefers essays to articles, he is also exaggerating the case to make his point. Indeed, much of your writing in college will be articles in the language and conventions of the particular subjects you study—critical interpretations of literature, position papers in philosophy or political science, interpretive presentations of information in history, case histories in psychology or business or law, explanations of processes in computer science or auto mechanics. For instance Thomas S. Kuhn's "The Route to Normal Science" (221–33) explains and interprets the complex process of how scientists do their work, while in the course of explaining what's "Inside the Engine" (233–40), master mechanics Tom and Ray Magliozzi tell readers how and why motor oil keeps the engine humming smoothly. Dr. Martin Luther

King, Jr., in "Letter from Birmingham Jail" (596–616) uses evidence from world religions, his own life experience and that of numerous other African-Americans, theology, history and the law to make the case for civil disobedience. And Stephanie Coontz interprets American public policy as it affects numerous aspects of everyday life from home mortgages to education subsidies to show how such policy makes the vast American middle class "A Nation of Welfare Families" (294–301).

Gass's preference for essays notwithstanding, articles such as these do not have to be dry, dull, and devoid of a point of view. For instance, the science writings of Isaac Asimov (208–20), Vicki Hearne (560–72), and Natalie Angier (381–88) are known for their reader-friendly clarity as well as their absolute accuracy. And we can count on them to have a point of view—Angier invariably favors what is moderate and healthful. Even academic essays don't have to be deadly serious (or dull), plodding along under the weight of obscure jargon. Both Brenda Murphy's "Willy Loman: Icon of Business Culture" (741–52) and Valerie M. Smith's "Death of a Salesman's Wife" (752–58) are clear, interesting, and to the point. Who would have known, if Murphy's historical research hadn't told us, that, for instance, businessmen's organizations were so offended by Arthur Miller's presentation of the defeated salesman that they mounted counter-offensive propaganda campaigns?

Why a person writes often determines his or her point of view on a particular subject. George Orwell claims that people write for four main reasons: "sheer egoism," "esthetic enthusiasm," "historical impulse," and—his primary motive—"political purpose, the desire to push the world in a certain direction." Joan Didion, echoing Orwell, believes that writers are always pushing and nagging and tugging at their readers, saying *"listen to me, see it my way, change your mind."* In "Why I Write: Making No Become Yes" (53–60), Elie Wiesel interprets *"see it my way,"* as the role of the writer as witness. The survivor of imprisonment in several Nazi concentration camps, Wiesel explains, "I was duty-bound to give meaning to my survival, to justify each moment of my life. . . . Not to transmit an experience is to betray it." In this eloquent essay Wiesel, winner of the 1986 Nobel Peace Prize, demonstrates his continuing commitment to make survivors, the entire world, continually remember the meaning of the Holocaust: "Why do I write? To wrench those victims from oblivion. To help the dead vanquish death."

If you wish, you can use the definitions of *essay* and *article* provided here. Or for simplicity's sake you can consider all the writings in this book to be *essays*. No matter what you call them, we hope you'll find them engaging, provocative, stimulating examples of minds at work, ideas at play, artistry in action.

E. B. WHITE

Born in peaceful Mount Vernon, New York, in 1899, White was editor of the Cornell *Daily Sun* during his senior year in college, 1920–1921. In 1927, he joined the staff of the year-old *New Yorker*, writing "Talk of the Town" and "Notes and Comments" columns. Over the next thirty years he also wrote an estimated thirty thousand witty rejoinders to "newsbreaks," mangled sentences and misprints that filled out *New Yorker* columns and appeared under headings that White invented, such as "Letters We Never Finished Reading." In 1957 the Whites moved permanently to Allen Cove, Maine, where White wrote until his death in 1985. His distinguished works include the essays collected in *One Man's Meat* (1944), *The Second Tree from the Corner* (1954), and *The Points of My Compass* (1962); landmark advice on how to write clear, plain prose, *The Elements of Style* (rev. 1973), with his Cornell professor, William Strunk; and three classic children's books, *Stuart Little* (1945), *Charlotte's Web* (1952), and *The Trumpet of the Swan* (1970).

In this essay White amplifies upon Samuel Johnson's definition of the familiar, personal essay as "an irregular, undigested piece" of writing. He underestimates the skill of essayists, including himself, in considering them self-consigned to "second-class citizenship" in comparison with novelists, poets, and playwrights. In fact, the essays in this book are skillful works of thought and art, carefully controlled in structure, substance, language, and tone. In many essays the writer appears as a character or persona in his or her own work, speaking in a distinctive voice and interpreting the subject from an equally individualist—some would say idiosyncratic—point of view, as White does here and in all of his essays.

The Essayist and the Essay[1]

1   The essayist is a self-liberated man, sustained by the childish belief that everything he thinks about, everything that happens to him, is of general interest. He is a fellow who thoroughly enjoys his work, just as people who take bird walks enjoy theirs.

---

[1] Title supplied.

Each new excursion of the essayist, each new "attempt," differs
from the last and takes him into new country. This delights him.
Only a person who is congenitally self-centered has the effrontery
and the stamina to write essays.

There are as many kinds of essays as there are human atti-   2
tudes or poses, as many essay flavors as there are Howard Johnson
ice creams. The essayist arises in the morning and, if he has work
to do, selects his garb from an unusually extensive wardrobe: he
can pull on any sort of shirt, be any sort of person, according to his
mood or his subject matter—philosopher, scold, jester, raconteur,
confidant, pundit, devil's advocate, enthusiast. I like the essay,
have always liked it, and even as a child was at work, attempting
to inflict my young thoughts and experiences on others by putting
them on paper. I early broke into print in the pages of *St. Nicholas.*
I tend still to fall back on the essay form (or lack of form) when an
idea strikes me, but I am not fooled about the place of the essay in
twentieth-century American letters—it stands a short distance
down the line. The essayist, unlike the novelist, the poet, and the
playwright, must be content in his self-imposed role of second-
class citizen. A writer who has his sights trained on the Nobel
Prize or other earthly triumphs had best write a novel, a poem, or
a play and leave the essayist to ramble about, content with living
a free life and enjoying the satisfactions of a somewhat undisciplined existence. (Dr. Johnson called the essay "an irregular, undigested piece"; this happy practitioner has no wish to quarrel
with the good doctor's characterization.)

There is one thing the essayist cannot do, though—he cannot   3
indulge himself in deceit or in concealment, for he will be found
out in no time. Desmond MacCarthy, in his introductory remarks
to the 1928 E. P. Dutton & Company edition of Montaigne, observes that Montaigne "had the gift of natural candour. . . ." It is
the basic ingredient. And even the essayist's escape from discipline is only a partial escape: the essay, although a relaxed form,
imposes its own disciplines, raises its own problems, and these
disciplines and problems soon become apparent and (we all hope)
act as a deterrent to anyone wielding a pen merely because he en-
tertains random thoughts or is in a happy or wandering mood.

I think some people find the essay the last resort of the egoist,   4
a much too self-conscious and self-serving form for their taste;
they feel that it is presumptuous of a writer to assume that his little

excursions or his small observations will interest the reader. There is some justice in their complaint. I have always been aware that I am by nature self-absorbed and egoistical; to write of myself to the extent I have done indicates a too great attention to my own life, not enough to the lives of others. I have worn many shirts, and not all of them have been a good fit. But when I am discouraged or downcast I need only fling open the door of my closet, and there, hidden behind everything else, hangs the mantle of Michel de Montaigne, smelling slightly of camphor.

Content

1. How can the writer avoid the deceit or concealment that White says is impossible for an essayist, and nevertheless engage in any sort of pose he wants, as White claims in paragraph 2?

2. If you are familiar with some of the essays in this book, refer to them in commenting on White's assertion that essayists are "by nature self-absorbed and egoistical" (¶ 4).

Strategies/Structures

3. What kind of a person does White appear to be in this essay? Does he in fact seem to be "self-absorbed and egoistical"? Does he seem to be the sort of person who would write essays, as he defines them?

Language

4. White refers to essayists as self-imposed second-class citizens (¶ 2). Explain why you agree or disagree.

5. Is the essay "an irregular, undigested piece," as Dr. Samuel Johnson remarked, or expressive of "a ramble" through "a free life . . . of a somewhat undisciplined existence"?

For Writing

6. Like love, the essay may be a form that everyone recognizes but that is hard to define; like love, the essay may have as many definitions as there are practitioners. For readers and writers of essays, write a definition of the essay that is broad enough to encompass some of its characteristic types.

7. Explain how an essay is a work of revelation, concealment, and shaping (or manipulation) of facts. Use a specific essay, preferably one from *The Essay Connection*, to illustrate your analysis.

LOUISE ERDRICH

Erdrich, a poet and novelist, writes out of her heritage. She was born in 1954 in Little Falls, Minnesota, the daughter of a Chippewa nation mother and a German-American father who taught for the Bureau of Indian Affairs. Erdrich graduated from Dartmouth College in 1976, a member of the first class that admitted women, and earned an M.A. from Johns Hopkins University in 1979. Returning to Dartmouth as writer-in-residence, she collaborated with Michael Dorris, first director of Dartmouth's Native American studies department, on a prize-winning short story, "The World's Greatest Fisherman," which the couple later expanded as *Love Medicine* (1984, again expanded 1993). Erdrich subsequently published two other volumes of this prize-winning trilogy, *The Beet Queen* (1986) and *Tracks* (1988).

Erdrich and Dorris married in 1981; they collaborated on Dorris's *A Yellow Raft in Blue Water* (1988)—about his adoption of a child with learning disabilities as a result of Fetal Alcohol Syndrome—and on other works. Their unusual collaborative process left confusion about who actually was the author, although the couple was very clear about how they worked. Whoever had the original idea for the book wrote the first draft and was identified as the author; the other person edited it and another draft was written; then they repeated the process five or six more times. Finally they read the entire work aloud, never allowing a single manuscript to leave their home without, as Dorris said, "consensus on every word."

The appearance of ideal collaboration, indeed of a blissful though complicated life, is sustained throughout *The Blue Jay's Dance: A Birth Year* (1995), of which "Leap Day, the Baby-sitter, Dream, and Walking" are sections. In Erdrich's book about the process of being, concurrently and inseparably, a mother and a writer, the baby is a composite of the couple's youngest three children whom Erdrich "cared for in a series of writing offices" in a household on a New Hampshire farm with three older adopted Native American children. "I am not . . . the best or worst mother," says Erdrich, "but a writer only, a woman constantly surprised." Of enormous surprise—and sorrow—to the couple's close friends as well as their reading public was Dorris's suicide in 1997.

Leap Day, the Baby-sitter, Dream, Walking

Leap Day

1   As I write this, my left hand rests lightly on baby's back. She's trying to sleep but doesn't want me to put her down. With two fingers, I stroke the hair above her aching ear. If I take the fingers away, she wakes, she wails, as if my hand served a medicinal purpose. My arm below the elbow feels enormous, throbs with blood, seems almost to hum with electricity. It's a toss-up which will first lose consciousness: my arm or her head. At her inoculation last week, our four-year-old shrieked in surprise at the sudden pain of the needle. Then, to take the hurt away, she put the sting against my bare arm, held our skin together. Her tears stopped. My flesh still had magic. I could absorb her pain by touch.

The Baby-sitter

2   As our baby grows more into her own life, so I recover mine, but it is an ambiguous blessing. With one hand I drag the pen across the page and with the other, the other hand, I cannot let go of hers. There comes a day when we're at odds. I look at her, she looks at me. I put her down in a playpen filled with toys but she wants me and me alone after five minutes. I take her from the playpen, hold her, but she's not a lap baby for long anymore and wants to move, move anywhere. Soon she is bumping, creeping, undulating, standing, making her way through the little house on a hazardous obstacle course of delight.

There is a time in a baby's life when parents practically live   3
at a crouch. She wants to move no matter what, to engage with
the world. She is not a sleeper, but naps in short drops and then
is ready for the adventure of me. I've just begun a thought, I'm
writing my way in, when she laughs herself awake and bolts up,
expectant, her grin wide, her eyes wild and magnetic, and electricity of hope rising off her, a thrill of mirth.

Her smile is so touching, so alight. I put my head down on   4
my desk and within the dark cave of my hands a shout gathers.
I'm at the moment. I will turn to her and lay aside this story, but
with loss. I will play with her but part of me won't be there. Conflict has entered our perfect circle in a new set of clothes, and I'm
torn between wanting to be with her always and needing to be—
through writing and through concentration—who I am.

How perfectly, how generously she fits into my arms, how   5
comfortably I receive her. How unsurpassed and fine. She props
herself up on a chair and roams it, standing and dragging herself
around its edges, nearly pulling it over onto herself. She dives for
the woodstove tongs. I lunge after her, remove them. She creeps
for the light socket. I divert her. She tries eagerly to stuff carpet
lint, shoelaces, marbles, cat foot, dustpan, bark, paper clip, fork,
ancient noodle, the cat herself, gravel, shoe, mop board, book, toy
into her mouth. I remove these things from her spit damp fists.
She makes for me, won't let me hold her. Goes hell-bent for the
bathroom where she once found a toilet pond. She goes after table
legs with teeth, puts her hands under rockers, grabs, clutches,
falls, screams, goes blue, comes up laughing in my arms.

When she's had enough and I can nurse her, when she's tense   6
with eager hunger in my arms and then quieter, quieter, regrouping
for her next set of bold charges and forays, when at last I can hold
her for a space of time, I finally talk. I finally tell her I need help.

The first half day with the baby-sitter is a misery. Jean is a kind   7
and forthright woman licensed for day care in her home. A small
mother with dark eyes and a sweet smile, a woman who had been
caring for babies for many years, even Jean is surprised by how
long our baby manages to cry. Scream. Wail. Fret. I know the water
torture and I hope Jean can wait it out. One hour. Another half.
Two. My breasts burn, blood pumps hard in my temples. I call.

Behind Jean's voice our baby's roar, continual and harsh as the sea, breaks and falls, over and over.

8   I get into the car and pick baby up. The experiment is not repeated for a short while—then, then, the change. A hard week of teething, the first sudden breakthrough in language, and we try again. Little by little, she looks forward to this new routine. It happens. One day a week, two, finally three, she grows more out of my life and into her own.

9   The hours stretch wide on the mornings I work alone. Time expands in a blue haze. I am lighter, fuller, ballooning with stunned surprise. I constantly possess the feeling we usually have only momentarily, the where-was-I that causes us to slap at our foreheads. I'm trying to jostle out the thoughts. *Where was I? Where was I?* Of course, I know. I was in an ambiguous heaven, a paradise both difficult and temporary, the only kind on earth we know.

10   I ease into the day making noise, banging the tea kettle, rich in my aloneness again. Outside, the hoarfrost glitters, chickadees flip through the air, the weeds and branches of the trees are outlines with a fine brilliance. I am ready now to finish this book of scraps, of jottings, of notes and devotions taken at another time, another era in our lives. The little cat reclaims my lap and curls possessively beneath my hands, as I begin. . . .

Dream

11 One day, one night, I'll dream a dream, perhaps like any other dream, except that I won't know it is the last dream of my life.

12 I am keeping track for baby, waiting for her to dream something that she can put into words. There are spaces on the baby calendar for the first tooth, the first smile, the first word, but nowhere to record the first dream. I leave space in the margins and wait. She has been dreaming all along, there is no question watching her face complex in sleep, her eyes moving under delicate, violet-pink, sunrise lids.

13   Grand elk moving underneath the grand sky. Tyrant blue jays. Cats loping bannerlike across the fields. Moths fanning their pale wings against the light. Spiders. Brown recluse, marked like a violin. The beating of a heart perhaps, moving in, moving out.

My own voice—perhaps she dreams my own voice as I dream hers—starting out of sleep, awake, certain that she's cried out.

For years now I have been dreaming the powerful anxiety dreams of all parents. Something is lost, something must be protected. A baby swims in an aquarium, a baby sleeps in a suitcase. The suitcase goes astray, the airline company will not return it. I spend all night arguing with people at a baggage claims desk. Parents endure exhausting nights searching drawers and running through corridors and town streets and emptying laundry baskets looking for their missing babies. Mine is hiding in a washing machine or behind a Corinthian column or out in the long grass, the endless grass. Mine is running toward the nameless sky.

Now, as I move into the pages of manuscripts, I fall asleep anxious but embark on no tiring searches through piles of bricks and trains stations. The dream junk and dream treasure, the excess bliss and paranoia, goes into the pages of books. I do not dream when I am writing.

Walking

To pull herself upright, to strain upward, to climb, has been baby's obsession for the past three months and now, on her first birthday, it is that urge I celebrate and fear. She has pulled herself erect by the strings of her sister's hair, by using my clothes, hands, earrings, by the edges and the rungs and the unstable handles of the world. She has yanked herself up, stepped, and it is clear from her grand excitement that walking is one of the most important things we ever do. It is raw power to go forward, to lunge, catching at important arms and hands, to take control of the body, tell it what to do, to leave behind the immobility of babyhood. With each step she swells, her breath goes ragged and her eyes darken in a shine of happiness. A glaze of physical joy covers her, moves through her, more intense than the banged forehead, bumped chin, the bruises and knocks and losses, even than the breathtaking falls and solid thumps, joy more powerful than good sense.

It would seem she has everything she could want—she is fed, she is carried, she is rocked, put to sleep. But no, *walking* is the thing, the consuming urge to seize control. She has to walk to gain entrance to the world. From now on, she will get from here to there more and more by her own effort. As she goes, she will notice worn grass, shops or snow or the shapes of trees. She will walk for reasons other than to get somewhere in particular. She'll walk to think or not to think, to leave the body, which is often the same as becoming at one with it. She will walk to ward off anger in its many forms. For pleasure, purpose, or to grieve. She'll walk until her feet hurt, her muscles tremble, until her eyes are numb with looking. She'll walk until her sense of balance is the one thing left and the rest of the world is balanced, too, and eventually, if we do the growing up right, she will walk away from us.

Content

1. How, if at all, is it possible to combine the demands of parenting a very young child with the demands of being a writer? What qualities are needed for performing each role? Are these demands at all compatible? If so, in what ways? If not, why not?

2. Would a father's answer to question 1 be any different than a mother's? Why or why not?

3. What does Erdrich mean when she says, "The dream junk and dream treasure, the excess bliss and paranoia, goes into the pages of books. I do not dream when I am writing" (¶ 15)?

Strategies/Structures

4. "Leap Day" has one paragraph, "The Baby-sitter" has nine, "Dream" has five, and "Walking" has two. Is each section self-contained? Why or why not?

5. Although each section focuses on the topic of its title, each subsequent section gains in perspective and complexity from its predecessors. Explain how organization of prior sections enables the enrichment of succeeding sections. Should Erdrich have tried to make the sections equal in length?

6. Could the sections have been arranged in any other order? Why or why not?

Language

7. Writing about babies, small children, and other little things (tiny objects, small animals) often elicits sentimental (overly emotional) language from the writer, who expects the reader to respond with equal sentimentality. Is this desirable? Why or why not?

8. Does Erdrich treat her subject sentimentally (don't confuse *sentimentality* with *sentiment*)? If so, where, and with what effect? If not, why not? What are the effects of straightforward (though loving) writing on a potentially sentimental topic?

For Writing

9. It is clear that Erdrich loves her baby, and that she also loves writing: "As our baby grows more into her own life, so I recover mine, but it is an ambiguous blessing. With one hand I drag the pen across the page and with the other, the other hand, I cannot let go of hers" (¶ 2). How is it possible to devote appropriate time and thought to writing (or to any other compelling creative endeavor—say, that of playing an instrument or playing a sport) amidst life's other demands? Determine what's most important in your life and work out a plan to balance two or three competitive, perhaps conflicting, demands on your time, thought, and energy. (For a variety of perspectives, see the essays in Part I, and also Richard Wright's "The Power of Books" (425–35) and Judy Brady's "I Want a Wife" (506–10).)

10. Erdrich says, "The dream junk and dream treasure, the excess bliss and paranoia, goes into the pages of books" (¶ 15). How can a writer, in particular, sort out the "dream junk" from the "dream treasure"? At what stage in your writing does this sorting occur—before or during the writing of a particular draft? What do you need to enable you to do your best work—of any kind? Make a list (with the most important items at the top) and explain the order of the list and why each item is necessary.

ELIE WIESEL

Wiesel, a survivor of the Holocaust, explains, "For me, literature abolishes the gap between [childhood and death]. . . . Auschwitz marks the decisive, ultimate turning point . . . of the human adventure. Nothing will ever again be as it was. Thousands and thousands of deaths weigh upon every word. How speak of redemption after Treblinka? and how speak of anything else?" As a survivor, he became a writer in order to become a witness: "I believed that, having survived by chance, I was duty-bound to give meaning to my survival, to justify each moment of my life. I knew the story had to be told. Not to transmit an experience is to betray it." Wiesel has developed a literary style that reflects the distilled experience of concentration camps, in which "a sentence is worth a page, a word is worth a sentence. The unspoken weighs heavier than the spoken. . . . Say only the essential—say only what no other would say . . . a style sharp, hard, strong, in a word, pared. Suppress the imagination. And feeling, and philosophy. Speak as a witness on the stand speaks. With no indulgence to others or oneself."

In May 1944, when he was fifteen, Wiesel was forcibly removed from his native town of Sighet, Hungary ("which no longer exists," he says, "except in the memory of those it expelled"), to the first of several concentration camps. Although six million Jews died in the camps, including members of his family, Wiesel was liberated from Buchenwald in April 1945 and sent to Paris, where he studied philosophy. For twenty years "of exploration and apprenticeship" he worked as a journalist for Jewish newspapers, but the turning point in his career as a writer came in 1954 when he met novelist François Mauriac, who urged him to speak on behalf of the children in concentration camps. This encouraged Wiesel (who has lived in New York since 1956) to write some thirty books of fiction, nonfiction, poetry, and drama, starting in 1958 with *Night*, which opens, "In the beginning was faith, confidence, illusion." Wiesel, true citizen of the world, has been named to the French Legion of Honor, has been awarded a Congressional Gold Medal, and has received innumerable literary and humanitarian honors, including the Council of Jewish Organizations' Humanitarian of the Century award. In 1986 this "messenger to mankind" received the Nobel Peace Prize for his efforts epitomized in "Why I Write: Making No Become Yes," originally published in the *New York Times Book Review,* April 14, 1986.

Why I Write:
Making No Become Yes

1   Why do I write?

2   Perhaps in order not to go mad. Or, on the contrary, to touch the bottom of madness. Like Samuel Beckett, the survivor expresses himself "en désepoir de cause"—out of desperation.

3   Speaking of the solitude of the survivor, the great Yiddish and Hebrew poet and thinker Aaron Zeitlin addresses those—his father, his brother, his friends—who have died and left him: "You

have abandoned me," he says to them. "You are together, without me. I am here. Alone. And I make words."

So do I, just like him. I also say words, write words, reluctantly.   4

There are easier occupations, far more pleasant ones. But   5
for the survivor, writing is not a profession, but an occupation, a duty. Camus calls it "an honor." As he puts it: "I entered literature through worship." Other writers have said they did so through anger, through love. Speaking for myself, I would say— through silence.

It was by seeking, by probing silence that I began to dis-   6
cover the perils and power of the word. I never intended to be a philosopher, or a theologian. The only role I sought was that of witness. I believed that, having survived by chance, I was duty-bound to give meaning to my survival, to justify each moment of my life. I knew the story had to be told. Not to transmit an experience is to betray it. This is what Jewish tradition teaches us. But how to do this? "When Israel is in exile, so is the word," says the Zohar. The word has deserted the meaning it was intended to convey—impossible to make them coincide. The displacement, the shift, is irrevocable.

This was never more true than right after the upheaval. We   7
all knew that we could never, never say what had to be said, that we could never express in words, coherent, intelligible words, our experience of madness on an absolute scale. The walk through flaming night, the silence before and after the selection, the mo notonous praying of the condemned, the Kaddish of the dying, the fear and hunger of the sick, the shame and suffering, the haunted eyes, the demented stares. I thought that I would never be able to speak of them. All words seemed inadequate, worn, foolish, lifeless, whereas I wanted them to be searing.

Where was I to discover a fresh vocabulary, a primeval lan-   8
guage? The language of night was not human, it was primitive, almost animal—hoarse shouting, screams, muffled moaning, savage howling, the sound of beating. A brute strikes out wildly, a body falls. An officer raises his arm and a whole community walks toward a common grave. A soldier shrugs his shoulders, and a thousand families are torn apart, to be reunited only by death. This was the concentration camp language. It negated all other language and took its place. Rather than a link, it became a

wall. Could it be surmounted? Could the reader be brought to the other side? I knew the answer was negative, and yet I knew that "no" had to become "yes." It was the last wish of the dead.

9   The fear of forgetting remains the main obsession of all those who have passed through the universe of the damned. The enemy counted on people's incredulity and forgetfulness. How could one foil this plot? And if memory grew hollow, empty of substance, what would happen to all we had accumulated along the way? Remember, said the father to his son, and the son to his friend. Gather the names, the faces, the tears. We had all taken an oath: "If, by some miracle, I emerge alive, I will devote my life to testifying on behalf of those whose shadow will fall on mine forever and ever."

10   That is why I write certain things rather than others—to remain faithful.

11   Of course, there are times of doubt for the survivor, times when one gives in to weakness, or longs for comfort. I hear a voice within me telling me to stop mourning the past. I too want to sing of love and of its magic. I too want to celebrate the sun, and the dawn that heralds the sun. I would like to shout, and shout loudly: "Listen, listen well! I too am capable of victory, do you hear? I too am open to laughter and joy! I want to stride, head high, my face unguarded, without having to point to the ashes over there on the horizon, without having to tamper with facts to hide their tragic ugliness. For a man born blind, God himself is blind, but look, I see, I am not blind." One feels like shouting this, but the shout changes to a murmur. One must make a choice; one must remain faithful. A big word, I know. Nevertheless, I use it, it suits me. Having written the things I have written, I feel I can afford no longer to play with words. If I say that the writer in me wants to remain loyal, it is because it is true. This sentiment moves all survivors; they owe nothing to anyone, but everything to the dead.

12   I owe them my roots and my memory. I am duty-bound to serve as their emissary, transmitting the history of their disappearance, even if it disturbs, even if it brings pain. Not to do so would be to betray them, and thus myself. And since I am incapable of communicating their cry by shouting, I simply look at them. I see them and I write.

13   While writing, I question them as I question myself. I believe I have said it before, elsewhere. I write to understand as much as

to be understood. Will I succeed one day? Wherever one starts, one reaches darkness. God? He remains the God of darkness. Man? The source of darkness. The killers' derision, their victims' tears, the onlookers' indifference, their complicity and complacency— the divine role in all that I do not understand. A million children massacred—I shall never understand.

Jewish children—they haunt my writings. I see them again 14 and again. I shall always see them. Hounded, humiliated, bent like the old men who surround them as though to protect them, unable to do so. They are thirsty, the children, and there is no one to give them water. They are hungry, but there is no one to give them a crust of bread. They are afraid, and there is no one to re-assure them.

They walk in the middle of the road, like vagabonds. They are 15 on the way to the station, and they will never return. In sealed cars, without air or food, they travel toward another world. They guess where they are going, they know it, and they keep silent. Tense, thoughtful, they listen to the wind, the call of death in the distance.

All these children, these old people, I see them. I never stop 16 seeing them. I belong to them.

But they, to whom do they belong? 17

People tend to think that a murderer weakens when facing 18 a child. The child reawakens the killer's lost humanity. The killer can no longer kill the child before him, the child inside him.

But with us it happened differently. Our Jewish children had 19 no effect upon the killers. Nor upon the world. Nor upon God.

I think of them, I think of their childhood. Their childhood 20 is a small Jewish town, and this town is no more. They frighten me; they reflect an image of myself, one that I pursue and run from at the same time—the image of a Jewish adolescent who knew no fear, except the fear of God, whose faith was whole, comforting, and not marked by anxiety.

No, I do not understand. And if I write, it is to warn the 21 reader that he will not understand either. "You will not under-stand, you will never understand," were the words heard every-where during the reign of night. I can only echo them. You, who never lived under a sky of blood, will never know what it was like. Even if you read all the books ever written, even if you listen to all the testimonies ever given, you will remain on this side of the wall, you will view the agony and death of a people from afar, through the screen of a memory that is not your own.

22   An admission of impotence and guilt? I do not know. All I know is that Treblinka and Auschwitz cannot be told. And yet I have tried. God knows I have tried.

23   Have I attempted too much or not enough? Among some twenty-five volumes, only three or four penetrate the phantasmagoric realm of the dead. In my other books, through my other books, I have tried to follow other roads. For it is dangerous to linger among the dead, they hold on to you and you run the risk of speaking only to them. And so I have forced myself to turn away from them and study other periods, explore other destinies and teach other tales—the Bible and the Talmud, Hasidism and its fervor, the shtetl and its songs, Jerusalem and its echoes, the Russian Jews and their anguish, their awakening, their courage. At times, it has seemed to me that I was speaking of other things with the sole purpose of keeping the essential—the personal experience—unspoken. At times I have wondered: And what if I was wrong? Perhaps I should not have heeded my own advice and stayed in my own world with the dead.

24   But then, I have not forgotten the dead. They have their rightful place even in the works about the Hasidic capitals Ruzhany and Korets, and Jerusalem. Even in my biblical and Midrashic tales, I pursue their presence, mute and motionless. The presence of the dead then beckons in such tangible ways that it affects even the most removed characters. Thus they appear on Mount Moriah, where Abraham is about to sacrifice his son, a burnt offering to their common God. They appear on Mount Nebo, where Moses enters solitude and death. They appear in Hasidic and Talmudic legends in which victims forever need defending against forces that would crush them. Technically, so to speak, they are of course elsewhere, in time and space, but on a deeper, truer plane, the dead are part of every story, of every scene.

25   "But what is the connection?" you will ask. Believe me, there is one. After Auschwitz everything brings us back to Auschwitz. When I speak of Abraham, Isaac and Jacob, when I invoke Rabbi Yohanan ben Zakkai and Rabbi Akiba, it is the better to understand them in the light of Auschwitz. As for the Maggid of Mezeritch and his disciples, it is in order to encounter the followers of their fol-

lowers that I reconstruct their spellbound, spellbinding universe. I like to imagine them alive, exuberant, celebrating life and hope. Their happiness is as necessary to me as it was once to themselves.

And yet—how did they manage to keep their faith intact? How did they manage to sing as they went to meet the Angel of Death? I know Hasidim who never vacillated—I respect their strength. I know others who chose rebellion, protest, rage—I respect their courage. For there comes a time when only those who do not believe in God will not cry out to him in wrath and anguish. 26

Do not judge either group. Even the heroes perished as martyrs, even the martyrs died as heroes. Who would dare oppose knives to prayers? The faith of some matters as much as the strength of others. It is not ours to judge, it is only ours to tell the tale. 27

But where is one to begin? Whom is one to include? One meets a Hasid in all my novels. And a child. And an old man. And a beggar. And a madman. They are all part of my inner landscape. The reason why? Pursued and persecuted by the killers, I offer them shelter. The enemy wanted to create a society purged of their presence, and I have brought some of them back. The world denied them, repudiated them, so I let them live at least within the feverish dreams of my characters. 28

It is for them that I write, and yet the survivor may experience remorse. He has tried to bear witness; it was all in vain. 29

After the liberation, we had illusions. We were convinced that a new world would be built upon the ruins of Europe. A new civilization would see the light. No more wars, no more hate, no more intolerance, no fanaticism. And all this because the witnesses would speak. And speak they did, to no avail. 30

They will continue, for they cannot do otherwise. When man, in his grief, falls silent, Goethe says, then God gives him the strength to sing his sorrows. From that moment on, he may no longer choose not to sing, whether his song is heard or not. What matters is to struggle against silence with words, or through another form of silence. What matters is to gather a smile here and there, a tear here and there, a word here and there, and thus justify the faith placed in you, a long time ago, by so many victims. 31

Why do I write? To wrench those victims from oblivion. To help the dead vanquish death. 32

(Translated from the French by Rosette C. Lamont)

Content

1. Wiesel says, "The only role I sought [as a writer] was that of witness" (¶ 6). What does he mean by "witness"? Find examples of this role throughout the essay.

2. What does Wiesel mean by "not to transmit an experience is to betray it" (¶ 6)? What experience does his writing transmit? Why is this important to Wiesel? To humanity?

3. Does "Why I Write" fulfill Wiesel's commitment to "make no become yes" (¶ 8)? Explain.

Strategies/Structures

4. Identify some of Wiesel's major ethical appeals in this essay. Does he want to move his readers to action as well as to thought?

5. Why would Wiesel use paradoxes in an effort to explain and clarify? Explain the meaning of the following paradoxes:
   a. "No, I do not understand. And if I write, it is to warn the reader that he will not understand either" (¶ 21).
   b. I write "to help the dead vanquish death" (¶ 32).

6. For what audience does Wiesel want to explain "Why I Write"? What understanding of Judaism does Wiesel expect his readers to have? Of World War II? Of the operation of concentration camps? Why does he expect his reasons to matter to these readers, whether or not they have extensive knowledge of any of them?

Language

7. Does Wiesel's style here fulfill his goals of a style that is "sharp, hard, strong, pared"? Why is such a style appropriate to the subject?

8. Explain the meaning of "concentration camp language" (¶ 8). Why did it negate all other language and take its place (¶ 8)?

For Writing

9. Write an essay for someone who doesn't like to write comparing Elie Wiesel's and Amy Tan's reasons for writing as expressed in their essays "Why I Write" (53–60) and "Mother Tongue" (17–25).

10. Write an essay exploring for yourself how you know when you get ideas that are interesting or otherwise compelling enough to write about. If you're devoid of ideas, what are some ways you might go about getting some? In addition to the essays by White and Wiesel, consider the essays by Lamott and Least Heat-Moon in Chapter 3, and the Writers' Notebooks (109–119).

3 | *Getting Started*

To expect some people to learn to write by showing them a published essay or book is like expecting novice bakers to learn to make a wedding cake from looking at the completed confection, resplendent with icing and decorations. Indeed, the completed product in each case offers a model of what the finished work of art should look like—in concept, organization, shape, and style. Careful examination of the text exposes the intricacies of the finished sentences, paragraphs, logic, illustrative examples, and nuances of style. The text likewise provides cues about the context (intellectual, political, aesthetic . . .) in which it originated, its purpose, and its intended audience. But no matter how hard you look, it's almost impossible to detect in a completed, professionally polished work much about the process by which it was composed—the numerous visions and revisions of ideas and expression; the effort, frustration, even exhilaration. Blood, sweat, and tears don't belong on the printed page any more than they belong in the gymnast's flawless public performance on the balance beam. The audience doesn't want to agonize over the production but to enjoy the result.

Becoming a Writer

You've been training to become a writer all your life. Whether you want to become a professional writer or merely to write well enough to survive in college or on the job, your senses (particularly of sight and hearing) were functioning—even before you could interpret and understand in words the stimuli they conveyed. Indeed, the three sections of Eudora Welty's *One Writer's*

Beginnings focus on the topics "Listening" (excerpted on 34–39), "Learning to See," and "Finding a Voice"—a perspective that also governs Linda Hogan's "Hearing Voices" (67–72). Both Welty, who comes from a Western Christian tradition, and Hogan, who comes from a Chickasaw Indian background, reflect their culture's respect for their environment, natural and human. Their works show how important *listening* is to a writer's development, listening not just to the words but to the music, literal and figurative, which, as Hogan says, "teaches me, leads me places I never knew I was heading. It is about a new way of living, of being in the world."

Getting started for many people is the most difficult part of writing. It's hard to begin if you don't know what to write about. In "Polaroids" (72–77) Anne Lamott illustrates a good way to find a subject, analogous to "watching a Polaroid develop. You can't," she says, "know exactly what the picture is going to look like until it has finished developing." Indeed, you're "not supposed to know" at the outset what you'll find when you begin to focus; the picture emerges as you immerse yourself in the subject and begin to identify themes, individuals, revealing details. And gradually the overall shape and structure appear. Aha!

Making "A List of Nothing in Particular" (77–82), as William Least Heat-Moon did when he drove his van through the "barren waste" of west Texas on a circuit of the country, can enable one to extract some meaning, some significance even out of a territory where "'there's nothing out there.'" Heat-Moon's list has an eclectic span, seemingly random until it snaps into focus, ranging from "mockingbird" to "jackrabbit (chewed on cactus)" to "wind (always)." Talking with others, making an "idea tree," brainstorming, reading, thinking—even dreaming or daydreaming—all of these can provide you with something to write about, if you remain receptive to the possibilities.

Arthur Miller's method of starting to write—doing something entirely different while contemplating the writing task at hand—is fairly common, as you may have discovered if you've floundered about for a subject or a focus for your writing while doing a repetitive task such as exercising or housework. Nevertheless, as Miller's "Building and Writing" (82–88) and John Lahr's

"Making Willy Loman" (722–32) reveal, the task Miller undertook before he actually sat down to write *Death of a Salesman*—building a small cabin to write in—is most unusual. It is as if while Miller learned to solve the problems of physical construction, he prepared his mind to tackle analogous problems of literary construction.

Writers' Notebooks

Keeping a writer's diary or notebook, whether you do it with pencil, pen, typewriter, or word processor, can be a good way to get started—and even to keep going. Writing regularly—and better yet, at a regular time of the day or week—in a notebook or its equivalent, as Mark Twain did throughout the fifty-five years of his adult life, beginning long before he became a professional writer, can give you a lot to think about while you're writing, and a lot to expand on later. You could keep an account of what you do every day (6:30–7:30, swimming laps, shower; 7:30–8:15, breakfast—toasted English muffin, orange juice, raspberry yogurt . . .), but if your life is routine that might get monotonous.

The notebook entries included in this section were written in a variety of circumstances. The excerpts from Anne Frank's *The Diary of a Young Girl* (97–104) reveal to Frank—and ultimately to the audience of posterity for whom she intended this diary— what she could not tell the people she was living with, day in and day out, in confined quarters. In "Margot's Diary" (104–08), S. L. Wisenberg presents a sympathetic, though imaginary, portrait of Anne Frank's sister, a shadow to her posthumously famous sibling because she left no written record of her fleeting life. Twain made the entries "Aboard a Mississippi River Steamboat" (89–96) during the nostalgic trip he took in 1882 in preparation for expanding the seven installments of *Old Times on the Mississippi* into *Life on the Mississippi* (1883). "Selections from Student Writers' Notebooks" (109–20) met not only course requirements but were also obviously outlets for many types of expressions and explorations ranging from the meaning of education, race, and sexuality to the importance of family, music, an ordered environment, and writing.

A provocative and potentially useful writer's notebook might contain any or all of the following types of writing, and more:

- Reactions to one's reading: "I should pick up *Mansfield Park* again. Reading Austen or anyone that good reminds me of what I could be saying, and of the work that has to be put into it" (Loftus 110).
- Provocative quotations—invented, read, or overheard; appealing figures of speech; dialogue, dialect: "They have *Irish* whiskey [in Ireland]. . . . But I don't use much mesilf [sic]. I am not a hard drinker, sir. Give an Irishman lager beer for one month and he's a dead man. An Irishman is lined inside with copper and the lager beer corrodes it" (Twain 91).
- Lists—including sights, sounds, scents: "On one wall [of the living room] was a dart board with no darts and the wall behind pocked with holes. The lining had been torn from the bottom of a yellow Chippendale sofa and stuffing poked through . . . On the carpet . . . was a bowl of milk with Cheerios floating" (King 115).
- Memorable details—of clothing, animals, objects, settings, phenomena, processes: "The camp seems loudest at night. A huge, dulled murmur flows up from the valleys with hacking, rattling coughs, unending moaning like mantras, mules braying, wails, and shrieks like a child stepped on a nail. Clank tap-tapping, metal pots clanking and wood chopping sounds but no sounds of laughter" (Ryan 118).
- Personal aspirations, fears, joy, anger: "I can't imagine having to live like Mother . . . and all the women who go about their work and are then forgotten. I need to have something besides a husband and children to devote myself to! I don't want to have lived in vain like most people. I want to be useful or bring enjoyment to all people, even those I've never met. . . . When I write I can shake off all my cares. . . . But, and that's a big question, will I ever be able to write something great . . . ? (Frank 103).
- Sketches of people, either intrinsically interesting or engaged in intriguing activities, whether novel or familiar: "One of the 3 mates on this boat is of the ancient tribe. He is one of

the old-fashioned, God-damn-your-soul kind. Very affable and sociable. . . . (This man talks like the machine Barnum had around with his circus for a while. Has that same guttural indistinct, jumbling, rasping way of talking. But this mate can out-swear the machine)" (Twain 93).

- Analyses of friendships, family relationships: "My parents are getting divorced. . . . We did not put up a [Christmas] tree. . . . This year [since dad was gone] mom said we could eat when we wanted. But we never did. I ate a beans n franks dinner [by myself]. My brother went to drink his gift certificate" (Weast 114).
- Commentary on notable events, current or past, national or more immediate: "In California thongs are still Nipper Flippers or Jap Slaps. . . . December seventh is the Ides of March. I'm asked how I can see, is my field of vision narrowed?" (Watanabe 117).
- Possibilities for adventure, exploration, conflict: "Today in class Dudley said he's 'tired of racial issues in class.' Well— if he's tired of them, how does he think I feel? For years I have been the only Black (or at most one of two or three) in class and I have had to deal with white negativism towards Blacks" (Coles 115).
- Jokes, anecdotes, and humorous situations, characters, comic mannerisms, punch lines, provocative settings: "Stopped at Arkansas City April 24. This is a Hell of a place. One or two streets full of mud; 19 different stenches at the same time. A thriving place nevertheless" (Twain 96).

You'll need to put enough explanatory details in your notebook to remind yourself three weeks—or three years—later what something meant when you wrote it down, as the notebook keepers here have done. As all of these notebook entries reveal, those of the student writers in particular, in a writer's notebook you can be most candid, most off guard, for there you're writing primarily for yourself. You're also writing for yourself when you're freewriting—writing rapidly, with or without a particular subject, without editing, while you're in the process of generating ideas. As you freewrite you can free-associate, thinking of connections among like and unlike things or ideas, exploring their implications. Anything goes into the notebook, but not every-thing stays in later drafts if you decide to turn some of your most focused discussion into an essay. If you get into the habit of writing regularly on paper, you may find that you're also hearing the "voices in your head" that professional writers often experience. As James Thurber explained to an interviewer, "I never quite know when I'm not writing. Sometimes my wife comes up to me at a party and says, 'Dammit, Thurber, stop writing.' Or my daughter will look up from the dinner table and ask, 'Is he sick?' 'No,' my wife says, 'he's writing something.'"

Playing around with words and ideas in a notebook or in your head can also lead to an entire essay: a narrative, character sketch, reminiscence, discussion of how to do it, an argument, review, or some other form suitable for an extended piece of writing. After several drafts (148–54), Mary Ruffin's evocative portrait of her mother, who died when Mary was thirteen, emerged from fragments in her writer's notebook to become the polished "Mama's Smoke" (154–58), sophisticated in concept and techniques.

No matter what you write about, rereading a notebook entry or a freewriting can provide some material to start with. Ask your-self, "What do I want to write about?" "What makes me particu-larly happy—or angry?" (Don't write about something that seems bland, like a cookie without sugar. If it doesn't appeal to you, it won't attract your readers either.) As you write you will almost automatically be using description, narration, comparison and contrast, and other rhetorical techniques to express yourself, even if you don't attach labels to them. Enjoy.

LINDA HOGAN

Hogan is a Chickasaw Indian, born in Denver in 1947. She earned an M.A. at the University of Colorado, Boulder, in 1978 and was a professor of American and American Indian studies at the University of Minnesota before joining the faculty of the University of Colorado. Her reputation as a poet is based on six volumes, the most recent of which is *Book of Medicines* (1993). Hogan's fourth poetry collection, *Seeing Through the Sun* (1985), received an American Book Award. She has also published short stories and three novels, *Mean Spirit* (1990) and *Solar Storms* (1995), and *Power* (1998).

Hogan says of her work, "I have considered my writing to come from close observation of the life around me, a spoken connection with the earth and with the histories of the earth. More and more I find that my writing comes from a sense of traditional indigenous relationship with the land and its peoples, from the animals and plants of tribal histories, stories, and knowledge. I am trying to speak this connection, stating its spirit, adding to it the old stories that have come to a new language. My influences are sometimes the language of ceremony and transformation, sometimes science. I research my work and try to think of how to translate a world view, a different way to live with this world." That Hogan is also an ardent conservationist is clear from "Hearing Voices," which amplifies these views. Here she emphasizes how important it is to listen, as Indians do, to the literal "language of this continent," the stories of this earth, "the stones giving guidance, the trees singing, the corn telling of inner earth, the dragonfly offering up a tongue."

Hearing Voices

When Barbara McClintock was awarded a Nobel Prize for her work on gene transposition in corn plants, the most striking thing about her was that she made her discoveries by listening to what the corn spoke to her, by respecting the life of the corn and "letting it come." 1

McClintock says she learned "the stories" of the plants. She "heard" them. She watched the daily green journeys of growth 2 from earth toward sky and sun. She knew her plants in the way a healer or mystic would have known them, from the inside, the inner voices of corn and woman speaking to one another.

3   As an Indian woman, I come from a long history of people who have listened to the language of this continent, people who have known that corn grows with the songs and prayers of the people, that it has a story to tell, that the world is alive. Both in oral traditions and in mythology—the true language of inner life—account after account tells of the stones giving guidance, the trees singing, the corn telling of inner earth, the dragonfly offering up a tongue. This is true in the European traditions as well: Psyche received direction from the reeds and the ants, Orpheus knew the languages of earth, animals, and birds.

4   This intuitive and common language is what I seek for my writing, work in touch with the mystery and force of life, work that speaks a few of the many voices around us, and it is important to me that McClintock listened to the voices of corn. It is important to the continuance of life that she told the truth of her method and that it reminded us all of where our strength, our knowing, and our sustenance come from.

5   It is also poetry, this science, and I note how often scientific theories lead to the world of poetry and vision, theories telling us how atoms that were stars have been transformed into our living, breathing bodies. And in these theories, or maybe they should be called stories, we begin to understand how we are each many people, including the stars we once were, and how we are in essence the earth and the universe, how what we do travels clear around the earth and returns. In a single moment of our living, there is our ancestral and personal history, our future, even our deaths planted in us and already growing toward their fulfillment. The corn plants are there, and like all the rest we are forever merging our borders with theirs in the world collective.

6   Our very lives might depend on this listening. In the Chernobyl nuclear accident, the wind told the story that was being suppressed by the people. It gave away the truth. It carried the story of danger to other countries. It was a poet, a prophet, a scientist.

7   Sometimes, like the wind, poetry has its own laws speaking for the life of the planet. It is a language that wants to bring back together what the other words have torn apart. It is the language of life speaking through us about the sacredness of life.

This life speaking life is what I find so compelling about the 8 work of poets such as Ernesto Cardenal, who is also a priest and was the Nicaraguan Minister of Culture. He writes: "The armadilloes are very happy with this government. . . . Not only humans desired liberation/the whole ecology wanted it." Cardenal has also written "The Parrots," a poem about caged birds who were being sent to the United States as pets for the wealthy, how the cages were opened, the parrots allowed back into the mountains and jungles, freed like the people, "and sent back to the land we were pulled from."

How we have been pulled from the land! And how poetry 9 has worked hard to set us free, uncage us, keep us from split tongues that mimic the voices of our captors. It returns us to our land. Poetry is a string of words that parades without a permit. It is a lockbox of words to put an ear to as we try to crack the safe of language, listening for the right combination, the treasure inside. It is life resonating. It is sometimes called Prayer, Soothsaying, Complaint, Invocation, Proclamation, Testimony, Witness. Writing is and does all these things. And like that parade, it is illegitimately insistent on going its own way, on being part of the miracle of life, telling the story about what happened when we were cosmic dust, what it means to be stars listening to our human atoms.

But don't misunderstand me. I am not just a dreamer. I am 10 also the practical type. A friend's father, watching the United States stage another revolution in another Third World country, said, "Why doesn't the government just feed people and then let the political chips fall where they may?" He was right. It was easy, obvious, even financially more reasonable to do that, to let democracy be chosen because it feeds hunger. I want my writing to be that simple, that clear and direct. Likewise, I feel it is not enough for me just to write, but I need to live it, to be informed by it. I have found over the years that my work has more courage than I do. It has more wisdom. It teaches me, leads me places I never knew I was heading. And it is about a new way of living, of being in the world.

I was on a panel recently where the question was raised 11 whether we thought literature could save lives. The audience, book people, smiled expectantly with the thought. I wanted to say, Yes, it saves lives. But I couldn't speak those words. It saves spirits maybe, hearts. It changes minds, but for me writing is an incredible privilege. When I sit down at the desk, there are other women who are hungry, homeless. I don't want to forget that, that the world of matter is still there to be reckoned with. This writing is a form of freedom most other people do not have. So, when I write, I feel a responsibility, a commitment to other humans and to the animal and plant communities as well.

12   Still, writing has changed me. And there is the powerful need we all have to tell a story, each of us with a piece of the whole pattern to complete. As Alice Walker says, We are all telling part of the same story, and as Sharon Olds has said, Every writer is a cell on the body politic of America.

13   Another Nobel Prize laureate is Betty William, a Northern Ireland co-winner of the 1977 Peace Prize. I heard her speak about how, after witnessing the death of children, she stepped outside in the middle of the night and began knocking on doors and yelling, behaviors that would have earned her a diagnosis of hysteria in our own medical circles. She knocked on doors that might have opened with weapons pointing in her face, and she cried out, "What kind of people have we become that we would allow children to be killed on our streets?" Within four hours the city was awake, and there were sixteen thousand names on petitions for peace. Now, that woman's work is a lesson to those of us who deal with language, and to those of us who are dealt into silence. She used language to begin the process of peace. This is the living, breathing power of the word. It is poetry. So are the names of those who signed the petitions. Maybe it is this kind of language that saves lives.

14   Writing begins for me with survival, with life and with freeing life, saving life, speaking life. It is work that speaks what can't be easily said. It originates from a compelling desire to live and be alive. For me, it is sometimes the need to speak for other forms of life, to take the side of human life, even our sometimes frivolous living, and our grief-filled living, our joyous living, our violent living, busy living, our peaceful living. It is about possibility. It is based in the world of matter. I am interested in how something small turns into an image that is large and strong with resonance, where the ordinary becomes beautiful. I believe the divine, the magic, is here in the weeds at our feet, unacknowledged. What a world this is. Where else could water rise up to the sky, turn into snow crystals, magnificently brought together, fall from the sky

all around us, pile up billions deep, and catch the small sparks of sunlight as they return again to water?

These acts of magic happen all the time; in Chaco Canyon, 15 my sister has seen a kiva, a ceremonial room in the earth, that is in the center of the canyon. This place has been uninhabited for what seems like forever. It has been without water. In fact, there are theories that the ancient people disappeared when they journeyed after water. In the center of it a corn plant was growing. It was all alone and it had been there since the ancient ones, the old ones who came before us all, those people who wove dog hair into belts, who witnessed the painting of flute players on the seeping canyon walls, who knew the stories of corn. And there was one corn plant growing out of the holy place. It planted itself yearly. With no water, no person to care for it, no overturning of the soil, this corn plant rises up to tell its story, and that's what this poetry is.

Content

1. What does Hogan mean by "the language of this continent" (¶ 3)? Even if we listen intently, respectfully, how can we be sure that what we're hearing is "the true language of inner life" (¶ 3)? How can we understand—and interpret—what we hear?

2. How can a person's writing "have more wisdom" than the writer? Hogan says her writing "teaches me, leads me places I never knew I was heading" (¶ 10)? How does this process work for Hogan? How might it work for you?

3. "We are all telling part of the same story," says Hogan, quoting Alice Walker with approval (¶ 12). What is that story?

4. Why does Hogan associate writing with "survival, with life and with freeing life, saving life" (¶ 14)?

Strategies/Structures

5. Why does Hogan begin with the illustration of Barbara McClintock, who made her Nobel prize–winning discoveries "by listening to what the corn spoke to her" (¶ 1)? Where else does Hogan use the corn plant in this essay? Why does she conclude with the image of the solitary corn plant, "growing out of the holy place," without water or cultivation (¶ 15)?

6. How do these concrete illustrations help to explain the intuitive process of writing poetry (see especially ¶ 15)?

Language

7. What does Hogan mean by the metaphors she uses to define poetry, as "a string of words that parades without a permit," "a lockbox of words to put an ear to as we try to crack the safe of language," "life resonating" (¶ 9)?
8. Hogan says she seeks "intuitive and common language" (¶ 4) that is "simple," "clear," "direct" (¶ 10). How does she define these terms? Do your definitions agree with hers? Has she written "Hearing Voices" in the language she values?

For Writing

9. Select an object or an experience that symbolizes the meaning of something very important to you, such as life, freedom, writing, truth, or justice. Describe the object or explain the experience, interpreting it to make clear the connection between its concrete and symbolic meanings.
10. Have you ever heard a life-saving story, told either through words or through indirect means, such as the wind that spread the story of the Chernobyl nuclear disaster (¶ 6)? If so, tell that story, either orally or in writing, to a group of your peers—who will, in turn, share their stories with you. Or, tell the story out loud first, get feedback and answer questions from your audience; then write the story in a way that accommodates both your initial and more recent understanding of its significance.

ANNE LAMOTT

Lamott, born in San Francisco in 1954, is the daughter of a writer father and a lawyer mother. She dropped out of Goucher College after two years to return to Marin County, California, and write fiction. Although she published four novels in the 1980s, *Hard Laughter, Rosie, Joe Jones,* and *All New People,* her nonfiction has drawn the most attention—and affection—for its author. *Operating Instructions: A Journal of My Son's First Year* (1993) is an ironically witty account of her first months as a single parent at age thirty-six, including sleep deprivation, financial anxieties, speculations on what she will tell Sam when he asks about his absent father, and her appreciation of the friends and relatives whose involvement expands the definition of *family.*

But the book serious writers take comfort, as well as good advice from, is *Bird by Bird: Instructions on Writing and Life* (1994), of which "Polaroids" is an early chapter. Her explanation of the book's title serves also as an explanation of the metaphorical connection between the process of pictures emerging in Polaroid photographs and the way controlling ideas gradually emerge from a writer's experience and come into focus with slow precision. She says,

> Thirty years ago my older brother, who was ten years old at the time, was trying to get a report on birds written that he'd had three months to write. [It] was due the next day. We were out at our family cabin in Bolinas, and he was at the kitchen table close to tears, surrounded by binder paper and pencils and unopened books on birds, immobilized by the hugeness of the task ahead. Then my father sat down beside him, put his arm around my brother's shoulder, and said, "Bird by bird, buddy. Just take it bird by bird."

Polaroids

W riting a first draft is very much like watching a Polaroid develop. You can't—and, in fact, you're not supposed to— know exactly what the picture is going to look like until it has finished developing. First you just point at what has your attention and take the picture. In the last chapter, for instance, what had my attention were the contents of my lunch bag. But as the picture developed, I found I had a really clear image of the boy against the fence. Or maybe *your* Polaroid was supposed to be a picture of that boy against the fence, and you didn't notice until the last minute that a family was standing a few feet away from him. Now, maybe it's his family, or the family of one of the kids in his class, but at any rate these people are going to be in the photograph, too. Then the film emerges from the camera with a grayish green murkiness that gradually becomes clearer and clearer, and finally your see the husband and wife holding their baby with two children standing beside them. And at first it all seems very sweet, but then the shadows begin to appear, and then you start to see the animal tragedy, the baboons baring their teeth. And then you see a flash of bright red flowers in the bottom left quadrant that you didn't even know were in the picture when you took it, and these flowers evoke a time or a memory that moves you mysteriously. And finally, as the portrait comes into focus, you begin to notice all the props surrounding these people, and you begin to understand how props define us and comfort us, and show us what we value and what we need, and who we think we are.

2   You couldn't have had any way of knowing what this piece of work would look like when you first started. You just knew that there was something about these people that compelled you, and you stayed with that something long enough for it to show you what it was about.

3   Watch this Polaroid develop:

4   Six or seven years ago I was asked to write an article on the Special Olympics. I had been going to the local event for years, partly because a couple of friends of mine compete. Also, I love sports, and I love to watch athletes, special or otherwise. So I showed up this time with a great deal of interest but no real sense of what the finished article might look like.

5   Things tend to go very, very slowly at the Special Olympics. It is not like trying to cover the Preakness. Still, it has its own exhilaration, and I cheered and took notes all morning.

6   The last track-and-field even before lunch was a twenty-five-yard race run by some unusually handicapped runners and walkers, many of whom seemed completely confused. They lumped and careened along, one man making a snail-slow break for the strands, one heading out toward the steps where the winners receive their medals; both of them were shepherded back. The race took just about forever. And here it was nearly noon and we were all so hungry. Finally, though, everyone crossed over the line, and those of us in the stands got up to go—when we noticed that way down the track, four or five yards from the starting line, was another runner.

7   She was a girl of about sixteen with a normal-looking face above a wracked and emaciated body. She was on metal crutches, and she was just plugging along, one tiny step after another, moving one crutch forward two or three inches, then moving a leg, then moving the other crutch two or three inches, then moving the other leg. It was just excruciating. Plus, I was starving to death. Inside I was going, Come on, come on, come on, swabbing at my

forehead with anxiety, while she kept taking these two- or three-inch steps forward. What felt like four hours later, she crossed the finish line, and you could see that she was absolutely stoked, in a shy, girlish way.

A tall African American man with no front teeth fell into 8 step with me as I left the bleachers to go look for some lunch. He tugged on the sleeve of my sweater, and I looked up at him, and he handed me a Polaroid someone had taken of him and his friends that day. "Look at us," he said. His speech was difficult to understand, thick and slow as a warped record. His two friends in the picture had Down's syndrome. All three of them looked extremely pleased with themselves. I admired the picture and then handed it back to him. He stopped, so I stopped, too. He pointed to his own image. "That," he said, "is one cool man."

And this was the image from which an article began form- 9 ing, although I could not have told you exactly what the piece would end up being about. I just knew that something had started to emerge.

After lunch I wandered over to the auditorium, where it 10 turned out a men's basketball game was in progress. The African American man with no front teeth was the star of the game. You could tell that he was because even though no one had made a basket yet, his teammates almost always passed him the ball. Even the people on the *other* team passed him the ball a lot. In lieu of any scoring, the men stampeded in slow motion up and down the court, dribbling the ball thunderously. I had never heard such a loud game. It was all sort of crazily beautiful. I imagined describing the game for my article and then for my students: the loudness, the joy. I kept replaying the scene of the girl on crutches making her way up the track to the finish line—and all of a sudden my article began to appear out of the grayish green murk. And I could see that it was about tragedy transformed over the years into joy. It was about the beauty of sheer effort. I could see it almost as clearly as I could the photograph of that one cool man and his two friends.

The auditorium bleachers were packed. Then a few minutes 11 later, still with no score on the board, the tall black man dribbled slowly from one end of the court to the other, and heaved the ball up into the air, and it dropped into the basket. The crowd roared, and all the men on both teams looked up wide-eyed at the hoop, as if it had just burst into flames.

12   You would have loved it, I tell my students. You would have felt like you could write all day.

Content

1. In what ways is participating in the Special Olympics like finding one's way into writing about a particular topic? Is it possible to be both a spectator (appreciating what's going on, including the out-of-control parts, but sometimes getting frustrated by the slow pace [¶s 5–7]) and a participant concurrently?

2. What is Lamott's attitude toward the participants in the Special Olympics? How does she convey this? What clues does she give to indicate that she expects her readers to share her point of view? Would the families of Special Olympics participants have a similar point of view? Would the participants themselves?

3. In this essay about "the beauty of sheer effort" (¶ 10), intended as advice for beginning writers, why doesn't Lamott spend more time actually talking about writing?

Strategies/Structures

4. Why does Lamott use the relation of the gradual development of a Polaroid picture (¶s 1–3) as a metaphor for the process of writing? How does this relate to the actual Polaroid photograph (¶ 8) that appears in the essay? Why is the first paragraph so much longer than those that immediately follow it?

5. Only paragraph 10 is of comparable length to the opening paragraph. Why is it located where it is? In it, Lamott uses two scenes, an enactment of a basketball game in action and her replay of "the scene of the girl on crutches making her way . . . to the finish line." How do these scenes contribute to the author's "Aha!" moment, her sudden insight as the meaning of the essay snaps into place?

6. Lamott's technique is to present a collage of many snapshots to illustrate her point. Identify some of these snapshots and explain how they reinforce her concept of "Polaroids."

Language

7. Identify some of the ways in which Lamott conveys the slow pace of the Special Olympics and indicates her changing attitude toward this pace.

For Writing

8. Use an extended metaphor coupled with a series of illustrations to explain to newcomers how to perform a process (see Dolman's "Learning to Drive" [196–200] and the Magliozzis' "Inside the Engine" [233–40] for examples).

9. In many areas of academic research today, ethical questions are raised about who has the right to speak for whom. In "Polaroids," as in many other essays in this book (see those by Kozol [283–94], Coontz [294–301], and Barry [670–75]), the author speaks on behalf of people who can't always speak articulately for themselves. With other classmates, compose a set of guidelines for a writer's ethical behavior in representing such people, and include your rationale for these guidelines.

WILLIAM LEAST HEAT-MOON

William Least Heat-Moon, as William Trogdon renamed himself to acknowledge his Osage Indian ancestry, was born in 1939 in Kansas City, Missouri. He earned four degrees from the University of Missouri–Columbia, including a B.A. in photojournalism (1978) and a Ph.D. in literature (1973). His most recent book is *PrairyErth* (1991). On one cold day in February, 1979, "a day of canceled expectations," Least Heat-Moon lost both his wife ("the Cherokee") and his part-time job teaching English at a Missouri college.

True to the American tradition, to escape he took to the road, the "blue highways"—back roads on the old road maps—in the van that would be home as he circled the United States clockwise "in search of places where change did not mean ruin and where time and men and deeds connected." His account of his trip, *Blue Highways* (1982), is an intimate exploration of America's small towns, "Remote, Oregon; Simplicity, Virginia; New Freedom, Pennsylvania; New Hope, Tennessee; Why, Arizona; Whynot, Mississippi; Igo, California (just down the road from Ono). . . ." Though he tried to lose himself as a stranger in a strange land, as he came to know and appreciate the country through its back roads and small towns, Least Heat-Moon came inevitably to know and come to terms with himself. "The mere listing of details meaningless in themselves, at once provides them with significance which one denies in vain," says novelist Steven Millhauser. "The beauty of irrelevance fades away, accident darkens into design." Consequently, traveling—moving along a linear route—lends itself to list making, a good way to impose design on happenstance, to remember where you're going, where you've been, whom you've met, what you've seen or done.

A List of Nothing in Particular

1 S traight as a chief's countenance, the road lay ahead, curves so long and gradual as to be imperceptible except on the map. For nearly a hundred miles due west of Eldorado, not a single town. It was the Texas some people see as barren waste when they cross it, the part they later describe at the motel bar as "nothing." They say, "There's nothing out there."

2 Driving through the miles of nothing, I decided to test the hypothesis and stopped somewhere in western Crockett County on the top of a broad mesa, just off Texas 29. At a distance, the land looked so rocky and dry, a religious man could believe that the First Hand never got around to the creation in here. Still, somebody had decided to string barbed wire around it.

3 No plant grew higher than my head. For a while, I heard only miles of wind against the Ghost; but after the ringing in my ears stopped, I heard myself breathing, then a bird note, an answering call, another kind of birdsong, and another: mockingbird, mourning dove, an enigma. I heard the high zizz of flies the color of gray flannel and the deep buzz of a blue bumblebee. I made a list of nothing in particular:

1. mockingbird
2. mourning dove
3. enigma bird (heard not saw)
4. gray flies
5. blue bumblebee
6. two circling buzzards (not yet, boys)
7. orange ants
8. black ants
9. orange-black ants (what's been going on?)

10. three species of spiders
11. opossum skull
12. jackrabbit (chewed on cactus)
13. deer (left scat)
14. coyote (left tracks)
15. small rodent (den full of seed hulls under rock)
16. snake (skin hooked on cactus spine)
17. prickly pear cactus (yellow blossoms)
18. hedgehog cactus (orange blossoms)
19. barrel cactus (red blossoms)
20. devil's pincushion (no blossoms)
21. catclaw (no better name)
22. two species of grass (neither green, both alive)
23. yellow flowers (blossoms smaller than peppercorns)
24. sage (indicates alkali-free soil)
25. mesquite (three-foot plants with eighty-foot roots to reach water that fell as rain two thousand years ago)
26. greasewood (oh, yes)
27. joint fir (steeped stems make Brigham Young tea)
28. earth
29. sky
30. wind (always)

That was all the nothing I could identify then, but had I waited until dark when the desert really comes to life, I could have done better. To say nothing is out here is incorrect; to say the desert is stingy with everything except space and light, stone and earth is closer to the truth.

I drove on. The low sun turned the mesa rimrock to silhou- 4 ettes, angular and weird and unearthly; had someone said the far side of Saturn looked just like this, I would have believed him. The road dropped to the Pecos River, now dammed to such docility I couldn't imagine it formerly demarking the western edge of a rudimentary white civilization. Even the old wagonmen felt the unease of isolation when they crossed the Pecos, a small but once serious river that has had many names: Rio de las Vacas (River of Cows—perhaps a reference to bison), Rio Salado (Salty River), Rio Puerco (Dirty River).

West of the Pecos, a strangely truncated cone rose from the 5 valley. In the oblique evening light, its silhouette looked like a

Mayan temple, so perfect was its symmetry. I stopped again, started climbing, stirring a panic of lizards on the way up. From the top, the rubbled land below—veined with the highway and arroyos, topographical relief absorbed in the dusk—looked like a roadmap.

6   The desert, more than any other terrain, shows its age, shows time because so little vegetation covers the ancient erosions of wind and storm. What appears is tawny grit once stone and stone crumbling to grit. Everywhere rock, earth's oldest thing. Even desert creatures come from a time older than the woodland animals, and they, in answer to the arduousness, have retained prehistoric coverings of chitin and lapped scale and primitive defenses of spine and stinger, fang and poison, shell and claw.

7   The night, taking up the shadows and details, wiped the face of the desert into a simple, uncluttered blackness until there were only three things: land, wind, stars. I was there too, but my presence I felt more than saw. It was as if I had been reduced to mind, to an edge of consciousness. Men, ascetics, in all eras have gone into deserts to lose themselves—Jesus, Saint Anthony, Saint Basil, and numberless medicine men—maybe because such a losing happens almost as a matter of course here if you avail yourself. The Sioux once chanted, "All over the sky a sacred voice is calling."

8   Back to the highway, on with the headlamps, down Six Shooter Draw. In the darkness, deer, just shadows in the lights, began moving toward the desert willows in the wet bottoms. Stephen Vincent Benét:

> *When Daniel Boone goes by, at night,*
> *The phantom deer arise*
> *And all lost, wild America*
> *Is burning in their eyes.*

9   From the top of another high mesa: twelve miles west in the flat valley floor, the lights of Fort Stockton blinked white, blue, red, and yellow in the heat like a mirage. How is it that desert towns look so fine and big at night? It must be that little is hidden. The glistening ahead could have been a golden city of Cibola. But the reality of Fort Stockton was plywood and concrete block and the plastic signs of Holiday Inn and Mobil Oil.

10   The desert had given me an appetite that would have made carrion crow stuffed with saltbush taste good. I found a Mexican

cafe of adobe, with a whitewashed log ceiling, creekstone fireplace, and jukebox pumping out mariachi music. It was like a bunk-house. I ate burritos, chile rellenos, and pinto beans, all ladled over with a fine, incendiary sauce the color of sludge from an old steel drum. At the next table sat three big, round men: an Indian wearing a silver headband, a Chicano in a droopy Pancho Villa mustache, and a Negro in faded overalls. I thought what a litany of grievances that table could recite. But the more I looked, the more I believed they were someone's vision of the West, maybe someone making ads for Levy's bread, the ads that used to begin "You don't have to be Jewish."

Content

1. What details of the desert landscape does Least Heat-Moon use to describe it? How clearly can you visualize this place? Although this desert can be precisely located on a highway map, do you need to know its exact location in order to imagine it? What does it have in common with other deserts? Does it have any particularly unique features?

2. Travel writer Paul Theroux says, "The journey, not the arrival, matters." Is that true for Least Heat-Moon? Explain your answer.

Strategies/Structures

3. Least Heat-Moon structures this chapter from *Blue Highways* according to time (daylight to night) and distance. How does the structure relate to the subject matter?

4. What is the effect of ending this trip through the desert with the image of "three big, round men"—an Indian, a Chicano, and a black (¶ 10)? Does the reference to Levy's Jewish rye bread in the last sentence trivialize this example?

5. What kind of character does Least Heat-Moon play in his own narrative? Is this character identical to the author who is writing the essay?

Language

6. Least Heat-Moon includes many place names. With what effect? Do you need to read the essay with a map in hand?

7. Why are the parentheses in the list? Why do they appear beside some items and not others?

For Writing

8. Make a list of "nothing in particular" that you observe in a place so familiar that you take its distinguishing features for granted: your yard, your refrigerator, your clothes closet, your desk, a supermarket or other store, a library, or any other ordinary place. Write down as many specific details as you can, in whatever order you see them. (Use parenthetical remarks, too, if you wish.) Then, organize them according to some logical or psychologically relevant pattern (such as closet to farthest away, most to least dominant impression, largest to smallest, whatever) and put them into a larger context. For instance, how does the closet or the refrigerator relate to the rest of your house? Does organizing the list stimulate you to include even more details? What can you do to keep your essay from sounding like a collection of miscellaneous trivia?

9. Write an essay about some portion of a trip you have taken, where you have been a stranger in a strange land. Characterize yourself as a traveler, possibly an outsider, with a particular relationship to the place you're in (enjoyment, curiosity, boredom, loneliness, fear, fatigue, a desire to move on, or any combination of emotions you want to acknowledge).

ARTHUR MILLER

Miller was born in New York City in 1915. When his father's coat manufacturing business went bankrupt during the Depression, he worked his way through the University of Michigan (B.A. 1938), reporting labor union news for the *Michigan Daily* and writing plays that won prestigious Hopwood awards. As his autobiography *Timebends: A Life* (1987) makes clear, he envisions life in dramatic scenes, complete with characters, dialogue, and events drawn from real life. Thus the 1692 Salem witchcraft trials and their parallel to Senator Joseph McCarthy's Cold War "witch-hunting" investigations of Communism formed the basis for *The Crucible* (1953); his second wife, Marilyn Monroe, was the model for the heroine in the autobiographical *After the Fall* (1964). Although his later plays never achieved the success of his earlier, award-winning works (Emmy, Tony, and Peabody awards), he retains his reputation as a major American playwright.

In *Timebends*, Miller tells the story of how before he began *Death of a Salesman* he felt compelled to build a cabin to write in, "where I could block out the world and bring into focus what was still stuck in the corners of my eyes." He had in mind "the first two lines and a death" that would become the story not only of the composite salesmen who were his relatives in Depression-ridden America but also of middle American culture of the entire nation. "It was a purely instinctive act," he says, "I had never built a building in my life"—as the play's central character Willy Loman would say, "A salesman doesn't build anything, he don't put a bolt to a nut or a seed in the ground. A man who doesn't build anything must be liked." Once the house was built, with difficulty, Miller sat down and, as he describes in the excerpt from *Timebends* that follows, wrote the entire first act in less than twenty-four hours. Never again would the writing be that easy, that close to immortality: "It's all right," says Willy, exhausted, returning from a road trip, "I came back."

Building and Writing

Returning to New York, I felt speeded up, in motion now. With   1
Streetcar, Tennessee had printed a license to speak at full throat, and it helped strengthen me as I turned to Willy Loman, a salesman always full of words, and better yet, a man who could never cease trying, like Adam, to name himself and the world's wonders. I had known all along that this play could not be encompassed by conventional realism, and for one integral reason: in Willy the past was as alive as what was happening at the moment, sometimes even crashing in to completely overwhelm his mind. I wanted precisely the same fluidity in the form, and now it was clear to me that this must be primarily verbal. The language would of course have to be recognizably his to begin with, but it seemed possible now to infiltrate it with a kind of super-consciousness. The play, after all, involved the attempts of his sons and his wife and Willy himself to understand what was killing him. And to understand meant to lift the experience into emergency speech of an unashamedly open kind rather than to proceed by the crabbed dramatic hints and pretexts of the "natural." If the structure had to mirror the psychology as directly as could be done, it was still a psychology hammered into its strange shape by

society, the business life Willy had lived and believed in. The play could reflect what I had always sensed as the unbroken tissue that was man and society, a single unit rather than two.

2   By April of 1948 I felt I could find such a form, but it would have to be done, I thought, in a single sitting, in a night or a day, I did not know why. I stopped making my notes in our Grace Court house in Brooklyn Heights and drove up alone one morning to the country house we had bought the previous year. We had spent one summer there in that old farmhouse, which had been modernized by its former owner, a greeting card manufacture named Philip Jaffe, who as a sideline published a thin magazine for China specialists called *Amerasia*. Mary worked as one of his secretaries and so had the first news that he wanted to sell the place. In a year or two he would be on trial for publishing without authorization State Department reports from John Stewart Service, among a number of other China experts who recognized a Mao victory as inevitable and warned of the futility of America continuing to back her favorite, Chiang Kai-shek. *Amerasia* had been a vanity publication, in part born of Jaffe's desire for a place in history, but it nevertheless braved the mounting fury of the China lobby against any opinion questioning the virtues of the Chiang forces. At his trial, the government produced texts of conversations that Jaffe claimed could only have been picked up by long-range microphone as he and his friends walked the isolated backcountry roads near this house. Service was one of many who were purged from the State Department, leaving it blinded to Chinese reality but ideologically pure.

3   But all that was far from my mind this day; what I was looking for on my land was a spot for a little shack I wanted to build, where I could block out the world and bring into focus what was still stuck in the corners of my eyes. I found a knoll in the nearby woods and returned to the city, where instead of working on the play I drew plans for the framing, of which I really had very vague knowledge and no experience. A pair of carpenters could have put up this ten-by-twelve-foot cabin in two days at most, but for reasons I still do not understand it had to be my own hands that gave it form, on this ground, with a floor that I had made, upon which to sit to begin the risky expedition into myself. In reality, all I had was the first two lines and a death—"Willy!"

and "It's all right. I came back." Further than that I dared not, would not, venture until I could sit in the completed studio, four walls, two windows, a floor, a roof, and a door.

"It's all right. I came back" rolled over and over in my head 4 as I tried to figure out how to join the roof rafters in air unaided, until I finally put them together on the ground and swung them into position all nailed together. When I closed in the roof it was a miracle, as though I had mastered the rain and cooled the sun. And all the while afraid I would never be able to penetrate past those two first lines. I started writing one morning—the tiny studio was still unpainted and smelled of raw wood and sawdust, and the bags of nails were still stashed in a corner with my tools. The sun of April had found my windows to pour through, and the apple buds were moving on the wild trees, showing their first pale blue petals. I wrote all day until dark, and then I had dinner and went back and wrote until some hour in the darkness between midnight and four. I had skipped a few areas that I knew would give me no trouble in the writing and gone for the parts that had to be muscled into position. By the next morning I had done the first half, the first act of two. When I lay down to sleep I realized I had been weeping—my eyes still burned and my throat was sore from talking it all out and shouting and laughing. I would be stiff when I woke, aching as if I had played four hours of football or tennis and now had to face the start of another game. It would take some six more weeks to complete Act II.

My laughter during the writing came mostly at Willy's con ∍ tradicting himself so arrantly, and out of the laughter the title came one afternoon. *Death Comes for the Archbishop*, the *Death and the Maiden* Quartet—always austere and elevated was death in titles. Now it would be claimed by a joker, a bleeding mass of contradictions, a clown, and there was something funny about that something like a thumb in the eye, too. Yes, and in some far corner of my mind possibly something political; there was the smell in the air of a new American Empire in the making, if only because, as I had witnessed, Europe was dying or dead, and I wanted to set before the new captains and the so smugly confident kings the corpse of a believer. On the play's opening night a woman who shall not be named was outraged, calling it "a time bomb under American capitalism"; I hoped it was, or at least under the bullshit of capitalism, this pseudo life that thought to touch the clouds by standing on top of a refrigerator, waving a paid-up mortgage at the moon, victorious at last.

6   But some thirty-five years later, the Chinese reaction to my Beijing production of *Salesman* would confirm what had become more and more obvious over the decades in the play's hundreds of productions throughout the world: Willy was representative everywhere, in every kind of system, of ourselves in this time. The Chinese might disapprove of his lies and his self-deluding exaggerations as well as his immorality with women, but they certainly saw themselves in him. And it was not simply as a type but because of what he wanted. Which was to excel, to win out over anonymity and meaninglessness, to love and be loved, and above all, perhaps, to *count*. When he roared out, "I am not a dime a dozen! *I am Willy Loman, and you are Biff Loman!*" it came as a nearly revolutionary declaration after what was now thirty-four years of leveling. (The play was the same age as the Chinese revolution.) I did not know in 1948 in Connecticut that I was sending a message of resurgent individualism to the China of 1983—especially when the revolution had signified, it seemed at the time, the long-awaited rule of reason and the historic ending of chaotic egocentricity and selfish aggrandizement. Ah, yes. I had not reckoned on a young Chinese student saying to a CBS interviewer in the theatre lobby, "We are moved by it because we also want to be number one, and to be rich and successful." What else is this but human unpredictability, which goes on escaping the nets of unfreedom?

7   I did not move far from the phone for two days after sending the script to Kazan. By the end of the second silent day I would have accepted his calling to tell me that it was a scrambled egg, an impenetrable, unstageable piece of wreckage. And his tone when he finally did call was alarmingly somber.

8   "I've read your play." He sounded at a loss as to how to give me the bad news. "My God, it"s so sad."

9   "It's supposed to be."

10   "I just put it down. I don't know what to say. My father . . ." He broke off, the first of a great many men—and women—who would tell me that Willy was their father. I still thought he was letting me down easy. "It's a great play, Artie. I want to do it in the

fall or winter. I'll start thinking about casting." He was talking as though someone we both knew had just died, and it filled me with happiness. Such is art.

For the first time in months, as I hung up the phone, I could see my family clearly again. As was her way, Mary accepted the great news with a quiet pride, as though something more expressive would spoil me, but I too thought I should remain an ordinary citizen, even an anonymous one (although I did have a look at the new Studebaker convertible, the Raymond Lowey design that was the most beautiful American car of the time, and bought one as soon as the play opened). But Mary's mother, who was staying the week with us, was astonished. "*Another* play?" she said, as though the success of *All My Sons* had been enough for one lifetime. She had unknowingly triggered that play when she gossiped about a young girl somewhere in central Ohio who had turned her father in to the FBI for having manufactured faulty aircraft parts during the war. 11

Content

1. Why did Miller have to build a "little shack"—which he didn't know how to do and had to learn as he went along—before he could begin to write *Death of a Salesman* (¶s 3–4)?

2. How could Miller write a whole play with only "the first two lines and a death" in mind—"'Willy!' and 'It's all right. I came back'" (¶s 3–4)?

3. How could Miller write so fast, the entire first half of a play in less than 24 hours (¶ 4)? If it's unrealistic to expect most writers to write this rapidly and well without much revising, what's the point of asking prospective writers to read Miller's account of his writing process?

Strategies/Structures

4. What evidence does the arrangement of ideas and paragraphs in "Building and Writing" provide that this is an excerpt from Miller's autobiography, *Timebends*, rather than a conventional essay?

5. Who does Miller imagine as the audience for *Timebends* (first published in 1987)? What does he expect his readers to know and be familiar with? Can Miller (or any writer) expect readers of a different generation to know and understand the same things he and his contemporaries do? Does it matter whether they understand?

Language

6. Why does Miller say that closing in the roof was "a miracle, as though I had mastered the rain and cooled the sun" (¶ 4)?

For Writing

7. As one would expect of a playwright, Miller has the ability to create realistic dialogue (¶s 3, 8–11). For practice, try writing some conversation that you've either invented or overheard. Read it out loud to hear whether you've got it right. Then identify several principles of writing dialogue that works.

8. Examine the activities you engage in before beginning a major work project, whether they involve writing or not. Write a paper explaining for an audience of actual or potential procrastinators how one can discriminate between procrastination and warming up. To prepare for your paper, compare your behavior, and your interpretation of it, with that of several others you know. Can you reach any generalizations?

9. Miller explains that the Chinese, like people all over the world, loved *Death of a Salesman* because in Willy Loman they "saw themselves in him," recognizing the desire "to excel, to win out over anonymity and meaninglessness, to love and be loved, and above all, perhaps to *count*" (¶ 6). After you read *Death of a Salesman,* look at some of the other reviews and essays on this play—by Lahr (722–32), Atkinson (732–36), Brantley (736–41), Murphy (741–52), and Smith (752–58)—and see if you can explain, for American playgoers (or playgoers from your native country, if it's not the United States) why this play has been a favorite in many cultures for over half a century.

❄ *Writers' Notebooks*

There are no study questions for the notebook entries of either professional or student writers because these were not intended to be finished, unified artistic works. You can read these entries for diversity of content, tone, modes of expression, point of view, self-characterization, and persona. You can also consider how each entry might be a springboard for a full-blown essay.

MARK TWAIN

Mark Twain (a riverman's term for "two fathoms deep," the pen name of Samuel Clemens) celebrated in his writing a life-long love affair with the Mississippi River, which he regarded as "the great Mississippi, the majestic, the magnificent Mississippi, rolling its mile-wide tide along, shining in the sun." In *The Adventures of Tom Sawyer* (1876) and *The Adventures of Huckleberry Finn* (1885) he immortalized the riverfront town of Hannibal, Missouri, where he was born (1835) and whose folkways he absorbed. In 1875 he published *Old Times on the Mississippi*, a zestful account of his apprenticeship and experiences as a steamboat pilot, when he fulfilled a "permanent childhood ambition." He returned with great pleasure to the Mississippi in 1882 for the nostalgic trip downriver, recorded in the notebook entries reprinted here, partly to collect the material he used to expand *Old Times* into *Life on the Mississippi* (1883).

Even before he became a professional writer, Twain kept writer's notebooks, beginning in 1855, when he was twenty, and composing forty-nine volumes between 1855 and his death in 1910. (They have been published in a scholarly edition as *Mark Twain's Notebooks and Journals.*) Many of the entries are fragmentary—memorable names (some with comic possibilities) of people and places, epigrams or quotations provocative either for their dialect or their substance ("Paris papers small & dirty are dated a day ahead & contain last week's news"), ideas for later expansion ("My dream—talk with the Devil"). Longer entries record conversations, jokes, incidents, or other material that often emerged in Twain's published writing. The entries that follow exhibit these characteristics and epitomize a trip that was particularly happy when Twain was allowed to pilot the boat. He recalled, "When we got down below Cairo, and there was a big, full river—for it was high-water season and there was no danger of the boat hitting anything. . . I had her most of the time on [Lem Gray's] watch. He would . . . leave me there to dream that the years had not slipped away; that there had been no [Civil] war, no mining days, no literary adventures; that I was still a pilot, happy and care-free as I had been twenty years before."

Aboard a Mississippi River Steamboat[1]

New York to St. Louis
Apl. 18, 1882

1   The grace and picturesqueness of female dress seem to disappear as one travels west away from N. York. . . .

Scene near Greenville, O.

2   Tendency to the esthetic:—A rather plain, white-painted wooden house[;][2] facing the R.R. In the yard two composition Dogs guarding the walk; both with glass eyes—one with a fire-red head & ears; nearer the door two [lions] Lions couchant, regarding [pas] our train and other passing events with a ferocious smile/rigid ferocity; aspect of the dogs more benignant;—half a dozen [a] urns and vases;—near the center a cast-iron swan, not dying but evidently pretty sick. All these and other adornments in a door yard barely 50 feet square!

April 19th —

3   This morning struck into the region of full "goatees"—sometimes in company with moustaches, but usually not.

4   All the R.R. station loafers west of Pittsburgh carry *both* hands in their pockets. Further east one hand is sometimes out of doors. Here never. This is an important fact in Geography. . . .

Apl. 20th A.M.

5   The companionway was less than 2 inches deep in dirt, showing that she had n't been washed down for perhaps a couple of days. The saloon round about the stove was guttered up and splintered, showing that she had n't been repaired as to floors since I was in St. Louis last.

---

[1] Title supplied.
[2] Bracketed material denotes cancellations in Twain's original notebook. Footnotes are those of the Twain editors unless indicated by LZB.

Four iron spittoons around the stove—not particularly clean, but clean enough to show that there hadn't been any passengers aboard this year. Green, wooden chairs, cane seated, all more or less venerable; a venerable colored chambermaid;—everything venerable. No decoration except a painted, pale-green diamond over the state room doors. This boat built by Fulton; has not been repaired since.

Mem:—Comparative scarcity of steam boats now. In old days the 6
boats lay simply with their *noses* against the wharf, wedged in, stern out in the river[.], side by side like sardines in a box. Now the boats lie end to end.—The "Anchor Line" appears to [line] monopolise

Boarded the "Gold Dust" 5 p.m. Apl. 20th. 7

Encountered on the deck before starting a vender of books 8
and papers. His name is Sullivan—of pure Irish extraction. He says he came into the world on the 23^d Sept 1800. Has lived here 34 years and never crossed the Miss. Says if you meet an Irishman *prove* he is an Irishmn. Not an Irishmn because he is born in Ireland no more than a man is a horse because he's born in a stable. Thousands born in Ireland who are not Irishmen. His ancestors came to Ireland 300 years after the flood and he gave their names. Referring to his business of vending literature, he says:—"I read quite a little in my youthful days. Some say a person has no right to read fiction but I tell ye that all the great men of the day read fiction. I niver met a great man who didnt rade fiction. When you rade the Greek and Latin languages you're rading fiction. Go to-night and rade the firmament; the stars, [are] ivery [o] wan of 'em tells of fiction. Indade, its necessary for a man to rade fiction to be a scholar."

(By Johnson)[3] "Do they have Scotch whiskey in Ireland?" 9
"They have *Irish* whiskey sir. They have the best kind. ["] 10
But I don't use much mesilf. I am not a hard drinker, sir. Give an Irishman lager beer for one month and he's a dead man. An Irishman is lined inside with copper and the lager beer corrodes it."

---

[3] Mark Twain was trying out fictional names for his traveling companions.

11   (By Sampson) "I suppose the whiskey, on the other hand, tends to polish off the copper."

12   "Bedad that's the truth of it, sir." . . .

April 21 —

13   Landed at 6 o'clock this morning at a God forsaken rocky point where there was an old stone warehouse, gradually crumbling to ruin; two or three decayed dwelling houses, and nothing else suggestive of human life visible. X[4] Nobody put in an appearance except a tallow-faced [man o(f)] beardless man of about 30 carrying one cubic foot of baggage tied up in a red handkchf. As he came aboard his eye caught our Mr. Johnson seated on the forward deck. Something in the stern aspect of Johnson convinced this passenger that he was actually gazing upon the Captain of the Boat. [and a] A self-deprecatory look immediately overspread his features and he quickly crept in out of range of Johnson's eagle glances. X

14   We put ashore a gentleman and a lady, well-dressed[,] with good Russia leather bags; also two very nicely dressed lady like young girls. There was no carriage awaiting and they marched off down the road to go God knows where. It seemed a strange place for civilized folks to land. But the mystery was explained when we got under way again for these people were evidently bound for a large town which lay in behind a towhead two miles below the landing. I couldn't remember that town; couldn't place it; couldnt call its name; couldn't remember ever to have seen it before; couldn't imagine what the damned place might be. I guessed that it might be St. Genevieve—and that proved to be correct. The town is completely fenced in. Even at this [stage] excellent stage of the water a boat can't land within two miles of it. It is one of the oldest towns in Mo. Built on high ground, handsomely situated; once had good river privileges, but [is] it is no longer a river town. It is town out in the country. . . .

15   Went up to the pilothouse when we were approaching Chester (where the big Illinois penitentiary is located). Found everything familiar in the pilothouse except that they blow the

---

4 Twain's marks. [LZB]

whistle with a foot-treadle and have a bell-pull that I wasn't acquainted with to call for the electric light, and a big speaking tube under the breast board, whose use I don't know.

Something which suggests short packet lines and quick   16 trips is the absence of spars.

Another brand new thing is the suspending of the "stages"   17 from derricks, letting them swing in the air projecting forward. Admirable contrivance both for quickness and convenience in handling. There is no nighthawk on the jack staff. There is an electric light where it used to be, and that is used in place of the ancient torchbasket. There is an electric headlight over the companionway which can be turned in any direction by the Capt. from his position on deck—so that the landing of a steamboat at night is as easy work as in the day time. They couldnt use the nighthawk lamp to land by because it would blind the pilot.

The officers of this line will go into uniform on the 1ˢᵗ of   18 May. They are quiet and dignified according to the ancient custom. Also the mates; whereas it used to be required of the mate to rip and curse by way of emphasizing orders. One of the 3 mates on this boat is of the ancient tribe. He is one of the old-fashioned, God-damn-your-soul kind. Very affable and sociable. Pointed out a country residence saying, "There, that's a God damned fine place. That place was built out of the profits of the flesh brokerage business in St. Louis. The old bitch that owns that place has the biggest [h] whore house in St. Louis. She don't know how much she's worth. Brings the girls down here into the country to freshen them up for work. A man told me he had seen 47 "shimmies" hanging on one line there. She's got a husband and if he don't go straight she licks him. She makes him do as she God damn pleases.

This other place down here is owned by old what's-his-   19 name. He's got an income of $100,000. a month. *He* don't give a God-damn. He Don't know how much he's worth."

(This man talks like the machine Barnum had around with   20 his circus for a while. Has that same guttural indistinct, jumbling, rasping way of talking. But this mate can out-swear the machine.)

Our passenger from Nebraska thinks the dinner on the boat   21 was the best he ever "sot" down to. Soup & fish & two kinds of meat and several kinds of *Pie!*

22   He said to Phelps to-day, "Say, that friend of yours is up in the pilot house. I jest heard him talking & he's an old pilot himself. Now, he's been giving me taffy, representing that he didnt know much about this river. Judging by his conversation I think he knows *all* about it."

Friday Eve'g Apl 21ˢᵗ.

23   Visited the pilot house this morning to get warm, and was betrayed by one of the boys—the pilot on watch. He said, "I have seen somebody sometime or other who resembled you very strongly and a great many years ago I heard a man use your voice. He is sometimes called Mark Twain—or Sam Clemens."

24   I said, "Then don't give me away" and made no further effort to keep up the shallow swindle. The pilot said he recognized me partly by my voice and face and this was confirmed by my habit of running my hands up thro my hair.

25   The river is so thoroughly changed that I can't bring it back to mind even when the changes have been pointed out to me. It is like a man pointing out to me a place in the sky where a cloud has been. I can't reproduce the cloud. Yet as unfamiliar as all the aspects have been to-day I have felt as much at home and as much as in my proper place in the pilot house as if I had never been out of the pilot house. I have felt as if I might be informed any moment it was my watch to take a trick at the wheel.

26   To-night when some idiot approaching Cairo didn't answer our whistle but rounded to across our bows and came near getting himself split in two I felt an old-time hunger to be at the wheel and cut him in two,—knowing I had fulfilled the law and it would be his fault. By shipping up and backing we saved him, to my considerable regret—for it would have made good practical literature if we had got him.

27   Found Cairo looking very natural by the light of the gas and our own electric light from the pilot house, and concluded to wait till morning and go ashore and examine it.

28   Found government lights everywhere all down the river. This is too much. It takes away [all the] a great deal of the agony of piloting and must make it even more enjoyable than it used to be,—and it was always enjoyable enough. . . . Birds Point looked

as it always looked, except that the river has moved Mr. Bird's house ¾ mile nearer to the front than it used to be.

Mem:

The only thing that remains to me now of the technical edu-   29
cation which I got on the river is the faculty of remembering numbers, streets and addresses,—which I trace to the automatic remembering of the depths of water by the lead. . . .

Napoleon, Ark. Apl. 24.

The town (2000 inhab.) used to be where the river now is.   30
Washed entirely away by a cut-off and not a vestige of it re-mains—except one little house and the chimney of another which were out in the suburbs once.

The Captain's[5] Story.

Senator Bogy of Mo.[6] had a son a pompous sort of fellow. His name   31
was Joe. Joe was fond of being known as the son of Senator Bogy, and liked to be introduced at parties and gatherings as "Mr. Bogy son of Senator Bogy."

That ancient mariner went up thro the [shoot] chute down   32
the river up thro the [shoot] chute and down again all thro' his watch. Supposed was going down the river all the time. A darkey saw the boat passing so often and said, "Clar to gracious! I reckon dar must be a whole line o' dem ar Skylarks."

The "Eclipse" was [th] noted as being the fastest boat.[7] She   33
had just passed an old darkey on shore who happened not to rec-ognize her name. Presently some one asked him, "Any boat gone up?" "Yes sah." "Was she going fast?" "Oh, so-so, loafing along." "Now, do you know what boat that was?"

"No, sah."   34

---

5 John T. McCord entertained Clemens with the three anecdotes which follow.
6 Lewis Vital Bogy, a Saint Louis attorney and businessman, had served as United States senator from 1872 until his death in 1877.
7 In 1852 and 1853 the *Eclipse* made record runs from New Orleans to Natchez, Cairo, and other upstream ports. Mark Twain described her exploits in "Old Times on the Mississippi" (*Atlantic Monthly*, August 1875) in a section pub-lished as chapter 16 of *Life on the Mississippi*.

35   "Well, that was the Eclipse."

36   "Oh, well, she just went by here a sparkling!"

37   The pilot thinking I was a greenhorn put up a great deal of remarkable river information on me.

38   The Capt. said that if this boat were to sink right here (Ark. section) in less than one hour there would be a hundred pirates out here in skiffs after plunder.

39   Down here we are in the region of boots again. They don't wear shoes.

Fence-rail quarrel.

40   During the high water one man's fence rails washed down on another mans ground and the latter's rails around on to former's ground. Kind of exchange of rails. In the eddy they got mixed somehow. One said to the other "[let]Let it remain so; I will use your rails & you mine." But the other wouldn't have it so. One day the first man came down on the other's place to get his rails. The other said "I'll kill you, you son of a bitch," and went for him with a revolver. The other said "I'm not armed" and the assailant threw down his revolver and came at him with a knife, cut his throat all around but not severing the jugular vein or arteries. Struggling around the man whose throat was cut got hold of the other's revolver on the ground and shot him dead[.], but survived his own injuries.

Another.

41   Two shop-keepers in adjoining stores had a quarrel. One of them put his hand back in his hip pocket to get some documents. The other thought he was going for a weapon, drew his pistol and began firing. The first called out "Im not armed; don't kill an unarmed man." But the other kept on firing and killed him. Was acquitted by the jury. . . .

42   Neither this country nor any other can ever prosper until the votes of the two parties are nearly equal

43   Stopped at Arkansas City April 24. This is a Hell of a place. One or two streets full of mud; 19 different stenches at the same time. A thriving place nevertheless. A R.R. here—the Little Rock, Miss. river & Texas R.R.

ANNE FRANK

Anne Frank's *The Diary of a Young Girl* (first published in 1947) is the most widely read document ever written about Nazi crimes, says Melissa Müller, Frank's biographer. Its publication transformed the young author into "a universal symbol of the oppressed in a world of violence and tyranny," for the name of Anne Frank "invokes humanity, tolerance, human rights and democracy; her image is the epitome of optimism and the will to live."

The diary was a precious thirteenth birthday gift, begun on June 12, 1942, with Anne's comment, "I hope I will be able to confide everything to you, as I have never been able to confide in anyone, and I hope you will be a great source of comfort and support." Although Otto Frank, Anne's father, titled the work *The Diary of a Young Girl,* this spirited, evocative work provides a memorable self-presentation, not of an icon of innocence but of a teen-ager in the process of growing into a young woman. Anne, her parents, her older sister Margot, and four others, were confined for two years in "the Secret Annex" of a protector's house in Amsterdam, in hiding from the S.S., who were determined to round up all Jews and deport them to concentration camps. Nevertheless, as the *Diary* clearly reveals, even with the "approaching thunder" of the Holocaust echoing in the Nazi bombings of the city outside her window, the author juxtaposes attempts to negotiate new, mature relationships with her family with dreams of romantic love and aspirations to become a distinguished writer. Indeed, when she was fourteen and fifteen Anne revised her diary extensively, in hopes of publishing it after the war.[1] She expanded it by 30 percent, providing more interpretive commentary and explanations for an audience unfamiliar with the constrained circumstances of life in hiding.

On August 4, 1944, on an informer's tip, the S.S. raided the Annex and sent the inhabitants to concentration camps on the last train to leave the Netherlands for Auschwitz. Anne and her sister, separated from their parents, died of a typhus epidemic in Bergen-Belsen six weeks before the British liberated the camp in April, 1945. Only Otto Frank survived.

---

[1] The excerpts printed here are from *The Diary of a Young Girl,* "The Definitive Edition," ed. Otto H. Frank and Miriam Pressler, new translation by Susan Massotty (New York: Doubleday, 1995).

from The Diary of a Young Girl

SUNDAY, MAY 2, 1943

1   When I think about our lives here, I usually come to the conclusion that we live in a paradise compared to the Jews who aren't in hiding. All the same, later on, when everything has returned to normal, I'll probably wonder how we, who always lived in such comfortable circumstances, could have "sunk" so low. With respect to manner, I mean. For example, the same oilcloth has covered the dining table ever since we've been here. After so much use, it's hardly what you'd call spotless. I do my best to clean it, but since the dishcloth was also purchased before we went into hiding and consists of more holes than cloth, it's a thankless task. The van Daans have been sleeping all winter long on the same flannel sheet, which can't be washed because detergent is rationed and in short supply. Besides, it's of such poor quality that it's practically useless. Father is walking around in frayed trousers, and his tie is also showing signs of wear and tear. Mama's corset snapped today and is beyond repair, while Margot is wearing a bra that's two sizes too small. Mother and Margot have shared the same three undershirts the entire winter, and mine are so small they don't even cover my stomach. These are all things that can be overcome, but I sometimes wonder: how can we, whose every possession, from my underpants to Father's shaving brush, is so old and worn, ever hope to regain the position we had before the war?

SUNDAY, MAY 2, 1943

2   *Mr. van Daan.* In the opinion of us all, this revered gentleman has great insight into politics. Nevertheless, he predicts we'll have to stay here until the end of '43. That's a very long time, and yet it's possible to hold out until then. But who can assure us that this war, which has caused nothing but pain and sorrow, will then be over? And that nothing will have happened to us and our helpers long before that time? No one! That's why each and every day is filled with tension. Expectation and hope generate tension, as does fear—for example, when we hear a noise inside or outside

the house, when the guns go off or when we read new "procla-
mations" in the paper, since we're afraid our helpers might be
forced to go into hiding themselves sometime. These days everyone is talking about having to hide. We don't know how many
people are actually in hiding; of course, the number is relatively
small compared to the general population, but later on we'll no
doubt be astonished at how many good people in Holland were
willing to take Jews and Christians, with or without money, into
their homes. There're also an unbelievable number of people with
false identity papers.

TUESDAY, MAY 18, 1943

Dearest Kit,

  I recently witnessed a fierce dogfight between German and   3
English pilots. Unfortunately, a couple of Allied airmen had to
jump out of their burning plane. Our milkman, who lives in
Halfweg, saw four Canadians sitting along the side of the road,
and one of them spoke fluent Dutch. He asked the milkman if he
had a light for his cigarette, and then told him the crew had consisted of six men. The pilot had been burned to death, and the
fifth crew member had hidden himself somewhere. The German
Security Police came to pick up the four remaining men, none of
whom were injured. After parachuting out of a flaming plane,
how can anyone have such presence of mind?

  Although it's undeniably hot, we have to light a fire every   4
other day to burn our vegetable peelings and garbage. We can't
throw anything into the trash cans, because the warehouse employees might see it. One small act of carelessness and we're
done for!

  All college students are being asked to sign an official state-   5
ment to the effect that they "sympathize with the Germans and
approve of the New Order." Eighty percent have decided to obey
the dictates of their conscience, but the penalty will be severe.
Any student refusing to sign will be sent to a German labor camp.
What's to become of the youth of our country if they've all got to
do hard labor in Germany?

  Last night the guns were making so much noise that Mother   6
shut the window;

SATURDAY, MARCH 4, 1944

Dear Kitty,

7   This is the first Saturday in months that hasn't been tiresome, dreary and boring. The reason is Peter. This morning as I was on my way to the attic to hang up my apron, Father asked whether I wanted to stay and practice my French, and I said yes. We spoke French together for a while and I explained something to Peter, and then we worked on our English. Father read aloud from Dickens, and I was in seventh heaven, since I was sitting on Father's chair, close to Peter.

8   I went downstairs at quarter to eleven. When I went back up at eleven-thirty, Peter was already waiting for me on the stairs. We talked until quarter to one. Whenever I leave the room, for example after a meal, and Peter has a chance and no one else can hear, he says, "Bye, Anne, see you later."

9   Oh, I'm so happy! I wonder if he's going to fall in love with me after all? In any case, he's a nice boy, and you have no idea how good it is to talk to him!

10   Mrs. van D. thinks it's all right for me to talk to Peter, but today she asked me teasingly, "Can I trust you two up there?"

11   "Of course," I protested. "I take that as an insult!" Morning, noon and night, I look forward to seeing Peter.

Yours, Anne M. Frank

TUESDAY, MARCH 7, 1944

Dearest Kitty,

12   When I think back to my life in 1942, it all seems so unreal. The Anne Frank who enjoyed that heavenly existence was completely different from the one who has grown wise within these walls. Yes, it was heavenly. Five admirers on every street corner, twenty or so friends, the favorite of most of my teachers, spoiled rotten by Father and Mother, bags full of candy and a big allowance. What more could anyone ask for?

13   You're probably wondering how I could have charmed all those people. Peter says it's because I'm "attractive," but that isn't it entirely. The teachers were amused and entertained by my clever answers, my witty remarks, my smiling face and my critical mind. That's all I was: a terrible flirt, coquettish and amusing. I had a few plus points, which kept me in everybody's good

graces: I was hardworking, honest and generous. I would never have refused anyone who wanted to peek at my answers, I was magnanimous with my candy, and I wasn't stuck-up.

Would all that admiration eventually have made me over- 14
confident? It's a good thing that, at the height of my glory, I was suddenly plunged into reality. It took me more than a year to get used to doing without admiration.

How did they see me at school? As the class comedian, the 15
eternal ringleader, never in a bad mood, never a crybaby. Was it any wonder that everyone wanted to bicycle to school with me or do me little favors?

I look back at that Anne Frank as a pleasant, amusing, but 16
superficial girl, who has nothing to do with me. What did Peter say about me? "Whenever I saw you, you were surrounded by a flock of girls and at least two boys, you were always laughing, and you were always the center of attention!" He was right.

What's remained of that Anne Frank? Oh, I haven't forgot- 17
ten how to laugh or toss off a remark, I'm just as good, if not better, at raking people over the coals, and I can still flirt and be amusing, if I want to be . . .

But there's the catch. I'd like to live that seemingly carefree 18
and happy life for an evening, a few days, a week. At the end of that week I'd be exhausted, and would be grateful to the first per-son to talk to me about something meaningful. I want friends, not admirers. People who respect me for my character and my deeds, not my flattering smile. The circle around me would be much smaller, but what does that matter, as long as they're sincere?

In spite of everything, I wasn't altogether happy in 1942; I 19
often felt I'd been deserted, but because I was on the go all day long, I didn't think about it. I enjoyed myself as much as I could, trying consciously or unconsciously to fill the void with jokes.

Looking back, I realize that this period of my life has irrevo- 20
cably come to a close; my happy-go-lucky, carefree schooldays are gone forever. I don't even miss them. I've outgrown them. I can no longer just kid around, since my serious side is always there.

I see my life up to New Year's 1944 as if I were looking 21
through a powerful magnifying glass. When I was at home, my life was filled with sunshine. Then, in the middle of 1942, everything changed overnight. The quarrels, the accusations—I couldn't take

it all in. I was caught off guard, and the only way I knew to keep my bearings was to talk back.

22   The first half of 1943 brought crying spells, loneliness and the gradual realization of my faults and shortcomings, which were numerous and seemed even more so. I filled the day with chatter, tried to draw Pim closer to me and failed. This left me on my own to face the difficult task of improving myself so I wouldn't have to hear their reproaches, because they made me so despondent.

23   The second half of the year was slightly better. I became a teenager, and was treated more like a grown-up. I began to think about things and to write stories, finally coming to the conclusion that the others no longer had anything to do with me. They had no right to swing me back and forth like a pendulum on a clock. I wanted to change myself in my own way. I realized I could manage without my mother, completely and totally, and that hurt. But what affected me even more was the realization that I was never going to be able to confide in Father. I didn't trust anyone but myself.

24   After New Year's the second big change occurred: my dream, through which I discovered my longing for . . . a boy; not for a girl-friend, but for a boyfriend. I also discovered an inner happiness underneath my superficial and cheerful exterior. From time to time I was quiet. Now I live only for Peter, since what happens to me in the future depends largely on him!

25   I lie in bed at night, after ending my prayers with the words *"Ich danke dir für all das Gute und Liebe und Schöne,"** and I'm filled with joy. I think of going into hiding, my health and my whole being as *das Gute;* Peter's love (which is still so new and fragile and which neither of us dares to say aloud), the future, happiness and love as *das Liebe;* the world, nature and the tremendous beauty of everything, all that splendor, as *das Schöne.*

26   At such moments I don't think about all the misery, but about the beauty that still remains. This is where Mother and I differ greatly. Her advice in the face of melancholy is: "Think about all the suffering in the world and be thankful you're not part of it." My advise is "Go outside, to the country, enjoy the sun and all nature has to offer. Go outside and try to recapture the

---

*Thank you, God, for all that is good and dear and beautiful.

happiness within yourself; think of all the beauty in yourself and in everything around you and be happy."

I don't think Mother's advice can be right, because what are you supposed to do if you become part of the suffering? You'd be completely lost. On the contrary, beauty remains, even in misfortune. If you just look for it, you discover more and more happiness and regain your balance. A person who's happy will make others happy; a person who has courage and faith will never die in misery!

Yours, Anne M. Frank 27

WEDNESDAY, APRIL 5, 1944

I finally realized that I must do my schoolwork to keep from being ignorant, to get on in life, to become a journalist, because that's what I want! I *know* I can write. A few of my stories are good, my descriptions of the Secret Annex are humorous, much of my diary is vivid and alive, but . . . it remains to be seen whether I really have talent. 28

"Eva's Dream" is my best fairy tale, and the odd thing is that I don't have the faintest idea where it came from. Parts of "Cady's Life" are also good, but as a whole it's nothing special. I'm my best and harshest critic. I know what's good and what isn't. Unless you write yourself, you can't know how wonderful it is; I always used to bemoan the fact that I couldn't draw, but now I'm overjoyed that at least I can write. And if I don't have the talent to write books or newspaper articles, I can always write for myself. But I want to achieve more than that. I can't imagine having to live like Mother, Mrs. van Daan and all the women who go about their work and are then forgotten. I need to have something besides a husband and children to devote myself to! I don't want to have lived in vain like most people. I want to be useful or bring enjoyment to all people, even those I've never met. I want to go on living even after my death! And that's why I'm so grateful to God for having given me this gift, which I can use to develop myself and to express all that's inside me! 29

When I write I can shake off all my cares. My sorrow disappears, my spirits are revived! But, and that's a big question, will I ever be able to write something great, will I ever become a journalist or a writer? 30

31   I hope so, oh, I hope so very much, because writing allows me to record everything, all my thoughts, ideals and fantasies.

32   I have one outstanding character trait that must be obvious to anyone who's known me for any length of time: I have a great deal of self-knowledge. In everything I do, I can watch myself as if I were a stranger. I can stand across from the everyday Anne and, without being biased or making excuses, watch what she's doing, both the good and the bad. This self-awareness never leaves me, and every time I open my mouth, I think, "You should have said that differently" or "That's fine the way it is." I condemn myself in so many ways that I'm beginning to realize the truth of Father's adage: "Every child has to raise itself." Parents can only advise their children or point them in the right direction. Ultimately, people shape their own characters. In addition, I face life with an extraordinary amount of courage. I feel so strong and capable of bearing burdens, so young and free! When I first realized this, I was glad, because it means I can more easily withstand the blows life has in store.

S. L. WISENBERG

S[andi] L. Wisenberg (born, 1955) lived in Houston before earning a degree from Northwestern University's prestigious journalism program (1979) and an M.F.A. from the University of Iowa Writer's Workshop. I'm your basic descendant of the (Jewish) huddled masses," she says, "three of my grandparents [were] born in Eastern Europe," as were the parents of the fourth. She has been a reporter on the *Miami Herald* (1983–1985) and has taught writing classes and women's studies at Northwestern and other schools. "I knew early on I wanted to be a writer," she explains. "When I was growing up my two heroes were Anne Frank and Louisa May Alcott. I really identified with Anne Frank because she was Jewish and a writer." Creative nonfiction editor of *Another Chicago Magazine*, Wisenberg has published fiction and nonfiction (including Holocaust pieces) in many places, among them the *New Yorker*, *Tikkun*, *North American Review*, and *Pushcart Prize*.

"Margot's Diary" is based on information Wisenberg gleaned from visits in 1992 to the Anne Frank Huis in Amsterdam, the Anne Frank house in Frankfurt, from which the Franks moved in 1933 to escape persecution, and Anne Frank's diary. "I usually write quickly, put the piece aside, and go back and revise over several years," Wisenberg says. Here she imagines an alternative to Anne Frank's interpretation of life in the Secret Annex, as it might have been viewed by her older sister, Margot (see preceding selection): "She is the sister of. The shadow. The first child who made way for the second, the important one. Who is more alive." *Creative Nonfiction,* where the piece first appeared in 1998, "almost didn't publish it because it seemed so fictional, but I thought I'd made it clear that I was speculating on what Margot had written—the magic 'perhaps.' It was just chance that Anne's diary was saved and not Margot's, and I wondered what her diary was like. No matter how much we speculate, we don't know what she or Anne were really like, or the other six million."

Margot's Diary

Photos: Anne, 1941; Margot, 1941:   1
    They both part their hair on the left side, wear a watch on the same wrist, have the same eyebrows, same open-mouthed smile. Their noses and eyes are different, the shape of their faces, the cut of their hair, the fall of it. Books are open in front of each of them. One photo we glance past. Because she is unknown. We don't care what she looks like—she's vaguely familiar. Not the real one. She is the sister of. The shadow. The first child who made way for the second, the important one. Who is more alive. Whose photo is crisp in contrasts, not blurry.

The diaries: 2
    Margot kept one, you know. She was the daughter known to be smart, studious, reflective. Hers was lost. Among the many items lost in the war, among millions. Perhaps her diary was darker—she was older, quieter, frailer. More naturally introspective. Perhaps she did not write that she believed that people were good at heart. Perhaps she did not rejoice in nature. Perhaps she

wrote: "There must be something wrong with us or else they would not be after us. We are cooped up here like mice. Anne is the only one who seems not to know we are doomed but she may be the bravest of all. We learn our French for what. In order to learn our French. We will be so warped upon our exit here that if we ever do escape, if there ever is freedom, we will not be able to live among the others. We shall be marked more than by the outline of the yellow badges."

3   Why we like them:

They were suburban and then urban. They had bicycles and birthday parties. We know how to put both of those things together. Or whom to call to arrange them. Just like us—the thrill of the avalanche missed.

Not that we would ever sacrifice someone else —

4   In the Anne Frank *Huis*, Amsterdam:

Which was not a house, but an apartment over the office where her father had been in business selling pectin for making jellies, and spices for making sausages. In July 1992, a young girl on a tour smiles in recognition of Anne's familiar face in a photo. On the wall are French vocabulary words Anne copied out:

> *la poudre à canon*
> *le voleur*
> *la maison de commerce*
> *le conseil*
> *de retour*
> *le glute (het glure)*
> *le musée*
> *la cause*
> *le bouquet*
> *l'éducation*
> *envie*
> *après-demain*
> *avant-hier*
> *le sang*

(gun-powder, thief, business-firm?, advice, returning back, glue?, museum, cause, bouquet, education, desire, the day after tomorrow, the day before yesterday, blood)

Five thousand visitors a year stream into the old narrow 5
house. Often, there are lines.

In Frankfurt: 6
   There's a plaque on the door of the duplex of the first Anne
Frank house, which the family left the year of Hitler's election.
They went west, to Aachen, then Amsterdam, for safety. Someone
lives in the house still; it's private, not open to the public. The
neighborhood is outside the center city, an area where young families set up hopeful households in the late 1920s and early 1930s.
Streets named for poets, three-story stucco buildings. Cars are
parked all along both sides of the street. You can hear TVs, dogs,
birds, children playing. Occasionally a bike rider glides past. I
wonder if it was as leafy 60 years ago. There should be plaques on
houses throughout Europe: A Jew lived here and was taken away.
Or: People lived here and then Death took them away. Anne was
4 when they left in 1933; Margot was 6.

Perhaps Margot remembered: 7
   "Frankfurt, the house, the neighborhood, the protected
feeling of it, safe, bright, like in the country, but the excitement,
too, the newness of it. The best of everything, said my mother:
Brand-new sturdy outside, delicate antiques inside. In Amsterdam, we learned to see vertically, to look up and down. All is
narrow and the streets are crooked and thin. Contained. I was
sorry to move away from everything familiar. From my native
language. Everything in Amsterdam is approximate. And old.
Compare and contrast. In Amsterdam we find what is already
here. Someone else has already named everything. Anne, I don't
think, really understands what is happening. We brought our old
grandfather clock with us here, because it too is tall and thin.
Ticks like a soft heartbeat, brooding over us."

Perhaps Margot grieved: 8
   "July 1942. To leave yet again another house, in Amsterdam.
They have named me. The Nazis have found me. They know I am
here. A postcard ordering me to pack my winter clothes and appear for a transport to Germany. Instead I left the house, rode my
bicycle with Miep to what became the Annex. Rain protected us;
no one stopped us. And we arrived. I was the first one in the family to enter it that day. The boxes were already there. Night fell.

"July 1943. Over time I grew quieter and quieter, they said. My thoughts raged inside then slowed. Everything slowed. I followed the course for French, for shorthand. At night we went downstairs to file and alphabetize for the company—for its benefit, for ours, a slender thread connecting us to the real world, commerce.

"We could not get away from the chime of the Westertoren clock, every quarter hour. It surprised me each time; nothing seemed predictable about it. I missed the steady ticking of our clock at home, imagined it slowing down to match the winding down of my thoughts. My stomach throbbed, my head. My heartbeat pounded in code: It is time to die. That's why I was so quiet, in order to hear the heart's message. I couldn't tolerate Anne's chatter. I abhored singing."

9   Margot didn't write:

"Of the day they came for us, Aug. 4, 1944. It was late morning, happened fast. I gathered some bread, a Bible, a threadbare sweater—buttons missing. We tramped out, like machines set in motion. The sun hit us for a moment before we were herded into the car. Silent, of course, on the way to the station. Anne couldn't bear to look out the window. I did. Hungry for the familiar but impersonal landmarks. Signs in Dutch and German. German, the language we no longer memorized. Everyone was thin. But their hair shone. Wind riffled through skirts. That's what we'd been missing: the benign unpredictability of the breeze.

"You can imagine the rest."

10   At Bergen-Belsen, winter 1945:

Margot ran out of language. Everything seeped from her. She was barely 18. Her name appeared on lists of people who didn't come back. The day of death unmarked. She left no papers behind that were gathered up and stored in a file drawer in a maison de commerce in Amsterdam, then translated, promulgated. Of her family, only her father came *de retour*. The Annex is now a *musée*. It is a center for *l'éducation*, to search for *la cause*. Margot has lost her *envie*. It no longer matters if it is *après-demain* or *avant-hier*, she has lost today, the glue that binds one minute to the next, as once marked by the German-made grandfather clock. Her *sang* is as dry as *poudrà de canon*. Time is the *voleur*. She offers no *conseil*. This is not her *bouquet*.

Selections from Student Writers' Notebooks

RICHARD LOFTUS, JILL WOOLLEY, ART GREENWOOD,
BARBARA SCHOFIELD, SUSAN YORITOMO,
BETTY J. WALKER, TAMMY WEAST, KRISTIN KING,
ROSALIND BRADLEY COLES, CHERYL WATANABE,
STEPHEN E. RYAN

The students who kept these writers' notebooks in courses at the
University of Connecticut, Virginia Commonwealth University,
and the College of William and Mary in recent years majored in
a variety of subjects: King, Loftus, Ryan, and Watanabe, English;
Woolley, archaeology; Greenwood, general studies; Schofield,
education; Yoritomo, filmmaking; Walker, human resource management; Weast, mass communications; Coles, biology and
creative writing. All share a love of the sounds as well as the
sense of words, all like to play around with the language; some
read omnivorously while others focus on visual images. All bring
creativity to their work, which ranges from assisting on archaeo-
logical digs to personnel administration to pharmacological
laboratory research to editing publications for a hospital and
for the Wolf Trap music foundation.

The selections from their notebooks reflect a range of interests and moods as varied as the writers. Reactions to keeping a
notebook ("It's better to do it than to talk about it"), a satiric
recipe ("Oh, Mom, was there ever a worse cook than you?"),
self-analysis ("I could get by, looking good"), an attempt at
self-improvement ("I've been trying to put cigarettes down for
six years now"), explorations of sound ("HE'LL BANG EM
AND HIS CYMBALS CRASH AND HISS"), analysis of an
apartment style that mirrors the writer's personal style ("My
apartment is stark. I'm stark"), a humorous tirade against
housework ("I hate it"), the devastating impact of a divorce on
a family's Christmas ("I ate a beans n franks dinner later. My
brother went to drink his gift certificate"), reactions to being
black in a white world (Coles), homosexual in a straight world
(Loftus), Asian in America (Watanabe). And a joyous reaction

to the writer's first publication—"and not in the Letters to the Editor column, either."

These entries offer just a hint of the infinite potential of writers' notebooks.

Richard Loftus

1   I read something in some book from some new author in some bookshop somewhere to the effect that writer's block is "reading old fat novels instead of making new skinny ones." My secret is out.

• • •

2   I don't feel like writing now. I should pick up *Mansfield Park* again. Reading Austen or anyone that good reminds me of what I could be saying, and of the work that has to be put into it. How often have I begun a journal and stopped because two days later it didn't seem so good? I suppose I saved myself from some self-flagellation, but also from a record of growth. There are some people in the class who write often, and though their perceptions are no more acute or their difficulties in writing no less than my own, I feel that they're ahead. I must remember what Susan said to me, that "It's better to do it than talk about it." This is doing it, huh? This is getting it down on paper. Knowing that I have to keep this record is the best part.

• • •

Green Bean Surprise Casserole

1 can green beans, drained
1 can cream of mushroom soup
1 box cheez-bits

Layer ingredients—beans, then soup and cheez-bits—in greased casserole. Place casserole in preheated 350° oven. Bake forty-five minutes. Serve.

3   I'm telling you something I've never told anyone. Never, through the long years of dinners made possible by the invention of the electric can opener and the publication of Peg Bracken's *The*

I Hate to Cook Cookbook. Never, though the mention of meatloaf still conjures images of a dark, brick-like thing, ketchup glazed and gurgling angrily in a sea of orangish drippings in a pyrex baking dish. Never, even when her mantra spun in my brain like an old forty-five: "Some people live to eat, Richard (my name spoken with accusative gravity), *I* eat to live." Oh, Mom, was there ever a worse cook than you?

Jill Woolley

I don't want to be a scholar. I run on intuition. My pleasure is in 4 creating. . . . I hate collecting information and acting like I have something new and exciting to say about any of it. I'm not an organizer. Maybe I'm not a synthesizer. I'm all talent and no discipline. I can get away with some sweat and inspiration. I can get by with bullshit because my bull is better than 85% of everybody else's hard work. But I know what's coming off the top of my head. I know I'm a phony. At least that's how I feel. No substance. I've disconnected my soul. I've sold myself out because I could get by, looking good.

• • •

I meant to throw these boots away. I had them in a box for the 5 Salvation Army pick-up. Somehow they worked their way back on to my feet. It's the same with so many things—boots, men, cigarettes—you try to get them out of your life and they keep coming out on top.

I've been trying to put cigarettes down for six years now, on 6 and off. Still, day after day, I pay my [money] for a pack of poison. Why is it easier to smoke than to not smoke? It certainly isn't easier to exercise than to not exercise. It isn't easier to work hard than to not work hard. So why is it easier to smoke?

I try all kinds of tricks. I count how many cigarettes I've 7 smoked in a day. I wait until dark to light up. I brush my teeth after every cigarette. But these gimmicks soon fall away and again I'm chain smoking from the time I get up until I retire.

I guess I'll keep trying though. Tomorrow, the boots go back 8 on the pile for the Salvation Army. It's a start.

Art Greenwood

9   I live in an apartment with two musicians. Stan is a black man with a deep voice and a mild relaxed demeanor, who plays the drums. Meloni is his complement, fair-skinned and youthful, she sings and she plays the guitar. The are both rock musicians, perhaps, but their types of music are very different. STANLEY—HE PLAYS HIS DRUMS, SOMETIMES, AND HE BANGS EM, HE BANGS EM AND HE BANGS EM, HE'LL ROLL EM, BACK AND FORTH AND BACK REAL QUICK WITH A BASE THUMP, AND HE'LL BANG EM AND HE'LL BANG EM AND HIS CYMBALS CRASH AND HISS WHILE HE BANGS EM AND THE BASE THUMPS. And when he does this it's loud, and the place gets filled, and it feels good, as if you were in your own heart while it was beating. Meloni's music, though, is as different from his as she is, physically, from him. The deep rhythm of his drums doesn't surface in the trickling stream of her singsong. He puts you in your heart, but she leads you through your head. When you listen to her it's like the breeze in the trees or butterflies in springtime: light, airy, and hopeful.

Barbara Schofield

10   Sitting in class I realized that I would never be more naked than when I shared my writing. It is painful; it is frightening, because you open your very soul to acceptance or rejection by your peers. All this attempt to communicate with others is complicated by each individual's understanding of language; we try to present ourselves to others with as much clarity and understanding as is possible for another human being to comprehend of another.

11   In my mind's eye, I see all my physical, and thus symbolically, mental scars and deformities, and I wonder. Do my classmates see the moles on my neck? Do they see the puffy rolls of my flesh, my stretch-marked belly reminiscent of three pregnancies? Do they see the eight inch long scars down the sides of each thigh that resemble railroad tracks? What about the broken blood vessel at the back of my left knee that came with the stress of the second hip surgery? Do they see the peculiar scar on the first digit of my right hand, a constant reminder of the day I

sliced a piece of me off with the salami onto the deli scale? If they do, do they recognize these things for what they are, representations of someone's life? Do they accept all this? Do they reject it? And if they do, does it really matter? Have they not come naked to this class also, and aren't their scars just as visible? Of course they are, or so I tell myself, but it barely soothes me enough to honestly write about who I am, and how I came to be the way I am, today.

Susan Yoritomo

I want to be safe, so I'll hide in my apartment. I'm always hiding   12
in my apartment. I love my apartment. I can see the sunset from one window and sunrise from another. And it's not really hiding, there's no one after me. It's isolation. It's windows and doors and walls and floors and ceilings, the physical barriers I cherish. I have plants. I wonder and worry and care for them, but it's very technical. There's no love. I like them because they soften the sterile interior of my apartment. As a friend said, they are the "bare minimum" in the way of plants. I have to agree. They are the pointy, blade-like plants which are called tropical but are reminiscent of the desert. Stark. My apartment is stark. I'm stark. I strive for starkness. I hate those irresponsible, indulgent feminine traits that are me, the real me. I want my masculine, minimal, logical, problem-solving self to dominate. I want that hard, durable exterior that is not unlike a wall. A cool marble wall that endures.

Betty J. Walker

HOUSEWORK—Housework—I hate it. I have tried for the past   13
20 years to learn to like it but to no avail. It is so boring. It is repetitive and stagnates the mind. Anyone can do it; it requires no real talent except the willingness to do the same thing over and over again.

   Now take dusting . . . an exercise in sheer futility. You take   14
a cloth and spray some type of polish on it. You move it around on the surface of the table or chair or whatever and pick up the dust on the rag. You move around the room dusting whatever

level surface there is available that does not move. You move on from room to room. After a lapsed period of perhaps 20 minutes, you return to the room you dusted first. What do you find there . . . dust!

15   How about dishwashing and cooking. Those two things will drive you crazy. The cooking goes on forever and you no sooner get one meal completed then it is time to begin another. . . . Over the years I have developed a standard menu of things I can prepare that I don't burn or cause people to be poisoned. My family has learned that if it's Tuesday, it must be hamburgers. Or, if it's Friday, it must mean that we'll eat out. You see, I don't cook on Fridays. . . .

16   Lest you form the opinion that I am lazy, let me reassure you—I am. I will work all day at something I enjoy doing. Writing or sewing or creating something keeps me interested and busy and I am never bored. But the repetitive things drive me up the walls. The trouble with housework is that once you have it all done and the house is all clean and shining, six months later you have to do it all over again.

Tammy Weast

17   What makes Christmas Christmas? It is not the carols, the decorations, nor the cold weather. It is not even Santa Claus or turkey advertisements on TV. It must be something in the mind. That's it. Christmas is a state of mind.

18   My parents are getting divorced. This was the first Christmas my mom, brother, and I have spent without my dad. We did not put up a tree. I got the decorations out of the attic though. The first box I opened contained dad's stocking. Mom cried so I put it all away.

19   December 25th was weird. I did not get up until 11 A.M. The whole world had opened their presents while I slept. My brother gave me a leather briefcase. I gave him a $50 gift certificate from Darryl's restaurant. He goes there and drinks a lot lately.

20   Dinnertime has always been around 3 P.M. on holidays. That was because my dad liked to watch the football games. This year mom said we could eat when we wanted. But we never did. I ate a beans n franks dinner later. My brother went to drink his gift certificate.

I worked the day after Christmas. All the secretaries in my 21
office had new gold necklaces from men. They all cooed about
what a wonderful holiday they had had. I got nauseous because
everyone was asking me, "How was your holiday, Tammy?" or
"What did Santa bring you?" or "How long will you be eating
turkey leftovers?"

I went home early. Mom and my brother were all early too. 22
We each seemed to have upset stomachs. It must have been something we didn't eat. Or maybe it was just our state of mind.

Kristin King

They lived in a three-hundred-thousand-dollar house that looked 23
like a sty. I remember walking into the living room once and seeing the abuse. On one wall was a dart board with no darts and the
wall behind pocked with holes. The lining had been torn from the
bottom of a yellow Chippendale sofa and stuffing poked through
where the buttons had been ripped off. In front of the sofa was
a cherry table with a half-finished model spread out and a tube
of glue dripping. There were several high-backed chairs in the
room, one Windsor without an arm, another with a torn velvet
cover. On the carpet in front of the chair was a bowl of milk with
Cheerios floating. An empty pop bottle lay on the brick hearth.
Someone had tossed a crumpled McDonald's bag on the ashes of
last winter's fires. A Steinway stretched underneath a broad picture window. Water rings spoiled the finish and a tinker toy was
wedged between two keys. The piano bench, loaded with *Sports
Illustrated*, was pushed against the wall. A china bureau, filled
with Wedgwood and Lenox, stood in the corner next to the door.
A lacrosse stick was propped against one of its broken panes. A
black woman in a blue housecoat was attempting to compensate
for the absence of a cat's litter box by pushing a vacuum back and
forth over the stained carpet.

Rosalind Bradley Coles

Today in class Dudley said he's "tired of racial issues in class." 24
Well—if he's tired of them, how does he think I feel? For years I
have been the only Black (or at most one of two or three) in class
and I have had to deal with white negativism towards Blacks. . . .

Every time I've taken writing classes I've had to deal with some white person who had to put a Black person in their story— unfortunately the Black person is never a professional or middle class person, but illiterate, poor, kitchen workers or country hicks or rapists. Even Dudley in his first essay continuously used the word nigger derogatorily (although that's the only way whites can use it). . . . In the same week Grace had a sentence in her essay about a rural man who "knew the difference between a nigger and a colored man." Buffy is writing a story about two Blacks (with college degrees) who interact with a white lawyer. She is trying to adopt a Black dialect for her characters that has rhythm. What she has produced are illiterate Blacks.

25   Sometimes I wonder if these stories are written simply because it was what the author wanted to tell, or if it is a personal attack against me (which really isn't fair to assume, but it has happened so often). It's easy for Dudley to be tired of racial issues when he's white and surrounded mostly by whites. But what about me? Dudley's tired of racial issues. Well, I'm tired of having to see only the negative side of my people portrayed by my peers.

Richard Loftus, again

26   Should I write about sex? Not to be sensational. That's purposeless. I don't think it would be wrong to write about sex, because sex is so personal a subject that to use it is akin to plowing up earth. In the wake of the plow you find things you would not have expected to find, fragments of bone, earthworms, snakes, an old boot, strange rocks, an old wristwatch. Talking about sex digs down and throws up old lies, new lies, guilt, excess, happy memories, all manner of self perceptions ranging from the most superficial to most basic. So sex becomes the catalyst towards some reaction.

27   I think I see my own sexuality—my homosexuality—as the thing that made me a better listener. Because it was at thirteen something unpleasant to own up to. Can you imagine having to admit to yourself that you're black? Almost amusing, because I can remember little of my self-consciousness of that particular time, but it was definitely the experience of being the outsider,

living through my friends' heterosexual fumblings, being the uninvolved sexless sage. Later, having come out, an experience that has now been appropriated by ostomites, alcoholics, barren parents and anorexics, I was learning the joys of rhetoric. Gay politics is nothing if not rich in rhetoric. The difference between homosexual and gay? Homosexual is what the *New York Times* calls you; gay is what you earn the right to call yourself.

It was always surprising to listen to others, if somehow they 28 were aware of my sexuality, if, somehow, the subject came up. Listening to them as they revealed their positions, feigned acceptance, gushed too readily their acceptance, or guarded their words, or condemned—it seemed always to be an exercise in measuring and dissecting. They say this, they mean that. It made me even more careful to choose words that expressed my own individual sense and that told the truth. It also made me aware of how to lie, without *really* lying (hah!). Through listening, nuance is learned.

Cheryl Watanabe

After the homes were lost, the businesses destroyed, after the fur- 29 niture was sold or stolen, after the fathers were taken away and the rights of the land-born children erased you come—to offer money and recognition. Deeds not willing to be forgotten haunt you: Utah or California, horse stalls for hotels, manure for freshener, the death of our sons in Italy whose parents, buried deep in the desert, watered the brush with tears. But your offer comes too late. The children have grown, the night classes paid for, the businesses reestablished, and prominence regained. We have wealth enough to forgive with charity. Just put it in the textbooks, you never put it in the textbooks.

In California thongs are still Nipper Flippers or Jap Slaps. 30 People imitate Japanese (or is it Chinese?) when I walk by. December seventh is the Ides of March. I'm asked how I can see, is my field of vision narrowed? Would I like to go to Japan? Only after I've seen Europe and Israel. Do I speak Japanese? No. How come? Do you, being fourth generation French, Polish, Greek, speak French, Polish, or Greek? "I was hoping you'd be Buddhist." "Say some Japanese for me." "Play for me, dance for me, sing for me, cook for me—I love rice." Prejudice is the spear of Ignorance. "You write English very well. Where are you going for vacation?" Back to California. "Have you ever been there?" Yes, I was born in San Mateo and raised in San Jose.

Stephen E. Ryan

Refugee Camp 2
Turk/Iraqi Border
Company A, 2nd Battalion, 10th Special Forces Group (Airborne)
April, 1991
Day 6

31   The camp seems loudest at night. A huge, dulled murmur flows up from the valleys with hacking, rattling coughs, unending moaning like mantras, mules braying, wails and shrieks like a child stepped on a nail. Clank tap-tapping, metal pots clanking and wood chopping sounds but no sounds of laughter. The footsteps and shifting of thousands make a pressure on the ear just below the level of a sound. And no strong wind whistles close distractions or carries the sound away. Rising to the hill in the middle of 85,000 Kurdish refugees, the sounds articulate our mission.

32   In the morning, A–10 jets fly across in a low, slow demonstration. The screaming whine of their turbofans demands acknowledgement of their habitual, matin visits. The men look up out of makeshift tents with squinted eyes in a fearful reflex drawn from the sound. They have been down south where the wells still burn. Former conscripts twice fleeing, they fled Coalition destruction and then fled Saddam's genocide. But they and we and the Iraqi division beneath the border know the jet's other sound; the harsh, ripping bellow of the main gun, the tank killer. Welcome, sweet, fearsome companion.

33   Under the wide, banking circles, the women walk the morning road carrying clutched bundles pressed close. The bundles are soft-wrapped like cocoons, the folds unlike the sharp creases in the strained faces of the mothers' dry, silent anguish carrying children to graves. Behind them, men carry angular, longer, wrapped burdens as the dust rises.

Above, a rhythmic, tympanic beat from the north begins the 34
helos' arrivals. They approach the small landing pad at full
power remonstrating loudly at their heavy loads in the thin, high
altitude air. They settle in ungraceful bobs and tilts as wheels un-
evenly touch down and sag with rotor blade slowing, drooping,
giving back their cargo's weight to the ground. Today's arrival of
rations, medicine and plastic-bottled water is too late for some,
desperate hope for many.

Betty J. Walker, again

GOOD NEWS. . . . When it first happened, I was so excited I 35
wanted to just jump up and down and hug the world. I felt like a
balloon being blown up and up and up until I was about ready to
explode—a feeling of excitement and satisfaction, a pleased-with-
myself feeling. I wanted to tell everyone, but at the same time I
wanted to keep it as a delicious secret. . . . I am going to have
something that I have written published in the newspaper, and
not in the Letters to the Editor column, either.

Content

1. In "Margot's Diary" (104–08) Wisenberg uses Anne Frank's diary and
information gained from houses where the Franks lived in Amsterdam
and Frankfurt to re-create the life and mind of Margot Frank, Anne's
sister. Nevertheless, in an interview she concludes, "No matter how
much we speculate, we don't know what she or Anne were really like, or
the other six million." Is this an overstatement? What sorts of evidence
does Anne's diary provide about the kind of person Margot was, about
the life she lived? In what ways does the information in "Margot's
Diary" supplement this?
2. What clues in Anne's diary (97–104) indicate she is writing for an external audience? Although Anne could not have known at the time she
wrote the diary that anyone else would read it, let alone that her audience
would endure for decades, what features make the diary understandable
to people of different eras, different cultures?
3. Even many people who haven't read Mark Twain's notebooks
(89–96) or Anne Frank's diary (97–107) know something about the authors
because of the enormous reputation their work has gained over the years.

To what extent is your reading of these works influenced by prior information, perhaps stereotyping, you have of the authors? Does your reading reaffirm or dispel this prior information?

4. Compare your reading of diaries by people with well-known reputations with the way you read the student writers' notebooks. To what extent does external information, about the authors, their other work, or the conditions of their lives and writing, influence your reading of a particular diary segment—or other writing for that matter?

Strategies/Structures

5. What differences exist between writing an essay and keeping a diary or notebook, given that diary or notebook entries are short and written at daily or longer intervals, but are not necessarily self-contained or artistically complete?

Language

6. What clues in the language can tell readers whether the writer meant to keep the work private or meant for other people to read it?

For Writing

7. Keep a diary or writer's notebook, writing three to four times a week for fifteen minutes at a time. Use it as a place to jot down ideas for present or future writing. These may include:
   a. Sketches of people you know well or whom you've recently met
   b. Minidramas of people in action, discussion, or conflict
   c. Reactions to news events or to your reading, other writing, media viewing, or internet messages
   d. Thoughts you've had or decisions you're pondering
   e. Colorful or otherwise memorable language—read, overheard, seen in ads, on menus, on packages or elsewhere
   f. Events or issues that evoke a strong reaction from you, positive or negative—but not lukewarm
   g. Anything else you want

4 Writing: Re-Vision and Revision

The pun is intentional. *Re-vision* and *revision* both mean, literally, "to see again." The introduction to this book's first part, "On Writing," briefly identified some of the dramatic changes in the ways we currently think about reading and writing, our own and others' works (1–4).

The examples of revision by Donald Murray and student Mary Ruffin reveal the passionate commitment writers make to their work. Because they are fully invested in their writing, mind, heart, and spirit, they care enough about it to be willing to rewrite again and again and again until they get it right—in subject and substance, structure and style.

Of course, these examples are meant to inspire you, as well, to be willing "to see again." When you take a second, careful look at what you wrote as a freewriting or a first draft, chances are you'll decide to change it. If and when you do, you're approaching the process that most professional writers use—and your own work will be one step closer to professional. As playwright Neil Simon says, "Rewriting is when writing really gets to be fun. . . . In baseball you only get three swings and you're out. In rewriting, you get almost as many swings as you want and you know, sooner or later, you'll hit the ball."

Many people think that revision means correcting the spelling and punctuation of a first—and only—draft. Writers who care about their work know that such changes, though necessary, are editorial matters remote from the heart of real revising. For to revise is to rewrite. And rewrite. Novelist Toni Morrison affirms,

"The best part of all, the absolutely most delicious part, is finishing it and then doing it over. . . . I rewrite a lot, over and over again, so that it looks like I never did. I try to make it look like I never touched it, and that takes a lot of time and a lot of sweat."

When you rewrite, you're doing what computer language identifies as *add, delete, move* (reorganize), and *edit*. The concept of "draft" may have become elusive for people writing on a computer; one part of a given document may have been revised extensively, other parts may be in various stages of development, while others have yet to be written. For simplicity's sake, I'll use the term *draft* throughout *The Essay Connection* to refer to one particular version of a given essay (whether the writer considers it finished or not), as opposed to other versions of that same document. Even if you're only making a grocery list, you might add and subtract material, or change the organization. If your original list identified the items in the order they occurred to you, as lists often do, you could regroup them by categories of similar items, easier to shop for: produce, staples, meat, dairy products. You might provide specially detailed emphasis on the essentials, "a pound of Milagro super-hot green chilies," and "a half gallon of double chocolate extra fudge swirl ice cream."

Some writers compose essentially in their minds.* They work through their first drafts in their heads, over and over, before putting much—if anything—down on paper. As Joyce Carol Oates says, "If you are a writer, you locate yourself behind a wall of silence and no matter what you are doing, driving a car or walking or doing housework . . . you can still be writing." There's a lot of revising going on, but it's mostly mental. What appears on the paper the first time is what stays on the paper, with occasional minor changes. This writing process appears to work best with short pieces that can easily be held in the mind—a poem, a writing with a fixed and conventional format (such as a lab report), a short essay with a single central point, a narrative in which each point in the sequence reminds the writer of what comes next, logically, chronologically, psychologically. If you write that way,

---

* *Note:* Some material on 121–25 is adapted from Lynn Z. Bloom, *Fact and Artifact: Writing Nonfiction,* 2nd ed. (Englewood Cliffs, N.J.: Blair Press [Prentice Hall], 1994), 51–53.

then what we say about revising on paper should apply to your mental revising, as well.

Other writers use a first draft, and sometimes a second, and a third, and more, to enable themselves to think on paper. Novelist E. M. Forster observed, "How do I know what I think until I see what I say?" How you wrote the first draft may provide cues about what will need special attention when you revise. If you use a first draft to generate ideas, in revising you'll want to prune and shape to arrive at a precise subject and focus and an organization that reinforces your emphasis, as Mary Ruffin did between the ninth draft and final version of "Mama's Smoke" (148–58). Or your first draft may be a sketch, little more than an outline in paragraph form, just to get down the basic ideas. In revising you'd aim to flesh out this bare-bones discussion by elaborating on these essential points, supplying illustrations, or consulting references that you didn't want to look up the first time around. On the other hand, you may typically write a great deal more than you need, just to be sure of capturing random and stray ideas that may prove useful. Your revising of such an ample draft might consist in part of deleting irrelevant ideas and redundant illustrations.

In *Write to Learn* (New York: Holt, 1999), Donald Murray suggests a three-stage revising process that you might find helpful in general, whether or not you've settled on your own particular style of revising:

1. A quick first reading "to make sure that there is a single dominant meaning" and enough information to support that meaning.
2. A second quick reading, only slightly slower than the first, to focus on the overall structure and pace.
3. A third reading, "slow, careful, line-by-line editing of the text . . . here the reader cuts, adds, and reorders, paragraph by paragraph, sentence by sentence, word by word" (167).

First you look at the forest, then at the shape and pattern of the individual trees, then close up, at the branches and leaves. Although this may sound slow and cumbersome, if you try it, you'll find that it's actually faster and easier than trying to catch everything in one laborious reading, alternating between panoramic views and close-ups.

John Trimble, in *Writing with Style* (Englewood Cliffs, N.J.: Prentice Hall, 1975), offers a number of suggestions for writing in a very readable style that work equally well for first drafts as well as for revision. Trimble's cardinal principles are these: (1) Write as if your reader is a "companionable friend" who appreciates straightforwardness and has a sense of humor. (2) Write as if you were "talking to that friend," but had enough time to express your thoughts in a concise and interesting manner. He also suggests that if you've written three long sentences in a row, make the fourth sentence short. Even very short. Use contractions. Reinforce abstract discussions with "graphic illustrations, analogies, apt quotations, and concrete details." To achieve continuity, he advises, make sure each sentence is connected with those preceding and following it. And, most important, "Read your prose aloud. *Always* read your prose aloud. If it sounds as if it's come out of a machine or a social scientist's report . . . spare your reader and rewrite it" (82).

Two pieces in this section illustrate the dramatic effects of re-vision, re-seeing, reconfiguring one's subject. Garry Trudeau's "The Draft: My Story/My Story: The Holes" (137–41) illustrates how Trudeau's decision to finally tell the truth about how and why he did not serve in the army during the Vietnam War made him re-examine the evidence and his motives. This radical reappraisal led him to question what he had for years assured himself was honorable and lawful behavior and to replace "spin-doctoring" with something closer to the truth. In contrast, Maxine Hong Kingston's "On Discovery" (141–43) makes a metaphor literal. Here she shows how a man's perspective on the world becomes utterly transformed when Tang Ao, a traditional Chinese male, is obliged to live and act as a woman. John Trimbur's "Guidelines for Collaborating in Groups" (144–48) illustrates the enrichment that a variety of perspectives can bring to the writing process when several people are involved, such as a group leader, mediator, notetaker, critic, timekeeper.

Ernest Hemingway has said that he "rewrote the ending of *A Farewell to Arms,* the last page of it, thirty-nine times before I was satisfied"—which means a great deal of rewriting, even if you don't think he kept exact count.

"Was there some technical problem?" asked an interviewer. "What had you stumped?"

"Getting the words right," said Hemingway.

That is the essence of revision.

STRATEGIES FOR REVISING

1. Does my draft have a *thesis*, a focal point? Does the thesis cover the entire essay, and convey my attitude toward the subject?
2. Does my draft contain sufficient *information, evidence* to support that meaning? Is the writing developed sufficiently, or do I need to provide additional information, steps in an argument, illustrations, or analysis of what I've already said?
3. Who is my intended *audience*? Will they understand what I've said? Do I need to supply any background information? Will I meet my readers as friends, antagonists, or on neutral ground? How will this relationship determine what I say, the order in which I say it, and the language I use?
4. Do the *form* and *structure* of my writing suit the subject? (For instance, would a commentary on fast-food restaurants be more effective in an essay or description, comparison and contrast, analysis, some combination of the three—or as a narrative or satire?) Does the *proportioning* reinforce my emphasis (in other words, do the most important points get the most space)? Or do I need to expand some aspects and condense others?
5. Is the writing recognizably mine in *style, voice,* and *point of view*? Is the body of my prose like that of an experienced runner: tight and taut, vigorous, self-contained, and supple? Do I like what I've said? If not, am I willing to change it?

DONALD M. MURRAY

Murray was a successful writer long before he began teaching others to write. Born in Boston in 1924, he was educated at the University of New Hampshire (B.A., 1948) and Boston University. He wrote editorials for the *Boston Herald*, 1948–1954, for which he won a Pulitzer Prize in 1954; in retirement, he now writes a weekly column for the *Boston Globe*. During his quarter-century of teaching at the University of New Hampshire, Murray wrote numerous essays, volumes of short stories, poetry, and a novel, *The Man Who Had Everything* (1964). *A Writer Teaches Writing* (1964, rev. 1985), an explanation of how people really write (as opposed to how the rule books say they should), has been highly influential in persuading writing teachers to encourage their students to focus on the process of writing, rather than on the finished product. His most recent book is *The Craft of Revision* (1997).

Revision, in Murray's view, is central to the writing process: "Good writing is essentially rewriting." Murray offers a straightforward account of just how writers move through the process of revising, by making changes—in content, in form and in proportion, and finally in voice and word choice—that will substantially improve their work, even though "the words on a page are never finished." The history of this essay illustrates his points. Murray completely rewrote the essay twice before it was first published in *The Writer* in 1973. Then, for an anthology, Murray "re-edited, re-revised, re-read, re-re-edited" it again. A draft of the first twelve paragraphs of the "re-edited, revised" version, with numerous changes is reprinted below. As you examine both versions, note that many changes appear in the final ("re-re-edited") version that are not in the "revised" draft.

THE MAKER'S EYE: REVISING YOUR OWN
MANUSCRIPTS* by DONALD M. MURRAY

When ~~the beginning writer~~ [a students] completes ~~his~~ [a] first draft, ~~he~~ [they] 1
~~usually reads it through to correct typographical errors and~~
[-- and their teachers too often agree.]
consider the job of writing done. When ~~the~~ professional
writers completes ~~his~~ [the] first draft, ~~he~~ [they] usually feels ~~he is~~ [they are] at
the start of the writing process. ~~Now that he has~~ [when] a draft,
~~he can begin~~ writing / [can begin]. [(is completed, the job of]

That difference in attitude is the difference between 2
amateur and professional, inexperience and experience,
journeyman and craftsman. Peter F. Dru[c]ker, the prolific
business writer, for example, calls his first draft "the
zero draft"--after that he can start cou[n]ting. Most
~~productive~~ writers share the feeling ~~that~~ the first draft,
and ~~most of those~~ [all] which follow ~~is an~~ [are] opportunit[ies] to discover
what they have to say and how they can best say it.

~~Detachment and caring~~

To produce a progression of drafts, each of which says 3
more and says it better, the writer has to develop a special
[Kind of] reading skill. In school we are taught to ~~read~~ [decode] what ~~is~~ [appears] on
the page [as finished writing.] ~~We try to comprehend what the author has said,~~
~~what he meant and what are the implications of his words.~~

[Writers, however, face a different category of possibility 4
and responsibility. To them, the words are never finished
on the page. Each can be changed, rearranged, set off
a chain reaction of confusion or clarified meaning.
This is a different kind of reading, possibly more
difficult and certainly more exciting.]

---

* A different version of this article was published in *The Writer,* October 1973.

5   ~~The~~ **Writers** ~~writers of such drafts~~ must **learn to** be ~~his~~ **their** own best enemy. ~~He~~ **Writers** must accept the criticism of others **--especially teachers--** and be suspicious of it; ~~he~~ **they** must accept the praise of others **--especially teachers--** and be even more suspicious of it. ~~He~~ **Writers** cannot depend on others. ~~He~~ **They** must detach ~~himself~~ **themselves** from ~~his~~ **their** own pages so that ~~he~~ **they** can apply both ~~his~~ **their** caring and ~~his~~ **their** craft to ~~his~~ **their** own work.

6   Detachment is not easy. Science fiction writer Ray Bradbury supposedly puts each manuscript away for a year and then rereads it as a stranger. Not many writers can afford the time to do this. We must read when our judgment may be at its worst, when we are close to the euphoric moment of creation. The writer "should be critical of everything that seems to him most delightful in his style," advises novelist Nancy Hale. "He should excise what he most admires, because he wouldn't thus admire it if he weren't . . . in a sense protecting it from criticism."

7   ~~The writer must learn to protect himself from his own ego, when it takes the form of uncritical pride or uncritical self-destruction.~~ As poet John Ciardi points out, ". . . the last act of the writing must be to become one's own reader. It is, I suppose, a schizophrenic process, to begin passionately and to end critically, to begin hot and to end cold; and, more important, to be passion-hot and critic-cold at the same time." **unproductive** ~~Just as dangerous as the protective writer is the despairing one, who thinks everything he does is terrible, dreadful, awful. If he is to publish, he must save what is effective on his page while he cuts away what doesn't work. The writer must hear and respect his own voice.~~

Remember [how the] ~~how each~~ craftsman you have seen--the carpenter   9
[looking at the lie] ~~eyeing the level~~ of a shelf, the mechanic listening to the
motor--takes the instinctive step back. This is what ~~the~~
writer[s] [have to] ~~has to~~ do when ~~he~~ [they] read[s] ~~his~~ [their] own work. "The writer
must survey his work critically, coolly, and as though he
were a stranger to it," says children's book writer Eleanor
Estes. "He must be willing to prune, expertly and hard-
heartedly. At the end of each revision, a manuscript may
look like a battered old hive, worked over, torn apart,
pinned together, added to, deleted from, words changed and
words changed back. Yet the book must maintain its
original freshness and spontaneity."

¶ We are aware of ~~the~~ writers who think everything   8
they have written is literature but a more ~~serious~~
frequent and serious problem ~~is the~~ are writers ~~is~~ who
are ~~overly~~ overly critical of each page, tear[s] up each
page and never complete[s] a draft. The ~~cut~~ writer
must cut what is bad to ~~save~~ reveal what is good.

~~It is far easier for most~~ beginning writers ~~to~~   10
~~understand the need for rereading and rewriting than it is to~~
~~understand how to go about it. The publishing writer doesn't~~
~~necessarily break down the various stages of rewriting and~~
~~editing; he just goes ahead and does it.~~ ¶ ~~One of our most~~
[in the English-speaking world,]
prolific ~~fiction~~ writer[s], (Anthony Burgess,) says, "I might
revise a page twenty times." Short story and children's
writer Roald Dahl states, "By the time I'm nearing the end
of a story, the first part will have been reread and altered
and corrected at least 150 times. . . . Good writing is
essentially rewriting. I am positive of this."

11   ~~There is nothing~~ ~~itself about~~ ~~virtuous in~~ the rewriting process, *isn't virtuous* It is

simply an essential condition of life for most writers. There

are *a few* writers who do very little rewriting, mostly because they

have the capacity and experience to create and review a large

number of invisible drafts in their minds before they get to

the page. And ~~many~~ *some* writers ~~perform~~ *who slowly produce finished pages, performing* all ~~of~~ the tasks of revision

simultaneously, page by page, rather than draft by draft. But

it is still possible to break down the process of rereading

one's own work into the sequence most published writers follow

most of the time. ~~as he studies his own page.~~

~~Seven elements~~

12   Many writers ~~at first just~~ scan their manuscript, reading

as quickly as possible ~~for~~ *to catch the larger* problems of subject and form. ~~In this~~ *They take the*

craftsman's step back ~~way, they stand back~~ from the more ~~technical~~ *superficial* details of language

the larger problems in writing.

so they can spot ~~any weaknesses in content or in organization.~~

Then as they reread — and reread and ~~the reader~~ reread — *they*

~~when the writer reads his manuscript, he is usually looking~~

move in closer in a logical sequence which usually ~~must~~ *involves,*

~~for~~ *seven elements.*

13   The first is subject. ~~As a writer~~ ~~Do you have anything to say?~~ ~~If~~

Sometimes writers are lucky, they ~~you are lucky, you will find~~ ~~that~~ *Writers look first to discover if they have* indeed ~~you do~~ have something to

that they ~~anything to say~~ *said*

say, perhaps a little more than you expected. If the subject *anything*

writers know they can't write. *nothing,*

is not clear, or if it is not yet limited or defined enough

for you to handle, don't go on. What you have to say is *SAVE*

always more important than how you say it.

Novelist Elizabeth Janeway says, "I think there's a nice cooking word ~~which~~ *that explains a little of what happens while (the manuscript is) standing. It clarifies, like a consommé perhaps."*

The Maker's Eye: Revising Your Own Manuscripts

W hen students complete a first draft, they consider the job of   1
writing done—and their teachers too often agree. When
professional writers complete the first draft, they usually feel they
are at the start of the writing process. When a draft is completed,
the job of writing can begin.

That difference in attitude is the difference between amateur   2
and professional, inexperience and experience, journeyman and
craftsman. Peter F. Drucker, the prolific business writer, calls his
first draft "the zero draft"—after that he can start counting. Most
writers share the feeling the first draft, and all which follow, are
opportunities to discover what they have to say and how they can
best say it.

To produce a progression of drafts, each of which says more   3
and says it more clearly, the writer has to develop a special kind
of reading skill. In school we are taught to decode what appears
on the page as finished writing. Writers, however, face a different category of possibility and responsibility when they read
their own drafts. To them the words on the page are never finished. Each can be changed and rearranged, can set off a chain
reaction of confusion or clarified meaning. This is a different
kind of reading which is possibly more difficult and certainly
more exciting.

. Writers must learn to be their own best enemy. They must   4
accept the criticism of others and be suspicious of it; they must accept the praise of others and be even more suspicious of it. Writers
cannot depend on others. They must detach themselves from their
own pages so that they can apply both their caring and their craft
to their own work.

Such detachment is not easy. Science fiction writer Ray   5
Bradbury supposedly puts each manuscript away for a year to
the day and then rereads it as a stranger. Not many writers have
the discipline or the time to do this. We must read when our judgment may be at its worst, when we are close to the euphoric moment of creation.

6   Then the writer, counsels novelist Nancy Hale, "should be critical of everything that seems to him most delightful in his style. He should excise what he most admires, because he wouldn't thus admire it if he weren't . . . in a sense protecting it from criticism." John Ciardi, the poet, adds, "The last act of the writing must be to become one's own reader. It is, I suppose, a schizophrenic process, to begin passionately and to end critically, to begin hot and to end cold; and, more important, to be passion-hot and critic-cold at the same time."

7   Most people think that the principal problem is that writers are too proud of what they have written. Actually, a greater problem for most professional writers is one shared by the majority of students. They are overly critical, think everything is dreadful, tear up page after page, never complete a draft, see the task as hopeless.

8   The writer must learn to read critically but constructively, to cut what is bad, to reveal what is good. Eleanor Estes, the children's book author, explains: "The writer must survey his work critically, coolly, as though he were a stranger to it. He must be willing to prune, expertly and hard-heartedly. At the end of each revision, a manuscript may look . . . worked over, torn apart, pinned together, added to, deleted from, words changed and words changed back. Yet the book must maintain its original freshness and spontaneity."

9   Most readers underestimate the amount of rewriting it usually takes to produce spontaneous reading. This is a great disadvantage to the student writer, who sees only a finished product and never watches the craftsman who takes the necessary step back, studies the work carefully, returns to the task, steps back, returns, steps back, again and again. Anthony Burgess, one of the most prolific writers in the English-speaking world, admits, "I might revise a page twenty times." Roald Dahl, the popular children's writer, states, "By the time I'm nearing the end of a story, the first part will have been reread and altered and corrected at least 150 times. . . . Good writing is essentially rewriting. I am positive of this."

10   Rewriting isn't virtuous. It isn't something that ought to be done. It is simply something that most writers find they have to do to discover what they have to say and how to say it. It is a condition of the writer's life.

There are, however, a few writers who do little formal re- 11
writing, primarily because they have the capacity and experience
to create and review a large number of invisible drafts in their
minds before they approach the page. And some writers slowly
produce finished pages, performing all the tasks of revision
simultaneously, page by page, rather than draft by draft. But it is
still possible to see the sequence followed by most writers most of
the time in rereading their own work.

Most writers scan their drafts first, reading as quickly as pos- 12
sible to catch the larger problems of subject and form, then move
in closer and closer as they read and write, reread and rewrite.

The first thing writers look for in their drafts is *information*. 13
They know that a good piece of writing is built from specific,
accurate, and interesting information. The writer must have an
abundance of information from which to construct a readable
piece of writing.

Next writers look for *meaning* in the information. The spe- 14
cifics must build to a pattern of significance. Each piece of specific
information must carry the reader toward meaning.

Writers reading their own drafts are aware of *audience*. They 15
put themselves in the reader's situation and make sure that they
deliver information which a reader wants to know or needs to
know in a manner which is easily digested. Writers try to be sure
that they anticipate and answer the questions a critical reader will
ask when reading the piece of writing.

Writers make sure that the *form* is appropriate to the subject 16
and the audience. Form, or genre, is the vehicle which carries meaning to the reader, but form cannot be selected until the writer has
adequate information to discover its significance and an audience
which needs or wants that meaning.

Once writers are sure the form is appropriate, they must 17
then look at the *structure*, the order of what they have written.
Good writing is built on a solid framework of logic, argument,
narrative, or motivation which runs through the entire piece of
writing and holds it together. This is the time when many writers
find it most effective to outline as a way of visualizing the hidden
spine by which the piece of writing is supported.

The element on which writers may spend a majority of their 18
time is *development*. Each section of a piece of writing must be

adequately developed. It must give readers enough information so that they are satisfied. How much information is enough? That's as difficult as asking how much garlic belongs in a salad. It must be done to taste, but most beginning writers underdevelop, underestimating the reader's hunger for information.

19   As writers solve development problems, they often have to consider questions of *dimension.* There must be a pleasing and effective proportion among all the parts of the piece of writing. There is a continual process of subtracting and adding to keep the piece of writing in balance.

20   Finally, writers have to listen to their own voices. *Voice* is the force which drives a piece of writing forward. It is an expression of the writer's authority and concern. It is what is between the words on the page, what glues the piece of writing together. A good piece of writing is always marked by a consistent, individual voice.

21   As writers read and reread, write and rewrite, they move closer and closer to the page until they are doing line-by-line editing. Writers read their own pages with infinite care. Each sentence, each line, each clause, each phrase, each word, each mark of punctuation, each section of white space between the type has to contribute to the clarification of meaning.

22   Slowly the writer moves from word to word, looking through language to see the subject. As a word is changed, cut, or added, as a construction is rearranged, all the words used before that moment and all those that follow that moment must be considered and reconsidered.

23   Writers often read aloud at this stage of the editing process, muttering or whispering to themselves, calling on the ear's experience with language. Does this sound right—or that? Writers edit, shifting back and forth from eye to page to ear to page. I find I must do this careful editing in short runs, no more than fifteen to twenty minutes at a stretch, or I become too kind with myself. I begin to see what I hope is on the page, not what actually is on the page.

24   This sounds tedious if you haven't done it, but actually it is fun. Making something right is immensely satisfying, for writers begin to learn what they are writing about by writing. Language leads them to meaning, and there is the joy of discovery, of under-

standing, of making meaning clear as the writer employs the technical skills of language.

Words have double meanings, even triple and quadruple   25
meanings. Each word has its own potential for connotation and denotation. And when writers rub one word against the other, they are often rewarded with a sudden insight, an unexpected clarification.

The maker's eye moves back and forth from word to phrase   26
to sentence to paragraph to sentence to phrase to word. The maker's eye sees the need for variety and balance, for a firmer structure, for a more appropriate form. It peers into the interior of the paragraph, looking for coherence, unity, and emphasis, which make meaning clear.

I learned something about this process when my first bifo-   27
cals were prescribed. I had ordered a larger section of the reading portion of the glass because of my work, but even so, I could not contain my eyes with this new limit of vision. And I still find myself taking off my glasses and bending my nose towards the page, for my eyes unconsciously flick back and forth across the page, back to another page, forward to still another, as I try to see each evolving line in relation to every other line.

When does this process end? Most writers agree with the   28
great Russian writer Tolstoy, who said, "I scarcely ever reread my published writings, if by chance I come across a page, it always strikes me: all this must be rewritten; this is how I should have written it."

The maker's eye is never satisfied, for each word has the   29
potential to ignite the new meaning. This article has been twice written all the way through the writing process, and it was published four years ago. Now it is to be republished in a book. The editors made a few small suggestions, and then I read it with my maker's eye. Now it has been re-edited, re-revised, re-read, re-re-edited, for each piece of writing to the writer is full of potential and alternatives.

A piece of writing is never finished. It is delivered to a dead-   30
line, torn out of the typewriter on demand, sent off with a sense of accomplishment and shame and pride and frustration. If only there were a couple more days, time for just another run at it, perhaps then. . . .

Content

1. Why does Murray say that when a first "draft is completed, the job of writing can begin" (¶ 1)? If you thought before you read the essay that one draft was enough, has Murray's essay convinced you otherwise?

2. How does Murray explain John Ciardi's analysis of the "schizophrenic process" of becoming one's own reader, "to be passion-hot and critic-cold at the same time" (¶ 6)? Why does he consider it so important for writers to be both?

3. What are writers looking for when they revise? How can writers be sure that their "maker's eye" has in revision an accurate perception of the "need for variety and balance, for a firmer structure, for a more appropriate form. . . . for coherence, unity, and emphasis" (¶ 26)? How do you, as a writer, know whether your writing is good or not?

Strategies/Structures

4. Many of Murray's revisions are for greater conciseness. For example, the first sentence of paragraph 11 initially read, "There is nothing virtuous in the rewriting process." Murray then revised it to "The rewriting process isn't virtuous." The published version says, "Rewriting isn't virtuous." What are the effects of these successive changes? And of other comparable changes?

5. Compare and contrast the deleted paragraph 8 of the original version and the rewritten paragraphs 8 and 9 of the typescript with paragraphs 7 and 8 in the printed version. Why did Murray delete the original paragraph 8? Which ideas did he salvage? Why did he delete the first two sentences of the original paragraph 9? Are the longer paragraphs of the printed version preferable to the shorter paragraphs of the original?

Language

6. In many places in the revision typescript (see ¶s 1, 5) Murray has changed masculine pronouns (he, his) to the plural (they, their). What is the effect of these changes? What occurred in America between 1973, when the essay was first written, and 1980, when it was again revised, to affect this usage?

7. In the typescript Murray has added references to students and teachers which were not in the original published version. For whom was the original version intended? What do the additions reveal about the intended readers of the revision?

For Writing

8. Prepare a checklist of the points Murray says that writers look for in revising a manuscript: information, meaning, audience, form, structure, development, dimension, voice (¶s 13–20). Add others appropriate to your writing, and use the checklist as a guide in revising your own papers.

GARRY TRUDEAU

Trudeau, born in New York City in 1948, launched his comic strip, *Doonesbury,* in 1969 when he was twenty-one, a year before he graduated from Yale. The strip was an instant hit; the characters of Zonker, Boopsie, Lacey, Duke, and Joanie Caucus have become as familiar to the American public as the characters in *Peanuts,* though they operate in a different register. Known for its consistent satire of contemporary events, politics, personalities, and lifestyles, the strip is also critical of the economically privileged class in which Trudeau grew up. Indeed, many newspapers print the strip on their editorial pages rather than with the rest of the comics; in 1975 he won a Pulitzer Prize for editorial cartooning. "Satire is an ungentlemanly art," says Trudeau. "It's lacking in balance. It's unfair." The cartoonist and his family, Jane Pauley and three children, live an exceptionally well-balanced, decidedly low-key life in Manhattan.

Trudeau scans the news for ideas, keeping them in files and notebooks. He writes and draws in pencil, so he can easily erase and rewrite. Then—following a common practice among cartoonists—he faxes the strips to an inker, who redraws the strip in ink with exact fidelity to the original. In "The Draft: My Story/My Story: The Holes" Trudeau offers two versions of how and why he received a draft deferment in 1970. For more than twenty years he told the honorable, public version of the story (¶s 1–6) but in 1992 he decided to come clean and provide alternative interpretations of all the facts relevant to the decision (¶s 7–18). The *New York Times* published Trudeau's explanation in September 1992 as an op-ed article at a time when Bill Clinton, then running for his first term as president, was being called on to explain why he did not serve in the military during the Vietnam War even though he, like Trudeau, was eligible for the draft.

The Draft: My Story

1   In 1966, the Selective Service granted me a 2-S student defer-ment, which remained in effect until I graduated from college in 1970. One night in December 1969, I learned from the radio that I had received the number 27 in the draft lottery. I returned to my dorm room where for the next two hours I received a series of highly emotional phone calls from concerned family members and friends.

2   In January, I wrote my draft board and requested a defer-ment on grounds of national security, citing my involvement with a magazine for the "international community" in Washington. I asked for an interview with my draft board, for which occasion I received a memorable haircut. At the same time, I made in-quiries at my local National Guard unit, where I received assur-ances of an opening.

3   In March, 1970, I reported for my draft physical. Confronted with a written exam, I did what I had been trained to do my entire life—my best. I do not recall why. During the physical exam, I did not try to fake a disqualifying affliction for one reason alone—and this I distinctly remember—it would have been wrong.

4   Later, in examining my options, I ruled out applying for conscientious-objector status because I was able to imagine sce-narios in which I would be capable of taking life, and I assumed that my draft board would be able to imagine those scenarios, too.

5   In June 1970, I was reclassified as 1-A. Returning home, I ac-cepted my physician father's advice to have an X-ray at our local hospital. The X-ray revealed evidence of a past ulcer. At the urging of my lawyer, I sent the film to a doctor in New Hampshire, and in August 1970, just days before I had been ordered to report for induction, I was granted a permanent medical deferment.

This account was prepared without benefit of consultation   6
of existing records.

My Story: The Holes

My story of the draft, recounted in unvarying language for more   7
than 20 years, was initially conceived for two purposes—first, to
fulfill the autobiographical requirements of the examined life,
and, secondly, to grant myself permission to move on, secure in
my assessment that I had acted honorably and lawfully.

Had I, in fact? After writing the above, I talked to family   8
members, examined the record of my draft correspondence and
revisited memories that were called forth in the process.

Here is some of what I learned: 9

1. I did receive a student deferment in 1966. But it lasted   10
only until June 1967, when it had to be renewed.

2. No family member or friend recalls telephoning me the   11
night of the lottery. Did I imagine their concern? Possibly, since I
also now remember going out that evening for a few beers.

3. I applied for an occupational deferment, not a "national   12
security" deferment. Did I really believe that editing a glorified
tourist magazine was grounds for legitimate exemption? No one
can say, since I never actually appeared before the board in 1970.
The memorable haircut never happened.

4. I applied to the Guard in May, not in January. I also ap-   13
parently applied to two different Army Reserve units, where I
was placed on the waiting list.

5. I now recall why I tried to do well in the written exam. I   14
reasoned that a good score might earn me a desk job. And while
I did indeed feel that to fake an injury was wrong, it should be
added I was also pretty sure I couldn't pull it off.

6. Another reason I did not apply for C.O. status, I now re-   15
call, was the amount of paperwork. I felt it prohibitive.

7. I was reclassified 1-A on July 22, not in June. While my   16
X-ray did indeed show evidence of an ulcer, I have discovered that
my father wrote the cover letter to the radiologist's report. In it, he

noted a three-year history of gastric distress. I only recall one such year. Was my father spin-doctoring?

17   8. Lastly, in order to qualify for a New Hampshire physician's exam (reportedly the most lenient in the country), one was required to reside in that state, which I didn't. I must have known a resident who was willing to lend me his address.

18   If I ever run for public office, I'm sure I'll hear from him.

Content

1.   Trudeau provides two different interpretations of how and why he secured a draft deferment during the Vietnam War. Which is the most credible? Why?

2.   Readers generally trust the author of nonfiction writing unless there are cues that the work is satiric or in other ways patently false. Are such cues present in either version of Trudeau's story?

3.   Why did Trudeau wait twenty-one years to tell the second version of this story?

Strategies/Structures

4.   When we think of revision we often think of changing individual words or sentence structures, adding or deleting material, or reorganizing larger sections of the work. Rarely do we consider telling a completely different story, as Trudeau does here. What elements, major and minor, does he revise? With what effects?

5.   Why does Trudeau let the positive interpretation precede the negative one? In general, what is the effect on the reader or hearer of encountering something first? Second? Or later?

Language

6.   What is the attitude of Trudeau the author to Trudeau the character in each version of the story? What clues in the tone and language support your interpretation?

For Writing

7.   Write a paper in which you tell two or more versions of a story, using the same information in each but interpreting it very differently. Write as if you expect your readers to believe each version. To aid your thinking,

consider Akira Kurosawa's film *Rashōmon,* which tells four different accounts of the same sexual infidelity, Trudeau's draft story, or multiple accounts of an event in your own life as you might present the information to your parents, your best friend, a teacher, an audience of fellow students, the people where you work. . . . The possibilities are infinite.

8. Have you ever done something that you later told about in ways calculated, as Trudeau says, to reassure yourself—and others—that you "acted honorably and lawfully"? When you examined the evidence still later, could you find equally plausible, alternative interpretations much less favorable to yourself? Did these result from different ways of looking at the facts or from discovering different facts altogether? If so, write a paper presenting two (or even more) alternative versions, and explain why—as Trudeau does—these differ so much from one another.

==========

MAXINE HONG KINGSTON

Kingston's autobiographical writings are haunted by questions of gender and identity and belonging: what relation has she and the others she writes about to China, to other family members, to America, how much to herself alone? And what belongs to her? Kingston was born in Stockton, California, in 1940, the eldest American-born child of recent Chinese immigrants. At home she learned Chinese, her only language until she started first grade (which caused her to score "zero" on her first I.Q. test, in English), and Chinese customs from stories exchanged in her parents' laundry. She graduated from the University of California at Berkeley in 1962, married actor Earll Kingston, had a son, and taught school in Hawaii before returning to Berkeley. She publishes poetry, stories, and essays in national magazines, but is best known for her autobiography, *The Woman Warrior: Memoirs of a Girlhood Among Ghosts* (1975), winner of the National Book Critics Circle Award for nonfiction, and *China Men* (1980), winner of the American Book Award. Her most recent book is a novel, *Tripmaster Monkey: His Fake Book* (1989). Since 1990 she has been a Chancellor's Distinguished Professor at the University of California, Berkeley.

China Men focuses primarily on the meaning of immigration, cultural displacement, and cultural assimilation for Chinese men who emigrated to America, the "Gold Mountain" of Chinese legend. Its opening section, "On Discovery," is a parable in which a traditional Chinese man arrives by accident in the Land of Women, where he is forced into looking and behaving like a woman through the painful processes of having his ears pierced, his foot bones broken and bound, his eyebrows plucked and face made up—much to his embarrassment and shame. This metaphorical definition of a Chinese woman implies an equation: Chinese women are to Chinese men as Chinese men are to Americans. And this equation defines China men (note the connotation of fragility) in America. Metaphors and parables are useful devices for making meaning—explaining, discovering, or inventing new significance.

On Discovery

1   Once upon a time, a man, named Tang Ao, looking for the Gold Mountain, crossed an ocean, and came upon the Land of Women. The women immediately captured him, not on guard against ladies. When they asked Tang Ao to come along, he followed; if he had had male companions, he would've winked over his shoulder.

2   "We have to prepare you to meet the queen," the women said. They locked him in a canopied apartment equipped with pots of makeup, mirrors, and a woman's clothes. "Let us help you off with your armor and boots," said the women. They slipped his coat off his shoulders, pulled it down his arms, and shackled his wrists behind him. The women who kneeled to take off his shoes chained his ankles together.

3   A door opened, and he expected to meet his match, but it was only two old women with sewing boxes in their hands. "The less you struggle, the less it'll hurt," one said, squinting a bright eye as she threaded her needle. Two captors sat on him while another held his head. He felt an old woman's dry fingers trace his ear; the long nail on her little finger scraped his neck. "What are you doing?" he asked. "Sewing your lips together," she joked, blackening needles in a candle flame. The ones who sat on him bounced with laughter. But the old women did not sew his lips together. They pulled his earlobes taut and jabbed a needle through each of

them. They had to poke and probe before puncturing the layers of skin correctly, the hole in the front of the lobe in line with the one in back, the layers of skin sliding about so. They worked the needle through—a last jerk for the needle's wide eye ("needle's nose" in Chinese). They strung his raw flesh with silk threads; he could feel the fibers.

The women who sat on him turned to direct their attention 4 to his feet. They bent his toes so far backward that his arched foot cracked. The old ladies squeezed each foot and broke many tiny bones along the sides. They gathered his toes, toes over and under one another like a knot of ginger root. Tang Ao wept with pain. As they wound the bandages tight and tighter around his feet, the women sang footbinding songs to distract him: "Use aloe for binding feet and not for scholars."

During the months of a season, they fed him on women's 5 food: the tea was thick with white chrysanthemums and stirred the cool female winds inside his body; chicken wings made his hair shine; vinegar soup improved his womb. They drew the loops of thread through the scabs that grew daily over the holes in his earlobes. One day they inserted gold hoops. Every night they unbound his feet, but his veins had shrunk, and the blood pumping through them hurt so much, he begged to have his feet re-wrapped tight. They forced him to wash his used bandages, which were embroidered with flowers and smelled of rot and cheese. He hung the bandages up to dry, streamers that dropped and draped wall to wall. He felt embarrassed; the wrappings were like underwear, and they were his.

One day his attendants changed his gold hoops to jade studs 6 and strapped his feet to shoes that curved like bridges. They plucked out each hair on his face, powdered him white, painted his eyebrows like a moth's wings, painted his cheeks and lips red. He served a meal at the queen's court. His hips swayed and his shoulders swiveled because of his shaped feet. "She's pretty, don't you agree?" the diners said, smacking their lips at his dainty feet as he bent to put dishes before them.

In the Women's Land there are no taxes and no wars. Some 7 scholars say that the country was discovered during the reign of Empress Wu (A.D. 694–705), and some earlier than that, A.D. 441, and it was in North America.

JOHN TRIMBUR

Trimbur, born in San Francisco in 1946, grew up in Modesto, California, in the San Joaquin Valley and earned a B.A. in history at Stanford, followed by a Ph.D. in English at the State University of New York at Buffalo (1982). His teaching career began in basic writing programs in inner-city community colleges in Philadelphia and Baltimore. He then directed writing programs and writing centers at Rutgers in Camden, New Jersey, and at Rhode Island College before becoming director of the Technical, Scientific, and Professional Communication Program at Worcester Polytechnic Institute, where he is now Distinguished Professor of Humanities. His professional papers and books focus on writing theory and cultural studies of literacy, as is clear in the co-edited, prize-winning *The Politics of Writing Instruction* (1993). His most recent textbook is *The Call to Write* (1999), from which "Guidelines for Collaborating in Groups" is taken.

Trimbur explains his divergent views on writing alone and on collaborative writing, which he calls "co-writing." "I like to do both," he says, "in part because they're different. Co-writing gives me a lot of energy and accountability. There's less anxiety because you can pass a text back and forth, building and changing it along the way, believing that your team is eventually going to get it into a shape that everyone can live with." In contrast, he says, when I'm writing by myself I sometimes wonder "whether what I'm saying makes any sense or holds together in a public way. I keep wondering whether I'm adequate to the task, whereas in co-writing I'm confident we'll eventually get it right."

Guidelines for Collaborating in Groups

1   Any group of people working together on a project will face certain issues, and a group collaborating on a writing project is no exception. The following guidelines are meant to keep a group running smoothly and to forestall some common problems.

Recognize that Group Members Need to Get Acquainted and that Groups Take Time to Form

People entering new groups sometimes make snap judgments 2 without getting to know the other people or giving the group time to form and develop. Initial impressions are rarely reliable indicators of how a group will be. Like individuals, groups have life histories, and one of the most awkward and difficult moments is getting started. Group members may be nervous, defensive, or overly assertive. It takes some time for people to get to know one another and to develop a sense of connectedness to the group.

Clarify Group Purposes and Individual Roles

Much of people's initial discomfort and anxiety has to do with 3 their uncertainty about what the purpose of the group is and what their role in the group will be. Group members need to define their collective task and develop a plan to do it. This way, members will know what to expect and how the group will operate.

Recognize that Members Bring Different Styles to the Group

. . . Individual styles of composing can vary considerably. The 4 same is true of individuals' styles of working in groups. For example, individuals differ in the way they approach problems. Some people like to spend a lot of time formulating problems, exploring the complexities, contradictions, and nuances of a situation. Others want to define problems quickly and then spend their time figuring out how to solve them. By the same token people have different styles of interacting in groups. Some people like to develop their ideas by talking, while others prefer to decide what they think before speaking. So successful groups learn to incorporate the strengths of all these styles, making sure that even the most reticent members participate.

Recognize that You May Not Play the Same Role in Every Group

5   In some instances you may be the group leader, but in other instances the role you'll need to play is that of the mediator, helping members negotiate their differences, or the critic, questioning the others' ideas, or the timekeeper, prompting the group to stick to deadlines. You may play different roles in the same group from meeting to meeting or even within a meeting. For a group to be successful, members must be willing and able to respond flexibly to the work at hand.

Monitor Group Progress and Reassess Goals and Procedures

6   It's helpful to step back periodically to take stock of what has been accomplished and what remains to be done. Groups also need to look at their own internal workings, to see if the procedures they have set up are effective and if everyone is participating.

Quickly Address Problems in Group Dynamics

7   Problems arise in group work. Some members may dominate and talk too much. Others may withdraw and not contribute. Still others may fail to carry out assigned tasks. If a group avoids confronting these problems, the problems will only get worse. Remember, the point of raising a problem is not to blame individuals but to promote an understanding about what's expected of each person and what the group can do to encourage everyone's participation.

Encourage Differences of Opinion

8   One of the things that makes groups productive is the different perspectives individual members bring to group work. In fact, groups of like-minded people who share basic assumptions are often not as creative as groups where there are differences among members. At the same time, group members may feel that there are ideas or feelings they can't bring up in the group because to do so would threaten group harmony. This feeling is understandable.

Sometimes it's difficult to take a position that diverges from what other members of the group think and believe. But groups are not forms of social organization to enforce conformity; they are working bodies that need to consider all the available options and points of view. For this reason, groups need to encourage the discussion of differences and to look at conflicting viewpoints.

Division of Labor or Integrated Team?

Some groups approach collaborative projects by developing a division of labor that assigns particular tasks to group members who complete them individually and then bring the results back to the group. This has been the traditional model for collaborative work in business, industry, and government. It is an efficient method of work, especially when groups are composed of highly skilled members. Its limitations are that weak group members can affect the quality of the overall work and that group members may lose sight of the overall project because they are so caught up in their own specialized work.   9

More recently, groups have begun to explore an integrated approach in which group members all work together through each stage of the project. An integrated-team approach involves members more fully in the work and helps them maintain an overall view of the project's goals and progress. But it also takes more time—time must be devoted to meetings and, often, to developing good working relations among members.   10

These two models of group work are not mutually exclusive. In fact many groups function along integrated-team lines when they are planning and reviewing work, but also farm out particular tasks to individuals or subgroups. So you need to discuss and develop some basic guidelines on group functioning.   11

Content

1. Why has Trimbur arranged the principles for collaborating in groups in the order in which they appear here?

2. In what ways can these principles be adapted to the interests and abilities of the group at hand? To what sorts of activities in addition to writing might these principles apply?

3. Discuss—preferably with a group—how Trimbur's principles might apply to writing a particular document, for instance, a report or other presentation of information.

For Writing

4. Form a group, draw up some principles of collaboration, and follow your group's guidelines to write a collaborative document. Then revise the principles to reflect your experience of collaborative writing and revise the document.

MARY RUFFIN

Ruffin was born in Richmond, Virginia, in 1964. She earned a B.A. in English and philosophy from Virginia Commonwealth University in 1984 and an M.A. in 1986. Her mother, an artist and aspiring writer, died when Ruffin was thirteen. As a college student, Ruffin attempted for several years in her writing to come to terms with the meaning of her mother's life and death. The nine notebook entries that follow show the genesis and evolution of "Mama's Smoke" over a two-month period. They include one freewriting (#1), three drafts of a poem (#2, 3, 7), a playful free association of words (#6), and the completed poem (#8)—with which she was "never happy." In retrospect, she found the poem's first draft "far better than [its] final draft . . . because the VOICE IS REAL! I killed it."

The three preliminary prose versions (#4, 5, 9) developed from the original freewriting. The ninth and tenth (final) versions both included the same topics and most of the same language. However, at her classmates' suggestions during group discussion, Ruffin decided to revise the paper so that the opening paragraphs reinforced the theme of the title and the ultimate message of the essay. Note that Ruffin tried dramatically different modes of writing—poetry, free association, and prose—in the process of discovering the version that best suited her and her subject.

"Mama's Smoke," the resulting combination of epitaph, eulogy, and portrait, is a tribute to the continuing complexity of their relationship. Ruffin's characterization of her mother epitomizes her own complicated narrative technique and illustrates the poetic aspects of her prose: "She is something like a sequel to herself, elliptical and confusing, out of context. She speaks in fragments, interrupting in the middle of my own sentences, giving to others the illusion that I have spoken her words. But the others don't know her, don't know her words from mine. The illusion is mine." As the smoke through which Ruffin imagines her mother swirls and eddies, the image of her mother emerges with precision, the different aspects of her activities and of her relationship with her daughter coalescing through the catalyst of love.

❄ Writer's Notebook Entries: The Evolution of "Mama's Smoke"

2/23   #1
Freewriting

A frcewrite is all I can do again because the page is glaring, more ominous even than its traditional blank stare.

The poetry won't come. I've killed it with the spearhead of desire to be Outstanding English Major.

The prose won't come because it can't break out of the stillborn poetry.

The academics won't come because they're forced into the name-dropping realm of pretension. . . . Plus, I hate traditional white male southern writers. With those accents that sound like my mother but aren't my mother at all. . . .

There must be a starting point somewhere—a thread to grasp.

Can't do it all. Must at least reach out to the part that reaches back.

Mama.

2/24   #2
Writer's Notebook, first poem draft

Mama had fierce green eyes and black hair
I know from the black and white pictures
forty years old and more
and the salt and pepper I remember
and the tired hazel that I ~~be~~ inherited
for she could have been my grandma.

Jet black hair so thick the sheen
Matched the fierceness of green eyes
That were my Mama I know cause I've
heard tell and seen the faded black and
white pictures stuffed in the cookie tin
she had for twenty some odd years
and I've kept for ten, and the memory
of the permed salt and pepper I played
in dangling my feet in mid air hung
over the chair back and the tired
hazel nestled in the hooded lids,
I inherited her eyes but without
the green snap

2/25   #3
Writer's Notebook, second poem draft

<u>Rites</u>

Back
~~when~~
~~Back~~ When
It was cool to smoke, she did, and was
I imagine, of course not able to remember,
the picture of glamourousness. It was
In the days before that surgeon general
Determined the hazardousness

that ~~immediately~~ ~~to~~ ~~rings in my ears in unison~~ is now as immediate as
with "once upon a time", ~~steeped in~~ possessing
The familiarity of ~~what raised~~ reared. that with which
Unfiltered *Camels in* we were ~~raised.~~ Or ~~reared,~~ ~~She was never without~~
An ivory holder I've heard tell
and seen the legendary
~~the~~ flash of her fierce green eyes
~~in the wrinkled~~ rusted ~~yellowed~~
yellowing and wrinkled in the cookie tin of black and
snapshots
white ~~photos~~ she hung onto for
twenty some odd years, and I now
for ten. difficult
The lid is ~~not easy~~ to pry open.
~~She passed on a spark to me, hazel~~
~~eyes~~ miraculously
The spark ~~somehow~~ passed on,
Miscellaneous barely discernible in my hazel,
~~itches~~ mediated by ~~brown~~ *by chromosomes* and the bloodshot
of Menthol Virginia Slim Lights
~~itches, smolders and goes cold.~~ incessant.
Itches ~~a dry itch, beyond my years.~~

2/27   #4
Writer's Notebook, first prose draft

She was a smoker, but that began in the days when it was cool to smoke. Long before that surgeon general determined the hazardousness of the habit, and the behaviorists blasted it as an infantile fixation, she was glamorous. It was unfiltered Camels in the beginning, though by the time I was around she had gone to Merits, clunky with thick filters wrapped in blotchy brown.

My mother was an artist. She used to paint, in a turquoise studio smock, portraits of everyone she knew. Though I don't remember her ever painting herself—that is except for the red polish on her toenails. Her fingernails stayed natural yellow, she said because of the turpentine, but I think nicotine contributed to the hue. I've heard that when she was young she was never without her ivory cigarette holder. She readily admitted to her vanity.

later, 2/27
Writer's Notebook, first prose draft, second installment (excerpt)

She comes to me in the middle of the night, or rather I come to her, chase her even, through strange landscapes and insidescapes. Sometimes she is an old crone, witch-like, her black hair full of salt and her green eyes bloodshot knifeslits. . . .

3/3/85   #5
Writer's Notebook, second prose draft

She can surface without warning, anytime, anyplace. Sometimes she comes and goes so quickly that I hardly notice her presence. The other day, for instance, I stood in the kitchen staring at the can of Crisco and a tattered, encrusted cookbook page. Spoon in hand, I wondered blankly for a moment how to measure solid shortening. When the idea of displacement struck me and I filled the cup half full with water, I thought it was the ghost of a physics text. By the time I realized that it had been her, she was long gone and I had to shake my head. That's the way it happens frequently.

She never answers to her name—she almost seems to run away when she comes to mind. She is called Peggy, the only nickname for Margaret she could ever tolerate. She told me once that was why I had such a simple name, something virtually unalterable, to have forever. I resemble Peggy slightly, but just like the futility of calling her, when I look for the resemblance in the mirror it isn't there—It's those other times, catching an unexpected glimpse of my reflection out of the corner of my eye, that she suddenly appears.

3/10   #6
Writer's Notebook, "playing" (free association)

Dragons

Cookie tin——shining armor——rusty knight
Desert— -fire——camels——dragons
Green dragons
Slain dragons & fair maidens

Dark fair maidens——unfair damsels
Once upon atime hazardousness——dragon
Dragon——take a "drag on" a cigarette
Smoke——cool smoke——hot smoke——smoke breath
Dragon's lair——womb——cave
cookies & stories——yellowing green
eyes & hazel bloodshot
Grendel's mother
Damsel in distress
Legend——spark of the divine
Glamourousness——amourousness——clamourousness
Reptiles——evolution —snake——fake——fang
Red nails——red lips—— glamour is dark— beauty light
Medieval- —Middle Ages——
Middle age——
The Tale——the monomyth——hero's journey
Separation— Initiation——Return
Smoke——illusion
Birthrite— legacy——heir——air——smoke
Glamour as aloof passion——cool hotness——
artifice——surface image——imagination
hard——glamour = armor- —defense mechanism
Smoking as oral fixation
Smoking as magic
Fairy tales——scales——fear in fairy tails——wicked
stepmother——poison

3/17   #7
Writer's Notebook, third poem draft (excerpt)

Rites

Back when it was cool to smoke, she did, and was
I imagine, of course not able to remember, the picture
of glamourousness. It was in the days before the surgeon
general determined the dreadful gnawing
hazardousness that is now as immediate as
once-upon-a-time, possessing the familiarity
of that with which we were reared. . . .

3/28/85   #8
Writer's Notebook, final poem

Once Upon a Time

Back when it was cool to smoke, she did, and was
I imagine, of course not able to remember, the picture
of glamourousness.
Chains of unfiltered Camels, never without the ivory
holder between blood-red nails, I've heard tell
and seen the legendary flash of her fierce green
eyes yellowing and wrinkled in the rusted
cookie tin filled to brimming with brittle
undated black and white snapshots she hung onto
for twenty-some-odd years, and I still keep.

It is difficult to pry open the lid.

Once I caught her in the mirror, her tears
a simple bewilderment to me then,
turning more complex. Now
I catch her only on the edges
of my own reflection. Her spark in my hazel,
barely discernable, bloodshot
itches, runs, waters, burns
incessant.

4/2   #9
Writer's Notebook, third prose draft
(excerpt of entire essay)

Mama's Smoke

   "Not 'plain'! Pure and ageless, incorruptible! That's what
your name is. I always hated mine with a passion! When people
called me 'Margaret' I felt squeamish. And 'Maggie'—ugh—a
literal punch in the stomach! But it's awkward to go through life
with a nickname. It makes you feel always like you're not quite
ever really yourself. I didn't want that for you."

   Peggy wanted only the best for me, the best being an abstraction she pondered incessantly. When I was little, I would sit on the

ancient wobbly wooden stool in the corner of the kitchen, rocking and squeaking, listening to her. I liked that spot because it was right over the heat duct in the winter, and caught the breeze from the screen door in the utility room in the summer. Evenings, I asked her all kinds of questions—never afraid to broach any subject—and her answers usually took off miraculously, soaring.

Sometimes I just listened to the rhythm of her plastic-soled slippers. . . .

4/23   Mama's Smoke #10
final prose version (whole essay, revised and completed)

Mama's Smoke

I never thought I would smoke. With her it was different— she started way back when it was cool to smoke—had been the very picture of glamour. But that was before the surgeon general determined the hazardousness that is as immediate in the origins of my consciousness as once-upon-a-time.   1

Myths are absorbing. I've been told of the chains of unfil- tered Camels she used to smoke, never without the legendary ivory holder between fingers with blood-red nails. By the time I was around she had switched to Merits.   2

Peggy thrived on craving. She wanted only the best for me, the best being an abstraction she pondered incessantly. When I was little I would sit on the ancient wobbly wooden stool in the corner of the kitchen, rocking and squeaking, listening to her. I liked the spot because it was right over the heat duct in the winter, and caught the breeze through the screen door in the utility room in the summer. Evenings, I asked her all kinds of questions—never afraid to broach any subject—and her answers usually took off miraculously, soaring.   3

"Not 'plain'! Pure and ageless, incorruptible! That's what your name is. That's why I gave it to you. I always hated mine with a passion! When people called me 'Margaret' I felt squea- mish. And 'Maggie'—ugh—a literal punch in the stomach! But it's awkward to go through life with a nickname. It makes you feel always like you're not quite ever really yourself. I didn't want that for you."   4

5   If I didn't understand the songs she sang, I knew the syllables by heart. Sometimes I would just listen to the rhythm of her plastic-soled slippers. I creaked my stool in time as her slippers slid on the red and white tiles, moving from one end of the long counter to the other and back, to the sink, ice box, sink again, stove, counter. There was a regularity to the irregularity that soothed me.

6   As I draw deeply on my menthol Virginia Slims Light, looking through the yellowing black and white snapshots in the rusty old cookie tin she held onto for twenty-some-odd years, I wonder what happened to make me start smoking. The lid is difficult to open. Inside there are faces, one face altered over and over, with fierce green eyes flashing, despite the brittle fadedness of the images. My hazel eyes have the spark, but only enough of a spark to torment me, to always make me seem not quite all me. Peggy stays away when I look at the pictures of her—maybe she doesn't identify with them anymore herself. She certainly used to.

7   But she also used to answer me when I called, and she no longer does that either. Often deep in my sleep I glimpse her and chase her through strange insidescapes, but she always refuses to recognize me. Once recently she consented to meet me in an abandoned ice rink. When I skated in late, she simply stared down my apologies. Suddenly busying herself with an old movie projector, her back to me, she became a flailing chaos of limbs in the darkness of the rink. I gave in to the oppression of futility and seated myself behind her. At first the picture jumped and lurched on the screen, out of focus, broke once, and then smoothed out. Peggy danced a vaudeville set in our old kitchen, twirling whisks and spatulas to the soundtrack of "Clementine." When the lights came on she had disappeared, and I was alone shivering, with the distorted tune ringing in my ears.

8   Usually she surfaces so briefly and unobtrusively that I'm not sure she has been there until after she's gone. Sometimes she appears an old haggard crone, the salt in her hair so thick that the pepper looks like dirt streaks washing away. Other times she is vital, younger than I am, the sheen of her black hair almost blinding. In the buttered daylight of my kitchen, as I stand blankly staring at the can of Crisco and the Pyrex measuring cup, I guess it is the sudden memory of a physics lesson that makes me think

of using water to measure the solid substance. Displacement. Only later, as I gently knead the biscuit dough, careful not to bruise it, I realize that she has been there. Her smirk of disgust at the soybean powder in the open cabinet gave her away—she couldn't resist a mild "eee-gad" under her breath.

Peggy is steeped in colloquialism, figures of speech that barely escape the shallows of cliché. She wrote a novel once, some kind of sequel to *Gone with the Wind* and now she comes to me at the typewriter sometimes, though rarely at the notebook stage, and whispers more criticism than commentary. She burned it, burned it in a fit of rage. Justified, for they wouldn't make her known. One attempt, one refusal. The only grace is to make a clean break.

She is something like a sequel to herself, elliptical and confusing, out of context. She speaks in fragments, interrupting in the middle of my own sentences, giving to others the illusion that I have spoken her words. But that's not exactly accurate either. The others don't know her, don't know her words from mine. The illusion is mine.

The hiss of the word "fixatif" on a spray can evokes a frustrated whimper of reminiscence. The bite of turpentine and linseed oil draws her. She is a painter of portraits and has rendered a likeness of almost everyone she is close to at one time or another, I believe, with the exception of herself. When I pick up a piece of charcoal she jumps in and jerks my hand, refusing to let me catch an image clearly. I have forsaken our art and she will not let me be forgiven so easily. But when I settle back and contemplate my own regrets, she relents. I feel her take her dry brush in hand and trace my features, a delicious tickle I revered as a child.

The legacy of paint stains on her pale turquoise smock, like the rhythm of the shuffle of her slippers on the floor, is her highest art. She denies it, of course, as obstinately as she refuses to appear when I look for her in the mirror. But she proves it as she shows up at those moments when I catch my reflection unexpectedly out of the corner of my eye.

The conversations we have now in black coffee cups and clouds of smoke are the closest we come to shared sustenance. They are always late, the times when it's most conspicuous to be awake. We plan the colors for the drapes and the throw pillows to furnish some future studio. The studio gradually takes shape, perfect, and then shatters in a coughing fit. I hear her in another room, hacking, fading, and then she's gone.

14   Just as she never stays, she never stays away for long. She was beautiful in her day and she still preens, still believes underneath in the ultimate importance of surfaces.

15   At parties, her old acquaintances appear as her friends. They ask me if I'm in art school and the flinching negative reply is overridden by their awe at my study of "philosophy."

16   "So like her! Right down to the hair and eyes, though not quite so dark, not quite so green. But underneath, Peggy *was* a philosopher, she was, so wise. . . ."

17   And Peggy surfaces and "eee-gads" so loudly in my ear that the friends' politenesses go under and my own return politenesses are just-not-quite-right. I sip my wine and kick Peggy in the shin. The acquaintances wander off whispering, "Almost the spitting image, except not nearly so . . . *genuine*. . . . This new generation. . . ."

18   Later, Peggy and I have pillow fights. The pillows are wet. The stains in the morning are on my face in the angry mirror. My eyes are hazel, murky. Peggy's eyes are clear, stinging green. When the lids began to droop, right before they closed for good, she cried bitterly in the mirror. Then I felt simple bewilderment, turning more complex. She still will not understand that her spattered smock is finer than the portraits. We light up. We cough out our truce.

For Writing

These various drafts of notebook, poetry, freewriting, and prose demonstrate the evolution of Mary Ruffin's "Mama's Smoke." You can compare and analyze these for evidence of development of character, style, narrative persona, changes in organization, incorporation of poetic language into the prose versions, and control over tone and relationship between the mother and daughter. You might also want to try to write a poem as a preliminary draft of a prose paper. Just play around with words, ideas, images, and sounds until they coalesce.

Part II

Determining Ideas in a Sequence

5 | *Narration*

Narration, telling a story, is a particularly attractive mode of writing. Ours is a storytelling culture. It is as old as Indian legends, Br'er Rabbit, Grimm's fairy tales, and the stories of Edgar Allan Poe. It is as new as speakers' warm-up jokes ("A funny thing happened on my way to . . .") and anecdotal leads to otherwise impersonal news stories. Thus *Newsweek* begins a lead article, "The Agony of Pan Am Flight 73," with a dramatic vignette that starts

> It was hot inside the cabin and the lights were growing dim. Four jittery gunmen had herded 374 passengers and 15 crew members into the center of the Boeing 747. Then at 9:55 p.m. the lights went out for good. The terrorists opened fire. Two grenades exploded. Shouting "Jihad! Jihad!" the gunmen randomly fired their automatic weapons into the panic-stricken pack of innocents.

This paragraph contains the major elements of a narrative: *characters* (in this case, the bad guys, "four jittery gunmen," and the good guys, "374 passengers and 15 crew members"); the *conflict* (evil versus good); the *motives* (hijacking versus safety/survival);

the *plot* (which side will win or prevail? how?); the *setting* (the hot interior of a Boeing 747 at 9:55 P.M.; *point of view* (the third-person account of a nonparticipant—in this case, not even an eyewitness); even a bit of *dialogue* ("Jihad! Jihad!"). All these features make the above incident or any vivid narrative a particularly easy form of writing for readers to remember. As this narration reveals, a narrative does *not* necessarily have to be a personal essay.

Narratives can be whole novels, stories, essays, or segments of other types of writings. They can be as long and complicated as Charles Dickens's novels or an account of the Watergate break-in, trial, and aftermath. Or they can be as short and to the point as the following narrative by student Myrna Greenfield, complete in a single paragraph:

> now every dream i'd ever dreamed about college room-mates said they are your best friends and the two of you fall in love with two men who are best friends and you get married after college to the best friends and you move to minneapolis or new rochelle and live next door and you have kids who grow up to be best friends with your best friend's kids. but kim was coolish and i was warmish and kim loved beethoven and i loved beatles and kim was neat and i was sloppy and kim was quiet and i was noisy as all hell broke loose. so much for the dream.

Myrna, as an author writing in the first person, has efficiently (although with unconventional punctuation) narrated two stories. The first, structured by a unified chronological progression, relates the myth of a college woman's stereotyped life history. The second, emphasizing variations on the theme of incompatibility, tells the story of the actual relationship between the author and her roommate. There are two main characters in the first story: Myrna's idealized version of herself and Kim. The two characters in the second story are the actual roommates. Each story has a setting: college and the suburbs in the first; college in the second. Each story covers a period of time—the entire life span in the first; the recent past in the second. The second sentence negates the first and leads to the short, punchy emotional climax, "so much for the dream."

A narrative need not be fictional, as the above examples and the essays in this section indicate. When you're writing a narrative based on real people, actual incidents, you shape the material to emphasize the *point of view, sequence of action* (a chase, an exploration), a *theme* (greed, pleasure), a *particular relationship between characters* (love, antagonism), or the *personalities of the people involved* (vigorous, passive). This shaping—supplying information or other specific details where necessary, deleting trivial or irrelevant material—is essential in transforming skeletal diary entries (see Twain in Chapter 3) into three-dimensional configurations.

A narrative can *exist for its own sake*. As sixteenth-century poet and courtier Sir Philip Sidney observed, such writing can attract "children from play and old men from the chimney corner." Though Ann Upperco Dolman's comic tale of "Learning to Drive" (196–200) typifies the experiences of thousands of new teenage drivers, it won't improve anyone's learning curve—but everyone who has ever survived driving lessons will enjoy it. Through a narrative you can also *illustrate or explore a personality or an idea*. In the classic "Once More to the Lake" (171–79), E. B. White uses his own experiences on a timeless summer vacation to explore the continuity of generations of parents and children, embedding short narrative vignettes into the overarching narrative structure.

In "The Inheritance of Tools" (186–96) Scott Russell Sanders uses a comparable narrative technique to interpret the character of his father. As Sanders's essay becomes a tribute to his father, and to the extended family of which his father was a member, Sanders describes his legacy, the carpenters' tools ("the hammer [that] had belonged to him, and to his father before him") and the knowledge of how to use them, transmitted through years of patient teaching and an insistence on high-quality work, "making sure before I drove the first nail that every line was square and true." This type of description consists of stories embedded within stories: How Sanders's father taught him to use the hammer (¶s 6, 9), the saw (¶s 10, 12), the square (¶s 14–16). Still more stories incorporate the current use to which Sanders puts this knowledge (he's building a bedroom in the basement), the incident of the gerbil escaping behind the new bedroom wall (¶s 17, 22), learning of his father's death (¶s 26, 28)—all embedded in the matrix of the stories of four generations of the Sanders family.

If you wish to write a personal narrative you can *present a whole or partial biography or autobiography,* as does Frederick Douglass in "Resurrection"(164–70), an excerpt from his *Life and Times* that recounts a single narrative incident in the life of a slave. Here Douglass tells the story of how he defied—in a two-hour fist-fight—a Simon Legree–like overseer who had determined to break his spirit through repeated beatings. This, explains Douglass, was "the turning-point in my career as a slave. . . . It recalled the departed self-confidence, and inspired me again with a determination to be free. . . . It was a glorious resurrection, from the tomb of slavery, to the heaven of freedom."

Through narration you can *impart information* or *an account of historical events,* either from an impartial or—more likely—an engaged eyewitness point of view, as Zitkala-Sa does in excerpts from *The School Days of an Indian Girl* (273–83). Through narration you can, as Zitkala-Sa also does, *present a powerful argument, overt or implicit.* Lynda Barry's "The Sanctuary of School" (670–75) also uses the example of herself (and her brother—"children with the sound turned off") to present the implied argument that for neglected youngsters public schools are a lifeline and should be funded at a level that reflects their vital importance. Fables, parables, and other *morality* or *cautionary tales* are as old as Aesop, as familiar as the Old and New Testaments, as contemporary as Judith Ortiz Cofer's narrative about storytelling itself, "*Casa:* A Partial Remembrance of a Puerto Rican Childhood" (179–86). Here, the process of telling and interpreting a story with a moral reinforces the close female community of tellers and listeners.

To write a narrative you can ask, What do I want to demonstrate? Through what characters, performing what actions or thinking what thoughts? In what setting and time frame? From what point of view do I want to tell the tale? Do I want to use a first-person involved narrator who may also be a character in the story, as are the narrators of all the essays in this section? Or a third-person narrator, either on the scene or depending on the reports of other people, as in the *Newsweek* account quoted on page 159? An easy way to remember these questions is to ask yourself

1. *Who* participated?
2. *What* happened?

3. *Why* did this event/these phenomena happen?
4. *When* did it (or they) happen?
5. *Where* did it (or they) happen?
6. *How* did it (or they) happen? Under what circumstances?

Narratives have as many purposes, as many plots, as many characters as there are people to write them. You have but to examine your life, your thoughts, your experiences, to find an unwritten library of narratives yet to tell. Therein lie a thousand tales. Or a thousand and one. . . .

STRATEGIES FOR WRITING— NARRATION

1. You'll need to consider, "What is the purpose of my narrative?" Am I telling the tale for its own sake, or using it to make a larger point?
2. For what audience am I writing this? What will they have experienced or be able to understand, and what will I need to explain? How do I want my audience to react?
3. What is the focus, the conflict of my narrative? How will it begin? Gain momentum and develop to a climax? End? What emphasis will I give each part, or separate scenes or incidents within each part?
4. Will I write from a first- or third-person point of view? Will I be a major character in my narrative? As a participant or as an observer? Or both, if my present self is observing my past self?
5. What is my attitude toward my material? What tone do I want to use? Will it be consistent throughout, or will it change during the course of events?

FREDERICK DOUGLASS

Douglass (1817–1895) was born a slave in Talbot County, Maryland. Unlike many slaves, he learned to read, and the power of this accomplishment coupled with an iron physique and the will to match, enabled him to escape to New York in 1838. For the next twenty-five years he toured the country as a powerful spokesperson for the abolitionist movement, serving as an adviser to Harriet Beecher Stowe, author of *Uncle Tom's Cabin,* and to President Lincoln, among others. After the war he campaigned for civil rights for African-Americans and women. In 1890 his political significance was acknowledged in his appointment as minister to Haiti.

Slave narratives, written or dictated by the hundreds in the nineteenth century, provided memorable accounts of the physical, geographical, and psychological movement from captivity to freedom, from dependence to independence. Douglass's autobiography, an abolitionist document like many other slave narratives, is exceptional in its forthright language and absence of stereotyping of either whites or blacks; his people are multi-dimensional. Crisis points, and the insights and opportunities they provide, are natural topics for personal narratives (see also Richard Rodriguez's "None of This Is Fair" [398–405], and Richard Wright's "The Power of Books" [425–35]). This episode, taken from the first version (of four) of *The Narrative of the Life of Frederick Douglass, an American Slave* (1845), explains the incident that was "the turning point in my career as a slave," for it enabled him to make the transformation from slave to human being.

Resurrection

1   I have already intimated that my condition was much worse, during the first six months of my stay at Mr. Covey's, than in the last six. The circumstances leading to the change in Mr. Covey's course toward me form an epoch in my humble history. You have seen how a man was made a slave; you shall see how a slave was made a man. On one of the hottest days of the month of August, 1833, Bill Smith, William Hughes, a slave named Eli, and myself,

were engaged in fanning wheat. Hughes was clearing the fanned wheat from before the fan. Eli was turning, Smith was feeding, and I was carrying wheat to the fan. The work was simple, requiring strength rather than intellect; yet, to one entirely unused to such work, it came very hard. About three o'clock of that day, I broke down; my strength failed me; I was seized with a violent aching of the head, attended with extreme dizziness; I trembled in every limb. Finding what was coming, I nerved myself up, feeling it would never do to stop work. I stood as long as I could stagger to the hopper with grain. When I could stand no longer, I fell, and felt as if held down by an immense weight. The fan of course stopped; every one had his own work to do; and no one could do the work of the other, and have his own go on at the same time.

Mr. Covey was at the house, about one hundred yards from the treading-yard where we were fanning. On hearing the fan stop, he left immediately, and came to the spot where we were. He hastily inquired what the matter was. Bill answered that I was sick, and there was no one to bring wheat to the fan. I had by this time crawled away under the side of the post and rail-fence by which the yard was enclosed, hoping to find relief by getting out of the sun. He then asked where I was. He was told by one of the hands. He came to the spot, and, after looking at me awhile, asked me what was the matter. I told him as well as I could, for I scarce had strength to speak. He then gave me a savage kick in the side, and told me to get up. I tried to do so, but fell back in the attempt. He gave me another kick, and again told me to rise. I again tried, and succeeded in gaining my feet; but, stooping to get the tub with which I was feeding the fan, I again staggered and fell. While down in this situation, Mr. Covey took up the hickory slat with which Hughes had been striking off the half-bushel measure, and with it gave me a heavy blow upon the head, making a large wound, and the blood ran freely; and with this again told me to get up. I made no effort to comply, having now made up my mind to let him do his worst. In a short time after receiving this blow, my head grew better. Mr. Covey had now left me to my fate. At this moment I resolved, for the first time, to go to my master, enter a complaint, and ask his protection. In order to do this, I must that afternoon walk seven miles; and this, under the circumstances, was truly a severe undertaking. I was exceedingly feeble; made so as much by the kicks and blows which I received, as by the severe fit of sickness to which I had been subjected. I, however, watched my chance, while Covey was looking in an opposite direction, and started for St. Michael's: I succeeded in getting a considerable distance on my way to the woods, when Covey discovered me, and called after me to come back, threatening what he would do if I did not come. I disregarded both his calls and his threats, and made my way to the woods as fast as my feeble state would allow; and thinking I might be overhauled by him if I kept to the road, I walked through the woods, keeping far enough from the road to avoid detection, and near enough to prevent losing my way. I had not gone far before my little strength again failed me. I could go no farther. I fell down, and lay for a considerable time. The blood was yet oozing from the wound on my head. For a time I thought I should bleed to death; and think now that I should have done so, but that the blood so matted my hair as to stop the wound. After lying there about three quarters of an hour, I nerved myself up again, and started on my way, through bogs and briers, barefooted and bareheaded, tearing my feet sometimes at nearly every step; and after a journey of about seven miles, occupying some five hours to perform it, I arrived at master's store. I then presented an appearance enough to affect any but a heart of iron. From the crown of my head to my feet, I was covered with blood. My hair was all clotted with dust and blood; my shirt was stiff with blood. My legs and feet were torn in sundry places with briers and thorns, and were also covered in blood. I suppose I looked like a man who had escaped a den of wild beasts, and barely escaped them. In this state I appeared before my master, humbly entreating him to interpose his authority for my protection. I told him all the circumstances as well as I could, and it seemed, as I spoke, at times to affect him. He would then walk the floor, and seek to justify Covey by saying he expected I deserved it. He asked me what I wanted. I told him, to let me get a new home; that as sure as I lived with Mr. Covey again, I should live with but to die with him; that Covey would surely kill me; he was in a fair way for it. Master Thomas ridiculed the idea that there was any danger of Mr. Covey's killing me, and said that he knew Mr. Covey, that he was a good man, and that he could not think of taking me from him; that, should he do so, he would lose the whole year's wages;

that I belonged to Mr. Covey for one year, and that I must go back to him, come what might; and that I must not trouble him with any more stories, or that he would himself *get hold of me*. After threatening me thus, he gave me a very large dose of salts, telling me that I might remain in St. Michael's that night, (it being quite late,) but that I must be off back to Mr. Covey's early in the morning; and that if I did not, he would *get hold of me*, which meant that he would whip me. I remained all night, and, according to his orders, I started off to Covey's in the morning, (Saturday morning,) wearied in body and broken in spirit. I got no supper that night, or breakfast that morning. I reached Covey's about nine o'clock; and just as I was getting over the fence that divided Mrs. Kemp's fields from ours, out ran Covey with his cowskin, to give me another whipping. Before he could reach me, I succeeded in getting to the cornfield; and as the corn was very high, it afforded me the means of hiding. He seemed very angry, and searched for me a long time. My behavior was altogether unaccountable. He finally gave up the chase, thinking, I suppose, that I must come home for something to eat; he would give himself no further trouble in looking for me. I spent that day mostly in the woods, having the alternative before me—to go home and be whipped to death, or stay in the woods and be starved to death. That night, I fell in with Sandy Jenkins, a slave with whom I was somewhat acquainted. Sandy had a free wife who lived about four miles from Mr. Covey's; and it being Saturday, he was on his way to see her. I told him my circumstances, and he very kindly invited me to go home with him. I went home with him, and talked this whole matter over, and got his advice as to what course it was best for me to pursue. I found Sandy an old adviser. He told me, with great solemnity, I must go back to Covey; but that before I went, I must go with him into another part of the woods, where there was a certain *root*, which, if I would take some of it with me, carrying it *always on my right side*, would render it impossible for Mr. Covey, or any other white man, to whip me. He said he had carried it for years; and since he had done so, he had never received a blow, and never expected to while he carried it. I at first rejected the idea, that the simple carrying of a root in my pocket would have any such effect as he had said, and was not disposed to take it; but Sandy impressed the necessity with much earnestness, telling me it could do no harm, if it did no good. To please him, I at length took the root, and, according to his direction, carried it upon my right side. This was Sunday morning. I immediately started for home; and upon entering the yard gate, out came Mr. Covey on his way to meeting. He spoke to me very kindly, bade me drive the pigs from a lot near by, and passed on towards the church. Now, this singular conduct of Mr. Covey really made me begin to think that there was something in the *root* which Sandy had given me; and had it been on any other day than Sunday, I could have attributed the conduct to no other cause than the influence of that root; and as it was, I was half inclined to think the *root* to be something more than I at first had taken it to be. All went well till Monday morning. On this morning, the virtue of the *root* was fully tested. Long before daylight, I was called to go and rub, curry, and feed, the horses. I obeyed, and was glad to obey. But whilst thus engaged, whilst in the act of throwing down some blades from the loft, Mr. Covey entered the stable with a long rope; and just as I was half out of the loft, he caught hold of my legs, and was about tying me. As soon as I found what he was up to, I gave a sudden spring, and as I did so, he holding to my legs, I was brought sprawling on the stable floor. Mr. Covey seemed now to think he had me, and could do what he pleased; but at this moment—from whence came the spirit I don't know—I resolved to fight; and, suiting my action to the resolution, I seized Covey hard by the throat; and as I did so, I rose. He held on to me, and I to him. My resistance was so entirely unexpected, that Covey seemed taken all aback. He trembled like a leaf. This gave me assurance, and I held him uneasy, causing the blood to run where I touched him with the ends of my fingers. Mr. Covey soon called out to Hughes for help. Hughes came, and while Covey held me, attempted to tie my right hand. While he was in the act of doing so, I watched my chance, and gave him a heavy kick close under the ribs. This kick fairly sickened Hughes, so that he left me in the hands of Mr. Covey. This kick had the effect of not only weakening Hughes, but Covey also. When he saw Hughes bending over with pain, his courage quailed. He asked me if I meant to persist in my resistance. I told him I did, come what might; that he had used me like a brute for six months, and that I was determined to be used so no longer. With that, he strove to drag me to a stick that was lying just out of the stable door. He meant to knock me down. But just as he was leaning over to get the stick, I seized him with both hands by his collar, and brought him by a sudden snatch to the ground. By this time, Bill came. Covey called upon him for assistance. Bill wanted to know what he could do. Covey said, "Take hold of him, take hold of him!" Bill said his master hired him out to work, and not to help whip me; so he left Covey and myself to fight our own battle out. We were at it for nearly two hours. Covey at length let me go, puffing and blowing at a great rate, saying that if I had not resisted, he would not have whipped me half so much. The truth was, that he had not whipped me at all. I considered him as getting entirely the worst end of the bargain; for he had drawn no blood from me, but I had from him. The whole six months afterwards, that I spent with Mr. Covey, he never laid the weight of his finger upon me in anger. He would occasionally say, he didn't want to get hold of me again. "No," thought I, "you need not; for you will come off worse than you did before."

This battle with Mr. Covey was the turning-point in my ₃ career as a slave. It rekindled the few expiring embers of freedom, and revived within me a sense of my own manhood. It recalled the departed self-confidence, and inspired me again with a determination to be free. The gratification afforded by the triumph was a full compensation for whatever else might follow, even death itself. He only can understand the deep satisfaction which I experienced, who has himself repelled by force the bloody arm of slavery. I felt as I never felt before. It was a glorious resurrection, from the tomb of slavery, to the heaven of freedom. My long-crushed spirit rose, cowardice departed, bold defiance took its place; and I now resolved that, however long I might remain a slave in form, the day had passed forever when I could be a slave in fact. I did not hesitate to let it be known of me, that the white man who expected to succeed in whipping, must also succeed in killing me.

Content

1. Twelve years after he successfully defied Mr. Covey, Douglass identified this incident as "the turning-point in my career as a slave" (¶ 3). Why? Would Douglass have been able to recognize its significance at the time or only in retrospect?

2. What, if anything, does Douglass expect his audience to do about slavery, as a consequence of having read his narrative?

Strategies/Structures

3. Douglass's account begins with Friday afternoon and ends with Monday morning, but some events receive considerable emphasis while others are scarcely mentioned. Which ones does he focus on? Why?

4. Why is paragraph 2 so long? Should it have been divided into shorter units, or is the longer unit preferable? Justify your answer.

5. Douglass provides considerable details about his appearance after his first beating by Covey (¶ 2), but scarcely any about the appearance of either Covey or Master Thomas. Why?

6. Would slave owners have been likely to read Douglass's autobiography? Why or why not? Would Douglass's emphasis have been likely to change for an audience of Northern post–Civil War blacks? Southern antebellum whites?

Language

7. How sophisticated is Douglass's level of diction? Is it appropriate for the narrative he tells? How is this related to his self-characterization?

8. Why does Douglass explain his changed self-image as a "resurrection, from the tomb of slavery, to the heaven of freedom"?

For Writing

9. Write a narrative in which you recount and explain the significance of an event in which you participated that provided you with an important change of status in the eyes of others. (See Rodriguez's "None of This Is Fair," 398–405, and Wright's "The Power of Books," 425–35.) Provide enough specific details so readers unfamiliar with either you or the situation can experience it as you did. Be sure to depict the personalities of the central characters; their physical appearance may not be nearly as significant.

10. Write a narrative intended to inspire your readers in which you recount an incident expressing the difficulties of a minority or oppressed person or group. (See essays by Rodriguez and Wright mentioned in the previous question.) You can also try to move your readers to take action concerning the problem. Try to move them by example rather than through preaching or an excess of emotion. Understatement is usually more appealing than overstatement.

E. B. WHITE

"Once More to the Lake," a narrative of father and son, timeless generations in the eternal Maine countryside, conveys significant intangibles (love—parental and filial; the importance of nature; the inevitability of growth, change, and death) through memorably specific details. White leads us to the lake itself ("cool and motionless"), down the path to yesteryear, where the continuity of generations intermingles past, present, and future until they become almost indistinguishable: "The years were a mirage and there had been no years. . . ." Everywhere White's son, thoroughly identified with his father, does the same things White had done at the same lake as a boy—putting about in the same boat, catching the same bass, drinking the same soda pop, enjoying the same ritualistic swim after the same summer thunderstorm (see also Scott Russell Sanders's "The Inheritance of Tools," 186–96). The mood of "peace and goodness and jollity" that White recreates indelibly shifts, however, as the cosmic chill of the last sentence reminds us of the inevitable passing of generations. (For a biographical sketch of E. B. White, see page 44.)

Once More to the Lake

O ne summer, along about 1904, my father rented a camp on a lake in Maine and took us all there for the month of August. We all got ringworm from some kittens and had to rub Pond's Extract on our arms and legs night and morning, and my father rolled over in a canoe with all his clothes on; but outside of that the vacation was a success and from then on none of us ever thought there was any place in the world like that lake in Maine. We returned summer after summer—always on August 1st for one month. I have since become a salt-water man, but sometimes in summer there are days when the restlessness of the tides and the fearful cold of the sea water and the incessant wind which blows across the afternoon and into the evening make me wish for the placidity of a lake in the woods. A few weeks ago this feeling got so strong I bought myself a couple of bass hooks and a spinner and returned to the lake where we used to go, for a week's fishing and to revisit old haunts.

2   I took along my son, who had never had any fresh water up his nose and who had seen lily pads only from train windows. On the journey over to the lake I began to wonder what it would be like. I wondered how time would have marred this unique, this holy spot—the coves and streams, the hills that the sun set behind, the camps and the paths behind the camps. I was sure the tarred road would have found it out and I wondered in what other ways it would be desolated. It is strange how much you can remember about places like that once you allow your mind to return into the grooves which lead back. You remember one thing, and that suddenly reminds you of another thing. I guess I remembered clearest of all the early mornings, when the lake was cool and motionless, remembered how the bedroom smelled of the lumber it was made of and of the wet woods whose scent entered through the screen. The partitions in the camp were thin and did not extend clear to the top of the rooms, and as I was always the first up I would dress softly so as not to wake the others, and sneak out into the sweet outdoors and start out in the canoe, keeping close along the shore in the long shadows of the pines. I remembered being very careful never to rub my paddle against the gunwale for fear of disturbing the stillness of the cathedral.

3   The lake had never been what you would call a wild lake. There were cottages sprinkled around the shores, and it was in farming country although the shores of the lake were quite heavily wooded. Some of the cottages were owned by nearby farmers, and you would live at the shore and eat your meals at the farmhouse. That's what our family did. But although it wasn't wild, it was a fairly large and undisturbed lake and there were places in it which, to a child at least, seemed infinitely remote and primeval.

4   I was right about the tar: it led to within half a mile of the shore. But when I got back there, with my boy, and we settled into a camp near a farmhouse and into the kind of summertime I had known, I could tell that it was going to be pretty much the same as it had been before—I knew it, lying in bed the first morning, smelling the bedroom, and hearing the boy sneak quietly out and go off along the shore in a boat. I began to sustain

the illusion that he was I, and therefore by simple transposition, that I was my father. This sensation persisted, kept cropping up all the time we were there. It was not an entirely new feeling, but in this setting it grew much stronger. I seemed to be living a dual existence. I would be in the middle of some simple act, I would be picking up a bait box or laying down a table fork, or I would be saying something, and suddenly it would be not I but my father who was saying the words or making the gesture. It gave me a creepy sensation.

We went fishing the first morning. I felt the same damp 5 moss covering the worms in the bait can, and saw the dragonfly alight on the tip of my rod as it hovered a few inches from the surface of the water. It was the arrival of this fly that convinced me beyond any doubt that everything was as it always had been, that the years were a mirage and there had been no years. The small waves were the same, chucking the rowboat under the chin as we fished at anchor, and the boat was the same boat, the same color green and the ribs broken in the same places, and under the floor-boards the same fresh-water leavings and debris—the dead helgramite, the wisps of moss, the rusty discarded fishhook, the dried blood from yesterday's catch. We stared silently at the tips of our rods, at the dragonflies that came and went. I lowered the tip of mine into the water, tentatively, pensively dislodging the fly, which darted two feet away, poised, darted two feet back, and came to a rest again a little farther up the rod. There had been no years between the ducking of this dragonfly and the other one— the one that was part of memory. I looked at the boy, who was silently watching his fly, and it was my hands that held his rod, my eyes watching. I felt dizzy and didn't know which rod I was at the end of.

We caught two bass, hauling them in briskly as though they 6 were mackerel, pulling them over the side of the boat in a businesslike manner without any landing net, and stunning them with a blow on the back of the head. When we got back for a swim before lunch, the lake was exactly where we had left it, the same number of inches from the dock, and there was only the merest suggestion of a breeze. This seemed an utterly enchanted sea, this lake you could leave to its own devices for a few hours and come back to, and find that it had not stirred, this constant and trustworthy body of water. In the shallows, the dark, water-soaked sticks and twigs, smooth and old, were undulating in clusters on the bottom against the clean ribbed sand, and the track of the mussel was plain. A school of minnows swam by, each minnow with its small individual shadow, doubling the attendance, so clear and sharp in the sunlight. Some of the other campers were in swimming, along the shore, one of them with a cake of soap, and the water felt thin and clear and unsubstantial. Over the years there had been this person with the cake of soap, this cultist, and here he was. There had been no years.

7   Up to the farmhouse to dinner through the teeming, dusty field, the road under our sneakers was only a two-track road. The middle track was missing, the one with the marks of the hooves and the splotches of dried, flaky manure. There had always been three tracks to choose from in choosing which track to walk in; now the choice was narrowed down to two. For a moment I missed terribly the middle alternative. But the way led past the tennis court, and something about the way it lay there in the sun reassured me; the tape had loosened along the backline, the alleys were green with plantains and other weeds, and the net (installed in June and removed in September) sagged in the dry noon, and the whole place steamed with midday heat and hunger and emptiness. There was a choice of pie for dessert, and one was blueberry and one was apple, and the waitresses were the same country girls, there having been no passage of time, only the illusion of it as in a dropped curtain—the waitresses were still fifteen; their hair had been washed, that was the only difference—they had been to the movies and seen the pretty girls with the clean hair.

8   Summertime, oh summertime, pattern of life indelible, the fade-proof lake, the wood unshatterable, the pasture with the sweetfern and the juniper forever and ever, summer without end; this was the background, and the life along the shore was the design, the cottages with their innocent and tranquil design, their tiny docks with the flagpole and the American flag floating against the white clouds in the blue sky, the little paths over the roots of the trees leading from camp to camp and the paths leading back to the outhouses and the can of lime for sprinkling, and

at the souvenir counters at the store the miniature birchbark canoes and the post cards that showed things looking a little better than they looked. This was the American family at play, escaping the city heat, wondering whether the newcomers in the camp at the head of the cove were "common" or "nice," wondering whether it was true that the people who drove up for Sunday dinner at the farmhouse were turned away because there wasn't enough chicken.

It seemed to me, as I kept remembering all this, that those 9 times and those summers had been infinitely precious and worth saving. There had been jollity and peace and goodness. The arriving (at the beginning of August) had been so big a business in itself, at the railway station the farm wagon drawn up, the first smell of the pine-laden air, the first glimpse of the smiling farmer, and the great importance of the trunks and your father's enormous authority in such matters, and the feel of the wagon under you for the long ten-mile haul, and at the top of the last long hill catching the first view of the lake after eleven months of not seeing this cherished body of water. The shouts and cries of the other campers when they saw you, and the trunks to be unpacked, to give up their rich burden. (Arriving was less exciting nowadays, when you sneaked up in your car and parked it under a tree near the camp and took out the bags and in five minutes it was all over, no fuss, no loud wonderful fuss about trunks.)

Peace and goodness and jollity. The only thing that was 10 wrong now, really, was the sound of the place, an unfamiliar nervous sound of the outboard motors. This was the note that jarred, the one thing that would sometimes break the illusion and set the years moving. In those other summertimes all motors were inboard; and when they were at a little distance, the noise they made was a sedative, an ingredient of summer sleep. They were one-cylinder and two-cylinder engines, and some were make-and-break and some were jump-spark, but they all made a sleepy sound across the lake. The one-lungers throbbed and fluttered, and the twin-cylinder ones purred and purred, and that was a quiet sound too. But now the campers all had outboards. In the daytime, in the hot mornings, these motors made a petulant, irritable sound; at night, in the still evening when the afterglow lit the water, they whined about one's ears like mosquitoes. My boy loved our rented outboard, and his great desire was to achieve singlehanded mastery over it, and authority, and he soon learned the trick of choking it a little (but not too much), and the adjustment of the needle valve. Watching him I would remember the things you could do with the old one-cylinder engine with the heavy flywheel, how you could have it eating out of your hand if you got really close to it spiritually. Motor boats in those days didn't have clutches, and you would make a landing by shutting off the motor at the proper time and coasting in with a dead rudder. But there was a way of reversing them, if you learned the trick, by cutting the switch and putting it on again exactly on the final dying revolution of the flywheel, so that it would kick back against compression and begin reversing. Approaching a dock in a strong following breeze, it was difficult to slow up sufficiently by the ordinary coasting method, and if a boy felt he had complete mastery over his motor, he was tempted to keep it running beyond its time and then reverse it a few feet from the dock. It took a cool nerve, because if you threw the switch a twentieth of a second too soon you would catch the flywheel when it still had speed enough to go up past center, and the boat would leap ahead, charging bull-fashion at the dock.

11   We had a good week at the camp. The bass were biting well and the sun shone endlessly, day after day. We would be tired at night and lie down in the accumulated heat of the little bedrooms after the long hot day and the breeze would stir almost imperceptibly outside and the smell of the swamp drift in through the rusty screens. Sleep would come easily and in the morning the red squirrel would be on the roof, tapping out his gay routine. I kept remembering everything, lying in bed in the mornings—the small steamboat that had a long rounded stern like the lip of a Ubangi, and how quietly she ran on the moonlight sails, when the older boys played their mandolins and the girls sang and we ate doughnuts dipped in sugar, and how sweet the music was on the water in the shining night, and what it had felt like to think about girls then. After breakfast we would go up to the store and the things were in the same place—the minnows in a bottle, the plugs and spinners, disarranged and pawed over by the youngsters from the boys' camp, the Fig Newtons and the Beeman's gum.

Outside, the road was tarred and cars stood in front of the store. Inside, all was just as it had always been, except there was more Coca-Cola and not so much Moxie and root beer and birch beer and sarsaparilla. We would walk out with a bottle of pop apiece and sometimes the pop would backfire up our noses and hurt. We explored the streams, quietly, where the turtles slid off the sunny logs and dug their way into the soft bottom; and we lay on the town wharf and fed worms to the tame bass. Everywhere we went I had trouble making out which was I, the one walking at my side, the one walking in my pants.

One afternoon while we were there at that lake a thunder-   12
storm came up. It was like the revival of an old melodrama that I had seen long ago with childish awe. The second-act climax of the drama of the electrical disturbance over a lake in America had not changed in any important respect. This was the big scene, still the big scene. The whole thing was so familiar, the first feeling of oppression and heat and a general air around camp of not wanting to go very far away. In midafternoon (it was all the same) a curious darkening of the sky, and a lull in everything that had made life tick; and then the way the boats suddenly swung the other way at their moorings with the coming of a breeze out of the new quarter, and the premonitory rumble. Then the kettle drum, then the snare, then the bass drum and cymbals, then crackling light against the dark, and the gods grinning and licking their chops in the hills. Afterward the calm, the rain steadily rustling in the calm lake, the return of light and hope and spirits, and the campers running out in joy and relief to go swimming in the rain, their bright cries perpetuating the deathless joke about how they were getting simply drenched, and the children screaming with delight at the new sensation of bathing in the rain, and the joke about getting drenched linking the generations in a strong indestructible chain. And the comedian who waded in carrying an umbrella.

When the others went swimming my son said he was going   13
in too. He pulled his dripping trunks from the line where they had hung all through the shower, and wrung them out. Languidly, and with no thought of going in, I watching him, his hard little body, skinny and bare, saw him wince slightly as he pulled up around

his vitals the small, soggy, icy garment. As he buckled the swollen belt suddenly my groin felt the chill of death.

Content

1. Characterize White's son. Why is he referred to as "my son" and "the boy" but never by name?
2. How do the ways in which the boy and his father relate to the lake environment emphasize their personal relationship? In which ways are these similar to the relationship between the narrator and his father, the boy's grandfather? Are there any significant differences, stated or implied?
3. White emphasizes the "peace and goodness and jollity" of the summers at the lake. What incidents and details reinforce this emphasis? Why, then, does White end with "As he buckled the swollen belt suddenly my groin felt the chill of death" (¶ 13)?

Strategies/Structures

4. Many narratives proceed chronologically from the beginning to the end of the time period they cover, relating the events of that period in the sequence in which they occurred. Instead, White organizes this narrative topically. What are the major topics? Why do they come in the order they do, concluding with the thunderstorm and its aftermath?
5. What are the effects of White's frequent repetition of phrases ("there had been no years") and words ("same")? What details or incidents does he use to illustrate the cycle of time?

Language

6. What language contributes to the relaxed mood of this essay? In what ways does the mood fit the subject?
7. Beginning writers are often advised when writing description to be sparing of adjectives and adverbs—to put the weight on nouns and verbs instead. Does White do this? Consistently? Pick a paragraph and analyze it to illustrate your answer.

For Writing

8. Tell the story of your experiences in a particular place—school building, restaurant, vacation spot, hometown, place visited—that emphasizes

the influence of the place on your experiences and on your understanding of them. Identify what makes it memorable, but do not describe it in the picture-pretty manner of a travel brochure.

9. Write a narrative in which you focus on a significant relationship between yourself at a particular age and another member of your family of a different generation, either older or younger. If you emphasize its specific features you will probably capture some of its common or universal elements as well.

JUDITH ORTIZ COFER

"I grew up in two worlds, the tropical island and the cold city, and that would later surface in my dreams and in my poetry," says Cofer, born in Puerto Rico in 1952. She spent her bicultural, bilingual childhood shuttling between Paterson, New Jersey, and Puerto Rico, where her career Navy father was stationed until he retired and the family moved to Georgia. Cofer earned a B.A. from Augusta College (1974), an M.A. from Florida Atlantic University (1977), and studied at Oxford. She returned to Florida to teach English and write the poetry that soon won critical acclaim and a staff position at the Bread Loaf Writers' Conference; she now teaches creative writing at the University of Georgia. Her work includes poetry: *Peregrina* (1986); *Reaching for the Mainland* (1987); and *Terms of Survival* (1987); a novel, *The Line of the Sun* (1909), a collection of poetry and essays, *The Latin Deli* (1993); and a collection of stories, *An Island Like You* (1995); and a collection of poetry and stories, *The Year of Our Revolution* (1998).

In her poetry, as in *"Casa:* A Partial Remembrance of a Puerto Rican Childhood," originally published in *Prairie Schooner* in 1989 and reprinted in *Silent Dancing* (1990), Cofer is concerned with the instability of relationships between men, absent and elusive, and the women whose stability and community are the heart of the household. Although she writes in English, the Spanish bleeds through into the text, reinforcing the animated blending of Puerto Rican and North American cultures in what she calls the "habit of movement." "The Woman Who Was Left at the Altar" (1987), presents in poetry the same story of solitary, mad Maria who is the subject of the climactic, cautionary tale Cofer's grandmother tells as a warning to young women not to be trapped or defeated by love. *"Casa,"* then, is a true story about storytelling, where the *facts* are not important, but the message of the *cuentos* is, embedded in the closeness of teller and listeners, their heritage and future.

Casa: *A Partial Remembrance of a Puerto Rican Childhood*

1   At three or four o'clock in the afternoon, the hour of *café con leche*, the women of my family gathered in Mamá's living room to speak of important things and retell familiar stories meant to be overheard by us young girls, their daughters. In Mamá's house (everyone called my grandmother Mamá) was a large parlor built by my grandfather to his wife's exact specifications so that it was always cool, facing away from the sun. The doorway was on the side of the house so no one could walk directly into her living room. First they had to take a little stroll through and around her beautiful garden where prize-winning orchids grew in the trunk of an ancient tree she had hollowed out for that purpose. This room was furnished with several mahogany rocking chairs, acquired at the births of her children, and one intricately carved rocker that had passed down to Mamá at the death of her own mother.

2   It was on these rockers that my mother, her sisters, and my grandmother sat on these afternoons of my childhood to tell their stories, teaching each other, and my cousin and me, what it was like to be a woman, more specifically, a Puerto Rican woman. They talked about life on the island, and life in *Los Nueva Yores*, their way of referring to the United States from New York City to California: the other place, not home, all the same. They told real-life stories though, as I later learned, always embellishing them with a little or a lot of dramatic detail. And they told *cuentos*, the morality and cautionary tales told by the women in our family for generations: stories that became a part of my subconscious as I grew up in two worlds, the tropical island and the cold city, and that would later surface in my dreams and in my poetry.

One of these tales was about the woman who was left at the   3
altar. Mamá liked to tell that one with histrionic intensity. I remember the rise and fall of her voice, the sighs, and her constantly
gesturing hands, like two birds swooping through her words. This
particular story usually would come up in a conversation as a
result of someone mentioning a forthcoming engagement or wedding. The first time I remember hearing it, I was sitting on the floor
at Mamá's feet, pretending to read a comic book. I may have been
eleven or twelve years old, at that difficult age when a girl was no
longer a child who could be ordered to leave the room if the
women wanted freedom to take their talk into forbidden zones,
nor really old enough to be considered a part of their conclave. I
could only sit quietly, pretending to be in another world, while absorbing it all in a sort of unspoken agreement of my status as silent
auditor. On this day, Mamá had taken my long, tangled mane of
hair into her ever-busy hands. Without looking down at me and
with no interruption of her flow of words, she began braiding my
hair, working at it with the quickness and determination that characterized all her actions. My mother was watching us impassively
from her rocker across the room. On her lips played a little ironic
smile. I would never sit still for *her* ministrations, but even then, I
instinctively knew that she did not possess Mamá's matriarchal
power to command and keep everyone's attention. This was never
more evident than in the spell she cast when telling a story.

"It is not like it used to be when I was a girl," Mamá an-   4
nounced. "Then, a man could leave a girl standing at the church
altar with a bouquet of fresh flowers in her hands and disappear
off the face of the earth. No way to track him down if he was from
another town. He could be a married man, with maybe even two
or three families all over the island. There was no way to know.
And there were men who did this. Hombres with the devil in their
flesh who would come to a pueblo, like this one, take a job at one
of the haciendas, never meaning to stay, only to have a good time
and to seduce the women."

The whole time she was speaking, Mamá would be weaving   5
my hair into a flat plait that required pulling apart the two sections of hair with little jerks that made my eyes water; but knowing how grandmother detested whining and *boba* (sissy) tears, as
she called them, I just sat up as straight and stiff as I did at La

Escuela San Jose, where the nuns enforced good posture with a flexible plastic ruler they bounced off of slumped shoulders and heads. As Mamá's story progressed, I noticed how my young Aunt Laura lowered her eyes, refusing to meet Mamá's meaningful gaze. Laura was seventeen, in her last year of high school, and already engaged to a boy from another town who had staked his claim with a tiny diamond ring, then left for Los Nueva Yores to make his fortune. They were planning to get married in a year. Mamá had expressed serious doubts that the wedding would ever take place. In Mamá's eyes, a man set free without a legal contract was a man lost. She believed that marriage was not something men desired, but simply the price they had to pay for the privilege of children and, of course, for what no decent (synonymous with "smart") woman would give away for free.

6   "María La Loca was only seventeen when *it* happened to her." I listened closely at the mention of this name. María was a town character, a fat middle-aged woman who lived with her old mother on the outskirts of town. She was to be seen around the pueblo delivering the meat pies the two women made for a living. The most peculiar thing about María, in my eyes, was that she walked and moved like a little girl though she had the thick body and wrinkled face of an old woman. She would swing her hips in an exaggerated, clownish way, and sometimes even hop and skip up to someone's house. She spoke to no one. Even if you asked her a question, she would just look at you and smile, showing her yellow teeth. But I had heard that if you got close enough, you could hear her humming a tune without words. The kids yelled out nasty things at her, calling her *La Loca,* and the men who hung out at the bodega playing dominoes sometimes whistled mockingly as she passed by with her funny, outlandish walk. But María seemed impervious to it all, carrying her basket of *pasteles* like a grotesque Little Red Riding Hood through the forest.

7   María La Loca interested me, as did all the eccentrics and crazies of our pueblo. Their weirdness was a measuring stick I used in my serious quest for a definition of normal. As a Navy brat shuttling between New Jersey and the pueblo, I was constantly made to feel like an oddball by my peers, who made fun of my two-way accent: a Spanish accent when I spoke English, and when I spoke Spanish I was told that I sounded like a *Gringa.* Being the

outsider had already turned my brother and me into cultural chameleons. We developed early on the ability to blend into a crowd, to sit and read quietly in a fifth story apartment building for days and days when it was too bitterly cold to play outside, or, set free, to run wild in Mamá's realm, where she took charge of our lives, releasing Mother for a while from the intense fear for our safety that our father's absences instilled in her. In order to keep us from harm when Father was away, Mother kept us under strict surveillance. She even walked us to and from Public School No. 11, which we attended during the months we lived in Paterson, New Jersey, our home base in the states. Mamá freed all three of us like pigeons from a cage. I saw her as my liberator and my model. Her stories were parables from which to glean the *Truth*.

"María La Loca was once a beautiful girl. Everyone thought 8 she would marry the Méndez boy." As everyone knew, Rogelio Méndez was the richest man in town. "But," Mamá continued, knitting my hair with the same intensity she was putting into her story, "this *macho* made a fool out of her and ruined her life." She paused for the effect of her use of the word "macho," which at that time had not yet become a popular epithet for an unliberated man. This word had for us the crude and comical connotation of "male of the species," stud; a *macho* was what you put in a pen to increase your stock.

I peeked over my comic book at my mother. She too was 9 under Mamá's spell, smiling conspiratorially at this little swipe at men. She was safe from Mamá's contempt in this area. Married at an early age, an unspotted lamb, she had been accepted by a good family of strict Spaniards whose name was old and respected, though their fortune had been lost long before my birth. In a rocker Papá had painted sky blue sat Mamá's oldest child, Aunt Nena. Mother of three children, stepmother of two more, she was a quiet woman who liked books but had married an ignorant and abusive widower whose main interest in life was accumulating wealth. He too was in the mainland working on his dream of returning home rich and triumphant to buy the *finca* of his dreams. She was waiting for him to send for her. She would leave her children with Mamá for several years while the two of them slaved away in factories. He would one day be a rich man, and she a sadder woman. Even now her life-light was dimming. She spoke little, an aberration in

Mamá's house, and she read avidly, as if storing up spiritual food for the long winters that awaited her in Los Nueva Yores without her family. But even Aunt Nena came alive to Mamá's words, rocking gently, her hands over a thick book in her lap.

10   Her daughter, my cousin Sara, played jacks by herself on the tile porch outside the room where we sat. She was a year older than I. We shared a bed and all our family's secrets. Collaborators in search of answers, Sara and I discussed everything we heard the women say, trying to fit it all together like a puzzle that, once assembled, would reveal life's mysteries to us. Though she and I still enjoyed taking part in boys' games—chase, volleyball, and even *vaqueros*, the island version of cowboys and Indians involving cap-gun battles and violent shoot-outs under the mango tree in Mamá's backyard—we loved best the quiet hours in the afternoon when the men were still at work, and the boys had gone to play serious baseball at the park. Then Mamá's house belonged only to us women. The aroma of coffee perking in the kitchen, the mesmerizing creaks and groans of the rockers, and the women telling their lives in *cuentos* are forever woven into the fabric of my imagination, braided like my hair that day I felt my grandmother's hands teaching me about strength, her voice convincing me of the power of storytelling.

11   That day Mamá told how the beautiful María had fallen prey to a man whose name was never the same in subsequent versions of the story; it was Juan one time, José, Rafael, Diego, another. We understood that neither the name nor any of the *facts* were important, only that a woman had allowed love to defeat her. Mamá put each of us in Mariá's place by describing her wedding dress in loving detail: how she looked like a princess in her lace as she waited at the altar. Then, as Mamá approached the tragic denouement of her story, I was distracted by the sound of my Aunt Laura's violent rocking. She seemed on the verge of tears. She knew the fable was intended for her. That week she was going to have her wedding gown fitted, though no firm date had been set for the marriage. Mamá ignored Laura's obvious discomfort, digging out a ribbon from the sewing basket she kept by her rocker while describing María's long illness, "a fever that would not break for days." She spoke of a mother's despair: "that woman climbed the church steps on her knees every morning, wore only black as a *promesa* to

the Holy Virgin in exchange for her daughter's health." By the time María returned from her honeymoon with death, she was ravished, no longer young or sane. "As you can see, she is almost as old as her mother already," Mamá lamented while tying the ribbon to the ends of my hair, pulling it back with such force that I just knew I would never be able to close my eyes completely again.

"That María's getting crazier every day." Mamá's voice would take a lighter tone now, expressing satisfaction, either for the perfection of my braid, or for a story well told—it was hard to tell. "You know that tune María is always humming?" Carried away by her enthusiasm, I tried to nod, but Mamá still had me pinned between her knees.   12

"Well that's the wedding march." Surprising us all, Mamá sang out, "Da, da, dara . . . da, da, dara." Then lifting me off the floor by my skinny shoulders, she would lead me around the room in an impromptu waltz—another session ending with the laughter of women, all of us caught up in the infectious joke of our lives.   13

Content

1. How does the community of Puerto Rican women, grandmother, mother, and aunts, use storytelling to teach the young girls in their family "what it [is] like to be a woman, more specifically, a Puerto Rican woman" (¶ 2)? Are there comparable informal communities in which boys learn what it means to be men?

2. What features of the storytelling context (such as where it takes place, the storyteller's status and authority) reinforce the messages of the *cuentos?*

3. Under what circumstances is Cofer an outsider as a child (see ¶ 7)? An insider?

4. How does Cofer's dual status as an insider/outsider contribute to her childhood understanding of the story of María La Loca (¶s 6–13)? Does the fact that she is writing the story as an adult contribute any new dimensions, understanding to the tale?

Strategies/Structures

5. In *"Casa,"* Cofer conveys a number of points of view: her own, as a child and as an adult, her grandmother's, her mother's, Aunt Nena's, and Aunt Laura's—the seventeen-year-old fiancée at whom the cautionary

tale is directed. In what ways does she do this, even though some characters, such as Nena and Laura, never speak?

Language

6. *"Casa"* is written primarily in English, with a sprinkling of Spanish words. Where do these come? With what effect? Under what circumstances does the author define them? When does she expect the reader to infer their meaning?

7. What does an author gain or lose by incorporating foreign words and phrases into a primarily English text? (Assume that the author is not using these to show off!)

For Writing

8. Tell, for an audience of your peers or for younger teenagers or adolescents, a real-life cautionary tale drawn preferably from your own experience or that of someone you know well. Let the characterization and the plot make the point; you don't have to state the moral explicitly.

9. Retell for the same audience as in the previous writing suggestion a well-known fable (such as one by Aesop, Joel Chandler Harris, or James Thurber) in a contemporary context, substituting characters you know for those in the original tale.

10. Have you ever felt, as Cofer did, "like an oddball" (¶ 7)? Did you try to fit in, were you pleased to be different, or were you ambivalent about your status? How do you feel about the same characteristics—of yourself, your language or dialect, your culture, your family—now? Tell a story, for people who don't know you, that depicts yourself as an outsider and that illustrates your past and present feelings about your status.

SCOTT RUSSELL SANDERS

Sanders (born, 1945) grew up in Ohio, earned a Ph.D. in English from Cambridge University in 1971, and has taught ever since at Indiana University. His dozen books include fiction, science fiction, a biography of Audubon, and several collections of personal essays. The essay collections, *In Limestone Country* (1985), *Secrets of the Universe* (1991), *Staying Put* (1993), and *Writing from the*

Center (1995), focus on living and writing in the Midwest. Sanders interprets his seemingly diverse work as an integrated whole: "I have long been divided, in my life and in my work, between science and the arts." As a novelist, Sanders focused on "many of the fundamental questions that scientists ask," seeking "to understand our place in nature, trace the sources of our violence, and speculate about the future evolution of our species. My writing . . . is bound together by a web of questions," which he continues to ask in personal essays dealing with "the ways in which human beings come to terms with the practical problems of living on a small planet, in nature . . . in marriages and families and towns. . . ."

The elegiac "The Inheritance of Tools" appeared in the award-winning *The Paradise of Bombs* (1987), a collection of personal essays mainly about the American culture of violence. This essay reveals Sanders's concerns, as a writer and as a son, husband, and father, with the inheritance of skills and values through the generations.

In this essay, narration is explanation, as it is in a companion piece, "Skill" (*Georgia Review* 1998). Sanders shows how tools become not just extensions of the hand and brain, but of the human heart, as the knowledge of how to use and care for them is transmitted from grandfather to father to son to grandchildren—a girl as well as a boy. The ways in which people use tools, and think about tools and care for them, reflect their values and personalities; "each hammer and level and saw is wrapped in a cloud of knowing."

The Inheritance of Tools

A t just about the hour when my father died, soon after dawn 1
one February morning when ice coated the windows like cataracts, I banged my thumb with a hammer. Naturally I swore at the hammer, the reckless thing, and in the moment of swearing I thought of what my father would say: "If you'd try hitting the nail it would go in a whole lot faster. Don't you know your thumb's not as hard as that hammer?" We both were doing carpentry that day, but far apart. He was building cupboards at my brother's place in Oklahoma; I was at home in Indiana, putting up a wall in the basement to make a bedroom for my daughter. By the time my mother called with news of his death—the long distance wires

whittling her voice until it seemed too thin to bear the weight of what she had to say—my thumb was swollen. A week or so later a white scar in the shape of a crescent moon began to show above the cuticle and month by month it rose across the pink sky of my thumbnail. It took the better part of a year for the scar to disappear, and every time I noticed it I thought of my father.

2   The hammer had belonged to him, and to his father before him. The three of us have used it to build houses and barns and chicken coops, to upholster chairs and crack walnuts, to make doll furniture and bookshelves and jewelry boxes. The head is scratched and pockmarked, like an old plowshare that has been working rocky fields, and it gives off the sort of dull sheen you see on fast creek water in the shade. It is a finishing hammer, about the weight of a bread loaf, too light, really, for framing walls, too heavy for cabinet work, with a curved claw for pulling nails, a rounded head for pounding, a fluted neck for looks, and a hickory handle for strength.

3   The present handle is my third one, bought from a lumberyard in Tennessee, down the road from where my brother and I were helping my father build his retirement house. I broke the previous one by trying to pull sixteen-penny nails out of floor joists—a foolish thing to do with a finishing hammer, as my father pointed out. "You ever hear of a crowbar?" he said. No telling how many handles he and my grandfather had gone through before me. My grandfather used to cut down hickory trees on his farm, saw them into slabs, cure the planks in his hayloft, and carve handles with a drawknife. The grain in hickory is crooked and knotty, and therefore tough, hard to split, like the grain in the two men who owned this hammer before me.

4   After proposing marriage to a neighbor girl, my grandfather used this hammer to build a house for his bride on a stretch of river bottom in northern Mississippi. The lumber for the place, like the hickory for the handle, was cut on his own land. By the day of the wedding he had not quite finished the house, and so right after the ceremony he took his wife home and put her to work. My grandmother had worn her Sunday dress for the wedding, with a fringe of lace tacked on around the hem in honor of the occasion. She removed this lace and folded it away before going out to help my grandfather nail siding on the house. "There

she was in her good dress," he told me some fifty-odd years after that wedding day, "holding up them long pieces of clapboard while I hammered, and together we got the place covered up before dark." As the family grew to four, six, eight, and eventually thirteen, my grandfather used this hammer to enlarge his house room by room, like a chambered nautilus expanding its shell.

By and by the hammer was passed along to my father. One day he was up on the roof of our pony barn nailing shingles with it, when I stepped out the kitchen door to call him for supper. Before I could yell, something about the sight of him straddling the spine of that roof and swinging the hammer caught my eye and made me hold my tongue. I was five or six years old, and the world's commonplaces were still news to me. He would pull a nail from the pouch at his waist, bring the hammer down, and a moment later the *thunk* of the blow would reach my ears. And that is what had stopped me in my tracks and stilled my tongue, that momentary gap between seeing and hearing the blow. Instead of yelling from the kitchen door, I ran to the barn and climbed two rungs up the ladder—as far as I was allowed to go—and spoke quietly to my father. On our walk to the house he explained that sound takes time to make its way through air. Suddenly the world seemed larger, the air more dense, if sound could be held back like any ordinary traveler.

By the time I started using this hammer, at about the age when I discovered the speed of sound, it already contained houses and mysteries for me. The smooth handle was one my grandfather had made. In those days I needed both hands to swing it. My father would start a nail in a scrap of wood, and I would pound away until I bent it over.

"Looks like you got ahold of some of those rubber nails," he would tell me. "Here, let me see if I can find you some stiff ones." And he would rummage in a drawer until he came up with a fistful of more cooperative nails. "Look at the head," he would tell me. "Don't look at your hands, don't look at the hammer. Just look at the head of that nail and pretty soon you'll learn to hit it square."

Pretty soon I did learn. While he worked in the garage cutting dovetail joints for a drawer or skinning a deer or tuning an engine, I would hammer nails. I made innocent blocks of wood look like porcupines. He did not talk much in the midst of his tools, but he kept up a nearly ceaseless humming, slipping in and out of a dozen tunes in an afternoon, often running back over the same stretch of melody again and again, as if searching for a way out. When the humming did cease, I knew he was faced with a task requiring great delicacy or concentration, and I took care not to distract him.

9   He kept scraps of wood in a cardboard box—the ends of two-by-fours, slabs of shelving and plywood, odd pieces of molding—and everything in it was fair game. I nailed scraps together to fashion what I called boats or houses, but the results usually bore only faint resemblance to the visions I carried in my head. I would hold up these constructions to show my father, and he would turn them over in his hands admiringly, speculating about what they might be. My cobbled-together guitars might have been alien spaceships, my barns might have been models of Aztec temples, each wooden contraption might have been anything but what I had set out to make.

10   Now and again I would feel the need to have a chunk of wood shaped or shortened before I riddled it with nails, and I would clamp it in a vise and scrape at it with a handsaw. My father would let me lacerate the board until my arm gave out, and then he would wrap his hand around mine and help me finish the cut, showing me how to use my thumb to guide the blade, how to pull back on the saw to keep it from binding, how to let my shoulder do the work.

11   "Don't force it," he would say, "just drag it easy and give the teeth a chance to bite."

12   As the saw teeth bit down, the wood released its smell, each kind with its own fragrance, oak or walnut or cherry or pine—usually pine because it was the softest, easiest for a child to work. No matter how weathered and gray the board, no matter how warped and cracked, inside there was this smell waiting, as of something freshly baked. I gathered every smidgen of sawdust and stored it away in coffee cans, which I kept in a drawer of the workbench. When I did not feel like hammering nails, I would dump my sawdust on the concrete floor of the garage and landscape it into highways and farms and towns, running miniature cars and trucks along miniature roads. Looming as huge as a colossus, my father worked over and around me, now and again bending down to inspect my work, careful not to trample my creations. It was a landscape that smelled dizzyingly of wood.

Even after a bath my skin would carry the smell, and so would my father's hair, when he lifted me for a bedtime hug.

I tell these things not only from memory but also from recent 13 observation, because my own son now turns blocks of wood into nailed porcupines, dumps cans full of sawdust at my feet and sculpts highways on the floor. He learns how to swing a hammer from the elbow instead of the wrist, how to lay his thumb beside the blade to guide a saw, how to tap a chisel with a wooden mallet, how to mark a hole with an awl before starting a drill bit. My daughter did the same before him, and even now, on the brink of teenage aloofness, she will occasionally drag out my box of wood scraps and carpenter something. So I have seen my apprenticeship to wood and tools reenacted in each of my children, as my father saw his own apprenticeship renewed in me.

The saw I use belonged to him, as did my level and both of 14 my squares, and all four tools had belonged to his father. The blade of the saw is the bluish color of gun barrels, and the maple handle, dark from the sweat of hands, is inscribed with curving leaf designs. The level is a shaft of walnut two feet long, edged with brass and pierced by three round windows in which air bubbles float in oil-filled tubes of glass. The middle window serves for testing if a surface is horizontal, the others for testing if a surface is plumb or vertical. My grandfather used to carry this level on the gun rack behind the seat in his pickup, and when I rode with him I would turn around to watch the bubbles dance. The larger of the two squares is called a framing square, a flat steel elbow, so beat up and tarnished you can barely make out the rows of numbers that show how to figure the cuts on rafters. The smaller one is called a try square, for marking right angles, with a blued steel blade for the shank and a brass-faced block of cherry for the head.

I was taught early on that a saw is not to be used apart from 15 a square: "If you're going to cut a piece of wood," my father insisted, "you owe it to the tree to cut it straight."

Long before studying geometry, I learned there is a mystical 16 virtue in right angles. There is an unspoken morality in seeking the level and the plumb. A house will stand, a table will bear weight, the sides of a box will hold together, only if the joints are square and the members upright. When the bubble is lined up between two marks etched in the glass tube of a level, you have aligned yourself with the forces that hold the universe together. When you miter the corners of a picture frame each angle must be exactly forty-five degrees, as they are in the perfect triangles of Pythagoras, not a degree more or less. Otherwise the frame will hang crookedly, as if ashamed of itself and of its maker. No matter if the joints you are cutting do not show. Even if you are butting two pieces of wood together inside a cabinet, where no one except a wrecking crew will ever see them, you must take pains to ensure that the ends are square and the studs are plumb.

17   I took pains over the wall I was building on the day my father died. Not long after that wall was finished—paneled with tongue-and-groove boards of yellow pine, the nail holes filled with putty and the wood all stained and sealed—I came close to wrecking it one afternoon when my daughter ran howling up the stairs to announce that her gerbils had escaped from their cage and were hiding in my brand new wall. She could hear them scratching and squeaking behind her bed. Impossible! I said. How on earth could they get inside my drum-tight wall? Through the heating vent, she answered. I went downstairs, pressed my ear to the honey-colored wood, and heard the *scritch scritch* of tiny feet.

18   "What can we do?" my daughter wailed. "They'll starve to death, they'll die of thirst, they'll suffocate."

19   "Hold on," I soothed. "I'll think of something."

20   While I thought and she fretted, the radio on her bedside table delivered us the headlines: Several thousand people had died in a city in India from a poisonous cloud that had leaked overnight from a chemical plant. A nuclear-powered submarine had been launched. Rioting continued in South Africa. An airplane had been hijacked in the Mediterranean. Authorities calculated that several thousand homeless people slept on the streets within sight of the Washington Monument. I felt my usual helplessness in the face of all these calamities. But here was my daughter, weeping because her gerbils were holed up in a wall. This calamity I could handle.

21   "Don't worry," I told her. "We'll set food and water by the heating vent and lure them out. And if that doesn't do the trick, I'll tear the wall apart until we find them."

22   She stopped crying and gazed at me. "You'd really tear it apart? Just for my gerbils? The *wall*?" Astonishment slowed her down only for a second, however, before she ran to the workbench

and began tugging at drawers, saying, "Let's see, what'll we need? Crowbar. Hammer. Chisels. I hope we don't have to use them— but just in case."

We didn't need the wrecking tools. I never had to assault my 23 handsome wall, because the gerbils eventually came out to nibble at a dish of popcorn. But for several hours I studied the tongue- and-groove skin I had nailed up on the day of my father's death, considering where to begin prying. There were no gaps in that wall, no crooked joints.

I had botched a great many pieces of wood before I mas- 24 tered the right angle with a saw, botched even more before I learned to miter a joint. The knowledge of these things resides in my hands and eyes and the webwork of muscles, not in the tools. There are machines for sale—powered miter boxes and radial-arm saws, for instance—that will enable any casual soul to cut proper angles in boards. The skill is invested in the gadget instead of the person who uses it, and this is what distinguishes a machine from a tool. If I had to earn my keep by making furniture or building houses, I suppose I would buy powered saws and pneumatic nailers; the need for speed would drive me to it. But since I car- penter only for my own pleasure or to help neighbors or to remake the house around the ears of my family, I stick with hand tools. Most of the ones I own were given to me by my father, who also taught me how to wield them. The tools in my workbench are a double inheritance, for each hammer and level and saw is wrapped in a cloud of knowing.

All of these tools are a pleasure to look at and to hold. Mer- 25 chants would never paste NEW NEW NEW! signs on them in stores. Their designs are old because they work, because they serve their purpose well. Like folk songs and aphorisms and the grainy bits of language, these tools have been pared down to essentials. I look at my claw hammer, the distillation of a hundred generations of carpenters, and consider that it holds up well beside those other classics—Greek vases, Gregorian chants, *Don Quixote*, barbed fish hooks, candles, spoons. Knowledge of hammering stretches back to the earliest humans who squatted beside fires, chipping flints. Anthropologists have a lovely name for those unworked rocks that served as the earliest hammers. "Dawn stones," they are called. Their only qualification for the work, aside from hardness, is that they fit the hand. Our ancestors used them for grinding corn, tapping awls, smashing bones. From dawn stones to this claw hammer is a great leap in time, but no great distance in design or imagination.

26   On that iced-over February morning when I smashed my thumb with the hammer, I was down in the basement framing the wall that my daughter's gerbils would later hide in. I was thinking of my father, as I always did whenever I built anything, thinking how he would have gone about the work, hearing in memory what he would have said about the wisdom of hitting the nail instead of my thumb. I had the studs and plates nailed together all square and trim, and was lifting the wall into place when the phone rang upstairs. My wife answered, and in a moment she came to the basement door and called down softly to me. The stillness in her voice made me drop the framed wall and hurry upstairs. She told me my father was dead. Then I heard the details over the phone from my mother. Building a set of cupboards for my brother in Oklahoma, he had knocked off work early the previous afternoon because of cramps in his stomach. Early this morning, on his way into the kitchen of my brother's trailer, maybe going for a glass of water, so early that no one else was awake, he slumped down on the linoleum and his heart quit.

27   For several hours I paced around inside my house, upstairs and down, in and out of every room, looking for the right door to open and knowing there was no such door. My wife and children followed me and wrapped me in arms and backed away again, circling and staring as if I were on fire. Where was the door, the door, the door? I kept wondering. My smashed thumb turned purple and throbbed, making me furious. I wanted to cut it off and rush outside and scrape away at the snow and hack a hole in the frozen earth and bury the shameful thing.

28   I went down into the basement, opened a drawer in my workbench, and stared at the ranks of chisels and knives. Oiled and sharp, as my father would have kept them, they gleamed at me like teeth. I took up a clasp knife, pried out the longest blade, and tested the edge on the hair of my forearm. A tuft came away cleanly, and I saw my father testing the sharpness of tools on his own skin, the

blades of axes and knives and gouges and hoes, saw the red hair shaved off in patches from his arms and the backs of his hands. "That will cut bear," he would say. He never cut a bear with his blades, now my blades, but he cut deer, dirt, wood. I closed the knife and put it away. Then I took up the hammer and went back to work on my daughter's wall, snugging the bottom plate against a chalk line on the floor, shimming the top plate against the joists overhead, plumbing the studs with my level, making sure before I drove the first nail that every line was square and true.

Content

1. Sanders characterizes his father, and grandfather, and himself by showing how they used tools and transmitted this knowledge to their children. What characteristics do they have in common? Why does he omit any differences they might have, focusing on their similarities?

2. Sanders distinguishes between a machine and a tool, saying "The skill is invested in the gadget instead of the person who uses it" (¶ 24). Why does he favor tools over machines? Do you agree with his definition? With his preference?

Strategies/Structures

3. What is the point of this essay? Why does Sanders begin and end with the relation between banging his thumb with a hammer and his father's death?

4. Why does Sanders include the vignette of his daughter and her gerbils, which escaped inside the "drum-tight wall" he had just built (¶s 17–23)? Would he really have wrecked the wall to get the gerbils out?

5. For what audience is Sanders writing? Does it matter whether or not his readers know how to use tools?

Language

6. Sanders occasionally quotes his father's advice (¶s 7, 11, 15). What do these quotations reveal about his father?

7. Show, through specific examples, how Sanders's language fits his subject, tools, and the people who use them. Consider phrases such as "ice coated the windows like cataracts" (¶ 1) and "making sure before I drove the first nail that every line was square and true" (¶ 28).

For Writing

8. Sanders defines the "inheritance" of tools as, "So I have seen my apprenticeship to wood and tools re-enacted in each of my children, as my father saw his own apprenticeship renewed in me." (¶ 13). Tell the story of your own apprenticeship with a tool or collection of tools (kitchen utensils, art supplies, a sewing machine, computer, skis, or other equipment). The explanation of your increasing skill in learning to use it should be intertwined with your relationship with the person who taught you how to use it (not necessarily a family member) and the manner of the teaching—and of the learning. How many generations of teachers and learners does your inheritance involve? If you have taught others how to use it, incorporate this as well.

9. Sanders's father is central figure in two essays in *The Essay Connection*, "The Inheritance of Tools" and "Under the Influence" (441–56). Each uses a series of stories, narratives, to characterize this significant figure in Sanders's life, yet the father of "Inheritance" is a very different character from the father in "Under the Influence." Write an essay in which you compare and contrast Sanders's portraits of his father to show the different ways of presenting the same person. Or—for an audience who doesn't know your subject—write a portrait of someone you know well, or of a public figure you know a great deal about. Use stories to present two or more significant—perhaps contradictory—sides of the same person.

ANN UPPERCO DOLMAN

> Ann Upperco Dolman (born, 1960) grew up in Arlington, Virginia, and majored in religion at the College of William and Mary (B.A., 1982). She then worked in Chicago as a textbook editor, and after marriage and a move to Wilson, North Carolina, as communications manager for the local Chamber of Commerce, where she wrote all the time—brochures, a newsletter, "even speeches. . . . I've come a long way from my undergraduate days when crying over writing papers was almost as natural to me as breathing. A big help," she says, "is the use of a word processor [for I] realize that whatever I have written is not engraved in stone. I can experiment with a variety of organizational schemes and words with just a push of a few buttons, so editing has

become a breeze." In 1996 she earned a master's degree in library science from the University of North Carolina.

Dolman had been a highly anxious writer, procrastinating for long periods of time and then spending miserable, long hours trying to grind out a paper in time to meet a deadline. However, in writing "Learning to Drive" for an undergraduate composition course, she explains, "I wrote it at one sitting, then revised it. I think this method of sitting down and writing something and then going back to revise is what enabled me to get over my fear of writing." She says, "I had originally intended to write a series of comic vignettes on the individual driving styles of each member of my family. But the more I thought about it, the more comfortable I felt with the idea of poking fun at myself instead. . . . Writing this essay was almost fun."

Dolman has captured a common set of experiences participated in by a set of familiar figures, comical to contemplate from the safe distance of time, however painful the traumas of a new driver may have been when they occurred. The tense, skittish novice driver is counterpointed against the patient teacher, her reassuring father, with the nervous figure of her mother hovering uneasily in the background.

❄ Learning to Drive

G reater love hath no man for his children than to teach them   1
how to drive. As soon as I turned 15 years and 8 months—the requisite age for obtaining a learner's permit—my father took me around our neighborhood to let me get a feel for the huge Chevrolet we own. The quiet, tree-shaded, narrow streets of the neighborhood witnessed the blunders of yet another new driver: too-wide (or too-narrow) turns; sudden screeching halts (those power brakes take some getting used to); defoliation of low-hanging trees by the radio antenna or the car too close to the curb; driving on the wrong side of the street to avoid the parked cars on the right side.

Through it all my father murmured words of advice and   2
encouragement, drawing on a seemingly bottomless well of patience which I never before knew he possessed. One day while

driving on the highway, I drifted dangerously close to a car in the lane to my right, almost scraping the shiny chrome strip right off its side. Dad looked nonchalantly into the terrified face of the other driver—a mere six inches away—then turned back to me and said, "You might want to steer to the left a bit; you're just a little close on this side." A mile further down the road, Dad chuckled and said, "I think you gave that poor lady a scare—her eyes were as big as golfballs!" Here was he, not only unperturbed, but actually amused by the whole incident while I watched my whole life pass before my eyes.

3   Not long after this incident I had another near miss, this time while intentionally changing lanes. I still was not accustomed to using the rearview mirror, so Dad had told me to glance over my shoulder to make sure all was clear. Being right-handed, I automatically looked over my right shoulder, and not seeing anything, proceeded to veer left. Not until I almost plowed into another car did I realize that when turning left, I needed to glance over my left shoulder to avoid causing a wreck. Despite the danger, Dad stuck it out, continuing to give me tips to improve my driving.

4   Confident now of my driving prowess, I cajoled my parents into letting me drive every chance I got. Dad usually sat up front with me, to the relief of Mom, an uneasy driver herself whose nerves were still recovering from my brother's driving apprenticeship two years earlier. This arrangement suited me perfectly; Mom's behavior in the front seat tended to make me a trifle nervous. Gripping the dashboard as if it would fall off if she let go, and frequently pressing to the floor the nonexistent brake on her side of the car, Mom would periodically utter spine-chilling gasps at the slightest provocation—none of which increased my newly-won confidence behind the wheel. Whether Dad never suffered from such a case of jitters or whether he merely hid it better, I'm not sure. But whatever the reasons, he managed to remain calm, at least outwardly, when riding with me.

5   When I had mastered (in a manner of speaking) the skill of driving our full-size, power-steering, power-brake tank, Dad proceeded to show me the secrets of operating the small, standard-shift rattle-trap-of-a-Pinto which adorned the curb in front of our house. Had I known at the time the humiliation and tribulation I'd have to endure at the wheel of that car, I'm not sure I would have

embarked as willingly on the adventure. But Dad, glutton for punishment that he is, knew what was in store; as he buckled his seat
belt he braced both feet against the floor and said, "Okay, let's give
it a try." For at least an hour, I lurched up and down our driveway,
trying to get a feel for "slipping the clutch." (Poor Dad didn't
realize I hardly even knew which was the clutch, much less what
"slipping" it entailed.) After one particularly violent jolt that
almost sent us through the garage door, Dad decided to let me try
taking the car around the block. Ostensibly, he wanted me to practice driving in all four gears, though I really think he was more
concerned about the fate of the garage door than anything else.

Once out on the street (after a bristly encounter with the   6
forsythia bush which unfortunately stood at the end of the driveway), I embarrassed myself completely. To keep from stalling, I'd
rev the engine while I tried to slip the clutch. I couldn't even pretend to be a racing driver; the car didn't have the decency to sound
like a high-powered race car, it just roared like an outraged lion
with a thorn in its paw. Feeling conspicuous about making all this
noise, I let the clutch out too soon, which either stalled the car, or,
worse still, made it jerk down the street like a bucking bronco. The
poor car looked like a seesaw with the front end first taking a
nose-dive while the rear end flew up, then leaping into the air as
the rear end came back down. Jolting around the block with tires
screeching and rubber burning, I provided my neighbors with the
best free entertainment they'd seen in a long time, since the days
when my brother was learning how to drive that beastly little car.

With this display of ineptitude, I tumbled from the pedestal   7
of special privilege which a driver's permit had given me; once
again the kids too young to drive regarded me as simply the klutz
I was. Good ol' Dad stuck by me through the ignominy of it all,
assuring me that everybody who learned to drive a stick-shift
underwent the same ordeal. It still amazes me that with all that
lurching around, he was willing to go with me again.

Now that I have several years' experience behind me, I ac-   8
tually enjoy driving—especially driving a stick-shift. I'll often take
to the road to relax, emptying my mind by concentrating on the
mechanics of driving. Had it not been for Dad's patient, calm perseverance, I might still be the public menace today that I was three
years ago. As for Dad, he lucked out—I'm the last kid in the family.

Content

1. This essay combines the telling of a story with the explanation of a process. Which is dominant? How do you know?

2. Could one learn how to drive—or how not.to drive—from reading this essay? If not, what is its point?

3. What is the point of the last paragraph? What impact does the fact that not only did Dolman learn to drive but to enjoy it have on the rest of the essay?

Strategies/Structures

4. How can you tell that Dolman is writing from the perspective of someone who has mastered the skill of driving, rather than from the viewpoint of a learner? What effect does this have on the tone of the essay?

5. Much of Dolman's humor is visual. What comic scenes does she create and how does she help readers to see them? Why should close escapes from accidents provoke laughter instead of terrified relief?

Language

6. What does Dolman's terminology reveal about her intended readers? Are they experienced drivers? Novices? Unable to drive at all?

7. Find some instances where Dolman uses overstated language, understated language, and slang to enhance the humor. What is the effect of the occasional direct quotation of Mr. Upperco's comments (¶s 2, 5)?

For Writing

8. Write an essay in which you explain the process by which you learned or are still learning to do something fairly complicated. You can write it either (1) to explain to your readers how to do the same thing or (2) to entertain your readers by showing, as Dolman does, the amusing pitfalls of the learning process.

9. Write a narrative essay in which you at your present age and level of maturity are narrating an incident in which you at a younger age and a different level of maturity are one of the principal characters. See Sanders, "Under the Influence" (441–56), Zitkala-Sa, excerpts from *The School Days of an Indian Girl* (273–83), and White, "Once More to the Lake" (171–79). You may use this dual characterization and split point of view as the basis for humor, though the essay could also be serious.

Additional Topics for Writing

Narration (For strategies for writing narration, see 162–63)

1. Write two versions of the earliest experience you can remember that involved some fright, danger, discovery, or excitement. Write the first version as the experience appeared to you at the time it happened. Then, write another version interpreting how the experience appears to you now.

2. Write a narrative of an experience you had that taught you a difficult lesson (see Ning Yu, "Red and Black, or One English Major's Beginning," 405–18). You can either make explicit the point of the lesson, or imply it through your reactions to the experience.

3. Sometimes a meaningful incident or significant relationship with someone can help us to mature, easily or painfully, as Douglass explains in "Resurrection" (164–70). Tell the story of such an incident or relationship in your own life or in the life of someone you know well.

4. Have you ever witnessed an event important to history, sports, science, or some other field of endeavor? If so, tell the story either as an eyewitness, or from the point of view of someone looking back on it and more aware now of its true meaning.

5. If you have ever been to a place that is particularly significant to you, narrate an incident to show its significance through specified details. (See White, 171–79, Ozick, 316–30, and Tschannerl, 360–67.)

6. Have you ever worshipped someone as a hero or heroine, or modeled yourself after someone? Or been treated as someone's particular favorite (or nemesis)? Tell the story of this special relationship you have (or had) with a parent or grandparent, brother or sister, friend or antagonist, spouse, employer, teacher. Through narrating one or two typical incidents to convey its essence, show why this relationship has been beneficial or harmful to you. (See White, "Once More to the Lake," 171–79; Douglass, "Resurrection," 164–70; Ruffin, "Mama's Smoke," 148–58; Swanson, "The Turning Point," 249–52; or Barry, "The Sanctuary of School," 670–75. Control your language carefully to control the mood and tone.

7. If you have had a "watershed experience"—made an important discovery, survived a major traumatic event, such as an automobile accident, a natural disaster, a flood, or a family breakup; met a person who has changed your life—that has changed your life or your thinking about life significantly, narrate the experience and analyze its effects, short- or long-term. You will need to explain enough of what you were like beforehand so readers can recognize the effects of the experience. (See Douglass, "Resurrection," 164–70, or Grealy, "Masks," 349–60.)

8.   Explain what it's like to be a typical student or employee (on an assembly line, in a restaurant or store, or elsewhere) through an account of "A Day in the Life of . . . ." If you find that life to be boring or demeaning, your narrative might be an implied protest or an argument for change.

9.   Write a fairy tale or fable, a story with a moral. Make it suitable for children (but don't talk down to them) or for people of your own age.

10.   Write a pseudo-diary, an imaginary account of how you would lead a day in your life if all your wishes were fulfilled—or if all your worst fears were realized.

11.   Imagine that you're telling a major news event of the day (or of your lifetime) to someone fifty years from now. What details will you have to include and explain to make sure your reader understands it?

12.   Through using your own experiences or those of someone you know well, write an essay showing the truth or falsity of an adage about human nature, such as

   a.   Quitters never win. Or do they?
   b.   Try hard and you'll succeed. Or will you?
   c.   It doesn't matter whether you win or lose, it's how you play the game.
   d.   Absence makes the heart grow fonder—or, Out of sight out of mind.

6 | Process Analysis

Analysis involves dividing something into its component parts and explaining what they are, on the assumption that it is easier to consider and to understand the subject in smaller segments than in a large, complicated whole (see Division and Classification, (370–74). To analyze the human body, you could divide it into systems —skeletal, circulatory, respiratory, digestive, neurological— before identifying and defining the components of each. Of the digestive system, for instance, you would discuss the mouth, pharynx, esophagus, stomach, and large and small intestines.

You can analyze a process in the same way, focusing on *how* rather than *what*. A *directive process analysis* identifies the steps in how to make or do something: how to sail a catamaran; how to get to Kuala Lumpur; how to make brownies; how to collaborate in a writing group "to keep a group running smoothly and to forestall some common problems," as John Trimbur advises in "Guidelines for Working in Groups" (144–48).

An *informative process analysis* can identify the stages by which something is created or formed, or how something is done. In "Those Crazy Ideas" (208–20), Isaac Asimov analyzes two "styles" of scientific investigation by comparing and contrasting the ways in which Charles Darwin (see also 483–90) and Alfred Russel Wallace arrived "independently and simultaneously" at the theory of evolution. A process analysis can also explain how something functions or works, as Tom and Ray Magliozzi do in "Inside the Engine" (233–40); "overfilling [your car oil] is just as bad as underfilling. . . . if you're a quart and a half . . . overfilled, you could have so much oil in the crankcase that the spinning crankshaft is going to hit the oil and turn it into suds. It's impossible for the pump to pump suds, so you'll ruin the motor. It's kind of like a front-loading washing machine that goes berserk and spills suds all over the floor when you put too much detergent in." Or a process analysis can explain the meanings and implications of a concept, system, or mechanism as the basis for a philosophy that incorporates the process in question. Thus in the process of explaining the medical processes involved in a "Code Blue" alert (520–25), Jasmine Innerarity offers not only a philosophy of life-saving, but a philosophy of life.

A process analysis can incorporate an explanation and appreciation of a way of life, as Ntozake Shange does in "What Is It We Really Harvestin' Here?" (240–49). Shange explains how to grow potatoes, mustard greens, and watermelon, and how to cook "Mama's rice"; in the process, she offers a joyous interpretation not only of "'colored' cuisine," but of the people who cultivate, prepare, and eat this nourishment for the soul as well as the body. An analysis can also incorporate a critique of a process, sometimes as a way to advocate an alternative, as Scott Russell Sanders does in showing the deleterious effects of alcoholism on alcoholics' families in "Under the Influence" (441–56). "Harvest of Gold, Harvest of Shame" (675–83) provides both an overt explanation of a process—how tobacco is harvested—and an implied critique of the exploitation of the migrant workers who do the backbreaking labor. Each worker must "must tie [a burlap sack] around his waist as a source of protection against the dirt and rocks that he will be dragging himself through for the next eight hours."

To write an informative analysis of how the digestive system works, you could explain the process by which food is ingested and broken down as it passes through the esophagus, stomach, and small and large intestines. The complexity of your analysis would depend on the sophistication of your audience. For general readers you might explain the peristaltic movement as "a strong, wave-like motion that forces food through the digestive tract." Medical students would require a far more detailed explanation of the same phenomenon—in far more technical language.

The following suggestions for writing an essay of process analysis are in themselves—you guessed it—a process analysis.

To write about a process, for whatever audience, you first have to *make sure you understand it yourself.* If it's a process you can

perform, such as parallel parking or hitting a good tennis fore-
hand, try it out before you begin to write, and note the steps and
possible variations from start to finish.

Early on you'll need to *identify the purpose or function of the
process and its likely outcome:* "How to lose twenty pounds in ten
weeks." Then the steps or stages in the process occur in a given
sequence; it's helpful to *list them in their logical or natural order* and
to *provide time markers* so your readers will know what comes first,
second, and thereafter. "First have a physical exam. Next: work
out a sensible diet, under medical supervision. Then. . . ."

If the process involves many simultaneous operations, for
clarity you may need to *classify all aspects of the process and discuss
each one separately.* For instance, since playing the violin requires
bowing with the right hand and fingering with the left, it makes
sense to consider each by itself. After you've done this, however, be
sure to *indicate how all of the separate elements of the process fit together.*
To play the violin successfully the right hand has to know what
the left hand is doing. If the process you're discussing is cyclic or
circular—as in the life cycle of a plant, or the water cycle, involving evaporation, condensation, and precipitation—start with whatever seems to you most logical or most familiar to your readers.

If you're using specialized or technical language, *define your
terms* unless you're writing for an audience of experts. You'll also
need to *identify specialized equipment* and *be explicit about whatever
techniques and measurements your readers need to know.* For example,
an essay on how to throw a pot would need to tell a reader who
had never potted what the proper consistency of the clay should
be before one begins to wedge it, or how to tell when all the air
bubbles have been wedged out. But how complicated should an
explanation be? The more your reader knows about your subject,
the more sophisticated your analysis can be, with less emphasis,
if any, on the basics. How thin can the pot's walls be without col-
lapsing? Does the type of clay (white, red, with or without grog)
make any difference? The reverse is true if you're writing for
novices—keep it simple to start with.

If subprocesses are involved in the larger process, you can
either *explain these where they would logically come in the sequence,* or
consider them in footnotes or an appendix. You don't want to side-
track your reader from the main thrust. For instance, if you were

to explain the process of Prank Day, an annual ritual at Cal Tech, you might begin with the time by which all seniors have to be out of their residence halls for the day, 8 A.M. You might then follow a typical prank from beginning to end: the selection of a senior's parked car to disassemble; the transportation of its parts to the victim's dorm room; the reassembling of the vehicle; the victim's consternation when he encounters it in his room with the motor running. If the focus is on the process of playing the prank, you probably wouldn't want to give directions on how to disassemble and reassemble the car; to do so would require a hefty manual. But you might want to supplement your discussion with helpful hints on how to pay (or avoid paying) for the damage.

After you've finished your essay, if it explains how to perform a process, ask a friend, preferably one who's unfamiliar with the subject, to try it out. (Even people who know how to tie shoelaces can get all tangled up in murky directions.) She can tell you what's unclear, what needs to be explained more fully—and even point out where you're belaboring the obvious. If your paper is an informative analysis of a process, as is Thomas S. Kuhn's "The Route to Normal Science" (221–33), ask your reader to tell you how well she understands what you've said. If, by the end, she's still asking you what the fundamental concept is, you'll know you've got to run the paper through your typewriter or computer once again.

Process analysis can serve as a vehicle for explaining personal relationships. For example, an analysis of the sequential process of performing some activity can serve as the framework for explaining a complicated relationship among the people involved in performing the same process or an analogous one. In such essays the relationship among the participants or the character of the person performing the process is more important than the process itself; whether or not the explanation is sufficient to enable the readers to actually perform the process is beside the point. Craig Swanson's "The Turning Point" (249–52) is typical of such writing. In this case, making a pot is the catalytic activity uniting Swanson, the admiring son, and his father, the potter. Although Mr. Swanson's process of pot-making is described in detail, readers would still need more information about potting itself to be able to learn to wedge the clay and throw the pot (as indicated above [205]).

Writing parodies of processes, particularly those that are complicated, mysterious, or done badly—may be the ideal revenge of the novice learner (see Ann Upperco Dolman's "Learning to Drive" [196–200]) or the person obsessed with or defeated by a process, as in Craig Swanson's "It's the Only Video Game My Mom Lets Me Chew" (253–55). Parodies such as these may include a critique of the process, a satire of the novice or victim (often the author), or both.

STRATEGIES FOR WRITING— PROCESS ANALYSIS

1. Is the purpose of my essay to provide directions—a step-by-step explanation of how to do or make something? Or is the essay's purpose informative—to explain how something happens or works? Do I know my subject well enough to explain it clearly and accurately?
2. If I'm providing directions, how much does my audience already know about performing the process? Should I start with definitions of basic terms ("sauté," "dado") and explanations of subprocesses, or can I focus on the main process at hand? Should I simplify the process for a naive audience, or are my readers sophisticated enough to understand its complexities? Likewise, if I'm providing an informative explanation, where will I start? How complicated will my explanation become? The assumed expertise of my audience will help determine my answers.
3. Have I presented the process in logical or chronological sequence (first, second, third . . .)? Have I furnished an overview so that my readers will have the outcome (or desired results) and major aspects of the process in mind before they immerse themselves in the particulars of the individual steps?
4. Does my language fit both the subject, however general or technical, and the audience? Do I use technical terms when necessary? Which of these do I need to define or explain for my intended readers?
5. What tone will I use in my essay? A serious or matter-of-fact tone will indicate that I'm treating my subject "straight." An ironic, exaggerated, or understated tone will indicate that I'm treating it humorously.

ISAAC ASIMOV

Asimov (1920–1992) said that his talent lay in his ability to "read a dozen dull books and make one interesting book out of them." He amplified, "I'm on fire to explain, and happiest when it's something reasonably intricate which I can make clear step by step." From these motives, Asimov wrote nearly five hundred books, averaging one every six weeks for over thirty-five years. Although Asimov held a doctorate in chemistry from Columbia University (1948), his subjects ranged from astronomy, biology, biochemistry, mathematics, and physics, to history, literature, the Bible, limericks, and a two-volume autobiography. Nevertheless, he is probably best known for his science fiction—stories and novels; "Nightfall" has been called "the best science fiction work of all time." In 1973 he won both the Hugo and Nebula Awards.

Even before the advent of word processors, Asimov wrote ninety words a minute, up to twelve hours a day, a superhuman pace. His demanding schedule allowed two—and only two—drafts of everything, the first on a typewriter, and in his final years, the second on a computer. He said, "But I have a completely unadorned style. I aim to be accurate and clear—whether for an audience of sci-fi fans or general readers, including children." Asimov has been praised for being "encyclopedic, witty, with a gift for colorful and illuminating examples and explanations"—qualities apparent in "Those Crazy Ideas." There he explains the creative processes by which two scientists, Charles Darwin and Alfred Russel Wallace, arrived independently at the theory of evolution. Then he analyzes how they worked to illustrate the common characteristics of the creative process, a combination of education, intelligence, intuition, courage—and luck.

Those Crazy Ideas

1   Time and time again I have been asked (and I'm sure others who have, in their time, written science fiction have been asked too): "Where do you get your crazy ideas?"

2   Over the years, my answers have sunk from flattered confusion to a shrug and a feeble smile. Actually, I don't really know,

and the lack of knowledge doesn't really worry me, either, as long as the ideas keep coming.

But then some time ago, a consultant firm in Boston, en- 3 gaged in a sophisticated space-age project for the government, got in touch with me.

What they needed, it seemed, to bring their project to a 4 successful conclusion were novel suggestions, startling new principles, conceptual breakthroughs. To put it into the nutshell of a well-turned phrase, they needed "crazy ideas."

Unfortunately, they didn't know how to go about getting 5 crazy ideas, but some among them had read my science fiction, so they looked me up in the phone book and called me to ask (in essence), "Dr. Asimov, where do you get your crazy ideas?"

Alas, I still didn't know, but as speculation is my profession, 6 I am perfectly willing to think about the matter and share my thoughts with you.

The question before the house, then, is: How does one go 7 about creating or inventing or dreaming up or stumbling over a new and revolutionary scientific principle?

For instance—to take a deliberately chosen example—how 8 did Darwin come to think of evolution?

To begin with, in 1831, when Charles Darwin was twenty- 9 two, he joined the crew of a ship called the *Beagle*. This ship was making a five-year voyage about the world to explore various coast lines and to increase man's geographical knowledge. Darwin went along as ship's naturalist, to study the forms of life in far-off places.

This he did extensively and well, and upon the return of the 10 *Beagle* Darwin wrote a book about his experiences (published in 1840) which made him famous. In the course of this voyage, numerous observations led him to the conclusion that species of living creatures changed and developed slowly with time; that new species descended from old. This, in itself, was not a new idea. Ancient Greeks had had glimmerings of evolutionary notions. Many scientists before Darwin, including Darwin's own grandfather, had theories of evolution.

The trouble, however, was that no scientist could evolve an 11 explanation for the *why* of evolution. A French naturalist, Jean Baptiste de Lamarck, had suggested in the early 1800s that it came about by a kind of conscious effort or inner drive. A tree-grazing animal, attempting to reach leaves, stretched its neck over the years and transmitted a longer neck to its descendants. The process was repeated with each generation until a giraffe in full glory was formed.

12   The only trouble was that acquired characteristics are not inherited and this was easily proved. The Lamarckian explanation did not carry conviction.

13   Charles Darwin, however, had nothing better to suggest after several years of thinking about the problem.

14   But in 1798, eleven years before Darwin's birth, an English clergyman named Thomas Robert Malthus had written a book entitled *An Essay on the Principle of Population*. In this book Malthus suggested that the human population always increased faster than the food supply and that the population had to be cut down by either starvation, disease, or war; that these evils were therefore unavoidable.

15   In 1838 Darwin, still puzzling over the problem of the development of species, read Malthus's book. It is hackneyed to say "in a flash" but that, apparently, is how it happened. In a flash, it was clear to Darwin. Not only human beings increased faster than the food supply; all species of living things did. In every case, the surplus population had to be cut down by starvation, by predators, or by disease. Now no two members of any species are exactly alike; each has slight individual variations from the norm. Accepting this fact, which part of the population was cut down?

16   Why—and this was Darwin's breakthrough—those members of the species who were less efficient in the race for food, less adept at fighting off or escaping from predators, less equipped to resist disease, went down.

17   The survivors, generation after generation, were better adapted, on the average, to their environment. The slow changes toward a better fit with the environment accumulated until a new (and more adapted) species had replaced the old. Darwin thus postulated the reason for evolution as being the action of *natural selection*. In fact, the full title of his book is *On the Origin of Species by Means of Natural Selection, or the Preservation of Favoured Races in the Struggle for Life*. We just call it *The Origin of Species* and miss the full flavor of what it was he did.

18   It was in 1838 that Darwin received this flash and in 1844 that he began writing his book, but he worked on for fourteen

years gathering evidence to back up his thesis. He was a methodical perfectionist and no amount of evidence seemed to satisfy him. He always wanted more. His friends read his preliminary manuscripts and urged him to publish. In particular, Charles Lyell (whose book *Principles of Geology,* published in 1830–1833, first convinced scientists of the great age of the earth and thus first showed there was *time* for the slow progress of evolution to take place) warned Darwin that someone would beat him to the punch.

While Darwin was working, another and younger English 19 naturalist, Alfred Russel Wallace, was traveling in distant lands. He too found copious evidence to show that evolution took place and he too wanted to find a reason. He did not know that Darwin had already solved the problem.

He spent three years puzzling, and then in 1858, he too came 20 across Malthus's book and read it. I am embarrassed to have to become hackneyed again, but in a flash he saw the answer. Unlike Darwin, however, he did not settle down to fourteen years of gathering and arranging evidence.

Instead, he grabbed pen and paper and at once wrote up his 21 theory. He finished this in two days.

Naturally, he didn't want to rush into print without having 22 his notions checked by competent colleagues, so he decided to send it to some well-known naturalist. To whom? Why, to Charles Darwin. To whom else?

I have often tried to picture Darwin's feeling as he read 23 Wallace's essay which, he afterward stated, expressed matters in almost his own words. He wrote to Lyell that he had been forestalled "with a vengeance."

Darwin might easily have retained full credit. He was well- 24 known and there were many witnesses to the fact that he had been working on his project for a decade and a half. Darwin, however, was a man of the highest integrity. He made no attempt to suppress Wallace. On the contrary, he passed on the essay to others and arranged to have it published along with a similar essay of his own. The year after, Darwin published his book.

Now the reason I chose this case was that here we have two 25 men making one of the greatest discoveries in the history of science independently and simultaneously and under precisely the same stimulus. Does that mean *anyone* could have worked out the theory of natural selection if they had but made a sea voyage and combined that with reading Malthus?

26   Well, let's see. Here's where the speculation starts.

27   To begin with, both Darwin and Wallace were thoroughly grounded in natural history. Each had accumulated a vast collection of facts in the field in which they were to make their breakthrough. Surely this is significant.

28   Now every man in his lifetime collects facts, individual pieces of data, items of information. Let's call these "bits" (as they do, I think, in information theory). The "bits" can be of all varieties: personal memories, girls' phone numbers, baseball players' batting averages, yesterday's weather, the atomic weights of the chemical elements.

29   Naturally, different men gather different numbers of different varieties of "bits." A person who has collected a larger number than usual of those varieties that are held to be particularly difficult to obtain—say, those involving the sciences and the liberal arts—is considered "educated."

30   There are two broad ways in which the "bits" can be accumulated. The more common way, nowadays, is to find people who already possess many "bits" and have them transfer those "bits" to your mind in good order and in predigested fashion. Our schools specialize in this transfer of "bits" and those of us who take advantage of them receive a "formal education."

31   The less common way is to collect "bits" with a minimum amount of live help. They can be obtained from books or out of personal experience. In that case you are "self-educated." (It often happens that "self-educated" is confused with "uneducated." This is an error to be avoided.)

32   In actual practice, scientific breakthroughs have been initiated by those who were formally educated, as for instance by Nicolaus Copernicus, and by those who were self-educated, as for instance by Michael Faraday.

33   To be sure, the structure of science has grown more complex over the years and the absorption of the necessary number of "bits" has become more and more difficult without the guidance of someone who has already absorbed them. The self-educated genius is therefore becoming rarer, though he has still not vanished.

However, without drawing any distinction according to the $_{34}$ manner in which "bits" have been accumulated, let's set up the first criterion for scientific creativity:

1) The creative person must possess as many "bits" of infor- $_{35}$ mation as possible; i.e., he must be educated.

Of course, the accumulation of "bits" is not enough in itself. $_{36}$ We have probably all met people who are intensely educated, but who manage to be abysmally stupid, nevertheless. They have the "bits," but the "bits" just lie there.

But what is there one can do with "bits"? $_{37}$

Well, one can combine them into groups of two or more. $_{38}$ Everyone does that; it is the principle of the string on the finger. You tell yourself to remember *a* (to buy bread) when you observe *b* (the string). You enforce a combination that will not let you forget *a* because *b* is so noticeable.

That, of course, is a conscious and artificial combination of $_{39}$ "bits." It is my feeling that every mind is, more or less uncon- sciously, continually making all sorts of combinations and permu- tations of "bits," probably at random.

Some minds do this with greater facility than others; some $_{40}$ minds have greater capacity for dredging the combinations out of the unconscious and becoming consciously aware of them. This results in "new ideas," in "novel outlooks."

The ability to combine "bits" with facility and to grow con- $_{41}$ sciously aware of the new combinations is, I would like to sug- gest, the measure of what we call "intelligence." In this view, it is quite possible to be educated and yet not intelligent.

Obviously, the creative scientist must not only have his "bits" $_{42}$ on hand but he must be able to combine them readily and more or less consciously. Darwin not only observed data, he also made deductions—clever and far-reaching deductions—from what he observed. That is, he combined the "bits" in interesting ways and drew important conclusions.

So the second criterion of creativity is: $_{43}$

2) The creative person must be able to combine "bits" with $_{44}$ facility and recognize the combinations he has formed; i.e., he must be intelligent.

Even forming and recognizing new combinations is insuffi- $_{45}$ cient in itself. Some combinations are important and some are

trivial. How do you tell which are which? There is no question
but that a person who cannot tell them apart must labor under a
terrible disadvantage. As he plods after each possible new idea,
he loses time and his life passes uselessly.

46   There is also no question but that there are people who
somehow have the gift of seeing the consequences "in a flash" as
Darwin and Wallace did; of feeling what the end must be without
consciously going through every step of the reasoning. This, I
suggest, is the measure of what we call "intuition."

47   Intuition plays more of a role in some branches of scientific
knowledge than others. Mathematics, for instance, is a deductive
science in which, once certain basic principles are learned, a large
number of items of information become "obvious" as merely consequences of those principles. Most of us, to be sure, lack the
intuitive powers to see the "obvious."

48   To the truly intuitive mind, however, the combination of the
few necessary "bits" is at once extraordinarily rich in consequences. Without too much trouble they see them all, including
some that have not been seen by their predecessors.[1]

49   It is perhaps for this reason that mathematics and mathematical physics has seen repeated cases of first-rank breakthroughs
by youngsters. Evariste Galois evolved group theory at twenty-
one. Isaac Newton worked out calculus at twenty-three. Albert
Einstein presented the theory of relativity at twenty-six, and so on.

50   In those branches of science which are more inductive and
require larger numbers of "bits" to begin with, the average age of
the scientists at the time of the breakthrough is greater. Darwin
was twenty-nine at the time of his flash, Wallace was thirty-five.

51   But in any science, however inductive, intuition is necessary
for creativity. So:

52   3) The creative person must be able to see, with as little
delay as possible, the consequences of the new combinations of
"bits" which he has formed; i.e., he must be intuitive.

53   But now let's look at this business of combining "bits" in a
little more detail. "Bits" are at varying distances from each other.

---

[1] The Swiss mathematician, Leonhard Euler, said that to the true mathematician,
it is at once obvious that $e^{\pi i} = -1$.

The more closely related two "bits" are, the more apt one is to be reminded of one by the other and to make the combination. Consequently, a new idea that arises from such a combination is made quickly. It is a "natural consequence" of an older idea, a "corollary." It "obviously follows."

The combination of less related "bits" results in a more startling idea; if for no other reason than that it takes longer for such a combination to be made, so that the new idea is therefore less "obvious." For a scientific breakthrough of the first rank, there must be a combination of "bits" so widely spaced that the random chance of the combination being made is small indeed. (Otherwise, it will be made quickly and be considered but a corollary of some previous idea which will then be considered the "breakthrough.")

But then, it can easily happen that two "bits" sufficiently widely spaced to make a breakthrough by their combination are not present in the same mind. Neither Darwin nor Wallace, for all their education, intelligence, and intuition, possessed the key "bits" necessary to work out the theory of evolution by natural selection. Those "bits" were lying in Malthus's book, and both Darwin and Wallace had to find them there.

To do this, however, they had to read, understand, and appreciate the book. In short, they had to be ready to incorporate other people's "bits" and treat them with all the ease with which they treated their own.

It would hamper creativity, in other words, to emphasize intensity of education at the expense of broadness. It is bad enough to limit the nature of the "bits" to the point where the necessary two would not be in the same mind. It would be fatal to mold a mind to the point where it was incapable of accepting "foreign bits."

I think we ought to revise the first criterion of creativity, then, to read:

1) The creative person must possess as many "bits" as possible, falling into as wide a variety of types as possible; i.e., he must be broadly educated.

As the total amount of "bits" to be accumulated increases with the advance of science, it is becoming more and more difficult to gather enough "bits" in a wide enough area. Therefore, the practice of "brain-busting" is coming into popularity; the notion of collecting thinkers into groups and hoping that they will cross-fertilize one another into startling new breakthroughs.

61   Under what circumstances could this conceivably work? (After all, anything that will stimulate creativity is of first importance to humanity.)

62   Well, to begin with, a group of people will have more "bits" on hand than any member of the group singly since each man is likely to have some "bits" the others do not possess.

63   However, the increase in "bits" is not in direct proportion to the number of men, because there is bound to be considerable overlapping. As the group increases, the smaller and smaller addition of completely new "bits" introduced by each additional member is quickly outweighed by the added tensions involved in greater numbers; the longer wait to speak, the greater likelihood of being interrupted, and so on. It is my (intuitive) guess that five is as large a number as one can stand in such a conference.

64   Now of the three criteria mentioned so far, I feel (intuitively) that intuition is the least common. It is more likely that none of the group will be intuitive than that none will be intelligent or none educated. If no individual in the group is intuitive, the group as a whole will not be intuitive. You cannot add non-intuition and form intuition.

65   If one of the group is intuitive, he is almost certain to be intelligent and educated as well, or he would not have been asked to join the group in the first place. In short, for a brain-busting group to be creative, it must be quite small and it must possess at least one creative individual. But in that case, does that one individual need the group? Well, I'll get back to that later.

66   Why did Darwin work fourteen years gathering evidence for a theory he himself must have been convinced was correct from the beginning? Why did Wallace send his manuscript to Darwin first instead of offering it for publication at once?

67   To me it seems that they must have realized that any new idea is met by resistance from the general population who, after all, are not creative. The more radical the new idea, the greater the dislike and distrust it arouses. The dislike and distrust aroused by a first-class breakthrough are so great that the author must be prepared for unpleasant consequences (sometimes for expulsion

from the respect of the scientific community; sometimes, in some societies, for death).

Darwin was trying to gather enough evidence to protect 68
himself by convincing others through a sheer flood of reasoning. Wallace wanted to have Darwin on his side before proceeding.

It takes courage to announce the results of your creativity. 69
The greater the creativity, the greater the necessary courage in much more than direct proportion. After all, consider that the more profound the breakthrough, the more solidified the previous opinions; the more "against reason" the new discovery seems, the more against cherished authority.

Usually a man who possesses enough courage to be a scien- 70
tific genius seems odd. After all, a man who has sufficient courage or irreverence to fly in the face of reason or authority must be odd, if you define "odd" as "being not like most people." And if he is courageous and irreverent in such a colossally big thing, he will certainly be courageous and irreverent in many small things so that being odd in one way, he is apt to be odd in others. In short, he will seem to the non-creative, conforming people about him to be a "crackpot."

So we have the fourth criterion: 71

4) The creative person must possess courage (and to the 72
general public may, in consequence, seem a crackpot).

As it happens, it is the crackpottery that is most often most 73
noticeable about the creative individual. The eccentric and absent-minded professor is a stock character in fiction; and the phrase "mad scientist" is almost a cliché.

(And be it noted that I am never asked where I get my inter- 74
esting or effective or clever or fascinating ideas. I am invariably asked where I get my *crazy* ideas.)

Of course, it does not follow that because the creative indi- 75
vidual is usually a crackpot, that any crackpot is automatically an unrecognized genius. The chances are low indeed, and failure to recognize that the proposition cannot be so reversed is the cause of a great deal of trouble.

Then, since I believe that combinations of "bits" take place 76
quite at random in the unconscious mind, it follows that it is quite possible that a person may possess all four of the criteria I have mentioned in superabundance and yet may never happen to make

the necessary combination. After all, suppose Darwin had never read Malthus. Would he ever have thought of natural selection? What made him pick up the copy? What if someone had come in at the crucial time and interrupted him?

77   So there is a fifth criterion which I am at a loss to phrase in any other way than this:

78   5) A creative person must be lucky.

79   To summarize:

80   A creative person must be 1) broadly educated, 2) intelligent, 3) intuitive, 4) courageous, and 5) lucky.

81   How, then, does one go about encouraging scientific creativity? For now, more than ever before in man's history, we must; and the need will grow constantly in the future.

82   Only, it seems to me, by increasing the incidence of the various criteria among the general population.

83   Of the five criteria, number 5 (luck) is out of our hands. We can only hope; although we must also remember Louis Pasteur's famous statement that "Luck favors the prepared mind." Presumably, if we have enough of the four other criteria, we shall find enough of number five as well.

84   Criterion 1 (broad education) is in the hands of our school system. Many educators are working hard to find ways of increasing the quality of education among the public. They should be encouraged to continue doing so.

85   Criterion 2 (intelligence) and 3 (intuition) are inborn and their incidence cannot be increased in the ordinary way. However, they can be more efficiently recognized and utilized. I would like to see methods devised for spotting the intelligent and intuitive (particularly the latter) early in life and treating them with special care. This, too, educators are concerned with.

86   To me, though, it seems that it is criterion 4 (courage) that receives the least concern, and it is just the one we may most easily be able to handle. Perhaps it is difficult to make a person more courageous than he is, but that is not necessary. It would be equally effective to make it sufficient to be less courageous; to adopt an attitude that creativity is a permissible activity.

87   Does this mean changing society or changing human nature? I don't think so. I think there are ways of achieving the end that do

not involve massive change of anything, and it is here that brain-busting has its greatest chance of significance.

Suppose we have a group of five that includes one creative individual. Let's ask again what that individual can receive from the non-creative four.   88

The answer to me, seems to be just this: Permission!   89

They must permit him to create. They must tell him to go ahead and be a crackpot.[2]   90

How is this permission to be granted? Can four essentially non-creative people find it within themselves to grant such permission? Can the one creative person find it within himself to accept it?   91

I don't know. Here, it seems to me, is where we need experimentation and perhaps a kind of creative breakthrough about creativity. Once we learn enough about the whole matter, who knows—I may even find out where I get those crazy ideas.   92

Content

1. How does Asimov define "crazy ideas"? Is he using "crazy idea" as a synonym for a "new and revolutionary scientific principle"? How would Asimov (or you) distinguish between a "crazy idea" and a "crackpot" idea? Or the insane notion of a "mad scientist"?

2. Compare and contrast the creative processes by which Charles Darwin and Alfred Russel Wallace arrived independently at the theory of evolution.

3. How appropriate is it for Asimov to generalize about scientific creativity on the basis of two examples from a particular field?

4. Identify the five qualities Asimov says are necessary for the creative process to operate. Has he covered all the essentials? To what extent must the "climate be right" for the creative process to function effectively? What becomes of "crazy ideas" too advanced for their time?

---

[2] AUTHOR'S NOTE: Always with the provision, of course, that the crackpot creation that results survives the test of hard inspection. Though many of the products of genius seem crackpot at first, very few of the creations that seem crackpot turn out, after all, to be products of genius.

Strategies/Structures

5. Show how Asimov's essay is an example of inductive reasoning—beginning with evidence, assessing that evidence, and drawing conclusions from it.

6. Although Asimov identifies the fifth quality in a successful creative process as luck (¶ 78), he doesn't define it, says it's "out of our hands" (¶ 83), and blithely assures us that "if we have enough of the four other criteria" we'll find enough luck as well (¶ 83). Is Asimov irresponsible here?

Language

7. Asimov uses a conversational tone and vocabulary, as well as two extended narrative examples (of Darwin and Wallace). Would you expect to find such literary techniques in scientific writing? If so, for what kind of audience? (Compare Darwin, "Understanding Natural Selection" [483–90] and Gould, "Evolution as Fact and Theory" [550–60].)

8. Asimov always identifies the scientists to whom he is referring when he first introduces them (Lamarck, ¶ 11; Malthus, ¶ 14; Lyell, ¶ 18). What does this practice reveal about the amount of scientific knowledge Asimov expects his readers to have?

For Writing

9. What does it take to be successful? Identify and define the essential criteria (four or five items) for an outstanding performance in one of the fields or roles below. Illustrate your definition with a detailed example or two from the lives of successful people in that field or role, perhaps people you know:

   a. Parent or grandparent
   b. Medicine (doctor, nurse, social worker, medical researcher)
   c. Politics, military, and the law (police or military officer, lawyer, elected official, bureaucrat, judge)
   d. Athletics (player of team or individual sports, coach)
   e. Education (student, teacher, or administrator)
   f. The fine arts (painter, sculptor, musician, writer)
   g. Business (self-made man or woman, salesperson, manager, executive, accountant, broker)
   h. Another profession or occupation of your choice.

THOMAS S. KUHN

Kuhn's writings as a professor of philosophy and history of science approach the ways scientists think and work from a philosophical and humanistic perspective. Kuhn (1922–1996) was educated as a physicist at Harvard (B.A., 1943; M.A., 1946; Ph.D., 1949), and taught at Harvard (1948–1956), the University of California, Berkeley (1958–1964), Princeton (1964–1979), and thereafter at the Massachusetts Institute of Technology. His illuminating books, profoundly influential on the ways scientists and humanists alike understand their own and each other's work, include *The Copernican Revolution: Planetary Astronomy in the Development of Western Thought* (1957) and *The Essential Tension* (1977). The idea for *The Structure of Scientific Revolutions* (1962), from which this classic essay is taken, had been germinating for fifteen years, beginning when Kuhn as a graduate student taught historical case studies of scientists and concluded that Aristotle's physics were not "bad Newton," but simply different. "I sweated blood and blood and blood, and finally I had a breakthrough," he said.

Nothing is as practical as a good theory, or in this case, a good definition of a theory. Kuhn begins by defining paradigms—structures or patterns that allow scientists to share a common set of assumptions, theories, laws, applications as they look at their fields. Scientists whose research is based on shared paradigms, who "learned the bases of their field from the same concrete models . . . are committed to the same rules and standards for scientific practice" and do not disagree over the fundamentals. The rest of this essay explains how and why this is so, and shows the random state of any scientific field before the emergence of a workable paradigm, the effects of competing paradigms on the discipline, and the consequences to the field of shifting from one paradigm to another.

The Route to Normal Science

In this essay, "normal science" means research firmly based upon one or more past scientific achievements, achievements that some particular scientific community acknowledges for a time as supplying the foundation for its further practice. Today such achievements are recounted, though seldom in their original form, by science textbooks, elementary and advanced. These textbooks expound the body of accepted theory, illustrate many or all of its successful applications, and compare these applications with exemplary observations and experiments. Before such books became popular early in the nineteenth century (and until even more recently in the newly matured sciences), many of the famous classics of science fulfilled a similar function. Aristotle's *Physica,* Ptolemy's *Almagest,* Newton's *Principia* and *Opticks,* Franklin's *Electricity,* Lavoisier's *Chemistry,* and Lyell's *Geology*—these and many other works served for a time implicitly to define the legitimate problems and methods of a research field for succeeding generations of practitioners. They were able to do so because they shared two essential characteristics. Their achievement was sufficiently unprecedented to attract an enduring group of adherents away from competing modes of scientific activity. Simultaneously, it was sufficiently open-ended to leave all sorts of problems for the redefined group of practitioners to resolve.

2   Achievements that share these two characteristics I shall henceforth refer to as "paradigms," a term that relates closely to "normal science." By choosing it, I mean to suggest that some accepted examples of actual scientific practice—examples which include law, theory, application, and instrumentation together— provide models from which spring particular coherent traditions of scientific research. These are the traditions which the historian describes under such rubrics as "Ptolemaic astronomy" (or "Copernican"), "Aristotelian dynamics" (or "Newtonian"), "corpuscular optics" (or "wave optics"), and so on. The study of paradigms, including many that are far more specialized than those named illustratively above, is what mainly prepares the student for membership in the particular scientific community with which he will later practice. Because he there joins men who learned the bases of their field from the same concrete models, his subsequent practice will seldom evoke overt disagreement over fundamentals. Men whose research is based on shared paradigms are committed to the same rules and standards for scientific practice. That commitment and the apparent consensus it produces are prerequisites for normal science, i.e., for the genesis and continuation of a particular research tradition.

Because in this essay the concept of a paradigm will often 3
substitute for a variety of familiar notions, more will need to be
said about the reasons for its introduction. Why is the concrete scientific achievement, as a locus of professional commitment, prior
to the various concepts, laws, theories, and points of view that
may be abstracted from it? In what sense is the shared paradigm a
fundamental unit for the student of scientific development, a unit
that cannot be fully reduced to logically atomic components which
might function in its stead? There can be a sort of scientific research without paradigms, or at least without any so unequivocal
and so binding as the ones named above. Acquisition of a paradigm and of the more esoteric type of research it permits is a sign
of maturity in the development of any given scientific field.

If the historian traces the scientific knowledge of any se- 4
lected group of related phenomena backward in time, he is likely
to encounter some minor variant of a pattern here illustrated from
the history of physical optics. Today's physics textbooks tell the
student that light is photons, i.e., quantum-mechanical entities
that exhibit some characteristics of waves and some of particles.
Research proceeds accordingly, or rather according to the more
elaborate and mathematical characterization from which this
usual verbalization is derived. That characterization of light is,
however, scarcely half a century old. Before it was developed by
Planck, Einstein, and others early in this century, physics texts
taught that light was transverse wave motion, a conception
rooted in a paradigm that derived ultimately from the optical
writings of Young and Fresnel in the early nineteenth century.
Nor was the wave theory the first to be embraced by almost all
practitioners of optical science. During the eighteenth century the
paradigm for this field was provided by Newton's *Opticks*, which
taught that light was material corpuscles. At that time physicists
sought evidence, as the early wave theorists had not, of the pressure exerted by light particles impinging on solid bodies.

These transformations of the paradigms of physical optics 5
are scientific revolutions, and the successive transition from one
paradigm to another via revolution is the usual developmental
pattern of mature science. It is not, however, the pattern characteristic of the period before Newton's work, and that is the contrast that concerns us here. No period between remote antiquity

and the end of the seventeenth century exhibited a single generally accepted view about the nature of light. Instead there were
a number of competing schools and sub-schools, most of them
espousing one variant or another of Epicurean, Aristotelian, or
Platonic theory. One group took light to be particles emanating
from material bodies; for another it was a modification of the
medium that intervened between the body and the eye; still another explained light in terms of an interaction of the medium with
an emanation from the eye; and there were other combinations and
modifications besides. Each of the corresponding schools derived
strength from its relation to some particular metaphysic, and each
emphasized, as paradigmatic observations, the particular cluster
of optical phenomena that its own theory could do most to explain.
Other observations were dealt with by *ad hoc* elaborations, or they
remained as outstanding problems for further research.

6   At various times all these schools made significant contributions to the body of concepts, phenomena, and techniques from
which Newton drew the first nearly uniformly accepted paradigm
for physical optics. Any definition of the scientist that excludes at
least the more creative members of these various schools will exclude their modern successors as well. Those men were scientists.
Yet anyone examining a survey of physical optics before Newton
may well conclude that, though the field's practitioners were
scientists, the net result of their activity was something less than
science. Being able to take no common body of belief for granted,
each writer on physical optics felt forced to build his field anew
from its foundations. In doing so, his choice of supporting observation and experiment was relatively free, for there was no standard set of methods or of phenomena that every optical writer felt
forced to employ and explain. Under these circumstances, the dialogue of the resulting books was often directed as much to the
members of other schools as it was to nature. That pattern is not
unfamiliar in a number of creative fields today, nor is it incompatible with significant discovery and invention. It is not, however,
the pattern of development that physical optics acquired after
Newton and that other natural sciences make familiar today.

7   The history of electrical research in the first half of the
eighteenth century provides a more concrete and better known
example of the way a science develops before it acquires its first
universally received paradigm. During that period there were

almost as many views about the nature of electricity as there were important electrician experimenters, men like Haukshee, Gray, Desaguliers, Du Fay, Nollett, Watson, Franklin, and others. All their numerous concepts of electricity had something in common—they were partially derived from one or another version of the mechanico-corpuscular philosophy that guided all scientific research of the day. In addition, all were components of real scientific theories, of theories that had been drawn in part from experiment and observation that partially determined the choice and interpretation of additional problems undertaken in research. Yet though all the experiments were electrical and though most of the experimenters read each other's works, their theories had no more than a family resemblance.

One early group of theories, following seventeenth-century practice, regarded attraction and frictional generation as the fundamental electrical phenomena. This group tended to treat repulsion as a secondary effect due to some sort of mechanical rebounding and also to postpone for as long as possible both discussion and systematic research on Gray's newly discovered effect, electrical conduction. Other "electricians" (the term is their own) took attraction and repulsion to be equally elementary manifestations of electricity and modified their theories and research accordingly. (Actually, this group is remarkably small—even Franklin's theory never quite accounted for the mutual repulsion of two negatively charged bodies.) But they had as much difficulty as the first group in accounting simultaneously for any but the simplest conduction effects. Those effects, however, provided the starting point for still a third group, one which tended to speak of electricity as a "fluid" that could run through conductors rather than as an "effluvium" that emanated from non-conductors. This group, in its turn, had difficulty reconciling its theory with a number of attractive and repulsive effects. Only through the work of Franklin and his immediate successors did a theory arise that could account with something like equal facility for very nearly all these effects and that therefore could and did provide a subsequent generation of "electricians" with a common paradigm for its research.

Excluding those fields, like mathematics and astronomy, in which the first firm paradigms date from prehistory and also those, like biochemistry, that arose by division and recombination of specialties already matured, the situations outlined above are historically typical. Though it involves my continuing to employ the unfortunate simplification that tags an extended historical episode with a single and somewhat arbitrarily chosen name (e.g., Newton or Franklin), I suggest that similar fundamental disagreements characterized, for example, the study of motion before Aristotle and of statics before Archimedes, the study of heat before Black, of chemistry before Boyle and Boerhaave, and of historical geology before Hutton. In parts of biology—the study of heredity, for example—the first universally received paradigms are still more recent; and it remains an open question what parts of social science have yet acquired such paradigms at all. History suggests that the road to a firm research consensus is extraordinarily arduous.

10   History also suggests, however, some reasons for the difficulties encountered on the road. In the absence of a paradigm or some candidate for paradigm, all of the facts that could possibly pertain to the development of a given science are likely to seem equally relevant. As a result, early fact-gathering is a far more nearly random activity than the one that subsequent scientific development makes familiar. Furthermore, in the absence of a reason for seeking some particular form of more recondite information, early fact-gathering is usually restricted to the wealth of data that lie ready to hand. The resulting pool of facts contains those accessible to casual observation and experiment together with some of the more esoteric data retrievable from established crafts, medicine, calendar making, and metallurgy. Because the crafts are one readily accessible source of facts that could not have been casually discovered, technology has often played a vital role in the emergence of new sciences.

11   But though this sort of fact-collecting has been essential to the origin of many significant sciences, anyone who examines, for example, Pliny's encyclopedic writings or the Baconian natural histories of the seventeenth century will discover that it produces a morass. One somehow hesitates to call the literature that results scientific. The Baconian "histories" of heat, color, wind, mining, and so on, are filled with information, some of it recondite. But they juxtapose facts that will later prove revealing (e.g., heating by mixture) with others (e.g., the warmth of dung heaps) that will for some time remain too complex to be integrated with theory at

all. In addition, since any description must be partial, the typical natural history often omits from its immensely circumstantial accounts just those details that later scientists will find sources of important illumination. Almost none of the early "histories" of electricity, for example, mention that chaff, attracted to a rubbed glass rod, bounces off again. That effect seemed mechanical, not electrical. Moreover, since the casual fact-gatherer seldom possesses the time or the tools to be critical, the natural histories often juxtapose descriptions like the above with others, say, heating by antiperistasis (or by cooling), that we are now quite unable to confirm.[1] Only very occasionally, as in the case of ancient statics, dynamics, and geometrical optics, do facts collected with so little guidance from pre-established theory speak with sufficient clarity to permit the emergence of a first paradigm.

This is the situation that creates the schools characteristic of the early stages of a science's development. No natural history can be interpreted in the absence of at least some implicit body of intertwined theoretical and methodological belief that permits selection, evaluation, and criticism. If that body of belief is not already implicit in the collection of facts—in which case more than "mere facts" are at hand—it must be externally supplied, perhaps by a current metaphysic, by another science, or by personal and historical accident. No wonder, then, that in the early stages of the development of any science different men confronting the same range of phenomena, but not usually all the same particular phenomena, describe and interpret them in different ways. What is surprising, and perhaps also unique in its degree to the fields we call science, is that such initial divergences should ever largely disappear.

For they do disappear to a very considerable extent and then apparently once and for all. Furthermore, their disappearance is usually caused by the triumph of one of the pre-paradigm schools, which, because of its own characteristic beliefs and preconceptions, emphasized only some special part of the too sizable and inchoate pool of information. Those electricians who thought

12

13

---

[1] Bacon [in the *Novum Organum*] says, "Water slightly warm is more easily frozen than quite cold"; *antiperistasis*: an old word meaning a reaction caused by the action of an opposite quality or principle — here, heating through cooling.

electricity a fluid and therefore gave particular emphasis to conduction provide an excellent case in point. Led by this belief,
which could scarcely cope with the known multiplicity of attractive and repulsive effects, several of them conceived the idea of
bottling the electrical fluid. The immediate fruit of their efforts
was the Leyden jar, a device which might never have been discovered by a man exploring nature casually or at random, but
which was in fact independently developed by at least two inves-
tigators in the early 1740's. Almost from the start of his electrical
researches, Franklin was particularly concerned to explain that
strange and, in the event, particularly revealing piece of special
apparatus. His success in doing so provided the most effective of
the arguments that made his theory a paradigm, though one that
was still unable to account for quite all the known cases of electrical repulsion.[2] To be accepted as a paradigm, a theory must seem
better than its competitors, but it need not, and in fact never does,
explain all the facts with which it can be confronted.

14   What the fluid theory of electricity did for the subgroup
that held it, the Franklinian paradigm later did for the entire
group of electricians. It suggested which experiments would be
worth performing and which, because directed to secondary or
to overly complex manifestations of electricity, would not. Only
the paradigm did the job far more effectively, partly because the
end of interschool debate ended the constant reiteration of fundamentals and partly because the confidence that they were on
the right track encouraged scientists to undertake more precise,
esoteric, and consuming sorts of work.[3] Freed from the concern
with any and all electrical phenomena, the united group of electricians could pursue selected phenomena in far more detail,
designing much special equipment for the task and employing it

---

[2] The troublesome case was the mutual repulsion of negatively charged bodies.
[3] It should be noted that the acceptance of Franklin's theory did not end quite all
debate. In 1759 Robert Symmer proposed a two-fluid version of that theory, and
for many years thereafter electricians were divided about whether electricity was
a single fluid or two. But the debates on this subject only confirm what has been
said above about the manner in which a universally recognized achievement
unites the profession. Electricians, though they continued divided on this point,
rapidly concluded that no experimental tests could distinguish the two versions
of the theory and that they were therefore equivalent. After that, both schools
could and did exploit all the benefits that the Franklinian theory provided.

more stubbornly and systematically than electricians had ever done before. Both fact collection and theory articulation became highly directed activities. The effectiveness and efficiency of electrical research increased accordingly, providing evidence for a societal version of Francis Bacon's acute methodological dictum: "Truth emerges more readily from error than from confusion."

We shall be examining the nature of this highly directed or paradigm-based research in the next section, but must first note briefly how the emergence of a paradigm affects the structure of the group that practices the field. When, in the development of a natural science, an individual or group first produces a synthesis able to attract most of the next generation's practitioners, the older schools gradually disappear. In part their disappearance is caused by their members' conversion to the new paradigm. But there are always some men who cling to one or another of the older views, and they are simply read out of the profession, which thereafter ignores their work. The new paradigm implies a new and more rigid definition of the field. Those unwilling or unable to accommodate their work to it must proceed in isolation or attach themselves to some other group.[4] Historically, they have often simply stayed in the departments of philosophy from which so many of the special sciences have been spawned. As these indications hint, it is sometimes just its reception of a paradigm that transforms a group previously interested merely in the study of nature into a profession or, at least, a discipline. In the sciences (though not in fields like medicine, technology, and law, of which the principal *raison d'être* is an external social need), the formation of specialized journals, the foundation of specialists' societies, and the claim for a special place in the curriculum have usually been associated with a group's first reception of a single paradigm. At least this was the case between the time, a century and a

---

[4] The history of electricity provides an excellent example which could be duplicated from the careers of Priestley, Kelvin, and others. Franklin reports that Nollet, who at mid-century was the most influential of the Continental electricians, "lived to see himself the last of his Sect, except Mr. B. — his *Eleve* [pupil] and immediate Disciple." More interesting, however, is the endurance of whole schools in increasing isolation from professional science. Consider, for example, the case of astrology, which was once an integral part of astronomy. Or consider the continuation in the late eighteenth, and early nineteenth centuries of a previously respected tradition of "romantic" chemistry.

half ago, when the institutional pattern of scientific specialization
first developed and the very recent time when the paraphernalia
of specialization acquired a prestige of their own.

16   The more rigid definition of the scientific group has other
consequences. When the individual scientist can take a paradigm
for granted, he need no longer, in his major works, attempt to
build his field anew, starting from first principles and justifying
the use of each concept introduced. That can be left to the writer
of textbooks. Given a textbook, however, the creative scientist can
begin his research where it leaves off and thus concentrate exclusively upon the subtlest and most esoteric aspects of the natural
phenomena that concern his group. And as he does this, his
research communiqués will begin to change in ways whose evolution has been too little studied but whose modern end products
are obvious to all and oppressive to many. No longer will his researches usually be embodied in books addressed, like Franklin's
Experiments . . . on Electricity or Darwin's *Origin of Species,* to anyone who might be interested in the subject matter of the field.
Instead they will usually appear as brief articles addressed only to
professional colleagues, the men whose knowledge of a shared
paradigm can be assumed and who prove to be the only ones able
to read the papers addressed to them.

17   Today in the sciences, books are usually either texts or retro-
spective reflections upon one aspect or another of the scientific
life. The scientist who writes one is more likely to find his professional reputation impaired than enhanced. Only in the earlier, pre-
paradigm, stages of the development of the various sciences did
the book ordinarily possess the same relation to professional
achievement that it still retains in other creative fields. And only in
those fields that still retain the book, with or without the article, as
a vehicle for research communication are the lines of professionalization still so loosely drawn that the layman may hope to follow
progress by reading the practitioners' original reports. Both in
mathematics and astronomy, research reports had ceased already
in antiquity to be intelligible to a generally educated audience. In
dynamics, research became similarly esoteric in the latter Middle
Ages, and it recaptured general intelligibility only briefly during
the early seventeenth century when a new paradigm replaced the
one that had guided medieval research. Electrical research began

to require translation for the layman before the end of the eighteenth century, and most other fields of physical science ceased to be generally accessible in the nineteenth. During the same two centuries similar transitions can be isolated in the various parts of the biological sciences. In parts of the social sciences they may well be occurring today. Although it has become customary, and is surely proper, to deplore the widening gulf that separates the professional scientist from his colleagues in other fields, too little attention is paid to the essential relationship between that gulf and the mechanisms intrinsic to scientific advance.

Ever since prehistoric antiquity one field of study after another has crossed the divide between what the historian might call its prehistory as a science and its history proper. These transitions to maturity have seldom been so sudden or so unequivocal as my necessarily schematic discussion may have implied. But neither have they been historically gradual, coextensive, that is to say, with the entire development of the fields within which they occurred. Writers on electricity during the first four decades of the eighteenth century possessed far more information about electrical phenomena than had their sixteenth-century predecessors. During the half-century after 1740, few new sorts of electrical phenomena were added to their lists. Nevertheless, in important respects, the electrical writings of Cavendish, Coulomb, and Volta in the last third of the eighteenth century seem further removed from those of Gray, Du Fay, and even Franklin than are the writings of these early eighteenth-century electrical discoverers from those of the sixteenth century.[5] Sometime between 1740 and 1780, electricians were for the first time enabled to take the foundations of their field for granted. From that point they pushed on to more concrete and recondite problems, and increasingly they then reported their results in articles addressed to other electricians rather than in books addressed to the learned world at large. As a group they achieved what had been gained by astronomers in antiquity and

18

---

[5] The post-Franklinian developments include an immense increase in the sensitivity of charge detectors, the first reliable and generally diffused techniques for measuring charge, the evolution of the concept of capacity and its relation to a newly refined notion of electric tension, and the quantification of electrostatic force.

by students of motion in the Middle Ages, of physical optics in the late seventeenth century, and of historical geology in the early nineteenth. They had, that is, achieved a paradigm that proved able to guide the whole group's research. Except with the advantage of hindsight, it is hard to find another criterion that so clearly proclaims a field a science.

Content

1. What does Kuhn mean by "normal science" (¶ 1 and elsewhere)? What is "the route to normal science," as he explains it in this essay?

2. What does Kuhn mean by a "paradigm" in science (¶ 2 and elsewhere)? What is the relation of "paradigm" to "normal science" (¶ 2 and elsewhere)?

3. What is a pre-paradigmatic state (¶s 10–13)? What is the relation of the development of a paradigm and the emergence of "some implicit body of intertwined theoretical and methodological belief that permits selection, evaluation, and criticism" (¶ 12)?

4. What is the process by which one paradigm replaces another (¶ 15)?

5. What is the relation of innovative scientists to writers of textbooks (¶s 16–17)? Who reads scientific articles? Who reads textbooks of science (¶s 16–17)?

Language

6. Why is it necessary for Kuhn to define his key terms, "paradigms" and "normal science" (¶ 2) before he proceeds with the rest of the essay? Paraphrase them to make sure you understand what he's talking about.

7. Kuhn uses relatively nontechnical language throughout to explain complicated and technical phenomena. What does this choice of language reveal about Kuhn's intended audience?

8. When Kuhn does use such illustrative concepts as "photons," he defines them immediately afterward (¶ 4). Is this adequate for nonscientific readers?

For Writing

9. Explain in your own words the prevailing paradigm in one of the sciences Kuhn uses for illustrative purposes in this essay: physics, chemistry, biology, psychology. What is the prevailing paradigm in another science you know about? Use a scientific article in a field of your choice to help illustrate your analysis. How does the search for or finding of

paradigms in the sciences help you (or people new to the field) understand the field? Or explain the prevailing paradigm in another field you know, such as business, education, engineering, a fine art, or a humanistic subject.

10. Explain what Kuhn means by the following: "When the individual scientists can take a paradigm for granted, he need no longer, in his major works, attempt to build his field anew, starting from first principles and justifying the use of each concept introduced. That can be left to the writer of textbooks" (¶ 16). What paradigms do your natural science, social science, or other textbooks exemplify?

TOM AND RAY MAGLIOZZI

Tom (born, 1938) and Ray (born, 1947) Magliozzi were born in East Cambridge, Massachusetts, and educated at the Massachusetts Institute of Technology. Tom worked in marketing; Ray was a VISTA volunteer, and taught junior high school. In 1973 the brothers opened the Good News garage in Cambridge, which Ray continues to operate while Tom teaches business at Suffolk University. Three years later their career as Click and Clack, the Tappet Brothers, began with a local call-in radio show on car repair, "Car Talk," which was syndicated through National Public Radio in 1987.

Speaking, as one commentator has observed, "pure Bostonese that sounds a lot like a truck running over vowels," and with considerable humor, including unrestrained (some say "maniacal") laughter at their own jokes, the brothers dispense realistic, easy-to-understand advice about how cars work and what to do when they don't, both on the radio and in *Car Talk* (1991), in which the following explanation of "Inside the Engine" appears.

Inside the Engine

A customer of ours had an old Thunderbird that he used to drive back and forth to New York to see a girlfriend every other weekend. And every time he made the trip he'd be in the shop the following Monday needing to get something fixed because the car was such a hopeless piece of trash. One Monday he failed to show up and Tom said, "Gee, that's kind of unusual." I said jokingly, "Maybe he blew the car up."

2   Well, what happened was that he was on the Merritt Parkway in Connecticut when he noticed that he had to keep the gas pedal all the way to the floor just to go 30 m.p.h., with this big V-8 engine, and he figured something was awry.

3   So he pulled into one of those filling stations where they sell gasoline and chocolate-chip cookies and milk. And he asked the attendant to look at the engine and, of course, the guy said, "I can't help you. All I know is cookies and milk." But the guy agreed to look anyway since our friend was really desperate. His girlfriend was waiting for him and he needed to know if he was going to make it. Anyway, the guy threw open the hood and jumped back in terror. The engine was glowing red. Somewhere along the line, probably around Hartford, he must have lost all of his motor oil. The engine kept getting hotter and hotter, but like a lot of other things in the car that didn't work, neither did his oil pressure warning light. As a result, the engine got so heated up that it fused itself together. All the pistons melted, and the cylinder heads deformed, and the pistons fused to the cylinder walls, and the bearings welded themselves to the crankshaft—oh, it was a terrible sight! When he tried to restart the engine, he just heard a *click, click, click* since the whole thing was seized up tighter than a drum.

4   That's what can happen in a case of extreme engine neglect. Most of us wouldn't do that, or at least wouldn't do it knowingly. Our friend didn't do it knowingly either, but he learned a valuable lesson. He learned that his girlfriend wouldn't come and get him if his car broke down. Even if he offered her cookies and milk.

5   The oil is critical to keeping things running since it not only acts as a lubricant, but it also helps to keep the engine cool. What happens is that the oil pump sucks the oil out of what's called the sump (or the crankcase or the oil pan), and it pushes that oil, under pressure, up to all of the parts that need lubrication.

6   The way the oil works is that it acts as a cushion. The molecules of oil actually separate the moving metal parts from one another so that they don't directly touch; the crankshaft *journals,* or the hard parts of the crankshaft, never touch the soft connecting-

rod *bearings* because there's a film of oil between them, forced in there under pressure. From the pump.

It's pretty high pressure too. When the engine is running at 7 highway speed, the oil, at 50 or 60 pounds or more per square inch (or about 4 bars, if you're of the metric persuasion—but let's leave religion out of this), is coursing through the veins of the engine and keeping all these parts at safe, albeit microscopic, distances from each other.

But if there's a lot of dirt in the oil, the dirt particles get 8 embedded in these metal surfaces and gradually the dirt acts as an abrasive and wears away these metal surfaces. And pretty soon the engine is junk.

It's also important that the motor oil be present in sufficient 9 quantity. In nontechnical terms, that means there's got to be enough of it in there. If you have too little oil in your engine, there's not going to be enough of it to go around, and it will get very hot, because four quarts will be doing the work of five, and so forth. When that happens, the oil gets overheated and begins to burn up at a greater than normal rate. Pretty soon, instead of having four quarts, you have three and a half quarts, then three quarts doing the work of five. And then, next thing you know, you're down to two quarts and your engine is glowing red, just like that guy driving to New York, and it's chocolate-chip cookie time.

In order to avoid this, some cars have gauges and some 10 have warning lights; some people call them "idiot lights." Actually, we prefer to reverse it and call them "idiot gauges." I think gauges are bad. When you drive a car—maybe I'm weird about this—I think it's a good idea to look at the road most of the time. And you can't look at the road if you're busy looking at a bunch of gauges. It's the same objection we have to these stupid radios today that have so damn many buttons and slides and digital scanners and so forth that you need a copilot to change stations. Remember when you just turned a knob?

Not that gauges are bad in and of themselves. I think if you 11 have your choice, what you want is idiot lights—or what we call "genius lights"—and gauges too. It's nice to have a gauge that you can kind of keep an eye on for an overview of what's going on. For example, if you know that your engine typically runs at 215 degrees and on this particular day, which is not abnormally hot, it's running at 220 or 225, you might suspect that something is wrong and get it looked at before your radiator boils over.

12   On the other hand, if that gauge was the only thing you had to rely on and you didn't have a light to alert you when something was going wrong, then you'd look at the thing all the time, especially if your engine had melted on you once. In that case, why don't you take the bus? Because you're not going to be a very good driver, spending most of your time looking at the gauges.

13   Incidentally, if that oil warning light ever comes on, shut the engine off! We don't mean that you should shut it off in rush-hour traffic when you're in the passing lane. Use all necessary caution and get the thing over to the breakdown lane. But don't think you can limp to the next exit, because you can't. Spend the money to get towed and you may save the engine.

14   It's a little-known fact that the oil light does *not* signify whether or not you have oil in the engine. The oil warning light is really monitoring the oil *pressure.* Of course, if you have no oil, you'll have no oil pressure, so the light will be on. But it's also possible to have plenty of oil and an oil pump that's not working for one reason or another. In this event, a new pump would fix the problem, but if you were to drive the car (saying, "It must be a bad light, I just checked the oil!") you'd melt the motor.

15   So if the oil warning light comes on, even if you just had an oil change and the oil is right up to the full mark on the dipstick and is nice and clean—don't drive the car!

16   Here's another piece of useful info. When you turn the key to the "on" position, all the little warning lights *should light up:* the temperature light, the oil light, whatever other lights you may have. Because that is the *test mode* for these lights. If those lights *don't* light up when you turn the key to the "on" position (just before you turn it all the way to start the car), does that mean you're out of oil? No. It means that something is wrong with the warning light itself. If the light doesn't work then, it's not going to work at all. Like when you need it, for example.

17   One more thing about oil: overfilling is just as bad as underfilling. Can you really have too much of a good thing? you ask. Yes. If you're half a quart or even a quart overfilled, it's not a big

deal, and I wouldn't be afraid to drive the car under those circumstances. But if you're a quart and a half or two quarts or more overfilled, you could have so much oil in the crankcase that the spinning crankshaft is going to hit the oil and turn it into suds. It's impossible for the pump to pump suds, so you'll ruin the motor. It's kind of like a front-loading washing machine that goes berserk and spills suds all over the floor when you put too much detergent in. That's what happens to your motor oil when you overfill it.

With all this talk about things that can go wrong, let's not forget [18] that modern engines are pretty incredible. People always say, "You know, the cars of yesteryear were wonderful. They built cars rough and tough and durable in those days."

Horsefeathers. [19]

The cars of yesteryear were nicer to look at because they [20] were very individualistic. They were all different, and some were even beautiful. In fact, when I was a kid, you could tell the year, make, and model of a car from a hundred paces just by looking at the taillights or the grille.

Nowadays, they all look the same. They're like jellybeans [21] on wheels. You can't tell one from the other. But the truth is, they've never made engines as good as they make them today. Think of the abuse they take! None of the cars of yesteryear was capable of going 60 or 70 miles per hour all day long and taking it for 100,000 miles.

Engines of today—and by today I mean from the late '60s on [22] up —are far superior. What makes them superior is not only the design and the metallurgy, but the lubricants. The oil they had thirty years ago was lousy compared to what we have today. There are magic additives and detergents and long-chain polymers and what-have-you that make them able to hold dirt in suspension and to neutralize acids and to lubricate better than oils of the old days.

There aren't too many things that will go wrong, because the [23] engines are made so well and the tolerances are closer. And aside from doing stupid things like running out of oil or failing to heed the warning lights or overfilling the thing, you shouldn't worry.

But here's one word of caution about cars that have timing [24] belts: Lots of cars these days are made with overhead camshafts. The camshaft, which opens the valves, is turned by a gear and gets its power from the crankshaft. Many cars today use a notched rubber *timing belt* to connect the two shafts instead of a chain because it's cheaper and easy to change. And here's the caveat: *if you don't change it and the belt breaks, it can mean swift ruin to the engine.* The pistons can hit the valves and you'll have bent valves and possibly broken pistons.

25   So you can do many hundreds of dollars' worth of damage by failing to heed the manufacturer's warning about changing the timing belt in a timely manner. No pun intended. For most cars, the timing belt replacement is somewhere between $100 and $200. It's not a big deal.

26   I might add that there are many cars that have rubber timing belts that will *not* cause damage to the engine when they break. But even if you have one of those cars, make sure that you get the belt changed, at the very least, when the manufacturer suggests it. If there's no specific recommendation and you have a car with a rubber belt, we would recommend that you change it at 60,000 miles. Because even if you don't do damage to the motor when the belt breaks, you're still going to be stuck somewhere, maybe somewhere unpleasant. Maybe even Cleveland! So you want to make sure that you don't fall into that situation.

27   Many engines that have rubber timing belts also use the belt to drive the water pump. On these, don't forget to change the water pump when you change the timing belt, because the leading cause of premature belt failure is that the water pump seizes. So if you have a timing belt that drives the water pump, get the water pump out of there at the same time. You don't want to put a belt in and then have the water pump go a month later, because it'll break the new belt and wreck the engine.

28   The best way to protect all the other pieces that you can't get to without spending a lot of money is through frequent oil changes. The manufacturers recommend oil changes somewhere between seven and ten thousand miles, depending upon the car. We've always recommended that you change your oil at 3,000 miles. We realize for some people that's a bit of an inconvenience, but look at it as cheap insurance. And change the filter every time too.

29   And last but not least, I want to repeat this because it's important: Make sure your warning lights work. The oil pressure and

engine temperature warning lights are your engine's lifeline. Check them every day. You should make it as routine as checking to see if your zipper's up. You guys should do it at the same time.

What you do is, you get into the car, check to see that your zipper's up, and then turn the key on and check to see if your oil pressure and temperature warning lights come on.   30

I don't know what women do.   31

Content

1. Are you convinced that the Magliozzi brothers know their subject? Does their explanation of how a car engine works contain sufficient information for you to trust their authority? Why or why not?
2. What assumptions do the authors make about their readers' technical knowledge? Why do they provide basic information (such as how oil works in an engine, ¶s 5–9)? How are they able to do this without either offending their readers' intelligence or boring them?
3. Why do the Magliozzi brothers make a point of dispelling myths about "the cars of yesteryear" in comparison with the "engines of today" (¶s 18–22)?

Strategies/Structures

4. Why do the authors begin their explanation of a process with a story—in this case, a cautionary tale of the guy whose beat-up old Thunderbird had a meltdown on the Merritt Parkway?
5. When writing about science and technology, why is it important to define fundamental terms, even terms readers have heard—and used—many times, such as *motor oil* (¶s 5–9), *gauges* (or *idiot gauges* ¶s 10–12), and *oil warning light* (¶s 13–15)?
6. What part do cookies and milk play in this story? Does the author's use of humor reinforce or undermine the authority of their explanations? Does their humor help you to understand how an engine works?

Language

7. Typical of science writers, the authors use a number of analogies to explain how oil keeps an engine in good working order ("cushion," ¶ 6; "veins," ¶ 7; "front-loading washing machine" and "suds," ¶ 17). If these analogies help you to understand the subject, explain why they do. If they don't help, why don't they?

8. The authors give commands, such as "Don't drive the car!" when the oil warning light is on (¶ 15), and "Make sure your warning lights work" (¶ 29). Why can they expect readers to react to such commands without being offended?

9. There are two authors. Sometimes they refer to themselves in the plural ("A customer of ours," ¶ 1); but most of the time they use the singular pronoun "I" (¶s 11, 20, and throughout). With what effect? What's the effect of addressing their readers as "you")?

For Writing

10. Write an essay for a nonspecialized audience explaining how a tool, mechanical object, or more abstract process (about which you know a great deal) works and how to get maximum performance from it. Possible topics include: a racing bicycle, a particular exercise machine, a power tool, a kitchen implement, a spread sheet, a particular computer program, management of a particular small business, an election campaign.

11. Authors in the physical or social sciences customarily work in teams, reporting on their collaborative research. In the spirit of this model, collaborate with another equally knowledgeable person or team to explain a technical process for a specialized audience in the same field.

NTOZAKE SHANGE

In 1971, the year after she graduated from Barnard with a B.A. in American Studies, Paulette Williams, daughter of a noted St. Louis surgeon and a social worker, adopted the Zulu name Ntozake Shange (en-toh-ZAH-kee SHAHN-gay), Ntozake meaning "she who comes with her own things" and Shange, "who walks like a lion." "As a feminist I thought it was ridiculous to be named after a boy," she says. Within three years of earning an M.A. from the University of Southern California (1973), her first and most memorable play had been produced, *for colored girls who have considered suicide/when the rainbow is enuf.* It received an Obie award for the best play of 1977 and Tony and Grammy award nominations, and it established Shange as a writer as well as a dancer and an actress who performed in her own work.

Shange's works include over a dozen other plays and dramatic adaptations, ranging from *Boogie Woogie Landscapes* (1978) to an Obie award-winning adaptation of Bertolt Brecht's *Mother Courage and Her Children* (1981). She has written four novels; the most recent is *Liliane. Resurrection of the Daughter* (1994), seven volumes of poetry, of which *Nappy Edges* (1978) is the best known, and numerous short stories and essays. "What Is It We Really Harvestin' Here?" published in *Creative Nonfiction* in 1998, is characteristic of Shange's free-flowing form and fast-paced conversational style, simultaneously lyrical, comical, and satiric. In the process of explaining how to grow sweet potatoes, mustard greens, and watermelon, Shange incorporates African-American history, social commentary, autobiography, and recipes—American studies with attitude.

What Is It We Really Harvestin' Here?

We got a sayin', "The blacker the berry, the sweeter the juice," which is usually meant as a compliment. To my mind, it also refers to the delectable treats we as a people harvested for our owners and for our own selves all these many years, slave or free. In fact, we knew something about the land, sensuality, rhythm and ourselves that has continued to elude our captors—puttin' aside all our treasures in the basement of the British Museum, or the Met, for that matter. What am I talkin' about? A different approach to the force of gravity, to our bodies, and what we produce: a reverence for the efforts of the group and the intimate couple. Harvest time and Christmas were prime occasions for courtin'. A famine, a drought, a flood or Lent do not serve as inspiration for couplin', you see. 1

The Juba, a dance of courtin' known in slave quarters of North America and the Caribbean, is a phenomenon that stayed with us through the jitterbug, the wobble, the butterfly, as a means of courtin' that's apparently very colored, and very "African." In fact we still have it and we've never been so "integrated"—the *Soul Train* dancers aren't all black anymore, but the dynamic certainly is. A visitor to Cuba in Lynne Fauley Emery's "Dance Horizon Book" described the Juba as a series of challenges. 2

A woman advances and commencing a slow dance, made up of shuffling of the feet and various contortions of the body, thus challenges a rival from among the men. One of these, bolder than the rest, after a while steps out, and the two then strive which shall tire the other; the woman performing many feats which the man attempts to rival, often excelling them, amid the shouts of the rest. A woman will sometimes drive two or three successive beaux from the ring, yielding her place at length to some impatient belle.

3   John Henry went up against a locomotive, but decades before we simply were up against ourselves and the elements. And so we are performers in the fields, in the kitchens, by kilns, and for one another. Sterling Stuckey points out, in "Slave Culture," however, that by 1794 "it was illegal to allow slaves to dance and drink on the premises . . . without the written consent of their owners," the exceptions being Christmas and the burials, which are communal experiences. And what shall we plant and harvest, so that we might "Hab big times duh fus hahves, and duh fus ting wut growed we take tuh duh church so as ebrybody could hab a pieces ub it. We pray over it and shout. Wen we hab a dance, we use tuh shout in a rinig. We ain't have wutyuh call a propuh dance tuday."

4   Say we've gone about our owners' business. Planted and harvested his crop of sugar cane, remembering that the "ratio of slaves/sugar was ten times that of slaves/tobacco and slaves/cotton." That to plant a sugar crop we have to dig a pit 3 feet square and a few inches deep into which one young plant is set. Then, of course, the thing has to grow. A mature sugar-cane plant is 3–9 feet tall. That's got to be cut at exactly the right point. Then we've got to crush it, boil it, refine it, from thick black syrup to fine white sugar, to make sure, as they say in Virginia, that we "got the niggah out." Now it's time to tend to our own gardens. Let's grow some sweet potatoes to "keep the niggah alive."

Sweet Potatoes

5   *Like everything else, we have to start with something. Now we need a small piece of potato with at least one of those scraggly roots hanging about for this native Central American tuber. This vegetable will stand more heat than almost any other grown in the United States. It does not*

take to cool weather, and any kind of frost early or seasonal will kill the leaves, and if your soil gets cold the tubers themselves will not look very good. Get your soil ready at least two weeks before planting, weeding, turning, and generally disrupting the congealed and solid mass we refer to as dirt, so that your hands and the tubers may move easily through the soil, as will water and other nutrients.

Once the soil is free of winter, two weeks after the last frost, plant   6
the potato slips in 6–12 inch ridges, 3–4.5 feet apart. Separate the plants by 9–12 inches. If we space the plants more than that, our tubers may be grand, but way too big to make good use of in the kitchen. We should harvest our sweet potatoes when the tubers are not quite ripe, but of good size, or we can wait until the vines turn yellow. Don't handle our potatoes too roughly, which could lead to bruising and decay. If a frost comes upon us unexpectedly, take those potatoes out the ground right away. Our potatoes will show marked improvement during storage, which allows the starch in them to turn to sugar. Nevertheless let them lie out in the open for 2 to 3 hours to fully dry. Then move them to a moist and warm storage space. The growing time for our crop'll vary from 95 to 125 days.

The easiest thing to do with a sweet potato is to bake it. In its skin.   7
I coat the thing with olive oil, or butter in a pinch. Wrap it in some aluminum foil, set it in the oven at 400 degrees. Wait till I hear sizzling, anywhere from 45 minutes to an hour after, in a very hot oven. I can eat it with my supper at that point or I can let it cool off for later. (One of the sexiest dates I ever went on was to the movies to see "El Mariachi." My date brought along chilled baked sweet potatoes and ginger beer. Much nicer than canola-sprayed "buttered" popcorn with too syrupy Coca-Cola, wouldn't you say?)

Mustard Greens

No, they are not the same as collards. We could say they, with their frilly   8
edges and sinuous shapes, have more character, are more flirtatious, than collards. This green can be planted in the spring or the fall, so long as the soil is workable (not cold). It's not a hot weather plant, preferring short days and temperate climates. We can use the same techniques for mustard greens that we use for lettuce. Sowing the seeds in rows 12–18 inches apart, seedlings 4–8 inches apart. These plants should get lots of fertilizer to end up tender, lots of water, too. They should be harvested

before they are fully mature. Now, you've got to be alert, because mustard greens grow fast, 25–40 days from the time you set them in the soil to harvest. When it comes time to reap what you've sown, gather the outer leaves when they are 3–4 inches long, tender enough; let the inner leaves then develop more or wait till it's hot and harvest the whole plant.

9   *Now we cook the mustard greens just like the collards, or we don't have to cook it at all. This vegetable is fine in salads or on sandwiches and soups. If you shy away from pungent tastes, mix these greens with some collards, kale, or beet greens. That should take some of the kick out of them. I still like my peppers and vinegar, though. If we go back, pre-Columbus, the Caribs did, too. According to Spanish travelers, the Caribs, who fancied vegetables, added strong peppers called aji-aji to just about everything. We can still find aji-aji on some sauces from Spanish-speaking countries if we read the labels carefully. Like "La Morena." So appropriate.*

Watermelon

10   *The watermelon is an integral part of our actual life as much as it is a feature of our stereotypical lives in the movies, posters, racial jokes, toys, and early American portraits of the "happy darky." We could just as easily been eatin' watermelon in D. W. Griffith's "Birth of a Nation" as chicken legs. The implications are the same. Like the watermelon, we were a throwback of "African" pre-history, which isn't too off, since Lucy, the oldest Homo sapiens currently known is from Africa, too.*

11   *But I remember being instructed not to order watermelon in restaurants or to eat watermelon in any public places because it makes white people think poorly of us. They already did that, so I don't see what the watermelon was going to precipitate. Europeans brought watermelon with them from Africa anyway. In Massachusetts by 1629 it was recorded as "abounding." In my rebelliousness as a child, I got so angry about the status of the watermelon, I tried to grow some in the flower box on our front porch in Missouri. My harvest was minimal to say the least.*

12   *Here's how you can really grow you some watermelon. They like summer heat, particularly sultry, damp nights. If we can grow watermelons, we can grow ourselves almost any other kind of melon. The treatment is the same. Now, these need some space, if we're looking for a refrigerator-sized melon or one ranging from 25–30 pounds. Let them have a foot between plants in between rows 4–6 feet apart. They need a*

*lot of fertilizer, especially if the soil is heavy and doesn't drain well.
When the runners (vines) are a foot to a foot-and-a-half long, fertilize
again about 8 inches from the plant itself. Put some more fertilizer when
the first melons appear. Watermelons come in different varieties, but I'm
telling you about the red kind. I have no primal response to a golden or
blanched fleshed melon. Once your melons set on the vines and start to
really take up some space, be sure not to forget to water the vines during
the ripening process.*

When is your watermelon ripe? You can't tell by thumping it nor 13
*by the curly tail at the point where the melon is still on the vine. The best
way to know if your melon is ready is by looking at the bottom. The center turns from a light yellow to deep amber. Your melon'll have a powdery
or mushy tasteless sorta taste if you let it ripen too long.*

Surely you've seen enough pictures or been to enough picnics to 14
*know how to eat a watermelon, so I won't insult you with that informa-
tion. However, there is a fractious continuing debate about whether to
sprinkle sugar or salt on your watermelon slice. I am not going to take
sides in this matter.*

Some of us were carried to the New World specifically because 15
we knew 'bout certain crops, know 'bout the groomin' and harvestin' of rice, for instance.

> Plantation owners were perfectly aware of the superiority
> . . . of African slaves from rice country. Littlefield (jour-
> nalist) writes that "as early as 1700 ships from Carolina
> were reported in the Gambia River." . . . In a letter dated
> 1756, Henry Laurens, a Charleston merchant, wrote, "The
> slaves from the River Gambia are prefer'd to all others
> with us save the Gold Coast." The previous year he had
> written: "Gold Coast or Gambias are best; next to them
> the Windward Coast are prefer'd to Angolas."

These bits of information throw an entirely different, more 16
dignified light on "colored" cuisine, for me. Particularly since I
was raised on rice and my mother's people on both sides are in-
defatigable Carolinians, South, to be exact, South Carolinians. To
some, our "phrenologically immature brains" didn't have consequence until our mastery of the cultivation of "cargo," "patna,"
"joponica," and finally Carolina rice, "small-grained, rather long

and wiry, and remarkably white" was transferred to the books and records of our owners. Nevertheless, our penchant for rice was not dampened by its relationship to our bondage. Whether through force or will, we held on to our rice-eatin' heritage. I repeat, I was raised on rice. If I was Joe Williams, insteada singin' "Every day, every day, I sing the blues," I'd be sayin', "Oh, every day, almost any kinda way, I get my rice."

17   My poor mother, Eloise, Ellie, for short, made the mistake of marrying a man who was raised by a woman from Canada. So every day, he wanted a potato, some kinda potato, mashed, boiled, baked, scalloped, fried, just a potato. Yet my mother was raising a sixth generation of Carolinians, which meant we had to eat some kinda rice. Thus, Ellie was busy fixing potato for one and rice for all the rest every day, until I finally learnt how to do one or the other and gave her a break. I asked Ellie Williams how her mother, Viola, went about preparing the rice for her "chirren"—a Low-country linguistic lapse referring to off-spring like me. Anyway, this is what Mama said.

Mama's Rice

18   *"We'd buy some rice in a brown paper bag (this is in The Bronx). Soak it in a bit of water. Rinse it off and cook it the same way we do now." "How is that, Ma?" I asked. "Well, you boil a certain amount of water. Let it boil good. Add your rice and let it boil till tender. Stirring every so often because you want the water to evaporate. You lift your pot. You can tell if your rice is okay because there's no water there. Then you fluff it with a fork. You want every kind, extra, extra, what you call it. No ordinary olive oil will do.*

19   *"Heat this up. Just a little bit of it. You don't want no greasy rice, do you? Heat this until, oh, it is so hot that the smoke is coming quick. Throw in 3–4 cloves garlic, maybe 1 cup chopped onion too, I forgot. Let that sizzle and soften with ½ cup each cilantro, pimiento, and everything. But don't let this get burned, no. So add your 4 cups water and 2 cups rice. Turn up the heat some more till there's a great boiling of rice, water, seasonings. The whole thing. Then leave it alone for a while with the cover on so all the rice cooks even. Now, when you check and see there's only a small bit of water left in the bottom of the pot, stir it all up. Turn the heat up again and wait. When there's no water left at all, at all. Just*

watch the steam coming up. Of course you should have a good pegau *by now, but the whole pot of your rice should be delicioso, ready even for my table. If you do as I say."*

For North Americans, a pot with burnt rice on the bottom is a scary concept. But all over the Caribbean, it's a different story entirely. In order to avoid making *asopao*—a rice moist and heavy with the sofrito or tomato-achiote mixture, almost like a thick soup where the rice becomes one mass instead of standing, each grain on its own—it is necessary to let the rice on the bottom of the pot get a crustlike bottom, assuring that all moisture has evaporated. My poor North American mother, Ellie, chastises me frequently for "ruining" good rice with all this spice. Then I remind her that outside North America we Africans were left to cook in ways that reminded us of our mother's cooking, not Jane Austen's characters. The rice tastes different, too. But sometimes I cheat and simply use Goya's Sazon—after all, I'm a modern woman. I shouldn't say that too loudly, though. Mathilde can hear all the way from her front porch any blasphemous notion I have about good cooking. No, it is her good cooking that I am to learn. I think it is more than appropriate that we know something about some of the crops that led to most of us African descendants of the Diaspora, being here, to eat anything at all.

But rather than end on a sour note, I am thinking of my classes with the great Brazilian dancer, choreographer and teacher Mercedes Baptista at the now legendary Clark Center. We learned a harvest dance, for there are many, but the movements of this celebratory ritual were lyrical and delicate, far from the tortured recounts of EuroAmericans to our "jigaboo" gatherings; no gyrations, repetitive shuffling that held no interest. Indeed, the simple movement of the arms, which we worked on for days until we got it, resembled a tropical port-à-bras worthy of any ballerina. Our hip movements, ever so subtle, with four switches to the left, then four to the right, all the while turning and covering space. The head leaning in the direction of the hips, the arms moving against it, till the next hip demanded counterpoint.

A healthy respect for the land, for what we produce for the blessing of a harvest begot dances of communal joy. On New Year's Eve in the late fifties, we danced the Madison; today it's a burning rendition of "The Electric Slide." Eighty-years-olds jammin' with toddlers after the weddin' toast. No, we haven't changed so much.

Content

1. What's the point of Shange's title? What *is* it "we really harvestin'"?
2. Shange gives directions on how to grow, prepare, and eat several foods—sweet potatoes, mustard greens, watermelon—and how to cook "Mama's Rice." Like many other directions written by experts, these seem easy to follow and the results seem assured. Why are most directions written so simply and positively?
3. "What Is It We Really Harvestin' Here?" was published in *Creative Nonfiction,* a publication usually read by creative writers, not in a home or cooking magazine. Why might this piece appeal to readers who are writers? Or to any readers who don't garden? Or cook? Or eat much "'colored' cusine"?

Strategies/Structures

4. Shange's planting instructions are presented in a matrix of African-American political and social history (¶s 1–4), family history (¶s 16–17), and autobiography (¶s 20–22). How do these elements make the reading different from the usual instructions on how to perform a process, such as following a recipe or planting a garden?

Language

5. Whom does Shange include in *we?* Is the *we* of the title and "We got a sayin'" (¶ 1, sentence 1), the same as the *we* of "*we* as a people" (¶ 1, sentence 2)? The same as the *we* of "And so we are performers in the fields" (¶ 3, sentence 2)? Why does it matter, to writer and readers, who *we* are?
6. In this essay that is largely written in standard English, what are the effects of using dialect spelling (as in *chirren* [¶ 7]), or omitting the -*g* at the end of *ing* words, as in *puttin'* (¶ 1)? Why does Shange quote entire sentences in dialect: "Wen we hab a dance . . ." (¶ 3)?
7. Why does Shange use dialect much more extensively in the first four paragraphs of the essay than later on? What happens when she inserts a conversational spelling into an otherwise fairly formal sentence: "Yet my mother was raising a sixth generation of Carolinians, which meant we had to eat some kinda rice? (¶ 17, sentence 3)?
8. How does Shange's style suit her subject?

For Writing

9. If you're a competent cook, write out a favorite recipe so others less experienced than you can prepare it. Identify unusual ingredients, the major steps to follow, and also any subprocesses that need to be done to prepare the dish. Have someone read (better yet, try out) your recipe. What questions do they ask? Incorporate the information from your answers into the recipe as you revise it.

10. Explain how to do or make something that's integral to your culture or subculture (such as how to interpret or perform a particular religious ritual, celebrate a particular holiday, do a particular dance step, play a particular game, perform a specific athletic activity, engage in a flirtation or courtship). Embed your instructions, as Shange does, in a matrix of cultural, family, or personal history—tell some true stories to provide a context for the instructions that will help to explain why certain things are done in a certain way, as well as how.

CRAIG SWANSON

Swanson says of his life, "I was born in Ridgewood, New Jersey, in the year 1961. Not since 1881 has there been a year that can be read the same upside-down as right side up. And there won't be another until 6009. I grew up in the rural town of Hopewell, New Jersey, strikingly similar to the Lionel Train town, Plasticville. I studied at Rutgers and Syracuse universities before completing my bachelor's of mathematics/computer science at Virginia Commonwealth University in 1984. If I could write all day long"—he wrote the following essays as an undergraduate—"I'd be a very happy man. But alas, one cannot write all day, presuming he has financial obligations," so Swanson returned to Virginia Commonwealth University for graduate work in artificial intelligence. Both of the following essays, one serious, one satiric, devote most of their space to explaining processes, though in each the discussion of the process itself is the means to a different end.

Ostensibly, "The Turning Point" is an essay about making a pot; indeed, directions for the process occupy two-thirds of the text. With the addition of a few more specific details, such as what was used for the slip (¶ 6), and what the "finishing touches" were (¶ 8), the process is fairly complete. But the essay is about much more than potting. Sometimes writers describe a process in great detail as a way of focusing on the person performing it or on the people affected by either the process or the performance. Here, the activity of making the pot is the catalyst that draws the son and his father together. The first two paragraphs place the father's potting in its painful context; the potter's wheel is the consolation for the loss of his job, and he can engage in the potting itself because he has no formal claim on his time. Through Swanson's appreciation of his father's skill as a potter we recognize his respect, love, and concern for the man who performs this process so well. And so we come to appreciate the pain and the pleasure, as well as the process, in this essay with the wonderfully ambiguous title.

❄ *The Turning Point*

1   Dad lost his job last summer. They say that it was due to political reasons. After twenty years in the government it was a shock to us all. Dad never talked much about what he did at work, although it took up enough of his time. All I really know was his position: Deputy Assistant Commissioner of the State Department of Education. I was impressed by his title, though he rarely seemed to enjoy himself. Just the same, it was a job. These days it's hard enough to support a family without being out of work.

2   Apparently his co-workers felt so badly about the situation that they held a large testimonial dinner in his honor. People came from all over the east coast. I wish I could have gone. Everyone who went said it was really nice. It's a good feeling to know that your Dad means a lot to so many people. As a farewell present they gave Dad a potter's wheel. Dad says it's the best wheel he's ever seen, and to come from someone who's done pottery for as long as he has, that's saying a lot. Over the years Dad used to borrow potter's wheels from friends. That's when I learned how to "throw" a pot.

3   When I came home for Thanksgiving vacation the first thing I did was rush down to the basement to check it out. I was quite surprised. Dad had fixed the whole corner of the basement with a big table top for playing with the clay; an area set up for preparing the clay, including a plaster bat and a wedging board; the kiln

Walt built for Dad one Christmas; one hundred and fifty pounds of clay; nine different glazes; hand tools for sculpting, and the brand new potter's wheel. It had a tractor seat from which you work the clay. It could be turned manually or by motor, and it offered lots of surface area, which always comes in handy. Dad was right, it was beautiful. He had already made a couple dozen pots. I couldn't wait to try it.

The next day I came down into the basement to find Dad in his old gray smock preparing the clay. I love to watch Dad do art, whether it's drawing, painting, lettering, or pottery. I stood next to him as he wedged a ball of clay the size of a small canteloupe. He'd slice it in half on the wire and slam one half onto the wedging board, a canvas-covered slab of plaster; then he'd slam the other half on top of the first. He did this to get all the air bubbles out of the clay. You put a pot with air bubbles in the kiln, the pot'll explode in the heat and you've got yourself one heck of a mess to clean up. Dad wedged the clay, over and over. 4

When he was finished he sat down, wet the wheelhead, and pressed the clay right in the center of the wheel. Dad hit the accelerator and the clay started turning. He wet his hands and leaned over the clay. Bracing his elbows on his knees he began centering the clay. Steady right hand on the sides of the clay. Steady left hand pushing down on the clay. Centering the clay is the toughest part for me. The clay spins around and around and you have to shape it into a perfectly symmetric form in the center by letting the wheel do all the moving. Your hands stay motionless until the clay is centered. It takes me ten or fifteen minutes to do this. It takes Dad two. I shake my head and smile in amazement. 5

Dad's hands cup the clay, thumbs together on top. He wets his hands again and pushes down with his thumbs. Slowly, steadily. Once he's as far down as he wants to go he makes the bottom of the pot by spreading his thumbs. His hands relax and he pulls them out of the pot. Every motion is deliberate. If you move your hands quickly or carelessly you can be sure you will have to start again. Dad wipes the slip, very watery clay, off his hands with a sponge. It is extremely messy. 6

To make the walls Dad hooks his thumbs and curls all of his fingers except for his index fingers. Holding them like forceps, he reaches into the pot to mold the walls to just the right thickness. 7

He starts at the bottom and brings them up slowly, making the walls of the pot thin and even all the way up, about twelve inches.

8   Dad sponges off his hands, wets them, and then cups his hands around the belly of the pot. Slowly, as the pot spins around, he squeezes his hands together, causing it to bevel slightly. Dad spends five minutes on the finishing touches. He's got himself a real nice skill.

9   It is a rare treat to watch Dad do something that he enjoys so much.

Content

1. What are the meanings of the title, "The Turning Point"? How do they reinforce one another? What is the essay's main subject? Its secondary subject?

2. What other information would Swanson need to provide to complete his explanation of the process of making a pot? Given the essay's main subject, does it matter whether he explains the process of making a pot as fully as he could?

Strategies/Structures

3. In what ways does Swanson convey his attitude toward his father? Why doesn't he just come right out and say directly that he loves him and feels sorry for him?

4. How does Swanson's attitude toward his father function as a catalyst to integrate the main and secondary subjects?

Language

5. What is the tone of this essay? Why has Swanson chosen understatement rather than a more emotional means to make his point?

For Writing

6. Explain how to make or do something for an audience unfamiliar with the process. This may be the primary focus of your paper or, as in "The Turning Point," an explanation of the process may be subordinate to your discussion of something else—a relationship between the performer of the process and another person (as in Swanson and his father), or a group of people (see Zitkala-Sa, 273–83) or animals (see Hearne, 560–72).

In the following essay Swanson presents himself as a character addicted to the very process he criticizes, as we realize from the opening salvo with its implicit comparison of the video parlor to a men's room. Although his intellectual focus is on the process whereby video games extract money from the hapless player "as long as his twenty-five cent pieces last," Swanson's emotional focus is on the mindless possibility of winning: "bonus gobblers, shooters, racers, fighters. . . ."

❄ It's the Only Video Game My Mom Lets Me Chew[1]

E ven before I walk into the room I feel the electronic presence   1
sink to my bones. The beeps, twoozers, fanfares, and fugues of the video games compete for dominance. As I enter the game room I notice how much the machines look like urinals. People fill the room, each playing "their" game.

My game is Tron. It is the only video game that is also a   2
movie. I do expect, however, to someday see a series of Pacman films—"The Return of the Son of Pacman," Part II. Although I play Tron often, I have never seen the movie. I just don't have the money. I place my two hundredth quarter on the control panel to reserve the next game.

Before it's my turn I have some time to watch the other   3
people within the parlor. All video players develop their own ways of playing the games. Inexperienced players handle the controls spasmodically and nervously. To make up for their slow reaction time they slam the joystick much harder than necessary, under the assumption that if they can't beat the machine through skill, then they'll win out of brute strength. This often includes kicking the coin return or beating upon the screen. Of course this is exactly what the machine wants. The sarcastic whines or droning catcalls that accompany the flashing "game over" sign are designed to

---

[1] The title is a takeoff on a sugarless gum commercial.

antagonize the player. The angrier you get when you play these games, the worse you play. The worse you play the more games you play. Determined to get even, you pop quarter after quarter into the gaping coin slot.

4   A more experienced video player rarely shows emotion. A casual stance, a plop of the coin, a flip of an eyebrow, and he's ready. If he happens to win bonus gobblers, shooters, racers, fighters, markers, flippers, diggers, jugglers, rollers, or air ships, he does not carry on with a high-pitched, glass-shattering scream. When he loses a man, he doesn't get worked up or display fits of violence. He simply stares mindlessly into the video screen as long as his twenty-five-cent pieces last.

5   In goes my quarter. The machine sings out its familiar song of thanks, remarkably similar to Bach's Toccata in D-Minor. I am then attacked by spider-like "grid-bugs," an army of tanks, zooming "light cycles," and descending blocks that disintegrate me into a rainbow of dust particles. When my last player is played, Tron tells me the game is over by casting out the celebrated raspberry, then slowly droning out "Taps."

6   I walk out relieved. My pockets are quarterless. My vision is distorted and I am devoid of all intelligent thought. I step out, ready to avoid reality for another day.

Content

1. Is Swanson writing this to criticize video parlors? To criticize himself for his addiction to Tron? To help himself overcome his addiction? To caution others? To entertain his readers? Or some combination of these?

2. Is there a danger that explaining a process, even if one despises or has problems with it, will teach readers how to perform an offensive or problematic action? Explain your answer.

Strategies/Structures

3. What does the title signal to readers about the subject? About the way Swanson will treat the subject?

4. What kind of character is Swanson in this narrative? How do you know that Swanson as an author is exaggerating this character? Is he really "devoid of all intelligent thought"?

Language

5. In what respects is the narrator's language—precise, varied, and vivid throughout—at variance with video-game jargon? How does this discrepancy add to the humor and convince us of the narrator's analytic ability (see ¶ 3, for instance)?

For Writing

6. Write a parody of a process that others use straightforwardly, as a way to warn them against a mindless or self-destructive practice.

7. The technique of self-satire enables many writers to criticize potentially sensitive subjects; if they show themselves to be personally affected by the problem, their critique may seem more valid. Write a paper in which you satirize yourself in the process of providing a critique of some social, political, educational, or other phenomenon. It doesn't matter whether your intended audience knows you, but if they are unfamiliar with the object of your satire you'll need to provide enough information to make your essay self-contained.

Additional Topics for Writing Process Analysis

(For strategies for writing process analysis, see 207)

1. Write an essay in which you provide directions on how to perform a process—how to do or make something at which you are particularly skilled. In addition to the essential steps, you may wish to explain your own special technique or strategy that makes your method unique or better. Some possible subjects (which may be narrowed or adapted as you and your instructor wish) are these:

    a. How to get a good job, permanent or summer
    b. How to reduce stress
    c. How to scuba dive, hang-glide, rappel, jog, lift weights, train for a marathon or triathlon
    d. How to make a good first impression (on a prospective employer, on a date, on your date's parents)
    e. How to study for a test
    f. How to be happy
    g. How to build a library of books, tapes, videocassettes, or CDs
    h. How to lose (or gain) weight
    i. How to shop at a garage sale or secondhand store
    j. How to repair your own car, bicycle, or other machine
    k. How to live cheaply (but enjoyably)
    l. How to rope a calf, drive a tractor, ride a horse
    m. How to administer first aid for choking, drowning, burns, or some other medical emergency
    n. How to get rich
    o. Anything else you know that others might want to learn

2. Write an informative essay in which you explain how one of the following occurs or works. Although you should pick a subject you know something about, you may need to supplement your information by consulting outside sources.

    a. How I made a major decision (to be—or not to be—a member of a particular profession, to practice a particular religion or lifestyle...)
    b. How a computer (or amplifier, piano, microwave oven, or other machine) works
    c. How a solar (or other) heating system works
    d. How a professional develops skill in his or her chosen field; i.e., how one becomes a skilled electrical engineer, geologist, chef, tennis coach, surgeon . . . ; pick a field in which you're interested

  e. How birds fly (or learn to fly), or some other process in the nat-
      ural world
  f. How a system of the body (circulatory, digestive, respiratory,
      skeletal, neurological) works
  g. How the earth (or the solar system) was formed
  h. How the scientific method (or a particular variation of it) functions
  i. How a well-run business (pick one of your choice—manufac-
      turing, restaurant, clothing or hardware store, television repair
      service . . .) functions
  j   How advertisers appeal to prospective customers
  k. How our federal government (or your particular local or state
      government) came into existence, or has changed over time
  l. How a particular drug or other medicine was developed
  m. How a great idea (on the nature of love, justice, truth, beauty . . .)
      found acceptance
  n. How a particular culture (ethnic, regional, tribal, religious) or
      subculture (preppies, yuppies, pacifists, punk rockers, motor-
      cycle gangs . . .) developed

3. Write a humorous paper explaining a process of the kind identified
below. You will need to provide a serious analysis of the method you
propose, even though the subject itself is intended to be amusing.

  a. How to get good grades without actually studying
  b. How to be popular
  c. How to survive in college
  d. How to withstand an unhappy love affair
  e. How to be a model babysitter/son/daughter/student/
      employee/lover/spouse/parent
  f. How to become a celebrity
  g. Any of the topics in Writing Suggestions 1 or 2 above

4. Write a seemingly objective account of a social phenomenon or some
other aspect of human behavior of which you actually disapprove, either
because the form and context seem at variance (see Joan Didion's interpretation of Las Vegas weddings, [330–35]), or because the phenomenon
itself seems to you wrong, or to cause problems, or otherwise inappropriate. Justify your opinion (and convince your readers) through your
choice of details and selection of a revealing incident or several vignettes
(brief glimpses of scenes or actions, such as Swanson provides in "It's the
Only Video Game . . ." [253–55]). Social and cultural phenomena are particularly suitable subjects for such an essay—nerd or geek or yuppie or
twentysomething behavior, ways of spending money and leisure time
(and foolish, trivial, or wasteful things to spend it on).

7 | *Cause and Effect*

Writers concerned with cause and effect relationships ask, "*Why* did something happen?" or "*What* are its consequences?" or both. Why did the United States develop as a democracy rather than as some other form of government? What have the effects of this form of government been on its population? Or you, as a writer may choose to examine a chain reaction in which, like a Rube Goldberg cartoon device, Cause *A* produces Effect *B* which in turn causes *C* which produces Effect *D*: Peer pressure (Cause *A*) causes young men to drink to excess (Effect *B*), which causes them to drive unsafely (Cause *C*, a corollary of Effect *B*) and results in high accident rates in unmarried males under twenty-five (Effect *D*).

Although process analysis also deals with events or phenomena in sequence, it's concerned with the *how* rather than the *why*. To focus on the process of drinking and driving would be to explain, as an accident report might, how Al C. O'Hall became intoxicated (he drank seventeen beers and a bourbon chaser in two hours at the Dun Inn); how he then roared off at 120 miles an hour, lost control of his lightweight sports car on a curve, and plowed into an oncoming sedan.

Two conditions have to be met to prove a given cause:

B cannot occur without *A*.
Whenever *A* occurs, *B* must also occur.

Thus a biologist who observed, repeatedly, that photosynthesis (*B*) occurred in green plants whenever a light source (*A*) was present, and that it only occurred under this condition could infer that light causes photosynthesis. This would be the immediate cause. The more *remote* or *ultimate cause* might be the source of the light if it were natural (the sun). Artificial light (electricity) would have a yet more remote cause, such as water or nuclear power.

But don't be misled by a coincidental time sequence. Just because *A* preceded *B* in time doesn't necessarily mean that *A* caused *B*. Although it may appear to rain every time you wash your car, the car wash doesn't cause the rain. To blame the car wash would be an example of the *post hoc, ergo propter hoc* fallacy (Latin for "after this, therefore because of this").

Indeed, in cause and effect papers ultimate causes may be of greater significance than immediate ones, especially when you're considering social, political, or psychological causes rather than exclusively physical phenomena. Looking for possible causes from multiple perspectives is a good way to develop ideas to write about. It's also a sure way to avoid oversimplification, attributing a single cause to an effect that results from several. Thus if you wanted to probe the causes of Al C. O'Hall's excessive drinking, looking at the phenomenon from the following perspectives would give you considerable breadth for discussion.

Perspective	*Reason (Attributed cause)*
Al, a twenty-one-year-old unmarried male:	"Because I like the taste."
Al's best friend:	"Because he thinks drinking is cool."
Al's mother:	"Because Al wants to defy me."
Al's father:	"Because Al wants to be my pal."
Physician:	"Because Al is addicted to alcohol. There's a strong probability that this is hereditary."
Sociologist:	"Because 79.2 percent of American males twenty-one and under drink at least once a week. It's a social trend encouraged by peer pressure."
Criminologist:	"Because Al derives antisocial pleasure from breaking the law."
Brewer or distiller:	"Because of my heavy advertising campaign."

All of these explanations may be partly right; none—not even the genetic explanation—is in itself sufficient. (Even if Al were genetically predisposed to alcoholism as the child of an alcoholic parent, he'd have to drink to become an alcoholic.) Taken together they, and perhaps still other explanations, can be considered the complex cause of Al's behavior. To write a paper on the subject, using Al as a case in point, you might decide to discuss all the causes. Or you might concentrate on the most important causes and weed out those that seem irrelevant or less significant. Or, to handle a large, complex subject in a short paper you could limit your discussion to a particular cause or type of causes, say, the social or the psychological. You have the same options for selectivity in discussing multiple effects.

The essays that follow treat cause and effect in a variety of ways. Because causes and effects are invariably intertwined, writers usually acknowledge the causes even when they're emphasizing the effects, and vice versa.

Four of the five essays in this section deal with the causes and effects of education, formal and informal, on the students involved; and with the consequences of that education—or lack of it—not only to the individual but to society. In "I Just Wanna Be Average" (263–73), Mike Rose reflects on the social, cultural, psychological, and educational causes that singly but more likely in combination would make a student decide he just wanted to be average, rather than to be the high achiever that middle-class society assumes and expects its children to be. "If you're a working-class kid in the vocational track," says Rose, your options are constrained: "You're defined by your school as 'slow'" and treated as slow by teachers and other students; "you're placed in a curriculum that isn't designed to liberate you but to occupy you" or to train you for work "society does not esteem" (269). All these factors have to change for students to be able to change their mind, self-image, and aspirations. Zitkala-Sa's excerpts from *The School Days of an Indian Girl* (273–83) illustrate other constraints that are placed on Native American children uprooted from their homes and sent far away to boarding schools run by whites. Whether the efforts to acclimate these children to white middle-class culture (symbolized by cutting off their braids, making them wear Anglo clothing, and obliging them to speak English rather than their tribal languages) were made from benign or more sinister motives, the effects were the same: alienation from and marginalization in both cultures. In re-creating the child's point of view, intended to represent all children in such schools, the author does not offer solutions, though she implies them.

Jonathan Kozol's "The Human Cost of an Illiterate Society" (283–94) focuses on the enormous social costs—effects—of illiteracy on the 16 million Americans who cannot read or do math well enough to read or interpret prescriptions, insurance policies, medical warnings, bank regulations, telephone books, cookbooks, and a host of other printed materials that provide directions and information for everyday living. Illiteracy causes people to involuntarily relinquish their freedom of choice, their independence, their self-respect, their citizenship. The costs, in human, ethical, social, economic, and political terms, are enormous. In "Framing My Father" (301–08), Leslie Moore offers a portrait of a complex man, "who has made a name for himself as a son-of-a-bitch." His uncompromising perfectionism as a teacher of his young daughter produces contradictory effects—anger, exhaustion, resistance— and in the process, a high level of learning and respect.

In "A Nation of Welfare Families" (294–301), Stephanie Coontz argues that for two centuries Americans have confused effect with cause, and altogether denied the cause of the country's success. The American myth, that "dependence reflects some kind of individual or family failure, and that the ideal family is the self-reliant unit of traditional lore" is contradicted by the facts. The reality is that government policies help everybody (the rich far more than the poor) through the "abolition of child labor," putting governmental "pressure on industrialists to negotiate with unions, federal arbitration, expansion of compulsory schooling," federal subsidies of home mortgages, settlement lands, and highways. The *effect*, a seemingly self-reliant, independent citizenry, should appropriately be attributed to its *cause*, the variety of federal government policies in the nineteenth and twentieth centuries that have supported the "the well-being of its citizens."

A paper of cause and effect analysis requires you, as a thoughtful and careful writer, to know your subject well enough to avoid oversimplification and to shore up your analysis with specific, convincing details. You won't be expected to explain all the causes or effects of a particular phenomenon; that might be impossible for most humans, even the experts. But you can do a sufficiently thorough job with your chosen segment of the subject to satisfy yourself and help your readers to see it your way. Maybe they'll even come to agree with your interpretation. Why? Because. . . .

STRATEGIES FOR WRITING—
CAUSE AND EFFECT

1. What is the purpose of my cause and effect paper? Will I be focusing on the cause(s) of something, or its effect(s), short- or long-term? Will I be using cause and effect to explain a process? Analyze a situation? Present a prediction or an argument?
2. How much does my audience know about my subject? Will I have to explain some portions of the cause and effect relationship in more detail than others to compensate for their lack of knowledge? Or do they have sufficient background so I can focus primarily on new information or interpretations?
3. Is the cause and effect relationship I'm writing about valid? Or might there be other possible causes (or effects) that I'm overlooking? If I'm emphasizing causes, how far back do I want to go? If I'm focusing on effects, how many do I wish to discuss, and with how many examples?
4. Will I be using narration, description, definition, process analysis, argument, or other strategies in my explanation or analysis of cause(s) and effect(s)?
5. How technical or nontechnical will my language be? Will I need to qualify any of my claims or conclusions with "probably," or "in most cases," or other admissions that what I'm saying is not absolutely certain? What will my tone be—explanatory, persuasive, argumentative, humorous?

MIKE ROSE

In the award-winning *Lives on the Boundary* (1989), Mike Rose (born, 1944) explains his firsthand understanding of the book's subtitle, *The Struggles and Achievements of America's Underprepared.* Its sequel *Possible Lives* (1995) focuses on, as the subtitle indicates, *The Promise of Public Education in America.* He was reared in the 1950s in Los Angeles in a poor neighborhood. Rose remembers his early years, when his father was ill and disabled and his mother worked as a waitress, as "a peculiar mix of physical warmth and barrenness"—"quiet, lazy, lonely." Only reading "opened up the world." For two years Rose was mistakenly placed in the bottom level vocational track, amidst classmates who could claim, with sincere indifference, "I just wanna be average." The vocational curriculum, "a dumping ground for the disaffected," was designed not to liberate the students but to occupy their time. As "I Just Wanna Be Average" makes clear, Rose and his peers reacted defensively, using their collective indifference as a defense against learning.

It took a tough, demanding, caring teacher to crack this armor of ignorance. Prodded by his sophomore biology teacher, who recognized his intellectual potential, Rose switched from the vocational to the college prep track, graduated in 1966 from Loyola University (Los Angeles), and earned a Ph.D. in education (1981) from UCLA. Rose, now a professor, has remained at UCLA ever since, directing the UCLA Writing Programs. At UCLA he tutored veterans and Chicano, Asian, and African-American students, which provided firsthand research for *Lives on the Boundary.* This excerpt is taken from Chapter 2, "I Just Wanna Be Average."

"I Just Wanna Be Average"

M y rhapsodic and prescientific astronomy carried me into my teens, consumed me right up till high school, losing out finally, and only, to the siren call of pubescence—that endocrine hoodoo that transmogrifies nice boys into gawky flesh fiends. My mother used to bring home *Confidential* magazine, a peep-show

rag specializing in the sins of the stars, and it beckoned me
mercilessly: Jayne Mansfield's cleavage, Gina Lollobrigida's eyes,
innuendos about deviant sexuality, ads for Frederick's of Hollywood—spiked heels, lacy brassieres, the epiphany of silk panties
on a mannequin's hips. Along with Phil Everly, I was through
with counting the stars above.

2   Budding manhood. Only adults talk about adolescence budding. Kids have no choice but to talk in extremes; they're being
wrenched and buffeted, rabbit-punched from inside by systemic
thugs. Nothing sweet and pastoral here. Kids become ridiculous
and touching at one and the same time: passionate about the
trivial, fixed before the mirror, yet traversing one of the most important rites of passage in their lives—liminal people, silly and
profoundly human. Given my own expertise, I fantasized about
concocting the fail-safe aphrodisiac that would bring Marianne
Bilpusch, the cloakroom monitor, rushing into my arms or about
commanding a squadron of bosomy, linguistically mysterious
astronauts like Zsa Zsa Gabor. My parents used to say that their
son would have the best education they could afford. Maybe I
would be a doctor. There was a public school in our neighborhood and several Catholic schools to the west. They had heard
that quality schooling meant private, Catholic schooling, so they
somehow got the money together to send me to Our Lady of
Mercy, fifteen or so miles southwest of Ninety-first and Vermont.
So much for my fantasies. Most Catholic secondary schools then
were separated by gender.

3   It took two buses to get to Our Lady of Mercy. The first
started deep in South Los Angeles and caught me at midpoint. The
second drifted through neighborhoods with trees, parks, big
lawns, and lots of flowers. The rides were long but were livened
up by a group of South L.A. veterans whose parents also thought
that Hope had set up shop in the west end of the county. There was
Christy Biggars, who, at sixteen, was dealing and was, according to
rumor, a pimp as well. There were Bill Cobb and Johnny Gonzales,
grease-pencil artists extraordinaire, who left Nembutal-enhanced
swirls of "Cobb" and "Johnny" on the corrugated walls of the bus.
And then there was Tyrrell Wilson. Tyrrell was the coolest kid I
knew. He ran the dozens like a metric halfback, laid down a rap
that outrhymed and outpointed Cobb, whose rap was good but

not great—the curse of a moderately soulful kid trapped in white skin. But it was Cobb who would sneak a radio onto the bus, and thus underwrote his patter with Little Richard, Fats Domino, Chuck Berry, the Coasters, and Ernie K. Doe's mother-in-law, an awful woman who was "sent from down below." And so it was that Christy and Cobb and Johnny G. and Tyrrell and I and assorted others picked up along the way passed our days in the back of the bus, a funny mix brought together by geography and parental desire.

Entrance to school brings with it forms and releases and   4 assessments. Mercy relied on a series of tests, mostly the Stanford-Binet, for placement, and somehow the results of my tests got confused with those of another student named Rose. The other Rose apparently didn't do very well, for I was placed in the vocational track, a euphemism for the bottom level. Neither I nor my parents realized what this meant. We had no sense that Business Math, Typing, and English-Level D were dead ends. The current spate of reports on the schools criticizes parents for not involving themselves in the education of their children. But how would someone like Tommy Rose, with his two years of Italian schooling, know what to ask? And what sort of pressure could an exhausted waitress apply? The error went undetected, and I remained in the vocational track for two years. What a place.

My homeroom was supervised by Brother Dill, a troubled   5 and unstable man who also taught freshman English. When his class drifted away from him, which was often, his voice would rise in paranoid accusations, and occasionally he would lose control and shake or smack us. I hadn't been there two months when one of his brisk, face-turning slaps had my glasses sliding down the aisle. Physical education was also pretty harsh. Our teacher was a stubby ex-lineman who had played old-time pro ball in the Midwest. He routinely had us grabbing our ankles to receive his stinging paddle across our butts. He did that, he said, to make men of us. "Rose," he bellowed on our first encounter; me standing geeky in line in my baggy shorts. "'Rose'? What the hell kind of name is that?"

"Italian, sir," I squeaked.   6

"Italian! Ho. Rose, do you know the sound a bag of shit   7 makes when it hits the wall?"

8   "No, sir."

9   "Wop!"

10   Sophomore English was taught by Mr. Mitropetros. He was a large, bejeweled man who managed the parking lot at the Shrine Auditorium. He would crow and preen and list for us the stars he'd brushed against. We'd ask questions and glance knowingly and snicker, and all that fueled the poor guy to brag some more. Parking cars was his night job. He had little training in English, so his lesson plan for his day work had us reading the district's required text, *Julius Caesar,* aloud for the semester. We'd finish the play way before the twenty weeks was up, so he'd have us switch parts again and again and start again: David Snyder, the fastest guy at Mercy, muscling through Caesar to the breathless squeals of Calpurnia, as interpreted by Steve Fusco, a surfer who owned the school's most envied paneled wagon. Week ten and Dave and Steve would take on new roles, as would we all, and render a water-logged Cassius and a Brutus that are beyond my powers of description.

11   Spanish I—taken in the second year—fell into the hands of a new recruit. Mr. Montez was a tiny man, slight, five foot six at the most, soft-spoken and delicate. Spanish was a particularly rowdy class, and Mr. Montez was as prepared for it as a doily maker at a hammer throw. He would tap his pencil to a room in which Steve Fusco was propelling spitballs from his heavy lips, in which Mike Dweetz was taunting Billy Hawk, a half-Indian, half-Spanish, reed-thin, quietly explosive boy. The vocational track at Our Lady of Mercy mixed kids traveling in from South L.A. with South Bay surfers and a few Slavs and Chicanos from the harbors of San Pedro. This was a dangerous miscellany: surfers and hodads and South-Central blacks all ablaze to the metronomic tapping of Hector Montez's pencil.

12   One day Billy lost it. Out of the corner of my eye I saw him strike out with his right arm and catch Dweetz across the neck. Quick as a spasm, Dweetz was out of his seat, scattering desks, cracking Billy on the side of the head, right behind the eye. Snyder and Fusco and others broke it up, but the room felt hot and close and naked. Mr. Montez's tenuous authority was finally ripped to shreds, and I think everyone felt a little strange about that. The charade was over, and when it came down to it, I don't

think any of the kids really wanted it to end this way. They had pushed and pushed and bullied their way into a freedom that both scared and embarrassed them.

Students will float to the mark you set. I and the others in the vo- 13 cational classes were bobbing in pretty shallow water. Vocational education has aimed at increasing the economic opportunities of students who do not do well in our schools. Some serious programs succeed in doing that, and through exceptional teachers— like Mr. Gross in *Horace's Compromise*—students learn to develop hypotheses and troubleshoot, reason through a problem, and communicate effectively—the true job skills. The vocational track, however, is most often a place for those who are just not making it, a dumping ground for the disaffected. There were a few teachers who worked hard at education; young Brother Slattery, for example, combined a stern voice with weekly quizzes to try to pass along to us a skeletal outline of world history. But mostly the teachers had no idea of how to engage the imaginations of us kids who were scuttling along at the bottom of the pond.

And the teachers would have needed some inventiveness, 14 for none of us was groomed for the classroom. It wasn't just that I didn't know things—didn't know how to simplify algebraic fractions, couldn't identify different kinds of clauses, bungled Spanish translations—but that I had developed various faulty and inadequate ways of doing algebra and making sense of Spanish. Worse yet, the years of defensive tuning out in elementary school had given me a way to escape quickly while seeming at least half alert. During my time in Voc. Ed., I developed further into a mediocre student and a somnambulant problem solver, and that affected the subjects I did have the wherewithal to handle: I detested Shakespeare; I got bored with history. My attention flitted here and there. I fooled around in class and read my books indifferently—the intellectual equivalent of playing with your food. I did what I had to do to get by, and I did it with half a mind.

But I did learn things about people and eventually came into 15 my own socially. I liked the guys in Voc. Ed. Growing up where I did, I understood and admired physical prowess, and there was an abundance of muscle here. There was Dave Snyder, a sprinter and halfback of true quality. Dave's ability and his quick wit gave him a natural appeal, and he was welcome in any clique, though he always kept a little independent. He enjoyed acting the fool and could care less about studies, but he possessed a certain maturity and never caused the faculty much trouble. It was a testament to this independence that he included me among his friends—I eventually went out for track, but I was no jock. Owing to the Latin alphabet and a dearth of *R*s and *S*s, Snyder sat behind Rose, and we started exchanging one-liners and became friends.

16   There was Ted Richard, a much-touted Little League pitcher. He was chunky and had a baby face and came to Our Lady of Mercy as a seasoned street fighter. Ted was quick to laugh and he had a loud, jolly laugh, but when he got angry he'd smile a little smile, the kind that simply raises the corner of the mouth a quarter of an inch. For those who knew, it was an eerie signal. Those who didn't found themselves in big trouble, for Ted was very quick. He loved to carry on what we would come to call philosophical discussions: What is courage? Does God exist? He also loved words, enjoyed picking up big ones like *salubrious* and *equivocal* and using them in our conversations—laughing at himself as the word hit a chuckhole rolling off his tongue. Ted didn't do all that well in school—baseball and parties and testing the courage he'd speculated about took up his time. His textbooks were *Argosy* and *Field and Stream,* whatever newspapers he'd find on the bus stop—from the *Daily Worker* to pornography—conversations with uncles or hobos or businessmen he'd meet in a coffee shop, *The Old Man and the Sea.* With hindsight, I can see that Ted was developing into one of those rough-hewn intellectuals whose sources are a mix of the learned and the apocryphal, whose discussions are both assured and sad.

17   And then there was Ken Harvey. Ken was good-looking in a puffy way and had a full and oily ducktail and was a car enthusiast . . . a hodad. One day in religion class, he said the sentence that turned out to be one of the most memorable of the hundreds of thousands I heard in those Voc. Ed. years. We were talking about the parable of the talents, about achievement, working hard, doing the best you can do, blah-blah-blah, when the teacher called on the restive Ken Harvey for an opinion. Ken thought about it, but just for a second, and said (with studied, minimal affect), "I just wanna be average." That woke me up. Average?! Who wants to

be average? Then the athletes chimed in with clichés that make you want to laryngectomize them, and the exchange became a platitudinous melee. At the time, I thought Ken's assertion was stupid, and I wrote him off. But his sentence has stayed with me all these years, and I think I am finally coming to understand it.

Ken Harvey was gasping for air. School can be a tremendously disorienting place. No matter how bad the school, you're going to encounter notions that don't fit with the assumptions and beliefs that you grew up with—maybe you'll hear these dissonant notions from teachers, maybe from the other students, and maybe you'll read them. You'll also be thrown in with all kinds of kids from all kinds of backgrounds, and that can be unsettling—this is especially true in places of rich ethnic and linguistic mix, like the L.A. basin. You'll see a handful of students far excel you in courses that sound exotic and that are only in the curriculum of the elite: French, physics, trigonometry. And all this is happening while you're trying to shape an identity, your body is changing, and your emotions are running wild. If you're a working-class kid in the vocational track, the options you'll have to deal with this will be constrained in certain ways: You're defined by your school as "slow"; you're placed in a curriculum that isn't designed to liberate you but to occupy you, or, if you're lucky, train you, though the training is for work the society does not esteem; other students are picking up the cues from your school and your curriculum and interacting with you in particular ways. If you're a kid like Ted Richard, you turn your back on all this and let your mind roam where it may. But youngsters like Ted are rare. What Ken and so many others do is protect themselves from such suffocating madness by taking on with a vengeance the identity implied in the vocational track. Reject the confusion and frustration by openly defining yourself as the Common Joe. Champion the average. Rely on your own good sense. Fuck this bullshit. Bullshit, of course, is everything you—and the others—fear is beyond you: books, essays, tests, academic scrambling, complexity, scientific reasoning, philosophical inquiry. 18

The tragedy is that you have to twist the knife in your own gray matter to make this defense work. You'll have to shut down, have to reject intellectual stimuli or diffuse them with sarcasm, have to cultivate stupidity, have to convert boredom from a malady 19 into a way of confronting the world. Keep your vocabulary simple, act stoned when you're not or act more stoned than you are, flaunt ignorance, materialize your dreams. It is a powerful and effective defense—it neutralizes the insult and the frustration of being a vocational kid and, when perfected, it drives teachers up the wall, a delightful secondary effect. But like all strong magic, it exacts a price.

20   My own deliverance from the Voc. Ed. world began with sophomore biology. Every student, college prep to vocational, had to take biology, and unlike the other courses, the same person taught all sections. When teaching the vocational group, Brother Clint probably slowed down a bit or omitted a little of the fundamental biochemistry, but he used the same book and more or less the same syllabus across the board. If one class got tough, he could get tougher. He was young and powerful and very handsome, and looks and physical strength were high currency. No one gave him any trouble.

21   I was pretty bad at the dissecting table, but the lectures and the textbook were interesting: plastic overlays that, with each turned page, peeled away skin, then veins and muscle, then organs, down to the very bones that Brother Clint, pointer in hand, would tap out on our hanging skeleton. Dave Snyder was in big trouble, for the study of life—versus the living of it—was sticking in his craw. We worked out a code for our multiple-choice exams. He'd poke me in the back: once for the answer under *A*, twice for *B*, and so on; and when he'd hit the right one, I'd look up to the ceiling as though I were lost in thought. Poke: cytoplasm. Poke, poke: methane. Poke, poke, poke: William Harvey. Poke, poke, poke, poke: islets of Langerhans. This didn't work out perfectly, but Dave passed the course, and I mastered the dreamy look of a guy on a record jacket. And something else happened. Brother Clint puzzled over this Voc. Ed. kid who was racking up 98s and 99s on his tests. He checked the school's records and discovered the error. He recommended that I begin my junior year in the College Prep program. According to all I've read since, such a shift, as one report put it, is virtually impossible. Kids at that level rarely cross tracks. The telling thing is how chancy both my placement into and exit from Voc. Ed. was; neither I nor my parents had anything to do with it. I lived in one world during spring

semester, and when I came back to school in the fall, I was living in another.

Switching to College Prep was a mixed blessing. I was an 22 erratic student. I was undisciplined. And I hadn't caught onto the rules of the game: Why work hard in a class that didn't grab my fancy? I was also hopelessly behind in math. Chemistry was hard; toying with my chemistry set years before hadn't prepared me for the chemist's equations. Fortunately, the priest who taught both chemistry and second-year algebra was also the school's athletic director. Membership on the track team covered me; I knew I wouldn't get lower than a C. U.S. history was taught pretty well, and I did okay. But civics was taken over by a football coach who had trouble reading the textbook aloud—and reading aloud was the centerpiece of his pedagogy. College Prep at Mercy was certainly an improvement over the vocational program—at least it carried some status—but the social science curriculum was weak, and the mathematics and physical sciences were simply beyond me. I had a miserable quantitative background and ended up copying some assignments and finessing the rest as best I could. Let me try to explain how it feels to see again and again material you should once have learned but didn't.

You are given a problem. It requires you to simplify alge- 23 braic fractions or to multiply expressions containing square roots. You know this is pretty basic material because you've seen it for years. Once a teacher took some time with you, and you learned how to carry out these operations. Simple versions, anyway. But that was a year or two or more in the past, and these are more complex versions, and now you're not sure. And this, you keep telling yourself, is ninth- or even eighth-grade stuff.

Next it's a word problem. This is also old hat. The basic ele- 24 ments are as familiar as story characters: trains speeding so many miles per hour or shadows of buildings angling so many degrees. Maybe you know enough, have sat through enough explanations, to be able to begin setting up the problem: "If one train is going this fast . . ." or "This shadow is really one line of a triangle. . . ." Then: "Let's see . . ." "How did Jones do this?" "Hmmmm." "No." "No, that won't work." Your attention wavers. You wonder about other things: a football game, a dance, that cute new checker at the market. You try to focus on the problem again. You scribble on paper for a while, but the tension wins out and your attention flits elsewhere. You crumple the paper and begin day-dreaming to ease the frustration.

25   The particulars will vary, but in essence this is what a number of students go through, especially those in so-called remedial classes. They open their textbooks and see once again the familiar and impenetrable formulas and diagrams and terms that have stumped them for years. There is no excitement here. *No* excitement. Regardless of what the teacher says, this is not a new challenge. There is, rather, embarrassment and frustration and, not surprisingly, some anger in being reminded once again of long-standing inadequacies. No wonder so many students finally attribute their difficulties to something inborn, organic: "That part of my brain just doesn't work." Given the troubling histories many of these students have, it's miraculous that any of them can lift the shroud of hopelessness sufficiently to make deliverance from these classes possible.

Content

1.   In Rose's view, what is there about school itself—student placement, courses, teachers' and students' expectations and attitudes—that causes students to be indifferent as to whether they learn anything or not? Do you agree? Why or why not?

2.   Rose demonstrates the immediate effects of deficient or inadequate schooling on the students in the classroom; these range from boredom to anarchy, and are not conducive to learning. What long-range effects, extending well beyond the schools themselves, does Rose project or imply as the consequences of short-term inadequacies?

3.   In what ways is this as much an essay about social class and economic marginality as it is about education? How are these themes intertwined?

Strategies/Structures

4.   Rose often re-creates the students' point of view ("I just wanna be average") to help his readers understand the learning problems typical of such disaffected, discouraged students (see, for instance, ¶s 24 and 25). What does this point of view reveal that the perspectives of teachers or parents are likely to miss?

5.   Rose personifies the problems of inadequate schools by characterizing some of their presumably typical teachers (Brother Dill, Mr. Mitropetros, Mr. Montez) and students (Mike Dweetz, Billy Hawk, Dave

Snyder, Ted Richard, Ken Harvey, and Rose himself). What are some of the problems associated with each character? Does such characterization make the problems more memorable? More understandable? Does it run the risk of oversimplifying them? Explain your answers.

6. Writings about education often portray one or two teachers as life-savers, rescuing their students who would otherwise drown in a sea of mediocrity, indifference, or worse. What teacher performs this function in "I Just Wanna Be Average"? Why is he successful?

Language

7. How can you tell that Rose cares passionately about whether or not students learn—and want to learn?

8. What is Rose's characteristic language in this essay? How does it reinforce his subject and his thesis? How compatible is this language with the speech of the high school students he's writing about?

For Writing

9. Explain, candidly, to readers who don't know your family or your hometown, what it was like to be a student in your high school. If you wish, compare your experiences with those of Zitkala-Sa (273–83), Shirley Lim (388–98), or Richard Wright (425–35). What factors, in your home, school, or community environment contributed to your decision to attend college? If there were any factors that worked against this decision, what were they, and how compelling did you find them? If you're convinced that you made the right decision, explain why, if not, why are you unconvinced or uncertain?

10. Have you ever dropped out of school? If so, why did you do so? What were the consequences? Why did you return to school? What do you expect the consequences, short- and long-range, to be?

ZITKALA-SA

Zitkala-Sa (1878–1938) was the first Native American woman to write her autobiography by herself, without the help of an intermediary, such as an ethnographer, translator, editor, or oral historian. This unmediated authenticity gives her work unusual authority. She was a Yankton, born on the Pine Ridge Reservation in South Dakota, daughter of a full-blooded Sioux and a white father.

Zitkala-Sa wrote a number of autobiographical essays to call attention to the cultural dislocation and hardships caused when whites sent Native American children to boarding schools hundreds of miles away from home and imposed white culture on them. In her own case, as she explains in "The Land of Red Apples" (274–77), at the age of eight she left the reservation to attend a boarding school in Wabash, Indiana, run by Quaker missionaries. On her return, "neither a wild Indian nor a tame one" (¶ 25), her distress and cultural displacement were acute, as "Four Strange Summers" (279–82) makes clear. These were originally published in *Atlantic Monthly* (1900), as portions of *Impressions of an Indian Childhood* and *The School Days of an Indian Girl*.

Zitkala-Sa remained unhappily on the reservation for four years, then returned to the Quaker school, and at nineteen enrolled in the Quaker-run Earlham College in Indiana. Her marriage to Raymond Bonnin, a Sioux, enhanced her activism for Indian rights. She served as secretary of the Society of American Indians, and also edited *American Indian Magazine*. As a lobbyist and spokesperson for the National Council of American Indians, which she founded in 1926, she helped to secure passage of the Indian Citizenship Bill and other reforms. Yet she was an integrationist, not a separatist, and attempted to forge meaningful connections between cultures.

from The School Days of an Indian Girl

I   The Land of Red Apples

1   There were eight in our party of bronzed children who were going East with the missionaries. Among us were three young braves, two tall girls, and we three little ones, Judéwin, Thowin, and I.

2   We had been very impatient to start on our journey to the Red Apple Country, which, we were told, lay a little beyond the great

circular horizon of the Western prairie. Under a sky of rosy apples we dreamt of roaming as freely and happily as we had chased the cloud shadows on the Dakota plains. We had anticipated much pleasure from a ride on the iron horse, but the throngs of staring palefaces disturbed and troubled us.

On the train, fair women, with tottering babies on each 3 arm, stopped their haste and scrutinized the children of absent mothers. Large men, with heavy bundles in their hands, halted near by, and riveted their glassy blue eyes upon us.

I sank deep into the corner of my seat, for I resented being 4 watched. Directly in front of me, children who were no larger than I hung themselves upon the backs of their seats, with their bold white faces toward me. Sometimes they took their forefingers out of their mouths and pointed at my moccasined feet. Their mothers, instead of reproving such rude curiosity, looked closely at me, and attracted their children's further notice to my blanket. This embarrassed me, and kept me constantly on the verge of tears.

I sat perfectly still, with my eyes downcast, daring only now 5 and then to shoot long glances around me. Chancing to turn to the window at my side, I was quite breathless upon seeing one familiar object. It was the telegraph pole which strode by at short paces. Very near my mother's dwelling, along the edge of a road thickly bordered with wild sunflowers, some poles like these had been planted by white men. Often I had stopped, on my way down the road, to hold my ear against the pole, and, hearing its low moaning, I used to wonder what the paleface had done to hurt it. Now I sat watching for each pole that glided by to be the last one.

In this way I had forgotten my uncomfortable surroundings, 6 when I heard one of my comrades call out my name. I saw the missionary standing very near, tossing candies and gums into our midst. This amused us all, and we tried to see who could catch the most of the sweet-meats. The missionary's generous distribution of candies was impressed upon my memory by a disastrous result which followed. I had caught more than my share of candies and gums, and soon after our arrival at the school I had a chance to disgrace myself, which, I am ashamed to say, I did.

Though we rode several days inside of the iron horse, I do 7 not recall a single thing about our luncheons.

8   It was night when we reached the school grounds. The lights from the windows of the large buildings fell upon some of the icicled trees that stood beneath them. We were led toward an open door, where the brightness of the lights within flooded out over the heads of the excited palefaces who blocked the way. My body trembled more from fear than from the snow I trod upon.

9   Entering the house, I stood close against the wall. The strong glaring light in the large whitewashed room dazzled my eyes. The noisy hurrying of hard shoes upon a bare wooden floor increased the whirring in my ears. My only safety seemed to be in keeping next to the wall. As I was wondering in which direction to escape from all this confusion, two warm hands grasped me firmly, and in the same moment I was tossed high in midair. A rosy-checked paleface woman caught me in her arms. I was both frightened and insulted by such trifling. I stared into her eyes, wishing her to let me stand on my own feet, but she jumped me up and down with increasing enthusiasm. My mother had never made a plaything of her wee daughter. Remembering this I began to cry aloud.

10   They misunderstood the cause of my tears, and placed me at a white table loaded with food. There our party were united again. As I did not hush my crying, one of the older ones whispered to me, "Wait until you are alone in the night."

11   It was very little I could swallow besides my sobs, that evening.

12   "Oh, I want my mother and my brother Dawée! I want to go to my aunt!" I pleaded; but the ears of the palefaces could not hear me.

13   From the table we were taken along an upward incline of wooden boxes, which I learned afterward to call a stairway. At the top was a quiet hall, dimly lighted. Many narrow beds were in one straight line down the entire length of the wall. In them lay sleeping brown faces, which peeped just out of the coverings. I was tucked into bed with one of the tall girls, because she talked to me in my mother tongue and seemed to soothe me.

14   I had arrived in the wonderful land of rosy skies, but I was not happy, as I had thought I should be. My long travel and the bewildering sights had exhausted me. I fell asleep, heaving deep,

tired sobs. My tears were left to dry themselves in streaks, because neither my aunt nor my mother was near to wipe them away.

II   The Cutting of My Long Hair

The first day in the land of the apples was a bitter-cold one; for the snow still covered the ground, and the trees were bare. A large bell rang for breakfast, its loud metallic voice crashing through the belfry overhead and into our sensitive ears. The annoying clatter of shoes on bare floors gave us no peace. The constant clash of harsh noises, with an undercurrent of many voices murmuring an unknown tongue, made a bedlam within which I was securely tied. And though my spirit tore itself in struggling for its lost freedom, all was useless.

A paleface woman, with white hair, came up after us. We were placed in a line of girls who were marching into the dining room. These were Indian girls, in stiff shoes and closely clinging dresses. The small girls wore sleeved aprons and shingled hair. As I walked noiselessly in my soft moccasins, I felt like sinking to the floor, for my blanket had been stripped from my shoulders. I looked hard at the Indian girls, who seemed not to care that they were even more immodestly dressed than I, in their tightly fitting clothes. While we marched in, the boys entered at an opposite door. I watched for the three young braves who came in our party. I spied them in the rear ranks, looking as uncomfortable as I felt.

A small bell was tapped, and each of the pupils drew a chair from under the table. Supposing this act meant they were to be seated, I pulled out mine and at once slipped into it from one side. But when I turned my head, I saw that I was the only one seated, and all the rest at our table remained standing. Just as I began to rise, looking shyly around to see how chairs were to be used, a second bell was sounded. All were seated at last, and I had to crawl back into my chair again. I heard a man's voice at one end of the hall, and I looked around to see him. But all the others hung their heads over their plates. As I glanced at the long chain of tables, I caught the eyes of a paleface woman upon me. Immediately I dropped my eyes, wondering why I was so keenly watched by the strange woman. The man ceased his mutterings, and then a third bell was tapped. Every one picked up his knife and fork and began eating. I began crying instead, for by this time I was afraid to venture anything more.

18   But this eating by formula was not the hardest trial in that first day. Late in the morning, my friend Judéwin gave me a terrible warning. Judéwin knew a few words of English; and she had overheard the paleface woman talk about cutting our long, heavy hair. Our mothers had taught us that only unskilled warriors who were captured had their hair shingled by the enemy. Among our people, short hair was worn by mourners, and shingled hair by cowards!

19   We discussed our fate some moments, and when Judéwin said, "We have to submit, because they are strong," I rebelled.

20   "No, I will not submit! I will struggle first!" I answered.

21   I watched my chance, and when no one noticed I disappeared. I crept up the stairs quietly as I could in my squeaking shoes,—my moccasins had been exchanged for shoes. Along the hall I passed, without knowing whither I was going. Turning aside to an open door, I found a large room with three white beds in it. The windows were covered with dark green curtains, which made the room very dim. Thankful that no one was there, I directed my steps toward the corner farthest from the door. On my hands and knees I crawled under the bed, and cuddled myself in the dark corner.

22   From my hiding place I peered out, shuddering with fear whenever I heard footsteps near by. Though in the hall loud voices were calling my name, and I knew that even Judéwin was searching for me, I did not open my mouth to answer. Then the steps were quickened and the voices became excited. The sounds came nearer and nearer. Woman and girls entered the room. I held my breath, and watched them open closet doors and peep behind large trunks. Some one threw up the curtains, and the room was filled with sudden light. What caused them to stoop and look under the bed I do not know. I remember being dragged out, though I resisted by kicking and scratching wildly. In spite of myself, I was carried downstairs and tied fast in a chair.

23   I cried aloud, shaking my head all the while until I felt the cold blades of the scissors against my neck, and heard them gnaw off one of my thick braids. Then I lost my spirit. Since the

day I was taken from my mother I had suffered extreme indignities. People had stared at me. I had been tossed about in the air like a wooden puppet. And now my long hair was shingled like a coward's! In my anguish I moaned for my mother, but no one came to comfort me. Not a soul reasoned quietly with me, as my own mother used to do: for now I was only one of many little animals driven by a herder. . . .

VI   Four Strange Summers[1]

After my first three years of school, I roamed again in the Western country through four strange summers.   24

During this time I seemed to hang in the heart of chaos, beyond the touch or voice of human aid. My brother, being almost ten years my senior, did not quite understand my feelings. My mother had never gone inside of a schoolhouse, and so she was not capable of comforting her daughter who could read and write. Even nature seemed to have no place for me. I was neither a wee girl nor a tall one; neither a wild Indian nor a tame one. This deplorable situation was the effect of my brief course in the East, and the unsatisfactory "teenth" in a girl's years.   25

It was under these trying conditions that, one bright afternoon, as I sat restless and unhappy in my mother's cabin, I caught the sound of the spirited step of my brother's pony on the road which passed by our dwelling. Soon I heard the wheels of a light buckboard, and Dawée's familiar "Ho!" to his pony. He alighted upon the bare ground in front of our house. Tying his pony to one of the projecting corner logs of the low-roofed cottage, he stepped upon the wooden doorstep.   26

I met him there with a hurried greeting, and, as I passed by, he looked a quiet "What?" into my eyes.   27

When he began talking with my mother, I slipped the rope from the pony's bridle. Seizing the reins and bracing my feet against the dashboard, I wheeled around in an instant. The pony was ever ready to try his speed. Looking backward, I saw Dawée waving his hand to me. I turned with the curve in the road and   28

---

[1] Sections III, IV, and V are omitted.

disappeared. I followed the winding road which crawled upward between the bases of little hillocks. Deep water-worn ditches ran parallel on either side. A strong wind blew against my cheeks and fluttered my sleeves. The pony reached the top of the highest hill, and began an even race on level lands. There was nothing moving within that great circular horizon of the Dakota prairies save the tall grasses, over which the wind blew and rolled off in long, shadowy waves.

29   Within this vast wigwam of blue and green I rode reckless and insignificant. It satisfied my small consciousness to see the white foam fly from the pony's mouth.

30   Suddenly, out of the earth a coyote came forth at a swinging trot that was taking the cunning thief toward the hills and the village beyond. Upon the moment's impulse, I gave him a long chase and a wholesome fright. As I turned away to go back to the village, the wolf sank down upon his haunches for a rest, for it was a hot summer day; and as I drove slowly homeward, I saw his sharp nose still pointed at me, until I vanished below the margin of the hilltops.

31   In a little while I came in sight of my mother's house. Dawée stood in the yard, laughing at an old warrior who was pointing his forefinger, and again waving his whole hand, toward the hills. With his blanket drawn over one shoulder, he talked and motioned excitely. Dawée turned the old man by the shoulder and pointed me out to him.

32   "Oh han!" (Oh yes) the warrior muttered, and went his way. He had climbed the top of his favorite barren hill to survey the surrounding prairies, when he spied my chase after the coyote. His keen eyes recognized the pony and driver. At once uneasy for my safety, he had come running to my mother's cabin to give her warning. I did not appreciate his kindly interest, for there was an unrest gnawing at my heart.

33   As soon as he went away, I asked Dawée about something else.

34   "No, my baby sister. I cannot take you with me to the party to-night," he replied. Though I was not far from fifteen, and I felt that before long I should enjoy all the privileges of my tall cousin, Dawée persisted in calling me his baby sister.

That moonlight night, I cried in my mother's presence when   35
I heard the jolly young people pass by our cottage. There were no
more young braves in blankets and eagle plumes, nor Indian
maids with prettily painted cheeks. They had gone three years to
school in the East, and had become civilized. The young men
wore the white man's coat and trousers, with bright neckties. The
girls wore tight muslin dresses, with ribbons at neck and waist.
At these gatherings they talked English. I could speak English
almost as well as my brother, but I was not properly dressed to be
taken along. I had no hat, no ribbons, and no close-fitting gown.
Since my return from school I had thrown away my shoes, and
wore again the soft moccasins.

While Dawée was busily preparing to go I controlled my   36
tears. But when I heard him bounding away on his pony, I buried
my face in my arms and cried hot tears.

My mother was troubled by my unhappiness. Coming to   37
my side, she offered me the only printed matter we had in our
home. It was an Indian Bible, given her some years ago by a missionary. She tried to console me. "Here, my child, are the white
man's papers. Read a little from them," she said most piously.

I took it from her hand, for her sake; but my enraged spirit   38
felt more like burning the book, which afforded me no help, and
was a perfect delusion to my mother. I did not read it, but laid it
unopened on the floor, where I sat on my feet. The dim yellow
light of the braided muslin burning in a small vessel of oil flick-
ered and sizzled in the awful silent storm which followed my
rejection of the Bible.

Now my wrath against the fates consumed my tears before   39
they reached my eyes. I sat stony, with a bowed head. My mother
threw a shawl over her head and shoulders, and stepped out into
the night.

After an uncertain solitude, I was suddenly aroused by a   40
loud cry piercing the night. It was my mother's voice wailing
among the barren hills which held the bones of buried warriors.
She called aloud for her brothers' spirits to support her in her
helpless misery. My fingers grew icy cold, as I realized that my
unrestrained tears had betrayed my suffering to her, and she was
grieving for me.

41   Before she returned, though I knew she was on her way, for she had ceased her weeping, I extinguished the light, and leaned my head on the window sill.

42   Many schemes of running away from my surroundings hovered about in my mind. A few more moons of such a turmoil drove me away to the Eastern school. I rode on the white man's iron steed, thinking it would bring me back to my mother in a few winters, when I should be grown tall, and there would be congenial friends awaiting me. . . .

Content

1. To an extent, leaving the security of home and its familiar culture to go to school, with its inevitably somewhat different culture, presents problems for any child. To what extent are Zitkala-Sa's memories of being uprooted and sent away to school similar to those of any child in a similar circumstance, and to what extent are they exacerbated by the alien culture to which she is expected to adapt?

2. What was the whites' rationale for sending Native American children away to boarding school? Why did parents allow their children to be sent away (see "The Land of Red Apples")? In what ways did this contribute to the adulteration and breakup of Native American culture (see all sections)?

3. Historically, the Quakers have a reputation for being respectful of civil rights and very sympathetic to the preservation of minority cultures. Quaker households, for instance, were often places of shelter for slaves escaping along the Underground Railway. Was the Quaker school to which Zitkala-Sa went an exception? What factors influenced her perception of the school when she was in residence and later when she wrote about it?

Strategies/Structures

4. Zitkala-Sa is writing in English for a white audience in 1900, many of whom might never have met a Native American, and who would have known very little about their schooling. What information does she need to supply to make the context of her narrative clear? Has she done this?

5. Zitkala-Sa's readers might be expected to share the viewpoint of the school personnel, in opposition to her own point of view, both as a character in her own story and the narrator of it. By what means does she try to win readers to her point of view? Is she successful?

Language

6. Why did Zitkala-Sa choose to write primarily in standard English, omitting the stereotypical features whites attribute, rightly or wrongly, to Native American speakers of English as a second language?

7. What are the effects of occasional passages in the language whites attribute to Native Americans? See, for example, "palefaces" (¶ 2 and *passim*); "A few *more moons* . . . I rode on the white man's *iron steed*, thinking it would bring me back to my mother in a *few winters*" (¶ 42).

8. Examine the language of the last paragraph of "The Cutting of My Long Hair" and analyze it in light of your answers to 1 and 2.

For Writing

9. Today many Native American children living on reservations can go to school there. On some reservations, college students can even earn degrees in such subjects as education. Write an essay for parents trying to decide what's best for their children in which you weigh the advantages of cultural integrity versus ghettoization that are inherent in this, or any system, of a closed-culture education—public or private (including parochial schooling). Feel free to draw on your own experiences in school. You may need to do some research on a particular school system to provide information for your argument.

10. As Zitkala-Sa does, tell the story of an experience of cultural displacement that you or someone you know well has experienced. Identify its causes and interpret its consequences, short- and long-term.

JONATHAN KOZOL

Kozol's first critique of American education, *Death at an Early Age: The Destruction of the Hearts and Minds of Negro Children in the Boston Public Schools* in 1967, won the National Book Award. Written during the civil rights and school desegregation movements in the 1960s, this book documents the repressive teaching methods in Boston's unintegrated public schools, designed, Kozol claimed, to reinforce a system that would keep the children separate but unequal. Kozol, himself a Harvard graduate (1958), Rhodes Scholar, and recipient of numerous prestigious fellowships (Gugenheim, Rockefeller, and Ford foundations), transcends his privileged background to address what he considers to be the failure of American education to reach minorities and the poor. Even his book on middle-class education, *The Night Is Dark and I Am Far from Home* (1975), expounds on his claim that because the schools reflect the inequities in society at large, the more affluent are educated at the expense of the poor. His recent books, *Savage Inequalities: Children in America's Schools* (1991) and *Amazing Grace: The Lives of Children and the Conscience of a Nation* (1995), extend and reinforce these concerns.

Illiterate America (1985) analyzes the nature, causes, and effects of illiteracy, the ultimate and pervasive failure that, says Kozol, denies sixty million people "significant participation" in the government that "is neither of, nor for, nor by, the people." Kozol concludes with a call to action, a nationwide army of neighborhood volunteers who would teach people to read. Part of his strategy in arousing his own readers to action is to make them understand what it's like to be illiterate, on which this chapter (reprinted in full) focuses. Characteristically, Kozol interprets both the causes of illiteracy and the effects—discussed here—in human, moral terms. Kozol says, "I write as a witness. . . . this is what we have done. This is what we have permitted."

The Human Cost of an Illiterate Society

1   *PRECAUTIONS. READ BEFORE USING.*
       Poison: Contains sodium hydroxide (caustic soda-lye).
       Corrosive: Causes severe eye and skin damage, may cause blindness.
       Harmful or fatal if swallowed.
       If swallowed, give large quantities of milk or water.
       Do not induce vomiting.
       Important: Keep water out of can at all times to prevent contents from violently erupting . . .

                                          WARNING ON A CAN OF DRĀNO

2   We are speaking here no longer of the dangers faced by passengers on Eastern Airlines or the dollar costs incurred by U.S. corporations and taxpayers. We are speaking now of human suffering and of the

ethical dilemmas that are faced by a society that looks upon such suffering with qualified concern but does not take those actions which its wealth and ingenuity would seemingly demand.

Questions of literacy, in Socrates' belief, must at length be   3
judged as matters of morality. Socrates could not have had in mind the moral compromise peculiar to a nation like our own. Some of our Founding Fathers did, however, have this question in their minds. One of the wisest of those Founding Fathers (one who may not have been most compassionate but surely was more prescient than some of his peers) recognized the special dangers that illiteracy would pose to basic equity in the political construction that he helped to shape.

"A people who mean to be their own governors," James   4
Madison wrote, "must arm themselves with the power knowledge gives. A popular government without popular information or the means of acquiring it, is but a prologue to a farce or a tragedy, or perhaps both."

Tragedy looms larger than farce in the United States today.   5
Illiterate citizens seldom vote. Those who do are forced to cast a vote of questionable worth. They cannot make informed decisions based on serious print information. Sometimes they can be alerted to their interests by aggressive voter education. More frequently, they vote for a face, a smile, or a style, not for a mind or character or body of beliefs.

The number of illiterate adults exceeds by 16 million the   6
entire vote cast for the winner in the 1980 presidential contest. If even one third of all illiterates could vote, and read enough and do sufficient math to vote in their self-interest, Ronald Reagan would not likely have been chosen president. There is, of course, no way to know for sure. We do know this: Democracy is a mendacious term when used by those who are prepared to countenance the forced exclusion of one third of our electorate. So long as 60 million people are denied significant participation, the government is neither of, nor for, nor by, the people. It is a government, at best, of those two thirds whose wealth, skin color, or parental privilege allows them opportunity to profit from the provocation and instruction of the written word.

The undermining of democracy in the United States is one   7
"expense" that sensitive Americans can easily deplore because it

represents a contradiction that endangers citizens of all political positions. The human price is not so obvious at first.

8   Since I first immersed myself within this work I have often had the following dream: I find that I am in a railroad station or a large department store within a city that is utterly unknown to me and where I cannot understand the printed words. None of the signs or symbols is familiar. Everything looks strange: like mirror writing of some kind. Gradually I understand that I am in the Soviet Union. All the letters on the walls around me are Cyrillic. I look for my pocket dictionary but I find that it has been mislaid. Where have I left it? Then I recall that I forgot to bring it with me when I packed my bags in Boston. I struggle to remember the name of my hotel. I try to ask somebody for directions. One person stops and looks at me in a peculiar way. I lose the nerve to ask. At last I reach into my wallet for an ID card. The card is missing. Have I lost it? Then I remember that my card was confiscated for some reason, many years before. Around this point, I wake up in a panic.

9   This panic is not so different from the misery that millions of adult illiterates experience each day within the course of their routine existence in the U.S.A.

10   Illiterates cannot read the menu in a restaurant.

11   They cannot read the cost of items on the menu in the *window* of the restaurant before they enter.

12   Illiterates cannot read the letters that their children bring home from their teachers. They cannot study school department circulars that tell them of the courses that their children must be taking if they hope to pass the SAT exams. They cannot help with homework. They cannot write a letter to the teacher. They are afraid to visit in the classroom. They do not want to humiliate their child or themselves.

13   Illiterates cannot read instructions on a bottle of prescription medicine. They cannot find out when a medicine is past the year of safe consumption; nor can they read of allergenic risks, warnings to diabetics, or the potential sedative effect of certain kinds of nonprescription pills. They cannot observe preventive health care admonitions. They cannot read about "the seven warning signs of cancer" or the indications of blood-sugar fluctuations or the risks of eating certain foods that aggravate the likelihood of cardiac arrest.

Illiterates live, in more than literal ways, an uninsured exis-   14
tence. They cannot understand the written details on a health insurance form. They cannot read the waivers that they sign preceding
surgical procedures. Several women I have known in Boston have
entered a slum hospital with the intention of obtaining a tubal
ligation and have emerged a few days later after having been
subjected to a hysterectomy. Unaware of their rights, incognizant
of jargon, intimidated by the unfamiliar air of fear and atmosphere of ether that so many of us find oppressive in the confines
even of the most attractive and expensive medical facilities, they
have signed their names to documents they could not read and
which nobody, in the hectic situation that prevails so often in
those overcrowded hospitals that serve the urban poor, had even
bothered to explain.

Childbirth might seem to be the last inalienable right of any   15
female citizen within a civilized society. Illiterate mothers, as we
shall see, already have been cheated of the power to protect their
progeny against the likelihood of demolition in deficient public
schools and, as a result, against the verbal servitude within which
they themselves exist. Surgical denial of the right to bear that child
in the first place represents an ultimate denial, an unspeakable
metaphor, a final darkness that denies even the twilight gleamings
of our own humanity. What greater violation of our biological, our
biblical, our spiritual humanity could possibly exist than that
which takes place nightly, perhaps hourly these days, within such
overburdened and benighted institutions as the Boston City Hospital? Illiteracy has many costs; few are so irreversible as this.

Even the roof above one's head, the gas or other fuel for   16
heating that protects the residents of northern city slums against
the threat of illness in the winter months become uncertain guarantees. Illiterates cannot read the lease that they must sign to live
in an apartment which, too often, they cannot afford. The cannot
manage check accounts and therefore seldom pay for anything by
mail. Hours and entire days of difficult travel (and the cost of bus
or other public transit) must be added to the real cost of whatever
they consume. Loss of interest on the check accounts they do not
have, and could not manage if they did, must be regarded as another of the excess costs paid by the citizen who is excluded from
the common instruments of commerce in a numerate society.

17   "I couldn't understand the bills," a woman in Washington, D.C., reports, "and then I couldn't write the checks to pay them. We signed things we didn't know what they were."

18   Illiterates cannot read the notices that they receive from welfare offices or from the IRS. They must depend on word-of-mouth instruction from the welfare worker—or from other persons whom they have good reason to mistrust. They do not know what rights they have, what deadlines and requirements they face, what options they might choose to exercise. They are half-citizens. Their rights exist in print but not in fact.

19   Illiterates cannot look up numbers in a telephone directory. Even if they can find the names of friends, few possess the sorting skills to make use of the yellow pages; categories are bewildering and trade names are beyond decoding capabilities for millions of nonreaders. Even the emergency numbers listed on the first page of the phone book—"Ambulance," "Police," and "Fire"—are too frequently beyond the recognition of nonreaders.

20   Many illiterates cannot read the admonition on a pack of cigarettes. Neither the Surgeon General's warning nor its reproduction on the package can alert them to the risks. Although most people learn by word of mouth that smoking is related to a number of grave physical disorders, they do not get the chance to read the detailed stories which can document this danger with the vividness that turns concern into determination to resist. They can see the handsome cowboy or the slim Virginia lady lighting up a filter cigarette; they cannot heed the words that tell them that this product is (not "may be") dangerous to their health. Sixty million men and women are condemned to be the unalerted, high-risk candidates for cancer.

21   Illiterates do not buy "no-name" products in the supermarkets. They must depend on photographs or the familiar logos that are printed on the packages of brand-name groceries. The poorest people, therefore, are denied the benefits of the least costly products.

22   Illiterates depend almost entirely upon label recognition. Many labels, however, are not easy to distinguish. Dozens of different kinds of Campbell's soup appear identical to the nonreader. The purchaser who cannot read and does not dare to ask for help, out of the fear of being stigmatized (a fear which is unfortunately

realistic), frequently comes home with something which she never wanted and her family never tasted.

Illiterates cannot read instructions on a pack of frozen food.   23 Packages sometimes provide an illustration to explain the cooking preparations; but illustrations are of little help to someone who must "boil water, drop the food—*within* its plastic wrapper—in the boiling water, wait for it to simmer, instantly remove."

Even when labels are seemingly clear, they may be easily   24 mistaken. A woman in Detroit brought home a gallon of Crisco for her children's dinner. She thought that she had bought the chicken that was pictured on the label. She had enough Crisco now to last a year—but no more money to go back and buy the food for dinner.

Recipes provided on the packages of certain staples some-   25 times tempt a semiliterate person to prepare a meal her children have not tasted. The longing to vary the uniform and often starchy content of low-budget meals provided to the family that relies on food stamps commonly leads to ruinous results. Scarce funds have been wasted and the food must be thrown out. The same applies to distribution of food-surplus produce in emergency conditions. Government inducements to poor people to "explore the ways" by which to make a tasty meal from tasteless noodles, surplus cheese, and powdered milk are useless to nonreaders. Intended as benevolent advice, such recommendations mock reality and foster deeper feelings of resentment and of inability to cope. (Those on the other hand, who cautiously refrain from "innovative" recipes in preparation of their children's meals must suffer the opprobrium of "laziness," "lack of imagination . . .")

Illiterates cannot travel freely. When they attempt to do so,   26 they encounter risks that few of us can dream of. They cannot read traffic signs and, while they often learn to recognize and to decipher symbols, they cannot manage street names which they haven't seen before. The same is true for bus and subway stops. While ingenuity can sometimes help a man or woman to discern directions from familiar landmarks, buildings, cemeteries, churches, and the like, most illiterates are virtually immobilized. They seldom wander past the streets and neighborhoods they know. Geographical paralysis becomes a bitter metaphor for their entire existence. They are immobilized in almost every sense we can imagine. They can't move up. They can't move out. They cannot see beyond. Illiterates may take an oral test for drivers' permits in most sections of America. It is a questionable concession. Where will they go? How will they get there? How will they get home? Could it be that some of us might like it better if they stayed where they belong?

27   Travel is only one of many instances of circumscribed existence. Choice, in almost all of its facets, is diminished in the life of an illiterate adult. Even the printed TV schedule, which provides most people with the luxury of preselection, does not belong within the arsenal of options in illiterate existence. One consequence is that the viewer watches only what appears at moments when he happens to have time to turn the switch. Another consequence, a lot more common, is that the TV set remains in operation night and day. Whatever the program offered at the hour when he walks into the room will be the nutriment that he accepts and swallows. Thus, to passivity, is added frequency—indeed, almost uninterrupted continuity. Freedom to select is no more possible here than in the choice of home or surgery or food.

28   "You don't choose," said one illiterate woman. "You take your wishes from somebody else." Whether in perusal of a menu, selection of highways, purchase of groceries, or determination of affordable enjoyment, illiterate Americans must trust somebody else: a friend, a relative, a stranger on the street, a grocery clerk, a TV copywriter.

29   "All of our mail we get, it's hard for her to read. Settin' down and writing a letter, she can't do it. Like if we get a bill . . . we take it over to my sister-in-law . . . My sister-in-law reads it."

30   Billing agencies harass poor people for the payment of the bills for purchases that might have taken place six months before. Utility companies offer an agreement for a staggered payment schedule on a bill past due. "You have to trust them," one man said. Precisely for this reason, you end up by trusting no one and suspecting everyone of possible deceit. A submerged sense of distrust becomes the corollary to a constant need to trust. "They are cheating me . . . I have been tricked . . . I do not know . . ."

31   *Not knowing:* This is a familiar theme. Not knowing the right word for the right thing at the right time is one form of subjugation. Not knowing the world that lies concealed behind those words is a more terrifying feeling. The longitude and latitude of

one's existence are beyond all easy apprehension. Even the hard, cold stars within the firmament above one's head begin to mock the possibilities for self-location. Where am I? Where did I come from? Where will I go?

"I've lost a lot of jobs," one man explains. "Today, even if 32 you're a janitor, there's still reading and writing . . . They leave a note saying, 'Go to room so-and-so . . .' You can't do it. You can't read it. You don't know."

"The hardest thing about it is that I've been places where I 33 didn't know where I was. You don't know where you are . . . You're lost."

"Like I said: I have two kids. What do I do if one of my kids 34 starts choking? I go running to the phone . . . I can't look up the hospital phone number. That's if we're at home. Out on the street, I can't read the sign. I get to a pay phone. 'Okay, tell us where you are. We'll send an ambulance.' I look at the street sign. Right there, I can't tell you what it says. I'd have to spell it out, letter for letter. By that time, one of my kids would be dead . . . These are the kinds of fears you go with, every single day . . ."

"Reading directions, I suffer with. I work with chemicals . . . 35 That's scary to begin with . . ."

"You sit down. They throw the menu in front of you. Where 36 do you go from there? Nine times out of ten you say, 'Go ahead. Pick out something for the both of us.' I've eaten some weird things, let me tell you!"

Menus. Chemicals. A child choking while his mother 37 searches for a word she does not know to find assistance that will come too late. Another mother speaks about the inability to help her kids to read: "I can't read to them. Of course that's leaving them out of something they should have. Oh, it matters. You *believe* it matters! I ordered all these books. The kids belong to a book club. Donny wanted me to read a book to him. I told Donny: 'I can't read.' He said: 'Mommy, you sit down. I'll read it to you.' I tried it one day, reading from the pictures. Donny looked at me. He said, 'Mommy, that's not right.' He's only five. He knew I couldn't read . . ."

A landlord tells a woman that her lease allows him to evict 38 her if her baby cries and causes inconvenience to her neighbors. The consequence of challenging his words conveys a danger which appears, unlikely as it seems, even more alarming than the danger of eviction. Once she admits that she can't read, in the desire to maneuver for the time in which to call a friend, she will have defined herself in terms of an explicit impotence that she cannot endure. Capitulation in this case is preferable to self-humiliation. Resisting the definition of oneself in terms of what one cannot do, what others take for granted, represents a need so great that other imperatives (even one so urgent as the need to keep one's home in winter's cold) evaporate and fall away in face of fear. Even the loss of home and shelter, in this case, is not so terrifying as the loss of self.

39   "I come out of school. I was sixteen. They had their meetings. The directors meet. They said that I was wasting their school paper. I was wasting pencils . . ."

40   Another illiterate, looking back, believes she was not worthy of her teacher's time. She believes that it was wrong of her to take up space within her school. She believes that it was right to leave in order that somebody more deserving could receive her place.

41   Children choke. Their mother chokes another way: on more than chicken bones.

42   People eat what others order, know what others tell them, struggle not to see themselves as they believe the world perceives them. A man in California speaks about his own loss of identity, of self-location, definition:

43   "I stood at the bottom of the ramp. My car had broke down on the freeway. There was a phone. I asked for the police. They was nice. They said to tell them where I was. I looked up at the signs. There was one that I had seen before. I read it to them: ONE WAY STREET. They thought it was a joke. I told them I couldn't read. There was other signs above the ramp. They told me to try. I looked around for somebody to help. All the cars was going by real fast. I couldn't make them understand that I was lost. The cop was nice. He told me: 'Try once more.' I did my best. I couldn't read. I only knew the sign above my head. The cop was trying to be nice. He knew that I was trapped. 'I can't send out a car to you if you can't tell me where you are.' I felt afraid. I nearly cried. I'm forty-eight years old. I only said: 'I'm on a one-way street . . .'"

44   Perhaps we might slow down a moment here and look at the realities described above. This is the nation that we live in. This is

a society that most of us did not create but which our President and other leaders have been willing to sustain by virtue of malign neglect. Do we possess the character and courage to address a problem which so many nations, poorer than our own, have found it natural to correct?

The answers to these questions represent a reasonable test 45 of our belief in the democracy to which we have been asked in public school to swear allegiance.

Content

1. In earlier eras, explanations for illiteracy often implied considerable blame for the victims—they were seen as stupid, lazy, shiftless, imprudent, living only for the day but with no concern for the future. To what extent do these explanations confuse the effects of illiteracy with the causes? In what ways does Kozol's essay refute these stereotypes? In his opinion, who's to blame?

2. How does Kozol's chapter illustrate his assertion that 60 million illiterates in America are "denied significant participation" in the government "of those two thirds whose wealth, skin color, or parental privilege allows them the opportunity to profit from the provocation and instruction of the written word" (¶ 6)? What's provocative about literacy?

Strategies/Structures

3. Why does Kozol begin his chapter on the costs of illiteracy with the warning on a can of Drāno (a caustic chemical to unclog drains)? Why doesn't he say anything more about it—or about a great many of his other examples? To what extent can these (or any) examples be counted on to speak for themselves?

4. Kozol constructs his argument by using a myriad of examples of the effects of illiteracy. What determines the order of the examples? Which are the most memorable? Where in this chapter do they appear?

Language

5. Why does Kozol use so many direct quotations from the illiterate people whose experiences he cites as examples?

6. What clues in Kozol's language let his readers know that he's sympathetic toward his subjects and angry at the conditions that cause the class of people his readers represent?

For Writing

7.   "Questions of literacy, in Socrates' belief, must at length be judged as matters of morality" (¶ 3). Write an essay in which you explain the connection between literacy and a moral society (and the converse, illiteracy and an immoral society), either for an audience you expect to agree with you or for readers who will disagree.

8.   In the concluding vignette of the man unable to read the road signs to guide the police to his disabled car on the freeway (¶s 42–43), Kozol implicitly equates literacy with a sense of self-identity, self-location, self-definition. Write an essay exploring the question, How does being literate enable one to become a full human being? When you're thinking about this, imagine what your life would be like if you couldn't read, write, or do math.

===

STEPHANIE COONTZ

Coontz (born, 1944) earned a B.A. at the University of California, Berkeley (1966), and an M.A. at the University of Washington (1970). A faculty member since 1975 at Evergreen State College in Olympia, Washington, her research in history and women's studies coalesce in work intended to correct misconceptions about American families. She is critical of the nostalgia that she sees as "very tempting to political and economic elitists who would like to avoid grappling with new demographic challenges. My favorite example," she told an interviewer, "is when people get nostalgic about the way elders were cared for in the past. Well, good Lord! Elders were the poorest, most abused sector of the population until the advent of Social Security."

The mythical American family, autonomous and independent, lives in legends from the early Puritans to the midwestern homesteaders to the rugged ranchers who "tamed" the Wild West. But people confuse the effect with the cause; the mythological characteristics of hard work and self-reliance are at odds with the facts—that the American family actually succeeded only with considerable outside help, particularly through federal policies. Thus in this essay, originally published in *Harper's Magazine* (1992) and in the book *The Way We Never Were: American Families and the Nostalgia Trap* (1992), Coontz identifies the numerous ways in which "assisting families is, simply, what government does." She looks again at families in *The Way We Really Are: Coming to Terms with America's Changing Families* (1997).

A Nation of Welfare Families

The current political debate over family values, personal responsibility, and welfare takes for granted the entrenched American belief that dependence on government assistance is a recent and destructive phenomenon. Conservatives tend to blame this dependence on personal irresponsibility aggravated by a swollen welfare apparatus that saps individual initiative. Liberals are more likely to blame it on personal misfortune magnified by the harsh lot that falls to losers in our competitive market economy. But both sides believe that "winners" in America make it on their own, that dependence reflects some kind of individual or family failure, and that the ideal family is the self-reliant unit of traditional lore—a family that takes care of its own, carves out a future for its children, and never asks for handouts. Politicians at both ends of the ideological spectrum have wrapped themselves in the mantle of these "family values," arguing over *why* the poor have not been able to make do without assistance, or whether aid has exacerbated their situation, but never questioning the assumption that American families traditionally achieve success by establishing their independence from the government. 1

The myth of family self-reliance is so compelling that our actual national and personal histories often buckle under its emotional weight. "We always stood on our own two feet," my grandfather used to say about his pioneer heritage, whenever he walked me to the top of the hill to survey the property in Washington State that his family had bought for next to nothing after it had been logged off in the early 1900s. Perhaps he didn't know that the land came so cheap because much of it was part of a federal subsidy originally allotted to the railroad companies, which had received 183 million acres of the public domain in the nineteenth century. These federal giveaways were the original source of most major Western logging companies' land, and when some of these 2 logging companies moved on to virgin stands of timber, federal lands trickled down to a few early settlers who were able to purchase them inexpensively.

3   Like my grandparents, few families in American history—whatever their "values"—have been able to rely solely on their own resources. Instead, they have depended on the legislative, judicial, and social support structures set up by governing authorities, whether those authorities were the clan elders of Native American societies, the church courts and city officials of colonial America, or the judicial and legislative bodies established by the Constitution.

4   At America's inception, this was considered not a dirty little secret but the norm, one that confirmed our social and personal interdependence. The idea that the family should have the sole or even primary responsibility for educating and socializing its members, finding them suitable work, or keeping them from poverty and crime was not only ludicrous to colonial and revolutionary thinkers but dangerously parochial.

5   Historically, one way that government has played a role in the well-being of its citizens is by regulating the way that employers and civic bodies interact with families. In the early twentieth century, for example, as a response to rapid changes ushered in by a mass-production economy, the government promoted a "family wage system." This system was designed to strengthen the ability of the male breadwinner to support a family without having his wife or children work. This family wage system was not a natural outgrowth of the market. It was a *political* response to conditions that the market had produced: child labor, rampant employment insecurity, recurring economic downturns, an earnings structure in which 45 percent of industrial workers fell below the poverty level and another 40 percent hovered barely above it, and a system in which thousands of children had been placed in orphanages or other institutions simply because their parents could not afford their keep. The state policies involved in the establishment of the family wage system included abolition of child labor, government pressure on industrialists to negotiate with unions, federal arbitration, expansion of compulsory schooling—and legislation discriminating against women workers.

But even such extensive regulation of economic and social 6
institutions has never been enough: government has always
supported families with direct material aid as well. The two best
examples of the government's history of material aid can be found
in what many people consider the ideal models of self-reliant families: the Western pioneer family and the 1950s suburban family. In
both cases, the ability of these families to establish and sustain
themselves required massive underwriting by the government.

Pioneer families, such as my grandparents, could never 7
have moved west without government-funded military mobiliza-
tions against the original Indian and Mexican inhabitants or state-
sponsored economic investment in transportation systems. In
addition, the Homestead Act of 1862 allowed settlers to buy 160
acres for $10—far below the government's cost of acquiring the
land—if the homesteader lived on and improved the land for five
years. In the twentieth century, a new form of public assistance
became crucial to Western families: construction of dams and
other federally subsidized irrigation projects. During the 1930s,
for example, government electrification projects brought pumps,
refrigeration, and household technology to millions of families.

The suburban family of the 1950s is another oft-cited ex- 8
ample of familial self-reliance. According to legend, after World
War II a new, family-oriented generation settled down, saved their
pennies, worked hard, and found well-paying jobs that allowed
them to purchase homes in the suburbs. In fact, however, the
1950s suburban family was far more dependent on government
assistance than any so-called underclass family of today. Federal
GI benefit payments, available to 40 percent of the male population between the ages of twenty and twenty-four, permitted a
whole generation of men to expand their education and improve
their job prospects without forgoing marriage and children. The
National Defense Education Act retooled science education in
America, subsidizing both American industry and the education
of individual scientists. Government-funded research developed
the aluminum clapboards, prefabricated walls and ceilings, and
plywood paneling that comprised the technological basis of the
postwar housing revolution. Government spending was also
largely responsible for the new highways, sewer systems, utility
services, and traffic-control programs that opened up suburbia.

9   In addition, suburban home ownership depended on an unprecedented expansion of federal regulation and financing. Before the war, banks often required a 50 percent down payment on homes and normally issued mortgages for five to ten years. In the postwar period, however, the Federal Housing Authority, supplemented by the GI bill, put the federal government in the business of insuring and regulating private loans for single-home construction. FHA policy required down payments of only 5 to 10 percent of the purchase price and guaranteed mortgages of up to thirty years at interest rates of just 2 to 3 percent. The Veterans Administration required a mere dollar down from veterans. Almost half the housing in suburbia in the 1950s depended on such federal programs.

10   The drawback of these aid programs was that although they worked well for recipients, nonrecipients—disproportionately poor and urban—were left far behind. While the general public financed the roads that suburbanites used to commute, the streetcars and trolleys that served urban and poor families received almost no tax revenues, and our previously thriving rail system was allowed to decay. In addition, federal loan policies, which were a boon to upwardly mobile white families, tended to systematize the pervasive but informal racism that had previously characterized the housing market. FHA redlining practices, for example, took entire urban areas and declared them ineligible for loans, while the government's two new mortgage institutions, the Federal National Mortgage Association and the Government National Mortgage Association (Fannie Mae and Ginny Mae) made it possible for urban banks to transfer savings out of the cities and into new suburban developments in the South and West.

11   Despite the devastating effects on families and regions that did not receive such assistance, government aid to suburban residents during the 1950s and 1960s produced in its beneficiaries none of the demoralization usually presumed to afflict recipients of government handouts. Instead, federal subsidies to suburbia encouraged family formation, residential stability, upward occupational mobility, and rising educational aspirations among youth who could look forward to receiving such aid. Seen in this light, the idea that government subsidies intrinsically induce

dependence, undermine self-esteem, or break down family ties is exposed as no more than a myth.

I am not suggesting that the way to solve the problems of poverty   12
and urban decay in America is to quadruple our spending on welfare. Certainly there are major reforms needed in our current aid policies to the poor. But the debate over such reform should put welfare in the context of *all* federal assistance programs. As long as we pretend that only poor or single-parent families need outside assistance, while normal families "stand on their own two feet," we will shortchange poor families, overcompensate rich ones, and fail to come up with effective policies for helping out families in the middle. Current government housing policies are a case in point. The richest 20 percent of American households receives three times as much federal housing aid—mostly in tax subsidies—as the poorest 20 percent receives in expenditures for low-income housing.

Historically, the debate over government policies toward   13
families has never been over *whether* to intervene but *how:* to rescue or to warehouse, to prevent or to punish, to moralize about values or mobilize resources for education and job creation. Today's debate, lacking such historical perspective, caricatures the real issues. Our attempt to sustain the myth of family self-reliance in the face of all the historical evidence to the contrary has led policymakers into theoretical contortions and practical miscalculations that are reminiscent of efforts by medieval philosophers to maintain that the earth and not the sun was the center of the planetary system. In the sixteenth century, leading European thinkers insisted that the planets and the sun all revolved around the earth—much as American politicians today insist that our society revolves around family self-reliance. When evidence to the contrary mounted, defenders of the Ptolemaic universe postulated all sorts of elaborate planetary orbits in order to reconcile observed reality with their cherished theory. Similarly, rather than admit that all families need some kind of public support, we have constructed ideological orbits that explain away each instance of middle-class dependence as "exception," an "abnormality," or even an illusion. We have distributed public aid to families through convoluted bureaucracies that have become impossible

to track; in some cases the system has become so cumbersome that it threatens to collapse around our ears. It is time to break through the old paradigm of self-reliance and substitute a new one that recognizes that assisting families is, simply, what government does.

Content

1. How could the Great American Myth—if myth it is—"that American families traditionally achieve success by establishing their independence from the government" (¶ 1) have arisen?
2. Why has this myth remained, in spite of the evidence to the contrary that Coontz cites throughout the essay?
3. What sorts of dependence on the government do Western pioneers and "the 1950s suburban family" (¶ 6) have in common (¶s 6–10)?
4. Is it accurate to say, as Coontz does, that "assisting families is, simply, what government does"? Explain your answer, in light of both this essay and your own experience.

Strategies/Structures

5. Coontz is a historian. How does her professional orientation govern the sorts of examples she uses? The way she organizes the essay?
6. Much of Coontz's evidence is expressed in percentages, as in paragraphs 8, 9, 12, and multiples, as in, "The richest 20 percent of American households receives three times as much federal housing aid—mostly in tax subsidies—as the poorest 20 percent receives in expenditures for low-income housing" (¶ 12). Is this evidence convincing? More or less convincing than evidence expressed in terms of numbers of people and dollar amounts?
7. The stereotype of welfare dependence is essentially negative. What sorts of evidence does Coontz use to replace this powerful stereotype with a positive one? Does she succeed in changing your mind?

Language

8. In what ways do the language and illustrations of the essay imply that Coontz is writing for an audience of the very same middle-class American families that she identifies as dependent on federal assistance?
9. Define "family values," "personal irresponsibility," "welfare," "family self-reliance" (used in the first two paragraphs and throughout the

essay) as they are used by one or another vested interest group and as Coontz uses them. To what extent are all these definitions value-laden? Can you think of any neutral definitions for these terms?

For Writing

10. Most people believe, says Coontz, that "'winners' in America make it on their own, that dependence reflects some kind of individual or family failure, and that the ideal family is the self-reliant unit of traditional lore—a family that takes care of its own, carves out a future for its children, and never asks for handouts" (¶ 1). Does "A Nation of Welfare Families" convince you that this is, as Coontz says, a "myth"? Write a paper for an audience that shares this belief, in which you either reinforce or dispute Coontz's claim. You will need to take into account the evidence she provides and to supplement it with evidence from your own and your family's experience.

11. Compare and contrast the conventional stereotypes of welfare recipients with the typical middle-class welfare family that Coontz describes. Do you think that the politicians who promise to end welfare as we know it have the middle class in mind? Explain, for a middle-class readership, using evidence from Coontz (feel free to consult her book, *The Way We Never Were*) and from either local or national politicians.

LESLIE S. MOORE

Moore (born, 1954) grew up in California and majored in English at the University of California at Santa Cruz and at Berkeley, earning a B.A. in 1976 and an M.A.T. in 1982. She has served twice in the Peace Corps, first teaching English in Korea, 1977–1979. Six years later, she and her husband joined the Peace Corps together and were sent to Bamako, Mali, to teach composition and literature at the Ecole Normale Supérieure. The Moores then moved to Princeton, Massachusetts, where Leslie worked as a newspaper writer and photographer and later taught high school English. They now live in Brooksville, Maine, where she works for a social service agency.

Two writers influenced Moore's prizewinning "Framing My Father," Eudora Welty (see 34–39) and Scott Russell Sanders. She explains, "I used what Welty said in *One Writer's Beginnings* about the increasing importance of framing scene, situation, implication, and finally, 'a single, entire human being,' as a challenge to push me beyond merely describing scenes and situations to considering implications and to capturing more of the entire human being. Thus, Welty provided the shape for my essay. Sanders taught me another lesson in point of view with his two essays about his father: 'The Inheritance of Tools' (186–95) and 'Under the Influence: Paying the Price of My Father's Booze' (441–55). By first eulogizing his father as a mentor in carpentry and then lamenting his father's alcoholism, Sanders showed me two ways of looking at the same man and the divergent lessons he taught his son. In 'Framing My Father,' I used Sanders' two-pronged approach in reverse, first presenting my father and the lessons he taught me in a negative light, then shifting my perspective to the positive."

❄ *Framing My Father*

The frame through which I viewed the world changed too, with time. Greater than scene, I came to see, is situation. Greater than situation is implication. Greater than all of these is a single, entire human being, who will never be confined in any frame.

EUDORA WELTY, *One Writer's Beginnings*

First Frame: The Scene

1   My father, fierce as ever, sits in the center of our living room folded into the low-slung chair, his long frame scooped to its elliptical contours, his thin shoulders hunched around his ears, his white beard bristling against his chest. He's reading *The Bourne Ultimatum* by Robert Ludlum. "#1 New York Times Bestseller" announces the front cover; "VINTAGE LUDLUM" proclaims the back. He's wearing white leather athletic shoes, gray warm-up pants, a red-knit shirt with the collar turned up, and black-rimmed reading glasses—full-sized, not half glasses. At his right elbow a computerized chess set stands ready, the little plastic players guarding their squares: black king on white, white king on black, queens, bishops, knights, castles, and pawns ranged around them. To his left the wood stove ticks.

Second Frame: The Situation

On his visit to New England from California with his wife of only 2
two months, my father commandeers the best chair in the house.
An heirloom from my husband's side of the family, the chair is a
citadel of security that no one vacates willingly. "Out!" my father
orders the Scottie and she thumps down with a suffering sidelong
glance. The Westie suffers his eviction with a great show of terrier
ferocity that delights my father. My stepmother keeps out of the
fray, opting for the second best chair in the house. Neither my
husband nor I have a minute to dispute the chair with my father.
My husband's not on vacation. When he's not reading or writing
or teaching, he's harvesting firewood, loading stove lengths into
the wheelbarrow in the woodlot then wheeling it to the woodshed
in our garage. And I'm too busy entertaining—orchestrating
meals and planning itineraries. I don't have the leisure to sit in
the chair. So my father monopolizes the house favorite for ten
days—from Friday, the eve of my April vacation, to Monday, the
day I go back to teaching school. He gets up early each morning,
brings one armload of wood in from the garage, stokes the stove
next to the chair, and folds into it. Then he shifts his attention
from bestsellers to chess problems.

Third Frame: The Implication

My father dominates our living room with his inertia. He forces us 3
to move around him—around his feet, his books, his games—
around a lifestyle that we don't share. Of course my husband and
I both read. We have to. We read for the courses we teach and take.
We read our students' papers. We read each other's writing. We
read with pencils in hand, underlining, taking notes, commenting
in the margins. We read as a discipline. My father reads to escape.
He has always read. He warned my mother early that marriage
wasn't going to get in the way of his reading; the marriage ended
in divorce. He reads widely and eclectically, balancing history, philosophy, and science on the one hand, science fiction, spy thrillers,
and mysteries on the other. He used to read with a drink in one
hand and a cigar in the other, but he has given up both—for health,
not sociability. He avoids what he calls "classical literature," the

sort I read. In a bookstore I point out Toni Morrison's *Beloved* but he ignores the suggestion and heads for the bestseller rack.

4   While my father sits folded into our favorite chair, my husband and I fret over the school work we have to get done this week. My husband is writing papers, working on images of pride in seventeenth-century country house poems and analyzing Hawthorne's rhetorical stance in the introduction to *The Scarlet Letter*. He wants me to critique his writing. I have to wrench my thoughts from hostess problems—how much fresh pasta it takes to feed four, whether my stepmother has enough Swiss almond coffee beans to last the week, when I'll get to the store to buy my father his newspapers—to concentrate on houses of pride and phrases embedded within phrases. Plus I have my own work to do—*Romeo and Juliet* papers to grade and a high school murder mystery I've promised my students I'd write with them—but I don't have the psychic space to start either. Meanwhile my father gives up another game of chess to the computer, stokes the fire, and goes back to *The Bourne Ultimatum*.

5   "Why doesn't he put on a sweater?" asks my husband. "We've burned more wood this week than we did in January."

6   We heat our house with wood that my husband cuts on our property. It's a process that he works at year long and enjoys—felling oak, hickory, and maple with his chainsaw, limbing the trees, pulling and piling the brush to burn later, cutting the wood into stove lengths, stacking it to dry, splitting the dry wood with a sledge and steel wedges, then wheeling it into the woodshed. Once he leaves the full wheelbarrow nosed half-way into the garage. My father doesn't offer to help unload it.

7   We wait for my father to take an interest in us—to ask what we are teaching, to inquire about books we have read, to wonder what we have written. Instead, near the end of his visit, he offers to buy us things. A microwave. We decline. A telephone answering machine. We shudder. We suggest rose bushes for our garden and he writes a check, then returns to his chair and his thriller.

Fourth Frame: The Human Being

8   My father has made a name for himself as a son-of-a-bitch. He has spent a lifetime cultivating a fierceness that intimidates adults and terrorizes children. That's one reason, I'm sure, he gave up

pediatrics to go into public health. He honed this fierceness on his own four children. When my brothers and I were growing up, his favorite phrase was "Stop crying or I'll spank you again." His favorite epithet was "You dumb stupe!" We cringed at the sound of his explosive "God-damn-it-all-to-hells!" and ducked out of the reach of his backhands. Recently my father admitted to me that the way he treated us as children would be considered child abuse today.

The lessons my father taught me were stamped in fear and 9 humiliation. Somehow I survived. Somehow the lessons stuck. Somehow I am grateful for the things I learned.

My father taught me how to body surf at Laguna Beach in 10 Southern California. One moment I would be patting wet sand onto a castle, the next I would be tucked under his arm like a football and carried full speed into the surf kicking and screaming and swallowing salt water. Yet I learned how to body surf. I learned how to get out past the breakers, diving under walls of thundering surf. I learned what to look for in a wave—the green swell on the horizon, the slow build, the fingers of foam tickling the top. I learned how to time my take-off, poised under the wave's foaming lip, arms cocked for their furious windmilling, feet set to kick. I learned how to let the wave take me, my body rigid and horizontal, head jutting out of the wave, one arm straight-fisted before me, the other clasped to my side. Finally I learned how to finish, tucking and rolling out of the breaker as it ground its way onto the shore.

When I was an awkward thirteen-year-old seeking accep- 11 tance in a new school, my father taught me to throw a softball so that I could try out for Miss Sparks' all-star team. He began our first lesson with an insult. "You throw the ball just like a girl," he told me. "Here!" he ordered. "Hold it like this. Like *this*, I said. *Look* at me!" He taught me to hold the ball between my thumb and two fingers, to draw it back behind my ear, cocking my elbow, curling my arm like a snake ready to strike, then whipping it from my shoulder to my wrist. He also taught me to catch: to scoop up the grounders that skittered across the pavement, to glove the fast balls without flinching, to judge the high flies and get underneath them, to dive for the balls that curved out of reach. Finally he taught me to catch and throw in the same instant, to fire the ball back at him faster than thought, only a short skip between the crack in my mitt and its sendoff.

12   I don't know when I first showed my father my school papers, but by the time I was in high school we had established regular editing sessions. I slaved over my manuscripts in longhand, leaving margins where my father wrote my literary pretensions clean off the page. He never commented on content—he'd rarely read the "classical literature" I was writing about—but he always had plenty to say about my style. None of it was complimentary. He muttered my sentences out loud, his pencil poised over the page, ready to attack my excesses—"You don't need *this*. Get rid of *that*."—my obscurities—"What in the hell is *that* supposed to mean?"—my stumblings—"You dumb stupe!"—my misspellings—"Look it up." He jabbed holes through the paper where I used big words to conceal incomplete thoughts and demanded that I sort out my ideas on the spot. And so we worked our way through my papers, paragraph by painful paragraph, page after painful page. By the end of an editing session with my father, my papers and my pretensions were returned to me, battered and bleeding, and I limped back to my room to start the rewrites.

13   My father's fierceness has cut both ways. It has cut all of his children, leaving scars on each. Some of the scars have healed. It has also cut him off, isolated him from human kindness, left him lonely and needy. And so, like King Lear in his retirement, my father invites himself to his grown children's houses. He commandeers the best chairs. He surrounds himself with books and games. And then he folds in upon himself. He has spent much of his fierceness and now he needs friends. Oscar Wilde says, "Children begin by loving their parents; then they judge them; sometimes they forgive them." As I trip over my father's feet in my living room, I wonder if I've forgiven him.

14   I remember those editing sessions—my father's lessons in brevity, clarity, grace, and precision. They were lessons in honesty, too. "Well then, why in the hell don't you say what you mean?" I can still hear my father demanding. And so I say it and I edit it and I rewrite it and I say it again.

15   I remember those softball practices—my father and I standing at opposite ends of stinging fast balls, the clap of leather against leather echoing off houses, our own special pattern of plays back and forth, the pain that numbed my throwing arm, yet still

the "Just a few more, Dad, please?" and the weight of acceptance that lone ball carried on its fleeting course from hand to glove.

And I remember my brothers and me at Laguna Beach, called out of the water at dusk and pleading to stay longer—"Just till the sun goes down, please, Daddy?" Then we'd bob out there past the breakers, watching the sun sigh into the Pacific, firing its dark surface with one last breath, until only a whisper of red remained, and we rode our last waves in triumphantly. 16

Content

1. Was Dr. Smith, Moore's father, a good or bad teacher of his own children? Does Moore view his lessons differently as an adult than she did at the time he was teaching her?
2. Is it possible to sort out single causes and single effects from among the complex factors that influence the ways we learn anything and everything? Explain your answer with reference to Moore's essay.
3. Moore says, "Recently my father admitted to me that the way he treated us as children would be considered child abuse today" (¶ 8). Do you agree? Why do you think Dr. Smith, a pediatrician and public health physician, treated his children so harshly? What was their reaction to him at the time?

Strategies/Structures

4. How does Moore's use, and labeling, of the four frames provide structure for her essay?
5. What does Moore think of her father? How do you know? Does she want you to share her opinion? Does her opinion actually change as the essay proceeds, or does she complicate it by showing more facets of a complicated parent-child relationship?

Language

6. Moore uses quotations from her father in all but the first of the essay's frames. What are these, how do they change as the essay proceeds, and what do they convey to you about the ambivalent relationship of Moore and her father?
7. If you (or anyone) had Dr. Smith for a writing tutor, would you have learned to write well? What is the effect of working one's way through a

paper, under a mentor's unforgiving scrutiny, "paragraph by painful paragraph, page after painful page"?

For Writing

8. What makes parents good, or bad, teachers of their own children? Can they be both concurrently? Address this question, for an audience that doesn't know your parents (or other significant mentor) by identifying two or three of your major personal characteristics (such as honesty, curiosity, perseverance, loyalty, athletic ability, whatever) and show how a parent or mentor strongly influenced these while you were growing up. Show, as Moore does, through some characteristic incidents, what this person did (or did not do) to cause these effects. Do you consider the results good, bad, or a mixture? Explain why.

9. Try writing an essay by using a series of several frames, as Moore does, to establish and interpret a relationship, either between an older and younger person or between two age peers—grandparent-grandchild, teacher-student, a married couple, two friends or enemies of the same or opposite sex, or others. Whether or not you write about yourself, you should know both of your subjects very well. The frames may be the same as Moore's (scene, situation, implication, character) or others of your own choice.

10. Throughout America's history, harshness has alternated with gentleness as being for children's own good. Is the adage "No pain, no gain" a valid assertion, in teaching children or in learning anything else? What teaching/learning style suits you best? Why?

Additional Topics for Writing
Cause and Effect

(For strategies for writing cause and effect, see 262.)

Write an essay, adapted to an audience of your choice, explaining either the causes or the effects of one of the following:

1. Substance abuse by teenagers, young adults, or another group
2. America's 50 percent divorce rate
3. Genetic engineering
4. Teenage pregnancy
5. The popularity of a given television show, movie or rock star, film, book, or type of book (such as romance, Gothic, Western)
6. Current taste in clothing, food, cars, architecture, interior decoration
7. The Civil War, the Great Depression, World War II, the Vietnam War, or other historical event
8. The popularity of a particular spectator or active sport
9. Your personality or temperament
10. Success in college or in business
11. Being "born again" or losing one's religious faith
12. Racial, sexual, or religious discrimination
13. An increasingly higher proportion of working women (or mothers of young children)
14. The computer revolution
15. The American Dream that "if you work hard you're bound to succeed"
16. America's disappearing farm land, and/or the decrease in the number of family farms (see Keifer, "The Death of a Farm" [636–39])
17. The actual or potential consequences of nuclear leaks, meltdowns
18. Vanishing animal or plant species; or the depletion of natural resources
19. Decrease in the number of people in training for skilled labor—electricians, plumbers, carpenters, tool and die makers, and others
20. A sudden change in personal status (from being a high school student to being a college freshman; from living at home to living away from home; from being dependent to being self-supporting; from being single to being married; from being childless to being a parent; from being married to being divorced . . .)

Part III

Clarifying Ideas

8 Description

When you describe a person, place, thing, or phenomenon, you want your readers to see it as you do, and to experience its sounds, tastes, smells, or textures. You may or may not wish to interpret it for them as well.

If you don't, you can describe something with seeming objectivity, impartially, sticking to the facts without evaluating them and letting your readers infer what they wish. (But bear in mind that by your very *selection and organization* of the facts you are implicitly evaluating them, deciding that some deserve emphasis, or mention, for whatever reasons, and others don't). Technical and scientific descriptions usually aim for objectivity, as would the author of a manual describing the components of a home computer, or an astronaut explaining the size, appearance, and composition of a newly discovered crater on the moon. So do some travel guides when describing places, for the authors cannot afford to let their personal preferences influence their presentations of Altoona and Oshkosh, which (bigosh!) must be described as impartially— or enthusiastically—as San Francisco and New Orleans.

If you do want to interpret something for your readers, your writing is bound to be subjective. For instance, Cynthia Ozick wants us to enter into "A Drugstore Eden" (316–30) and savor the pleasures of both the old-fashioned pharmacy and the garden of earthly delights in its backyard. Ozick's succulent description of the soda fountain appeals to our senses: "A pull at a long black handle [*touch and sight*] spurted out carbonated water [*touch, sound, and taste*]; a push at a tiny silver spout [*touch and sight*] drew forth curly drifts of whipped cream [*touch, sight, and taste*]. The air in this part of the drugstore was steamy with a deep coffee fragrance [*touch and smell*]. . . . Everything was fashioned of the same burnished chocolate-colored wood, except the fountain counters, which were heavy marble" [*sight and touch*]. In contrast is Joan Didion's "Marrying Absurd" (330–35), an indictment of Las Vegas weddings which condemns the place and its venal inhabitants as well as the practice mentioned in her judgmental title. The desert setting is a "moonscape of rattlesnakes and mesquite." Las Vegas, Didion says,

> is the most extreme and allegorical of American settlements, bizarre and beautiful in its venality and in its devotion to immediate gratification, a place the tone of which is set by mobsters and call girls and ladies' room attendants with amyl nitrite poppers in their uniform pockets. . . . There is no "time" in Las Vegas, no night and no day and no past and no future. . . .

Its values, she says, are hedonistic and money-oriented, as reflected by the only people she identifies, "mobsters," "call girls," and "ladies' room attendants." It is a place so "extreme," so weird, that even the ordinary measurements of time do not function. It is horrible, she implies.

In Didion's description of Las Vegas and Ozick's "Drugstore Eden" people are a significant part of the picture. The character of Las Vegas, a city operating "on the premise that marriage, like craps, is a game to be played when the table seems hot," is determined—in Didion's view—by people attracted and drawn into its illusions, the superficial elements of weddings that mimic "sincere" ceremonies with all the clichés, such as conventional organ music and fancy clothing, to reinforce the artificial sentiment of quickie weddings. The magical character of Ozick's pharmacy paradise emerges in distant contrast to its drab surroundings. Amidst Depression hardships a conscientious, hard-working husband and wife, whose industry nurtures the neighborhood and whose garden flourishes, provide a magical place where their daughter can read to her heart's content. The lush bulwark of flowers and vegetables keeps the ominous specter of World War II at bay.

Poignant events can occur anywhere, in places as familiar as one's own backyard or in exotic spots halfway around the world. In "One Remembers Most What One Loves" (360–67), Asiya Tschannerl recalls incidents from her early childhood in Beijing to depict her life as a foreign schoolchild, "a little black [American] kid" who soon learned to speak "perfect Mandarin." She juxtaposes these with images of Tiananmen Square, initially a place of happy socialization, later tainted with the bloody massacre of the Chinese people by Chinese soldiers. Having become acculturated to life in China, she undergoes culture shock on return to her native country, with its noise, racism, and lack of respect for elders.

Lucy Grealy experiences culture shock of a different sort. In "Masks" (349–60) she describes her life as a patient recovering from a two-year series of radiation treatments for cancer of the jaw. She doesn't tell us exactly what she looks like, but how she felt when childhood harassers called out, "Hey, girl, take off that monster mask—oops, she's not wearing a mask!'" A stranger in an increasingly strange land, she presents a series of snapshot scenes: wearing a costume on Halloween, feeling wonderful because "no one could see my face"; receiving an award for "bravery" at her elementary school graduation; attempting to camouflage herself in junior high to escape cruel remarks such as "*That* is the ugliest girl I have *ever* seen"; the increasingly macabre snapshots of her inner life. Grealy contrasts her state of mind, her ease of belonging "*Before*" her illness, with her fear, depression, and sense of ostracism *After* becoming a cancer victim.

Thus through details, carefully chosen and arranged, description offers an interpretation, an understanding of its varied subjects. The subjects may be *places:* geographic (China), natural (the Nevada desert surrounding Las Vegas), or constructed by humans (Las Vegas itself or the Park View Pharmacy). The subjects may be *people:* characters in their own right (Ozick's uncle Ruby) or in relation to others (Eric Liu in "Notes of a Native Speaker," 335–49). An Asian American, Liu fights against being stereotyped

Asian while he considers himself "white"—in lifestyle, values, clothing, jobs, ambition, language, groups he identifies with and respects. People are often described in relation to a particular place, role, occupation, or context. Like all the characters in this chapter, people are seen as experiencing change or understanding (or some other state of being) as a consequence of their reactions to or adventures in a particular setting or condition of life. The significance of descriptive details may be fairly obvious, whether stated or implied. Ozick's Edenic backyard contrasts the specific delights of the Parkview Pharmacy and its glorious backyard Eden with the barely glimpsed anti-Edenic forces of World War II and the Holocaust. Liu's self-description begins with an overview of who he is now (whether "'an honorary white'" or "' a banana,'" a person who has "become white inside" in his assimilation of American culture) and then proceeds in historical order from his childhood through elementary school, high school, and college to the present.

Rarely do any literary techniques occur in isolation. Although the organization of *The Essay Connection* is intended to highlight many of the major techniques of nonfiction writing, it would be unrealistic to present pure types, for they rarely exist. Even when you write an essay to experiment with a particular technique, such as description or narration, you're bound to employ others, as well.

Consequently, none of the essays in this chapter is purely descriptive. Note, for instance, the extensive comparisons and contrasts in people, territory, ways of life implied in the essays by Ozick, Didion, Liu, Grealy, and Tschannerl. All of these essays involve narration, as the writers tell of their personal involvement with the subject, through conversation, scene setting, and actions of individuals, groups, animals. Ozick, Liu, and Grealy use a great deal of exposition—explanations about their subject—and analyses to provide interpretations of themselves and their families, who are all rock-solid supportive of their children, and of where and how they live. In contrast to Ozick's and Tschannerl's loving interpretations of where they lived, whether Pelham Bay in the Bronx, or in Beijing, Didion uses extensive description to present implied arguments against what she sees as the dominant Las Vegas lifestyle and values: "Las Vegas seems to offer something other than 'convenience'; it is merchandising 'niceness,' the facsimile of proper ritual, to children who do not know how else to find it, how to make the arrangements, how to do it 'right.'"

There is a world of difference in descriptions, a compelling, complex world to explore.

STRATEGIES FOR WRITING— DESCRIPTION

1. What is my main purpose in writing this descriptive essay? To present and interpret factual information about the subject? To recreate its essence as I have experienced it, or the person, as I have known him or her? To form the basis for a narrative, or an argument—overt or implied? What mixture of objective information and subjective impressions will best fit my purpose?

2. If my audience is completely unfamiliar with the subject, how much and what kinds of basic information will I have to provide so they can understand what I'm talking about? (Can I assume that they've seen lakes, but not necessarily Lake Tahoe, the subject of my paper? Or that they know other grandmothers, but not mine, about whom I'm writing?) If my readers are familiar with the subject, in what ways can I describe it so they'll discover new aspects of it?

3. What particular characteristics of my subject do I wish to emphasize? Will I use in this description details revealed by the senses—sight, sound, taste, smell, touch? Any other sort of information, such as a person's characteristic behavior, gestures, ways of speaking or moving or dressing, values, companions, possessions, occupation, residence, style of spending money, beliefs, hopes, vulnerabilities? Nonsensory details will be particularly necessary in describing an abstraction, such as somebody's temperament or state of mind.

4. How will I organize my description? From the most dominant to the least dominant details? From the most to the least familiar aspects (or vice versa)? According to what an observer is likely to notice first, second . . . last? Or according to some other pattern?

5. Will I use much general language, or will my description be highly specific throughout? Do I want to evoke a clear, distinct image of the subject? Or a mood—nostalgic, thoughtful, happy, sad, or otherwise?

CYNTHIA OZICK

Ozick won notice as an American rarity, a public intellectual, before she achieved success as a novelist and essayist—*Art & Ardor* (1983), *Metaphor & Memory* (1989), *Family & Folly* (1996). A quintessential New Yorker, she was born in 1928, reared in the Bronx, and educated at Hunter College High School and New York University (B.A., 1949). After earning an M.A. (1950) at Ohio State, she returned to New York and has lived since her marriage (in 1952) in New Rochelle. Judaism is central to her life and work, "fired by Jewish culture, tradition, and controversy," and a commitment to Jewish survival, as a culture and in the State of Israel. "The term 'Jewish writer' is an oxymoron," she explains. "Being a good Jew means being a person of restraint, all the ethical things that a Jew stands for. The fiction writer must have total freedom of the imagination. The writer murders, rapes, is unkind, acerbic, and nasty. My father always said, 'Don't say what you think.' My mother had a flaming sense of social justice. I feel my mother and father at war in my genes."

Yet in "A Drugstore Eden" Ozick conveys a sense of peace, security, and tranquility in the idyllic ambience of her parents' drugstore in Pelham Bay, where she lived throughout her childhood and adolescence. In contrast to the Depression and World War II, which constituted the fabric of American life during this time, the drugstore provided a magical alternative. "Across the ocean synagogues were being torched," she writes, "refugees were in flight. On American movie screens Ginger Rogers and Fred Astaire whirled in and out of the March of Time's grim newsreels . . . the Sudetenland devoured, Poland invaded. Meanwhile, my mother's garden grew." Ozick's description of this lush haven abuzz with "ferocities of growth" incorporates familial and political history, autobiography, drugstore inventory; and she employs this entire microcosm as a metaphor for a time of life, a way of living that only memory can now recapture.

A Drugstore Eden

1   In 1929, my parents sold their drugstore in Yorkville—a neighborhood comprising Manhattan's East Eighties—and bought a pharmacy in Pelham Bay, in the northeast corner of the Bronx. It

was a move from dense city to almost country. Pelham Bay was at the very end of a relatively new stretch of elevated train track that extended from the subway of the true city all the way out to a small-town enclave of little houses and a single row of local shops: shoemaker's, greengrocer, drugstore, grocery, bait store. There was even a miniature five-and-ten where you could buy pots, housedresses, and thick lisle stockings for winter. Three stops down the line was the more populous Westchester Square, with its bank and post office, which old-timers still called "the village"—Pelham Bay had once lain outside the city limits, in Westchester County.

This lost little finger of the borough was named for the 2 broad but mild body of water that rippled across Long Island Sound to a blurry opposite shore. All the paths of Pelham Bay Park led down to a narrow beach of rough pebbles, and all the surrounding streets led, sooner or later, to the park, wild and generally deserted. Along many of these streets there were empty lots that resembled meadows, overgrown with Queen Anne's lace and waist-high weeds glistening with what the children termed "snake spit"; poison ivy crowded between the toes of clumps of sky-tall oaks. The snake spit was a sort of bubbly botanical excretion, but there were real snakes in those lots, with luminescent skins, brownish-greenish, crisscrossed with white lines. There were real meadows, too: acres of downhill grasses, in the middle of which you might suddenly come on a set of rusty old swings—wooden slats on chains—or a broken red-brick wall left over from some ruined and forgotten Westchester estate.

The Park View Pharmacy—the drugstore my parents 3 bought—stood on Colonial Avenue between Continental and Burr: Burr for Aaron Burr, the vice president who killed Alexander Hamilton in a duel. The neighborhood had a somewhat bloodthirsty Revolutionary flavor. You could still visit Spy Oak, the venerable tree, not far away, on which some captured Redcoats had been hanged; and now and then Revolutionary bullets were churned up a foot or so beneath the front lawn of the old O'Keefe house, directly across the street from the Park View Pharmacy. George Washington had watered his horses, it was believed, in the ancient sheds beyond Ye Olde Homestead, a local tavern that well after Prohibition was still referred to as "the speakeasy." All the same, there were no Daughters of the American Revolution here: Pelham Bay was populated by the children of German, Irish, Swedish, Scottish, and Italian immigrants, and by a handful of the original immigrants themselves. The greenhorn Italians, from Naples and Sicily, kept goats and pigs in their back yards and pigeons on their roofs. Pelham Bay's single Communist—you could tell from the election results that there was such a rare bird—was the Scotsman who lived around the corner, though only my parents knew this. They were privy to the neighborhood's opinions, ailments, and family secrets.

4   In those years, the drugstore seemed one of the world's permanent institutions. Who could have imagined that it would one day vanish into an aisle in the supermarket, or reemerge as a kind of supermarket itself? What passes for a pharmacy nowadays is all open shelves and ceiling racks of brilliant white neon suggesting perpetual indoor sunshine. The Park View, by contrast, was a dark cavern lined with polished wood cabinets rubbed nearly black and equipped with sliding glass doors and mirrored backs. The counters were heaped with towering ziggurats of lotions, potions, and packets, and under them ran glassed-in showcases of the same sober wood. There was a post office (designated a "substation") that sold penny postcards and stamps and money orders. The prescription area was in the rear, closed off from view: here were scores of labeled drawers of all sizes and rows of oddly shaped brown bottles. In one of those drawers traditional rock candy was stored, in two flavors, plain and maple; it dangled on long strings. And finally there was the prescription desk itself, a sloping, lecternlike affair on which the current prescription ledger always lay, like some scared text.

5   There was also a soda fountain. A pull at a long black handle spurted out carbonated water; a push at a tiny silver spout drew forth curly drifts of whipped cream. The air in this part of the drugstore was steamy with a deep coffee fragrance, and on wintry Friday afternoons the librarians from the Travelling Library, a green truck that arrived once a week, would linger, sipping and gossiping on the high-backed fountain chairs or else at the little glass-topped tables nearby, with their small three-cornered seats. Everything was fashioned of the same burnished chocolate-colored wood, except the fountain counters, which were heavy marble. Above the prescription area, sovereign over all, rose a

symbolic pair of pharmacy globes, one filled with red fluid, the other with blue. My father's diploma, class of 1917, was mounted on a wall; next to it hung a picture of the graduates. There was my very young father, with his round pale eyes and widow's peak— a fleck in a mass of black gowns.

Sometime around 1937, my mother said to my father, "Willie, if   6
we don't do it now we'll never do it."

It was the trough of the Great Depression. In the comics,   7
Pete the Tramp was swiping freshly baked pies set out to cool on windowsills, and in real life tramps (as the homeless were then called) were turning up in the Park View nearly every day. Sometimes they were city drunks—"Bowery bums"—who had fallen asleep downtown on the subway and ended up in Pelham Bay. Sometimes they were exhausted Midwesterners who had been riding the rails and had rolled off into the cattails of the Baychester marsh. But always my father sat them down at the fountain and fed them a sandwich and soup. They smelled bad, and their eyes were red and rheumy; often they were very polite. They never left without a meal and a nickel for carfare.

No one was worse off than the tramps, or more desolate   8
than the family who lived in an old freight car on the way to Westchester Square; but no one escaped the Depression. Seven days a week, the Park View opened at 9 A.M. and closed at two the next morning. My mother scurried from counter to counter, tended the fountain, unpacked cartons, climbed ladders; her varicose veins oozed through their strappings. My father patiently ground powders and folded the white dust into translucent paper squares with elegantly efficient motions. The drugstore was, besides, a public resource: my father bandaged cuts, took specks out of strangers' eyes, and once removed a fishhook from a man's cheek—though he sent him off to the hospital, on the other side of the Bronx, immediately afterward. My quiet father had cronies and clients, grim women and voluble men who flooded his understanding ears with the stories of their sufferings, of flesh or psyche. My father murmured and comforted, and later my parents would whisper sadly about who had "the big C," or, with an ominous gleam, they would smile over a geezer certain to have a heart attack: the geezer would be newly

married to a sweet young thing. (And usually they were right about the heart attack.)

9   Yet, no matter how hard they toiled, they were always in peril. There were notes to pay off: they had bought the Park View from a pharmacist named Robbins, and every month, relentlessly, a note came due. They never fell behind, and never missed a payment (and in fact were eventually awarded a certificate attesting to this feat), but the effort—the unremitting pressure, the endless anxiety—ground them down. "The note, the note," I would hear, a refrain that shadowed my childhood, though I had no notion of what it meant.

10   What it meant was that the Depression, which had already crushed so many, was about to crush my mother and father: suddenly their troubles intensified. The Park View was housed in a building owned by a woman my parents habitually referred to, whether out of familiarity or resentment, only as Tessie. The pharmacy's lease was soon to expire, and at this moment, in the cruellest hour of the Depression, Tessie chose to raise the rent. Her tiger's eyes narrowed to slits; no appeal could soften her.

11   It was because of those adamant tiger's eyes that my mother said, "Willie, if we don't do it now we'll never do it."

12   My mother was aflame with ambition, emotion, struggle. My father was reticent and far more resigned to the world as given. Once, when the days of the Travelling Library were over and a real library had been constructed at Westchester Square—you reached it by trolley—I came home elated, carrying a pair of books I had found side by side. One was called *My Mother Is a Violent Woman*, the other was *My Father Is a Timid Man*. These seemed a comic revelation of my parents' temperaments. My mother was all heat and enthusiasm. My father was all logic and reserve. My mother, unrestrained, could have run an empire of drugstores. My father was satisfied with one.

13   Together they decided to do something revolutionary, something virtually impossible in those raw and merciless times. One street over—past McCardle's sun-baked gas station, where there was always a Model A Ford with its hood open for repair, and past the gloomy bait store, ruled over by Mr. Isaacs, a dour and reclusive veteran of the Spanish-American War, who sat reading military histories all day under a mastless sailboat suspended from the

ceiling—lay an empty lot in the shape of an elongated lozenge. My parents' daring plan—for young people without means it was beyond daring— was to buy that lot and build on it, from scratch, a brand-new Park View Pharmacy.

They might as well have been dreaming of taking off in 14 Buck Rogers's twenty-fifth century rocket ship. The cost of the lot was a stratospheric $13,500, unchanged from the boom of 1928, just before the national wretchedness descended. And that figure was only for the land. Then would come the digging of a foundation and the construction of a building. What was needed was a miracle.

One sad winter afternoon, my mother was standing on a 15 ladder, concentrating on setting out some newly arrived drug items on a high shelf. (Although a typical drugstore stocked several thousand articles, the Park View's unit-by-unit inventory was never ample. At the end of every week, I would hear my father's melodious, impecunious chant on the telephone, as he ordered goods from the jobber: "A sixth of a dozen, a twelfth of a dozen . . .") A stranger wearing a brown fedora and a long overcoat entered, looked around, and appeared not at all interested in making a purchase; instead, he went wandering from case to case, picking things up and putting them down again, trying to be inconspicuous, asking an occasional question or two, all the while scrupulously observing my diligent parents. The stranger turned out to be a mortgage officer from the American Bible Society, and what he saw, he explained afterward, was a conscientious application of the work ethic; so it was the American Bible Society that supplied the financial foundation of my parents' Eden, the new Park View. They had entertained an angel unawares.

The actual foundation, the one to be dug out of the ground, 16 ran into instant biblical trouble: flood. An unemployed civil engineer named Levinson presided over the excavation; he was unemployed partly because the Depression had dried up much of the job market but mostly because engineering firms in those years were notorious for their unwillingness to hire Jews. Poor Levinson! The vast hole in the earth that was to become the Park View's cellar filled up overnight with water; the bay was near, and the water table was higher than the hapless Levinson had expected. The work halted. Along came Finnegan and rescued

Levinson: Finnegan the plumber, who for a painful fee of fifty dollars (somehow squeezed out of Levinson's mainly empty pockets) pumped out the sea.

17   After the Park View's exultant move, in 1939, the shell of Tessie's old place on Colonial Avenue remained vacant for years. No one took it over; the plate-glass windows grew murkier and murkier. Dead moths were heaped in decaying mounds on the inner sills. Tessie had lost more than the heartless increase she had demanded, and more than the monthly rent the renewed lease would have brought: there was something ignominious and luckless—tramplike—about that fly-specked empty space, now dimmer than ever. But, within its freshly risen walls, the Park View redux gleamed. Overhead, fluorescent tubes—an indoor innovation—shed a steady white glow, and a big square skylight poured down shifting shafts of brilliance. Familiar objects appeared clarified in the new light: the chocolate-colored fixtures, arranged in unaccustomed configurations, were all at once thrillingly revivified. Nothing from the original Park View had been left behind—everything was just the same, yet zanily out of order: the two crystal urns with their magical red and blue fluids suggestive of alchemy; the entire stock of syrups, pills, tablets, powders, pastes, capsules; tubes and bottles by the hundred; the fountain, with its marble top; the prescription desk and its sacrosanct ledger; the stacks of invaluable cigar boxes stuffed with masses of expired prescriptions; the locked and well-guarded narcotics cabinet; the post office and the safe in which the post office receipts were kept. Even the great, weighty, monosyllabically blunt hanging sign—"Drugs"—had been brought over and rehung, and it, too, looked different now. In the summer heat it dropped its black rectangular shadow over Mr. Isaac's already shadowy headquarters, where vials of live worms were crowded side by side with vials of nails and screws.

18 At around this time, my mother's youngest brother, my uncle Rubin, had come to stay with us—no one knew for how long—in our little house on St. Paul Avenue, a short walk from the Park View. Five of us lived in that house: my parents, my grandmother, my brother, and I. Rubin, who was called Ruby, was now the sixth. He was a bachelor and something of a family conundrum.

He was both bitter and cheerful; effervescence would give way to lassitude. He taught me how to draw babies and bunnies, and could draw anything himself; he wrote ingenious comic jingles, which he illustrated as adroitly, it struck me, as Edward Lear; he cooked up mouthwatering corn fritters and designed fruit salads in the shape of ravishing unearthly blossoms. When now and then it fell to him to put me to bed, he always sang the same heartbreaking lullaby—"Sometimes I fee-eel like a motherless child, a long, long way-ay from ho-ome"—in a deep and sweet quaver. In those days, he was mostly jobless; on occasion, he would crank up his tin lizzie and drive out to upper Westchester to prune trees. Once he was stopped at a police roadblock, under suspicion of being the Lindbergh-baby kidnapper—the back seat of his messy old Ford was strewn with ropes, hooks, and my discarded baby bottles.

Ruby had been disappointed in love, and was somehow a [19] disappointment to everyone around him. When he was melancholy or resentful, the melancholy was irritable and the resentment acrid. As a very young man, he had been single-minded in a way that none of his immigrant relations, or the snobbish mother of the girlfriend who had been coerced into jilting him, could understand or sympathize with. In czarist Russia's restricted Pale of Settlement, a pharmacist was the highest vocation a Jew could attain to. In a family of pharmacists, Ruby wanted to be a farmer. Against opposition, he had gone off to farm school in New Jersey—one of several Jewish agricultural projects sponsored by the German philanthropist Baron Maurice de Hirsch. Ruby was always dreaming up one sort of horticultural improvement or another, and sometimes took me with him to visit a certain Dr. McClean, at the New York Botanical Garden, whom he was trying to interest in one of his inventions. He was kindly received, but nothing came of it. Despite his energy and originality, all Ruby's hopes and strivings collapsed in futility.

His presence now was fortuitous: he could assist in the [20] move from Tessie's place to the new location. But his ingenuity, it would soon develop, was benison from the goddess Flora. The Park View occupied all the width but not the entire depth of the lot on which it was built. It had, of course, a welcoming front door, through which customers passed, but there was also a back door, past a little aisle adjoining the prescription room in the rear of the store, and well out of sight. When you walked out this back door, you were confronted by an untamed patch of weeds and stones, some of them as thick as boulders. At the very end of it lay a large flat rock, in the center of which someone had scratched a mysterious X. The X, it turned out, was a surveyor's sign; it had been there long before my parents bought the lot. It meant that the property extended to that point and no farther.

21   I was no stranger either to the lot or to its big rock. It was where the neighborhood children played—a sparse group in that sparsely populated place. Sometimes the rock was a pirate ship; sometimes it was a pretty room in a pretty house; in January it held a snow fort. But early one summer evening, when the red ball of the sun was very low, a little girl named Theresa, whose hair was as red as the sun's red ball, discovered the surveyor's X and warned me against stamping on it. If you stamp on a cross, she said, the Devil's helpers climb right out from inside the earth and grab you and take you away to be tortured. "I don't believe that," I said, and stamped on the X as hard as I could. Instantly, Theresa sent out a terrified shriek; chased by the red-gold zigzag of her hair, she fled. I stood there abandoned—suppose it was true? In the silence all around, the wavering green weeds seemed taller than ever before.

22   Looking out from the back door at those same high weeds, my mother, like Theresa, saw hallucinatory shapes rising out of the ground. But it was not the Devil's minions that she imagined streaming upward; it was their very opposite—a vision of celestial growths and fragrances, brilliant botanical hues, golden pears and yellow sunflower faces, fruitful vines and dreaming gourds. She imagined an enchanted garden. She imagined a secret Eden.

23   What she did not imagine was that Ruby, himself so un-peaceable, would turn out to be the viceroy of her peaceable kingdom. Ruby was angry at my mother; he was angry at everyone but me—I was too young to be held responsible for his lost loves and aspirations. But he could not be separated from his love of fecund dirt. Dirt—the brown dirt of the earth—inspired him; the feel and smell of dirt uplifted him; he took an artist's pleasure in the soil and all its generative properties. And though he claimed to scorn my mother, he became the subaltern of her passion. Like some

wizard commander of the stones—they were scattered everywhere in a wild jumble—he swept them into orderliness. A pack of stones was marshaled into a low wall. Five stones were transformed into a perfect set of stairs. Seven stones surrounded what was to become a flower bed. Stones were borders, stones were pathways, stones—placed just so—were natural sculptures. And, finally, Ruby commanded the stones to settle in a circle in the very center of the lot. Inside the circle there was to be a green serenity of grass, invaded only by the blunders of violets and wandering buttercups. Outside the circle, the earth would be a fructifying engine. It was a dreamer's circle, like the moon or the sun, or a fairy ring, or a mystical small Stonehenge, miniaturized by a spell.

The back yard was cleared, but it was not yet a garden. Like a merman combing a mermaid's weedy hair, my uncle Ruby had unraveled primeval tangles and brambles. He had set up two tall metal poles to accommodate a rough canvas hammock, with a wire strung from the top of one pole to the other. Over this wire a rain-faded old shop awning had been flung, so that the hammock became a tent or cave or darkened den. A backyard hammock! I had encountered such things only in storybooks. 24

And then my uncle was gone—drafted before the garden could be dug. German tanks were biting into Europe. Weeping, my grandmother pounded her breast with her fist: the British White Paper of 1939 had declared that ships packed with Jewish refugees would be barred from the beaches of Haifa and Tel Aviv, and returned to a Nazi doom. In P.S. 71, our neighborhood school, the boys were drawing cannons and warplanes; the girls were drawing figure skaters in tutus; both boys and girls were drawing the Trylon and the Perisphere. The Trylon was a three-sided pyramid. The Perisphere was a shining globe. They were already as sublimely legendary as the Taj Mahal. The "official" colors of the 1939 World's Fair were orange and blue: everyone knew this; everyone had ridden in the noiselessly moving armchairs of the Futurama into the fair's City of Tomorrow, where the elevated highways of the impossibly futuristic 1960s materialized among inconceivable suburbs. In the magical lanes of Flushing, you could watch yourself grin on a television screen as round and small as the mouth of a teacup. My grandmother, in that frail year of her dying, was taken to see the Jewish Palestine Pavilion. 25

26   Ruby sent a photograph of himself in army uniform and a muffled recording of his voice, all songs and jolly jingles, from a honky-tonk arcade in an unnamed Caribbean town. It was left to my mother to dig the garden. I have no inkling of when or how. I lived inside the hammock all that time, under the awning, enclosed; I read and read. Sometimes, for a treat, I would be given two nickels for carfare and a pair of quarters, and then I would climb the double staircase to the train and go all the way to Fifth-ninth Street: you could enter Bloomingdale's directly from the subway, without ever glimpsing daylight. I would run up the steps to the book department, on the mezzanine, moon over the Nancy Drew series in an agony of choosing (*Password to Larkspur Lane, The Whispering Statue,* each for fifty cents), and run down to the subway again with my lucky treasure. An hour and a half later I would be back in the hammock, under the awning, while the afternoon sun broiled on. But such a trip was rare. Mostly, the books came from the Travelling Library; inside my hammock cave the melting glue of new bindings sent out a blissful redolence. And now my mother would emerge from the back door of the Park View, carrying—because it was so hot under the awning—half a cantaloupe with a hillock of vanilla ice cream in its scooped-out center. (Have I ever been so safe, so happy since? Has consciousness ever felt so steady, so unimperiled, so immortal?)

27   Across the ocean, synagogues were being torched, refugees were in flight. On American movie screens Ginger Rogers and Fred Astaire whirled in and out of the March of Time's grim newsreels—Chamberlain with his defeatist umbrella, the Sudetenland devoured, Poland invaded. Meanwhile, my mother's garden grew. The wild raw field Ruby had regimented was ripening now into a luxuriant and powerful fertility: all around my uncle's talismanic ring of stones the ground swelled with thick, savory smells. Corn tassels hung down over the shut green-leaf lids of pearly young cobs. Fat tomatoes reddened on sticks. The bumpy scalps of cucumbers poked up. And flowers! First, as tall as the hammock poles, a flock of hunchbacked sunflowers, their heads too weighty for their shoulders—huge, heavy heads of seeds and a ruff of yellow petals. At their feet, rows of zinnias and marigolds, with tiny violets and the weedy pink buds of clover sidling between.

28   Now and then a praying mantis—a stiffly marching fake leaf—would rub its skinny forelegs together and stare at you with

two stern black dots. Or there would be a sudden blizzard of butterflies—mostly white and mothlike, but sometimes a great black-
veined monarch would alight on a stone, in perfect stillness. Year
by year, the shade of a trio of pear trees widened and deepened.

Did it rain? It must have rained—it must have thundered—   29
in those successive summers of my mother's garden, but I remember a perpetual sunlight, hot and honeyed, and the airless boil
under the awning, and the heart-piercing scalliony odor of library
glue (so explicit that I can this minute re-create it in my very tear
ducts, as a kind of mourning), and the fear of bees.

No one knew the garden was there. It was utterly hidden. You   30
could not see it, or suspect it, inside the Park View, and because it
was nestled in a wilderness of empty lots, it was altogether invisible from any surrounding street. It was a small secluded paradise.

And what vegetable chargings, what ferocities of growth,   31
the turbulent earth pushed out! Buzzings and dapplings. Birds
dipping their beaks in an orgy of seed lust. It was as if the ground
itself were crying peace, peace; and the war roared on. In Europe,
the German death factories were pumping out smoke and human
ash from a poisoned orchard of chimneys. In Pelham Bay, among
bees and white-wing flutterings, the sweet brown dirt pumped
ears of corn.

Though I was mostly alone there, I was never lonely in the garden.   32
But, on the other side of the door, inside the Park View, an unfamiliar churning had begun—a raucous teeming, the world turning
on its hinge. In the aftermath of Pearl Harbor, there was all at once
a job for nearly everyone, and money to spend in any cranny of
wartime leisure. The Depression was receding. On weekends, the
subway spilled out mobs of city picnickers into the green fields of
Pelham Bay Park, bringing a tentative prosperity to the neighborhood—especially on Sundays. I dreaded and hated this new Sunday frenzy, when the Park View seemed less a pharmacy than a
carnival stand, and my isolation grew bleak. Open shelves
sprouted in the aisles, laden with anomalous racks of sunglasses,
ice coolers, tubes of mosquito repellent and suntan lotion, paper
cups, colorful towers of hats—sailors' and fishermen's caps, cellu-
loid visors, straw topis and sombreros, headgear of every conceivable shape. Thirsty picnickers stood three deep at the fountain,
clamoring for ice cream cones or sodas. The low, serious drugstore

voices that accompanied the Park View's weekly decorum were swept away by revolving, laughing crowds—carnival crowds. And at the close of these frenetic summer Sundays my parents would anxiously count up the cash register in the worn night of their exhaustion, and I would hear their joyful disbelief: unimaginable riches, almost seventy-five dollars in a single day!

33   Then, when the safe was locked up and the long cords of the fluorescent lights pulled, they would drift in the dimness into the garden to breathe the cool fragrance. At this starry hour, the katydids were screaming in chorus, and fireflies bleeped like errant semaphores. In the enigmatic dark, my mother and father, with their heads together in silhouette, looked just then as I pictured them looking on the Albany night boat, on June 19, 1921, their wedding day. There was a serial photo from that long-ago time I often gazed at—a strip taken in an automatic photo booth in fabled, faraway Albany. It showed them leaning close, my young father quizzical, my young mother trying to smile, or else trying not to; the corners of her lips wandered toward one loveliness or the other. They had brought back a honeymoon souvenir: three sandstone monkeys joined at the elbows—see no evil, hear no evil, speak no evil. And now, in their struggling forties, standing in Ruby's circle of stones, they breathed in the night smells of the garden, onion grass and honeysuckle, and felt their private triumph. Seventy-five dollars in seventeen hours.

34   Nearly all the drugstores of the old kind are gone, in Pelham Bay and elsewhere. The Park View Pharmacy lives only in a secret Eden behind my eyes. Gone are Bernardini, Pressman, Weiss, the rival druggists on the way to Westchester Square. They all, like my father, rolled suppositories on glass slabs and ground powders with brass pestles. My mother's garden has returned to its beginning: a wild patch, though enclosed now by brick house after brick house. The houses have high stoops; they are city houses. The meadows are striped with highways. Spy Oak gave up its many ghosts long ago.

35   But under a matting of decayed pear pits and thriving ragweed back of what used to be the Park View, Ruby's circle of stones stands frozen. The earth, I suppose, has covered them over, as—far off, in an overgrown old cemetery on Staten Island—it

covers my dreaming mother, my father, my grandmother, my resourceful and embittered farmer uncle.

Content

1. Is Ozick's "Drugstore Eden" comprised of both the drugstore and the
garden? Does each have edenic elements? Or is only the garden an Eden?
2. Why is it important that this drugstore Eden be experienced by a
child? Would Ozick's parents have described their workplace, the Park
View Pharmacy and the garden in back, the way their daughter did?
Why or why not? How would the family's interpretations have differed
from those of Ruby, Ozick's "resourceful and embittered farmer uncle"
(¶s 18–24)?
3. Why do we sense all along what the last two paragraphs (¶s 34–35)
confirm, that the Park View Pharmacy, like other Edens, no longer exists?
How does our sense of nostalgia influence our interpretation of the scene
and its characters?

Strategies/Structures

4. Ozick's description often involves lists or catalogs of vegetation (¶s
2, 27), nationalities (¶ 3), drugstore furnishings (¶s 4–5), among many
other things. What kinds of details does she include to vary the lists and
keep them appealing?
5. In this largely descriptive account, Ozick provides characterizations
(of her parents, Uncle Ruby), many interpretations ("no matter how hard
[my parents] toiled, they were always in peril," ¶ 9), and narration of incidents (the visit of the mortgage officer from the American Bible Society,
¶ 15). Explain how these techniques contribute to the overall picture of
the pharmacy, inside and out.
6. How does Ozick avoid overwhelming her readers with details? Or
is the effect of the abundance of details in fact overpowering?

Language

7. Descriptions of the way things were in the good old days often become either sentimental—excessively emotional—unbelievable, or both.
Is either true of "The Drugstore Eden"?
8. Ozick uses the language of an adult to recall the drugstore and garden of her childhood. Find a typical passage in which she enables her
readers to see the experience as a child yet also implies or offers an adult's
interpretation.

For Writing

9.   Identify a place that had considerable significance—pleasant or unpleasant—for you as a child or an adolescent, and describe it for readers
unfamiliar with it so that you put them there. Use details of sight, sound,
smell, touch, taste, where appropriate, to help your readers experience it
as you did, in emotional as well as intellectual understanding.

10.   Pick an aspect of your childhood or adolescent relationship with a
parent, relative, or other adult or pick a critical experience in growing up,
in or out of school, in mainstream or minority culture, and describe it
so the reader not only shares your experience but interprets it as you
do. Compare, if you wish, with Welty (34–39), Cofer (179–86), Zitkala-Sa
(273–83), Liu (335–49), Soto (436–41), Barry (670–75).

JOAN DIDION

Novelist and essayist Didion was born (1934) in Sacramento,
California, and educated at the University of California, Berkeley.
Since 1964 she and her husband, writer John Gregory Dunne,
have collaborated on screenplays, including *A Star Is Born* (1976)
and *Up Close and Personal* (1996). In her novels, including *A Book
of Common Prayer* (1977) and *Democracy* (1984), and three essay
collections, *Slouching Towards Bethlehem* (1968), *The White Album*
(1979), and *After Henry* (1992). In many of her works, Didion
writes to confound the moral vacuum she finds in people es-
tranged from the traditional values of religion, family, and society.

Estrangement from tradition permeates "Marrying Absurd,"
as Didion focuses on the discrepancy between our exalted expectations of marriage as a sacrament and the reality of this
experience in Las Vegas, where "marriage, like craps, is a game
to be played when the table seems hot." Didion uses a number of
examples to make her point: the speedy judge who compresses
the ceremony from five minutes into three; the commercial Las
Vegas wedding chapels, as divorced from life in the rest of the
world as Las Vegas itself is; the 11 p.m. wedding of a drunken
bride rushing to perform in "the midnight show"; and the oddly
formal weddings of innocents who confuse the accessories (formal
clothes and pink champagne) with the essence of a personally
significant ceremony. Through vivid, compelling examples Didion

defines a city and a travesty of a ceremony—and the people who
partake of both. In accord with her own advice, *"listen to me, see it
my way, change your mind,"* Didion promotes her moral vision.

Marrying Absurd

T o be married in Las Vegas, Clark County, Nevada, a bride   1
must swear that she is eighteen or has parental permission
and a bridegroom that he is twenty-one or has parental permission. Someone must put up five dollars for the license. (On
Sundays and holidays, fifteen dollars. The Clark County Courthouse issues marriage licenses at any time of the day or night
except between noon and one in the afternoon, between eight and
nine in the evening, and between four and five in the morning.)
Nothing else is required. The State of Nevada, alone among these
United States, demands neither a premarital blood test nor a
waiting period before or after the issuance of a marriage license.
Driving in across the Mojave from Los Angeles, one sees the signs
way out on the desert, looming up from that moonscape of rattlesnakes and mesquite, even before the Las Vegas lights appear like
a mirage on the horizon: "GETTING MARRIED? Free License Information First Strip Exit." Perhaps the Las Vegas wedding industry
achieved its peak operational efficiency between 9·00 p.m. and
midnight of August 26, 1965, an otherwise unremarkable Thurs-
day which happened to be, by Presidential order, the last day on
which anyone could improve his draft status merely by getting
married. One hundred and seventy-one couples were pronounced
man and wife in the name of Clark County and the State of
Nevada that night, sixty-seven of them by a single justice of the
peace, Mr. James A. Brennan. Mr. Brennan did one wedding at the
Dunes and the other sixty-six in his office, and charged each
couple eight dollars. One bride lent her veil to six others. "I got it
down from five to three minutes," Mr. Brennan said later of his
feat. "I could've married them *en masse*, but they're people, not
cattle. People expect more when they get married."

What people who get married in Las Vegas actually do   2
expect—what, in the largest sense, their "expectations" are—

strikes one as a curious and self-contradictory business. Las Vegas is the most extreme and allegorical of American settlements, bizarre and beautiful in its venality and in its devotion to immediate gratification, a place the tone of which is set by mobsters and call girls and ladies' room attendants with amyl nitrite poppers in their uniform pockets. Almost everyone notes that there is no "time" in Las Vegas, no night and no day and no past and no future (no Las Vegas casino, however, has taken the obliteration of the ordinary time sense quite so far as Harold's Club in Reno, which for a while issued, at odd intervals in the day and night, mimeographed "bulletins" carrying news from the world outside); neither is there any logical sense of where one is. One is standing on a highway in the middle of a vast hostile desert looking at an eighty-foot sign which blinks "STARDUST" or "CAESAR'S PALACE." Yes, but what does that explain? This geographical implausibility reinforces the sense that what happens there has no connection with "real" life; Nevada cities like Reno and Carson are ranch towns, Western towns, places behind which there is some historical imperative. But Las Vegas seems to exist only in the eye of the beholder. All of which makes it an extraordinarily stimulating and interesting place, but an odd one in which to want to wear a candlelight satin Priscilla of Boston wedding dress with Chantilly lace insets, tapered sleeves and a detachable modified train.

3   And yet the Las Vegas wedding business seems to appeal to precisely that impulse. "Sincere and Dignified Since 1954," one wedding chapel advertises. There are nineteen such wedding chapels in Las Vegas, intensely competitive, each offering better, faster, and, by implication, more sincere services than the next: Our Photos Best Anywhere, Your Wedding on A Phonograph Record, Candlelight with Your Ceremony, Honeymoon Accommodations, Free Transportation from Your Motel to Courthouse to Chapel and Return to Motel, Religious or Civil Ceremonies, Dressing Rooms, Flowers, Rings, Announcements, Witnesses Available, and Ample Parking. All of these services, like most others in Las Vegas (sauna baths, payroll-check cashing, chinchilla coats for sale or rent) are offered twenty-four hours a day, seven days a week, presumably on the premise that marriage, like craps, is a game to be played when the table seems hot.

But what strikes one most about the Strip chapels, with their   4
wishing wells and stained-glass paper windows and their artificial bouvardia, is that so much of their business is by no means a
matter of simple convenience, of late-night liaisons between show
girls and baby Crosbys. Of course there is some of that. (One night
about eleven o'clock in Las Vegas I watched a bride in an orange
minidress and masses of flame-colored hair stumble from a Strip
chapel on the arm of her bridegroom, who looked the part of the
expendable nephew in movies like *Miami Syndicate*. "I gotta get
the kids," the bride whimpered. "I gotta pick up the sitter, I gotta
get to the midnight show." "What you gotta get," the bridegroom
said, opening the door of a Cadillac Coupe de Ville and watching
her crumple on the seat, "is sober.") But Las Vegas seems to offer
something other than "convenience"; it is merchandising "niceness," the facsimile of proper ritual, to children who do not know
how else to find it, how to make the arrangements, how to do it
"right." All day and evening long on the Strip, one sees actual
wedding parties, waiting under the harsh lights at a crosswalk,
standing uneasily in the parking lot of the Frontier while the
photographer hired by The Little Church of the West ("Wedding
Place of the Stars") certifies the occasion, takes the picture: the
bride in a veil and white satin pumps, the bridegroom usually in
a white dinner jacket, and even an attendant or two, a sister or a
best friend in hot-pink *peau de soie*, a flirtation veil, a carnation
nosegay. "When I Fall in Love It Will Be Forever," the organist
plays, and then a few bars of Lohengrin. The mother cries; the
stepfather, awkward in his role, invites the chapel hostess to join
them for a drink at the Sands. The hostess declines with a professional smile; she has already transferred her interest to the group
waiting outside. One bride out, another in, and again the sign goes
up on the chapel door: "One moment please—Wedding."

I sat next to one such wedding party in a Strip restaurant the   5
last time I was in Las Vegas. The marriage had just taken place; the
bride still wore her dress, the mother her corsage. A bored waiter
poured out a few swallows of pink champagne ("on the house")
for everyone but the bride, who was too young to be served.
"You'll need something with more kick than that," the bride's
father said with heavy jocularity to his new son-in-law; the ritual

jokes about the wedding night had a certain Panglossian charac-ter, since the bride was clearly several months pregnant. Another round of pink champagne, this time not on the house, and the bride began to cry. "It was just as nice," she sobbed, "as I hoped and dreamed it would be."

Content

1. How does Didion's essay illustrate her observation that "there is no 'time' in Las Vegas, no night and no day and no past and no future" (¶ 2)?

2. How does Didion illustrate her point that in Las Vegas there is no "logical sense of where one is" (¶ 2)? That Las Vegas is geographically implausible (¶ 2)?

3. Do you think that Didion agrees with the Las Vegas assumption that "marriage, like craps, is a game to be played when the table seems hot" (¶ 3)? What illustrations does she provide to demonstrate that the patrons of Las Vegas believe this?

4. Does the concluding illustration of the pregnant, underage bride sob-bing with pleasure at the "niceness" of her wedding (¶ 5) support Didion's assertion that Las Vegas is "merchandising 'niceness,' the facsimile of proper ritual, to children who do not know how else to find it" (¶ 4)?

Strategies/Structures

5. Why does Didion emphasize so early in the essay the juxtaposition of the "moonscape of rattlesnakes and mesquite" with the "Getting Married" signs (¶ 1)? The hasty weddings and the view of the justice of the peace who married sixty-seven couples in three hours (¶ 1)?

6. What is Didion's prevailing tone? Find some instances of it. Can she count on her readers to share her attitude toward Las Vegas weddings? Does Didion's intended audience include the kind of people who might get married in Las Vegas?

Language

7. What language is Didion imitating when she refers to "a candlelight satin Priscilla of Boston wedding dress with Chantilly lace insets, tapered sleeves and a detachable modified train" (¶ 2)? Why does she employ only one comma in this heavily modified sequence that might ordinarily use many more?

8. In paragraph 3 Didion quotes or paraphrases many advertising slogans. For what purposes? With what effects?

For Writing

9. Describe, for people who haven't been there, a place—either an entertainment spot, a college, a whole city or town—(as Didion does Las Vegas), or a family property (as Ozick does in "A Drugstore Eden" [316–29]). Through carefully selected details, convey not only an impression of the place, but your attitude toward it, favorable or otherwise.

10. Connect two or three anecdotes or vignettes to illustrate a thesis, as Didion does with the sixty-seven speedy weddings (¶ 1), the wedding of the showgirl and the "expendable nephew" (¶ 4), and the wedding of the underage pregnant bride (¶ 5).

ERIC LIU

Liu (born, 1968) grew up in Wappingers Falls, New York, near Poughkeepsie where his father, a Taiwanese immigrant, worked as an account executive at IBM until his recent death. His mother, also Taiwanese, is a computer programmer. A history major at Yale, Liu served a summer internship after his freshman year in the office of Senator Daniel Patrick Moynihan; he spent two subsequent summers at Marine officer candidates school in Quantico, Virginia, happy to have survived grueling drill sergeants and emerging with a "sense of common cause." After graduating in 1990, Liu worked as a legislative assistant to Senator David Boren and started a magazine of writings from people age twenty-four to thirty-two, positive views of society and politics designed to contradict the negative stereotypes of Generation X as self-centered hedonists (compiled in 1994 in *Next: Young American Writers on the New Generation*). Consequently, he became a speechwriter, first for Secretary of State Warren Christopher (1993), and then for President Bill Clinton, before entering Harvard Law School at age twenty-five.

In his autobiography *The Accidental Asian: Notes of a Native Speaker* (1998), published when he was twenty-nine, Liu (pronounced LOO) explores what it means to grow up as an Asian in America. Should he, like other children of immigrants, embrace, resist, or redefine assimilation? In "Notes of a Native Speaker" (a chapter from *The Accidental Asian*), Liu defines himself as an "accidental Asian," someone who has stumbled upon a sense of race and tries to describe it in order to define and live with it. This isn't always easy. "If Asians were shy and retiring," he says, "I'd try to be exuberant and jocular. If they were narrow-minded specialists, I'd be a well-rounded generalist." He realizes, "The irony is that in working so hard to defy stereotype, I became a slave to it. . . . I could have spared myself a great deal of heartache had I understood . . . that the choice of race is not simply 'embrace or efface.'"

Notes of a Native Speaker

1.

1   Here are some of the ways you could say I am "white":

I listen to National Public Radio.
I wear khaki Dockers.
I own brown suede bucks.
I eat gourmet greens.
I have few close friends "of color."
I married a white woman.
I am a child of the suburbs.
I furnish my condo à la Crate & Barrel.
I vacation in charming bed-and-breakfasts.
I have never once been the victim of blatant discrimination.
I am a member of several exclusive institutions.
I have been in the inner sanctums of political power.
I have been there as something other than an attendant.
I have the ambition to return.
I am a producer of the culture.
I expect my voice to be heard.
I speak flawless, unaccented English.
I subscribe to *Foreign Affairs.*
I do not mind when editorialists write in the first person plural.
I do not mind how white television casts are.
I am not too ethnic.
I am wary of minority militants.

I consider myself neither in exile nor in opposition.
I am considered "a credit to my race."

I never asked to be white. I am not literally white. That is, I do not
have white skin or white ancestors. I have yellow skin and yellow
ancestors, hundreds of generations of them. But like so many
other Asian Americans of the second generation, I find myself
now the bearer of a strange new status: white, by acclamation.
Thus it is that I have been described as an "honorary white," by
other whites, and as a "banana," by other Asians. Both the hon-
orific and the epithet take as a given this idea: to the extent that I
have moved away from the periphery and toward the center of
American life, I have become white inside. *Some are born white,
others achieve whiteness, still others have whiteness thrust upon them.*
This, supposedly, is what it means to assimilate.

There was a time when assimilation did quite strictly mean   2
whitening. In fact, well into the first half of this century, mimicry
of the stylized standards of the WASP gentry was the proper, dominant, perhaps even sole method of ensuring that your origins
would not be held against you. You "made it" in society not only
by putting on airs of anglitude, but also by assiduously bleaching
out the marks of a darker, dirtier past. And this bargain, stifling as
it was, was open to European immigrants almost exclusively; to
blacks, only on the passing occasion; to Asians, hardly at all.

Times have changed, and I suppose you could call it progress   3
that a Chinaman, too, may now aspire to whiteness. But precisely
because the times have changed, that aspiration—and the *imputa-
tion* of the aspiration—now seems astonishingly outmoded. The
meaning of "American" has undergone a revolution in the twenty-
nine years I have been alive, a revolution of color, class, and culture. Yet the vocabulary of "assimilation" has remained fixed all
this time: fixed in whiteness, which is still our metonym for power;
and fixed in shame, which is what the colored are expected to feel
for embracing the power.

I have assimilated. I am of the mainstream. In many ways I   4
fit the psychological profile of the so-called banana: imitative, im-
pressionable, rootless, eager to please. As I will admit in this essay,
I have at times gone to great lengths to downplay my difference,
the better to penetrate the "establishment" of the moment. Yet I'm

not sure that what I did was so cut-and-dried as "becoming white." I plead guilty to the charges above: achieving, learning the ways of the upper middle class, distancing myself from radicals of any hue. But having confessed, I still do not know my crime.

5   To be an accused banana is to stand at the ill-fated intersection of class and race. And because class is the only thing Americans have more trouble talking about than race, a minority's climb up the social ladder is often willfully misnamed and wrongly portrayed. There is usually, in the portrayal, a strong whiff of betrayal: the assimilist is a traitor to his kind, to his class, to his own family. He cannot gain the world without losing his soul. To be sure, something *is* lost in any migration, whether from place to place or from class to class. But something is gained as well. And the result is always more complicated than the monochrome language of "whiteness" and "authenticity" would suggest.

6   My own assimilation began long before I was born. It began with my parents, who came here with an appetite for Western ways already whetted by films and books and music and, in my mother's case, by a father who'd been to the West. My parents, who traded Chinese formality for the more laissez-faire stance of this country. Who made their way by hard work and quiet adaptation. Who fashioned a comfortable life in a quiet development in a second-tier suburb. Who, unlike your "typical" Chinese parents, were not pushy, status-obsessed, rigid, disciplined, or prepared. Who were haphazard about passing down ancestral traditions and "lessons" to their children. Who did pass down, however, the sense that their children were entitled to mix and match, as they saw fit, whatever aspects of whatever cultures they encountered.

7   I was raised, in short, to assimilate, to claim this place as mine. I don't mean that my parents told me to act like an American. That's partly the point: they didn't tell me to do anything except to be a good boy. They trusted I would find my way, and I did, following their example and navigating by the lights of the culture that encircled me like a dome. As a function of my parents' own half-conscious, half-finished acculturation, I grew up feeling that my life was Book II of an ongoing saga. Or that I was running the second leg of a relay race. *Slap!* I was out of the womb and sprinting, baton in hand. Gradually more sure of my stride,

my breathing, the feel of the track beneath me. Eyes forward, never backward.

Today, nearly seven years after my father's death and two   8 years after my marriage into a large white family, it is as if I have come round a bend and realized that I am no longer sure where I am running or why. My sprint slows to a trot. I scan the unfamiliar vista that is opening up. I am somewhere else now, somewhere far from the China that yielded my mother and father; far, as well, from the modest horizons I knew as a boy. I look at my limbs and realize I am no longer that boy; my gait and grasp exceed his by an order of magnitude. Now I want desperately to see my face, to see what time has marked and what it has erased. But I can find no mirror except the people who surround me. And they are mainly pale, powerful.

How did I end up here, standing in what seems the very   9 seat of whiteness, gazing from the promontory of social privilege? How did I cover so much ground so quickly? What was it, in my blind journey, that I felt I should leave behind? And what *did* I leave behind? This, the jettisoning of one mode of life to send another aloft, is not only the immigrant's tale; it is the son's tale, too. By coming to America, my parents made themselves into citizens of a new country. By traveling the trajectory of an assimilist, so did I.

2.

As a child, I lived in a state of "amoebic bliss," to borrow the   10 felicitous phrase of the author of *Nisei Daughter*, Monica Sone. The world was a gossamer web of wonder that began with life at home, extended to my friendships, and made the imaginary realm of daydream seem as immediate as the real. If something or someone was in my personal web of meaning, then color or station was irrelevant. I made no distinctions in fourth grade between my best friend, a black boy named Kimathi, and my next-best friend, a white boy named Charlie—other than the fact that one was number one, the other number two. I did not feel, or feel for, a seam that separated the textures of my Chinese life from those of my American life. I was not "bicultural" but omnicultural, and omnivorous, too. To my mind, I differed from others in only two ways that counted: I was a faster runner than most, and a better student. Thus did work blend happily with play, school with home, Western culture with Eastern: it was all the same to a self-confident boy who believed he'd always be at the center of his own universe.

11   As I approached adolescence, though, things shifted. Suddenly, I could no longer subsume the public world under my private concept of self. Suddenly, the public world was more complicated than just a parade of smiling teachers and a few affirming friends. Now I had to contend with the unstated, inchoate, but inescapable standards of *cool*. The essence of cool was the ability to conform. The essence of conformity was the ability to anticipate what was cool. And I wasn't so good at that. For the first time, I had found something that did not come effortlessly to me. No one had warned me about this transition from happy amoeboid to social animal; no one had prepared me for the great labors of fitting in.

12   And so in three adjoining arenas—my looks, my loves, my manners—I suffered a bruising adolescent education. I don't mean to overdramatize: there was, in these teenage banalities, usually something humorous and nothing particularly tragic. But in each of these realms, I came to feel I was not normal. And obtusely, I ascribed the difficulties of that age not to my age but to my color. I came to suspect that there was an order to things, an order that I, as someone Chinese, could perceive but not quite crack. I responded not by exploding in rebellion but by dedicating myself, quietly and sometimes angrily, to learning the order as best I could. I was never ashamed of being Chinese; I was, in fact, rather proud to be linked to a great civilization. But I was mad that my difference should matter now. And if it had to matter, I did not want it to defeat me.

13   Consider, if you will, my hair. For the first eleven years of my life, I sported what was essentially the same hairstyle: a tapered bowl cut, the handiwork of my mother. For those eleven joyful years, this low-maintenance do was entirely satisfactory. But in my twelfth year, as sixth grade got under way, I became aware—gradually at first, then urgently—that bangs were no longer the look for boys. This was the year when certain early bloomers first made the height-weight-physique distribution in our class seem startlingly wide—and when I first realized that I was lingering near the bottom. It was essential that I compensate for my childlike mien by cultivating at least a patina of teenage style.

This is where my hair betrayed me. For some readers the 14 words "Chinese hair" should suffice as explanation. For the rest, particularly those who have spent all your lives with the ability to comb back, style, and part your hair *at will*, what follows should make you count your blessings. As you may recall, 1980 was a vintage year for hair that was parted straight down the middle, then feathered on each side, feathered so immaculately that the ends would meet in the back like the closed wings of angels. I dreamed of such hair. I imagined tossing my head back casually, to ease into place the one or two strands that had drifted from their positions. I dreamed of wearing the fluffy, tailored locks of the blessed.

Instead, I was cursed. My hair was straight, rigid, and wiry. 15 Not only did it fail to feather back; it would not even bend. Worse still, it grew the wrong way. That is, it all emanated from a single swirl near the rear edge of my scalp. Parting my hair in any direction except back to front, the way certain balding men stage their final retreat, was a physical impossibility. It should go without saying that this was a disaster. For the next three years, I experimented with a variety of hairstyles that ranged from the ridiculous to the sublimely bad. There was the stringy pothead look. The mushroom do. Helmet head. Bangs folded back like curtains. I enlisted a blow-dryer, a Conair set on high heat, to force my hair into stiff postures of submission. The results, though sometimes innovative, fell always far short of cool.

I feigned nonchalance, and no one ever said anything about 16 it. But make no mistake: this was one of the most consuming crises of my inner life as a young teen. Though neither of my parents had ever had such troubles, I blamed this predicament squarely on my Chinese genes. And I could not abide my fate. At a time when homogeneity was the highest virtue, I felt I stood out like a pigtailed Manchu.

My salvation didn't come until the end of junior high, when 17 one of my buddies, in an epiphany as we walked past the Palace of Hair Design, dared me to get my head shaved. Without hesitation, I did it—to the tearful laughter of my friends and, soon afterward, the tearful horror of my mother. Of course, I had moments of doubt the next few days as I rubbed my peach-fuzzed skull. But what I liked was this: I had managed, without losing face, to rid myself of my greatest social burden. What's more, in the eyes of some classmates, I was now a bold (if bald) iconoclast. I've worn a crew cut ever since.

18   Well-styled hair was only one part of a much larger pre-occupation during the ensuing years: wooing girls. In this realm I experienced a most frustrating kind of success. I was the boy that girls always found "sweet" and "funny" and "smart" and "nice." Which, to my highly sensitive ear, sounded like "leprous." Time and again, I would charm a girl into deep friendship. Time and again, as the possibility of romance came within reach, I would smash into what I took to be a glass ceiling.

19   The girls were white, you see; such were the demographics of my school. I was Chinese. And I was convinced that this was the sole obstacle to my advancement. It made sense, did it not? I was, after all, sweet and funny and smart and nice. Hair notwithstanding, I was not unattractive, at least compared with some of the beasts who had started "going out" with girls. There was simply no other explanation. Yet I could never say this out loud: it would have been the whining of a loser. My response, then, was to secretly scorn the girls I coveted. It was *they* who were subpar, whose small-mindedness and veiled prejudice made them unworthy.

20   My response, too, was to take refuge in my talents. I made myself into a Renaissance boy, playing in the orchestra but also joining the wrestling team, winning science prizes but also editing the school paper. I thought I was defying the stereotype of the Asian American male as a one-dimensional nerd. But in the eyes of some, I suppose, I was simply another "Asian overachiever."

21   In hindsight, it's hard to know exactly how great a romantic penalty I paid for being Chinese. There may have been girls who would have had nothing to do with me on account of my race, but I never knew them. There were probably girls who, race aside, simply didn't like me. And then there were girls who liked me well enough but who also shied from the prospect of being part of an interracial couple. With so many boys out there, they probably reasoned, why take the path of greater resistance? Why risk so many status points? Why not be "just friends" with this Chinese boy?

22   Maybe this stigma was more imagined than real. But being an ABC ("American-born Chinese," as our parents called us) certainly affected me another way. It made me feel like something of a greenhorn, a social immigrant. I wanted so greatly to be liked. And

my earnestness, though endearing, was not the sort of demeanor that won girls' hearts. Though I was observant enough to notice how people talked when flirting, astute enough to mimic the forms, I was oblivious to the subterranean levels of courtship, blind to the more subtle rituals of "getting chicks" by spurning them. I held the view that if you were manifestly a good person, eventually someone of the opposite sex would do the rational thing and be smitten with you. I was clueless. Many years would pass before I'd wise up.

3.

I recently dug up a photograph of myself from freshman year of   23
college that made me smile. I have on the wrong shoes, the wrong socks, the wrong checkered shirt tucked the wrong way into the wrong slacks. I look like what I was: a boy sprung from a middle-brow burg who affected a secondhand preppiness. I look nervous. Compare that image to one from my senior-class dinner: now I am attired in a gray tweed jacket with a green plaid bow tie and a sensible button-down shirt, all purchased at the Yale Co-op. I look confident, and more than a bit contrived.

What happened in between those two photographs is that   24
I experienced, then overcame, what the poet Meena Alexander has called "the shock of arrival." When I was deposited at the wrought-iron gates of my residential college as a freshman, I felt more like an outsider than I'd thought possible. It wasn't just that I was a small Chinese boy standing at a grand WASP temple; nor simply that I was a hayseed neophyte puzzled by the refinements of college style. It was *both:* color and class were all twisted together in a double helix of felt inadequacy.

For a while I coped with the shock by retreating to a group   25
of my own kind—not fellow Asians, but fellow marginal public-school grads who resented the rah-rah Yalies to whom everything came so effortlessly. Aligning myself this way was bearable—I was hiding, but at least I could place myself in a long tradition of underdog exiles at Yale. Aligning myself by race, on the other hand, would have seemed too inhibiting.

I know this doesn't make much sense. I know also that college,   26
in the multicultural era, is supposed to be where the deracinated

minority youth discovers the "person of color" inside. To a point, I did. I studied Chinese, took an Asian American history course, a seminar on race politics. But ultimately, college was where the unconscious habits of my adolescent assimilation hardened into self-conscious strategy.

27   I still remember the moment, in the first week of school, when I came upon a table in Yale Station set up by the Asian American Student Association. The upperclassman staffing the table was pleasant enough. He certainly did not strike me as a fanatic. Yet, for some reason, I flashed immediately to a scene I'd witnessed days earlier, on the corner outside. Several Lubavitcher Jews, dressed in black, their faces bracketed by dangling side curls, were looking for fellow travelers at this busy crossroads. Their method was crude but memorable. As any vaguely Jewish-looking male walked past, the zealots would quickly approach, extend a pamphlet, and ask, "Excuse me, sir, are you Jewish?" Since most were not, and since those who weren't about to stop, the result was a frantic, nervous, almost comical buzz all about the corner: Excuse me, are you Jewish? Are you Jewish? Excuse me. Are you Jewish?

28   I looked now at the clean-cut Korean boy at the AASA table (I think I can distinguish among Asian ethnicities as readily as those Hasidim thought they could tell Gentile from Jew), and though he had merely offered an introductory hello and was now smiling mutely at me, in the back of my mind I heard only this: *Excuse me, are you Asian? Are you Asian? Excuse me. Are you Asian?* I took one of the flyers on the table, even put my name on a mailing list, so as not to appear impolite. But I had already resolved not to be active in any Asians-only group. I thought then: I would never *choose* to be so pigeonholed.

29   This allergic sensitivity to "pigeonholing" is one of the unhappy hallmarks of the banana mentality. What does the banana fear? That is, what did *I* fear? The possibility of being mistaken for someone more Chinese. The possibility of being known only, or even primarily, for being Asian. The possibility of being written off by whites as a self-segregating ethnic clumper. These were the threats—unseen and, frankly, unsubstantiated—that I felt I should keep at bay.

30   I didn't avoid making Asian friends in college or working with Asian classmates; I simply never went out of my way to do so.

This distinction seemed important—it marked, to my mind, the difference between self-hate and self-respect. That the two should have been so proximate in the first place never struck me as odd, or telling. Nor did it ever occur to me that the reasons I gave myself for dissociating from Asians as a group—that I didn't want to be part of a clique, that I didn't want to get absorbed and lose my individuality—were the very developments that marked my own assimilation. I simply hewed to my ideology of race neutrality and self-reliance. I didn't need that crutch, I told myself nervously, that crutch of racial affinity. What's more, I was vaguely insulted by the presumption that I might.

But again: Who was making the presumption? Who more 31 than I was taking the mere existence of Korean volleyball leagues or Taiwanese social sets or pan-Asian student clubs to mean that *all* people of Asian descent, myself included, needed such quasi-kinship groups? And who more than I interpreted this need as infirmity, as a failure to fit in? I resented the faintly sneering way that some whites regarded Asians as an undifferentiated mass. But whose sneer, really, did I resent more than my own?

I was keenly aware of the unflattering mythologies that at- 32 tach to Asian Americans: that we are indelibly foreign, exotic, math and science geeks, numbers people rather than people people, followers and not leaders, physically frail but devious and sneaky, unknowable and potentially treacherous. These stereotypes of Asian otherness and inferiority were like immense blocks of ice sitting before me, challenging me to chip away at them. And I did, tirelessly. All the while, though, I was oblivious to rumors of my *own* otherness and inferiority, rumors that rose off those blocks like a fog, wafting into my consciousness and chilling my sense of self.

As I had done in high school, I combated the stereotypes in 33 part by trying to disprove them. If Asians were reputed to be math and science geeks, I would be a student of history and politics. If Asians were supposed to be feeble subalterns, I'd lift weights and go to Marine officer candidate school. If Asians were alien, I'd be ardently patriotic. If Asians were shy and retiring, I'd try to be exuberant and jocular. If they were narrow-minded specialists, I'd be a well-rounded generalist. If they were perpetual outsiders, I'd join every establishment outfit I could and show that I, too, could run with the swift.

34   I overstate, of course. It wasn't that I chose to do all these things with no other purpose than to cut against a supposed convention. I was neither so Pavlovian nor so calculating that I would simply remake myself into the opposite of what people expected. I actually *liked* history, and wasn't especially good at math. As the grandson of a military officer, I *wanted* to see what officer candidates school would be like, and I enjoyed it, at least once I'd finished. I am *by nature* enthusiastic and allegiant, a joiner, and a bit of a jingo.

35   At the same time, I was often aware, sometimes even hopeful, that others might think me "exceptional" for my race. I derived satisfaction from being the "atypical" Asian, the only Chinese face at OCS or in this club or that.

36   The irony is that in working so duteously to defy stereotype, I became a slave to it. For to act self-consciously against Asian "tendencies" is not to break loose from the cage of myth and legend; it is to turn the very key that locks you inside. What spontaneity is there when the value of every act is measured, at least in part, by its power to refute a presumption about why you act? The *typical Asian* I imagined, and the *atypical Asian* I imagined myself to be, were identical in this sense: neither was as much a creature of free will as a human being ought to be.

37   Let me say it plainly, then: I am not proud to have had this mentality. I believe I have outgrown it. And I expose it now not to justify it but to detoxify it, to prevent its further spread.

38   Yet it would be misleading, I think, to suggest that my education centered solely on the discomfort caused by race. The fact is, when I first got to college I felt deficient compared with people of *every* color. Part of why I believed it so necessary to achieve was that I lacked the connections, the wealth, the experience, the sophistication that so many of my classmates seemed to have. I didn't get the jokes or the intellectual references. I didn't have the canny attitude. So in addition to all my coursework, I began to puzzle over this, the culture of the influential class.

39   Over time, I suppose, I learned the culture. My interests and vocabulary became ever more worldly. I made my way onto what Calvin Trillin once described as the "magic escalator" of a Yale education. Extracurriculars opened the door to an alumni internship, which brought me to Capitol Hill, which led to a job and a life

in Washington after commencement. Gradually, very gradually, I found that I was not so much of an outsider anymore. I found that by almost any standard, but particularly by the standards of my younger self, I was actually beginning to "make it."

It has taken me until now, however, to appraise the thoughts 40 and acts of that younger self. I can see now that the straitening path I took was not the only or even the best path. For while it may be possible to transcend race, *it is not always necessary to try.* And while racial identity is sometimes a shackle, it is not *only* a shackle. I could have spared myself a great deal of heartache had I understood this earlier, that the choice of race is not simply "embrace or efface."

I wonder sometimes how I would have turned out had I 41 been, from the start, more comfortable in my own skin. What did I miss by distancing myself from race? What friendships did I forgo, what self-knowledge did I defer? Had certain accidents of privilege been accidents of privation or exclusion, I might well have developed a different view of the world. But I do not know just how my view would have differed.

What I know is that through all those years of shadow- 42 dancing with my identity, something happened, something that had only partially to do with color. By the time I left Yale I was no longer the scared boy of that freshman photo. I had become more sure of myself and of my place—sure enough, indeed, to perceive the folly of my fears. And in the years since, I have assumed as sense of expectation, of access and *belonging*, that my younger self could scarcely have imagined. All this happened incrementally. There was no clear tipping point, no obvious moment of mutation. The shock of arrival, it would seem, is simply that I arrived.

Content

1. On what basis does Liu define himself as "white, by acclamation" (¶ 1)? Why is racial identification and definition so important to Liu? Why is he so concerned with defying Asian stereotypes?

2. Given the variability of white (or any) culture, what aspects of white culture does Liu claim he has assimilated? Is his assimilation more a matter of class than race (see ¶s 6–7)?

3. Why did the adolescent Liu's "bad hair" present so many problems (¶s 13–17)? Why as an adult, after he's solved the hair problem, does he devote so much space to discussing it?

4. Liu refers to people having a "choice of race" when he says "I could have spared myself a great deal of heartache had I understood . . . earlier, that the choice of race is not simply 'embrace or efface'" (¶ 40). Explain what he means by this. Does his essay compel you to agree with him? Why or why not?

Strategies/Structures

5. Is Liu writing primarily for himself? For an audience of white Americans? For Asians? For other immigrants? How can you tell?

6. Why does Liu begin by describing his present self (¶s 1–9) before moving back, first to his childhood (¶ 10) and then to his adolescence (¶s 11–21) and college years (¶s 23–39)? Why does he spend so little space on his childhood in comparison with the other periods of his life?

Language

7. Liu refers to himself as an "Asian American" (¶ 1), "'an honorary white'" (¶ 1), "'a banana'" (¶ 1), an "Asian" (¶ 2), "a Chinaman" (¶ 3), an "assimilist" (¶ 5). Do all these labels fit equally well? Or are some better than others? For what purposes? Which of these are labels that only the Chinese can use in talking about themselves?

8. In what places is this essay humorous? In ironic self-mockery, does Liu (or any other author who uses this technique) invite readers to laugh with him or to laugh at him? Can readers take him seriously if he's laughing at himself?

For Writing

9. "How did I cover so much ground so quickly [in my quest for assimilation]?" asks Liu. "What was it, in my blind journey, that I felt I should leave behind? And what *did* I leave behind? This, the jettisoning of one mode of life to send another aloft, is not only the immigrant's tale; it is the son's tale, too" (¶ 9). Identify a culture (of family, gender, race, class, occupation, nationality) that helped to shape you and which to an extent you have resisted. What did you take from it and what about it did you resist? If you have made deliberate choices, on what basis did you do so? If the shaping was unavoidable, explain why this was so. If

stereotyping played any role in either your acceptance or resistance, identify the stereotype and the nature of its influence.

10. Liu's list of the ways in which he is "'white'" (¶ 1) covers food, clothing, shelter, entertainment, affiliations, jobs, ambition, language, groups he identifies with and rejects, measures of self-esteem, and attitudes toward himself and his status. Why is he making this comparison? Make a list of the ways in which you address these same aspects of your own life, and other significant ones (note, for instance, that Liu omits a spiritual dimension). Write a paper of self-description in which you compare your list with Liu's, and show how each list defines the culture of its author.

LUCY GREALY

Born in Dublin in 1963, Grealy moved in 1967 with her parents and four siblings (her father was a television news producer) to Spring Valley, a New York City suburb. Grealy's *Autobiography of a Face* (1994) describes coming to terms with cancer of the jaw (Ewing's sarcoma) when she was nine, the ensuing cancer treatments "five days a week, every week, for two years of radiation and chemotherapy, then once a week for another half-year to finish out the chemotherapy." Thirty reconstructive procedures followed during her teens and twenties, in attempt after attempt to restore the lower quadrant of her ravaged face. During this time she graduated from Sarah Lawrence College (B.A., 1984), where she now teaches creative writing, and earned a M.F.A. in creative writing from the University of Iowa Writers' Workshop. She explains, "I spent five years of my life being treated for cancer, but since then I've spent fifteen years being treated for nothing other than looking different from everyone else. It was the pain from that, from feeling ugly, that I always viewed as the great tragedy in my life. That fact that I had cancer seemed minor in comparison."

In "Masks," from the middle chapter of *Autobiography of a Face,* Grealy describes with candor and unsentimentality (she never succumbs to "poor me") her realization in elementary school that wearing a mask at Halloween can be a respite from being trapped behind a damaged face in a culture that emphasizes beauty and wholeness, where boys in the lunchroom call out to their friends, "'*What* on earth is *that?' 'That* is the ugliest girl I have *ever* seen.'"

Masks

1   Having missed most of fourth grade and all but a week or so of fifth grade, I finally started to reappear at school sometime in sixth grade during my periodic "vacations" from chemotherapy. I'd mysteriously show up for a week or two weeks or sometimes even three or four, then disappear again for a couple of months.

2   Most of the sixth-grade class consisted of children I'd grown up with. They were, for the most part, genuinely curious about what had happened to me. They treated me respectfully, if somewhat distantly, though there was a clique of boys who always called me names: "Hey, girl, take off that monster mask—oops, she's not wearing a mask!" This was the height of hilarity in sixth grade, and the boys, for they were always and only boys, practically fell to the ground, besotted with their own wit. Much to their bewilderment and to the shock of my teachers, I retorted by calling out to them, "You stupid dildos."

3   Derek used to say that word all the time, and I thought it a wonderful insult, though I didn't have a clue as to what a dildo was. After being reprimanded enough times for wielding this powerful insult, I finally asked my brother what it meant: an artificial penis, he informed me. I gave up using the word. I'd known children in the hospital with artificial limbs, and I'd known children with urinary tract problems.

4   The school year progressed slowly. I felt as if I had been in the sixth grade for years, yet it was only October. Halloween was approaching. Coming from Ireland, we had never thought of it as a big holiday, though Sarah and I usually went out trick-or-treating. For the last couple of years I had been too sick to go out, but this year Halloween fell on a day when I felt quite fine. My mother was the one who came up with the Eskimo idea. I put on a winter coat, made a fish out of paper, which I hung on the end of a stick, and wrapped my face up in a scarf. My hair was growing I, and I loved the way the top of the hood rubbed against it. By this time my hat had become part of me; I took it off only at home. Sometimes kids would make fun of me, run past me, knock my hat off,and call me Baldy. I hated this, but I assumed

that one day my hair would grow in, and on that day the teasing would end.

We walked around the neighborhood with our pillowcase sacks, running into the other groups of kids and comparing notes: the house three doors down gave whole candy bars, while the house next to that gave only cheap mints. I felt wonderful. It was only as the night wore on and the moon came out and the older kids, the big kids, went on their rounds that I began to realize why I felt so good. No one could see me clearly. No one could see my face.

For the end of October it was a very warm night and I was sweating in my parka, but I didn't care. I felt such freedom: I waltzed up to people effortlessly and boldly, I asked questions and made comments the rest of my troupe were afraid to make. I didn't understand their fear. I hadn't realized just how meek I'd become, how self-conscious I was about my face until now that it was obscured. My sister and her friends never had to worry about their appearance, or so it seemed to me, so why didn't they always feel as bold and as happy as I felt that night?

Our sacks filled up, and eventually it was time to go home. We gleefully poured out our candy on the floor and traded off: because chewing had become difficult, I gave Sarah everything that was too hard for me, while she unselfishly gave me everything soft. I took off my Eskimo parka and went down to my room without my hat. Normally I didn't feel that I had to wear my hat around my family, and I never wore it when I was alone in my room. Yet once I was alone with all my candy, still hot from running around on that unseasonably warm night, I felt compelled to put my hat back on. I didn't know what was wrong. I ate sugar until I was ready to burst, trying hard to ignore everything except what was directly in front of me, what I could touch and taste, the chocolate melting brown beneath my fingernails, the candy so sweet it made my throat hurt.

The following spring, on one of the first warm days, I was playing with an old friend, Teresa, in her neat and ordered back yard when she asked, completely out of the blue, if I was dying. She looked at me casually, as if she'd just asked what I was doing later that day. "The other kids say that you're slowly dying, that you're 'wasting away.'" I looked at her in shock. Dying? Why on earth would anyone think I was dying? "No," I replied, in the tone of voice I'd have used if she'd asked me whether I was the pope, "I'm not dying."

9   When I got home I planned to ask my mother why Teresa would say such a thing. But just as I was coming through the front door, she was entering from the garage, her arms laden with shopping bags. She took a bright red shirt out of a bag and held it up against my chest. It smelled new and a price tag scratched my neck.

10   "Turtlenecks are very hard to find in short sleeves, so I bought you several."

11   I was still a tomboy at heart and cared little about what I wore, just so long as it wasn't a dress. But turtlenecks—why on earth would I want to wear turtlenecks in the spring? I didn't ask this out loud, but my mother must have known what I was thinking. She looked me straight in the eye: "If you wear something that comes up around your neck, it makes the scar less visible."

12   Genuinely bewildered, I took the bright-colored pile of shirts down to my room. Wouldn't I look even more stupid wearing a turtleneck in the summer? Would they really hide my "scar"? I hadn't taken a good long, objective look at myself since the wig fitting, but that seemed so long ago, almost two years. I remembered feeling upset by it, but I conveniently didn't remember what I'd seen in that mirror, and I hadn't allowed myself a close scrutiny since.

13   I donned my short-sleeved turtlenecks and finished out the few short months of elementary school. I played with my friend Jan at her wonderful home with its several acres of meadow and, most magnificent of all, a small lake. There was a rowboat we weren't allowed to take out by ourselves, but we did anyway. Rowing it to the far shore, a mere eighth of a mile away, we'd "land" and pretend we'd just discovered a new country. With notebooks in hand, we logged our discoveries, overturning stones and giving false Latin names to the newts and various pieces of slime we found under them.

14   Jan had as complex a relationship to her stuffed and plastic animals as I had to mine, and when I slept over we'd compare our intricate worlds. Sometimes, though not too frequently, Jan wanted

to talk about boys, and I'd sit on my sleeping bag with my knees tucked up under my nightgown, listening patiently. I never had much to offer, though I had just developed my very first crush. It was on Omar Sharif.

Late one night I'd stayed up and watched *Dr. Zhivago* on 15 television with my father. Curled up beside him, with my head against his big stomach, I listened to my father's heart, his breathing, and attentively watched the images of a remote world, a world as beautiful as it was deadly and cold. I thought I would have managed very well there, imagined that I would have remained true to my passions had I lived through the Russian Revolution. I, too, would have trudged across all that tundra, letting the ice sheet over me and crackle on my eyebrows. For weeks I pictured the ruined estate where Zhivago wrote his sonnets, aware that the true splendor of the house was inextricably bound to the fact that it was ruined. I didn't understand why this should be so, and I didn't understand why reimagining this scene gave me such a deep sense of fulfillment, nor why this fulfillment was mingled with such a sad sense of longing, nor why this longing only added to the beauty of everything else.

Elementary-school graduation day approached. I remembered 16 being in second grade and looking out on a group of sixth-graders preparing for graduation. It had seemed like an unimaginable length of time before I'd get there. But now I was out there mingling in the courtyard, remembering the day when I laid my head down on the desk and announced to the teacher, "I'll never make it." I could even see the classroom window I had gazed out of. So much had happened in four years. I felt so old, and I felt proud of being so old. During the ceremony I was shocked when the vice-principal started speaking about *me*, about how I should receive special attention for my "bravery." I could feel the heat rising in me as he spoke, my face turning red. Here I was, the center of attention, receiving the praise and appreciation I'd been fantasizing about for so many years, and all I could feel was intense, searing embarrassment. I was called up onto the platform. I know everyone was applauding, but I felt it more than heard it. In a daze I accepted the gift Mr. Schultz was presenting me with, a copy of *The Prophet*. I could barely thank him.

17   Later, alone in my room, I opened the book at random. The verse I read was about love, about how to accept the love of another with dignity. I shut the book after only a page. I wanted nothing to do with the world of love; I thought wanting love was a weakness to be overcome. And besides, I thought to myself, the world of love wanted nothing to do with me.

18 The summer passed, and junior high school loomed. Jan, Teresa, and Sarah were all very excited at the prospect of being "grown-ups," of attending different classes, of having their own locker. Their excitement was contagious, and the night before the first day of school, I proudly marked my assorted notebooks for my different subjects and secretly scuffed my new shoes to make them look old.

19   Everyone must have been nervous, but I was sure I was the only one who felt true apprehension. I found myself sidling through the halls I'd been looking forward to, trying to pretend that I didn't notice the other kids, almost all of them strangers from adjoining towns, staring at me. Having seen plenty of teen movies with their promise of intrigue and drama, I had been looking forward to going to the lunchroom. As it happened, I sat down next to a table full of boys.

20   They pointed openly and laughed, calling out loudly enough for me to hear, "*What* on earth is *that?*" "*That* is the ugliest girl I have *ever* seen." I knew in my heart that their comments had nothing to do with me, that it was all about them appearing tough and cool to their friends. But these boys were older than the ones in grade school, and for the very first time I realized they were passing judgment on my suitability, or lack of it, as a girlfriend. "I bet David wants to go kiss her, don't you, David?" "Yeah, right, then I'll go kiss your mother's asshole." "How'll you know which is which?"

21   My initial tactic was to pretend I didn't hear them, but this only seemed to spur them on. In the hallways, where I suffered similar attacks of teasing from random attackers, I simply looked down at the floor and walked more quickly, but in the lunchroom I was a sitting duck. The same group took to seeking me out and purposely sitting near me day after day, even when I tried to camouflage myself by sitting in the middle of a group. They grew

bolder, and I could hear them plotting to send someone to sit across the table from me. I'd look up from my food and there would be a boy slouching awkwardly in a red plastic chair, innocently asking me my name. Then he'd ask me how I got to be so ugly. At this the group would burst into laughter, and my inquisitor would saunter back, victorious.

After two weeks I broke down and went to my guidance   22
counselor to complain. I thought he would offer to reprimand them, but instead he asked if I'd like to come and eat in the privacy of his office. Surprised, I said yes, and that's what I did for the rest of the year whenever I was attending school. Every day I'd wait for him, the other guidance counselors, and the secretaries to go on their own lunch break. Then I'd walk through the empty outer office and sit down in his private office, closing the door behind me. As I ate the food in my brown paper bag, which crinkled loudly in the silence, I'd look at the drawings his own young children had made. They were taped to the wall near his desk, simplistic drawings in which the sky was a blue line near the top and the grass a green line near the bottom and people were as big as houses. I felt safe and secure in that office, but I also felt lonely, and for the very first time I definitively identified the source of my unhappiness as being ugly. A few weeks later I left school to reenter chemotherapy, and for the very first time I was almost glad to go back to it.

My inner life became ever more macabre. Vietnam was still   23
within recent memory, and pictures of the horrors of Cambodia loomed on every TV screen and in every newspaper. I told myself again and again how good I had it in comparison, what a wonder it was to have food and clothes and a home and no one torturing me. I told myself what fools those boys at school were, what stupid, unaware lives they led. How could they assume their own lives were so important? Didn't they know they could lose everything at any moment, that you couldn't take anything good or worthwhile for granted, because pain and cruelty could and would arrive sooner or later? I bombed and starved and persecuted my own suffering right out of existence.

I had the capacity of imagination to momentarily escape my   24
own pain, and I had the elegance of imagination to teach myself

something true regarding the world around me, but I didn't yet have the clarity of imagination to grant myself the complicated and necessary right to suffer. I treated despair in terms of hierarchy: if there was a more important pain in the world, it meant my own was negated. I thought I simply had to accept the fact that I was ugly, and that to feel despair about it was simply wrong.

25   Halloween came round again, and even though I was feeling a bit woozy from an injection I'd had a few days before, I begged my mother to let me go out. I put on a plastic witch mask and went out with Teresa. I walked down the streets suddenly bold and free: no one could see my face. I peered through the oval eye slits and did not see one person staring back at me, ready to make fun of my face. I breathed in the condensing, plastic-tainted air behind the mask and thought that I was breathing in normalcy, that this freedom and ease were what the world consisted of, that other people felt it all the time. How could they not? How could they not feel the joy of walking down the street without the threat of being made fun of? Assuming this was how other people felt all the time, I again named my own face as the thing that kept me apart, as the tangible element of what was wrong with my life and with me.

26   At home, when I took the mask off, I felt both sad and relieved. Sad because I had felt like a pauper walking for a few brief hours in the clothes of a prince and because I had liked it so much. Relieved because I felt no connection with that kind of happiness: I didn't deserve it and thus I shouldn't want it. It was easier to slip back into my depression and blame my face for everything.

27   Hannah was a cleaning woman in Dr. Woolf's office. She was quite old, or at least seemed old to me, and she wore a cardigan summer and winter. Her domain, when she wasn't polishing the hallway floors or disinfecting the metal furniture, was an oblong room off the main doctors' hallway, just a few doors down from Dr. Woolf's. I appreciated this room because it was painted pale blue, so unlike the sickly green that dominated the rest of the place. During the last year of chemotherapy I'd grown considerably weaker, and sometimes walking the few blocks to the parking lot after the injection seemed an insurmountable task. On particularly bad days my mother would leave me in Hannah's care while she went to fetch the car. Hannah would sit me down

in a chair next to a small table with a kettle and some cups on it, her own small island where she took breaks.

The routine never varied. She knelt in front of me and asked, "How do you feel?" I could hear her slip rubbing between her stockings and dress. Looking her straight in the eye I'd confidentially report, "My nose hurts." 28

It was always such a relief to be able to admit this to her. I later learned why the chemo affected my sinuses, but as far as I could tell, Hannah was the only one who believed this comic complaint. She'd nod sympathetically and offer me a cup of tea, and I would politely refuse. Then we would sit and stare at each other, waiting for my mother to return. I knew that beyond a cup of tea, there was nothing she could offer me. But her gaze soothed me. Normally I despised the looks of others, but with Hannah I felt a vague sense of camaraderie, imagining that both our little lives were made miserable by these unknowing, cloddish doctors. To her I was probably just one of many sick children who streamed in and out of the place, but in my mind I'd found a silent link with someone whose life was as difficult as I found my own. As ill as I felt, I always liked sitting there with her, imagining our parallel lives clicking quietly along like two trains beside each other, with similar routes but different destinations. 29

When I played with Jan or Teresa, my friends from the time now indelibly labeled *Before,* they treated me the same way they always had, though perhaps with an air of delicacy that seemed uncomfortable and unnatural for all of us. They asked me questions about the physical effects of my treatment—how much it hurt, why I was so skinny, when my hair would grow back. I loved to answer with vigor and embellishment. A third of my answers were shaped by the braggart's love of a good tale, another third by my instinctive knowledge that they'd never understand what it was really like, and a third by my own unawareness of what it was like a great deal of the time. I witnessed my life unfolding like someone who has awkwardly stumbled in after the movie has started. I sensed that something important had been revealed in the opening sequence, some essential knowledge everyone else was privy to that was being kept from me. 30

I could converse with well-intentioned neighbors, go the usual round of polite questions about my health, though I was 31 highly aware of how different these conversations were from the ones with my friends on Ward 10, my friends from *After.* People who weren't ill or involved in the daily flow of hospital life had their own ideas of what it was like to be ill. It seemed impossible to tell them how it really was, and I didn't particularly want to do so. I preferred to have strangers on the street imagine me as sickly, confident that as soon as I was back on Ward 10 my friends and I would redefine for each other what it was like to be sick.

32   I felt as if my illness were a blanket the world had thrown over me; all that could be seen from the outside was an indistinguishable lump. And somehow I transformed that blanket into a tent, beneath which I almost happily set up camp. I had no sense of how my life was *supposed* to be, only of how it was. Not that this meant I was actually happy, not in any normal definition of the word. Though I depended on my apocalyptic thoughts to keep my situation in perspective, they did imbue me with a rather depressed aura. "For God's sake, stop looking so morbid all the time" became a familiar phrase in my house. Whenever anyone else was present I felt incapable of being anything other than a depressed lump. It was only when I was alone that my ability to relish life surfaced.

33   Each week, with the first glimmer of returning strength after days of vomiting, I discovered that, for me, joy could be measured in negative terms: of what I *didn't* have, which was pain and weakness. My greatest happiness wasn't acquired through effort but was something I already had, deep and sonorous inside of me, found through a process of removing the walls of pain around it. I knew the walls were inside of me, and I saw that most people, never having experienced deep physical discomfort on a regular basis, didn't, couldn't, know this.

34   I viewed other people both critically and sympathetically. Why couldn't they just stop complaining so much, just let go and see how good they actually had it? Everyone seemed to be waiting for something to happen that would allow them to move forward, waiting for some shadowy future moment to begin their lives in earnest. Everybody, from my mother to the characters I read about in books (who were as actual and important as real people to me), was always looking at someone else's life and envying it, wishing to occupy it. I wanted them to stop, to see how

much they had already, how they had their health and their strength. I imagined how my life would be if I had half their fortune. Then I would catch myself, guilty of exactly the thing I was accusing others of. As clear-headed as I was, sometimes I felt that the only reason for this clarity was to see how hypocritically I lived my own life.

Once, during a week of intensive chemotherapy toward the end 35 of the two and a half years, I was sent to another ward, as 10 was already full when I checked in. My roommate was a girl who'd been run over by an iceboat; the blades had cut her intestines in two, and she'd had to have them sewn back together. She got a lot of attention, lots of calls from concerned relatives and school friends, and I was both a little jealous of her and a little contemptuous because she was taking her accident a bit too seriously for my taste. After all, she'd lived, hadn't she? She'd had one operation and they might do another one the next week, but after that it would be all over, so what was the big fuss about?

Content

1. What made the adolescent Lucy so sensitive to the importance of her physical appearance (see ¶ 20, for example, "'*That* is the ugliest girl I have *ever* seen.'")? Given the emphasis on beauty in the culture in which she was growing up, is there any way she could have escaped this? Would a boy's appearance have been equally problematic (see Liu's discussion of his hair in "Notes of a Native Speaker," 335–47)?

2. Why did wearing a mask on Halloween (¶s 4–5, 25–26) make Lucy so happy? Do *masks* as a concept have symbolic meanings, either in Lucy's life or the lives of others, yourself included? Under what circumstances are figurative masks most useful? For what purposes?

3. Given the fact that she was still in the process of chemotherapy for cancer of the jaw, what could Lucy (or her parents or teachers or classmates) have done to deemphasize her appearance and make her feel better about herself?

4. Contrast the freedom that people of normal appearance or physical ability (also see Lamott, "Polaroids," 72–77) take for granted with the constraints that physical challenges impose on those who have them (see ¶s 23–24, 33–35).

5. Could Grealy have written this account if the operations to restore her facial contours had not finally been successful?

Strategies/Structures

6. Like many who have suffered, Grealy tries to explain her experiences of pain and illness in a variety of ways the evoke sympathetic understanding but are devoid of self-pity. Identify some of these (¶s 26–35 contain many examples) and discuss whether or not she has succeeded.

Language

7. Grealy is a poet as well as an autobiographer. In what ways does "Masks" disclose her poetic ability?

For Writing

8. To what extent are we defined by our appearance, particularly our faces? What sorts of messages does our contemporary culture send that reinforce the importance of one's physical beauty? In what ways is it possible, if at all, for ordinary people (or even exceptionally beautiful people) to resist the pervasive emphasis on appearance? In what ways can we escape the stereotypes associated with appearance, such as "fat and lazy," "beautiful but dumb"? Focusing on one or a combination of these questions, write a paper in which you use one or two symbols (such as "masks") or incidents to clarify and illustrate your point.

9. Is beauty really only skin deep? To address this question for an audience that needs to be convinced of your point of view, describe an intangible "beauty"—character, intelligence, ethics, heroism, altruism, public service, ability to perform a particular skill (musical, artistic, athletic). Illustrate your definition by positive and perhaps negative examples, such as scenes that show people or ideas in action (see, for instance, Sanders, "The Inheritance of Tools," 186–96 and King, Jr., "Letter from Birmingham Jail," 596–616).

ASIYA S. TSCHANNERL

Asiya Tschannerl was adopted soon after her birth in Philadelphia in 1977 by parents of Indian and Austrian nationalities (her Austrian last name, *Tschannerl*, rhymes with *chunnel*, as in the name of the tunnel under the English Channel). Having lived in China,

India, and parts of Africa and Europe, she feels that her ethnicity extends well beyond her African-American roots. In 1998 she earned a B.Sc. in medical biochemistry from Royal Holloway, University of London, to which she has returned for graduate study in pursuit of a M.D. She is currently a certified emergency medical technician, as well as an artist, composer, singer, cellist, and writer.

Asiya believes that her best writing stems from subjects she knows well. As a consequence, she particularly enjoys writing short autobiographical pieces. As she composes these, she explains, she "retraces thoughts, smells, and touches from the past, since doing so usually brings a wealth of other memories along with the initial association." Indeed, through the "domino effect of remembrance," she claims even to remember her adoption at three months, the moment when her adoptive mother first held her. Her memories are evocative of the senses ("I remember leaning back against that wind and not being able to fall"), of pride, terror, disillusionment, and love. Through writing sketches such as "One Remembers Most What One Loves," Asiya hopes to "inspire readers with a willingness to embrace and love other cultures as their own."

❄ One Remembers Most What One Loves

I have often been commended for my memory. I can even remember being held when I was adopted at three months of age. Perhaps one only recalls events which profoundly change one's life.

I remember my youth very clearly. How the seasons would change! September would bring its chilly air and a nervous start of a new school year. November would be full of excitement, with its strong gusts of wind and swirling sandstorms. It was amazing to look at a grain of sand and know that it had come from over two thousand miles away, from the Gobi desert. I remember leaning back against that wind and not being able to fall. I can still see that stream of bicycles going to the city, every head clad with a thin scarf to protect against the sand.

3   How well I know that bitter coldness of the winter, bringing snowballs and ice-skating on the lake at the Summer Palace. February fireworks, noodles and mooncakes for the New Year, our home always filled with friendly visits. I remember the monsoon rains of April and how the rice fields behind our apartment would sway as if they had a life of their own. And how could I forget the long, hot summers of badminton, evening walks, and mosquito nets?

4   Perhaps my memory is fostered by the countless nights I spent memorizing Chinese characters, stroke after stroke. In any case, I cannot forget. I love my childhood. I love Beijing.

5   Bei sha tan nong ji xue yuan. This is the name of the Chinese compound we lived in, an agricultural mechanization institute on the outskirts of Beijing. During the day, my father worked there while I would accompany my mother into the city. My mother taught sociology at the Beijing Foreign Languages Institute and I attended its adjoining Chinese elementary school. At age nine, I was in a country I had not lived in since I was a toddler and my Chinese was very poor. Hence, I entered first grade having already had four years of American grade school.

6   I remember my apprehension when my teacher introduced me on the first day of school. A hush fell over the classroom as forty pairs of wide eyes beheld for the first time a person of African descent. After what seemed a long time, class went on as usual, and finding myself amidst a maze of unintelligible dialogue, I took out my coloring pencils and began to draw. The children around me smiled shyly at me, curious to see what I was drawing. Such was the beginning of enduring friendships.

7   As the months rolled by, the sea of gibberish slowly became a wealth of vocabulary. I never knew that a language could describe things so precisely—but this is not to be wondered at when one considers the 15,000 characters that comprise the Chinese language, of which one must know at least 3,000 to be literate.

8   There was a routine common to each day. Upon arriving at school in the morning, everyone assembled in the playground and did the morning exercises. This involved dance-like movements and several laps around the school, rain or shine. Once inside the building we would do a series of mental math computations as quickly as possible. Then everyone would assume the "correct

posture" of arms folded behind the back—a posture I found exceedingly uncomfortable at first. This position had to be maintained throughout class except when raising a hand, which was done by putting the right elbow on the desk.

Chinese class would involved reading passages from our ⁹ textbooks and learning new characters. Breaks between every class would be used to clean the classroom—sprinkling water on the concrete floor to dampen the famous Beijing dust before sweeping, washing the blackboards with wet cloths and neatening up the teacher's desk. One of these breaks was used for everyone to massage their heads while relaxing music wafted down from the announcement speaker attached to the ceiling. In the middle of the day, everybody went home to eat lunch and nap for a few hours, after which classes would continue till four in the afternoon.

After school I would always get a snack while I waited for ¹⁰ my mother to pick me up. In the fall there were glazed apple-like fruit which were put on sticks, kebab style. In the winter there were dried, seasoned fish slices, and dried plums. Summer always meant popsicles, peaches and watermelon. I would eat my snack on the way home, watching the city change into the corn and rice fields of our institute.

At first I found the idea of Saturday classes repelling but I ¹¹ soon forgot that I ever had a two-day weekend. Sundays I looked forward to the hour of Disney cartoons in Chinese. Every other weekend I visited a nearby cow farm and helped feed the cows and calves. I remember talking at length with a milkmaid who had never before heard of the African slave trade, and her subsequent wishful disbelief.

I remember the proud feeling of putting on my red scarf for ¹² the first time. By then, I had read a lot about Chairman Mao and talked to people about the history of China. I felt a nationalist pride wearing this scarf, as the Little Red Guards had forty years ago in helping to defeat the Japanese militarists. The red scarf meant that one was committed to helping all those in difficulty and I proceeded to do this with great zeal—picking up watermelons for a man whose wheelbarrow wheels had split, helping old people across busy roads, etc.

Third grade brought the advent of the English class. I was ¹³ inwardly amused by the children's accents but when I corrected them, I was astonished to find that my words differed very little from theirs. In fact, as a grain of desert sand that has traveled many miles is indistinguishable from surrounding indigenous earth, I felt no different from any other Chinese child.

14   I can still see the faces of shopkeepers who had had their backs turned when I had asked for an item and when they turned around, were astounded to see a little black kid speaking perfect Mandarin. I think I even delighted in shocking people, purposefully going on a raid of the local shops. But I found that people were genuinely touched that I had taken the time to study their difficult language. I was warmly embraced as one of their children.

15   Fourth grade brought the Tiananmen massacre. Before the shootings, my mother and I had gone every day to visit her students and friends at the square. My heart felt like it was bursting with love, so strong was the feeling of community. There were so many people there that every part of your body was in contact with someone else. Once I looked triumphantly at my mother and exclaimed, "See? When you're with the people, you can't fall!" I remember drawing an analogy between the people and the November winds I could lean back against. Of course it was also a political statement.

16   The night of the massacre, I could hear the firing of guns from our home. My mother, who had been in the square at the time, managed to get back safely. The silence the next day pervaded the whole city and the sadness was unbearable. I remember feeling betrayed. How could this happen to my people? For the first time in forty years, the army had gone against its people. The young said that this was what socialism had come to, but the elders, recognizing that this was a form of fascism, muttered softly that this would never have happened under Chairman Mao.

17   The vision of black marks on the roads made from burning vehicles is engraved in my mind. The pools of blood were quickly washed away, bullet holes patched and death tolls revised. Near our institute there was the distinct scent of decomposing bodies brought from the city. These may have been buried or set fire to— no one knew, no one asked or verified. No one dared to speak, but in everyone was a mixture of anger, anguish and horror.

18   My parents' following separation accentuated the sadness. I spent months trying to heal our broken family, almost believing

that that achievement would heal the outside world as well. Fourth grade ended early and I longed to get away from the sadness. It was at this point that my mother decided to return to the U.S. I dreaded leaving but I anticipated the change of atmosphere. I was in for a surprise.

For more than a year, I experienced culture shock. Everything was familiar but new—the clothes, hairstyles, houses, toilets. People had so many things they never used or took for granted, and yet they considered themselves not to be well-off. I was incensed how little respect my peers had for their parents and elders. How anyone could hear what the teachers were saying when classes were so noisy was beyond me. Everyone seemed arrogant and ignorant of other cultures. Kids wouldn't believe I was American because they thought I "spoke weird." They asked me, "Why can't you talk normal?" I grew tired of explaining. Even African Americans thought I was from elsewhere. The pride I had felt when I represented Black America in China suffered a pang. I was disgusted by the racism against the Orient which I discovered to be rampant. I found myself pining for the comfortable existence I had come from. 19

Seven years later, I still like to surprise Chinese people with my knowledge of the language when I happen to meet them. I think it is important to show that cultural gaps can be crossed, and without much difficulty as long as there is an open mind. I go back to China when money is available—I visit Beijing and the cow farm, reliving old memories and making new ones. Perhaps one remembers most what one loves. 20

Content

1. Is it necessary to believe Tschannerl's claim in paragraph 1—"I can even remember being held when I was adopted at three months of age"— to trust her memories of life in China?

2. If you were to form your understanding of China only from Tschannerl's description, what would your impression of the country be?

3. What kind of a character is Tschannerl herself? What details, what incidents does she specifically present (as, for example, "I can still see the faces of shopkeepers who had their backs turned when I had asked for an item and when they turned around, were astounded to see a little

black kid speaking perfect Mandarin," ¶ 14)? What else do you infer about her from reading between the lines?

4. Why did returning to the United States present such a culture shock (¶ 19) for Tschannerl?

Strategies/Structures

5. Throughout the essay (except for the last paragraph) Tschannerl appropriately sticks to her child's perspective. What would she have gained—or lost—if she had incorporated her more adult understanding of the country and the subject?

6. Based on your own experiences as identified in question 9 below, what can you conclude about the reliability of child witnesses? Do your conclusions affect the extent to which you trust other people's accounts of childhood incidents, not only Tschannerl's but those of Sanders (186–96 and 441–56), Grealy (349–60), and Barry (670–75)? Might they be true to the spirit of the memories but weak on the specific details? Or vice versa?

Language

7. The prevailing tone of Tschannerl's recollection of China is one of love. How does she manage to convey this while at the same time acknowledging the harshness of the political climate?

8. Tschannerl uses only a single Chinese expression, the name of the compound where her family lived (¶ 5), yet her immersion in China depends on fishing "a wealth of vocabulary" out of "a sea of gibberish" (¶ 7). This technique, of using a small fragment to indicate a much larger picture, delicate as a calligraphed scroll, conveys a wealth of meaning. Find other instances where she has used this technique effectively.

For Writing

9. Many of the essays in *The Essay Connection,* such as this one (see also Sanders [186–96 and 441–56], Grealy [349–60], and Barry [670–75]) rely on the memories of very young children for their details, incidents, even interpretations—though the meanings are often enhanced by the adult author's understanding. Drawing primarily on your childhood memories, describe a place that is important to you, providing sufficient detail to convey its significance to readers who are unfamiliar with it. Can you rely entirely on your own memory, or do you need to consult other sources? If so, for what kinds of information?

10. All of us are continually in the process of shaping and being shaped by a particular culture or cultures; identify some of the major features of this process and how this process works. For instance, if we live in a culture where high-tech material comforts (such as TVs, stereos, computers, cell phones, and much much more) are commonplace in everyday life—at home, at school, and at work—we take them for granted. Yet their presence influences in obvious and more subtle ways how we do our work and spend our leisure time, even as we make individual choices about how much time to devote daily or weekly to any or all of these devices and for what purposes, as when we decide what to call up on the Internet, and then what to do with what we've found.

In your answer you could refer not only to Tschannerl's essay but to essays by any of the following: Rose (263–73), Cofer (179–86), Zitkala-Sa (273–83), Liu (335–49), Soto (510–20), or Barry (670–75). How is this process complicated when a person is multicultural and has lived in more than one country or culture?

Additional Topics for Writing
Description   (For strategies for writing description, see 315.)

1. Places, for readers who haven't been there:

   a. Your dream house (or room)
   b. Your favorite spot on earth
   c. A ghost town, or a dying or decaying neighborhood
   d. A foreign city or country you have visited
   e. A shopping mall
   f. A factory, farm, store, or other place where you've worked
   g. The waiting room of a bus station, airport, hospital, or dentist's office
   h. A mountain, beach, lake, forest, desert, field, or other natural setting you know well
   i. Or, compare and contrast two places you know well—two churches, houses, restaurants, vacation spots, schools, or any of the places identified in parts a–h, above

2. People, for readers who don't know them:

   a. A close relative or friend
   b. A friend or relative with whom you were once very close but from whom you are presently separated, physically or psychologically
   c. An antagonist
   d. Someone with an occupation or skill you want to know more about—you may want to interview the person to learn what skills, training, and personal qualities the job or activity requires
   e. Someone who has participated, voluntarily or involuntarily, in a significant historical event
   f. A bizarre or eccentric person, a "character"
   g. A high achiever—in business, sports, the arts or sciences, politics, religion
   h. A person whose reputation, public or private, has changed dramatically, for better or worse

3. Situations or events, for readers who weren't there:

   a. A holiday, birthday, or community celebration
   b. A high school or college party
   c. A farmer's market, flea market, garage sale, swap meet, or auction

d. An athletic event
e. A performance of a play or concert
f. A ceremony—a graduation, wedding, christening, bar or bat mitzvah, an initiation, the swearing-in of a public official
g. A family or school reunion
h. A confrontation—between team members and referees or the coach, strikers and scabs, protesters and police

4. Experiences or feelings, for readers with analogous experiences:

   a. Love—romantic, familial, patriotic, or religious (see Kiefer, 636–39); Jefferson, 591–96)
   b. Isolation or rejection (see Grealy, 349–60; Soto, 436–41)
   c. Fear (see Barry, 670–75)
   d. Aspiration (see Rose, 263–73)
   e. Success (see Liu, 335–49)
   f. Anger (see Douglass, 164–69)
   g. Peace, contentment, or happiness (see White, 171–79)
   h. An encounter with birth or death (see Erdrich, 47–53)
   i. Coping with a handicap or disability—yours or that of someone close to you (see Lamott, 72–77; Mairs, 456–71)

9 | Division and Classification

To divide something is to separate it into its component parts. As a writer you can divide a large, complex subject into smaller segments, easier for you and your readers to deal with individually than to consider in a large, complicated whole. As the section on process analysis indicates (see 203–07), writers usually employ division to explain the individual stages of a process—how the earth was formed; how a professional jockey (or potter or surgeon) performs his or her job; how a heat pump works. Process analysis also underlies explanations of how to make or do something, how to train your dog, or make a cake, or cut gems.

You could also divide your subject in other ways—according to types of dogs, cakes, or gems. And there would be still different ways to divide a discussion of dogs—by their size (miniature, small, medium, large); by the length of their hair (short or long); or according to their suitability as working dogs, pets, or show dogs.

As you start to divide your subject, you almost naturally begin to *classify* it as well, to sort it into categories of groups or families. You'll probably determine the subcategories according to some logical principle or according to characteristics common to members of particular subgroups. Don't stretch to create esoteric groupings (dogs by hair color, for example) if your common sense suggests a more natural way. Some categories simply make more sense than others. A discussion of dogs by breeds could be logically arranged in alphabetical order—Afghan, borzoi, bulldog, collie, weimaraner. But a discussion that grouped dogs by type first and then breed would be easier to understand and more economical to write. For instance, you could consider all the common features of spaniels first, before dividing them into breeds of spaniels—cocker, springer, water—and discussing the differences.

Again, how minutely you refine the subcategories of your classification system depends on the length of your writing, your focus, and your emphasis. You could use a *binary* (two-part) *classification*. This is a favorite technique of classifiers who wish to sort things into two categories, those with a particular characteristic and those without it (drinkers and nondrinkers, swimmers and nonswimmers). Thus, in an essay discussing the components of a large structure or organization—a farm, a corporation, a university—a binary classification might lead you to focus on management and labor, or the university's academic and nonacademic functions. In "None of This Is Fair" (398–405), Richard Rodriguez adopts two binary classification systems, first dividing students into ethnic minorities and majorities to argue against affirmative action; then in the last two paragraphs dividing all children into two classes—the poor, irrespective of race, who "lack the confidence to assume their right to a good education," and all other people, who feel entitled to a good education. Likewise, Ning Yu's "Red and Black, or One English Major's Beginning" (405–18) uses the Chinese Communists' classification of Chinese citizens into "reds" (and therefore good, proletarian party loyalists) and "blacks" (and therefore subversive intellectuals and political dissenters) as the basis for showing two very different ways of teaching English to children who speak only Chinese. Embedded in these political labels are two very different cultures and sets of values, each claiming to promote what is good for China and its people.

Sometimes the divisions get more complicated because they are less clear-cut. In "Why Men Don't Last: Self-Destruction as a Way of Life" (381–88), Natalie Angier makes distinctions, based on biological and psychological research and statistical reports, between the self-destructive behavior of men and women—"women are about three times more likely than men to express suicidal thoughts or to attempt to kill themselves . . . but in the United States, four times more men than women die from the act each year." However, there are, she indicates, different ways to interpret these facts to show either that men are the greater risk takers ("given to showy displays of bravado, aggression and daring all for the sake of attracting a harem of mates") or that women are (because those who talk about suicide are more open to experience, including taking risks and seeking novelties). She makes other distinctions between men's and women's risk-taking behavior concerning homicide, alcohol and drug use, and gambling. For instance, while both men and women gamble, their "methods and preferences for throwing away big sums of money" are very different. Men try to "overcome the odds and beat the system" at table games "where they can feel powerful and omnipotent while everybody watches them," while women prefer "the solitary forms of gambling, the slot machines or video poker, where there isn't as much social scrutiny." Angier concludes by citing research that classifies boys by the extent to which they uphold traditional versus egalitarian views of masculinity; presumably the traditionalists would grow up to be more self-destructive than those who favored equal rights and responsibilities for women.

In "Pomegranates and English Education"(388–98), Shirley Geok-lin Lim, a Chinese born and reared in Malacca, Malaysia, examines the multiple influences on her elementary and high school education of the French-oriented convent school whose curriculum followed that of an English private school in which the students studied English books and therefore English culture. She writes, "No one asked why Indian, Eurasian, Malay, and Chinese children should be singing" Scottish and Irish ballads. "What was the place of Celt ballads in a Malayan future?" The nuns, European and Eurasian, exhibited a hierarchy of jobs and power which, "despite their uniform habits and sisterly titles," was "a ranking regulated by race." The same racial basis for status was replicated among the pupils, who valued above all European appearance and clothing. And why not? "To every schoolgirl," sensitive to all nuances and caste distinctions, "it was obvious that something about a white child made the good nuns benevolent." Only the orphans, "girls abandoned as babies on the convent doorsteps," had a lower status than the Chinese; they were "a class to be shunned."

Another type of classification is to construct three categories or subcategories. In "The Technology of Medicine" (375–81), Lewis Thomas classifies his subject as "nontechnology," "halfway technology," and the "genuinely decisive technology of modern medicine," arranged from the least to the most genuine technology. Each of these has specific functions, causes, and effects. As he classifies, Thomas also analyzes his subject by comparing the first two categories, which deal with medical problems after they have occurred and are very costly and difficult to deliver. He contrasts these with the last category; decisive technology, he demonstrates, is preventive, "relatively inexpensive and relatively easy to deliver."

Obviously, you can create as many categories and subcategories as are useful in enabling you and your readers to understand and interpret the subject. If you wanted to concentrate on the academic aspects of your own university, you might categorize them according to academic divisions—arts and sciences, business, education, music, public health. A smaller classification would examine the academic disciplines within a division—biology, English, history, mathematics. Or smaller yet, depending on your purpose—English literature, American literature, creative writing, linguistics—*ad infinitum*, as the anonymous jingle observes:

> Big fleas have little fleas, and these
> Have littler fleas to bite 'em,
> And these have fleas, and these have fleas,
> And so on *ad infinitum*.

In all five of the essays in this chapter, the classification system provides the basis for the overall organization; but here as in most essays, the authors use many other techniques of writing in addition—narration, definition, description, analysis, illustration, and comparison and contrast.

In writing essays based on division, you might ask the following questions to help organize your materials: What are the parts of the total unit? How can these be subdivided to make the subject more understandable to my readers? In essays of classification, where you're sorting or grouping two or more things, you can ask: Into what categories can I sort these items? According to what principles—of logic, common characteristics, "fitness"? Do I want my classification to emphasize the similarities among groups or their differences? Once I've determined the groupings, am I organizing my discussion of each category in the same way, considering the same features in the same order? In many instances divisions and classifications are in the mind of the beholder. Is the glass half full or half empty? Your job as a writer is to help your readers recognize and accept the order of your universe.

STRATEGIES FOR WRITING— DIVISION AND CLASSIFICATION

1. Am I going to explain an existing system of classification, or am I going to invent a new one? Do I want to define a system by categorizing its components? Explain a process by dividing it into stages? Argue in favor of one category or another? Entertain through an amusing classification?
2. Do my readers know my subject but not my classification system? Know both subject and system? Or are they unacquainted with either? How will their knowledge (or lack of knowledge) of the subject or system influence how much I say about either? Will this influence the simplicity or complexity of my classification system?
3. According to what principle am I classifying or dividing my subject? Is it sensible? Significant? Does it emphasize the similarities or the differences among groups? Have I applied the principle consistently with respect to each category? How have I integrated my paper (to keep it from being just a long list), through providing interconnections among the parts and transitions between the divisions?
4. Have I organized my discussion of each category in the same way, considering the same features in the same order? Have I illustrated each category? Are the discussions of each category the same length? Should they be? Why or why not?
5. Have I used language similar in vocabulary level (equally technical, or equally informal) in each category? Have I defined any needed terms?

LEWIS THOMAS

Thomas (1913–1993) who earned a B.S. from Princeton (1933) and an M.D. from Harvard (1937), was the author of some two hundred research papers on immunology and pathology. As he explained in his autobiography, *The Youngest Science* (1983), these were written "in the relentlessly flat style required for absolute unambiguity." He is better known to the public, however, for his witty monthly columns in the *New England Journal of Medicine* that have been collected in *The Lives of a Cell: Notes of a Biology Watcher* (1974), winner of a 1974 National Book Award; *The Medusa and the Snail: More Notes of a Biology Watcher* (1979); and *Late Night Thoughts on Listening to Mahler's Ninth Symphony* (1983). Writing late at night, "usually on the weekend two days after I'd already passed the deadline," never outlining "or planning in advance," Thomas created graceful, informal personal essays using scientific knowledge, particularly from cell biology, as a source of metaphors for understanding human experience and the natural world.

Thomas taught at Johns Hopkins, the School of Medicine at New York University, and the Yale Medical School; from 1973 to 1980 he was president of the Memorial Sloan-Kettering Cancer Center; thereafter, president emeritus.

This essay, from *The Lives of a Cell* (1974), categorizes three levels of medical technology (supportive, "halfway," and preventive) and demonstrates Thomas's talent for explaining medical phenomena in terms general readers—and potential beneficiaries of this technology—can understand. Thomas uses the classification he has established as the basis for his argument, that "the real high technology of medicine . . . comes as the result of a genuine understanding of disease mechanisms" and is the least dramatic, the least obtrusive, and "relatively inexpensive, and relatively easy to deliver."

The Technology of Medicine

T echnology assessment has become a routine exercise for the   1
scientific enterprises on which the country is obliged to spend
vast sums for its needs. Brainy committees are continually evaluating the effectiveness and cost of doing various things in space,

defense, energy, transportation, and the like, to give advice about prudent investments for the future.

2   Somehow medicine, for all the $80-odd billion that it is said to cost the nation, has not yet come in for much of this analytical treatment. It seems taken for granted that the technology of medicine simply exists, take it or leave it, and the only major technologic problem which policy-makers are interested in is how to deliver today's kind of health care, with equity, to all the people.

3   When, as is bound to happen sooner or later, the analysts get around to the technology of medicine itself, they will have to face the problem of measuring the relative cost and effectiveness of all the things that are done in the management of disease. They make their living at this kind of thing, and I wish them well, but I imagine they will have a bewildering time. For one thing, our methods of managing disease are constantly changing—partly under the influence of new bits of information brought in from all corners of biologic science. At the same time, a great many things are done that are not so closely related to science, some not related at all.

4   In fact, there are three quite different levels of technology in medicine, so unlike each other as to seem altogether different undertakings. Practitioners of medicine and the analysts will be in trouble if they are not kept separate.

5   1. First of all, there is a large body of what might be termed "nontechnology," impossible to measure in terms of its capacity to alter either the natural course of disease or its eventual outcome. A great deal of money is spent on this. It is valued highly by the professionals as well as the patients. It consists of what is sometimes called "supportive therapy." It tides patients over through diseases that are not, by and large, understood. It is what is meant by the phrases "caring for" and "standing by." It is indispensable. It is not, however, a technology in any real sense, since it does not involve measures directed at the underlying mechanism of disease.

6   It includes the large part of any good doctor's time that is taken up with simply providing reassurance, explaining to patients who fear that they have contracted one or another lethal disease that they are, in fact, quite healthy.

7   It is what physicians used to be engaged in at the bedside of patients with diphtheria, meningitis, poliomyelitis, lobar pneumonia, and all the rest of the infectious diseases that have since come under control.

It is what physicians must now do for patients with intract- 8
able cancer, severe rheumatoid arthritis, multiple sclerosis, stroke,
and advanced cirrhosis. One can think of at least twenty major
diseases that require this kind of supportive medical care because
of the absence of an effective technology. I would include a large
amount of what is called mental disease, and most varieties of
cancer, in this category.

The cost of this nontechnology is very high, and getting 9
higher all the time. It requires not only a great deal of time but also
very hard effort and skill on the part of physicians; only the very
best of doctors are good at coping with this kind of defeat. It also
involves long periods of hospitalization, lots of nursing, lots of involvement of nonmedical professionals in and out of the hospital.
It represents, in short, a substantial segment of today's expenditures for health.

2. At the next level up is a kind of technology best termed 10
"halfway technology." This represents the kinds of things that
must be done after the fact, in efforts to compensate for the inca-
pacitating effects of certain diseases whose course one is unable to
do very much about. It is a technology designed to make up for
disease, or to postpone death.

The outstanding examples in recent years are the transplan- 11
tations of hearts, kidneys, livers, and other organs, and the equally
spectacular inventions of artificial organs. In the public mind, this
kind of technology has come to seem like the equivalent of the
high technologies of the physical sciences. The media tend to present each new procedure as though it represented a breakthrough
and therapeutic triumph, instead of the makeshift that it really is.

In fact, this level of technology is, by its nature, at the same 12
time highly sophisticated and profoundly primitive. It is the kind
of thing that one must continue to do until there is a genuine
understanding of the mechanisms involved in disease. In chronic
glomerulonephritis, for example, a much clearer insight will be
needed into the events leading to the destruction of glomeruli by
the immunologic reactants that now appear to govern this disease,
before one will know how to intervene intelligently to prevent the
process, or turn it around. But when this level of understanding
has been reached, the technology of kidney replacement will not
be much needed and should no longer pose the huge problem of
logistics, cost, and ethics that it poses today.

13   An extremely complex and costly technology for the management of coronary heart disease has evolved—involving specialized ambulances and hospital units, all kinds of electronic
gadgetry, and whole platoons of new professional personnel—to
deal with the end results of coronary thrombosis. Almost everything offered today for the treatment of heart disease is at this
level of technology, with the transplanted and artificial hearts as
ultimate examples. When enough has been learned to know what
really goes wrong in heart disease, one ought to be in a position
to figure out ways to prevent or reverse the process, and when
this happens the current elaborate technology will probably be
set to one side.

14   Much of what is done in the treatment of cancer, by surgery,
irradiation, and chemotherapy, represents halfway technology, in
the sense that these measures are directed at the existence of already established cancer cells, but not at the mechanisms by
which cells become neoplastic.

15   It is a characteristic of this kind of technology that it costs an
enormous amount of money and requires a continuing expansion
of hospital facilities. There is no end to the need for new, highly
trained people to run the enterprise. And there is really no way
out of this, at the present state of knowledge. If the installation of
specialized coronary-care units can result in the extension of life
for only a few patients with coronary disease (and there is no
question that this technology is effective in a few cases), it seems
to me an inevitable fact of life that as many of these as can be will
be put together, and as much money as can be found will be
spent. I do not see that anyone has much choice in this. The only
thing that can move medicine away from this level of technology
is new information, and the only imaginable source of this information is research.

16   3. The third type of technology is the kind that is so effective
that it seems to attract the least public notice; it has come to be
taken for granted. This is the genuinely decisive technology of
modern medicine, exemplified best by modern methods for im-
munization against diphtheria, pertussis, and the childhood virus
diseases, and the contemporary use of antibiotics and chemotherapy for bacterial infections. The capacity to deal effectively
with syphilis and tuberculosis represents a milestone in human

endeavor, even though full use of this potential has not yet been made. And there are, of course, other examples: the treatment of endocrinologic disorders with appropriate hormones, the prevention of hemolytic disease of the newborn, the treatment and prevention of various nutritional disorders, and perhaps just around the corner the management of Parkinsonism and sickle-cell anemia. There are other examples, and everyone will have his favorite candidates for the list, but the truth is that there are nothing like as many as the public has been led to believe.

The point to be made about this kind of technology—the real high technology of medicine—is that it comes as the result of a genuine understanding of disease mechanisms, and when it becomes available, it is relatively inexpensive, and relatively easy to deliver. 17

Offhand, I cannot think of any important human disease for which medicine possesses the outright capacity to prevent or cure where the cost of the technology is itself a major problem. The price is never as high as the cost of managing the same diseases during the earlier stages of no-technology or halfway technology. If a case of typhoid fever had to be managed today by the best methods of 1935, it would run to a staggering expense. At, say, around fifty days of hospitalization, requiring the most demanding kind of nursing care, with the obsessive concern for details of diet that characterized the therapy of that time, with daily laboratory monitoring, and, on occasion, surgical intervention for abdominal catastrophe, I should think $10,000 would be a conservative estimate for the illness, as contrasted with today's cost of a bottle of chloramphenicol and a day or two of fever. The halfway technology that was evolving for poliomyelitis in the early 1950s, just before the emergence of the basic research that made the vaccine possible, provides another illustration of the point. Do you remember Sister Kenny, and the cost of those institutes for rehabilitation, with all those ceremonially applied hot fomentations, and the debates about whether the affected limbs should be totally immobilized or kept in passive motion as frequently as possible, and the masses of statistically tormented data mobilized to support one view or the other? It is the cost of that kind of technology, and its relative effectiveness, that must be compared with the cost and effectiveness of the vaccine. 18

19   Pulmonary tuberculosis had similar episodes in its history. There was a sudden enthusiasm for the surgical removal of infected lung tissue in the early 1950s, and elaborate plans were being made for new and expensive installations for major pulmonary surgery in tuberculosis hospitals, and then INH and streptomycin came along and the hospitals themselves were closed up.

20   It is when physicians are bogged down by their incomplete technologies, by the innumerable things they are obliged to do in medicine when they lack a clear understanding of disease mechanisms, that the deficiencies of the health-care system are most conspicuous. If I were a policy-maker, interested in saving money for health care over the long haul, I would regard it as an act of high prudence to give high priority to a lot more basic research in biologic science. This is the only way to get the full mileage that biology owes to the science of medicine, even though it seems, as used to be said in the days when the phrase still had some meaning, like asking for the moon.

Content

1. What is "supportive therapy" (¶ 5)? Why isn't it a technology?
2. Why does Thomas term the second level of technology "halfway technology" (¶ 10)? Why does this technology "make up for disease, or postpone death" (¶ 10)? Why is it "profoundly primitive" (¶ 12)?
3. Why does Thomas most strongly favor the third type of technology, the "genuinely decisive technology of modern medicine" (¶ 16)? Why does he say that preventive technology is unobtrusive, taken for granted?
4. What does Thomas mean by "basic research in biologic science" (¶ 20)? Why does he believe that basic research will ultimately save money for health care "over the long haul"? What evidence does he provide to demonstrate this?

Strategies/Structures

5. What is the basis for Thomas's three-part classification? Show how Thomas uses the three categories of technology (or nontechnology) in medicine as the three stages of an argument that he builds as the essay progresses. Could these have been arranged in any other order?
6. Thomas's thesis takes issue with the conventional views about health care delivery that he states in the first two paragraphs. Where does he state his thesis? Why does he wait until so late in the essay to present it?

Language

7. What does Thomas mean by the "technology" of medicine? Why does he continually use the term "technology" rather than "science" except in the last sentence of the essay?

8. Would a general audience understand the examples Thomas provides to illustrate each category? How does the simplicity or technicality of his language affect that understanding?

For Writing

9. Thomas refers briefly to past ("halfway technology") treatments of tuberculosis and polio and compares them to current ("high technology") treatments of the same disease. Pick a disease whose treatment and cure has changed dramatically over the years and analyze its history to illustrate the truth of Thomas's assertion about "The Technology of Medicine."

10. Write an essay, intended to convince skeptics, in which you explain and advocate the benefits of prevention (of alcoholism, drug abuse, unwanted pregnancies, obesity) over prolonged treatment or cure. If possible, interview one or two people who have benefited from a prevention program and incorporate the information from the interviews into your paper.

NATALIE ANGIER

Angier (born, 1958), grew up in New York City, attended the University of Michigan and graduated from Barnard College in 1978. After working as a magazine staff writer at *Discover* and *Time* and as an editor at *Savvy*, she taught journalism at New York University before becoming a reporter for the *New York Times* in 1990. Her work as a *Times* science correspondent led to a Pulitzer Prize in 1991 and the publication of a collection of her columns, *The Beauty of the Beastly: New Views on the Nature of Life* (1995). Her topics include evolutionary biology ("Mating for Life?" "The Urge to Cuddle"), DNA, scorpions, hyenas, fish, and central issues of life, death (by suicide or AIDS) and creativity. Her newest work, *Woman: An Intimate Geography* (1999) offers a spirited and controversial celebration of "the female body—its anatomy, its chemistry, its evolution, and its laughter," including both traditional (the womb, the egg) and nontraditional elements ("movement, strength, aggression, and fury"). Angier, who lists her hobby as "weightlifting," recently became a mother; her work reflects the strengths of both.

Angier's writing is characteristically clear, precise, and witty. She explains the unfamiliar in terms of the familiar, giving research a memorably human perspective: "If stretched to its full length, a single molecule of human DNA would extend more than three feet, the height of the average nursery school child. But when squeezed and coiled and crammed into its rightful place in the bosom of the cell, the molecule of life measures about a hundred-thousandth of an inch across." With comparable precision and clarity in "Why Men Don't Last," first published in the *New York Times* (Feb. 17, 1999), Angier examines significant differences between the biology of men and women, translating statistical and psychological research (on risk taking, compulsive gambling, suicidal behavior, masculinity) into language and concepts general readers can readily understand—without oversimplifying the subject or demeaning the audience.

Why Men Don't Last: Self-Destruction as a Way of Life

1   My father had great habits. Long before ficus trees met weight machines, he was a dogged exerciser. He did push-ups and isometrics. He climbed rocks. He went for long, vigorous walks. He ate sparingly and avoided sweets and grease. He took such good care of his teeth that they looked fake.

2   My father had terrible habits. He was chronically angry. He threw things around the house and broke them. He didn't drink often, but when he did, he turned more violent than usual. He didn't go to doctors, even when we begged him to. He let a big, ugly mole on his back grow bigger and bigger, and so he died of malignant melanoma, a curable cancer, at 51.

3   My father was a real man—so good and so bad. He was also Everyman.

4   Men by some measures take better care of themselves than women do and are in better health. They are less likely to be fat,

for example; they exercise more, and suffer from fewer chronic diseases like diabetes, osteoporosis and arthritis.

By standard measures, men have less than half the rate of 5 depression seen in women. When men do feel depressed, they tend to seek distraction in an activity, which, many psychologists say, can be a more effective technique for dispelling the mood than is a depressed woman's tendency to turn inward and ruminate. In the United States and many other industrialized nations, women are about three times more likely than men to express suicidal thoughts or to attempt to kill themselves.

And yet . . . men don't last. They die off in greater numbers 6 than women do at every stage of life, and thus their average life span is seven years shorter. Women may attempt suicide relatively more often, but in the United States, four times more men than women die from the act each year.

Men are also far more likely than women to die behind the 7 wheel or to kill others as a result of their driving. From 1977 to 1995, three and a half times more male drivers than female drivers were involved in fatal car crashes. Death by homicide also favors men; among those under 30, the male-to-female ratio is 8 to 1.

Yes, men can be impressive in their tendency to self- 8 destruct, explosively or gradually. They are at least twice as likely as women to be alcoholics and three times more likely to be drug addicts. They have an eightfold greater chance than women do of ending up in prison. Boys are much more likely than girls to be thrown out of school for a conduct or antisocial personality disorder, or to drop out on their own surly initiative. Men gamble themselves into a devastating economic and emotional pit two to three times more often than women do.

"Between boys' suicide rates, dropout rates and homicide 9 rates, and men's self-destructive behaviors generally, we have a real crisis in America," said William S. Pollack, a psychologist at Harvard Medical School and co-director of the Center for Men at McLean Hospital in Belmont, Mass. "Until recently, the crisis has gone unheralded."

It is one thing to herald a presumed crisis, though, and to cite 10 a ream of gloomy statistics. It is quite another to understand the crisis, or to figure out where it comes from or what to do about it. As those who study the various forms of men's self-destructive behaviors realize, there is not a single, glib, overarching explanation for the sex-specific patterns they see.

11   A crude evolutionary hypothesis would have it that men are natural risk-takers, given to showy displays of bravado, aggression and daring all for the sake of attracting a harem of mates. By this premise, most of men's self-destructive, violent tendencies are a manifestation of their need to take big chances for the sake of passing their genes into the river of tomorrow.

12   Some of the data on men's bad habits fit the risk-taker model. For example, those who study compulsive gambling have observed that men and women tend to display very different methods and preferences for throwing away big sums of money.

13   "Men get enamored of the action in gambling," said Linda Chamberlain, a psychologist at Regis University in Denver who specializes in treating gambling disorders. "They describe an overwhelming rush of feelings and excitement associated with the process of gambling. They like the feeling of being a player, and taking on a struggle with the house to show that they can overcome the odds and beat the system. They tend to prefer the table games, where they can feel powerful and omnipotent while everybody watches them."

14   Dr. Chamberlain noted that many male gamblers engage in other risk-taking behaviors, like auto racing or hang gliding. By contrast, she said, "Women tend to use gambling more as a sedative, to numb themselves and escape from daily responsibilities, or feelings of depression or alienation. Women tend to prefer the solitary forms of gambling, the slot machines or video poker, where there isn't as much social scrutiny."

15 Yet the risk-taking theory does not account for why men outnumber women in the consumption of licit and illicit anodynes. Alcohol, heroin and marijuana can be at least as numbing and sedating as repetitively pulling the arm of a slot machine. And some studies have found that men use drugs and alcohol for the same reasons that women often overeat: as an attempt to self-medicate when they are feeling anxious or in despair.

16   "We can speculate all we want, but we really don't know why men drink more than women," said Enoch Gordis, the head of the National Institute on Alcohol Abuse and Alcoholism. Nor does men's comparatively higher rate of suicide appear linked to

the risk-taking profile. To the contrary, Paul Duberstein, an assistant professor of psychiatry and oncology at the University of Rochester School of Medicine, has found that people who complete a suicidal act are often low in a personality trait referred to as "openness to experience," tending to be rigid and inflexible in their behaviors. By comparison, those who express suicidal thoughts tend to score relatively high on the openness-to-experience scale.

Given that men commit suicide more often than women, [17] and women talk about it more, his research suggests that, in a sense, women are the greater risk-takers and novelty seekers, while the men are likelier to feel trapped and helpless in the face of changing circumstances.

Silvia Cara Canetto, an associate professor of psychology at [18] Colorado State University in Fort Collins, has extensively studied the role of gender in suicidal behaviors. Dr. Canetto has found that cultural narratives may determine why women attempt suicide more often while men kill themselves more often. She proposes that in Western countries, to talk about suicide or to survive a suicidal act is often considered "feminine," hysterical, irrational and weak. To actually die by one's own hand may be viewed as "masculine," decisive, strong. Even the language conveys the polarized, weak-strong imagery: a "failed" suicide attempt as opposed to a "successful" one.

"There is indirect evidence that there is negative stigma to- [19] ward men who survive suicide," Dr. Canetto said. "Men don't want to 'fail,' even though failing in this case means surviving." If the "suicidal script" that identifies completing the acts as "rational, courageous and masculine" can be "undermined and torn to pieces," she said, we might have a new approach to prevention.

Dr. Pollack of the Center for Men also blames many of men's [20] self-destructive ways on the persistent image of the dispassionate, resilient, action-oriented male—the Marlboro Man who never even gasps for breath. For all the talk of the sensitive "new man," he argues, men have yet to catch up with women in expanding their range of acceptable emotions and behaviors. Men in our culture, Dr. Pollack says, are pretty much limited to a menu of three strong feelings: rage, triumph, lust. "Anything else and you risk being seen as a sissy," he said.

In a number of books, most recently "Real Boys: Rescuing [21] Our Sons From the Myths of Boyhood," he proposes that boys "lose their voice, a whole half of their emotional selves," beginning at age 4 or 5. "Their vulnerable, sad feelings and sense of need are suppressed or shamed out of them," he said—by their peers, parents, the great wide televised fist in their face.

22   He added: "If you keep hammering it into a kid that he has to look tough and stop being a crybaby and a mama's boy, the boy will start creating a mask of bravado."

23   That boys and young men continue to feel confused over the proper harmonics of modern masculinity was revealed in a study that Dr. Pollack conducted of 200 eighth-grade boys. Through questionnaires, he determined their scores on two scales, one measuring their "egalitarianism"—the degree to which they think men and women are equal, that men should change a baby's diapers, that mothers should work and the like—and the other gauging their "traditionalism" as determined by their responses to conventional notions, like the premise that men must "stand on their own two feet" and must "always be willing to have sex if someone asks."

24   On average, the boys scored high on both scales. "They are split on what it means to be a man," said Dr. Pollack.

25   The cult of masculinity can beckon like a siren song in baritone. Dr. Franklin L. Nelson, a clinical psychologist at the Fairbanks Community Mental Health Center in Alaska, sees many men who get into trouble by adhering to sentimental notions of manhood. "A lot of men come up here hoping to get away from a wimpy world and live like pioneers by old-fashioned masculine principles of individualism, strength and ruggedness," he said. They learn that nothing is simple; even Alaska is part of a wider, interdependent world and they really do need friends, warmth and electricity.

26   "Right now, it's 35 degrees below zero outside," he said during a January interview. "If you're not prepared, it doesn't take long at that temperature to freeze to death."

Content

1.   Angier uses several categories of division in this piece: the "so good and so bad" habits of "Everyman" (¶ 3); the self-destructive habits and rates of men versus women (throughout); the division between the rugged individual versus the egalitarian helpmeet roles today's men are

expected to play (¶s 23–25). Why do such divisions enable readers to clearly recognize similarities as well as differences?

2. Angier's explanations for these divisions are equally divided. What evidence does she offer to support the "crude evolutionary hypothesis" that "men are natural risk-takers, given to showy display of bravado, aggression and daring all for the sake of attracting a harem of mates" (¶ 11)? What evidence does she offer to contradict this hypothesis?

3. What do you make of the fact that women talk about committing suicide more than men do, but that men actually have a higher rate of suicide than women do (¶s 16–19)?

Strategies/Structures

4. Why does Angier begin this piece with a paragraph that lists her father's "great habits," followed by one listing his "terrible habits" (¶s 1–2)?

5. Why aren't the divisions and classifications Angier uses more clear cut? Is this a phenomenon of the research she cites, of her writing, of the way things are in real life, or of some combination of the three?

6. Angier is writing as a reporter of other people's research. Although her writing begins with the personal example of her father, do we know where she stands on the subject—which hypothesis for men's risk-taking behavior she believes? Is her essay slanted in favor of one opinion or another, either in terms of her examples or her language?

7. Should a reporter be neutral? Isn't the selection of evidence in itself a form of tipping the scale in favor of one side or another?

8. What are the dangers and difficulties of categorizing behavior by gender?

For Writing

9. Have you ever done anything risky or dangerous to avoid looking like a wimp or to avoid falling into one or another stereotypical role for either men or women? Write a paper for an audience different from yourself; for instance, if you're a risk-taking man, write for a more prudent audience of women or men (if it makes a difference to your argument, specify which gender).

10. Angier, like other science writers, had the difficult job of translating scientific research into language that newspaper readers can understand. From the following list of authors she cites on the role of gender in suicidal behaviors, choose one source and identify, with illustrations, the principles by which Angier works. Consider aspects such as document format, uses of evidence, presentation of data (via graphs, charts,

statistics), technicality of language, definitions of scientific terms, citation of supporting research.

Canetto, Silvia Sara, and David Lester. "Gender, Culture, and Suicidal Behavior." *Transcultural Psychiatry* 35.2 (1998): 163–90.

Canetto, Silvia Sara, and Issac Sakinofsky. "The Gender Paradox in Suicide." *Suicide and Life-Threatening Behavior* 28.1 (Spring 1998): 1–23.

Chamberlain, Linda, Michael R. Ruetz, and William G. McCown. *Strange Attractors: Chaos, Complexity, and the Art of Family Therapy*. New York: Wiley, 1997.

Duberstein, Paul R., Yeates Conwell, and Christopher Cox. "Suicide in Widowed Persons." *American Journal of Geriatric Psychiatry* 6.4 (Fall 1998): 328–34.

Gordis, Enoch. "Alcohol Problems in Public Health Policy." *Journal of the American Medical Association*. (Dec. 1997) 1781–87.

Pollack, William S. *Real Boys: Rescuing Our Sons from the Myths of Boyhood*. New York: Random, 1998.

Pollack, William S., and Ronald F. Levant, eds. *New Psychotherapy for Men*. New York: Wiley, 1998.

SHIRLEY GEOK-LIN LIM

Lim was born in 1944 in Malacca, Malaysia, and immigrated to the United States in 1969 after enrolling in Brandeis University, where she earned a Ph.D. in 1973. She married a Jewish-American professor in 1972 and has taught at Hostos Community College in New York City; at Westchester Community College, in Valhalla, New York; and since 1990 at the University of California, Santa Barbara. Ever conscious of her complicated heritage, "Chinese/Malaysian/American," she explains, "Much of my writing life is composed of negotiating multiple identities, multiple societies, multiple desires, and multiple genres." She has published poetry (*Crossing the Peninsula and Other Poems* won the Commonwealth Poetry Prize in 1980), short stories (*Another Country and Other Stories*, 1982), criticism, and an autobiography, *Among the White Moon Faces: An Asian-American Memoir of Homelands* (1996), of which "Pomegranates and English Education" is a partial chapter.

Although Lim as an adult insists on the importance of an integrated multicultural life, she grew up in a colonial society that was based on a distinct social and political hierarchy and thus embedded complicated systems of divisions and classifications. As she says, "My Chinese life in Malaysia up to 1969 was a pomegranate, thickly seeded"; she appropriated those aspects of "British colonial culture" that she learned from French-accented Chinese nuns in her convent school as a way to "break out of the pomegranate shell of being Chinese and girl."

Pomegranates and English Education

A pomegranate tree grew in a pot on the open-air balcony at   1
the back of the second floor. It was a small skinny tree, even to a small skinny child like me. It had many fruits, marble-sized, dark green, shiny like overwaxed coats. Few grew to any size. The branches were sparse and graceful, as were the tear-shaped leaves that fluttered in the slightest breeze. Once a fruit grew round and large, we watched it every day. It grew lighter, then streaked with yellow and red. Finally we ate it, the purple and crimson seeds bursting with a tart liquid as we cracked the dry tough skin into segments to be shared by our many hands and mouths.

We were many. Looking back it seems to me that we had   2
always been many. Beng was the fierce brother, the growly eldest son. Chien was the gentle second brother, born with a squint eye. Seven other children followed after me: Jen, Wun, Wilson, Hui, Lui, Seng, and Marie, the last four my half-siblings. I was third, the only daughter through a succession of eight boys and, as far as real life goes, measured in rice bowls and in the bones of morning, I have remained an only daughter in my memory.

We were as many as the blood-seeds we chewed, sucked, and   3
spat out, the indigestible cores pulped and gray while their juice ran down our chins and stained our mouths with triumphant color. I still hold that crimson in memory, the original color of Chinese prosperity and health, now transformed to the berry shine of wine, the pump of blood in test tubes and smeared on glass plates

to prophesy one's future from the wriggles of a virus. My Chinese life in Malaysia up to 1969 was a pomegranate, thickly seeded.

4   When Beng and Chien began attending the Bandar Hilir Primary School, they brought home textbooks, British readers with thick linen-rag covers, strong slick paper, and lots of short stories and poems accompanied by colorful pictures in the style of Aubrey Beardsley. The story of the three Billy Goats Gruff who killed the Troll under the bridge was stark and compressed, illustrated by golden kids daintily trotting over a rope bridge and a dark squat figure peering from the ravine below. Wee Willie Winkie ran through a starry night wearing only a white night cap and gown. The goats, the troll, and Willie Winkie were equally phantasms to me, for whoever saw anything like a flowing white gown on a boy or a pointy night cap in Malaya?

5   How to explain the disorienting power of story and picture? Things never seen or thought of in Malayan experience took on a vividness that ordinary life could not possess. These British childhood texts materialized for me, a five- and six-year-old child, the kind of hyper-reality that television images hold for a later generation, a reality, moreover, that was consolidated by colonial education.

6   At five, I memorized the melody and lyrics to "The Jolly Miller" from my brother's school rendition:

> There lived a jolly miller once
> Along the River Dee.
> He worked and sang from morn till night,
> No lark more blithe than he.
> And this the burden of his song
> As always used to be,
> I care for nobody, no not I,
> And nobody cares for me.

7   It was my first English poem, my first English song, and my first English lesson. The song ran through my head mutely, obsessively, on hundreds of occasions. What catechism did I learn as I sang the words aloud? I knew nothing of millers or of larks. As a preschool child, I ate bread, that exotic food, only on rare and unwelcome occasions. The miller working alone had no analogue in the Malayan world. In Malacca, everyone was surrounded by

everyone else. A hawker needed his regular customers, a storefront the stream of pedestrians who shopped on the move. Caring was not a concept that signified. Necessity, the relations between and among many and diverse people, composed the bonds of Malaccan society. Caring denoted a field of choice, of individual voluntary action, that was foreign to family, the place of compulsory relations. Western ideological subversion, cultural colonialism, whatever we call those forces that have changed societies under forced political domination, for me began with something as simple as an old English folk song.

The pomegranate is a fruit of the East, coming originally from   8 Persia. The language of the West, English, and all its many manifestations in stories, songs, illustrations, films, school, and government, does not teach the lesson of the pomegranate. English taught me the lesson of the individual, the miller who is happy alone, and who affirms the principle of not caring for community. Why was it so easy for me to learn that lesson? Was it because within the pomegranate's hundreds of seeds is also contained the drive for singularity that will finally produce one tree from one seed? Or was it because my grandparents' Hokkien and *nonya* societies had become irremediably damaged by British colonial domination, their cultural confidence never to be recovered intact, so that Western notions of the individual took over collective imaginations, making of us, as V. S. Naipaul has coined it, "mimic" people?

But I resist this reading of colonialist corruption of an origi-   9 nal pure culture. Corruption is inherent in every culture, if we think of corruption as a will to break out, to rupture, to break down, to decay, and thus to change. We are all mimic people, born to cultures that push us, shape us, and pummel us; and we are all agents, with the power of the subject, no matter how puny or inarticulate, to push back and to struggle against such shaping. So I have seen myself not so much sucking at the teat of British colonial culture as actively appropriating those aspects of it that I needed to escape that other familial/gender/native culture that violently hammered out only one shape for self. I actively sought corruption to break out of the pomegranate shell of being Chinese and girl.

It was the convent school that gave me the first weapons with   10 which to wreck my familial culture. On the first day, Ah Chan took me, a six-year-old, in a trishaw to the Convent of the Holy

Infant Jesus. She waited outside the classroom the entire day with a *chun*, a tiffin carrier, filled with steamed rice, soup, and meat, fed me this lunch at eleven-thirty, then took me home in a trishaw at two. I wore a starched blue pinafore over a white cotton blouse and stared at the words, *See Jane run. Can Jane run? Jane can run.* After the first week, I begged to attend school without Ah Chan present. Baba drove me to school after he dropped my older brothers at their school a mile before the convent; I was now, like my brothers, free of domestic female attachment.

11   The convent school stood quiet and still behind thick cement walls that hid the buildings and its inhabitants from the road and muffled the sounds of passing traffic. The high walls also serve to snuff out the world once you entered the gates, which were always kept shut except at the opening and closing of the school day. Shards of broken bottles embedded in the top of the walls glinted in the hot tropical sunshine, a provocative signal that the convent women were daily conscious of dangers intruding on their seclusion. For the eleven years that I entered through those gates, I seldom met a man on the grounds, except for the Jesuit brought to officiate at the annual retreat. A shared public area was the chapel, a small low dark structure made sacred by stained glass windows, hard wooden benches, and the sacristy oil lamp whose light was never allowed to go out. The community was allowed into the chapel every Sunday to attend the masses held for the nuns and the orphans who lived in the convent.

12   But if the convent closed its face to the town of men and unbelievers, it lay open at the back to the Malacca Straits. Every recess I joined hundreds of girls milling at the canteen counters for little plates of noodles, curry puffs stuffed with potatoes, peas and traces of meat, and vile orange-colored sugared drinks. The food never held me for long. Instead I spent recess by the sea wall, a stone barrier free of bristling glass. Standing before the sandy ground that separated the field and summer house from the water, I gazed at high tide as the waves threw themselves against the wall with the peculiar repeated whoosh and sigh that I never wearied of hearing. Until I saw the huge pounding surf of the Atlantic Ocean, I believed all the world's water to be dancing, diamond-bright surfaced, a hypnotic meditative space in which shallow and deep seemed one and the same. Once inside the convent gates, one

was overtaken by a similar sense of an overwhelming becalmed-
ness, as if one had fallen asleep, out of worldliness, and entered
the security of a busy dream.

During recess the little girls sang, "In and out the window, 13
in and out the window, as we have done before," and skipped in
and out of arching linked hands, in a mindless pleasure of repeated movement, repeating the desire for safety, for routine, and
for the linked circular enclosure of the women's community that
would take me in from six to seventeen.

I also learned to write the alphabet. At first, the gray pencil 14
wouldn't obey my fingers. When the little orange nub at the end
of the pencil couldn't erase the badly made letter, I wetted a
finger with spit, rubbed hard, and then blubbered at the hole I
had made in the paper. Writing was fraught with fear. I cried
silently as I wrestled with the fragile paper that wouldn't sit still
and that crushed and tore under my palm.

My teacher was an elderly nun of uncertain European 15
nationality, perhaps French, who didn't speak English well. She
spoke with a lisp, mispronounced my name, called me "chérie"
instead of "Shirley," and, perhaps accordingly, showed more
affection to me than to the other children in her class. Sister Josie
was the first European I knew. Even in her voluminous black
robes and hood, she was an image of powder-white and pink
smiles. Bending over my small desk to guide my fingers, and
peering into my teary eyes, she spoke my name with a tender
concern. She was my first experience of an enveloping, unconditional, and safe physical affection. She smelled sweet, like fresh
yeast, and as I grew braver each day and strayed from my desk,
she would upbraid me in the most remorseful of tones, "Chérie,"
which carried with it an approving smile.

In return I applied myself to Jane and Dick and Spot and 16
to copying the alphabet letter by letter repeatedly. Sister Josie
couldn't teach anything beyond the alphabet and simple vocabulary. In a few years, she was retired to the position of gatekeeper
at the chapel annex. When I visited her six years later, as a child
of twelve, at the small annex in which a store of holy pictures,
medals, and lace veils were displayed for sale, Sister Josie's smile
was still as fond. But to my mature ears, her English speech was

halting, her grammar and vocabulary fractured. It was only to a six-year-old new to English that dear Sister Josie could have appeared as a native speaker of the English language.

17   It was my extreme good fortune to have this early missionary mother. Her gentle, undemanding care remains memorialized as a type of human relation not found in the fierce self-involvements of my family. My narrowly sensory world broadened not only with the magical letters she taught that spelled lives beyond what my single dreaming could imagine, but differently with her gentle greetings, in her palpable affection.

18 Nurturing is a human act that overleaps categories, but it is not free of history. It is not innocent. For the next eleven years nuns like Sister Josie broke down the domain of my infancy. Leaving the Bata shop and entering the jagged-glass-edged walls of the convent, I entered a society far removed from Baba and Emak.

19   The nuns wore the heavy wool habit of the missionary, full black blouses with wide sleeves like bat wings, long voluminous black skirts, black stockings, and shoes. Deep white hoods covered their heads and fell over their shoulders, and a white skull cap came down over their brows. Inexplicably they were collectively named "the French Convent," like a French colony or the foreign legion, but they were not chiefly white or European. Even in the early 1950s, some were Chinese and Eurasian "sisters."

20   Yet, despite their uniform habits and sisterly titles, a ranking regulated by race was obvious, even to the youngest Malayan child. Mother Superior was always white. A few white sisters, Sister Sean, Sister Patricia, and Sister Peter, taught the upper grades; or they performed special duties, like Sister Maria who gave singing lessons, or Sister Bernadette, who taught cooking and controlled the kitchen and the canteen.

21   Sister Maria was the only woman who was recognizably French. Her accent was itself music to us as she led us through years of Scottish and Irish ballads. No one asked why "Ye Banks and Braes of Bonnie Doon" or "The Minstrel Boy" formed our music curriculum, why Indian, Eurasian, Malay, and Chinese children should be singing, off-key, week after week in a faintly French-accented manner the melancholic attitudes of Celtic gloom. What was the place of Celt ballads in a Malayan future?

What did they instruct of a history of feelings, of British blood-shed and patriotism? Or were the curriculum setters in the Colonial Office in London reproducing in fortissimo an imperial narrative—the tragedy of failed Scottish and Irish nationalism, the first of England's colonies—in the physical pulses of the newly colonized?

Of the nonmissionary teachers from Malacca, many were   22
Eurasian, and a few were Indian, and Chinese. The sole Malay teacher appeared only after the British ceded independence to the Federation of Malaya in 1957. Chik Guru taught us the Malay language in my last two years at the convent, just as now in the United States in many colleges and universities, the only African-American or Latino or Asian-American professor a student may meet teaches African-American or Latino or Asian-American studies. Up to the end of the 1950s, and perhaps right up to the violence of the May 13 race riots in 1969, the educational structure in Malaya was British colonial.

My first inkling of race preference was formed by these   23
earliest teachers. In primary school, my teachers were almost all European expatriates or native-born Eurasian Catholics bearing such Hispanic and Dutch names as De Souza, De Witt, Minjoot, Aerea, and De Costa. They were the descendants of Portuguese soldiers and sailors who had captured Malacca from the Malay Sultanate in 1511, when Portugal was a small, poorly populated state. Expanding into the Spice Islands in the East, the Governor-Generals of the Indies encouraged intermarriage between Portuguese males and native women, thus seeding the loyal settler population with Portuguese mestizos. The Portuguese governed Malacca for 130 years. When the forces of the Dutch East India Company captured the port and its fortress in 1641, they found a garrison there of some 260 Portuguese soldiers, reinforced with a mestizo population of about two to three thousand fighting men. For over four hundred years, the mestizos of Malacca had identi-fied themselves as Portuguese.

The Eurasian teachers were physically distinguished from   24
me. I learned this in Primary Two with Mrs. Damien, a white-haired, very large woman whose fat dimpled arms fascinated me. While she demonstrated how to embroider a daisy stitch as we

crowded around her chair, I poked my finger into the dimples and creases that formed in the pale flesh that flowed over her shoulders and sagged in her upper arms. She was a fair Eurasian who dressed as a British matron, in sleeveless flowered print frocks with square-cut collars for coolness. Her exposed arms and chest presented dazzling mounds of white flesh that aroused my ardent admiration. I do not remember learning anything else in her class.

25   A few Eurasian girls were among my classmates. While they were not as coddled as the white daughters of plantation managers, they had an air of ease and inclusion that I envied. Their hair, which often had a copper sheen to it, was braided, while we Chinese girls had black, pudding-bowl cropped hair. By the time we were twelve and thirteen, and still flatchested, they had budded into bosomy women whose presence in Sunday masses attracted the attention of young Catholic males. The royal blue pleated pinafores that covered our prim skinny bodies like cardboard folded teasingly over their chests and hips. The difference between us and the early maturity of Eurasian girls was a symptom of the difference between our Chinese Malaccan culture and that dangerous Western culture made visible in their lushness. They were overtly religious, controlled by their strict mothers and the Ten Commandments that we had all memorized by preadolescence. But their breasts and hips that made swing skirts swing pronounced them ready for that unspoken but pervasive excitement we knew simply as "boys."

26   The convent held a number of orphans, girls abandoned as babies on the convent doorsteps, or given over to the nuns to raise by relatives too poor to pay for their upkeep. During school hours these "orphaned" girls were indistinguishable from the rest of us. They wore the school uniforms, white short-sleeved blouses under sleeveless blue linen smocks that were fashioned with triple overpleats on both sides so that burgeoning breasts were multiply overlayered with folds of starched fabric. But once school hours were over they changed into pink or blue gingham dresses that buttoned right up to the narrow Peter Pan collars. Those loose shapeless dresses, worn by sullen girls who earned their keep by

helping in the kitchen and laundry, formed some of my early images of a class to be shunned.

Instead I longed to be like the privileged boarders, almost all of whom were British, whose parents lived in remote and dangerous plantations or administrative outposts in the interior. These girls wore polished black leather shoes and fashionable skirts and blouses after school. In our classes, they sang unfamiliar songs, showed us how to dance, jerking their necks like hieroglyphic Egyptians. In the convent classroom where silence and stillness were enforced as standard behavior, they giggled and joked, shifting beams of sunshine, and were never reprimanded. To every schoolgirl it was obvious that something about a white child made the good nuns benevolent.

Content

1. Lim explains her early life as dominated by numerous divisions and classifications—by race, ethnicity, gender, religion, age, educational status, family background. Explain in what ways these influenced her thinking, behavior, and self-esteem as she was growing up.

2. Why were Chinese children in a Malaysian Catholic school run by French nuns educated in British culture about "things never seen or thought of in Malayan experience" (¶ 5; see also ¶ 21)? What effects did such a school have on Lim as a girl?

3. Many Americans are descendants of colonial peoples, either the colonizers or the colonized. What, if any, connections might Lim's readers make between her experience of a colonial education (being obliged to learn the colonizers' language, literature, history, and values) and their own life history or cultural history?

Strategies/Structures

4. Lim uses the pomegranate tree (¶s 1, 3, 8) to symbolize her "Chinese life in Malaysia up to 1969" (¶ 3). Does this symbol do the work she expects it to? Why or why not? Identify other symbols (such as the nuns' missionary clothing, ¶ 19) and explain how they work to reinforce Lim's point about colonialism.

5. In one sense, Lim's school world is self-contained and cloistered from the rest of the world by "thick cement walls" with "shards of broken bottles embedded in the top" (¶ 11). In another sense, the internal world

is as full of categories and divisions as the outer world from which the schoolgirls are sheltered. Explain. Is the same true of any or all schools everywhere?

Language

6. In what language was Lim educated? In what culture? For what purposes?

7. In what language and for what readers does Lim write about her education? For what purposes?

For Writing

8. Lim says, "Corruption is inherent in every culture, if we think of corruption as a will to break out, to rupture, to break down, to decay, and thus to change. We are all mimic people, born to cultures that push us, shape us, and pummel us; and we are all agents, with the power . . . to push back and to struggle against such shaping" (¶ 9). Identify a culture (of family, gender, race, class, occupation, nationality) that shaped you and which to an extent you have resisted. What did you take from it and what about it did you resist? If you made deliberate choices, on what basis did you do so? If the shaping was unavoidable, explain why this was so.

9. All of us are continually in the process of shaping and being shaped by a particular culture or cultures; identify some of the major features of this process and explain how this process works. You could refer not only to Lim's essay, but to essays by any of the following: Rose (263–73), Zitkala-Sa (273–83), Sanders (186–96 and 441–56), Rodriguez (398–405).

====================

RICHARD RODRIGUEZ

How Richard Rodriguez, born in San Francisco in 1944, the son of Mexican immigrants, should and can deal with his dual heritage is the subject of his autobiographical *Hunger of Memory: The Education of Richard Rodriguez* (1982). He spoke Spanish at home and didn't learn English until he began grammar school in Sacramento. Although for a time he refused to speak Spanish, he studied that language in high school as if it were a foreign language. Nevertheless, classified as Mexican-American, Rodriguez benefited from Affirmative Action programs, and on scholarships he earned a B.A. from Stanford (1967), and an M.A. from Columbia (1969). After that he studied Renaissance literature at the University of California, Berkeley—the site of the climactic event described in the following essay, later incorporated into *Hunger of Memory*. In 1992 he published *Days of Obligation: An Argument with my Mexican Father*, another collection of autobiographical essays focusing on his complicated relations to the cultures of the Catholic Church, San Francisco's gay Castro District, and Mexico.

For two decades Rodriguez, now an educational consultant and freelance writer, has consistently—and controversially—argued against bilingual education, other programs that would separate minority students from the mainstream, and Affirmative Action. In this essay Rodriguez argues against the arbitrary—and divisive—classification of people into categories, by race, religion, or ethnic origin, for the purposes of Affirmative Action. But he concludes with a different classification of people on the basis of income, which lumps together "white, black, brown. Always poor. Silent." Hopeless. And untouched by Affirmative Action. He will be their spokesperson, too.

None of This Is Fair

M y plan to become a professor of English—my ambition 1 during long years in college at Stanford, then in graduate school at Columbia and Berkeley—was complicated by feelings of embarrassment and guilt. So many times I would see other Mexican-Americans and know we were alike only in race. And yet, simply because our race was the same, I was, during the last years of my schooling, the beneficiary of their situation. Affirmative Action programs had made it all possible. The disadvantages of others permitted my promotion; the absence of many Mexican-Americans from academic life allowed my designation as a "minority student."

For me opportunities had been extravagant. There were fel- 2 lowships, summer research grants, and teaching assistantships. After only two years in graduate school, I was offered teaching jobs by several colleges. Invitations to Washington conferences arrived and I had the chance to travel abroad as a "Mexican-American representative." The benefits were often, however, too gaudy to please. In three published essays, in conversations with teachers, in letters to politicians and at conferences, I worried the issue of Affirmative Action. Often I proposed contradictory opinions. Though consistent was the admission that—because of an early, excellent education—I was no longer a principal victim of racism or any other social oppression. I said that but still I continued to indicate on applications for financial aid that I was a Hispanic-American. It didn't really occur to me to say anything else, or to leave the question unanswered.

3   Thus I complied with and encouraged the odd bureaucratic logic of Affirmative Action. I let government officials treat the disadvantaged condition of many Mexican-Americans with my advancement. Each fall my presence was noted by Health, Education, and Welfare department statisticians. As I pursued advanced literary studies and learned the skill of reading Spenser and Wordsworth and Empson, I would hear myself numbered among the culturally disadvantaged. Still, silent, I didn't object.

4   But the irony cut deep. And guilt would not be evaded by averting my glance when I confronted a face like my own in a crowd. By late 1975, nearing the completion of my graduate studies at Berkeley, I was so wary of the benefits of Affirmative Action that I feared my inevitable success as an applicant for a teaching position. The months of fall—traditionally that time of academic job-searching—passed without my applying to a single school. When one of my professors chanced to learn this in late November, he was astonished, then furious. He yelled at me: Did I think that because I was a minority student jobs would just come looking for me? What was I thinking? Did I realize that he and several other faculty members had already written letters on my behalf? Was I going to start acting like some other minority students he had known? They struggled for success and then, when it was almost within reach, grew strangely afraid and let it pass. Was that it? Was I determined to fail?

5   I did not respond to his questions. I didn't want to admit to him, and thus to myself, the reason I delayed.

I merely agreed to write to several schools. (In my letter I 6
wrote: "I cannot claim to represent disadvantaged Mexican-
Americans. The very fact that I am in a position to apply for this
job should make that clear.") After two or three days, there were
telegrams and phone calls, invitations to interviews, then airplane trips. A blur of faces and the murmur of their soft questions.
And, over someone's shoulder, the sight of campus buildings
shadowing pictures I had seen years before when I leafed through
Ivy League catalogues with great expectations. At the end of each
visit, interviewers would smile and wonder if I had any questions. A few times I quietly wondered what advantage my race
had given me over other applicants. But that was an impossible
question for them to answer without embarrassing me. Quickly,
several persons insisted that my ethnic identity had given me no
more than a "foot inside the door"; at most, I had a "slight edge"
over other applicants. "We just looked at your dossier with extra
care and we like what we saw. There was never any question of
having to alter our standards. You can be certain of that."

In the early part of January, offers arrived on stiffly elegant 7
stationery. Most schools promised terms appropriate for any new
assistant professor. A few made matters worse—and almost more
tempting—by offering more: the use of university housing; an
unusually large starting salary; a reduced teaching schedule. As
the stack of letters mounted, my hesitation increased. I started
calling department chairmen to ask for another week, then 10
more days—"more time to reach a decision"—to avoid the decision I would need to make.

At school, meantime, some students hadn't received a single 8
job offer. One man, probably the best student in the department,
did not even get a request for his dossier. He and I met outside a
classroom one day and he asked about my opportunities. He
seemed happy for me. Faculty members beamed. They said they
had expected it. "After all, not many schools are going to pass up
getting a Chicano with a Ph.D. in Renaissance literature," somebody said laughing. Friends wanted to know which of the offers
I was going to accept. But I couldn't make up my mind. February
came and I was running out of time and excuses. (One chairman
guessed my delay was a bargaining ploy and increased his offer

with each of my calls.) I had to promise a decision by the 10th; the 12th at the very latest.

9   On the 18th of February, late in the afternoon, I was in the office I shared with several other teaching assistants. Another graduate student was sitting across the room at his desk. When I got up to leave, he looked over to say in an uneventful voice that he had some big news. He had finally decided to accept a position at a faraway university. It was not a job he especially wanted, he admitted. But he had to take it because there hadn't been any other offers. He felt trapped, and depressed, since his job would separate him from his young daughter.

10   I tried to encourage him by remarking that he was lucky at least to have found a job. So many others hadn't been able to get anything. But before I finished speaking I realized that I had said the wrong thing. And I anticipated his next question.

11   "What are your plans?" he wanted to know. "Is it true you've gotten an offer from Yale?"

12   I said that it was. "Only, I still haven't made up my mind."

13   He stared at me as I put on my jacket. And smiling, then un-smiling, he asked if I knew that he too had written to Yale. In his case, however, no one had bothered to acknowledge his letter with even a postcard. What did I think of that?

14   He gave me no time to answer.

15   "Damn!" he said sharply and his chair rasped the floor as he pushed himself back. Suddenly, it was to *me* that he was com-plaining. "It's just not right, Richard. None of this is fair. You've done some good work, but so have I. I'll bet our records are just about equal. But when we look for jobs this year, it's a different story. You get all of the breaks."

16   To evade his criticism, I wanted to side with him. I was about to admit the injustice of Affirmative Action. But he went on, his voice hard with accusation. "It's all very simple this year. You're a Chicano. And I am a Jew. That's the only real difference between us."

17   His words stung me: there was nothing he was telling me that I didn't know. I had admitted everything already. But to hear someone else say these things, and in such an accusing tone, was suddenly hard to take. In a deceptively calm voice, I responded

that he had simplified the whole issue. The phrases came like bubbles to the tip of my tongue: "new blood", "the importance of cultural diversity"; "the goal of racial integration." These were all the arguments I had proposed several years ago—and had long since abandoned. Of course the offers were unjustifiable. I knew that. All I was saying amounted to a frantic self-defense. I tried to find an end to a sentence. My voice faltered to a stop.

"Yeah, sure," he said. "I've heard all that before. Nothing   18 you say really changes the fact that Affirmative Action is unfair. You see that, don't you? There isn't any way for me to compete with you. Once there were quotas to keep my parents out of certain schools; now there are quotas to get you in and the effect on me is the same as it was for them."

I listened to every word he spoke. But my mind was really   19 on something else. I knew at that moment that I would reject all of the offers. I stood there silently surprised by what an easy conclusion it was. Having prepared for so many years to teach, having trained myself to do nothing else, I had hesitated out of practical fear. But now that it was made, the decision came with relief. I immediately knew I had made the right choice.

My colleague continued talking and I realized that he was   20 simply right. Affirmative Action programs *are* unfair to white students. But as I listened to him assert his rights, I thought of the seriously disadvantaged. How different they were from white, middle-class students who come armed with the testimony of their grades and aptitude scores and self-confidence to complain about the unequal treatment they now receive. I listen to them. I do not want to be careless about what they say. Their rights are important to protect. But inevitably when I hear them or their lawyers, I think about the most seriously disadvantaged, not simply Mexican-Americans, but of all those who do not ever imagine themselves going to college or becoming doctors: white, black, brown. Always poor. Silent. They are not plaintiffs before the court or against the misdirection of Affirmative Action. They lack the confidence (my confidence!) to assume their right to a good education. They lack the confidence and skills a good primary and secondary education provides and which are prerequisites for informed public life. They remain silent.

21   The debate drones on and surrounds them in stillness. They are distant, faraway figures like the boys I have seen peering down from freeway overpasses in some other part of town.

Content

1. What does Rodriguez mean by his fundamental premise, "None of this is fair" (¶ 15)?
2. What is Affirmative Action? What is reverse discrimination? What does Rodriguez's comparison of his job-seeking experience with those of his white male classmates illustrate about these terms?
3. Does Rodriguez intend that his readers generalize on the basis of the job-seeking experiences of himself and his two white male classmates, one Jewish?
4. What categories of people does Rodriguez claim are currently benefiting from Affirmative Action programs? What categories of people are the victims of reverse discrimination?
5. In Rodriguez's opinion, which people truly need Affirmative Action (¶ 20)? Why aren't they getting what they need? Why does he wait so long to get to this point?

Strategies/Structures

6. If Rodriguez believes that Affirmative Action doesn't benefit the "most seriously disadvantaged" of all races (¶ 20), why doesn't he illustrate the point with an example of such people? And devote more space to them?
7. Show how Rodriguez employs division and classification to conduct his argument.

For Writing

8. If you or someone you know has either benefited from Affirmative Action or experienced reverse discrimination, write an essay about that experience to illustrate a general point about it for readers unfamiliar with the issue.
9. Rodriguez has been attacked as an Uncle Juan (a Chicano Uncle Tom) for claiming that he and other middle-class minority students improperly benefit from Affirmative Action programs that do not aid "all those who never imagine themselves going to college or becoming doctors: white, black, brown. Always poor. Silent" (¶ 20). Discuss the issue with fellow students or other colleagues and write an essay on Rodriguez's position,

summarizing either the consensus or the main lines of debate on this subject and indicating your position, as well. Do you, either individually or collectively, agree either with Rodriguez or with his critics?

NING YU

Ning Yu was born in 1955 in Beijing, People's Republic of China, and came to the United States in 1986 for graduate study. He earned a Ph.D. in English from the University of Connecticut in 1993 and now teaches at Western Washington University.

Ning Yu recounts some of the significant events of his youth in the following prizewinning essay, "Red and Black, or One English Major's Beginning." When he was in fourth grade, his school was closed down as a consequence of the "Great Proletarian Cultural Revolution," which overturned the existing social order. The intellectual class (the "blacks," in Yu's classification scheme) to which Yu's family belonged because his father was a professor of Chinese language and literature, were replaced on their jobs by members of the People's Liberation Army, "the reds," whose status—as we can see from Ning Yu's teachers—was determined by their political loyalty rather than their academic training.

So Ning Yu learned one kind of English at school, the rote memorization of political slogans: "Long live Chairman Mao! Down with the Soviet Neo Czarists!" He explains that because the Cultural Revolution stifled originality of language, as of thought, "the Cultural Revolution was rightly called the decade of clichés, when people couldn't say what they really wanted to say and therefore used trite phrases to say what they didn't want to say. "Consequently," he says, "I used the clichés deliberately to create a realistic atmosphere for my story, and also ironically to attack the decade of clichés."

Ning Yu learned another kind of English, the rich, imaginative language of high-culture literature, from his father. On the verge of his fourth imprisonment as an intellectual (and therefore by definition subversive), Dr. Yu taught his teenage son the alphabet, some rules for pronunciation, spelling, and grammar, and how to use a dictionary. As he went to prison, he gave Yu a copy of Jane Austen's *Pride and Prejudice* and an old English-Chinese dictionary and told him to translate the novel—which Ning Yu

406 Division and Classification

"struggled through from cover to cover" during the nineteen months of his father's incarceration. Ning Yu's essay makes clear the relations among politics, social class, and education under the Maoist regime.

❄ Red and Black, or One English Major's Beginning

1 I have always told my friends that my first English teacher was my father. That is the truth, but not the whole truth. It was a freezing morning more than twenty years ago, we, some fifty-odd boys and girls, were shivering in a poorly heated classroom when the door was pushed open and in came a gust of wind and Comrade Chang Hong-gen, our young teacher. Wrapped in an elegant army overcoat, Comrade Chang strode in front of the blackboard and began to address us in outrageous gibberish. His gestures, his facial expressions, and his loud voice unmistakably communicated that he was lecturing us as a People's Liberation Army captain would address his soldiers before a battle—in revolutionary war movies, that is. Of course we didn't understand a word of the speech until he translated it into Chinese later:

> Comrades, red-guards, and revolutionary pupils:
> The Great Revolutionary Teacher Marx teaches us: "A foreign language is an important weapon in the struggle of human life." Our Great Leader, Great Teacher, Great Supreme-Commander, and Great Helmsman, Chairman Mao, has also taught us that it is not too difficult to learn a foreign language. "Nothing in the world is too difficult if you are willing to tackle it with the same spirit in which we conquered this mountain."
> Now, as you know, the Soviet Social Imperialists and the U.S. Imperialists have agreed on a venomous scheme to enslave China. For years the U.S. Imperialists have brought war and disaster to Vietnam; and you must have heard that the Soviet troops invaded our Jewel Island in Heilongjiang

Province last month. Their evil purpose is obvious—to invade China, the Soviets from the north and the Americans from the south through Vietnam.

We are not afraid of them, because we have the leadership of Chairman Mao, the invincible Mao Zedong Thought, and seven hundred million people. But we need to be prepared. As intellectual youth, you must not only prepare to sacrifice your lives for the Party and the Motherland, but also learn to stir up our people's patriotic zeal and to shatter the morale of the enemy troops. To encourage our own people, you must study Chairman Mao's works very hard and learn your lessons well with your teacher of Chinese; to crush the enemy, you must learn your English lessons well with me.

Then Comrade Chang paused, his face red and sweat beading on the tip of his nose. Though nonplussed, we could see that he was genuinely excited, but we were not sure whether his excitement was induced by "patriotic zeal" or the pleasure of hearing grandiose sounds issued from his own lips. For my part, I suspected that verbal intoxication caused his excitement. Scanning the classroom, he seemed to bask in our admiration rather than to urge us to sacrifice our lives for the Party. He then translated the speech into Chinese and gave us another dose of eloquence:

> From now on, you are not pupils anymore, but soldiers—young, intellectual soldiers fighting at a special front. Neither is each English word you learn a mere word anymore. Each new word is a bullet shot at the enemy's chest, and each sentence a hand grenade.

Comrade Chang was from a "red" family. His name *hong* means red in Chinese, and *gen* means root, so literally, he was "Chang of Red Root." Students said that his father was a major in the People's Liberation Army, and his grandfather a general, and that both the father and the grandfather had "contributed a great deal to the Party, the Motherland, and the Chinese working people." When the "Great Proletarian Cultural Revolution" started, Mr. Chang had just graduated from the Beijing Foreign Languages Institute, a prestigious university in the capital where some thirty languages were taught to people "of red roots." Red youngsters were trained there to serve in the Foreign Ministry, mostly in Chinese embassies and consulates in foreign countries. We understood that Comrade Chang would work only for a token period in our ghetto middle school. At the time, the Foreign Ministry was too busy with the Cultural Revolution to hire new translators, but as soon as the "Movement" was over and everything back to normal, Comrade Chang, we knew, would leave us and begin his diplomatic career.

4   In the late 1960s the Revolution defined "intellectual" as "subversive." So my father, a university professor educated in a British missionary school in Tianjin, was regarded as a "black" element, an enemy of the people. In 1967, our family was driven out of our university faculty apartment, and I found myself in a ghetto middle school, an undeserving pupil of the red expert Comrade Chang.

5   In a shabby and ill-heated schoolroom I began my first English lesson, not "from the very beginning" by studying the alphabet, but with some powerful "hand grenades":

> Give up; no harm!
> Drop your guns!
> Down with the Soviet Neo-Czarists!
> Down with U.S. Imperialism!
> Long live Chairman Mao!
> We wish Chairman Mao a long, long life!
> Victory belongs to our people!

6   These sentences turned out to be almost more difficult and more dangerous to handle than real grenades, for soon the words became mixed up in our heads. So much so that not a few "revolutionary pupils" reconstructed the slogans to the hearty satisfactions of themselves but to the horror of Comrade Chang:

> Long live the Soviet Neo-Czarists!
> Victory belongs to your guns!

Upon hearing this, Comrade Chang turned pale and shouted at us, "You idiots! Had you uttered anything like that in Chinese, young as you are, you could have been thrown into jail for years.

Probably me too! Now you follow me closely: Long live Chairman Mao!"

"Long live Chairman Mao!" we shouted back.   7

"Long live Chairman Mao!"   8

"Long live Chairman Mao!"   9

"Down with the Soviet Neo-Czarists!"   10

"Down with the Soviet Neo-Czarists!"   11

Comrade Chang decided that those two sentences were   12
enough for idiots to learn in one lesson, and he told us to forget the
other sentences for the moment. Then he wrote the two sentences
on the chalkboard and asked us to copy them in our English exercise books. Alas, how could anybody in our school know what
that was!

I wrote the two sentences on my left palm and avoided   13
putting my left hand in my pocket or mitten for the rest of the day.
I also remembered what Comrade Chang said about being
thrown into jail, for as the son of a "black, stinking bourgeois
intellectual," I grasped the truth in his warning. The two English
sentences were a long series of meaningless, unutterable sounds.
Comrade Chang had the power to impose some Chinese meaning
on my mind. So, before I forgot or confused the sounds, I invented
a makeshift transliteration in Chinese for the phonetically difficult
and politically dangerous parts of the sentences. I put the Chinese
words *qui, mian,* and *mao* (cut, noodle, hair) under "Chairman
Mao," and *niu za sui* (beef organ meat) under "Neo-Czarists."
"Down with" were bad words applied to the enemies; "long live"
were good words reserved for the great leader. These were easy to
remember. So I went home with a sense of security, thinking the
device helped me distinguish the Great Leader from the enemy.

The next morning, Comrade "Red Roots" asked us to try our   14
weapons before the blackboard. Nobody volunteered. Then Comrade Chang began calling us by name. My friend "Calf" was the
first to stand up. He did not remember anything. He didn't try to
learn the words, and he told me to "forget it" when I was trying
to memorize the weird sounds. In fact, none of my classmates
remembered the sentences.

My fellow pupils were all "red" theoretically. But they were   15
not Comrade Chang's type of red. Their parents were coolies,

candy-peddlers, or bricklayers. Poor and illiterate. Before the 1949 revolution, these people led miserable lives. Even the revolution didn't improve their lives much, and parents preferred their children to do chores at home rather than fool around with books, especially after the "Great Proletarian Cultural Revolution" started in 1966. Books were dangerous. Those who read books often ran into trouble for having ideas the Party didn't want them to have. "Look at the intellectuals," they said. "They suffer even more than us illiterates." They also knew that their children could not become "red experts" like Comrade Chang, because they themselves were working people who didn't contribute to the Party, the Motherland—or to the liberation of the working people themselves.

16   Thus my friends didn't waste time in remembering nonsense. Still Comrade Chang's questions had to be answered. Since I was the only one in class not from a red family, my opinion was always the last asked, if asked at all. I stood up when Comrade Chang called my name. I had forgotten the English sounds too, for I took Calf's advice. But before I repeated the apology already repeated fifty times by my friends, I glanced at my left palm and inspiration lit up my mind. "Long live *qie mian mao!* Down with *niu za sui!*" My friends stared, and Comrade Chang glared at me. He couldn't believe his ears. "Say that again." I did. This time my classmates burst into a roar of laughter. "Cut noodle hair! Beef organ meat!" they shouted again and again.

17   "Shut up!" Comrade Chang yelled, trembling with anger and pointing at me with his right index finger. "What do you mean by 'cut noodle hair'? That insults our great leader Chairman Mao." Hearing that, the class suddenly became silent. The sons and daughters of the "Chinese working people" knew how serious an accusation that could be. But Calf stood up and said: "Comrade Teacher, it is truly a bad thing that Ning Yu should associate Chairman Mao with such nonsense as 'cut noodle hair.' But he didn't mean any harm. He was trying to throw a hand grenade at the enemy. He also called the Soviets 'beef organ meat.' He said one bad thing (not enough respect for Chairman Mao) but then said a good thing (condemning the Soviets). One take away one is zero. So he didn't really do anything wrong, right?"

18   Again the room shook with laughter.

Now Comrade Chang flew into a rage and began to lecture   19
us about how class enemies often say good things to cover up evil
intentions. Calf, Chang said, was a red boy and should draw a line
between himself and me, the black boy. He also threatened to
report my "evil words" to the revolutionary committee of the
middle school. He said that in the "urgent state of war" what I
said could not be forgiven or overlooked. He told me to examine
my mind and conduct severe self-criticism before being punished.
"The great proletarian dictatorship," he said, "is all-powerful. All
good will be rewarded and all evil punished when the right time
comes." He left the classroom in anger without giving us any new
hand grenades.

I felt ruined. Destroyed. Undone. I could feel icy steel hand-   20
cuffs closing around my wrists. I could hear the revolutionary
slogans that the mobs would shout at me when I was dragged off
by the iron hand of the Proletarian Dictatorship. My legs almost
failed me on my way home.

Calf knew better. "You have nothing to worry about, Third   21
Ass."

I am the third child in my family, and it is a tradition of old   22
Beijing to call a boy by number. So usually my family called me
Thirdy. But in my ghetto, when the kids wanted to be really
friendly, they added the word "ass" to your number or name.
This address upset me when I first moved into the neighborhood.
I was never comfortable with that affix during the years I lived
there, but at that moment I appreciated Calf's kindness in using
that affix. Words are empty shells. It's the feeling that people
attach to a word that counts.

"I'll be crushed like a rotten egg by the iron fist of the Great   23
Proletarian Dictatorship," I said.

"No way. Red Rooty is not going to tell on you. Don't you   24
know he was more scared than you? He was responsible. How
could you say such things if he had not taught you? You get it?
You relax. *Qie mian mao!* You know, you really sounded like
Rooty." Calf grinned.

Although Calf's wisdom helped me to "get it," relax I could   25
not. My legs were as stiff as sticks and my heart beat against my
chest so hard that I could hardly breathe. For many years I had

tried to get rid of my "blackness" by hard work and good manners. But I could not succeed. No matter how hard I tried I could not change the fact that I was not "red." The Party denied the existence of intermediate colors. If you were not red, logically you could only be black. What Chang said proved what I guessed. But, when cornered, even a rabbit may bite. Comrade Chang, I silently imagined, if I have to be crushed, you can forget about your diplomatic career. I created a drama in which Comrade Chang, the red root, and I, the black root, were crushed into such fine powder that one could hardly tell the red from the black. All one could see was a dark, devilish purple.

26   The next morning, I went to school with a faltering heart, expecting to be called out of the classroom and cuffed. Nothing happened. Comrade Chang seemed to have forgotten my transgression and gave us three handfuls of new "bullets." He slowed down too, placing more emphasis on pronunciation. He cast the "bullets" into hand grenades only after he was sure that we could shoot the "bullets" with certainty.

27   Nothing happened to me that day, or the next day, or the week after. Calf was right. As weeks passed, my dislike of Chang dwindled and I began to feel something akin to gratitude to him. Before learning his English tongue twisters, we only recited Chairman Mao's thirty-six poems. We did that for so long that I memorized the annotations together with the text. I also memorized how many copies were produced for the first, the second, and the third printing. I was bored, and Teacher Chang's tongue twisters brought me relief. Granted they were only old slogans in new sounds. But the mere sounds and the new way of recording the sounds challenged me. Still, as an old Chinese saying goes, good luck never lasts long.

28   Forty hand grenades were as many as the Party thought proper for us to hold. Before I mastered the fortieth tongue twister—"Revolutionary committees are fine"—our "fine" revolutionary committee ordered Comrade Chang to stop English lessons and to make us dig holes for air raid shelters. Comrade Chang approached this new task with just as much "patriotic zeal" as he taught English. In truth he seemed content to let our "bullets" and "hand grenades" rust in the bottom of the holes we dug. But I was not willing to let my only fun slip away easily.

When digging the holes I repeated the forty slogans silently. I even said them at home in bed. One night I uttered a sentence as I climbed onto my top bunk. Reading in the bottom bunk, my father heard me and was surprised. He asked where I had learned the words. Then for the first time I told him about Comrade Chang's English lessons.

Now it may seem strange for a middle school boy not to turn to his family during a "political crisis." But at that time, it was not strange at all. By then my mother, my sister, and my brother had already been sent to the countryside in two different remote provinces. Getting help from them was almost impossible, for they had enough pressing problems themselves. Help from my father was even more impractical: he was already "an enemy of the people," and therefore whatever he said or did for me could only complicate my problems rather than resolve them. So I kept him in the dark. Since we had only each other in the huge city of eight million people, we shared many things, but not political problems.

Our home in the working class neighborhood was a single seventeen-square-meter room. Kitchen, bathroom, sitting room, study, bedroom, all in one. There was no ceiling, so we could see the black beams and rafters when we lay in bed. The floor was a damp and sticky dirt, which defied attempts at sweeping and mopping. The walls were yellow and were as damp as the dirt floor. To partition the room was out of the question. Actually my parents had sold their king-sized bed and our single beds, and bought two bunk beds in their stead. My mother and sister each occupied a top bunk, my father slept in one bottom bunk, and my brother and I shared the other. Red Guards had confiscated and burned almost all of my father's Chinese books, but miraculously they left his English books intact. The English books were stuffed under the beds on the dirt floor. We lived in this manner for more than a year till the family members were scattered all over China, first my siblings to a province in the northwest, and then my mother to southern China. They were a thousand miles from us and fifteen hundred miles from each other. After they left, I moved to the top bunk over my father, and we piled the books on the other bed. Thanks to the hard covers, only the bottom two layers of the books had begun to mold.

31   That evening, after hearing me murmuring in English, my father gestured for me to sit down on his bunk. He asked me whether I knew any sentences other than the one he had heard. I jumped at the opportunity to go through the inventory of my English arsenal. After listening to my forty slogans my father said: "You have a very good English teacher. He has an excellent pronunciation, standard Oxford pronunciation. But the sentences are not likely to be found in any books written by native English speakers. Did he teach you how to read?"

32   "I can read all those sentences if you write them out."

33   "If *I* write them? But can't *you* write them by yourself?"

34   "No."

35   "Did he teach you grammar?"

36   "No."

37   "Did he teach you the alphabet?"

38   "No."

39   My father looked amused. Slowly he shook his head, and then asked: "Can you recognize the words, the separate words, when they appear in different contexts?"

40   "I think so, but I'm not sure."

41   He re-opened the book that he was reading and turned to the first page and pointed with his index finger at the first word in the first sentence, signaling me to identify it.

42   I shook my head.

43   He moved the finger to the next word. I didn't know that either. Nor did I know the third word, the shortest word in the line, the word made up of a single letter. My father traced the whole sentence slowly, hoping that I could identify some words. I recognized the bullet "in" and at once threw a hand grenade at him: "Beloved Chairman Mao, you are the red sun *in* our hearts." Encouraged, my father moved his finger back to the second word in the sentence. This time I looked at the word more closely but couldn't recognize it. "It's an 'is,'" he said. "You know 'are' but not 'is'! The third word in this sentence is an 'a'. It means 'one.'" It is the first letter in the alphabet and you don't know that either! What a teacher! A well-trained one too!" He then cleared his throat and read the whole sentence aloud: "It is a truth universally acknowledged, that a man in possession of a good fortune, must be in want of a wife."

The sounds he uttered reminded me of Chang's opening 44
speech, but they flowed out of my father's mouth smoothly. Without bothering about the meaning of the sentence, I asked my
father to repeat it several times because I liked the rhythm. Pleased
with my curiosity, my father began to explain the grammatical
structure of the sentence. His task turned out to be much harder
than he expected, for he had to explain terms such as "subject,"
"object," "nouns," "verbs" and "adjectives." To help me understand the structure of the English sentence, he had to teach me
Chinese grammar first. He realized that the Great Proletarian
Culture Revolution had made his youngest son literally illiterate,
in Chinese as well as English.

That night, our English lessons started. He taught me the 45
letters A through F. By the end of the week, I had learned my
alphabet. Afterward he taught the basics of grammar, sometimes
using my hand grenades to illustrate the rules. He also taught me
the international phonetic symbols and the way to use a dictionary. For reading materials, he excerpted simple passages from
whatever books were available. Some were short paragraphs
while others just sentences. We started our lessons at a manage-
able pace, but after a couple of months, for reasons he didn't tell
me till the very last, he speeded up the pace considerably. The
new words that I had to memorize increased from twenty words
per day to fifty. To meet the challenge, I wrote the new words on
small, thin slips of paper and hid them in the little red book of
Chairman Mao, so that I could memorize them during the political study hours at school. In hole-digging afternoons I recited the
sentences and sometimes even little paragraphs—aloud when I
was sure that Chang was not around.

Before the sounds and shapes of English words became less 46
elusive, before I could confidently study by myself, my father told
me that I would have to continue on my own. He was going to join
the "Mao Zedong Thought Study Group" at his university. In
those years, "Mao Zedong Thought Study Group" was a broad
term that could refer to many things. Used in reference to my
father and people like him, it had only one meaning: a euphemism
for imprisonment. He had been imprisoned once when my mother
and siblings were still in Bejing. Now it had come again. I asked,
"Are you detained or arrested?" "I don't know," he said. "It's just

a Study Group." "Oh," I said, feeling the weight of the words. Legally, detention couldn't be any longer than fifteen days; arrest had to be followed by a conviction and a sentence, which also had a definite term. "Just a Study Group" could be a week or a lifetime. I was left on my own in a city of eight million people, my English lessons indefinitely postponed. What was worse, some people never returned alive from "Study Groups."

47   "When are you joining them?"

48   "Tomorrow."

49   I pretended to be "man" enough not to cry, but my father's eyes were wet when he made me promise to finish *Pride and Prejudice* by the time he came back.

50   After he left for the "Study Group," bedding roll on his shoulder, I took my first careful look at the book he had thrust into my hands. It was a small book with dark green cloth covers and gilt designs and letters on its spine. I lifted the front cover; the frontispiece had a flowery design and a woman figure on the upper right corner. Floating in the middle of the flowery design and as a mother, holding a baby, she held an armful of herbs, two apples or peaches, and a scroll. Her head tilted slightly toward her right, to an opened scroll intertwined with the flowers on the other side of the page. On the unrolled scroll, there were some words. I was thrilled to find that I could understand all the words in the top two lines with no difficulty except the last word: EVERYMAN, / I WILL GO WITH THEE. . . .

51   Two months after father entered the "Study Group," I stopped going to his university for my monthly allowance. The Party secretary of the bursar's office wore me out by telling me that my father and I didn't deserve to be fed by "working people." "Your father has never done any positive work," meaning the twenty years my father taught at the university undermined rather than contributed to socialist ideology. To avoid starvation, I picked up horse droppings in the streets and sold them to the farming communes in the suburb. Between the little cash savings my father left me and what I earned by selling dung, I managed an independent life. Meanwhile, I didn't forget my promise to my father. When I saw him again nineteen months later, I boasted of having thumbed his dictionary to shreds and struggled through

Austen's novel from cover to cover. I hadn't understood the story, but I had learned many words.

My father was not surprised to find that I took pleasure in 52 drudgery. He knew that looking up English words in a dictionary and wrestling with an almost incomprehensible text could be an exciting challenge. It provided an intellectual relief for a teenager living at a time when the entire country read nothing but Chairman Mao's works. "Don't worry whether you are red or black," my father said. "Just be yourself. Just be an ordinary everyman. Keep up with your good work, and when you learn English well enough, you'll be sure of a guide 'in your most need.'"

Content

1. An essay of division and classification often draws rigid boundaries between its categories, so that they are mutually exclusive. Is that true in Ning Yu's essay? Are the "reds" in total opposition to the "blacks"? If there is any overlap or intermingling among these groups, where does it occur (see, for instance, ¶ 15)? Explain your answer.

2. Ning Yu is writing this essay for an American audience that he assumes is relatively unfamiliar with Red Chinese culture. What sorts of information does he need to supply each time he introduces an unfamiliar concept? Has he done this successfully? (An examination of ¶s 1–3 will help focus your answer.)

Strategies/Structures

3. Ning Yu can count on his American readers to make implicit comparisons between his childhood, schooling, and living conditions and their own. What sorts of comparisons do you make, and how do these enhance your understanding of "Red and Black"?

4. Ning Yu depends on Western readers, for political and cultural reasons, to be on the side of those persecuted by the People's Liberation Army, such as his father and, as a consequence, himself. Is this assumption accurate? What evidence from the text corroborates your answer? In what ways do your sympathies determine how you react to the characters and events in Ning Yu's account?

5. This essay gradually shifts from humor to somberness. In what ways does Ning Yu prepare his readers for this shift, and consequently, for the essay's conclusion?

Language

6. Much of the humor in "Red and Black" depends on the students' lack of understanding of the English slogans they are obliged to memorize, and their teacher's failure to teach them how to learn the language. Find some examples of this linguistic humor; why would it strike English-speaking readers as funny, but not the pupils who are trying to memorize the slogans?

7. Ning Yu's essay was written in English, not Chinese. Does his writing give any clues that his native language was not English? Explain your answer.

For Writing

8. Have you ever been given a "label"—based on your race, social class, gender, political or religious affiliation, place of residence (street or area, city or town, state)? If so, what was (or is) that label? How accurate are its connotations? Are they favorable, unfavorable, or a mixture? Does the label stereotype or limit the ways people are expected to react to it? Did (or do) you feel comfortable with that label? If not, what can you do to change it? Write a paper exploring these issues for an audience which includes at least some people whom that label doesn't fit.

9. Have you or anyone you know well ever experienced persecution or harassment—intellectual, political, economic, racial, religious, or for other reasons? If so, write a paper explaining the causes, effects, and resolution (if any) of the problem. If it's extremely complex, select one or two aspects to concentrate on in your paper. Can you count on your audience to be sympathetic to your point of view? If not, what will you need to do to win them to your side?

Additional Topics for Writing
Division and Classification

(For strategies for writing division and classification, see 374)

1. Write an essay in which you use division to analyze one of the subjects below. Explain or illustrate each of the component parts, showing how each part functions or relates to the functioning or structure of the whole. Remember to adapt your analysis to your reader's assumed knowledge of the subject. Is it extensive? meager? or somewhere in between?

   a. The organization of the college or university you attend
   b. An organization of which you are a member— team, band or orchestra, fraternity or sorority, social or political action group
   c. A typical (or atypical) weekday or weekend in your life
   d. Your budget, or the federal budget
   e. Your family
   f. A farm, kibbutz, or factory
   g. Geologic periods
   h. A poem
   i. A provocative short story, novel, play, or television or film drama
   j. A hospital, city hall, bank, restaurant, supermarket, shopping mall

2. Write an essay, adapted to your reader's assumed knowledge of the subject, in which you classify members of one of the following subjects. Make the basis of your classification apparent, consistent, and logical. You may want to identify each group or subgroup by a name or relevant term, actual or invented.

   a. Types of cars (or sports cars), boats, or bicycles
   b. People's temperaments or personality types
   c. Vacations or holidays
   d. Styles of music, or types of a particular kind of music (classical, country and western, folk, rock)
   e. People's styles of spending money
   f. Types of restaurants, or subcategories (such as types of fast-food restaurants)
   g. Individual or family lifestyles
   h. Types of post–high school educational institutions, or types of courses a given school offers
   i. Clothing styles for your age group

j. Tennis players, skiers, golfers, runners, or other sports stars; or television or movie stars

k. Computers—types of hardware, software, or computer (or Internet) users

l. Types of stores or shopping malls

m. Some phenomenon, activity, types of people or literature or entertainment that you like or dislike a great deal

n. Social or political groups

10 Illustration and Example

If generalizations are an essay's superstructure, illustrations are its building blocks, reinforcing and filling in the skeletal outline. Writers use examples or illustrations to clarify a general point, to make abstractions concrete, to give their general ideas focus, to show readers what they have in mind rather than letting them guess. Suppose you're writing a paper with the general thesis, "Women have been a powerful force in twentieth-century politics." You'll need to identify some of the women you have in mind by adding, for instance, "among them are Eleanor Roosevelt, Golda Meir, Indira Gandhi, Margaret Thatcher, and Aung San Suu Kyi." Each of these references is an example.

But is a simple allusion sufficient? An illustration is meaningful to the extent that your readers understand it. Can you count on them to understand your reference to Eleanor Roosevelt? If not, you'll have to provide enough detail so they'll recognize why you've included her—perhaps because she was the first American ambassador to the United Nations. How much space you spend on the explanation depends on how important the example is to the point you're illustrating. It might warrant a sentence or two, or in an expanded version become the focus of the whole essay.

The essays in this section illustrate the variety of types of examples writers can use, and the varied techniques for using them. "The Power of Books" (425–35) could be seen as a single, extended narrative illustration of the crucial importance of reading on Richard Wright's development as an independent-minded thinker, writer, and human being who would rather die than lead

422 Illustration and Example

a slave's life in the South. This illustration itself incorporates a
number of significant examples of the particular books and authors who most strongly influenced Wright. H. L. Mencken gets
the most space, and consequently the greatest emphasis, because
his work was the first that Wright borrowed clandestinely from the
public library (which denied access to African-Americans), and its
impact was electrifying: "[T]he impulse to dream . . . surged up
again and I hungered for books, new ways of looking and seeing."
Sinclair Lewis's *Main Street*, the "first serious novel" Wright read,
gets the second largest amount of space. Except for including the
titles of two Dreiser novels which revived Wright's "vivid sense of
[his] mother's suffering," Wright does not differentiate among the
other books he read, but treats them as a group (and therefore as a
single example), concentrating on their collective impact: "Reading was like a drug, a dope. The novels created moods in which I
lived for days."

How many examples do you need to illustrate a point?
Enough to make it clear, without becoming redundant or boring.
Sometimes a single example, with or without interpretation or
analysis (depending on how obvious it is) will suffice. In "Under
the Influence" (441–56), Scott Russell Sanders uses the single case
of his father's alcoholism (and its many manifestations) and his
family's reaction to it to represent the problem of alcoholism as it
affects the entire alcoholic population of our country. Even
though the particulars may vary, Sanders implies, the characteristics of the alcoholic—the drinking, the bravado, the lying and
losing control—and of his cowering, continually betrayed family
are common enough to be representative of the entire population.

In contrast to the negative discoveries Sanders made about
his father's alcoholism and the ambiguous discoveries Wright
made in the process of learning to read, Gary Soto's discoveries in
"Like Mexicans" are ultimately more positive. In interpreting his
personal reaction to his family's advice to "marry a Mexican girl,"
he uses two examples—one general, about the Mexican girls he
admired when he was growing up ("I saw them and I dreamed
them"), the other specific—his courtship of Carolyn, a Japanese
girl. The real point of the advice struck him "like a baseball in the
back"—"my mother wanted me to marry someone of my own
social class—a poor girl." And in that respect Carolyn's family,

"farm workers and pull-yourself-up-by-your-bootstrap ranchers,"
was "like Mexicans, only different."

In "On Being a Cripple" (456–70), Nancy Mairs offers a series
of illustrations to show what it means to live with multiple sclerosis, and to demonstrate what she can do (cook, write, be a wife,
mother, teacher, and friend) and what she can't do (run, walk
easily, vacuum). Some of these have a narrative structure that
states a problem, shows the complications of the problem, and
resolves it—all within a paragraph, such as the paragraph that
opens the essay with a dramatic fall which Mairs transforms into
a comic pratfall—"the old beetle-on-its-back routine." Together
these illustrations comprise a partial autobiography that also incorporates thumbnail sketches of Mairs's husband and children. A
major aspect of Mairs's essay is her attitude toward MS; she treats
her subject as she treats herself, with honesty, anger, sardonic
humor, and considerable vigor. Mairs's own life, her reactions to
it, and her interpretations of it comprise her existential illustration
of multiple sclerosis.

In "The Great Campus Goof-Off Machine" (471–74), Nate
Stulman uses a series of illustrations to argue that "colleges and
universities should be wary of placing such an emphasis on the
use of computers and the Internet" because students use "their
top-of-the-line PC's and high-speed T-1 Internet connections" to
goof off. They play games, download music files, and engage
in other electronic frivolities rather than in serious computing.
Stulman offers no positive examples of student computer use,
only negative ones. In most instances, a one-sided argument—on
whatever issue, whatever side—is dangerous and ultimately un-
satisfying because readers are bound to provide contradictory
illustrations of their own and thereby undercut the force of the
author's examples, however powerful.

When you're seeking examples for your own writing, as the
motto of the state of Michigan advises, "look about you." Ask
"What do I want to illustrate?" "Why?" "Is this a good illustration?" If someone throws an abstraction at you—"What is Truth?
Beauty? Justice?"—you can toss it back, without striking out on the
curve, if you examine your own experience. Who is the most beautiful person you ever knew? Was the beauty skin-deep? Internal?
Or both? Why? What, in your view, is the most beautiful place on

earth (including perhaps your own home, a favorite grandparent's kitchen, or . . .)? What makes it so attractive? Other examples might come from what you know about the lives of your family and friends; from conversations, reading, radio, and television.

As the essays by Soto and Stulman remind us, examples can be partisan and misleading, and they can be subject to multiple interpretations—and misinterpretations. It's necessary to choose your examples with care, and anticipate in your analysis how others of differing points of view might interpret them. To control the illustrations, instead of leaving vague, general gaps for your readers to fill in, is to enable your readers to experience the subject your way. With revealing examples, carefully interpreted, you're in charge.

STRATEGIES FOR WRITING— ILLUSTRATION AND EXAMPLE

1. Is my essay a single, extended illustration? Or a combination of several? What am I using the illustration(s) for—to clarify a point? To make an abstraction or a relationship concrete? To provide a definition? To imply or promote an argument?
2. Is my audience familiar with my example(s) or not? How much detail and background information must I provide to be sure the audience understands what I'm saying? How many examples will make my point most effectively? When will they become redundant or boring? Have I chosen the most appropriate examples I could use?
3. What kinds of illustrations or examples am I using? Positive? Negative? Or both? Simple or complicated? What are the sources of my examples—my own or others' personal experiences, a knowledge of history or some other subject, reading? My imagination? Are they to be interpreted literally, symbolically, or on multiple levels?
4. If I'm using more than one illustration or example, in what order will I arrange them? From the most to the least memorable, or vice versa? From the simplest to the most elaborate, or the reverse? In the order in which they occur naturally, historically, or in which they are arranged spatially or geographically? Or by some other means?
5. Are the illustrations or examples self-evident? To what extent must I analyze them to explain their meaning? Does my analysis anticipate objections readers might have to the example(s) I've chosen? Will my language (sarcastic, nostalgic, sentimental, objective) help to provide an interpretation? Does the language fit the example?

RICHARD WRIGHT

Wright was born in 1908 in a sharecropper's cabin on a plantation near Natchez, Mississippi. After a childhood plagued by the poverty, violence, racial discrimination, and family instability that Wright movingly chronicled in *Black Boy* (1945), the first volume of his autobiography, he moved to Memphis and then to Chicago, where he worked in the post office. He found conditions in the North as discriminatory as those in the South, as *American Hunger* (1977), the second—and even angrier—part of his autobiography demonstrates. (Current editions of *Black Boy* include both parts.) In Chicago and later in New York he wrote for a time for radical left publications, the *New Masses* and the *Daily Worker,* but soon chose to concentrate instead on tales of individuals as a literary mode of social protest. His first works, *Uncle Tom's Children* (1938), a collection of short stories, and *Native Son* (1940), established the international reputation he maintained until his death in 1960 in Paris, to which he had expatriated in 1946 in search of a more congenial racial and political environment.

"The Power of Books," from *Black Boy,* powerfully illustrates the liberating effects of reading on Wright as a young man, particularly the works of social iconoclast H. L. Mencken. Fortunately, Wright was unaware of Mencken's racist and anti-Semitic attitudes, made explicit with the publication in 1989 of Mencken's *Diary.* Indeed, these attitudes were at variance with Mencken's own enduring friendships with Jews and with his support of Harlem cultural life in the 1920s.

The Power of Books[1]

O ne morning I arrived early at work and went into the bank   1
lobby where the Negro porter was mopping. I stood at a
counter and picked up the Memphis *Commercial Appeal* and began
my free reading of the press. I came finally to the editorial page
and saw an article dealing with one H. L. Mencken. I knew by
hearsay that he was the editor of the *American Mercury,* but aside

---

[1] Title supplied.

from that I knew nothing about him. The article was a furious denunciation of Mencken, concluding with one, hot, short sentence: Mencken is a fool.

2   I wondered what on earth this Mencken had done to call down upon him the scorn of the South. The only people I had ever heard denounced in the South were Negroes, and this man was not a Negro. Then what ideas did Mencken hold that made a newspaper like the *Commercial Appeal* castigate him publicly? Undoubtedly he must be advocating ideas that the South did not like. Were there, then, people other than Negroes who criticized the South? I knew that during the Civil War the South had hated northern whites, but I had not encountered such hate during my life. Knowing no more of Mencken than I did at that moment, I felt a vague sympathy for him. Had not the South, which had assigned me the role of a nonman, cast at him its hardest words?

3   Now, how could I find out about this Mencken? There was a huge library near the riverfront, but I knew that Negroes were not allowed to patronize its shelves any more than they were the parks and playgrounds of the city. I had gone into the library several times to get books for the white men on the job. Which of them would now help me to get books? And how could I read them without causing concern to the white men with whom I worked? I had so far been successful in hiding my thoughts and feelings from them, but I knew that I would create hostility if I went about this business of reading in a clumsy way.

4   I weighed the personalities of the men on the job. There was Don, a Jew; but I distrusted him. His position was not much better than mine and I knew that he was uneasy and insecure; he had always treated me in an offhand, bantering way that barely concealed his contempt. I was afraid to ask him to help me to get books; his frantic desire to demonstrate a racial solidarity with the whites against Negroes might make him betray me.

5   Then how about the boss? No, he was a Baptist and I had the suspicion that he would not be quite able to comprehend why a black boy would want to read Mencken. There were other white men on the job whose attitudes showed clearly that they were Kluxers or sympathizers, and they were out of the question.

6   There remained only one man whose attitude did not fit into an anti-Negro category, for I had heard the white men refer to him as a "Pope lover." He was an Irish Catholic and was hated by the

white Southerners. I knew that he read books, because I had got him volumes from the library several times. Since he, too, was an object of hatred, I felt that he might refuse me but would hardly betray me. I hesitated, weighing and balancing the imponderable realities.

One morning I paused before the Catholic fellow's desk.   7

"I want to ask you a favor," I whispered to him.   8

"What is it?"   9

"I want to read. I can't get books from the library. I wonder   10
if you'd let me use your card?"

He looked at me suspiciously.   11

"My card is full most of the time," he said.   12

"I see," I said and waited, posing my question silently.   13

"You're not trying to get me into trouble, are you, boy?" he   14
asked, starting at me.

"Oh, no, sir."   15

"What book do you want?"   16

"A book by H. L. Mencken."   17

"Which one?"   18

"I don't know. Has he written more than one?"   19

"He has written several."   20

"I didn't know that."   21

"What makes you want to read Mencken?"   22

"Oh, I just saw his name in the newspaper," I said.   23

"It's good of you to want to read," he said. "But you ought   24
to read the right things."

I said nothing. Would he want to supervise my reading?   25

"Let me think," he said. "I'll figure out something."   26

I turned from him and he called me back. He stared at me   27
quizzically.

"Richard, don't mention this to the other white men," he said.   28

"I understand," I said, "I won't say a word."   29

A few days later he called me to him.   30

"I've got a card in my wife's name," he said. "Here's mine."   31

"Thank you, sir."   32

"Do you think you can manage it?"   33

"I'll manage fine," I said.   34

"If they suspect you, you'll get in trouble," he said.   35

"I'll write the same kind of notes to the library that you   36
wrote when you sent me for books," I told him. "I'll sign your
name."

37   He laughed.

38   "Go ahead. Let me see what you get," he said.

39   That afternoon I addressed myself to forging a note. Now, what were the names of books written by H. L. Mencken? I did not know any of them. I finally wrote what I thought would be a fool-proof note: *Dear Madam: Will you please let this nigger boy*—I used the word "nigger" to make the librarian feel that I could not possibly be the author of the note—*have some books by H. L. Mencken?* I forged the white man's name.

40   I entered the library as I had always done when on errands for whites, but I felt that I would somehow slip up and betray myself. I doffed my hat, stood a respectful distance from the desk, look as unbookish as possible, and waited for the white patrons to be taken care of. When the desk was clear of people, I still waited. The white librarian looked at me.

41   "What do you want, boy?"

42   As though I did not possess the power of speech, I stepped forward and simply handed her the forged note, not parting my lips.

43   "What books by Mencken does he want?" she asked.

44   "I don't know, ma'am," I said, avoiding her eyes.

45   "Who gave you this card?"

46   "Mr. Falk," I said.

47   "Where is he?"

48   "He's at work, at the M——— Optical Company," I said. "I've been in here for him before."

49   "I remember," the woman said. "But he never wrote notes like this."

50   Oh, God, she's suspicious. Perhaps she would not let me have the books? If she had turned her back at that moment, I would have ducked out the door and never gone back. Then I thought of a bold idea.

51   "You can call him up, ma'am," I said, my heart pounding.

52   "You're not using these books, are you?" she asked pointedly.

53   "Oh, no, ma'am. I can't read."

54   "I don't know what he wants by Mencken," she said under her breath.

55   I knew now that I had won; she was thinking of other things and the race question had gone out of her mind. She went to the

shelves. Once or twice she looked over her shoulder at me, as though she was still doubtful. Finally she came forward with two books in her hand.

"I'm sending him two books," she said. "But tell Mr. Falk to come in next time, or send me the names of the books he wants. I don't know what he wants to read." 56

I said nothing. She stamped the card and handed me the books. Not daring to glance at them, I went out of the library, fearing that the woman would call me back for further questioning. A block away from the library I opened one of the books and read a title: *A Book of Prefaces*. I was nearing my nineteenth birthday and I did not know how to pronounce the word *preface*. I thumbed the pages and saw strange words and strange names. I shook my head, disappointed. I looked at the other book; it was called *Prejudices*. I knew what that word meant; I had heard it all of my life. And right off I was on guard against Mencken's books. Why would a man want to call a book *Prejudices?* The word was so stained with all my memories of racial hate that I could not conceive of anybody using it for a title. Perhaps I had made a mistake about Mencken? A man who had prejudices must be wrong. 57

When I showed the books to Mr. Falk, he looked at me and frowned. 58

"That librarian might telephone you," I warned him. 59

"That's all right," he said. "But when you're through reading those books, I want you to tell me what you get out of them." 60

That night in my rented room, while letting the hot water run over my can of pork and beans in the sink, I opened *A Book of Prefaces* and began to read. I was jarred and shocked by the style, the clear, clean, sweeping sentences. Why did he write like that? And how did one write like that? I pictured the man as a raging demon, slashing with his pen, consumed with hate, denouncing everything American, extolling everything European or German, laughing at the weaknesses of people, mocking God, authority. What was this? I stood up, trying to realize what reality lay behind the meaning of the words. . . . Yes, this man was fighting, fighting with words. He was using words as a weapon, using them as one would use a club. Could words be weapons? Well, yes, for here they were. Then, maybe, perhaps, I could use them as a weapon? No. It frightened me. I read on and what amazed 61 me was not what he said, but how on earth anybody had the courage to say it.

62   Occasionally I glanced up to reassure myself that I was alone in the room. Who were these men about whom Mencken was talking so passionately? Who was Anatole France? Joseph Conrad? Sinclair Lewis, Sherwood Anderson, Dostoevski, George Moore, Gustave Flaubert, Maupassant, Tolstoy, Frank Harris, Mark Twain, Thomas Hardy, Arnold Bennett, Stephen Crane, Zola, Norris, Gorky, Bergson, Ibsen, Balzac, Bernard Shaw, Dumas, Poe, Thomas Mann, O. Henry, Dreiser, H. G. Wells, Gogol, T. S. Eliot, Gide, Baudelaire, Edgar Lee Masters, Stendhal, Turgenev, Huneker, Nietzsche, and scores of others? Were these men real? Did they exist or had they existed? And how did one pronounce their names?

63   I ran across many words whose meanings I did not know, and I either looked them up in a dictionary or, before I had a chance to do that, encountered the word in a context that made its meaning clear. But what strange world was this? I concluded the book with the conviction that I had somehow overlooked something terribly important in life. I had once tried to write, had once reveled in feeling, had let my crude imagination roam, but the impulse to dream had been slowly beaten out of me by experience. Now it surged up again and I hungered for books, new ways of looking and seeing. It was not a matter of believing or disbelieving what I read, but of feeling something new, of being affected by something that made the look of the world different.

64   As dawn broke I ate my pork and beans, feeling dopey, sleepy. I went to work, but the mood of the book would not die; it lingered, coloring everything I saw, heard, did. I now felt that I knew what the white men were feeling. Merely because I had read a book that had spoken of how they lived and thought, I identified myself with that book, I felt vaguely guilty. Would I, filled with bookish notions, act in a manner that would make the whites dislike me?

65   I forged more notes and my trips to the library became frequent. Reading grew into a passion. My first serious novel was Sinclair Lewis's *Main Street*. It made me see my boss, Mr. Gerald, and identify him as an American type. I would smile when I saw him lugging his golf bags into the office. I had always felt a vast

distance separating me from the boss, and now I felt closer to him, though still distant. I felt now that I knew him, that I could feel the very limits of his narrow life. And this had happened because I had read a novel about a mythical man called George F. Babbitt.

The plots and stories in the novels did not interest me so   66
much as the point of view revealed. I gave myself over to each novel without reserve, without trying to criticize it; it was enough for me to see and feel something different. And for me, everything was something different. Reading was like a drug, a dope. The novels created moods in which I lived for days. But I could not conquer my sense of guilt, my feeling that the white men around me knew that I was changing, that I had begun to regard them differently.

Whenever I brought a book to the job, I wrapped it in news-   67
paper— a habit that was to persist for years in other cities and under other circumstances. But some of the white men pried into my packages when I was absent and they questioned me.

"Boy, what are you reading those books for?"   68
"Oh, I don't know, sir."   69
"That's deep stuff you're reading, boy."   70
"I'm just killing time, sir."   71
"You'll addle your brains if you don't watch out."   72

I read Dreiser's *Jennie Gerhardt* and *Sister Carrie* and they   73
revived in me a vivid sense of my mother's suffering; I was overwhelmed, I grew silent, wondering about the life around me. It would have been impossible for me to have told anyone what I derived from these novels, for it was nothing less than a sense of life itself. All my life had shaped me for the realism, the naturalism of the modern novel, and I could not read enough of them.

Steeped in new moods and ideas, I bought a ream of paper   74
and tried to write; but nothing would come, or what did come was flat beyond telling. I discovered that more than desire and feeling were necessary to write and I dropped the idea. Yet I still wondered how it was possible to know people sufficiently to write about them? Could I ever learn about life and people? To me, with my vast ignorance, my Jim Crow station in life, it seemed a task impossible of achievement. I now knew what being a Negro meant. I could endure the hunger. I had learned to live with hate. But to feel that there were feelings denied me, that the

very breath of life itself was beyond my reach, that more than anything else hurt, wounded me. I had a new hunger.

75   In buoying me up, reading also cast me down, made me see what was possible, what I had missed. My tension returned, new, terrible, bitter, surging, almost too great to be contained. I no longer *felt* that the world about me was hostile, killing; I *knew* it. A million times I asked myself what I could do to save myself, and there were no answers. I seemed forever condemned, ringed by walls.

76   I did not discuss my reading with Mr. Falk, who had lent me his library card; it would have meant talking about myself and that would have been too painful. I smiled each day, fighting desperately to maintain my old behavior, to keep my disposition seemingly sunny. But some of the white men discerned that I had begun to brood.

77   "Wake up there, boy!" Mr. Olin said one day.

78   "Sir!" I answered for the lack of a better word.

79   "You act like you've stolen something," he said.

80   I laughed in the way I knew he expected me to laugh, but I resolved to be more conscious of myself, to watch my every act, to guard and hide the new knowledge that was dawning within me.

81   If I went north, would it be possible for me to build a new life then? But how could a man build a life upon vague, unformed yearnings? I wanted to write and I did not even know the English language. I bought English grammars and found them dull. I felt that I was getting a better sense of the language from novels than grammars. I read hard, discarding a writer as soon as I felt that I had grasped his point of view. At night the printed page stood before my eyes in sleep.

82   Mrs. Moss, my landlady, asked me one Sunday morning:

83   "Son, what is this you keep on reading?"

84   "Oh, nothing. Just novels."

85   "What you get out of 'em?"

86   "I'm just killing time," I said.

87   "I hope you know your own mind," she said in a tone which implied that she doubted if I had a mind.

88   I knew of no Negroes who read the books I liked and I wondered if any Negroes ever thought of them. I knew that there were Negro doctors, lawyers, newspapermen, but I never saw any of

them. When I read a Negro newspaper I never caught the faintest echo of my preoccupation in its pages. I felt trapped and occasionally, for a few days, I would stop reading. But a vague hunger would come over me for books, books that opened up new avenues of feeling and seeing, and again I would forge another note to the white librarian. Again I would read and wonder as only the naive and unlettered can read and wonder, feeling that I carried a secret, criminal burden about with me each day.

That winter my mother and brother came and we set up 89
housekeeping, buying furniture on the installment plan, being cheated and yet knowing no way to avoid it. I began to eat warm food and to my surprise found the regular meals enabled me to read faster. I may have lived through many illnesses and survived them, never suspecting that I was ill. My brother obtained a job and we began to save toward the trip north, plotting our time, setting tentative dates for departure. I told none of the white men on the job that I was planning to go north; I knew that the moment they felt I was thinking of the North they would change toward me. It would have made them feel that I did not like the life I was living, and because my life was completely conditioned by what they said or did, it would have been tantamount to challenging them.

I could calculate my chances for life in the South as a Negro 90
fairly clearly now.

I could fight the southern whites by organizing with other 91
Negroes, as my grandfather had done. But I knew that I could never win that way; there were many whites and there were but few blacks. They were strong and we were weak. Outright black rebellion could never win. If I fought openly I would die and I did not want to die. News of lynchings were frequent.

I could submit and live the life of a genial slave, but that was 92
impossible. All of my life had shaped me to live by my own feelings and thoughts. I could make up to Bess and marry her and inherit the house. But that, too, would be the life of a slave; if I did that, I would crush to death something within me, and I would hate myself as much as I knew the whites already hated those who had submitted. Neither could I ever willingly present myself to be kicked, as Shorty had done. I would rather have died than do that.

I could drain off my restlessness by fighting with Shorty and 93
Harrison. I had seen many Negroes solve the problem of being

black by transferring their hatred of themselves to others with a black skin and fighting them. I would have to be cold to do that, and I was not cold and I could never be.

94   I could, of course, forget what I had read, thrust the whites out of my mind, forget them; and find release from anxiety and longing in sex and alcohol. But the memory of how my father had conducted himself made that course repugnant. If I did not want others to violate my life, how could I voluntarily violate it myself?

95   I had no hope whatever of being a professional man. Not only had I been so conditioned that I did not desire it, but the fulfillment of such an ambition was beyond my capabilities. Well-to-do Negroes lived in a world that was almost as alien to me as the world inhabited by whites.

96   What, then, was there? I held my life in my mind, in my consciousness each day, feeling at times that I would stumble and drop it, spill it forever. My reading had created a vast sense of distance between me and the world in which I lived and tried to make a living, and that sense of distance was increasing each day. My days and nights were one long, quiet, continuously contained dream of terror, tension, and anxiety. I wondered how long I could bear it.

Content

1. This essay, a self-contained section of Wright's autobiography, is an extended illustration of "the power of books." What sorts of power did books hold and promise for Wright, a poor, black, undereducated teenage laborer in Memphis in the 1920s?

2. This essay is also an example of problem-solving. What is Wright's immediate problem (¶s 1–3)? How does he go about solving it? Why does the solution require lying, deception, and manipulation of others?

3. How does Wright expect his readers to react to this behavior? What moral standards does he expect them to apply? (Remember that he published this some twenty years before the passage of the 1964 Civil Rights Act; would his initial readers, southern or northern, have been receptive to his defiance of the law?)

4. How do both the problem and the solution reflect the larger problematic condition of Wright's life? In what ways does solving the immediate problem raise larger, profound issues that require long-term solutions? What options and possible solutions does he contemplate (¶s 90–95)?

Strategies/Structures

5. Why does Wright single out only H. L. Mencken, Sinclair Lewis, and Theodore Dreiser (¶s 61–73) for individual commentary as powerful influences on his "new ways of looking and seeing"? Why does he treat the rest of his vast reading collectively rather than individually?

6. Wright alternates between analytic narrative and scenes, short and long, involving characters and dialogue. Identify some of the key scenes and explain what each scene or character illustrates. What is the effect of these scenes, which show—rather than tell—us what happened?

Language

7. Wright saw Mencken "using words as a weapon, using them as one would use a club" (¶ 61). How does this influence his decision to become a writer? Why, having been overcome with "desire and feeling," can't he just plunge in and write (¶ 74)?

8. Reading gave Wright much of the vocabulary with which he has written "The Power of Books." Identify some words Wright the author uses here that the teenage Wright might not have known. Why does this more sophisticated vocabulary seem natural in the mature Wright's presentation of himself as a teenager?

For Writing

9. In this essay, Wright makes an implicit case for civil disobedience. (Compare this with King's explicit argument for civil disobedience in "Letter from Birmingham Jail" (596–616). Write an essay for a generally law-abiding audience in which, using an example from your life or the life of someone you know well (or perhaps have read about), you justify breaking the law (presumably, a "bad" civil law—you'll have to define that) or violating some accepted standards of conduct to support some higher moral principle. The principle(s) involved should be apparent from the example.

10. For Wright, the hard-won opportunity to read provocative and stimulating books not only revolutionized his thinking but gave him the energy to completely change his life. Write an essay on "the power of . . ." for people who would benefit from such power. Focus on a hard-won privilege, opportunity, or relationship and its implications for your life, actual or potential. If the implications have been realized (or are in the process of realization), what enabled you to accomplish them (your own efforts, help from others, luck)? (See Asimov, "Those Crazy Ideas," 208–20.)

GARY SOTO

"As a kid I imagined a dark fate," says Soto in his autobiographical *Living up the Street* (1985), winner of the American Book Award. He was born in 1952 to working-class Mexican-American parents in Fresno, California, in the heart of a rich agricultural area where as a teenager he and his family labored as migrant workers. He expected "to marry Mexican poor, work Mexican hours, and in the end die a Mexican death." However, his education, begun in 1970 at Fresno Community College, followed by a B.A. (Fresno State College, 1974) and a Master of Fine Arts in creative writing from the University of California, Irvine (1976), changed all that: "I didn't want to be poor—I'd had enough of that." Soto taught English and ethnic studies at Berkeley from 1979 to 1993, when he resigned his professorship to be a full-time writer. He remains happily married to Carolyn, whose courtship he illustrates in "Like Mexicans," originally published in the second volume of his autobiographical essays, *Small Faces* (1986). He has published several highly regarded volumes of poetry, including *Where Sparrows Work Hard* (1981) and *Black Hair* (1985), and, in the 1990s, a variety of books of stories and poems for children and adolescents, all focusing on Mexican-American culture.

Although both Soto's poetry and prose focus on his Mexican-American childhood and on the Mexican-American sense of community, his work transcends nationality. He once said, "I believe in the culture of the poor," a testament to the understanding that he expresses in "Like Mexicans."

Like Mexicans

1   M y grandmother gave me bad advice and good advice when I was in my early teens. For the bad advice, she said that I should become a barber because they made good money and listened to the radio all day. "Honey, they don't work como burros," she would say every time I visited her. She made the sound of donkeys braying. "Like that, honey!" For the good advice, she said that I should marry a Mexican girl. "No Okies, hijo"—she would say—"Look, my son. He marry one and they

fight every day about I don't know what and I don't know what."
For her, everyone who wasn't Mexican, black, or Asian were
Okies. The French were Okies, the Italians in suits were Okies.
When I asked about Jews, whom I had read about, she asked for a
picture. I rode home on my bicycle and returned with a calendar
depicting the important races of the world. "Pues si, son Okies
también!" she said, nodding her head. She waved the calendar
away and we went to the living room where she lectured me on
the virtues of the Mexican girl: first, she could cook and, second,
she acted like a woman, not a man, in her husband's home. She
said she would tell me about a third when I got a little older.

I asked my mother about it—becoming a barber and marry- 2
ing Mexican. She was in the kitchen. Steam curled from a pot of
boiling beans, the radio was on, looking as squat as a loaf of bread.
"Well, if you want to be a barber—they say they make good
money." She slapped a round steak with a knife, her glasses slipping down with each strike. She stopped and looked up. "If you
find a good Mexican girl, marry her of course." She returned to
slapping the meat and I went to the backyard where my brother
and David King were sitting on the lawn feeling the inside of
their cheeks.

"This is what girls feel like," my brother said, rubbing the 3
inside of his cheek. David put three fingers inside his mouth and
scratched. I ignored them and climbed the back fence to see my
best friend, Scott, a second-generation Okie. I called him and his
mother pointed to the side of the house where his bedroom was,
a small aluminum trailer, the kind you gawk at when they're
flipped over on the freeway, wheels spinning in the air. I went
around to find Scott pitching horseshoes.

I picked up a set of rusty ones and joined him. While we 4
played, we talked about school and friends and record albums.
The horseshoes scuffed up dirt, sometimes ringing the iron that
threw out a meager shadow like a sundial. After three argued-over
games we pulled two oranges apiece from his tree and started
down the alley still talking school and friends and record albums.
We pulled more oranges from the alley and talked about who we
would marry. "No offense, Scott," I said with an orange slice in my
mouth, "but I would never marry an Okie." We walked in step, almost touching, with a sled of shadows dragging behind us. "No

offense, Gary," Scott said, "but I would *never* marry a Mexican." I looked at him: a fang of orange slice showed from his munching mouth. I didn't think anything of it. He had his girl and I had mine. But our seventh-grade vision was the same: to marry, get jobs, buy cars and maybe a house if we had money left over.

5   We talked about our future lives until, to our surprise, we were on the downtown mall, two miles from home. We bought a bag of popcorn at Penneys and sat on a bench near the fountain watching Mexican and Okie girls pass. "That one's mine," I pointed with my chin when a girl with eyebrows arched into black rainbows ambled by. "She's cute," Scott said about a girl with yellow hair and a mouthful of gum. We dreamed aloud, our chins busy pointing out girls. We agreed that we couldn't wait to become men and lift them onto our laps.

6   But the woman I married was not Mexican but Japanese. It was a surprise to me. For years, I went about wide-eyed in my search for the brown girl in a white dress at a dance. I searched the playground at the baseball diamond. When the girls raced for grounders, their hair bounced like something that couldn't be caught. When they sat together in the lunchroom, heads pressed together, I knew they were talking about us Mexican guys. I saw them and dreamed them. I threw my face into my pillow, making up sentences that were good as in the movies.

7   But when I was twenty, I fell in love with this other girl who worried my mother, who had my grandmother asking once again to see the calendar of the Important Races of the World. I told her I had thrown it away years before. I took a much-glanced-at snapshot from my wallet. We looked at it together, in silence. Then grandma reclined in her chair, lit a cigarette, and said, "Es pretty." She blew and asked with all her worry pushed up to her forehead: "Chinese?"

8   I was in love and there was no looking back. She was the one. I told my mother who was slapping hamburger into patties. "Well, sure if you want to marry her," she said. But the more I talked, the more concerned she became. Later I began to worry. Was it all a mistake? "Marry a Mexican girl," I heard my mother say in my mind. I heard it at breakfast. I heard it over math problems, between Western Civilization and cultural geography. But then one afternoon while I was hitchhiking home from school, it

struck me like a baseball in the back: my mother wanted me to marry someone of my own social class—a poor girl. I considered my fiancee, Carolyn, and she didn't look poor, though I knew she came from a family of farm workers and pull-yourself-up-by-your-bootstraps ranchers. I asked my brother who was marrying Mexican poor that fall, if I should marry a poor girl. He screamed "Yeah" above his terrible guitar playing in his bedroom. I considered my sister who had married Mexican. Cousins were dating Mexican. Uncles were remarrying poor women. I asked Scott, who was still my best friend, and he said, "She's too good for you, so you better not."

I worried about it until Carolyn took me home to meet her 9 parents. We drove in her Plymouth until the houses gave way to farms and ranches and finally her house fifty feet from the highway. When we pulled into the drive, I panicked and begged Carolyn to make a U-turn and go back so we could talk about it over a soda. She pinched my cheek, calling me a "silly boy." I felt better, though, when I got out of the car and saw the house: the chipped paint, a cracked window, boards for a walk to the back door. There were rusting cars near the barn. A tractor with a net of spiderwebs under a mulberry. A field. A bale of barbed wire like children's scribbling leaning against an empty chicken coop. Carolyn took my hand and pulled me to my future mother-in-law who was coming out to greet us.

We had lunch: sandwiches, potato chips, and iced tea. 10 Carolyn and her mother talked mostly about neighbors and the congregation at the Japanese Methodist Church in West Fresno. Her father, who was in khaki work clothes, excused himself with a wave that was almost a salute and went outside. I heard a truck start, a dog bark, and then the truck rattle away.

Carolyn's mother offered another sandwich, but I declined 11 with a shake of my head and a smile. I looked around when I could, when I was not saying over and over that I was a college student, hinting that I could take care of her daughter. I shifted my chair, I saw newspapers piled in corners, dusty cereal boxes and vinegar bottles in corners. The wallpaper was bubbled from rain that had come in from a bad roof. Dust. Dust lay on lamp shades and window sills. These people are just like Mexicans, I thought. Poor people.

12   Carolyn's mother asked me through Carolyn if I would like a *sushi*. A plate of black and white things were held in front of me. I took one, wide-eyed, and turned it over like a foreign coin. I was biting into one when I saw a kitten crawl up the window screen over the sink. I chewed and the kitten opened its mouth of terror as she crawled higher, wanting in to paw the leftovers from our plates. I looked at Carolyn who said that the cat was just showing off. I looked up in time to see it fall. It crawled up, then fell again.

13   We talked for an hour and had apple pie and coffee, slowly. Finally, we got up with Carolyn taking my hand. Slightly embarrassed, I tried to pull away but her grip held me. I let her have her way as she led me down the hallway with her mother right behind me. When I opened the door, I was startled by a kitten clinging to the screen door, its mouth screaming "cat food, dog biscuits, *sushi*. . . ." I opened the door and the kitten, still holding on, whined in the language of hungry animals. When I got into Carolyn's car, I looked back: the cat was still clinging. I asked Carolyn if it were possibly hungry, but she said the cat was being silly. She started the car, waved to her mother, and bounced us over the rain-poked drive, patting my thigh for being her lover baby. Carolyn waved again. I looked back, waving, then gawking at a window screen where there were now three kittens clawing and screaming to get in. Like Mexicans, I thought. I remembered the Molinas and how the cats clung to their screens—cats they shot down with squirt guns. On the highway, I felt happy, pleased by it all. I patted Carolyn's thigh. Her people were like Mexicans, only different.

Content

1. Soto's grandmother considers "everyone who wasn't Mexican, black, or Asian" to be an "Okie" (¶ 1). What does she mean by this? Why does Soto use this example of her stereotyping generalization to begin "Like Mexicans"?

2. Who and what does Soto discover are "like Mexicans"? In what ways does Soto's lifetime experience of marginality and poverty prepare him for this discovery?

3. Why is it important for Soto's courtship that his fiancee's background be as poor as his own (¶s 8–13)?

Strategies/Structures

4. Why is there such a long windup, the first eight paragraphs, before the pitch—the last four paragraphs?
5. Which aspects of the analogy according to which "Like Mexicans" is structured, Soto is to Mexicans as Carolyn is to Japanese, require the most elaboration for readers unfamiliar with Mexican culture?

Language

6. In what ways does Soto let his readers know that he doesn't expect pity because he's poor?
7. Why doesn't Soto translate the Spanish he occasionally uses? What other ways do readers who don't know Spanish have to understand it?

For Writing

8. This essay makes explicit an analogy, Soto is to Mexican as Carolyn is to Japanese. Write an essay structured according to a comparable analogy, in which the equation, implied or expressed, illustrates your thesis. At least one major element of the analogy should be familiar to your readers.
9. Write an essay in which, like Soto, you use a great deal of natural-sounding conversation to characterize both people and the central issue of your paper.
10. If you have dated or married someone of a race, creed, color, ethnic background, nationality, or economic group dramatically different from your own, write an essay illustrating your experience for readers skeptical of the wisdom of this.

SCOTT RUSSELL SANDERS

"Under the Influence," from *Secrets of the Universe* (1991), is full of examples of the effects of alcoholism—on the alcoholic father, on his wife, alternately distressed and defiant, and on his children, cowering with guilt and fear. Sanders uses especially the example of himself, the eldest son, who felt responsible for his father's drinking, guilty because he couldn't get him to stop, and obligated to atone for his father's sins through his own perfection and accomplishment. Although at the age of forty-four Sanders knows that his father was "consumed by disease rather than by disappointment," he writes to understand "the corrosive mixture of helplessness, responsibility, and shame that I learned to feel as the son of an alcoholic." Through the highly specific example of his family's behavior, Sanders illustrates the general problem of alcoholism that afflicts some "ten or fifteen million people." He expects his readers to generalize and to learn from his understanding. (For more information about Sanders, see page 186).

Under the Influence: Paying the Price of My Father's Booze

1   My father drank. He drank as a gut-punched boxer gasps for breath, as a starving dog gobbles food—compulsively, secretly, in pain and trembling. I use the past tense not because he ever quit drinking but because he quit living. That is how the story ends for my father, age sixty-four, heart bursting, body cooling, slumped and forsaken on the linoleum of my brother's trailer. The story continues for my brother, my sister, my mother, and me, and will continue as long as memory holds.

2   In the perennial present of memory, I slip into the garage or barn to see my father tipping back the flat green bottles of wine, the brown cylinders of whiskey, the cans of beer disguised in paper bags. His Adam's apple bobs, the liquid gurgles, he wipes the sandy-haired back of a hand over his lips, and then, his bloodshot gaze bumping into me, he stashes the bottle or can inside his jacket, under the workbench, between two bales of hay, and we both pretend the moment has not occurred.

3   "What's up, buddy?" he says, thick-tongued and edgy.

4   "Sky's up," I answer, playing along.

5   "And don't forget prices," he grumbles. "Prices are always up. And taxes."

6   In memory, his white 1951 Pontiac with the stripes down the hood and the Indian head on the snout lurches to a stop in the driveway; or it is the 1956 Ford station wagon, or the 1963 Rambler

shaped like a toad, or the sleek 1969 Bonneville that will do 120 miles per hour on straightaways; or it is the robin's-egg-blue pickup, new in 1980, battered in 1981, the year of his death. He climbs out, grinning dangerously, unsteady on his legs, and we children interrupt our game of catch, our building of snow forts, our picking of plums, to watch in silence as he weaves past us into the house, where he drops into his overstuffed chair and falls asleep. Shaking her head, our mother stubs out a cigarette he has left smoldering in the ashtray. All evening, until our bedtimes, we tiptoe past him, as past a snoring dragon. Then we curl fearfully in our sheets, listening. Eventually he wakes with a grunt, Mother slings accusations at him, he snarls back, she yells, he growls, their voices clashing. Before long, she retreats to their bedroom, sobbing—not from the blows of fists, for he never strikes her, but from the force of his words.

Left alone, our father prowls the house, thumping into furni- 7 ture, rummaging in the kitchen, slamming doors, turning the pages of the newspaper with a savage crackle, muttering back at the late-night drivel from television. The roof might fly off, the walls might buckle from the pressure of his rage. Whatever my brother and sister and mother may be thinking on their own rumpled pillows, I lie there hating him, loving him, fearing him, knowing I have failed him. I tell myself he drinks to ease the ache that gnaws at his belly, an ache I must have caused by disappointing him somehow, a murderous ache I should be able to relieve by doing all my chores, earning A's in school, winning baseball games, fixing the broken washer and the burst pipes, bringing in the money to fill his empty wallet. He would not hide the green bottles in his tool-box, would not sneak off to the barn with a lump under his coat, would not fall asleep in the daylight, would not roar and fume, would not drink himself to death, if only I were perfect.

I am forty-four, and I know full well now that my father was 8 an alcoholic, a man consumed by disease rather than by disappointment. What had seemed to me a private grief is in fact, of course, a public scourge. In the United States alone, some ten or fifteen million people share his ailment, and behind the doors they slam in fury or disgrace, countless other children tremble. I comfort myself with such knowledge, holding it against the throb of memory like an ice pack against a bruise. Other people have keener

sources of grief: poverty, racism, rape, war. I do not wish to compete to determine who has suffered most. I am only trying to understand the corrosive mixture of helplessness, responsibility, and
shame that I learned to feel as the son of an alcoholic. I realize now
that I did not cause my father's illness, nor could I have cured it.
Yet for all this grownup knowledge, I am still ten years old, my
own son's age, and as that boy I struggle in guilt and confusion to
save my father from pain.

9   Consider a few of our synonyms for *drunk*: tipsy, tight, pickled,
soused, and plowed; stoned and stewed, lubricated and inebri-
ated, juiced and sluiced; three sheets to the wind, in your cups, out
of your mind, under the table; lit up, tanked up, wiped out; besotted, blotto, bombed, and buzzed; plastered, polluted, putrefied;
loaded or looped, boozy, woozy, fuddled, or smashed; crocked
and shit-faced, corked and pissed, snockered and sloshed.

10   It is a mostly humorous lexicon, as the lore that deals with
drunks—in jokes and cartoons, in plays, films and television
skits—is largely comic. Aunt Matilda nips elderberry wine from
the sideboard and burps politely during supper. Uncle Fred
slouches to the table glassy-eyed, wearing a lampshade for a hat
and murmuring, "Candy is dandy, but liquor is quicker." Inspired
by cocktails, Mrs. Somebody recounts the events of her day in a
fuzzy dialect, while Mr. Somebody nibbles her ear and croons a
bawdy song. On the sofa with Boyfriend, Daughter Somebody
giggles, licking gin from her lips, and loosens the bows in her hair.
Junior knocks back some brews with his chums at the Leopard
Lounge and stumbles home to the wrong house, wonders foggily
why he cannot locate his pajamas, and crawls naked into bed
with the ugliest girl in school. The family dog slurps from a
neglected martini and wobbles to the nursery, where he vomits
in Baby's shoe.

11   It is all great fun. But if in the audience you notice a few
laughing faces turn grim when the drunk lurches onstage, don't
be surprised, for these are the children of alcoholics. Over the
grinning mask of Dionysus, the leering face of Bacchus, these children cannot help seeing the bloated features of their own parents.
Instead of laughing, they wince, they mourn. Instead of celebrating the drunk as one freed from constraints, they pity him as one

enslaved. They refuse to believe *in vino veritas*, having seen their befuddled parents skid away from truth toward folly and oblivion. And so these children bite their lips until the lush staggers into the wings.

My father, when drunk, was neither funny nor honest; he   12
was pathetic, frightening, deceitful. There seemed to be a leak in him somewhere, and he poured in booze to keep from draining dry. Like a torture victim who refuses to squeal, he would never admit that he had touched a drop, not even in his last year, when he seemed to be dissolving in alcohol before our very eyes. I never knew him to lie about anything, ever, except about this one ruinous fact. Drowsy, clumsy, unable to fix a bicycle tire, balance a grocery sack, or walk across a room, he was stripped of his true self by drink. In a matter of minutes, the contents of a bottle could transform a brave man into a coward, a buddy into a bully, a gifted athlete and skilled carpenter and shrewd businessman into a bumbler. No dictionary of synonyms for *drunk* would soften the anguish of watching our prince turn into a frog.

Father's drinking became the family secret. While growing   13
up, we children never breathed a word of it beyond the four walls of our house. To this day, my brother and sister rarely mention it, and then only when I press them. I did not confess the ugly, bewildering fact to my wife until his wavering and slurred speech forced me to. Recently, on the seventh anniversary of my father's death, I asked my mother if she ever spoke of his drinking to friends. "No, no, never," she replied hastily. "I couldn't bear for anyone to know."

The secret bores under the skin, gets in the blood, into the   14
bone, and stays there. Long after you have supposedly been cured of malaria, the fever can flare up, the tremors can shake you. So it is with the fevers of shame. You swallow the bitter quinine of knowledge, and you learn to feel pity and compassion toward the drinker. Yet the shame lingers and, because of it, anger.

For a long stretch of my childhood we lived on a military reser-   15
vation in Ohio, an arsenal where bombs were stored underground in bunkers and vintage airplanes burst into flames and unstable artillery shells boomed nightly at the dump. We had the feeling, as children, that we played within a minefield, where a heedless

footfall could trigger an explosion. When Father was drinking, the house, too, became a minefield. The least bump could set off either parent.

16   The more he drank, the more obsessed Mother became with stopping him. She hunted for bottles, counted the cash in his wallet, sniffed at his breath. Without meaning to snoop, we children blundered left and right into damning evidence. On afternoons when he came home from work sober, we flung ourselves at him for hugs and felt against our ribs the telltale lump in his coat. In the barn we tumbled on the hay and heard beneath our sneakers the crunch of broken glass. We tugged open a drawer in his workbench, looking for screwdrivers or crescent wrenches, and spied a gleaming six-pack among the tools. Playing tag, we darted around the house just in time to see him sway on the rear stoop and heave a finished bottle into the woods. In his goodnight kiss we smelled the cloying sweetness of Clorets, the mints he chewed to camouflage his dragon's breath.

17   I can summon up that kiss right now by recalling Theodore Roethke's lines about his own father:

> The whiskey on your breath
> Could make a small boy dizzy;
> But I hung on like death:
> Such waltzing was not easy.

Such waltzing was hard, terribly hard, for with a boy's scrawny arms I was trying to hold my tipsy father upright.

18   For years, the chief source of those incriminating bottles and cans was a grimy store a mile from us, a cinderblock place called Sly's, with two gas pumps outside and a mangy dog asleep in the window. Inside, on rusty metal shelves or in wheezing coolers, you could find pop and Popsicles, cigarettes, potato chips, canned soup, raunchy postcards, fishing gear, Twinkies, wine, and beer. When Father drove anywhere on errands, Mother would send us along as guards, warning us not to let him out of our sight. And so with one or more of us on board, Father would cruise up to Sly's, pump a dollar's worth of gas or plump the tires with air, and then, telling us to wait in the car, he would head for the doorway.

19   Dutiful and panicky, we cried, "Let us go with you!"

20   "No," he answered. "I'll be back in two shakes."

21   "Please!"

"No!" he roared. "Don't you budge or I'll jerk a knot in your 22 tails!"

So we stayed put, kicking the seats, while he ducked inside. 23 Often, when he had parked the car at a careless angle, we gazed in through the window and saw Mr. Sly fetching down from the shelf behind the cash register two green pints of Gallo wine. Father swigged one of them right there at the counter, stuffed the other in his pocket, and then out he came, a bulge in his coat, a flustered look on his reddened face.

Because the mom and pop who ran the dump were neigh- 24 bors of ours, living just down the tar-blistered road, I hated them all the more for poisoning my father. I wanted to sneak in their store and smash the bottles and set fire to the place. I also hated the Gallo brothers, Ernest and Julio, whose jovial faces beamed from the labels of their wine, labels I would find, torn and curled, when I burned the trash. I noted the Gallo brothers' address in California and studied the road atlas to see how far that was from Ohio, because I meant to go out there and tell Ernest and Julio what they were doing to my father, and then, if they showed no mercy, I would kill them.

While growing up on the back roads and in the country schools 25 and cramped Methodist churches of Ohio and Tennessee, I never heard the word *alcoholic*, never happened across it in books or magazines. In the nearby towns, there were no addiction-treatment programs, no community mental-health centers, no Alcoholics Anonymous chapters, no therapists. Left alone with our grievous secret, we had no way of understanding Father's drinking except as an act of will, a deliberate folly or cruelty, a moral weakness, a sin. He drank because he chose to, pure and simple. Why our father, so playful and competent and kind when sober, would choose to ruin himself and punish his family we could not fathom.

Our neighborhood was high on the Bible, and the Bible was 26 hard on drunkards. "Woe to those who are heroes at drinking wine and valiant men in mixing strong drink," wrote Isaiah. "The priest and the prophet reel with strong drink, they are confused with wine, they err in vision, they stumble in giving judgment. For all tables are full of vomit, no place is without filthiness." We children had seen those fouled tables at the local truck stop where the notorious boozers hung out, our father occasionally among them.

"Wine and new wine take away the understanding," declared the prophet Hosea. We had also seen evidence of that in our father, who could multiply seven-digit numbers in his head when sober but when drunk could not help us with fourth-grade math. Proverbs warned: "Do not look at wine when it is red, when it sparkles in the cup and goes down smoothly. At the last it bites like a serpent and stings like an adder. Your eyes will see strange things, and your mind utter perverse things." Woe, woe.

27   Dismayingly often, these biblical drunkards stirred up trouble for their own kids. Noah made fresh wine after the flood, drank too much of it, fell asleep without any clothes on, and was glimpsed in the buff by his son Ham, whom Noah promptly cursed. In one passage—it was so shocking we had to read it under our blankets with flashlights—the patriarch Lot fell down drunk and slept with his daughters. The sins of the fathers set their children's teeth on edge.

28   Our ministers were fond of quoting St. Paul's pronouncement that drunkards would not inherit the kingdom of God. These grave preachers assured us that the wine referred to in the Last Supper was in fact grape juice. Bible and sermons and hymns combined to give us the impression that Moses should have brought down from the mountain another stone tablet, bearing the Eleventh Commandment: Thou shalt not drink.

29   The scariest and most illuminating Bible story apropos of drunkards was the one about the lunatic and the swine. We knew it by heart: When Jesus climbed out of his boat one day, this lunatic came charging up from the graveyard, stark naked and filthy, frothing at the mouth, so violent that he broke the strongest chains. Nobody would go near him. Night and day for years, this madman had been wailing among the tombs and bruising himself with stones. Jesus took one look at him and said, "Come out of the man, you unclean spirits!" for he could see that the lunatic was possessed by demons. Meanwhile, some hogs were conveniently rooting nearby. "If we have to come out," begged the demons, "at least let us go into those swine." Jesus agreed, the unclean spirits entered the hogs, and the hogs raced straight off a cliff and plunged into a lake. Hearing the story in Sunday school, my friends thought mainly of the pigs. (How big a splash did they make? Who paid for the lost pork?) But I thought of the redeemed

lunatic, who bathed himself and put on clothes and calmly sat at the feet of Jesus, restored—so the Bible said—to "his right mind."

When drunk, our father was clearly in his wrong mind. He became a stranger, as fearful to us as any graveyard lunatic, not quite frothing at the mouth but fierce enough, quick-tempered, explosive; or else he grew maudlin and weepy, which frightened us nearly as much. In my boyhood despair, I reasoned that maybe he wasn't to blame for turning into an ogre: Maybe, like the lunatic, he was possessed by demons.   30

If my father was indeed possessed, who would exorcise him? If he was a sinner, who would save him? If he was ill, who would cure him? If he suffered, who would ease his pain? Not ministers or doctors, for we could not bring ourselves to confide in them; not the neighbors, for we pretended they had never seen him drunk; not Mother, who fussed and pleaded but could not budge him; not my brother and sister, who were only kids. That left me. It did not matter that I, too, was only a child, and a be-wildered one at that. I could not excuse myself.   31

On first reading a description of delirium tremens—in a book on alcoholism I smuggled from a university library—I thought im-mediately of the frothing lunatic and the frenzied swine. When I read stories or watched films about grisly metamorphoses—Dr. Jekyll and Mr. Hyde, the mild husband changing into a werewolf, the kindly neighbor inhabited by a brutal alien—I could not help but see my own father's mutation from sober to drunk. Even today, knowing better, I am attracted by the demonic theory of drink, for when I recall my father's transformation, the emergence of his ugly second self, I find it easy to believe in being possessed by unclean spirits. We never knew which version of Father would come home from work, the true or the tainted, nor could we guess how far down the slope toward cruelty he would slide.   32

How far a man *could* slide we gauged by observing our back-road neighbors—the out-of-work miners who had dragged their families to our corner of Ohio from the desolate hollows of Appa-lachia, the tightfisted farmers, the surly mechanics, the balked and broken men. There was, for example, whiskey-soaked Mr. Jenkins, who beat his wife and kids so hard we could hear their screams from the road. There was Mr. Lavo the wino, who fell   33 asleep smoking time and again, until one night his disgusted wife bundled up the children and went outside and left him in his easy chair to burn; he awoke on his own, staggered out coughing into the yard, and pounded her flat while the children looked on and the shack turned to ash. There was the truck driver, Mr. Sampson, who tripped over his son's tricycle one night while drunk and got mad, jumped into his semi, and drove away, shifting through the dozen gears, and never came back. We saw the bruised children of these fathers clump onto our school bus, we saw the abandoned children huddle in the pews at church, we saw the stunned and battered mothers begging for help at our doors.

34   Our own father never beat us, and I don't think he beat Mother, but he threatened often. The Old Testament Yahweh was not more terrible in His rage. Eyes blazing, voice booming, Father would pull out his belt and swear to give us a whipping, but he never followed through, never needed to, because we could imagine it so vividly. He shoved us, pawed us with the back of his hand, not to injure, just to clear a space. I can see him grabbing Mother by the hair as she cowers on a chair during a nightly quarrel. He twists her neck back until she gapes up at him, and then he lifts over her skull a glass quart bottle of milk, and milk spilling down his forearm, and he yells at her, "Say just one more word, one goddamn word, and I'll shut you up!" I fear she will prick him with her sharp tongue, but she is terrified into silence, and so am I, and the leaking bottle quivers in the air, and milk seeps through the red hair of my father's uplifted arm, and the entire scene is there to this moment, the head jerked back, the club raised.

35   When the drink made him weepy, Father would pack, kiss each of us children on the head, and announce from the front door that he was moving out. "Where to?" we demanded, fearful each time that he would leave for good, as Mr. Sampson had roared away for good in his diesel truck. "Someplace where I won't get hounded every minute," Father would answer, his jaw quivering. He stabbed a look at Mother, who might say, "Don't run into the ditch before you get there," or "Good riddance," and then he would slink away. Mother watched him go with arms crossed over her chest, her face closed like the lid on a box of snakes. We children bawled. Where could he go? To the truck stop, that den of iniquity? To one of those dark, ratty flophouses

in town? Would he wind up sleeping under a railroad bridge or on a park bench or in a cardboard box, mummied in rags like the bums we had seen on our trips to Cleveland and Chicago? We bawled and bawled, wondering if he would ever come back.

He always did come back, a day or a week later, but each time there was a sliver less of him.   36

In Kafka's *Metamorphosis*, which opens famously with Gregor   37
Samsa waking up from uneasy dreams to find himself transformed into an insect, Gregor's family keep reassuring them-
selves that things will be just fine again "when he comes back to us." Each time alcohol transformed our father we held out the same hope, that he would really and truly come back to us, our authentic father, the tender and playful and competent man, and then all things would be fine. We had grounds for such hope. After his tearful departures and chapfallen returns, he would sometimes go weeks, even months, without drinking. Those were glad times. Every day without the furtive glint of bottles, every meal without a fight, every bedtime without sobs encouraged us to believe that such bliss might go on forever.

Mother was fooled by such a hope all during the forty-odd   38
years she knew Greeley Ray Sanders. Soon after she met him in a Chicago delicatessen on the eve of World War II and fell for his butter-melting Mississippi drawl and his wavy red hair, she learned that he drank heavily. But then so did a lot of men. She would soon coax or scold him into breaking the nasty habit. She would point out to him how ugly and foolish it was, this bleary drinking, and then he would quit. He refused to quit during their engagement, however, still refused during the first years of marriage, refused until my older sister came along. The shock of father-
hood sobered him, and he remained sober through my birth at the end of the war and right on through until we moved in 1951 to the Ohio arsenal. The arsenal had more than its share of alcoholics, drug addicts, and other varieties of escape artists. There I turned six and started school and woke into a child's flickering awareness, just in time to see my father begin sneaking swigs in the garage.

He sobered up again for most of a year at the height of the   39
Korean War, to celebrate the birth of my brother. But aside from that dry spell, his only breaks from drinking before I graduated

from high school were just long enough to raise and then dash our hopes. Then during the fall of my senior year—the time of the Cuban Missile Crisis, when it seemed that the nightly explosions at the munitions dump and the nightly rages in our household might spread to engulf the globe—Father collapsed. His liver, kidneys, and heart all conked out. The doctors saved him, but only by a hair. He stayed in the hospital for weeks, going through a withdrawal so terrible that Mother would not let us visit him. If he wanted to kill himself, the doctors solemnly warned him, all he had to do was hit the bottle again. One binge would finish him.

40   Father must have believed them, for he stayed dry the next fifteen years. It was an answer to prayer, Mother said, it was a miracle. I believe it was a reflex of fear, which he sustained over the years through courage and pride. He knew a man could die from drink, for his brother Roscoe had. We children never laid eyes on doomed Uncle Roscoe, but in the stories Mother told us he became a fairy-tale figure, like a boy who took the wrong turn in the woods and was gobbled up by the wolf.

41   The fifteen-year dry spell came to an end with Father's retirement in the spring of 1978. Like many men, he gave up his identity along with his job. One day he was a boss at the factory, with a brass plate on his door and a reputation to uphold; the next day he was a nobody at home. He and Mother were leaving Ontario, the last of the many places to which his job had carried them, and they were moving to a new house in Mississippi, his childhood stomping ground. As a boy in Mississippi, Father sold Coca-Cola during dances while the moonshiners peddled their brew in the parking lot; as a young blade, he fought in bars and in the ring, winning a state Golden Gloves championship; he gambled at poker, hunted pheasant, raced motorcycles and cars, played semiprofessional baseball, and, along with all his buddies—in the Black Cat Saloon, behind the cotton gin, in the woods—he drank hard. It was a perilous youth to dream of recovering.

42   After his final day of work, Mother drove on ahead with a car full of begonias and violets, while Father stayed behind to oversee the packing. When the van was loaded, the sweaty movers broke open a six-pack and offered him a beer.

43   "Let's drink to retirement!" they crowed. "Let's drink to freedom! to fishing! hunting! loafing! Let's drink to a guy who's going home!"

At least I imagine some such words, for that is all I can do, 44
imagine, and I see Father's hand trembling in midair as he thinks
about the fifteen sober years and about the doctors' warning, and
he tells himself, *Goddamnit, I am a free man*, and *Why can't a free man
drink one beer after a lifetime of hard work?* and I see his arm reaching, his fingers closing, the can tilting to his lips. I even supply a
label for the beer, a swaggering brand that promises on television
to deliver the essence of life. I watch the amber liquid pour down
his throat, the alcohol steal into his blood, the key turn in his brain.

Soon after my parents moved back to Father's treacherous stomp- 45
ing ground, my wife and I visited them in Mississippi with our
four-year-old daughter. Mother had been too distraught to warn
me about the return of the demons. So when I climbed out of the
car that bright July morning and saw my father napping in the
hammock, I felt uneasy, and when he lurched upright and blinked
his bloodshot eyes and greeted us in a syrupy voice, I was hurled
back into childhood.

"What's the matter with Papaw?" our daughter asked. 46
"Nothing," I said. "Nothing!" 47
Like a child again, I pretended not to see him in his stupor, 48
and behind my phony smile I grieved. On that visit and on the
few that remained before his death, once again I found bottles in
the workbench, bottles in the woods. Again his hands shook too
much for him to run a saw, to make his precious miniature furniture, to drive straight down back roads. Again he wound up in
the ditch, in the hospital, in jail, in the treatment center. Again he
shouted and wept. Again he lied. "I never touched a drop," he
swore. "Your mother's making it up."

I no longer fancied I could reason with the men whose names 49
I found on the bottles—Jim Beam, Jack Daniel's—but I was able
now to recall the cold statistics about alcoholism: ten million victims, fifteen million, twenty. And yet, in spite of my age, I reacted
in the same blind way as I had in childhood, by vainly seeking to
erase through my efforts whatever drove him to drink. I worked
on their place twelve and sixteen hours a day, in the swelter of
Mississippi summers, digging ditches, running electrical wires,
planting trees, mowing grass, building sheds, as though what
nagged at him was some list of chores, as though by taking his
worries upon my shoulders I could redeem him. I was flung back

into boyhood, acting as though my father would not drink himself to death if only I were perfect.

50   I failed of perfection; he succeeded in dying. To the end, he considered himself not sick but sinful. "Do you want to kill yourself?" I asked him. "Why not?" he answered. "Why the hell not? What's there to save?" To the end, he would not speak about his feelings, would not or could not give a name to the beast that was devouring him.

51   In silence, he went rushing off to the cliff. Unlike the biblical swine, however, he left behind a few of the demons to haunt his children. Life with him and the loss of him twisted us into shapes that will be familiar to other sons and daughters of alcoholics. My brother became a rebel, my sister retreated into shyness, I played the stalwart and dutiful son who would hold the family together. If my father was unstable, I would be a rock. If he squandered money on drink, I would pinch every penny. If he wept when drunk—and only when drunk—I would not let myself weep at all. If he roared at the Little League umpire for calling my pitches balls, I would throw nothing but strikes. Watching him flounder and rage, I came to dread the loss of control. I would go through life without making anyone mad. I vowed never to put in my mouth or veins any chemical that would banish my everyday self. I would never make a scene, never lash out at the ones I loved, never hurt a soul. Through hard work, relentless work, I would achieve something dazzling—in the classroom, on the basketball court, in the science lab, in the pages of books—and my achievement would distract the world's eyes from his humiliation. I would become a worthy sacrifice, and the smoke of my burning would please God.

52   It is far easier to recognize these twists in my character than to undo them. Work has become an addiction for me, as drink was an addiction for my father. Knowing this, my daughter gave me a placard for the wall: WORKAHOLIC. The labor is endless and futile, for I can no more redeem myself through work than I could redeem my father. I still panic in the face of other people's anger, because his drunken temper was so terrible. I shrink from causing sadness or disappointment even to strangers, as though I were still concealing the family shame. I still notice every twitch of emotion in those faces around me, having learned as a child to read the weather in faces, and I blame myself for their least pang

of unhappiness or anger. In certain moods I blame myself for everything. Guilt burns like acid in my veins.

I am moved to write these pages now because my own son, at the age of ten, is taking on himself the griefs of the world, and in particular the griefs of his father. He tells me that when I am gripped by sadness, he feels responsible; he feels there must be something he can do to spring me from depression, to fix my life and that crushing sense of responsibility is exactly what I felt at the age of ten in the face of my father's drinking. My son wonders if I, too, am possessed. I write, therefore, to drag into the light what eats at me—the fear, the guilt, the shame—so that my own children may be spared.

I still shy away from nightclubs, from bars, from parties where the solvent is alcohol. My friends puzzle over this, but it is no more peculiar than for a man to shy away from the lions' den after seeing his father torn apart. I took my own first drink at the age of twenty-one, half a glass of burgundy. I knew the odds of my becoming an alcoholic were four times higher than for the children of nonalcoholic fathers. So I sipped warily.

I still do—once a week, perhaps, a glass of wine, a can of beer, nothing stronger, nothing more. I listen for the turning of a key in my brain.

Content

1. This essay abounds in examples of alcoholism. Which examples are the most memorable? Are these also the most painful? The most powerful? Explain why.
2. Sanders says that in spite of all his "grown-up knowledge" of alcoholism, "I am still ten years old, my own son's age" (¶ 8) as he writes this essay. What does he mean by this? What kind of a character is Sanders in this essay? What kind of a character is his father? Is there any resemblance between father and son?

Strategies/Structures

3. Is Sanders writing for alcoholic readers? Their families? People unfamiliar with the symptoms of alcoholism? Or is he writing mostly for himself, to try to come to terms with the effects of his father's alcoholism on him then and now?

4. Each section of this essay (¶s 1–8, 9–14, 15–24, 25–31, 32–36, 37–44, 45–52, 53–55) focuses on a different sort of example. What are they, and why are they arranged in this particular order?

5. Why does Sanders wait until late in the essay (¶ 39) to discuss his father's sobriety, and then devote only three paragraphs to a state that lasted fifteen years?

Language

6. What is the tone of this essay? How does Sanders, one of the victims of alcoholism as both a child and an adult, avoid being full of self-pity? Is he angry at his father? How can you tell?

For Writing

7. "Father's drinking became the family secret," says Sanders (¶ 13). Every family has significant secrets. Explain one of your family secrets, illustrating its effects on various family members, particularly on yourself. If you wish to keep the secret, don't show your essay to anyone; the point of writing this is to help yourself understand or come to terms with the matter.

8. Define an economic, political, ecological, social, or personal problem (unemployment, waste disposal, AIDS, hunger, housing, racism, or another subject of your choice) so your readers can understand it from an unusual perspective—your own or that of your sources. Illustrate its causes, effects, or implications with several significant examples.

NANCY MAIRS

> Nancy Mairs (born, 1943) defies conventional autobiography as she defies conventional life. In her major works, *Plaintext* (1986), *Remembering the Bone House* (1989), and *Ordinary Time* (1993), and *Waist-high in the World* (1997), all autobiographical, this candid writer presents herself as bitchy, whiny, self-indulgent—but with a redeeming spirituality and wry humor. Married at nineteen, Mairs finished college (Wheaton, 1964), and bore two children. Her reaction to marriage and motherhood ("I didn't know how to do it") resulted in a suicidal mixture of agoraphobia and anorexia.

Hospitalized for six months, she has ever since coped with panic attacks and the worsening symptoms of multiple sclerosis. Yet she refuses to sentimentalize her physical state ("I hate it"), or to equate herself with MS: "I am not a disease. What I hate is not me but a disease."

In "On Being a Cripple" Mairs provides for an audience of healthy people a searing comprehensive definition of what it means to be "a cripple," the word she chooses to define herself— instead of "disabled," handicapped," or "differently abled." She examines head-on the symptoms from which those who can "pick up babies, play the piano" too often avert their eyes in embarrassment, ignorance, or fear. With humor and uncompromising integrity, this gutsy woman shows herself in action, grotesque ("I carry one arm bent in front of me, the fingers curled into a claw"), clumsy (falling over backward in a public toilet), fearful of others' pity: "If I had to have MS, by God I was going to do it well. This is a class act, ladies and gentlemen " In the process of explaining what it's like to live with MS, Mairs also shows what it's like to be a wife, a mother, a teacher, a writer. Her initial sense of "grief and fury and terror" has given way, over the years, to acceptance of the "change and loss" that are part of the human condition. Thus Mairs's thoroughly human definition of a particular disease expands to encompass a definition of what it means to be human.

On Being a Cripple

To escape is nothing. Not to escape is nothing.

LOUISE BOGAN

The other day I was thinking of writing an essay on being a cripple. I was thinking hard in one of the stalls of the women's room in my office building, as I was shoving my shirt into my jeans and tugging up my zipper. Preoccupied, I flushed, picked up my book bag, took my cane down from the hook, and unlatched the door. So many movements unbalanced me, and as I pulled the door open I fell over backward, landing fully clothed on the toilet seat with my legs splayed in front of me: the old beetle-on-its-back routine. Saturday afternoon, the building deserted, I was free to laugh aloud as I wriggled back to my feet, my voice bouncing off the yellowish tiles from all directions. Had anyone been there with me, I'd have been still and faint and hot with chagrin. I decided that it was high time to write the essay.

2   First, the matter of semantics. I am a cripple. I choose this word to name me. I choose from among several possibilities, the most common of which are "handicapped" and "disabled." I made the choice a number of years ago, without thinking, unaware of my motives for doing so. Even now, I'm not sure what those motives are, but I recognize that they are complex and not entirely flattering. People—crippled or not—wince at the word "cripple," as they do not at "handicapped" or "disabled." Perhaps I want them to wince. I want them to see me as a tough customer, one to whom the fates/gods/viruses have not been kind, but who can face the brutal truth of her existence squarely. As a cripple, I swagger.

3   But, to be fair to myself, a certain amount of honesty underlies my choice. "Cripple" seems to me a clean word, straightforward and precise. It has an honorable history, having made its first appearance in the Lindisfarne Gospel in the tenth century. As a lover of words, I like the accuracy with which it describes my condition: I have lost the full use of my limbs. "Disabled," by contrast, suggests any incapacity, physical or mental. And I certainly don't like "handicapped," which implies that I have deliberately been put at a disadvantage, by whom I can't imagine (my God is not a Handicapper General), in order to equalize chances in the great race of life. These words seem to me to be moving away from my condition, to be widening the gap between word and reality. Most remote is the recently coined euphemism "differently abled," which partakes of the same semantic hopefulness that transformed countries from "undeveloped" to "underdeveloped," then to "less developed," and finally to "developing" nations. People have continued to starve in those countries during the shift. Some realities do not obey the dictates of language.

4   Mine is one of them. Whatever you call me, I remain crippled. But I don't care what you call me, so long as it isn't "differently abled," which strikes me as pure verbal garbage designed, by its ability to describe anyone, to describe no one. I subscribe to George Orwell's thesis that "the slovenliness of our language makes it easier for us to have foolish thoughts." And I refuse to

participate in the degeneration of the language to the extent that I deny that I have lost anything in the course of this calamitous disease; I refuse to pretend that the only differences between you and me are the various ordinary ones that distinguish any one person from another. But call me "disabled" or "handicapped" if you like. I have long since grown accustomed to them; and if they are vague, at least they hint at the truth. Moreover, I use them myself. Society is no readier to accept crippledness than to accept death, war, sex, sweat, or wrinkles. I would never refer to another person as a cripple. It is the word I use to name only myself.

I haven't always been crippled, a fact for which I am soundly 5 grateful. To be whole of limb is, I know from experience, infinitely more pleasant and useful than to be crippled; and if that knowledge leaves me open to bitterness at my loss, the physical soundness I once enjoyed (though I did not enjoy it half enough) is well worth the occasional stab of regret. Though never any good at sports, I was a normally active child and young adult. I climbed trees, played hopscotch, jumped rope, skated, swam, rode my bicycle, sailed. I despised team sports, spending some of the wretchedest afternoons of my life, sweaty and humiliated, behind a field-hockey stick and under a basketball hoop. I tramped alone for miles along the bridle paths that webbed the woods behind the house I grew up in. I swayed through countless dim hours in the arms of one man or another under the scattered shot of light from mirrored balls, and gyrated through countless more as Tab Hunter and Johnny Mathis gave way to the Rolling Stones, Creedence Clearwater Revival, Cream. I walked down the aisle. I pushed baby carriages, changed tires in the rain, marched for peace.

When I was twenty-eight I started to trip and drop things. 6 What at first seemed my natural clumsiness soon became too pronounced to shrug off. I consulted a neurologist, who told me that I had a brain tumor. A battery of tests, increasingly disagreeable, revealed no tumor. About a year and a half later I developed a blurred spot in one eye. I had, at last, the episodes "disseminated in space and time" requisite for a diagnosis: multiple sclerosis. I have never been sorry for the doctor's initial misdiagnosis, however. For almost a week, until the negative results of tests were in, I thought that I was going to die right away. Every day for the past nearly ten years, then, has been a kind of gift. I accept all gifts.

7   Multiple sclerosis is a chronic degenerative disease of the central nervous system, in which the myelin that sheathes the nerves is somehow eaten away and scar tissue forms in its place, interrupting the nerves' signals. During its course, which is unpredictable and uncontrollable, one may lose vision, hearing, speech, the ability to walk, control of bladder and/or bowels, strength in any or all extremities, sensitivity to touch, vibration, and/or pain, potency, coordination of movements—the list of possibilities is lengthy and yes, horrifying. One may also lose one's sense of humor. That's the easiest to lose and the hardest to survive without.

8   In the past ten years, I have sustained some of these losses. Characteristic of MS are sudden attacks, called exacerbations, followed by remissions, and these I have not had. Instead, my disease has been slowly progressive. My left leg is now so weak that I walk with the aid of a brace and a cane; and for distances I use an Amigo, a variation on the electric wheelchair that looks rather like an electrified kiddie car. I no longer have much use of my left hand. Now my right side is weakening as well. I still have the blurred spot in my right eye. Overall, though, I've been lucky so far. My world has, of necessity, been circumscribed by my losses, but the terrain left me has been ample enough for me to continue many of the activities that absorb me: writing, teaching, raising children and cats and plants and snakes, reading, speaking publicly about MS and depression, even playing bridge with people patient and honorable enough to let me scatter cards every which way without sneaking a peek.

9   Lest I begin to sound like Pollyanna, however, let me say that I don't like having MS. I hate it. My life holds realities—harsh ones, some of them—that no right-minded human being ought to accept without grumbling. One of them is fatigue. I know of no one with MS who does not complain of bone-weariness; in a disease that presents an astonishing variety of symptoms, fatigue seems to be a common factor. I wake up in the morning feeling the way most people do at the end of a bad day, and I take it from there. As a result, I spend a lot of time *in extremis* and, impatient with limitation, I tend to ignore my fatigue until my body breaks down in some way and forces rest. Then I miss picnics, dinner parties, poetry readings, the brief visits of old friends from out of town. The offspring of a puritanical tradition of exceptional

venerability, I cannot view these lapses without shame. My life often seems a series of small failures to do as I ought.

I lead, on the whole, an ordinary life, probably rather like the 10 one I would have led had I not had MS. I am lucky that my predilections were already solitary, sedentary, and bookish—unlike the world-famous French cellist I have read about, or the young woman I talked with one long afternoon who wanted only to be a jockey. I had just begun graduate school when I found out something was wrong with me, and I have remained, interminably, a graduate student. Perhaps I would not have if I'd thought I had the stamina to return to a full-time job as a technical editor; but I've enjoyed my studies.

In addition to studying, I teach writing courses. I also teach 11 medical students how to give neurological examinations. I pick up freelance editing jobs here and there. I have raised a foster son and sent him into the world, where he has made me two grandbabies, and I am still escorting my daughter and son through adolescence. I go to Mass every Saturday. I am a superb, if messy, cook. I am also an enthusiastic laundress, capable of sorting a hamper full of clothes into five subtly differentiated piles, but a terrible housekeeper. I can do italic writing and, in an emergency, bathe an oil-soaked cat. I play a fiendish game of Scrabble. When I have the time and money, I like to sit on my front steps with my husband, drinking Amaretto and smoking a cigar, as we imagine our counterparts in Leningrad and make sure that the sun gets down once more behind the sharp childish scrawl of the Tucson Mountains.

This lively plenty has its bleak complement, of course, in all 12 the things I can no longer do. I will never run again, except in dreams, and one day I may have to write that I will never walk again. I like to go camping, but I can't follow George and the children along the trails that wander out of a campsite through the desert or into the mountains. In fact, even on the level I've learned never to check the weather or try to hold a coherent conversation: I need all my attention for my wayward feet. Of late, I have begun to catch myself wondering how people can propel themselves without canes. With only one usable hand, I have to select my clothing with care not so much for style as for ease of ingress and egress, and even so, dressing can be laborious. I can no longer do fine stitchery, pick up babies, play the piano, braid my hair. I am immobilized by acute attacks of depression, which may or may not be physiologically related to MS but are certainly its logical concomitant.

13   These two elements, the plenty and the privation, are never pure, nor are the delight and wretchedness that accompany them. Almost every pickle that I get into as a result of my weakness and clumsiness—and I get into plenty—is funny as well as maddening and sometimes painful. I recall one May afternoon when a friend and I were going out for a drink after finishing up at school. As we were climbing into opposite sides of my car, chatting, I tripped and fell, flat and hard, onto the asphalt parking lot, my abrupt departure interrupting him in mid-sentence. "Where'd you go?" he called as he came around the back of the car to find me hauling myself up by the door frame. "Are you all right?" Yes, I told him, I was fine, just a bit ratty, and we drove off to find a shady patio and some beer. When I got home an hour or so later, my daughter greeted me with "What have you done to yourself?" I looked down. One elbow of my white turtleneck with the green froggies, one knee of my white trousers, one white kneesock were bloodsoaked. We peeled off the clothes and inspected the damage, which was nasty enough but not alarming. That part wasn't funny: The abrasions took a long time to heal, and one got a little infected. Even so, when I think of my friend talking earnestly, suddenly, to the hot thin air while I dropped from his view as though through a trap door, I find the image as silly as something from a Marx Brothers movie.

14   I may find it easier than other cripples to amuse myself because I live propped by the acceptance and the assistance and, sometimes, the amusement of those around me. Grocery clerks tear my checks out of my checkbook for me, and sales clerks find chairs to put into dressing rooms when I want to try on clothes. The people I work with make sure I teach at times when I am least likely to be fatigued, in places I can get to, with the materials I need. My students, with one anonymous exception (in an end-of-the-semester evaluation), have been unperturbed by my disability. Some even like it. One was immensely cheered by the information that I paint my own fingernails; she decided, she told me, that if I could go to such trouble over fine details, she could

keep on writing essays. I suppose I became some sort of bright-fingered muse. She wrote good essays, too.

The most important struts in the framework of my existence, 15 of course, are my husband and children. Dismayingly few marriages survive the MS test, and why should they? Most twenty-two- and nineteen-year-olds, like George and me, can vow in clear conscience, after a childhood of chickenpox and summer colds, to keep one another in sickness and in health so long as they both shall live. Not many are equipped for catastrophe: the dismay, the depression, the extra work, the boredom that a degenerative disease can insinuate into a relationship. And our society, with its emphasis on fun and its association of fun with physical performance, offers little encouragement for a whole spouse to stay with a crippled partner. Children experience similar stresses when faced with a crippled parent, and they are more helpless, since parents and children can't usually get divorced. They hate, of course, to be different from their peers, and the child whose mother is tacking down the aisle of a school auditorium packed with proud parents like a Cape Cod dinghy in a stiff breeze jolly well stands out in a crowd. Deprived of legal divorce, the child can at least deny the mother's disability, even her existence, forgetting to tell her about recitals and PTA meetings, refusing to accompany her to stores or church or the movies, never inviting friends to the house. Many do.

But I've been limping along for ten years now, and so far 16 George and the children are still at my left elbow, holding tight. Anne and Matthew vacuum floors and dust furniture and haul trash and rake up dog droppings and button my cuffs and bake lasagna and Toll House cookies with just enough grumbling so I know that they don't have brain fever. And far from hiding me, they're forever dragging me by racks of fancy clothes or through teeming school corridors, or welcoming gaggles of friends while I'm wandering through the house in Anne's filmy pink babydoll pajamas. George generally calls before he brings someone home, but he does just as many dumb thankless chores as the children. And they all yell at me, laugh at some of my jokes, write me funny letters when we're apart—in short, treat me as an ordinary human being for whom they have some use. I think they like me. Unless they're faking. . . .

17   Faking. There's the rub. Tugging at the fringes of my consciousness always is the terror that people are kind to me only
because I'm a cripple. My mother almost shattered me once, with
that instinct mothers have—blind, I think, in this case, but un-
erring nonetheless—for striking blows along the fault-lines of
their children's hearts, by telling me, in an attack on my selfish-
ness, "We all have to make allowances for you, of course, because
of the way you are." From the distance of a couple of years, I have
to admit that I haven't any idea just what she meant, and I'm not
sure that she knew either. She was awfully angry. But at the time,
as the words thudded home, I felt my worst fear, suddenly realized. I could bear being called selfish: I am. But I couldn't bear the
corroboration that those around me were doing in fact what I'd
always suspected them of doing, professing fondness while
silently putting up with me because of the way I am. A cripple.
I've been a little cracked ever since.

18   Along with this fear that people are secretly accepting
shoddy goods comes a relentless pressure to please—to prove
myself worth the burdens I impose, I guess, or to build a substantial account of goodwill against which I may write drafts in times
of need. Part of the pressure arises from social expectations. In our
society, anyone who deviates from the norm had better find some
way to compensate. Like fat people, who are expected to be jolly,
cripples must bear their lot meekly and cheerfully. A grumpy
cripple isn't playing by the rules. And much of the pressure is self-
generated. Early on I vowed that, if I had to have MS, by God I
was going to do it well. This is a class act, ladies and gentlemen.
No tears, no recriminations, no faint-heartedness.

19   One way and another, then, I wind up feeling like Tiny Tim,
peering over the edge of the table at the Christmas goose, waving
my crutch, piping down God's blessing on us all. Only sometimes
I don't want to play Tiny Tim. I'd rather be Caliban, a most scurvy
monster. Fortunately, at home no one much cares whether I'm a
good cripple or a bad cripple as long as I make vichyssoise with
fair regularity. One evening several years ago, Anne was reading
at the dining-room table while I cooked dinner. As I opened a can
of tomatoes, the can slipped in my left hand and juice spattered
me and the counter with bloody spots. Fatigued and infuriated, I
bellowed, "I'm so sick of being crippled!" Anne glanced at me

over the top of her book. "There now," she said, "do you feel better?" "Yes," I said, "yes, I do." She went back to her reading. I felt better. That's about all the attention my scurviness ever gets.

Because I hate being crippled, I sometimes hate myself for being a cripple. Over the years I have come to expect—even accept—attacks of violent self-loathing. Luckily, in general our society no longer connects deformity and disease directly with evil (though a charismatic once told me that I have MS because a devil is in me) and so I'm allowed to move largely at will, even among small children. But I'm not sure that this revision of attitude has been particularly helpful. Physical imperfection, even freed of moral disapprobation, still defies and violates the ideal, especially for women, whose confinement in their bodies as objects of desire is far from over. Each age, of course, has its ideal, and I doubt that ours is any better or worse than any other. Today's ideal woman, who lives on the glossy pages of dozens of magazines, seems to be between the ages of eighteen and twenty-five; her hair has body, her teeth flash white, her breath smells minty, her underarms are dry, she has a career but is still a fabulous cook, especially of meals that take less than twenty minutes to prepare; she does not ordinarily appear to have a husband or children; she is trim and deeply tanned; she jogs, swims, plays tennis, rides a bicycle, sails, but does not bowl; she travels widely, even to out-of-the-way places like Finland and Samoa, always in the company of the ideal man, who possesses a nearly identical set of characteristics. There are a few exceptions. Though usually white and often blonde, she may be black, Hispanic, Asian, or Native American, so long as she is unusually sleek. She may be old, provided she is selling a laxative or is Lauren Bacall. If she is selling a detergent, she may be married and have a flock of strikingly messy children. But she is never a cripple.

Like many women I know, I have always had an uneasy relationship with my body. I was not a popular child, largely, I think now, because I was peculiar: intelligent, intense, moody, shy, given to unexpected actions and inexplicable notions and emotions. But as I entered adolescence, I believed myself unpopular because I was homely: my breasts too flat, my mouth too wide, my hips too narrow, my clothing never quite right in fit or style. I was not, in fact, particularly ugly, old photographs inform me, though

20

21

I was well off the ideal; but I carried this sense of self-alienation with me into adulthood, where it regenerated in response to the depredations of MS. Even with my brace I walk with a limp so pronounced that, seeing myself on the videotape of a television program on the disabled, I couldn't believe that anything but an inchworm could make progress humping along like that. My shoulders droop and my pelvis thrusts forward as I try to balance myself upright, throwing my frame into a bony S. As a result of contractures, one shoulder is higher than the other and I carry one arm bent in front of me, the fingers curled into a claw. My left arm and leg have wasted into pipe-stems, and I try always to keep them covered. When I think about how my body must look to others, especially to men, to whom I have been trained to display myself, I feel ludicrous, even loathsome.

22   At my age, however, I don't spend much time thinking about my appearance. The burning egocentricity of adolescence, which assures one that all the world is looking all the time, has passed, thank God, and I'm generally too caught up in what I'm doing to step back, as I used to, and watch myself as though upon a stage. I'm also too old to believe in the accuracy of self-image. I know that I'm not a hideous crone, that in fact, when I'm rested, well dressed, and well made up, I look fine. The self-loathing I feel is neither physically nor intellectually substantial. What I hate is not me but a disease.

23   I am not a disease.

24   And a disease is not—at least not singlehandedly—going to determine who I am, though at first it seemed to be going to. Adjusting to a chronic incurable illness, I have moved through a process similar to that outlined by Elizabeth Kübler-Ross in *On Death and Dying*. The major difference—and it is far more significant than most people recognize—is that I can't be sure of the outcome, as the terminally ill cancer patient can. Research studies indicate that, with proper medical care, I may achieve a "normal" life span. And in our society, with its vision of death as the ultimate evil, worse even than decrepitude, the response to such news is, "Oh well, at least you're not going to *die*." Are there worse things than dying? I think that there may be.

25   I think of two women I know, both with MS, both enough older than I to have served me as models. One took to her bed

several years ago and has been there ever since. Although she can sit in a high-backed wheelchair, because she is incontinent she refuses to go out at all, even though incontinent pants, which are readily available at any pharmacy, could protect her from embarrassment. Instead, she stays at home and insists that her husband, a small quiet man, a retired civil servant, stay there with her except for a quick weekly foray to the supermarket. The other woman, whose illness was diagnosed when she was eighteen, a nursing student engaged to a young doctor, finished her training, married her doctor, accompanied him to Germany when he was in the service, bore three sons and a daughter, now grown and gone. When she can, she travels with her husband; she plays bridge, embroiders, swims regularly; she works, like me, as a symptomatic-patient instructor of medical students in neurology. Guess which woman I hope to be.

At the beginning, I thought about having MS almost incessantly. And because of the unpredictable course of the disease, my thoughts were always terrified. Each night I'd get into bed wondering whether I'd get out again the next morning, whether I'd be able to see, to speak, to hold a pen between my fingers. Knowing that the day might come when I'd be physically incapable of killing myself, I thought perhaps I ought to do so right away, while I still had the strength. Gradually I came to understand that the Nancy who might one day lie inert under a bedsheet, arms and legs paralyzed, unable to feed or bathe herself, unable to reach out for a gun, a bottle of pills, was not the Nancy I was at present, and that I could not presume to make decisions for that future Nancy, who might well not want in the least to die. Now the only provision I've made for the future Nancy is that when the time comes— and it is likely to come in the form of pneumonia, friend to the weak and the old—I am not to be treated with machines and medications. If she is unable to communicate by then, I hope she will be satisfied with these terms.

Thinking all the time about having MS grew tiresome and intrusive, especially in the large and tragic mode in which I was accustomed to considering my plight. Months and even years went by without catastrophe (at least without one related to MS), and really I was awfully busy, what with George and children and snakes and students and poems, and I hadn't the time, let alone the inclination, to devote myself to being a disease. Too, the richer my life became, the funnier it seemed, as though there were some connection between largesse and laughter, and so my tragic stance began to waver until, even with the aid of a brace and cane, I couldn't hold it for very long at a time.

28   After several years I was satisfied with my adjustment. I had suffered my grief and fury and terror, I thought, but now I was at ease with my lot. Then one summer day I set out with George and the children across the desert for a vacation in California. Part way to Yuma I became aware that my right leg felt funny. "I think I've had an exacerbation," I told George. "What shall we do?" he asked. "I think we'd better get the hell to California," I said, "because I don't know whether I'll ever make it again." So we went on to San Diego and then to Orange, and up the Pacific Coast Highway to Santa Cruz, across to Yosemite, down to Sequoia and Joshua Tree, and so back over the desert to home. It was a fine two-week trip, filled with friends and fair weather, and I wouldn't have missed it for the world, though I did in fact make it back to California two years later. Nor would there have been any point in missing it, since in MS, once the symptoms have appeared, the neurological damage has been done, and there's no way to predict or prevent that damage.

29   The incident spoiled my self-satisfaction, however. It renewed my grief and fury and terror, and I learned that one never finishes adjusting to MS. I don't know now why I thought one would. One does not, after all, finish adjusting to life, and MS is simply a fact of my life—not my favorite fact, of course—but as ordinary as my nose and my tropical fish and my yellow Mazda station wagon. It may at any time get worse, but no amount of worry or anticipation can prepare me for a new loss. My life is a lesson in losses. I learn one at a time.

30   And I had best be patient in the learning, since I'll have to do it like it or not. As any rock fan knows, you can't always get what you want. Particularly when you have MS. You can't, for example, get cured. In recent years researchers and the organizations that fund research have started to pay MS some attention even though it isn't fatal; perhaps they have begun to see that life is something other than a quantitative phenomenon, that one may be very much alive for a very long time in a life that isn't worth living. The

researchers have made some progress toward understanding the mechanism of the disease: It may well be an autoimmune reaction triggered by a slow-acting virus. But they are nowhere near its prevention, control, or cure. And most of us want to be cured. Some, unable to accept incurability, grasp at one treatment after another, no matter how bizarre: megavitamin therapy, gluten-free diet, injections of cobra venom, hypothermal suits, lymphocyto-pharesis, hyperbaric chambers. Many treatments are probably harmless enough, but none are curative.

The absence of a cure often makes MS patients bitter toward   31 their doctors. Doctors are, after all, the priests of modern society, the new shamans, whose business is to heal, and many an MS patient roves from one to another, searching for the "good" doctor who will make him well. Doctors too think of themselves as healers, and for this reason many have trouble dealing with MS patients, whose disease in its intransigence defeats their aims and mocks their skills. Too few doctors, it is true, treat their patients as whole human beings, but the reverse is also true. I have always tried to be gentle with my doctors, who often have more at stake in terms of ego than I do. I may be frustrated, maddened, de-pressed by the incurability of my disease, but I am not dimin-ished by it, and they are. When I push myself up from my seat in the waiting room and stumble toward them, I incarnate the limi-tation of their powers. The least I can do is refuse to press on their tenderest spots.

This gentleness is part of the reason that I'm not sorry to be   32 a cripple. I didn't have it before. Perhaps I'd have developed it anyway—how could I know such a thing?—and I wish I had more of it, but I'm glad of what I have. It has opened and enriched my life enormously, this sense that my frailty and need must be mirrored in others, that in searching for and shaping a stable core in a life wrenched by change and loss, change and loss, I must rec-ognize the same process, under individual conditions, in the lives around me. I do not deprecate such knowledge, however I've come by it.

All the same, if a cure were found, would I take it? In a   33 minute. I may be a cripple, but I'm only occasionally a loony and never a saint. Anyway, in my brand of theology God doesn't give bonus points for a limp. I'd take a cure; I just don't need one. A friend who also has MS startled me once by asking, "Do you ever say to yourself, 'Why me, Lord?'" "No, Michael, I don't," I told him, "because whenever I try, the only response I can think of is 'Why not?'" If I could make a cosmic deal, who would I put in my place? What in my life would I give up in exchange for sound limbs and a thrilling rush of energy? No one. Nothing. I might as well do the job myself. Now that I'm getting the hang of it.

Content

1. Mairs uses a number of illustrations to compose her definition of "being a cripple," many of them involving physical failure or physical difficulty. Identify some of these. Given the fact that they represent recurring problems that will only get worse and will never be solved, how do you account for the ultimately positive, affirmative tone of the essay?
2. Mairs is very candid about her body, with which she has "always had an uneasy relationship" (¶ 21). What features of American culture and values cause people to be dissatisfied with their bodies? Is this as true of men as of women, of adults as well as teenagers? How has Mairs come to terms with her appearance, which is, in fact, continuing to deteriorate (¶ 22)? What could others, "crippled" or not, learn from her example?

Strategies/Structures

3. This essay involves considerable comparison and contrast, overt and implied, between being crippled and not crippled. Why is it important for Mairs to establish the fact that she "was a normally active child and young adult" (¶ 5)? How can we tell that she is writing for an audience "whole of limb," who will as they read be comparing their state with hers?
4. This essay is full of examples of Mairs in a variety of roles—wife, mother, friend, teacher, writer. What examples of activities does Mairs use to characterize herself in these roles as an adult with MS? Why are these varied examples important to her definition of "being crippled"?

Language

5. Why does Mairs choose for herself the label of "cripple" (¶s 2–4) rather than the alternative labels—"disabled," "handicapped," "differently abled"—that she rejects? Why does she put that word, sure to offend some readers, in the title?

6. Mairs wants our sympathetic understanding but not our pity. What language does she use to obtain this? What is her essay's prevailing tone? Is Mairs a person you'd like to know? Why or why not? Which of your reasons are related to her handicap?

For Writing

7. A disability of any kind makes the victim different from people without it. Mairs's essay shows the positive as well as negative effects of being different, and she also shows how these differences can be transcended, in spirit and in action. Have you ever felt different enough from your peers to be uncomfortable? If so, for mainstream readers, write a definition of "being different," and illustrate its effects, for better and/or worse. Make some connections between your case and larger groups. (see Lamott, "Polaroids" (72–77), for instance.)

8. Mairs says, "Every day for the past ten years," since her symptoms were diagnosed as MS rather than a malignant brain tumor, "has been a kind of gift" (¶ 6). If you (or someone you know well) have had an experience that has made you grateful for every day thereafter, explain the nature of that experience and show why its effects have been so profound.

NATE STULMAN

Stulman was a sophomore at Swarthmore College when he wrote "The Great Campus Goof-Off Machine," published as an op-ed article in the *New York Times*, March 15, 1999. To "question the wisdom" of supplying every college dorm room with "computers and the Internet," Stulman invites his readers to "take a walk through the residence halls of any college in the country." What they'll find becomes a series of illustrations that comprise most of the essay: students "playing Tomb Raider instead of going to chemistry class," students "tweaking the configurations of their machines instead of writing the paper due tomorrow," students "collecting mostly useless information from the World Wide Web instead of doing a math problem set," and students engaging in a host of other frivolous, nonacademic uses of the computer—playing games, collecting graphics or music, chatting by E-mail with people who live "10 feet down the hall." Stulman intends to provoke an argument by refusing to give the opposition equal time; he uses illustrations that reinforce the point of his cautionary tale.

❄ The Great Campus Goof-Off Machine

Swarthmore, Pa.

1   Conventional wisdom says that computers are a necessary tool for higher education. Many colleges and universities these days require students to have personal computers, and some factor the cost of one into tuition. A number of colleges have put high-speed Internet connections in every dorm room. But there are good reasons to question the wisdom of this preoccupation with computers and the Internet.

2   Take a walk through the residence halls of any college in the country and you'll find students seated at their desks, eyes transfixed on their computer monitors. What are they doing with their top-of-the-line PC's and high-speed T-1 Internet connections?

3   They are playing Tomb Raider instead of going to chemistry class, tweaking the configurations of their machines instead of writing the paper due tomorrow, collecting mostly useless information from the World Wide Web instead of doing a math problem set—a host of other activity that has little or nothing to do with traditional academic work.

4   I have friends who have spent whole weekends doing nothing but playing Quake or Warcraft or other interactive computer games. One friend sometimes spends entire evenings—six to eight hours—scouring the Web for images and modifying them just to have a new background on his computer desktop.

5   And many others I know have amassed overwhelming collections of music on their computers. It's the searching and finding that they seem to enjoy: some of them have more music files on their computers than they could play in months.

Several people who live in my hall routinely stay awake all 6
night chatting with dormmates on line. Why walk 10 feet down
the hall to have a conversation when you can chat on the computer—even if it takes three times as long?

You might expect that personal computers in dorm rooms 7
would be used for nonacademic purposes, but the problem is
not confined to residence halls. The other day I walked into the
library's reference department, and five or six students were
grouped around a computer—not conducting research, but playing Tetris. Every time I walk past the library's so-called research
computers, it seems that at least half are being used to play
games, chat or surf the Internet aimlessly.

Colleges and universities should be wary of placing such an 8
emphasis on the use of computers and the Internet. The Web may
be useful for finding simple facts, but serious research still means
a trip to the library.

For most students, having a computer in the dorm is more 9
of a distraction than a learning tool. Other than computer science
or mathematics majors, few students need more than a word processing program and access to E-mail in their rooms.

It is true, of course, that students have always procrastinated and 10
wasted time. But when students spend four, five, even ten hours
a day on computers and the Internet, a more troubling picture
emerges—a picture all the more disturbing because colleges
themselves have helped create the problem.

Content

1. What is Stulman's thesis? Is he justified in using only negative examples to illustrate it? Should an argument incorporate more balanced
evidence?

2. Is the computer the "great campus goof-off machine," as Stulman
says? Are there alternative labels that are more—or less—appropriate?
What are they?

3. Is Stulman accurate in saying, "Other than computer science or
mathematics majors, few students need more than a word processing
program and access to E-mail in their rooms" (¶ 9)? Explain your answer
with illustrations of students whose work and majors you know.

4. What does Stulman value in a college education? How can you tell?

Strategies/Structures

5. Although Stulman draws evidence for his argument from observing various students around his campus, he says nothing about his own use of computers. Why not?

6. Is Stulman justified in making assertions about "any college in the country" on the basis of his experience as a student at Swarthmore?

Language

7. Unusual for an essay on computers, Stulman writes without using any computer jargon. Should he have done so? Did you miss it?

For Writing

8. What does it mean to be computer literate? Address your essay to a particular group of computer users—highly specialized, moderately sophisticated, or novices—and make sure your illustrations and language are appropriate to the understanding of your audience.

9. Argue for or against the idea that given the rapid pace of technological change, college undergraduates shouldn't spend much time on the latest technological applications because these will soon become obsolete. Illustrate your argument with evidence of people and programs you know.

Additional Topics for Writing
Illustration and Example

(For strategies for writing with illustration and example, see 424)

1. Write an essay that takes as its thesis one of the general statements below, or your adaptation, variation, or disagreement with it. To make the point, use an extended illustration or several shorter ones, based on your own experience, reading, knowledge of history or current events, or other information. Assume that you have to convince a skeptical audience.

    a. Actions speak louder than words.
    b. To err is human.
    c. The only thing we have to fear is fear itself.
    d. And you shall know the truth and the truth shall set you free.
    e. Two heads are better than one.
    f. A house divided against itself cannot stand.
    g. You can lead a horse to water but you can't make him drink.
    h. Time is money.
    i. There never was a good war or a bad peace.
    j. The style is the person.
    k. Early to bed and early to rise, makes a man healthy, wealthy, and wise.
    l. Without justice, courage is weak.
    m. An ounce of prevention is worth a pound of cure.
    n. Self-love is the greatest of all flatterers.
    o. Those who can, do; those who can't, teach.
    p. Vision is the art of seeing things invisible.
    q. A little learning is a dangerous thing.
    r. Some books are to be tasted, others to be swallowed, and some few to be chewed and digested.
    s. Love is blind.
    t. Knowledge is power.
    u. All's fair in love and war.
    v. A winner never quits; a quitter never wins.

2. In an essay, for readers of the dominant ethnic majority, make a generalization about what it means (or meant) to be a member of an ethnic minority in the United States, either in the nineteenth or twentieth century, or before or after certain landmark events, such as the Civil War or the 1964 Civil Rights Act. Use illustrative examples from your own experience, from the experiences of people you know, from outside reading, or from

476   *Illustration and Example*

two or three of the following essays in *The Essay Connection:* Tan, "Mother Tongue," 17–25; Watanabe, "Selections from Student Writers' Notebooks," 117–118; Douglass, "Resurrection, 164–70; Cofer, "Casa," 179–86; Shange, "What Is It We Really Harvestin' Here?" 240–49; Zitkala-Sa, "School Days," 273–83; Liu, "Notes of a Native Speaker," 335–49; Tschannerl, "One Remembers Most What One Loves," 360–67; Lim, "Pomegrantes and English Education," 388–98; Yu, "Red and Black," 405–18; Wright, "The Power of Books," 425–35; Soto, "Black Hair," 436–41; King, Jr., "Letter from Birmingham Jail," 596–616; Guinier, "The Tyranny of the Majority," 616–24; Nocton, "Harvest of Gold," 675–83.

Or, write a comparable essay on what it means to be a writer, or to try to become a writer, for examples, see the essays in Chapters 1–4, and interview a writer you know, perhaps one of your teachers.

11 *Definition*

A definition can set limits or expand them. An objective definition may settle an argument; a subjective definition can provoke one. In either case, they answer the definer's fundamental question, What is X? The easiest way to define something is to identify it as a member of a class and then specify the characteristics that make it distinctive from all the other members of that class. You could define yourself as a "student," but that wouldn't be sufficient to discriminate between you as a college undergraduate and pupils in kindergarten, elementary, junior high, or high school, graduate students, or, for that matter, a person independently studying aardvarks, gourmet cooking, or the nature of the universe.

As you make any kind of writing more specific, you lower the level of abstraction, usually a good idea in definition. So you could identify—and thereby define—yourself by specifying "college student," or more specifically yet, your class status, "college freshman." That might be sufficient for some contexts, such as filling out an application blank. Or you might need to indicate where you go to school "at Cuyahoga Community College" or "Michigan State University." (Initials won't always work—readers might think MSU means Memphis State, or Mississippi, or Montana.)

But if you're writing an entire essay devoted to defining exactly what kind of student you are, a phrase or sentence will be insufficient, even if expanded to include "a computer science major" or "a business major with an accounting specialty, and a varsity diver." Although the details of that definition would separate and thereby distinguish you from, certainly, most other members of your class, they wouldn't convey the essence of what you as a person are like in your student role.

You could consider that sentence your core definition, and expand each key word into a separate paragraph to create an essay-length definition that could include "college student," "accounting major," and "varsity diver." By that still might not cover it. You could approach the subject through considering *cause-and-effect*. Why did you decide to go to college? Because you love to learn? Because you need to get specialized training for your chosen career? To get away from home? What have been the short-term effects of your decision to attend college? What are the long-term effects likely to be—on yourself, on your chosen field, perhaps on the world?

Or you might define yourself as a college student by *comparing and contrasting* your current life with that of a friend still in high school, or with someone who hasn't gone to college, or with a person you admire who has already graduated. If you work part- or full-time while attending college, you could write an *analysis* of its effect on your studying; or an *argument*, using yourself as an *extended example*, stating why it's desirable (or undesirable) for college students to work. Or, among many other possibilities, you could write a *narrative* of a typical week or semester at college. Each of these modes of writing could be an essay of definition. Each could be only partial, unless you wrote a book, for every definition is, by definition, selective. But each would serve your intended purpose. Each essay in this section represents a different common type of definition, but most use other types as well.

Definition According to Purpose. A definition according to purpose specifies the fundamental qualities an object, principle or policy, role, or literary or artistic work has—or should have—in order to fulfill its potential. Thus, such a definition might explicitly answer such questions as, What is the purpose of X? ("A parable is a simple story designed to teach a moral truth.") What is X for? ("Horror movies exist to scare the spectators.") Judy Brady's "I Want a Wife" (506–10) concentrates on two other aspects of definition according to purpose, What does X do? and What is the role of X? An ideal wife, says Brady, will serve as a wage-earner, secretary, housekeeper, "nurturant attendant" of the children, hostess, entertainer, and sexual companion, among other roles. Brady defines by both negative and positive examples: "I want a wife who will not bother me with rambling complaints about a wife's duties. But I want a wife who will listen to me when I feel the need to explain a rather difficult point I have come across in my course of studies." Because Brady is writing satirically, however, it is possible to interpret the positive examples as negative and vice versa, and still to agree with the emphatic conclusion of her definition, "My God, who *wouldn't* want a wife?"

Descriptive Definition. A descriptive definition identifies the distinctive characteristics of an individual or group that set it apart from others. Thus a descriptive definition may begin by *naming* something, answering the question, What is X called? A possible answer might be Eudora Welty (unique among all other women); a walnut (as opposed to all other species of nuts); or *The Sound and the Fury* (and no other novel by William Faulkner). A descriptive definition may also *specify the relationship among the parts of a unit or group*, responding to the questions, What is the structure of X? How is X organized? How is X put together or constituted? Jasmine Innerarity, in "Code Blue" (520–25) claims that Code Blue is "well organized and well executed."

Logical Definitions. Logical definitions answer two related questions: Into what general category does X fall? and How does it differ from all other members of that category? ("A porpoise is a marine mammal but differs from whales, seals, dolphins, and the others in its. . . .") Logical definitions are often used in scientific and philosophical writing, and indeed form the basis for the functional definition Howard Gardner presents in "Who Owns Intelligence?" (491–506).

There are five key principles for writing logical definitions:

1. For economy's sake, use the most specific category to which the item to be defined belongs, rather than broader categories. Thus Gardner confines his discussion to human beings, not animals nor even all primates.
2. Any division of a class must include all members of that class. *Negative definitions* explain what is excluded from a given classification and what is not.
3. Subdivisions must be smaller than the class divided. Intelligence, says Gardner, can be divided into various functional categories: "linguistic and logical-mathematical, musical, spatial, bodily-kinesthetic, naturalist, interpersonal, and intrapersonal."

4. Categories should be mutually exclusive; they should not overlap.
5. The basis for subdividing categories must be consistent throughout each stage of subdivision. Thus, claiming that Daniel Goleman, in his "otherwise admirable *Emotional Intelligence*," confuses emotional intelligence with "certain preferred patterns of behavior," Gardner prefers the term "emotional sensitivity" because this includes both "interpersonal and intrapersonal intelligences" and therefore applies to "people who are sensitive to emotions in themselves and in others."

Essential or Existential Definition.   An essential definition might be considered a variation of a descriptive definition as it answers the question, "What is the essence, the fundamental nature of X?"—love, beauty, truth, justice, for instance. An existential definition presents the essence of its subject by answering the question, "What does it mean to be X?" or "What does it mean to live as an X" or "in a state of X?"—perhaps Chinese, supremely happy, married, an AIDS victim, handicapped. Gary Soto's "Black Hair" (510–20) tells the story of a desperate runaway teenager who is living a life that provides a cluster of definitions learned the hard way from working at a particularly ugly menial, minimum-wage job. As he worked, living on the edge, refurbishing used tires for resale—lifting, hauling, buffing, grinding tires with machinery that could abrade fingers the same way it ground down tires—he came to understand in this degrading context the meanings of poverty, isolation, minority status, dirtiness, feelings of worthlessness, and social ostracism. Each definition is illustrated in revealing details or incidents, the meanings of which are summed up in "Nothing changes. You continue on in rags, with the sun still above you." Every detail becomes a form of protest.

Process Definitions.   These are concerned with how things or phenomena get to be the way they are. How is X produced? What causes X? How does it work? What does it do, or not do? With what effects? How does change affect X itself? Such questions are often the basis for scientific definitions, as Lewis Thomas's "The Technology of Medicine" (375–81) and Charles Darwin's "Understanding Natural Selection" (483–90) illustrate. Darwin's definition is composed of a series of illustrations of natural phenomena and processes (such as stags' horns, cocks' spurs, lions' manes, male peacocks' plumage) that lead to demonstrable effects, such as the propagation and survival of the species. The two essays on "Code Blue" provide very different definitions of a dramatic medical process. In "Code Blue: The Process," Jasmine Innerarity carefully explains, from her experience as a pediatric oncology nurse, the conditions for calling a "Code Blue," "the alert signal for a patient who has stopped breathing or whose heart has stopped." She identifies the medical personnel summoned in the process, the equipment needed, the processes involved ("sedating and intubating the patient"), the speed required, the decisions to be made (to take a patient to the operating room, or off a respirator), and the likely outcomes. Innerarity's language, precise and careful, identifies medical crises and explains the medical team's appropriate reactions—definition in the abstract. "Code Blue: The Story," Dr. Abraham Verghese's fast-paced narrative, takes readers into the emergency room for a breathless re-enactment of the race to snatch life from death—definition in action.

Ultimately, when you're writing an extended definition, you'll need to make it as clear, real, and understandable as possible. You could define a dog as "a clawed, domesticated carnivorous mammal, *Canis familiaris.*" But would that abstract, technical definition get at your intended focus on working dogs (for instance, sheepherding border collies or seeing-eye German shepherds), or convey the essence of the family setter, Serendipity, who rescued you from drowning when you were five and has been your security blanket ever since? Your choices of specific details, illustrations, analogies, anecdotes, and the like will enable your readers to accept your definition, the ways you see the subject, the boundaries you set.

STRATEGIES FOR WRITING— DEFINITION

1. What is the purpose of the definition (or definitions) I'm writing about? Do I want to explain the subject's particular characteristics? Identify its nature? Persuade readers of my interpretation of its meaning? Entertain readers with a novel, bizarre, or highly personal meaning? How

long will my essay be? (A short essay will require a restricted subject that you can cover in the limited space.)

2. For whom am I providing the definition? Why are they reading it? Do they know enough about the background of the subject to enable me to deal with it in a fairly technical way? Or must I stick to the basics—or at least begin there? If I wish to persuade or entertain my readers, can I count on them to have a pre-existing definition in mind against which I can match my own?

3. Will my entire essay be a definition, or will I incorporate definition(s) as part of a different type of essay? What proportion of my essay will be devoted to definition? Where will I include definitions? As I introduce new terms or concepts? Where else, if at all?

4. What techniques of definition will I use: naming; providing examples, brief or extended; comparing and contrasting; considering cause and effect; analysis; argument; narrative; analogy; or a mixture? Will I employ primarily positive or negative means (i.e., X is, or X is not)?

5. How much denotative (objective) definition will I use in my essay? How much connotative (subjective) definition? Will my tone be serious? Authoritative? Entertaining? Sarcastic? Or otherwise?

CHARLES DARWIN

Darwin (1809–1882) descended from a distinguished British scientific family; his father was a physician, and his grandfather was the renowned Erasmus Darwin, amateur naturalist. As a youth Darwin was most alert when studying natural phenomena, particularly beetles, even popping a rare specimen into his mouth to preserve it when his hands were full of other newly collected insects. So, despite his lackadaisical study of medicine at Edinburgh University (1825–1828) and equally indifferent preparation for the clergy at Cambridge (B.A., 1831), he shipped aboard the HMS *Beagle* on a scientific expedition around South America, 1831–1836. As the ship's naturalist, he recorded careful observations of plants, animals, and human behavior that were published in *The Voyage of the Beagle* (1839), and eventually led to his theories of natural selection (roughly translated as "the survival of the fittest") and evolution. The publication of the earthshaking *On the Origin of Species by Means of Natural Selection, or the Preservation of Favored Races in the Struggle for Life* (1859) was based on his painstaking observations of animals and plants, on land and sea and in the air.

"Understanding Natural Selection," a small portion of this work, contains the essence of Darwin's best-known and most revolutionary principles, that in natural selection those variations, "infinitesimally small inherited modifications," endure if they aid in survival. The claim that these modifications occur gradually, rather than being produced at a single stroke by a divine creator, is the basis for Darwin's theory of evolution, extended to humans in *The Descent of Man* (1871). Darwin's theories provoked the enormous controversy between theologians and scientists that continues to this day—as Gould's "Evolution as Fact and Theory" (550–60) makes clear.

Darwin's work continues to be read, as much for its clear and elegant literary style as for its content. Using the techniques of popular literature to explain sophisticated scientific concepts and to present mountains of detailed information, Darwin is a highly engaging writer. He uses the first person, metaphors, anecdotes, and numerous illustrations that overlap and reinforce one another—here as ways to define his subject. Because he is explaining a theory and concepts totally new to his audience, he has to ground them in the reality of numerous natural phenomena that can be seen and studied.

Understanding Natural Selection

1   I t may be said that natural selection is daily and hourly scruti-
nizing, throughout the world, every variation, even the slightest; rejecting that which is bad, preserving and adding up all that
is good; silently and insensibly working, whenever and wherever
opportunity offers, at the improvement of each organic being in
relation to its organic and inorganic conditions of life. We see
nothing of these slow changes in progress, until the hand of time
has marked the long lapses of ages, and then so imperfect is our
view into long past geological ages, that we only see that the
forms of life are now different from what they formerly were.

2   Although natural selection can act only through and for the
good of each being, yet characters and structures, which we are apt
to consider as of very trifling importance, may thus be acted on.
When we see leaf-eating insects green, and bark-feeders mottled-
grey; the alpine ptarmigan white in winter, the red-grouse the
color of heather, and the black-grouse that of peaty earth, we must
believe that these tints are of service to these birds and insects in
preserving them from danger. Grouse, if not destroyed at some
period of their lives, would increase in countless numbers; they
are known to suffer largely from birds of prey; and hawks are
guided by eyesight to their prey—so much so, that on parts of the
Continent persons are warned not to keep white pigeons, as being
the most liable to destruction. Hence I can see no reason to doubt
that natural selection might be most effective in giving the proper
color to each kind of grouse, and in keeping that color, when once
acquired, true and constant. Nor ought we to think that the occasional destruction of an animal of any particular color would produce little effect: we should remember how essential it is in a
flock of white sheep to destroy every lamb with the faintest trace
of black. In plants the down on the fruit and the color of the flesh
are considered by botanists as characters of the most trifling importance: yet we hear from an excellent horticulturist, Downing,
that in the United States smooth-skinned fruits suffer far more
from a beetle, a curculio, than those with down; that purple
plums suffer far more from a certain disease than yellow plums;
whereas another disease attacks yellow-fleshed peaches far more
than those with other colored flesh. If, with all the aids of art,

these slight differences make a great difference in cultivating the several varieties, assuredly, in a state of nature, where the trees would have to struggle with other trees and with a host of enemies, such differences would effectually settle which variety, whether a smooth or downy, a yellow or purple fleshed fruit, should succeed.

In looking at many small points of difference between species, which, as far as our ignorance permits us to judge, seem to be quite unimportant, we must not forget that climate, food, and so on probably produce some slight and direct effect. It is, however, far more necessary to bear in mind that there are many unknown laws of correlation to growth, which, when one part of the organization is modified through variation, and the modifications are accumulated by natural selection for the good of the being, will cause other modifications, often of the most unexpected nature.

As we see that those variations which under domestication appear at any particular period of life, tend to reappear in the offspring of the same period; for instance, in the seeds of the many varieties of our culinary and agricultural plants; in the caterpillar and cocoon stages of the varieties of the silkworm; in the eggs of poultry, and in the color of the down of their chickens; in the horns of our sheep and cattle when nearly adult; so in a state of nature, natural selection will be enabled to act on and modify organic beings at any age, by the accumulation of profitable variations at that age, and by their inheritance at a corresponding age. If it profit a plant to have its seeds more and more widely disseminated by the wind, I can see no greater difficulty in this being effected through natural selection, than in the cotton-planter increasing and improving by selection the down in the pods on his cotton-trees. Natural selection may modify and adapt the larva of an insect to a score of contingencies, wholly different from those which concern the mature insect. These modifications will no doubt affect, through the laws of correlation, the structure of the adult; and probably in the case of those insects which live only for a few hours, and which never feed, a large part of their structure is merely the correlated result of successive changes in the structure of their larvae. So, conversely, modifications in the adult will probably often affect the structure of the larva; but in all cases natural selection will ensure that modifications consequent on other modifications at a different period of life, shall not be in the least degree injurious: for if they became so, they would cause the extinction of the species.

5   Natural selection will modify the structure of the young in relation to the parent, and of the parent in relation to the young. In social animals it will adapt the structure of each individual for the benefit of the community; if each in consequence profits by the selected change. What natural selection cannot do, is to modify the structure of one species, without giving it any advantage, for the good of another species; and though statements to this effect may be found in works of natural history, I cannot find one case which will bear investigation. A structure used only once in an animal's whole life, if of high importance to it, might be modified to any extent by natural selection; for instance, the great jaws possessed by certain insects, and used exclusively for opening the cocoon—or the hard tip to the beak of nestling birds, used for breaking the egg. It has been asserted, that of the best short-beaked tumbler pigeons more perish in the egg than are able to get out of it; so that fanciers assist in the act of hatching. Now, if nature had to make the beak of a full-grown pigeon very short for the bird's own advantage, the process of modification would be very slow, and there would be simultaneously the most rigorous selection of the young birds within the egg, which had the most powerful and hardest beaks, for all with weak beaks would in-evitably perish: or, more delicate and more easily broken shells might be selected, the thickness of the shell being known to vary like every other structure.

Sexual Selection

6   Inasmuch as peculiarities often appear under domestication in one sex and become hereditarily attached to that sex, the same fact probably occurs under nature, and if so, natural selection will be able to modify one sex in its functional relations to the other sex, or in relation to wholly different habits of life in the two sexes, as is sometimes the case with insects. And this leads me to say a few words on what I call sexual selection. This depends, not on a struggle for existence, but on a struggle between the males for possession of the females; the result is not death to the unsuc-cessful competitor, but few or no offspring. Sexual selection is,

therefore, less rigorous than natural selection. Generally, the most vigorous males, those which are best fitted for their places in nature, will leave most progeny. But in many cases, victory will depend not on general vigor, but on having special weapons, confined to the male sex. A hornless stag or spurless cock would have a poor chance of leaving offspring. Sexual selection by always allowing the victor to breed might surely give indomitable courage, length to the spur, and strength to the wing to strike in the spurred leg, as well as the brutal cock-fighter, who knows well that he can improve his breed by careful selection of the best cocks. How low in the scale of nature this law of battle descends, I know not; male alligators have been described as fighting, bellowing, and whirling round, like Indians in a war dance, for the possession of the females; male salmons have been seen fighting all day long; male stag-beetles often bear wounds from the huge mandibles of other males. The war is, perhaps, severest between the males of polygamous animals, and these seem oftenest provided with special weapons. The males of carnivorous animals are already well armed; though to them and to others, special means of defence may be given through means of sexual selection, as the mane to the lion, the shoulder-pad to the boar, and the hooked jaw to the male salmon, for the shield may be as important for victory, as the sword or spear.

Amongst birds, the contest is often of a more peaceful char- 7 acter. All those who have attended to the subject, believe that there is the severest rivalry between the males of many species to attract by singing the females. The rock-thrush of Guiana, birds of Paradise, and some others, congregate; and successive males display their gorgeous plumage and perform strange antics before the females, which standing by as spectators, as last choose the most attractive partner. Those who have closely attended to birds in confinement well know that they often take individual preferences and dislikes: thus Sir R. Heron has described how one pied peacock was eminently attractive to all his hen birds. It may appear childish to attribute any effect to such apparently weak means: I cannot here enter on the details necessary to support this view; but if man can in a short time give elegant carriage and beauty to his bantams, according to his standard of beauty, I can see no good reason to doubt that female birds, by selecting, during thousands of generations, the most melodious or beautiful males, according to their standard of beauty, might produce a marked effect. I strongly suspect that some well-known laws with respect to the plumage of male and female birds, in comparison with the plumage of the young, can be explained on the view of plumage having been chiefly modified by sexual selection, acting when the birds have come to the breeding age or during the breeding season; the modifications thus produced being inherited at corresponding ages or seasons, either by the males alone, or by the males and females; but I have not space here to enter on this subject.

8   Thus it is, as I believe, that when the males and females of any animal have the same general habits of life, but differ in structure, color, or ornament, such differences have been mainly caused by sexual selection; that is, individual males have had, in successive generations, some slight advantage over other males, in their weapons, means of defence, or charms; and have transmitted these advantages to their male offspring. Yet, I would not wish to attribute all such sexual differences to this agency: for we see peculiarities arising and becoming attached to the male sex in our domestic animals (as the wattle in male carriers, horn-like protuberances in the cocks of certain fowls, and so on), which we cannot believe to be either useful to the males in battle, or attractive to the females. We see analogous cases under nature, for instance, the tuft of hair on the breast of the turkey-cock, which can hardly be either useful or ornamental to this bird; indeed, had the tuft appeared under domestication, it would have been called a monstrosity.

Illustration of the Action of Natural Selection

9   . . . Let us take the case of a wolf, which preys on various animals, securing some by craft, some by strength, and some by fleetness; and let us suppose that the fleetest prey, a deer for instance, had from any change in the country increased in numbers, or that other prey had decreased in numbers, during that season of the year when the wolf is hardest pressed for food. I can under such circumstances see no reason to doubt that the swiftest and slimmest wolves would have the best chance of surviving, and so be preserved or selected—provided always that they retain strength to master their prey at this or at some other period of the year, when

they might be compelled to prey on other animals. I can see no more reason to doubt this, than that man can improve the fleetness of his greyhounds by careful and methodical selection, or by that unconscious selection which results from each man trying to keep the best dogs without any thought of modifying the breed.

Even without any change in the proportional numbers of the animals on which our wolf preyed, a cub might be born with an innate tendency to pursue certain kinds of prey. Nor can this be thought very improbable; for we often observe great differences in the natural tendencies of our domestic animals; one cat, for instance, taking to catch rats, another mice; one cat . . . bringing home winged game, another hares or rabbits, and another hunting on marshy ground and almost nightly catching woodcocks or snipes. The tendency to catch rats rather than mice is known to be inherited. Now, if any slight innate change of habit or of structure benefited an individual wolf, it would have the best chance of surviving and of leaving offspring. Some of its young would probably inherit the same habits or structure, and by the repetition of this process, a new variety might be formed which would either supplant or coexist with the parent-form of wolf. Or, again, the wolves inhabiting a mountainous district, and those frequenting the lowlands, would naturally be forced to hunt different prey; and from the continued preservation of the individuals best fitted for the two sites, two varieties might slowly be formed. These varieties would cross and blend where they met; but to this subject of intercrossing we shall soon have to return. I may add, that . . . there are two varieties of the wolf inhabiting the Catskill Mountains in the United States, one with a light greyhoundlike form, which pursues deer, and the other more bulky, with shorter legs, which more frequently attacks the shepherd's flocks.

Content

1. What does Darwin mean by "natural selection" (¶s 1–5)? How does "natural selection" differ from "sexual selection" (¶s 6–8)?

2. Although Darwin doesn't use the term "evolution," this piece clearly illustrates that concept. Define that term, using some of Darwin's illustrations. Does your definition anticipate creationists' objections? Should it? If you believe in creationism, how does this belief influence the way you define "evolution"?

3. Distinguish between theory, opinion, and fact in Darwin's presentation of the concepts of natural selection (¶s 1–5, 9–10).

Strategies/Structures

4. Darwin offers arguments on behalf of both natural selection and sexual selection. Which argument has the better supporting evidence? Which argument makes its case more compellingly? Why?

5. Darwin builds his case for the existence of natural selection by using numerous illustrations. Identify some. Explain how an argument can also, as in this case, be a definition.

6. What kind of authorial persona does Darwin present? In what ways is this "scientist figure" familiar today? How does this persona differ from the stereotype of the "mad scientist"?

Language

7. Is Darwin writing for an audience of other scientists? For a general readership? Or for both? What aspects of his language (choice of vocabulary, familiar or unfamiliar language and illustrations), tone, and sentence structure reinforce your answer?

8. Are there features of Darwin's language, and sentence and paragraph structure, that indicates that this excerpt was written in the nineteenth rather than the twentieth century? Illustrate your answer.

For Writing

9. Write a definition of something (a natural phenomenon, human or animal behavior you have observed carefully over time) for an audience of nonscientists. If you are writing about the behavior of college students in a particular type of situation—for example, some aspect(s) of test-taking, dating, dressing, eating—record your observations in as objective and "scientific" a manner as you can.

10. Every definition is an argument, overt or implied, for the definer's particular way of looking at the subject (for example, see Gould's "Evolution as Fact and Theory" [550–60]). For readers who might disagree with you, write a controversial definition of a subject about which you feel passionate—friendship, love, marriage, violence, war, an ideal—you name it (place to live, job to have, family life, public policy). If you are dealing in abstractions, as you are likely to do in an extended definition, you will need to shore up your generalizations with specific information and illustrations.

HOWARD GARDNER

Gardner was born in 1943 to parents who had fled Nazi Germany five years earlier and emigrated to Scranton, Pennsylvania. He studied cognitive and social psychology at Harvard (B.A., 1965, Ph.D., 1971) and with David Perkins became codirector of Project Zero at the Harvard Graduate School of Education, studying the ways children and adults learn. He is currently the Hobbs Professor in Cognition and Education at Harvard and an adjunct research professor of neurology at Boston University School of Medicine.

Gardner has written nineteen books and hundreds of articles, most of them focusing on creativity and intelligence. In his best known book, *Frames of Mind: The Theory of Multiple Intelligences* (1983), he postulates that there are seven distinct cognitive realms in the human brain and that each governs a particular kind of intelligence. Those intelligences most commonly considered— and tested—by the American educational establishment are *linguistic,* the ability to communicate through language, and *logical-mathematical,* the ability to come up with and use abstract concepts. To these Gardner adds five other intelligences: *spatial,* the ability to perceive and re-image the physical world; *bodily-kinesthetic,* the ability to use the body in skilled or creative ways; *musical,* the ability to distinguish, remember, and manipulate tone, melody, and rhythm; *interpersonal,* the ability to understand other people; and *intrapersonal,* the ability to understand one's self and have a conscious awareness of one's emotions. A decade later Gardner added an eighth intelligence, *naturalist,* the ability to have an intuitive understanding about plants and animals. Despite criticism from people who say Gardner's multiple intelligences are really talents (something we can get along without, as opposed to traditionally defined intelligence, which is indispensable) and that they can't be easily measured, to many educators he evokes "the reverence teenagers lavish on a rock star." "Who Owns Intelligence?" first published in the *Atlantic Monthly* in February 1999, addresses these issues in attempting, once again, to pin down intelligence and who owns it—a particularly significant issue as the twenty-first century grapples with expanding concepts of intellectual property, ranging from book manuscripts, musical compositions, and mechanical inventions to web sites, applications of gene therapy, and esoteric chemical and technical processes.

Who Owns Intelligence?

1   A lmost a century ago Alfred Binet, a gifted psychologist, was asked by the French Ministry of Education to help determine who would experience difficulty in school. Given the influx of provincials to the capital, along with immigrants of uncertain stock, Parisian officials believed they needed to know who might not advance smoothly through the system. Proceeding in an empirical manner, Binet posed many questions to youngsters of different ages. He ascertained which questions when answered correctly predicted success in school, and which questions when answered incorrectly foretold school difficulties. The items that discriminated most clearly between the two groups became, in effect, the first test of intelligence.

2   Binet is a hero to many psychologists. He was a keen observer, a careful scholar, an inventive technologist. Perhaps even more important for his followers, he devised the instrument that is often considered psychology's greatest success story. Millions of people who have never heard Binet's name have had aspects of their fate influenced by instrumentation that the French psychologist inspired. And thousands of psychometricians—specialists in the measurement of psychological variables—earn their living courtesy of Binet's invention.

3   Although it has prevailed over the long run, the psychologists' version of intelligence is now facing its biggest threat. Many scholars and observers—and even some iconoclastic psychologists—feel that intelligence is too important to be left to the psychometricians. Experts are extending the breadth of the concept—proposing many intelligences, including emotional intelligence and moral intelligence. They are experimenting with new methods of ascertaining intelligence, including some that avoid tests altogether in favor of direct measures of brain activity. They are forcing citizens everywhere to confront a number of questions: What is intelligence? How ought it to be assessed? And how do our notions of intelligence fit with what we value about human beings? In short, experts are competing for the "ownership" of intelligence in the next century.

4   The outline of the psychometricians' success story is well known. Binet's colleagues in England and Germany contributed to the

conceptualization and instrumentation of intelligence testing—which soon became known as IQ tests. (An IQ, or intelligence quotient, designates the ratio between mental age and chronological age. Clearly we'd prefer that a child in our care have an IQ of 120, being smarter than average for his or her years, than an IQ of 80, being older than average for his or her intelligence). Like other Parisian fashions of the period, the intelligence test migrated easily to the United States. First used to determine who was "feeble-minded," it was soon used to assess "normal" children, to identify the "gifted," and to determine who was fit to serve in the Army. By the 1920s the intelligence test had become a fixture in educational practice in the United States and much of Western Europe.

Early intelligence tests were not without their critics. Many 5 enduring concerns were first raised by the influential journalist Walter Lippmann, in a series of published debates with Lewis Terman, of Stanford University, the father of IQ testing in America. Lippmann pointed out the superficiality of the questions, their possible cultural biases, and the risks of trying to determine a person's intellectual potential with a brief oral or paper-and-pencil measure.

Perhaps surprisingly, the conceptualization of intelligence 6 did not advance much in the decades following Binet's and Terman's pioneering contributions. Intelligence tests came to be seen, rightly or wrongly, as primarily a tool for selecting people to fill academic or vocational niches. In one of the most famous —if irritating—remarks about intelligence testing, the influential Harvard psychologist E. G. Boring declared, "Intelligence is what the tests test." So long as these tests did what they were supposed to do (that is, give some indication of school success), it did not seem necessary or prudent to probe too deeply into their meaning or to explore alternative views of the human intellect.

Psychologists who study intelligence have argued chiefly 7 about three questions. The first: Is intelligence singular, or does it consist of various more or less independent intellectual faculties? The purists—ranging from the turn-of-the-century English psychologist Charles Spearman to his latter-day disciples Richard J. Herrnstein and Charles Murray (of *The Bell Curve* fame)—defend the notion of a single overarching "g," or general intelligence. The pluralists—ranging from L. L. Thurstone, of the University of Chicago, who posited seven vectors of the mind, to J. P. Guilford, of the University of Southern California, who discerned 150 factors of the intellect—construe intelligence as composed of some or even many dissociable components. In his much cited *The Mismeasure of Man* (1981) the paleontologist Stephen Jay Gould argued that the conflicting conclusions reached on this issue reflect alternative assumptions about statistical procedures rather than the way the mind is. Still, psychologists continue the debate, with a majority sympathetic to the general-intelligence perspective.

8   The public is more interested in the second question: Is intelligence (or are intelligences) largely inherited? This is by and large a Western question. In the Confucian societies of East Asia individual differences in endowment are assumed to be modest, and differences in achievement are thought to be due largely to effort. In the West, however, many students of the subject sympathize with the view—defended within psychology by Lewis Terman, among others—that intelligence is inborn and one can do little to alter one's intellectual birthright.

9   Studies of identical twins reared apart provide surprisingly strong support for the "heritability" of psychometric intelligence. That is, if one wants to predict someone's score on an intelligence test, the scores of the biological parents (even if the child has not had appreciable contact with them) are more likely to prove relevant than the scores of the adoptive parents. By the same token, the IQs of identical twins are more similar than the IQs of fraternal twins. And, contrary to common sense (and political correctness), the IQs of biologically related people grow closer in the later years of life. Still, because of the intricacies of behavioral genetics and the difficulties of conducting valid experiments with human child-rearing, a few defend the proposition that intelligence is largely environmental rather than heritable, and some believe that we cannot answer the question at all.

10   Most scholars agree that even if psychometric intelligence is largely inherited, it is not possible to pinpoint the sources of differences in average IQ between groups, such as the fifteen-point difference typically observed between African-American and white populations. That is because in our society the contemporary—let alone the historical—experiences of these two groups cannot be equated. One could ferret out the differences (if any) between black and white populations only in a society that was truly color-blind.

One other question has intrigued laypeople and psychol- 11
ogists: Are intelligence tests biased? Cultural assumptions are
evident in early intelligence tests. Some class biases are obvious—
who except the wealthy could readily answer a question about
polo? Others are more subtle. Suppose the question is what one
should do with money found on the street. Although ordinarily
one might turn it over to the police, what if one had a hungry
child? Or what if the police force were known to be hostile to
members of one's ethnic group? Only the canonical response to
such a question would be scored as correct.

Psychometricians have striven to remove the obviously 12
biased items from such measures. But biases that are built into the
test situation itself are far more difficult to deal with. For example,
a person's background affects his or her reaction to being placed
in an unfamiliar locale, being instructed by someone dressed in a
certain way, and having a printed test booklet thrust into his or her
hands. And as the psychologist Claude M. Steele has argued in
these pages (see "Race and the Schooling of Black Americans,"
April, 1992), the biases prove even more acute when people know
that their academic potential is being measured and that their
racial or ethnic group is widely considered to be less intelligent
than the dominant social group. . . .

Paradoxically, one of the clearest signs of the success of 13
intelligence tests is that they are no longer widely administered.
In the wake of legal cases about the propriety of making consequential decisions about education on the basis of IQ scores,
many public school officials have become test-shy. By and large,
the testing of IQ in the schools is restricted to cases involving a
recognized problem (such as a learning disability) or a selection
procedure (determining eligibility for a program that serves
gifted children).

Despite this apparent setback, intelligence testing and the 14
line of thinking that underlies it have actually triumphed. Many
widely used scholastic measures, chief among them the SAT (renamed the Scholastic Assessment Test a few years ago), are thinly
disguised intelligence tests that correlate highly with scores on
standard psychometric instruments. Virtually no one raised in the
developed world today has gone untouched by Binet's seemingly
simple invention of a century ago.

Multiple Intelligences

15   The concept of intelligence has in recent years undergone its most robust challenge since the days of Walter Lippmann. Some who are informed by psychology but not bound by the assumptions of the psychometricians have invaded this formerly sacrosanct territory. They have put forth their own ideas of what intelligence is, how (and whether) it should be measured, and which values should be invoked in considerations of the human intellect. For the first time in many years the intelligence establishment is clearly on the defensive—and the new century seems likely to usher in quite different ways of thinking about intelligence.

16   One evident factor in the rethinking of intelligence is the perspective introduced by scholars who are not psychologists. Anthropologists have commented on the parochialism of the Western view of intelligence. Some cultures do not even have a concept called intelligence, and others define intelligence in terms of traits that we in the West might consider odd—obedience, good listening skills, or moral fiber, for example. Neuroscientists are skeptical that the highly differentiated and modular structure of the brain is consistent with a unitary form of intelligence. Computer scientists have devised programs deemed intelligent; these programs often go about problem-solving in ways quite different from those embraced by human beings or other animals.

17   Even within the field of psychology the natives have been getting restless. Probably the most restless is the Yale psychologist Robert J. Sternberg. A prodigious scholar, Sternberg, who is forty-nine, has written dozens of books and hundreds of articles, the majority of them focusing in one or another way on intelligence. Sternberg began with the strategic goal of understanding the actual mental processes mobilized by standard test items, such as the solving of analogies. But he soon went beyond standard intelligence testing by insisting on two hitherto neglected forms of intelligence: the "practical" ability to adapt to varying contexts (as we all must in these days of divorcing and downsizing), and the capacity to automate familiar activities so that we can deal effectively with novelty and display "creative" intelligence.

18   Sternberg has gone to greater pains than many other critics of standard intelligence testing to measure these forms of intelligence with the paper-and-pencil laboratory methods favored by

the profession. And he has found that a person's ability to adapt to diverse contexts or to deal with novel information can be differentiated from success at standard IQ-test problems. . . .

The psychologist and journalist Daniel Goleman has 19 achieved worldwide success with his book *Emotional Intelligence* (1995). Contending that this new concept (sometimes nicknamed EQ) may matter as much as or more than IQ, Goleman draws attention to such pivotal human abilities as controlling one's emotional reactions and "reading" the signals of others. In the view of the noted psychiatrist Robert Coles, author of *The Moral Intelligence of Children* (1997), among many other books, we should prize character over intellect. He decries the amorality of our families, hence our children; he shows how we might cultivate human beings with a strong sense of right and wrong, who are willing to act on that sense even when it runs counter to self-interest. Other, frankly popular accounts deal with leadership intelligence (LQ), executive intelligence (EQ or ExQ), and even financial intelligence.

Like Coles's and Goleman's efforts, my work on "multiple in- 20 telligences" eschews the psychologists' credo of operationalization and test-making. I began by asking two questions: How did the human mind and brain evolve over millions of years? and How can we account for the diversity of skills and capacities that are or have been valued in different communities around the world?

Armed with these questions and a set of eight criteria, I have 21 concluded that all human beings possess at least eight intelligences: linguistic and logical-mathematical (the two most prized in school and the ones central to success on standard intelligence tests), musical, spatial, bodily-kinesthetic, naturalist, interpersonal, and intrapersonal.

I make two complementary claims about intelligence. The 22 first is universal. We all possess these eight intelligences—and possibly more. Indeed, rather than seeing us as "rational animals," I offer a new definition of what it means to be a human being, cognitively speaking: *Homo sapiens sapiens* is the animal that possesses these eight forms of mental representation.

My second claim concerns individual differences. Owing to 23 the accidents of heredity, environment, and their interactions, no two of us exhibit the same intelligences in precisely the same proportions. Our "profiles of intelligence" differ from one another. This fact poses intriguing challenges and opportunities for our education system. We can ignore these differences and pretend that we are all the same; historically, that is what most education systems have done. Or we can fashion an education system that tries to exploit these differences, individualizing instruction and assessment as much as possible.

Intelligence and Morality

24   As the century of Binet and his successors draws to a close, we'd be wise to take stock of, and to anticipate, the course of thinking about intelligence. Although my crystal ball is no clearer than anyone else's (the species may lack "future intelligence"), it seems safe to predict that interest in intelligence will not go away.

25   To begin with, the psychometric community has scarcely laid down its arms. New versions of the standard tests continue to be created, and occasionally new tests surface as well. Researchers in the psychometric tradition churn out fresh evidence of the predictive power of their instruments and the correlations between measured intelligence and one's life chances. And some in the psychometric tradition are searching for the biological basis of intelligence: the gene or complex of genes that may affect intelligence, and neural structures that are crucial for intelligence, or telltale brain-wave patterns that distinguish the bright from the less bright.

26   Beyond various psychometric twists, interest in intelligence is likely to grow in other ways. It will be fed by the creation of machines that display intelligence and by the specific intelligence or intelligences. Moreover, observers as diverse as Richard Herrnstein and Robert B. Reich, President Clinton's first Secretary of Labor, have agreed that in coming years a large proportion of society's rewards will go to those people who are skilled symbol analysts— who can sit at a computer screen (or its technological successor), manipulate numbers and other kinds of symbols, and use the results of their operations to contrive plans, tactics, and strategies for enterprises ranging from business to science to war games. These people may well color how intelligence is conceived in decades to come—just as the need to provide good middle-level bureaucrats to run an empire served as a primary molder of intelligence tests in the early years of the century.

Surveying the landscape of intelligence, I discern three   27
struggles between opposing forces. The extent to which, and the
manner in which, these various struggles are resolved will influence the lives of millions of people. I believe that the three
struggles are interrelated; that the first struggle provides the key
to the other two; and that the ensemble of struggles can be resolved in an optimal way.

The first struggle concerns the breadth of our definition of   28
intelligence. One camp consists of the purists, who believe in a
single form of intelligence—one that basically predicts success in
school and in school-like activities. Arrayed against the purists
are the progressive pluralists, who believe that many forms of intelligence exist. Some of these pluralists would like to broaden the
definition of intelligence considerably, to include the abilities to
create, to lead, and to stand out in terms of emotional sensitivity
or moral excellence.

The second struggle concerns the assessment of intelligence.   29
Again, one readily encounters a traditional position. Once chiefly
concerned with paper-and-pencil tests, the traditionally oriented
practitioner is now likely to use computers to provide the same
information more quickly and more accurately. But other positions abound. Purists disdain psychological tasks of any complexity, preferring to look instead at reaction time, brain waves,
and other physiological measures of intellect. In contrast, simu-
lators favor measures closely resembling the actual abilities that
are prized. And skeptics warn against the continued expansion of
testing. They emphasize the damage often done to individual life
chances and self-esteem by a regimen of psychological testing,
and call for less technocratic, more humane methods—ranging
from self-assessment to the examination of portfolios of student
work to selection in the service of social equity.

The final struggle concerns the relationship between intelli-   30
gence and the qualities we value in human beings. Although no
one would baldly equate intellect and human worth, nuanced
positions have emerged on this issue. Some (in the *Bell Curve* mold)
see intelligence as closely related to a person's ethics and values;
they believe that brighter people are more likely to appreciate
moral complexity and to behave judiciously. Some call for a sharp
distinction between the realm of intellect on the one hand, and

character, morality, or ethics on the other. Society's ambivalence on this issue can be discerned in the figures that become the culture's heroes. For every Albert Einstein or Bobby Fischer who is celebrated for his intellect, there is a Forrest Gump or a Chauncey Gardiner who is celebrated for human—and humane—traits that would never be captured on any kind of intelligence test. . . .

The Borders of Intelligence

31   Writing as a scholar rather than as a layperson, I see two problems with the notion of emotional intelligence. First, unlike language or space, the emotions are not contents to be processed; rather, cognition has evolved so that we can make sense of human beings (self and others) that possess and experience emotions. Emotions are part and parcel of all cognition, though they may well prove more salient at certain times or under certain circumstances: they accompany our interactions with others, our listening to great music, our feelings when we solve—or fail to solve—a difficult mathematical problem. If one calls some intelligences emotional, one suggests that other intelligences are not—and that implication flies in the face of experience and empirical data.

32   The second problem is the conflation of emotional intelligence and a certain preferred pattern of behavior. This is the trap that Daniel Goleman sometimes falls into in his otherwise admirable *Emotional Intelligence.* Goleman singles out as emotionally intelligent those people who use their understanding of emotions to make others feel better, to solve conflicts, or to cooperate in home or work situations. No one would dispute that such people are wanted. However, people who understand emotion may not necessarily use their skills for the benefit of society.

33   For this reason I prefer the term "emotional sensitivity"—a term (encompassing my interpersonal and intrapersonal intelligences) that could apply to people who are sensitive to emotions in themselves and in others. Presumably, clinicians and salespeople excel in sensitivity to others, poets and mystics in sensitivity to themselves. And some autistic or psychopathological people seem completely insensitive to the emotional realm. I would insist, however, on a strict distinction between emotional sensitivity and being a "good" or "moral" person. A person may

be sensitive to the emotions of others but use that sensitivity to manipulate or to deceive them, or to create hatred.

I call, then, for a delineation of intelligence that includes the 34 full range of contents to which human beings are sensitive, but at the same time designates as off limits such valued but separate human traits as creativity, morality, and emotional appropriateness. I believe that such a delineation makes scientific and epistemological sense. It reinvigorates the elastic band without stretching it to the breaking point. It helps to resolve the two remaining struggles: how to assess, and what kinds of human beings to admire.

Once we decide to restrict intelligence to human informa- 35 tion-processing and product-making capacities, we can make use of the established technology of assessment. That is, we can continue to use paper-and-pencil or computer-adapted testing techniques while looking at a broader range of capacities, such as musical sensitivity and empathy with others. And we can avoid ticklish and possibly unresolvable questions about the assessment of values and morality that may well be restricted to a particular culture and that may well change over time.

Still, even with a limited perspective on intelligence, impor- 36 tant questions remain about which assessment path to follow— that of the purist, the simulator, or the skeptic. Here I have strong views. I question the wisdom of searching for a "pure" intelligence—be it general intelligence, musical intelligence, or interpersonal intelligence. I do not believe that such alchemical intellectual essences actually exist; they are a product of our penchant for creating terminology rather than determinable and measurable entities. Moreover, the correlations that have thus far been found between supposedly pure measures and the skills that we actually value in the world are too modest to be useful.

What does exist is the use of intelligences, individually and in 37 concert, to carry out tasks that are valued by a society. Accordingly, we should be assessing the extent to which human beings succeed in carrying out tasks of consequence that presumably involve certain intelligences. To be concrete, we should not test musical intelligence by looking at the ability to discriminate between two tones or timbres; rather, we should be teaching people to sing songs or play instruments or transform melodies and seeing how

readily they master such feats. At the same time, we should ab-
jure a search for pure emotional sensitivity—for example, a test
that matches facial expressions to galvanic skin response. Rather,
we should place (or observe) people in situations that call for
them to be sensitive to the aspirations and motives of others. For
example, we could see how they handle a situation in which they
and colleagues have to break up a fight between two teenagers, or
persuade a boss to change a policy of which they do not approve.

38   Here powerful new simulations can be invoked. We are now
in a position to draw on technologies that can deliver realistic situations or problems and also record the success of subjects in
dealing with them. A student can be presented with an unfamiliar tune on a computer and asked to learn that tune, transpose it,
orchestrate it, and the like. Such exercises would reveal much
about the student's intelligence in musical matters.

39   Turning to the social (or human, if you prefer) realm, subjects can be presented with simulated interactions and asked to
judge the shifting motivations of each actor. Or they can be asked
to work in an interactive hypermedia production with unfamiliar
people who are trying to accomplish some sort of goal, and to respond to their various moves and countermoves. The program
can alter responses in light of the moves of the subject. Like a
high-stakes poker game, such a measure should reveal much
about the interpersonal or emotional sensitivity of a subject.

40   A significant increase in the breadth—the elasticity—of our
concept of intelligence, then, should open the possibility for innovative forms of assessment far more realistic than the classic
short-answer examinations. Why settle for an IQ or an SAT test,
in which the items are at best remote proxies for the ability to design experiments, write essays, critique musical performances,
and so forth? Why not instead ask people actually (or virtually) to
carry out such tasks? And yet by not opening up the Pandora's
box of values and subjectivity, one can continue to make judicious
use of the insights and technologies achieved by those who have
devoted decades to perfecting mental measurement.

41   To be sure, one can create a psychometric instrument for any
conceivable human virtue, including morality, creativity, and emotional intelligence in its several senses. Indeed, since the publication of Daniel Goleman's book dozens of efforts have been made
to create tests for emotional intelligence. The resulting instruments

are not, however, necessarily useful. Such instruments are far more likely to satisfy the test maker's desire for reliability (a subject gets roughly the same score on two separate administrations of the test) than the need for validity (the test measures the trait that it purports to measure).

Such instruments-on-demand prove dubious for two rea- 42 sons. First, beyond some platitudes, few can agree on what it means to be moral, ethical, a good person: consider the differing values of Jesse Helms and Jesse Jackson, Margaret Thatcher and Margaret Mead. Second, scores on such tests are much more likely to reveal test-taking savvy (skills in language and logic) than fundamental character.

In speaking about character, I turn to a final concern: the 43 relationship between intelligence and what I will call virtue— those qualities that we admire and wish to hold up as examples for our children. No doubt the desire to expand intelligence to encompass ethics and character represents a direct response to the general feeling that our society is lacking in these dimensions; the expansionist view of intelligence reflects the hope that if we transmit the technology of intelligence to these virtues, we might in the end secure a more virtuous population.

I have already indicated my strong reservations about trying 44 to make the word "intelligence" all things to all people—the psychometric equivalent of the true, the beautiful, and the good. Yet the problem remains: how, in a post-Aristotelian, post-Confucian era in which psychometrics looms large, do we think about the virtuous human being?

My analysis suggests one promising approach. We should 45 recognize that intelligences, creativity, and morality—to mention just three desiderata—are separate. Each may require its own form of measurement or assessment, and some will prove far easier to assess objectively than others. Indeed, with respect to creativity and morality, we are more likely to rely on overall judgments by experts than on any putative test battery. At the same time, nothing prevents us from looking for people who combine several of these attributes—who have musical and interpersonal intelligence, who are psychometrically intelligent and creative in the arts, who combine emotional sensitivity and a high standard of moral conduct.

Let me introduce another analogy at this point. In college 46 admissions much attention is paid to scholastic performance, as measured by College Board examinations and grades. However, other features are also weighed, and sometimes a person with lower test scores is admitted if he or she proves exemplary in terms of citizenship or athletics or motivation. Admissions officers do not confound these virtues (indeed, they may use different scales and issue different grades), but they recognize the attractiveness of candidates who exemplify two or more desirable traits.

47   We have left the Eden of classical times, in which various intellectual and ethical values necessarily commingled, and we are unlikely ever to re-create it. We should recognize that these virtues can be separate and will often prove to be remote from one another. When we attempt to aggregate them, through phrases like "emotional intelligence," "creative intelligence," and "moral intelligence," we should realize that we are expressing a wish rather than denoting a necessary or even a likely coupling.

48   We have an aid in converting this wish to reality: the existence of powerful examples—people who succeed in exemplifying two or more cardinal human virtues. To name names is risky—particularly when one generation's heroes can become the subject of the next generation's pathographies. Even so, I can without apology mention Niels Bohr, George C. Marshall, Rachel Carson, Arthur Ashe, Louis Armstrong, Pablo Casals, Ella Fitzgerald.

49   In studying the lives of such people, we discover human possibilities. Young human beings learn primarily from the examples of powerful adults around them—those who are admirable and also those who are simply glamorous. Sustained attention to admirable examples may well increase the future incidence of people who actually do yoke capacities that are scientifically and epistemologically separate.

50   In one of the most evocative phrases of the century the British novelist E. M. Forster counseled us, "Only connect." I believe that some expansionists in the territory of intelligence, though well motivated, have prematurely asserted connections that do not exist. But I also believe that as human beings, we can help to forge connections that may be important for our physical and psychic survival.

51   Just how the precise borders of intelligence are drawn is a question we can leave to scholars. But the imperative to broaden our definition of intelligence in a responsible way goes well

beyond the academy. Who "owns" intelligence promises to be an issue even more critical in the next century than it has been in this era of the IQ test.

Content

1. What is intelligence? Compare and contrast some of the types Gardner refers to, which may be divided into two groups, the sort that "predicts success in school and in school-like activities" (¶s 4–10, 28) and all other kinds, including "the abilities to create, to lead, and to stand out in terms of emotional sensitivity or moral excellence" (¶ 28).

2. How can intelligence of a particular sort best be measured?

3. Who owns intelligence? The people who possess it? The society or social subgroup that determines what sorts of intelligence are valuable, necessary, appreciated—and those that aren't? The testers? How does Gardner's essay address this issue?

Strategies/Structures

4. Find examples in Gardner's essay of the following common techniques of definition, and comment on their effectiveness in conveying one or more meanings of intelligence:
   a. Illustration
   b. Comparison and contrast
   c. Negation (saying what something is not)
   d. Analysis
   e. Explanation of a process (how something is measured or works)
   f. Identification of causes or effects
   g. Simile, metaphor, or analogy
   h. Reference to authority or the writer's own expertise
   i. Reference to the writer's or others' personal experience or observation

5. Gardner's essay is full of arguments: for his definition of intelligence, against competing definitions; for various practical ways of measuring intelligence, against particular sorts of testing. Identify some of the assertions and evidence he uses to support his claims. Are they credible?

Language

6. Does Gardner believe it's possible to expand the definition of *intelligence* to include virtue (¶ 43), to make it encompass qualities he'd like it to have?

7. Can people change definitions of words to make them mean what they want them to mean? Or does every term have a border around it (¶ 50)? If so, who creates and enforces the boundaries?

For Writing

8. Write your own definition either of *intelligence* in general or of a specific type of intelligence such as one that Gardner discusses in his essay. You may need to define some of these yourself or consult other sources for the intelligences Gardner only touches on: a. psychometric intelligence (¶s 4–10); b. the "'practical'" ability to adapt to varying contexts (¶ 17); the "ability to deal with novel information" (¶ 18); emotional intelligence (¶s 19, 31–33); moral intelligence (¶s 19, 41–45); or creativity (¶s 41–45). Or define a form of intelligence on Gardner's personal list that includes: "linguistic, logical-mathematical, musical, spatial, bodily-kinesthetic, naturalist, interpersonal, and intrapersonal." (See Gardner's book *Frames of Mind* (1983) or any other of Gardner's numerous writings on the subject.) Use one or more techniques of definition identified in Strategies/Structures above, and, assuming that you yourself fulfill your own definition of *intelligent*, supplement your more general definition with a specific first-hand example.

9. Write a definition of an abstract concept for readers who may not have thought much about it—such as *love, truth, beauty, justice, greed, pride,* or *the good life*—but who have probably used it often in everyday life, something intangible that can be identified in terms of its effects, causes, manifestations, or other nonphysical properties. Use one or more techniques of definition identified in Strategies/Structures above and illustrate your definition with one or two specific examples with which you are familiar. Then use the examples as a basis for making generalizations that apply to other aspects of the concept.

JUDY BRADY

Brady was born in 1937 in San Francisco and earned a bachelor's degree in painting from the University of Iowa in 1962. Married in 1960 and now divorced, she raised two daughters as a "disenfranchised and fired housewife" while working full-time as a secretary and attending night school. Her activities in the women's movement led to political activism and a trip to Cuba in 1973 to study the influence of class relationships on social change.

Brady's definition of a wife, in the essay below, was first published in December 1971 in the inaugural issue of the feminist magazine *Ms.* That it has been widely reprinted ever since testifies to its appeal to a much wider audience than originally intended. This definition is comprehensive, though ironic, covering wifely behavior; temperament; domestic, social, and sexual tasks; and projected life span of eternal servitude; it justifies the title as well as the closing exclamation, "My God, who *wouldn't* want a wife?"

I Want a Wife

I belong to that classification of people known as wives. I am a   1
Wife. And, not altogether incidentally, I am a mother.

Not too long ago a male friend of mine appeared on the   2
scene fresh from a recent divorce. He had one child, who is, of course, with his ex-wife. He is obviously looking for another wife. As I thought about him while I was ironing one evening, it suddenly occurred to me that I, too, would like to have a wife. Why do I want a wife?

I would like to go back to school so that I can become eco-   3
nomically independent, support myself, and, if need be, support those dependent upon me. I want a wife who will work and send me to school. And while I am going to school I want a wife to take care of my children. I want a wife to keep track of the children's doctor and dentist appointments. And to keep track of mine, too. I want a wife to make sure my children eat properly and are kept clean. I want a wife who will wash the children's clothes and keep them mended. I want a wife who is a good nurturant attendant to my children, who arranges for their schooling, makes sure that they have an adequate social life with their peers, takes them to the park, the zoo, etc. I want a wife who takes care of the children when they are sick, a wife who arranges to be around when the children need special care, because, of course, I cannot miss classes at school. My wife must arrange to lose time at work and not lose the job. It may mean a small cut in my wife's income from time to time, but I guess I can tolerate that. Needless to say, my wife will arrange and pay for the care of the children while my wife is working.

4   I want a wife who will take care of *my* physical needs. I want a wife who will keep my house clean. A wife who will pick up after me. I want a wife who will keep my clothes clean, ironed, mended, replaced when need be, and who will see to it that my personal things are kept in their proper place so that I can find what I need the minute I need it. I want a wife who cooks the meals, a wife who is a *good* cook. I want a wife who will plan the menus, do the necessary grocery shopping, prepare the meals, serve them pleasantly, and then do the cleaning up while I do my studying. I want a wife who will care for me when I am sick and sympathize with my pain and loss of time from school. I want a wife to go along when our family takes a vacation so that someone can continue to care for me and my children when I need a rest and change of scene.

5   I want a wife who will not bother me with rambling complaints about a wife's duties. But I want a wife who will listen to me when I feel the need to explain a rather difficult point I have come across in my course of studies. And I want a wife who will type my papers for me when I have written them.

6   I want a wife who will take care of the details of my social life. When my wife and I are invited out by my friends, I want a wife who will take care of the babysitting arrangements. When I meet people at school that I like and want to entertain, I want a wife who will have the house clean, will prepare a special meal, serve it to me and my friends, and not interrupt when I talk about the things that interest me and my friends. I want a wife who will have arranged that the children are fed and ready for bed before my guests arrive so that the children do not bother us. I want a wife who takes care of the needs of my guests so that they feel comfortable, who makes sure that they have an ashtray, that they are passed the hors d'oeuvres, that they are offered a second helping of the food, that their wine glasses are replenished when necessary, that their coffee is served to them as they like it. And I want a wife who knows that sometimes I need a night out by myself.

7   I want a wife who is sensitive to my sexual needs, a wife who makes love passionately and eagerly when I feel like it, a wife who makes sure that I am satisfied. And, of course, I want a wife who will not demand sexual attention when I am not in the mood for it. I want a wife who assumes the complete responsibility for

birth control, because I do not want more children. I want a wife who will remain sexually faithful to me so that I do not have to clutter up my intellectual life with jealousies. And I want a wife who understands that *my* sexual needs may entail more than strict adherence to monogamy. I must, after all, be able to relate to people as fully as possible.

If, by chance, I find another person more suitable as a wife   8
than the wife I already have, I want the liberty to replace my present wife with another one. Naturally, I will expect a fresh, new
life; my wife will take the children and be solely responsible for
them so that I am left free.

When I am through with school and have a job, I want my   9
wife to quit working and remain at home so that my wife can
more fully and completely take care of a wife's duties.

My God, who *wouldn't* want a wife?   10

Content

1. Brady defines *wife* in terms of the purpose(s), activities, and personality traits of a person functioning in a wife's many roles. What are some
of these?
2. What is the purpose of Brady's definition of *wife*? How could she
expect her intended audience of feminist women to react to this definition? How would more traditional women be expected to respond to this
definition? Would men be expected to react in ways similar to those of
their female counterparts?

Strategies/Structures

3. In what order does Brady list the wife's expected services?
4. How do you know that Brady does not always mean what she says—
for instance, that she does not really favor the sexual double standard
identified in paragraphs 8 and 9?

Language

5. Brady always calls a *wife* by that label and never uses the pronouns
he or *she.* Why not?
6. Why does Brady use the short, simple (almost simplistic) phrase "I
want a wife," and why does she repeat it so often?

For Writing

7. Write your own ironic version of "I want a wife," or "I want a husband," aimed at your significant other, actual or imagined. Identify, as Brady does, the spouse's most important roles, activities, personality traits; this should imply or state the reciprocal way you would function as a spouse, for better or worse.

8. Write an essay in which you define the ideal relationship between husband and wife. How likely is this ideal to be realized? If you are married or engaged in a serious courtship, ask your partner to comment on a draft before you revise it.

GARY SOTO

> For biographical information see page 436.
> "Black Hair," reprinted here from *Living Up the Street: Narrative Recollections* (1985, reprint 1993) offers a cluster of definitions—of poverty, hard work, isolation, minority status, living on the edge, monotony, misery—and offers no foreseeable way out.

Black Hair

1   There are two kinds of work: One uses the mind and the other uses muscle. As a kid I found out about the latter. I'm thinking of the summer of 1969 when I was a seventeen-year-old runaway who ended up in Glendale, California, working for Valley Tire Factory. To answer an ad in the newspaper I walked miles in the afternoon sun, my stomach slowly knotting on a doughnut that was breakfast, my teeth like bright candles gone yellow.

2   I walked in the door sweating and feeling ugly because my hair was still stiff from a swim at the Santa Monica beach the day before. Jules, the accountant and part owner, looked droopily through his bifocals at my application and then at me. He tipped his cigar in the ashtray, asked my age as if he didn't believe I was seventeen, but finally, after a moment of silence, said, "Come back tomorrow. Eight-thirty."

I thanked him, left the office, and went around to the chain- ³
link fence to watch the workers heave tires into a bin; others
carted uneven stacks of tires on hand trucks. Their faces were
black from tire dust, and when they talked—or cussed—their
mouths showed a bright pink.

From there I walked up a commercial street, past a cleaners, ⁴
a motorcycle shop, and a gas station where I washed my face and
hands; before leaving I took a bottle that hung on the side of the
Coke machine, filled it with water, and stopped it with a scrap of
paper and a rubber band.

The next morning I arrived early at work. The assistant fore- ⁵
man, a potbellied Hungarian, showed me a time card and how to
punch in. He showed me the Coke machine and the locker room
with its slimy shower, and also pointed out the places where I
shouldn't go: the ovens where the tires were recapped and the
customer service area, which had a slashed couch, a coffee table
with greasy magazines, and an ashtray. He introduced me to
Tully, a fat man with one ear who worked the buffers that resur-
faced the whitewalls. I was handed an apron and a face mask and
shown how to use the buffer: Lift the tire and center it, inflate it
with a foot pedal, press the buffer against the white band until
cleaned, and then deflate and blow off the tire with an air hose.

With a paintbrush he stirred a can of industrial preserver. ⁶
"Then slap this blue stuff on." While he was talking a coworker
came up quietly behind him and goosed him with the air hose.
Tully jumped as if he had been struck by a bullet and then turned
around cussing and cupping his genitals in his hands as the other
worker walked away calling out foul names. When Tully turned
to me, smiling his gray teeth, I lifted my mouth into a smile because I wanted to get along. He has to be on my side, I thought.
He's the one who'll tell the foreman how I'm doing.

I worked carefully that day, setting the tires on the machine ⁷
as if they were babies, because it was easy to catch a finger in the
rim that expanded to inflate the tire. At the day's end we swept
up the tire dust and emptied the trash into bins.

At five the workers scattered for their cars and motorcycles ⁸
while I crossed the street to wash at a burger stand. My hair was
stiff with dust and my mouth showed pink against the backdrop
of my dirty face. I ordered a hotdog and walked slowly in the
direction of the abandoned house where I had stayed the night

before. I lay under the trees and within minutes was asleep. When I woke my shoulders were sore, and my eyes burned when I squeezed the lids together.

9   From the backyard I walked dully through a residential street, and as evening came on, the TV glare in the living rooms and the headlights of passing cars showed against the blue drift of dusk. I saw two children coming up the street with snow cones, their tongues darting at the packed ice. I saw a boy with a peach and wanted to stop him but felt embarrassed by my hunger. I walked for an hour, only to return and discover the house lit brightly. Behind the fence I heard voices and saw a flashlight poking at the garage door. A man on the back steps mumbled something about the refrigerator to the one with the flashlight.

10   I waited for them to leave but had the feeling they wouldn't because there was a commotion of furniture being moved. Tired, even more desperate, I started walking again with a great urge to kick things and tear the day from my life. I felt weak and my mind kept drifting because of hunger. I crossed the street to a gas station where I sipped at the water fountain and searched the Coke machine for change. I started walking again, first up a commercial street, then into a residential area where I lay down on someone's lawn and replayed a scene at home—my mother crying at the kitchen table, my stepfather yelling with food in his mouth. They're cruel, I thought, and warned myself that I should never forgive them. How could they do this to me?

11   When I got up from the lawn it was late. I searched out a place to sleep and found an unlocked car that seemed safe. In the backseat, with my shoes off, I fell asleep but woke up startled about four in the morning when the owner, a nurse on her way to work, opened the door. She got in and was about to start the engine when I raised my head to explain my presence. She screamed so loudly when I said "I'm sorry" that I sprinted from the car with my shoes in hand. Her screams faded, then stopped altogether, as I ran down the block, hid behind a trash bin, and waited for a police siren to sound. Nothing. I crossed the street to a church where I slept stiffly on cardboard in the balcony.

12   I woke up feeling tired and greasy. It was early and a few streetlights were still lit, the east growing pink with dawn. I washed myself from a garden hose and returned to the church to

break into what looked like a kitchen. Paper cups, plastic spoons, a coffee pot littered on a table. I found a box of Nabisco crackers and ate until I was full.

At work I spent the morning at the buffer, but was then told 13 to help Iggy, an old Mexican who was responsible for choosing tires that could be recapped without the risk of exploding at high speeds. Every morning a truck would deliver used tires, and after I unloaded them Iggy would step among the tires to inspect them for punctures and rips on the sidewalls.

With yellow chalk he marked circles and Xs to indicate dam- 14 age and called out "junk." Tires that could be recapped got a "goody" from Iggy, and I placed them on my hand truck. When I had a stack of eight I kicked the truck at an angle and balanced off to another work area, where Iggy again inspected the tires, scratching Xs and calling out "junk."

Iggy worked only until three in the afternoon, at which time 15 he went to the locker room to wash and shave and to dress in a two-piece suit. When he came out he glowed with a bracelet, watch, rings, and a shiny fountain pen in his breast pocket. His shoes sounded against the asphalt. He was the image of a banker stepping into sunlight with millions on his mind. He said a few low words to workers with whom he was friendly and none to people like me.

I was seventeen, stupid because I couldn't figure out the dif- 16 ference between an F78 14 and a 750 14 at sight. Iggy shook his head when I brought him the wrong tires, especially since I had expressed interest in being his understudy. "Mexican, how can you be so stupid?" he would yell at me, slapping a tire from my hands. But within weeks I learned a lot about tires, from sizes and makes to how they are molded in iron forms to how Valley stole from other companies. Now and then we received a truckload of tires, most of them new or nearly new and they were taken to our warehouse in the back, where the serial numbers were ground off with a sander. On those days the foreman handed out Cokes and joked with us as we worked to get the numbers off.

Most of the workers were Mexican or black, though a few 17 redneck whites worked there. The base pay was a dollar sixty-five but the average was three dollars. Of the black workers, I knew Sugar Daddy the best. His body carried 250 pounds and armfuls of scars, and he had a long knife that made me jump when he brought it out from his boot without warning. At one time he had been a singer and cut a record in 1967 called *Love's Chance,* which broke into the R & B charts. But nothing came of it. No big contract, no club dates, no tours. He made very little from record sales, only enough for an operation to pull a steering wheel from his gut when, drunk and mad at a lady friend, he slammed his Mustang into a row of parked cars.

18   "Touch it," he smiled at me one afternoon as he raised his shirt, his black belly kinked with hair. Scared, I traced the scar that ran from his chest to the left of his belly button, and I was repelled but hid my disgust.

19   Among the Mexicans I had few friends because I was different, a *pocho* who spoke bad Spanish. At lunch they sat in tires and laughed over burritos, looking up at me to laugh even harder. I also sat in tires while nursing a Coke and felt dirty and sticky because I was still living on the street and had not had a real bath in over a week. Nevertheless, when the border patrol came to round up the nationals, I ran with them as they scrambled for the fence or hid among the tires behind the warehouse. The foreman, who thought I was an undocumented worker, yelled at me to run, to get away. I did just that. At the time it seemed fun because there was no risk, only a good-hearted feeling of hide-and-seek, and besides, it meant an hour away from work on company time. When the police left we came back, and some of the nationals made up stories of how they were almost caught—how they outraced the police. Some of the stories were so convoluted and unconvincing that everyone laughed and shouted *"mentiras"* [lies], especially when one described how he overpowered a policeman, took his gun away, and sold the patrol car. We laughed and he laughed, happy to be there to make up such a story.

20   If work was difficult, so were the nights. I still had not gathered enough money to rent a room, so I spent the nights sleeping in parked cars or in the church balcony. After a week I found a newspaper ad for a room for rent, phoned, and was given directions. Finished with work, I walked the five miles down Mission Road looking back into the traffic with my thumb out. No rides. After eight hours of handling tires I was frightening to drivers, I suppose, since they seldom looked at me; if they did, it was a quick glance. For the next six weeks I would try to hitchhike, but

the only person to stop was a Mexican woman who gave me two dollars to take the bus. I told her it was too much and that no bus ran from Mission Road to where I lived, but she insisted that I keep the money and trotted back to her idling car. It must have hurt her to see me day after day walking in the heat and looking very much the dirty Mexican to the many minds that didn't know what it meant to work at hard labor. That woman knew. Her eyes met mine as she opened the car door, and there was a tenderness that was surprisingly true—one for which you wait for years but when it comes it doesn't help. Nothing changes. You continue on in rags, with the sun still above you.

I rented a room from a middle-aged couple whose lives 21 were a mess. She was a schoolteacher and he was a fireman. A perfect setup, I thought. But during my stay there they would argue for hours in their bedroom.

When I rang at the front door both Mr. and Mrs. Van Deusen 22 answered and didn't both to disguise their shock at how awful I looked. But they let me in all the same. Mrs. Van Deusen showed me around the house, from the kitchen and bathroom to the living room with its grand piano. On her fingers she counted out the house rules as she walked me to my room. It was a girl's room with lace curtains, scenic wallpaper of a Victorian couple enjoying a stroll, a canopied bed, and stuffed animals in a corner. Leaving, she turned and asked if she could do laundry for me. Feeling shy and hurt, I told her no; perhaps the next day. She left and I undressed to take a bath, exhausted as I sat on the edge of the bed probing my aches and my bruised places. With a towel around my waist I hurried down the hallway to the bathroom where Mrs. Van Deusen had set out an additional towel with a tube of shampoo. I ran water into the tub and sat on the closed toilet, watching the steam curl toward the ceiling. When I lowered myself into the tub I felt my body sting. I soaped a washcloth and scrubbed my arms until they lightened, even glowed pink, but I still looked unwashed around my neck and face no matter how hard I rubbed. Back in the room I sat in bed reading a magazine, happy and thinking of no better luxury that a girl's sheets, especially after nearly two weeks of sleeping on cardboard at the church.

I was too tired to sleep, so I sat at the window watching the 23 neighbors move about in pajamas, and, curious about the room, looked through the bureau drawers to search out personal things—

snapshots, a messy diary, and high-school yearbook. I looked up the Van Deusen's daughter, Barbara, and studied her face as if I recognized her from my own school—a face that said "promise," "college," "nice clothes in the closet." She was a skater and a member of the German Club; her greatest ambition was to sing at the Hollywood Bowl.

24   After a while I got into bed, and as I drifted toward sleep I thought about her. In my mind I played a love scene again and again and altered it slightly each time. She comes home from college and at first is indifferent to my presence in her home, but finally I overwhelm her with deep pity when I come home hurt from work, with blood on my shirt. Then there was another version: Home from college she is immediately taken with me, in spite of my work-darkened face, and invites me into the family car for a milkshake across town. Later, back at the house, we sit in the living room talking about school until we're so close I'm holding her hand. The truth of the matter was that Barbara did come home for a week but was bitter toward her parents for taking in boarders (two others besides me). During that time she spoke to me only twice: Once, while searching the refrigerator, she asked if we had any mustard; the other time she asked if I had seen her car keys.

25   But it was a place to stay. Work had become more and more difficult. I worked not only with Iggy but also with the assistant foreman, who was in charge of unloading trucks. After they backed in I hopped on top to pass the tires down, bouncing them on the tailgate to give them an extra spring so they would be less difficult to handle on the other end. Each truck was weighted down with more than two hundred tires, each averaging twenty pounds, so that by the time the truck was emptied and swept clean I glistened with sweat and my T-shirt stuck to my body. I blew snot threaded with tire dust onto the asphalt, indifferent to the customers who watched from the waiting room.

26   The days were dull. I did what there was to do from morning until the bell sounded at five; I tugged, pulled, and cussed at tires until I was listless and my mind drifted and caught on small things, from cold sodas to shoes to stupid talk about what we would do with a million dollars. I remember unloading a truck with Hamp, a black man.

"What's better than a sharp lady?" he asked me as I stood 27
sweaty on a pile of junked tires. "Water. With ice," I said.

He laughed with his mouth open wide. With his fingers he 28
pinched the sweat from his chin and flicked at me. "You be too
young, boy. A woman can make you a god."

As a kid I had chopped cotton and picked grapes, so I knew 29
work. I knew the fatigue and the boredom and the feeling that
there was a good possibility that you might have to do such work
for years, if not for a lifetime. In fact, as a kid I had imagined a
dark fate: to marry Mexican poor, work Mexican hours, and in the
end die a Mexican death, broke and in despair.

But this job at Valley Tire Company confirmed that there was 30
something worse than fieldwork, and I was doing it. We were all
doing it, from the foreman to the newcomers like me, and what I
felt heaving tires for eight hours a day was felt by everyone
black, Mexican, redneck. We all despised those hours but didn't
know what else to do. The workers were unskilled, some undocumented and fearful of deportation, and all struck with uncertainty at what to do with their lives. Although everyone bitched
about work, no one left. Some had worked there for twelve years;
some had sons working there. Few quit; no one was ever fired. It
amazed me that no one gave up when the border patrol jumped
from their vans, batons in hand, because I couldn't imagine any
work that could be worse—or any life. What was out there, in the
world, that made men run for the fence in fear?

Iggy was the only worker who seemed sure of himself. 31
After five hours of "junking," he brushed himself off, cleaned up
in the washroom, and came out gleaming with an elegance that
humbled the rest of us. Few would look him straight in the eye or
talk to him in our usual stupid way because he was so much
better. He carried himself as a man should—with Old World
"dignity"—while the rest of us muffed our jobs and talked dully
about dull things as we worked. From where he worked in his
open shed he would now and then watch us with his hands on
his hips. He would shake his head and click his tongue in disgust.

The rest of us lived dismally. I often wondered what the 32
others' homes were like; I couldn't imagine that they were much
better than our workplace. No one indicated that his outside
life was interesting or intriguing. We all looked defeated and

contemptible in our filth at the day's end. I imagined the average welcome at home: Rafael, a Mexican national who had worked at Valley for five years, returned to a beaten house full of kids dressed in mismatched clothes and playing kick the can. As for Sugar Daddy, he returned home to a stuffy room where he would read and reread old magazines. He ate potato chips, drank beer, and watched TV. There was no grace in dipping socks into a washbasin where later he would wash his cup and plate.

33   There was no grace at work. It was all ridicule. The assistant foreman drank Cokes in front of the newcomers as they laced tires in the afternoon sun. Knowing that I had a long walk home, Rudy, the college student, passed me waving and yelling "Hello" as I started down Mission Road on the way home to eat out of cans. Even our plump secretary got into the act by wearing short skirts and flaunting her milky legs. If there was love, it was ugly. I'm thinking of Tully and an older man whose name I can no longer recall fondling one another in the washroom. I had come in cradling a smashed finger to find them pressed together in the shower, their pants undone and partly pulled down. When they saw me they smiled with their pink mouths but didn't bother to push away.

34   How we arrived at such a place is a mystery to me. Why anyone would stay for years is an even deeper concern. You showed up, but from where? What broken life? What ugly past? The foreman showed you the Coke machine, the washroom, and the yard where you'd work. When you picked up a tire, you were amazed at the black it could give off.

Content

1. What is the significance of the title, "Black Hair"?
2. Is there any way out of the life for underclass unskilled workers that Soto describes in "Black Hair"?
3. What's the implied thesis of "Black Hair"? Why did Soto write such a negative, depressing piece? What reactions does he expect from his intended readers?
4. Soto begins with, "There are two kinds of work: One uses the mind and the other uses muscle" (¶ 1). Is this too simple a dichotomy? How does his essay complicate that definition?

Strategies/Structures

5. Pick a paragraph (such as 2, 3, 4, 5, 6, 8, 9, 10, or 11) and identify all the elements of a depressing, discouraging, dirty life that Soto incorporates in it. Each of these paragraphs could serve as a minidefinition of poverty. What techniques of definition (such as illustration, positive or negative example, analysis, explanation, comparison or contrast, personal experience) does Soto use in the paragraph you've chosen?

6. Why does Soto's essay remain pessimistic to the end? Why doesn't he entertain ways to leave the world of the Valley Tire Factory and give the piece a happy ending?

Language

7. Soto uses standard English to write about a work environment where people don't (as a rule) speak in standard English. Why doesn't he incorporate their actual language more extensively? What languages do Soto's intended readers speak in?

8. Does the fact that "Black Hair" is written in the past tense mean that Soto is no longer working at the Valley Tire Factory and living in the circumstances he's describing? If so, why doesn't he tell his readers how he escaped?

For Writing

9. Write an essay for college student readers in which you identify two or three features of life or culture that middle- and upper-class readers take for granted but which the underclass can't count on and may never experience. Your essay should elaborate on the implications of what having such aspects of life—such as a dependable family; assurance of a safe and comfortable place to live, the opportunity to attend and graduate from college—means for those who can count on them and for those whom these may be unattainable.

10. Write an essay in which you provide an extended definition of one of the following terms, explained in terms of what it is and what it's not: a good job (versus a terrible job or a mediocre job); dignity in life or in the workplace (versus a demeaning existence); hope (versus hopelessness); cleanliness (versus minor superficial dirtiness and intense dirtiness); self-respect (versus the absence of respect for oneself or from others); a healthful life (versus an unhealthful life). Ponder the examples in "Black Hair" and supply others from your own experience or the experiences of people you've known in real life or read about (see Sanders, "The Inheritance of

Tools," 186–96; Reich, 624–36; or in fiction such as John Steinbeck's *The Grapes of Wrath*). Consider the causes and effects, short and long term, of the positive and negative implications of the term you choose.

<hr>

JASMINE INNERARITY

Innerarity, born (1968) and raised in Jamaica, studied at the University of Toronto and earned from the University of Connecticut a B.S. in nursing (1989) and an M.S. in nursing/public health (1999). A pediatric oncology nurse, she has served as president of the Connecticut chapter of the Society of Pediatric Nurses and has written movingly of her compassionate care of young patients—those who would survive, and those who would not.

The writing of "Code Blue: The Process" presented problems for Innerarity. She wanted to present an accurate and precise definition of what happens during this emergency procedure that would be clear to an audience of undergraduates, who needed further definitions of terms such as "intubation," "crash cart," and "ambu bag." During the course of several revisions, to ensure that her writing was both accurate and ethical, she checked her work with nursing colleagues (was she revealing medical secrets? no!). She also provided additional definitions of key terms and more illustrations because of her realization that what she as a professional nurse could take for granted was not always common knowledge. To avoid giving the impression of medical infallibilty, her last revision was to include an example of the fact that despite a medical team's best efforts Code Blue procedures do not always succeed.

Code Blue: Two Definitions

❄ *Code Blue: The Process*

1   An unforgettable moment in caring for the sick in the hospital or any institutional setting is the Code Blue Process. Code Blue is the alert signal for a patient who has stopped breathing or whose heart has stopped. This signal is universal throughout

hospitals in the U.S. The alert is given via the physicians' private beepers and the overhead intercom within hospitals. This process is always associated with what seems like chaos to the outsider but to the health team, it is well organized and well executed.

Code Blue is usually initiated by the nurse. There are many 2 reasons for this. First, the nurse spends more time with the patient than any other member of the health team. In addition, the nurse is continuously assessing the patient's condition. The nurse usually detects small changes in vital signs or physical conditions at crucial times when other members of the health team are absent.

Within the hospital, a patient who has stopped breathing or 3 who is in cardiac arrest is quickly discovered because the circular arrangement of the floor allows all patients to be seen from the nursing station. In addition, those patients who are unstable are placed on cardiac monitors with audio alarms which alert the medical team to changes in their health status if medical personnel is not present in the room.

A cart which is equipped with all the necessary equipment 4 to initiate the Code Blue response is also placed in a central region on each hospital floor. This cart called the "Code cart," usually contains intravenous fluids, emergency medications, and equipment used for intubating the patient. In the event of a Code Blue, this cart is immediately brought into the patient's room.

Example of Code Blue Process

Timmy was a two-year-old boy. He was in the Intensive Care Unit 5 for a neurological condition which affects his breathing patterns. He has been doing well. I have been caring for him for the past week and have watched his progress with great joy. He was still being monitored before being released from the Intensive Care Unit to the regular Hospital Unit.

One morning, I walked in to see Timmy five minutes after 6 his mother had left the room. I had heard them playing together minutes before she left. As I entered the room, I noticed that Timmy was lying still and his lips were turning blue. "Timmy! Timmy!" I shouted, while shaking him. He did not respond. "I have a Code Blue," I called out.

My shout of "Code Blue!" was the warning to the rest of the 7 health team to get someone else into the room while the secretary announces the alert to the Code Blue team. In a Code Blue situation, a member from several different medical teams appears. The teams are designed to ensure that in an emergency situation, such as this one, each physician or health care member essential to getting this patient back to health is present. Although the medical personnel who arrive vary by hospitals, there is usually a surgeon, a cardiologist, a respiratory therapist, an anesthesiologist, an intensivist, and the patient's primary or attending physician for the day. The primary physician leads the Code team by getting a quick history of what precipitated the patient's cessation of breathing and tries to determine how to reverse this crisis. His role is to give the orders in the code.

8   The surgeon arrives to insert central lines—a plastic tubing going from the outside of the body to the inside that is used to infuse medication, fluids, and blood products quickly into the body and heart. A cardiologist has the role of prescribing medications to ensure that the most central organ in the body (the heart) is functioning.

9   The anesthesiologist has the role of sedating and intubating the patient who has stopped breathing. Intubation involves placing a plastic tubing through the patient's mouth and into his or her lungs. This process requires considerable skill, because one has to take care to insert the tube into the trachea, and not into the esophagus which leads to the stomach. Once the tube is placed into the lungs, an X-ray is taken of the chest to confirm that this tube is in fact where it belongs, in the lungs. The end of the tubing which projects from the mouth is connected to a respirator, a computerized machine that breathes for the patient. The respiratory therapist is in charge of monitoring the respirator.

10   Accessory personnel, such as members of the fire department or EMT team from the hospital, may arrive to assist in a Code Blue situation. In fact, it is not unusual after the initial assessment of the situation to ask some health personnel who are not needed to leave the room. The aim is to prevent clutter and maximize efficiency in responding to the Code.

11   A series of quick actions is executed within a minute of the Code Blue call. A team of health professionals rushes into the room. As I try to instill air into Timmy's lungs, using a mechanical device called an "ambu bag," another nurse feels for pulses, and the physician prepares to intubate Timmy. An ambu bag is a

pressure bag made of rubber (it looks like an inflated balloon) that has two ends. One end has a long plastic tubing which connects to an oxygen tank or oxygen outlet in the wall, and the other end has a mouthpiece which fits over the patient's face and mouth. When the middle part of the balloon is squeezed, oxygen is expelled into the patient's mouth and ultimately into the lungs.

The physician in charge of Timmy gives the orders: 12

"500 ml of I.V. fluids wide open stat!"
"What's his pressure?"
"Does he have a pulse?"
"Yes."
"Okay, let's have a blood gas."

Each member of the team rushes to fulfill their role.

The series of quick necessary motions, as well as the numer-   13
ous health professionals in the patient's room, give the impression of disorder. On the contrary, the process is very orderly: Blood is being drawn, phone calls are being made to get lab results quickly, and the physician is speaking loudly so that everyone can hear what to do and when. There is no time for mishaps. It is an assembly line and everyone must be alert. Each team member must mesh into this new team, the team of people trying to save the patient's life.

Timmy starts to cry after three minutes of resuscitation. His   14
lips are no longer blue. "Good job, team," says the physician.

The team rushes out and back to their original stations. The   15
nurses stay behind to do what they do best, care for Timmy and comfort his family. Timmy's mother has been brought down to the lounge during the code. Timmy will be in an oxygen tent for the night. "What's that?" she asks, pointing to the tent. The oxygen tent is made of plastic and is in the shape of a tent (hence the name). It delivers a continuous supply of oxygen to Timmy, which will help with his breathing overnight. I sit to explain to her what just happened to Timmy and to answer any questions she may have. Timmy's mother takes my hand, "Thanks for saving him."

The process of Code Blue in this instance is short, lasting for   16
fifteen minutes only. Timmy responded well to the medical interventions. In other cases, however, the outcome can be grave. Mark was a twelve-year-old boy with a brain tumor. His family had agonized about the decision to make him a "Do not resuscitate"

(DNR) patient. This status implies that if he should stop breathing, then the Code Blue process would not be initiated. DNR is attributed to patients who are gravely ill and for whom medical interventions have proven ineffective. The decision to make a patient a DNR however, is ultimately that of the family. Mark's parents wanted everything to be done for him despite the recommendation of DNR status by the physicians. Thus, Mark was not a DNR.

17   When Mark stopped breathing one evening, a Code Blue was called. Again the group of medical personnel arrived to save Mark's life. In this case and unlike Timmy, Mark responded poorly to the use of the ambu bag. His heart stopped. He was intubated by the anesthesiologist and was placed on a respirator. The private physician shouted: "We need to take him to the operating room (OR), he's bleeding." The physicians debated whether Mark's heart was strong enough for the OR. Despite several medications, Mark's heart would not return to the normal sinus rhythm.

18   The health team rushed to get blood into his body. The surgeons debated whether they could stop the bleeding, which they found was in his brain. After forty-five minutes of medications and mechanical ventilation, Mark still did not respond. The primary physician and the family talked about the grave outcome for Mark. After a half hour had passed since the Code Blue, the parents decided to let Mark go. He was taken off the respirator and died immediately.

19   The timing for the Code Blue process is as varied as the patients involved in the process. The two examples above showed the difference in response to medical interventions, which determine how long the process is continued. In many instances, the team will continue the process for up to an hour if the patient responds to medication. The patient will then be transferred to an Intensive Care Unit where he will be monitored closely until he is stable.

20   There are many emotions involved in a Code Blue process, depending on whether the outcome is good or poor. Initially, the team members experience a rush of adrenalin. This occurs because a Code Blue does not happen daily, so the nervousness, yet urgency of the situation takes one by surprise. There is also the continuous struggle with the ethical issues involved in Code Blue situations. For example, in each Code Blue situation, the determination must be made whether or not that patient is a DNR status.

Usually the primary nurse and physician are aware of this status. At times, however, the determination must be made immediately. Nurses as well as family members struggle with the decision to make someone a DNR or a full code status.

One of the biggest rewards in caring for the sick is the mir-   21 acle of seeing a person who has stopped breathing and who looks lifeless return to life. After ten years of being involved in the nursing process, my natural instinct is to care for those who are sick. I genuinely believe that caring for the sick makes them better. Of course, the Code Blue process shows that this is not always true. However, in my experience, the positive outcomes disproportionately overshadow the very small number of morbid outcomes.

―――――――――――――――――――――――――――――――――

ABRAHAM VERGHESE

Verghese was born in Addis Ababa, Ethiopia (1955), where his expatriate Indian parents were teachers, but he returned to India to study medicine (M.D., Madras University, 1979). In 1980 he began a three-year residency in internal medicine at East Tennessee State University, then switched to infectious diseases because, he says, "it offered the promise of a cure. In the early 1980s infectious disease was the one discipline where a cure was common." But in August, 1985, the local hospital in rural Johnson City treated its first AIDS patient, and soon the crisis that had once seemed an urban problem spread to the small town, as well. *My Own Country: A Doctor's Story* (1994) describes how Verghese, as a specialist in infectious diseases, gradually became drawn into the treatment of the "shocking number" of male and female patients who took over not only his professional life but also his compassionate imagination.

Of this experience, Verghese, now chief of infectious diseases at Texas Technological Regional Academic Health Center in El Paso, says, "Today I am a doctor who is unable to cure." He explains, "You're suddenly dealing with people your own age whose plight makes you reflect on your ideas about sex, about social issues and, of course, about your own mortality. Almost every emotion is magnified and brought into sharp relief with AIDS." He began writing nonfiction, now published in the *New Yorker* and many other places, aided by a year's Michener Fellowship to the Writers'

Workshop at the University of Iowa (1990–1991), as a way to deal with "some of my frustrations at work. I can't reverse death, I can't get into a patient's mind and think his thoughts. But with writing, the boundaries are virtually limitless," as Verghese's most recent book, *The Tennis Partner: A Doctor's Story of Friendship and Loss* (1998) also illustrates. "Code Blue: The Story" opens *My Own Country,* putting into dramatic action—with characters, dialogue, and frenetic activity—the definition that Innerarity has explained in a more formal manner.

Code Blue: Two Definitions

Code Blue: The Story

1   In the early evening of August 11, 1985, he was rolled into the emergency room (ER) of the Johnson City Medical Center— the "Miracle Center," as we referred to it when we were interns. Puffing like an overheated steam engine, he was squeezing in forty-five breaths a minute. Or so Claire Bellamy, the nurse, told me later. It had shocked her to see a thirty-two-year-old man in such severe respiratory distress.

2   He sat bolt upright on the stretcher, his arms propped behind him like struts that braced his heaving chest. His blond hair was wet and stuck to his forehead; his skin, Claire recalled, was gunmetal gray, his lips and nail beds blue.

3   She had slapped an oxygen mask on him and hollered for someone to pull the duty physician away from the wound he was suturing. A genuine emergency was at hand, something she realized, even as it overtook her, she was not fully comprehending. She knew what it was not: it was *not* severe asthma, status asthmaticus; it was *not* a heart attack. She could not stop to take it all in. Everything was happening too quickly.

4   With every breath he sucked in, his nostrils flared. The strap muscles of his neck stood out like cables. He pursed his lips when he exhaled, as if he was loath to let the oxygen go, hanging on to it as long as he could.

5   Electrodes placed on his chest and hooked to a monitor showed his heart fluttering at a desperate 160 beats per minute.

On his chest x-ray, the lungs that should have been dark as 6
the night were instead whited out by a veritable snowstorm.

My friend Ray, a pulmonary physician was immediately 7
summoned. While Ray listened to his chest, the phlebotomist
drew blood for serum electrolytes and red and white blood cell
counts. The respiratory therapist punctured the radial artery at
the wrist to measure blood oxygen levels. Claire started an intravenous line. And the young man slumped on the stretcher. He
stopped breathing.

Claire punched the "Code Blue" button on the cubicle wall 8
and an operator's voice sounded through the six-story hospital
building: "Code Blue, emergency room!"

The code team—an intern, a senior resident, two intensive 9
care unit nurses, a respiratory therapist, a pharmacist—thundered
down the hallway.

Patients in their rooms watching TV sat up in their beds; 10
visitors froze in place in the corridors.

More doctors arrived; some came in street clothes, having 11
heard the call as they headed for the parking lot. Others came in
scrub suits. Ray was "running" the code; he called for boluses of
bicarbonate and epinephrine, for a second intravenous line to be
secured, and for Claire to increase the vigor but slow down the
rate of her chest compressions.

The code team took their positions. The beefy intern with 12
Nautilus shoulders took off his jacket and climbed onto a step
stool. He moved in just as Claire stepped back, picking up the
rhythm of chest compressions without missing a beat, calling the
cadence out loud. With locked elbows, one palm over the back of
the other, he squished the heart between breastbone and spine,
trying to squirt enough blood out of it to supply the brain.

The ER physician unbuttoned the young man's pants and cut 13
away the underwear, now soiled with urine. His fingers reached
for the groin, feeling for the femoral artery to assess the adequacy
of the chest compressions.

A "crash cart" stocked with ampules of every variety, its de- 14
fibrillator paddles charged and ready, stood at the foot of the bed
as the pharmacist recorded each medication given and the exact
time it was administered.

The clock above the stretcher had been automatically zeroed 15
when the Code Blue was called. A code nurse called out the

elapsed time at thirty-second intervals. The resident and another nurse from the code team probed with a needle for a vein to establish the second "line."

16   Ray "bagged" the patient with a tight-fitting mask and hand-held squeeze bag as the respiratory therapist readied an endotracheal tube and laryngoscope.

17   At a signal from Ray, the players froze in midair while he bent the young man's head back over the edge of the stretcher. Ray slid the laryngoscope in between tongue and palate and heaved up with his left hand, pulling the base of the tongue up and forward until the leaf-shaped epiglottis appeared.

18   Behind it, the light at the tip of the laryngoscope showed glimpses of the voice box and the vocal cords. With his right hand, Ray fed the endotracheal tube alongside the laryngoscope, down the back of the throat, past the epiglottis, and past the vocal cords— this part done almost blindly and with a prayer—and into the trachea. Then he connected the squeeze bag to the end of the endotracheal tube and watched the chest rise as he pumped air into the lungs. He nodded, giving the signal for the action to resume.

19   Now Ray listened with his stethoscope over both sides of the chest as the respiratory therapist bagged the limp young man. He listened for the muffled *whoosh* of air, listened to see if it was equally loud over both lungs.

20   He heard sounds only over the right lung. The tube had gone down the right main bronchus, a straighter shot than the left.

21   He pulled the tube back an inch, listened again, and heard air entering both sides. The tube was sitting above the carina, above the point where the trachea bifurcates. He called for another chest x-ray; a radiopaque marker at the end of the tube would confirm its exact position.

22   With a syringe he inflated the balloon cuff at the end of the endotracheal tube that would keep it snugly in the trachea. Claire wound tape around the tube and plastered it down across the young man's cheeks and behind his neck.

23   The blue in the young man's skin began to wash out and a faint pink appeared in his cheeks. The ECG machine, which had spewed paper into a curly mound on the floor, now showed the original rapid heart rhythm restored.

24   At this point the young man was alive again, but just barely. The Code Blue had been a success.

Content

1. What is *Code Blue* according to Innerarity's definition?
2. Is it possible to infer a definition of *Code Blue* from Verghese's illustration of Code Blue in action? What additional information do you need?
3. After she had written several versions of "Code Blue" that contained only positive examples, Innerarity added a negative example—of Code Blue not working—at her teacher's insistence. Does the negative example undercut the positive?
4. Why, in medical and science writing, are there usually many more positive examples (successful processes and procedures) than negative ones? Do the essays by Innerarity and Verghese bear this out?

Strategies/Structures

5. Why would nonmedical people want to know the details of a procedure that can be performed only by a medical team?
6. Innerarity offers a textbook definition of the process, personnel, and equipment used to carry out a Code Blue. In contrast, Verghese shows Code Blue in action. Explain how his narrative also functions as a definition.
7. Which version of "Code Blue" are you more likely to remember? Why?

Language

8. Innerarity had difficulty translating medical terminology into everyday language and wrote several drafts to simplify and clarify the language. Has she succeeded? Has she used any terms that still need definition?

For Writing

9. Define a specialized technical or scientific term or process so a nonspecialist can understand it. See Kuhn (221–33), the Magliozzis (233–40), Thomas (375–81), Gardner (491–506), Brand (544–49).
10. Write a narrative (that is, tell a true story), as Innerarity and Verghese do, that through its characters and action implies a definition of a significant term—such as *love* (or *hate*), *beauty* (or *ugliness*), *fidelity* (or *betrayal*), *honesty* (or *dishonesty*)—or of a process (how to form or destroy a friendship, how to travel); or of some other concept that you expect to learn to understand in the process of writing about it.

Additional Topics for Writing
Definition   (For strategies for writing definition, see 481)

1. Write an extended definition of one or more of the following trends, concepts, abstractions, phenomena, or institutions. Be sure to identify your audience, limit your subject, and illustrate your essay with specific examples.

    a. Intelligence (see Gardner, 491–506)
    b. Physical fitness (see Lamott, 72–77; Mairs 456–71)
    c. Personality
    d. Character
    e. Optimism
    f. Depression (economic or psychological) (see Angier, 381–88)
    g. The nature of friendship
    h. Marriage (either, the ideal marriage, or the ideal versus the reality—see Brady, 506–10)
    i. Parenthood (see Erdrich, 47–53; White, 171–79; Sanders, 186–96 and 441–56; Spinner, 572–82)
    j. Education—formal or informal
    k. A good job or profession; work (see Miller, 82–88; Soto, 510–20)
    l. Comedy, tragedy, romance, or satire (see Chapter 16)
    m. A sport, game, hobby, or recreational activity
    n. A Northerner, Southerner, Midwesterner, Texan, Californian, or person from some other state or region
    o. A scientific or technical phenomenon of your choice (an eclipse, the "big bang" theory of creation, genetic engineering, DNA, the MX missile)

2. Explain a particular value system or belief system, such as:

    a. Democracy, communism, socialism, or some other political theory or form of government
    b. Protestantism (or a particular sect), Catholicism, Judaism (or a particular branch—Orthodox, Conservative, Reform), Buddhism (or a particular sort), Islam, or some other religion
    c. A theoretical system and some of its major ramifications (feminism, post-colonialism, Freudianism)

3. Prepare a dictionary of ten jargon or slang words used in your academic major, in your hobby, or in some other activity you enjoy, such as playing a particular sport or game, listening to a specific type of music, or working on a computer system.

12 Comparison and Contrast

Writers compare people, places, things, or qualities to identify their similarities, and contrast them to identify the differences. What you say about one subject usually helps to illuminate or explain the other; such explanations have the added advantage of answering questions that hinge on the similarities and differences under consideration. Your commentary can also provide the basis for judging the relative merits and demerits of the subject at hand.

For instance, comparison and contrast can help you determine whether to choose a liberal arts or technical education, and what your future will be like with whichever you select. It can help you explain the resemblances between the works of Faulkner and Hemingway, and the differences—and to justify your preference for one author over the other. Comparison and contrast can help you decide whom to vote for, what movie to see (or avoid), where to spend your next vacation, what car to buy, which person to marry. A thoroughgoing, detailed comparison and contrast of the reasons for the quality of life with and without handguns, conservation of natural resources, or nuclear power can provide a convincing argument for your choice.

But not everything will work. The subjects you select should have some obvious qualities in common to make the comparison and contrast fruitful. If you try to compare very dissimilar things, as the Mad Hatter does in *Alice in Wonderland* ("Why is a raven like a writing desk?"), you'll have to stretch for an answer ("Because they both begin with an *r* sound.") that may be either silly or irrelevant. But other comparisons by their very nature can command appropriate contrasts. Deborah Tannen's "Communication Styles" (536–44) is based on an extended exploration of differences in the way men and women students behave in the classroom. For instance, Tannen has found that men speak in class more often than women do. They're more at ease in the "public" classroom setting and enjoy the "debate-like form that discussion may take," while women students are "more comfortable speaking in private to a small group of people they know well" in non-confrontational dialogue.

Stewart Brand's "Written on the Wind" (544–49) and Jenny Spinner's "In Search of a Past" (572–82) abound in comparisons and contrasts, explicit and implied. Brand deals with life before and during the digital age; different stages of digital sophistication; digital continuity and discontinuity ("The great creator becomes the great eraser."); timeliness and obsolescence; a unified versus a fragmented network of computer systems; past, present, and future ("How can we invest in a future we know is structurally incapable of keeping faith with its past?"); and many more. Likewise, Spinner's essay explores the bonds and similarities between her twin sister and herself and her adoptive parents; fantasy versions of her birth parents in contrast with the unknown (to her) reality of their lives; negative comparisons between the twins and schoolmates certain of their ancestry; choosing to know and not know—all embedded in a narrative that proceeds chronologically through the essay, from before her birth, through her school and college years, to the present.

In writing an essay of comparison and contrast you'll need to justify your choice of subject, unless the grounds for comparison are obvious. Thus in "Evolution as Fact and Theory" (550–60), Stephen Jay Gould explains a contrast that is not necessarily apparent to general readers—that evolution as a theory and evolution as a fact are "different things, not rungs in a hierarchy of increasing certainty." Facts are the data which theories try to explain, as evolutionists have always made clear "from the very beginning, if only because we have always acknowledged how far we are from completely understanding the mechanisms (theory) by which evolution (fact) occurred." He then uses these definitions as the basis for refuting the contrasting view of "scientific creationism," a "self-contradictory, nonsense" set of beliefs.

You'll also have to limit your comparison. It would take a book or more to compare and contrast all the relevant aspects of the People's Republic of China and Taiwan. In an essay—short or long, or even treatise-length—on the subject you could focus instead on their relative educational systems, on their relations with the United Sates, or on the everyday life of the average worker in each country. Likewise, in a short paper, you're better off to compare the relevant aspects of two entities. The more items you add, the more complicated the comparison becomes, as you try to deal with the political system in the People's Republic of China, and Taiwan, and Russia, and Poland, and Romania, and. . . .

There are three common ways to organize an essay of comparison and contrast. Let's say you're in the market for a car and are writing an essay to help you make decisions on type (minivan, pickup, sportscar, sedan), make and model, age (new or used), cost, special features (four wheel drive, built-in CD player), and financing (buy or lease). If you've just begun to think about the subject, you could deal with each issue topic by topic, most usefully in the order listed here: type, make and model, etc. Or you could deal with each subject as a whole before moving on to the next. If you've already decided on the particular type and price of car, say, a small used vehicle costing between $6,000 and $8,000, then you might find it more useful to devote one section, say, to the Honda Civic, another to the GEO Prizm, and a third to the Toyota Celica, considering all features of each car in the same order: size, handling, reliability, fuel economy, safety, sportiness, and final cost. Why the same order for each car? Because you'll confuse yourself and your readers if you follow a different organizational pattern for each car; everyone needs to know where to look in each discussion to find comparable information. Another way to organize the information would be to group all the similarities about the cars in one section and all the differences in another, arranged in order from the most important (to you) to the least. Eventually, you'll summarize your conclusion: "While I like the first car better because it's sportier and more fun to drive, and the second is great on hills and curves, I guess I'm stuck with the third because I know I can get a good deal from my great uncle, who kept it in his garage all winter and never drove it over fifty."

The pattern of comparison and contrast that emerges may depend on how long the paper is; the longer the discussion, the less easy it is for readers to remember what they need to. Try out a sample section on members of your class or writing group and see whether they can understand the points of comparison you're trying to make; if they can't, then try another method of arrangement.

Whatever pattern of comparison and contrast you use, a topic outline can help you to organize such papers, and to make sure you've covered equivalent points for each item in the comparison. However you organize the paper, you don't have to give such equal emphasis to the similarities and to the differences; some may simply be more important than others. But you do have to make your chosen points of comparison relevant. Comparison and contrast is particularly useful as a technique in explanations. You can compare something that readers don't know much about (foreign sportscars) with something that's familiar (family sedans).

Contrast is also the basis of many types of argumentation; we tend to think in terms of a "right" versus a "wrong" side even when issues are more complicated than they might seem in a simple opposition. In "What's Wrong with Animal Rights?" (560–72), Vicki Hearne turns the conventional argument on its head. The animal rights advocates have "got it all wrong," she argues, for they build their advocacy "upon a misconceived premise that rights were created to prevent us from unnecessary suffering"; they view death, perhaps through a "humane" society, as positive, "the ultimate release." This sentimental stereotype of animals as "Helpless Fluff" and "Agonized Fluff" contrasts significantly with Hearne's experienced and unsentimental animal trainer's view that animals are ethical creatures who are happiest when doing good work. The appropriate rights for animals, in Hearne's view, are the positive Jeffersonian rights to "life, liberty, and the pursuit of happiness."

As we've seen, essays of comparison and contrast may include other types of writing, particularly description, narration, and analysis. Classification and division often determine the points to be covered in such essays: my actual life versus my ideal life, country living versus city living, life on the East (or West) coast versus life in the Midwest, middle-class life versus upper-class life. . . . And essays of comparison and contrast themselves become, at times, illustrations or arguments, direct or indirect, overt or more subtle. Long live the differences and the zest they provide.

STRATEGIES FOR WRITING—
COMPARISON AND CONTRAST

1. Will my essay focus on the similarities between two or more things (comparison) or the differences (contrast), or will I be discussing both similarities and differences? Why do I want to make the comparison or contrast? To find, explore, or deny overt or less apparent resemblances among the items? To decide which one of a pair or group is better or preferable? Or to use the comparison or contrast to argue for my preference?

2. Are my readers familiar with one or more of the objects of my comparison? If they are familiar with them all, then can I concentrate on the unique features of my analysis? (If they are familiar with only one item, start with the known before discussing the unknown. If they are unacquainted with everything, for purposes of explanation you might wish to begin with a comparison that focuses on the common elements among the items under discussion.)

3. How global or minute will my comparison be (i.e., do I want to make only a few points of comparison or contrast, or many)? Will my essay make more sense to my readers if I present each subject as a complete unit before discussing the next? Or will the comparison or contrast be more meaningful if I proceed point by point?

4. Have I ruled out trivial and irrelevant comparisons? Does each point have a counterpart that I have treated in an equivalent manner, through comparable analysis or illustration, length, and language?

5. Suppose I like or favor one item of the comparison or contrast over the others? Am I obliged to treat every item equally in language and tone, or can my tone vary to reinforce my interpretation?

DEBORAH TANNEN

Tannen, born in Brooklyn in 1945, was partially deafened by a childhood illness. Her consequent interest in nonverbal communication and other aspects of conversation led ultimately to a doctorate in linguistics (University of California, Berkeley, 1979) and professorship at Georgetown University. Tannen's numerous studies of gender-related speech patterns draw on the combined perspectives of anthropology, sociology, psychology, and women's studies, as well as linguistics. A poet and short story writer (*Greek Icons*) as well, Tannen brings a sensitive ear and keen analysis to *Gender and Conversational Interaction* (1993) among students from preschool through junior high, high school, and college. She also explores aspects of communication related to gender, power, and status in the best-selling *That's Not What I Meant!: How Conversational Style Makes or Breaks Your Relations with Others* (1986), *You Just Don't Understand: Women and Men in Conversation* (1990), *Talking from 9 to 5* (1994), and *The Argument Culture: Moving from Debate to Dialogue* (1998).

Much of Tannen's research, like her writing, is based on comparative analyses of the contrasting behavior of men and women in a variety of situations. "Communication Styles" was originally published as "Teachers' Classroom Strategies Should Recognize that Men and Women Use Language Differently" in the *Chronicle of Higher Education* (June 19, 1991). Here Tannen explores differences in the ways that men and women students interact, and how the size, informality, and composition of the group influences who speaks up and who remains silent.

Communication Styles

1   When I researched and wrote my book, *You Just Don't Understand: Women and Men in Conversation*, the furthest thing from my mind was reevaluating my teaching strategies. But that has been one of the direct benefits of having written the book.

2   The primary focus of my linguistic research always has been the language of everyday conversation. One facet of this is conversational style: how different regional, ethnic, and class backgrounds, as well as age and gender, result in different ways

of using language to communicate. *You Just Don't Understand* is about the conversational styles of women and men. As I gained more insight into typically male and female ways of using language, I began to suspect some of the causes of the troubling facts that women who go to single-sex schools do better in later life, and that when young women sit next to young men in classrooms, the males talk more. This is not to say that all men talk in class, nor that no women do. It is simply that a greater percentage of discussion time is taken by men's voices.

The research of sociologists and anthropologists such as 3 Janet Lever, Marjorie Harness Goodwin, and Donna Eder has shown that girls and boys learn to use language differently in their sex-separate peer groups. Typically, a girl has a best friend with whom she sits and talks, frequently telling secrets. It's the telling of secrets, the fact and the way that they talk to each other, that makes them best friends. For boys, activities are central: Their best friends are the ones they do things with. Boys also tend to play in larger groups that are hierarchical. High-status boys give orders and push low-status boys around. So boys are expected to use language to seize center stage: by exhibiting their skills, displaying their knowledge, and challenging and resisting challenges.

These patterns have stunning implications for classroom in- 4 teraction. Most faculty members assume that participating in class discussion is a necessary part of successful performance. Yet speaking in a classroom is more congenial to boys' language experience than to girls', since it entails putting oneself forward in front of a large group of people, many of whom are strangers and at least one of whom is sure to judge speakers' knowledge and intelligence by their verbal display.

Another aspect of many classrooms that makes them more 5 hospitable to most men than to most women is the use of debate-like formats as a learning tool. Our educational system, as Walter Ong argues persuasively in his book *Fighting for Life* (Cornell University Press, 1981), is fundamentally male in that the pursuit of knowledge is believed to be achieved by ritual opposition: public display followed by argument and challenge. Father Ong demonstrates that ritual opposition—what he calls "adversativeness" or "agonism"—is fundamental to the way most males approach almost any activity. (Consider, for example, the little boy who shows he likes a little girl by pulling her braids and shoving her.)

But ritual opposition is antithetical to the way most females learn and like to interact. It is not that females don't fight, but that they don't fight for fun. They don't *ritualize* opposition.

6   Anthropologists working in widely disparate parts of the world have found contrasting verbal rituals for women and men. Women in completely unrelated cultures (for example, Greece and Bali) engage in ritual laments: spontaneously produced rhyming couplets that express their pain, for example, over the loss of loved ones. Men do not take part in laments. They have their own, very different verbal ritual: a contest, a war of words in which they vie with each other to devise clever insults.

7   When discussing these phenomena with a colleague, I commented that I see these two styles in American conversation: Many women bond by talking about troubles, and many men bond by exchanging playful insults and put-downs, and other sorts of verbal sparring. He exclaimed: "I never thought of this, but that's the way I teach: I have students read an article, and then I invite them to tear it apart. After we've torn it to shreds, we talk about how to build a better model."

8   This contrasts sharply with the way I teach: I open the discussion of readings by asking, "What did you find useful in this? What can we use in our own theory building and our own methods?" I note what I see as weaknesses in the author's approach, but I also point out that the writer's discipline and purposes might be different from ours. Finally, I offer personal anecdotes illustrating the phenomena under discussion and praise students' anecdotes as well as their critical acumen.

9   These different teaching styles must make our classrooms wildly different places and hospitable to different students. Male students are more likely to be comfortable attacking the readings and might find the inclusion of personal anecdotes irrelevant and "soft." Women are more likely to resist discussion they perceive as hostile, and, indeed, it is women in my classes who are most likely to offer personal anecdotes.

10 A colleague who read my book commented that he had always taken for granted that the best way to deal with students' comments is to challenge them; this, he felt it was self-evident,

sharpens their minds and helps them develop debating skills. But he had noticed that women were relatively silent in his classes, so he decided to try beginning discussion with relatively open-ended questions and letting comments go unchallenged. He found, to his amazement and satisfaction, that more women began to speak up.

Though some women in his class clearly liked this better, 11 perhaps some of the men liked it less. One young man in my class wrote in a questionnaire about a history professor who gave students questions to think about and called on people to answer them: "He would then play devil's advocate . . . *i.e.,* he debated us. . . . That class *really* sharpened me intellectually. . . . We as students do need to know how to defend ourselves." This young man valued the experience of being attacked and challenged publicly. Many, if not most, women would shrink from such "challenge," experiencing it as public humiliation.

A professor at Hamilton College told me of a young man 12 who was upset because he felt his class presentation had been a failure. The professor was puzzled because he had observed that class members had listened attentively and agreed with the student's observations. It turned out that it was this very agreement that the student interpreted as failure: Since no one had engaged his ideas by arguing with him, he felt they had found them unworthy of attention.

So one reason men speak in class more than women is that 13 many of them find the "public" classroom setting more conducive to speaking, whereas most women are more comfortable speaking in private to a small group of people they know well. A second reason is that men are more likely to be comfortable with the debate-like form that discussion may take. Yet another reason is the different attitudes toward speaking in class that typify women and men.

Students who speak frequently in class, many of whom are 14 men, assume that it is their job to think of contributions and try to get the floor to express them. But many women monitor their participation not only to get the floor but to avoid getting it. Women students in my class tell me that if they have spoken up once or twice, they hold back for the rest of the class because they don't want to dominate. If they have spoken a lot one week, they will remain silent the next. These different ethics of participation are, of course, unstated, so those who speak freely assume that those who remain silent have nothing to say, and those who are reining themselves in assume that the big talkers are selfish and hoggish.

15   When I looked around my classes, I could see these differing ethics and habits at work. For example, my graduate class in analyzing conversation had 20 students, 11 women and 9 men. Of the men, four were foreign students: two Japanese, one Chinese, and one Syrian. With the exception of the three Asian men, all the men spoke in class at least occasionally. The biggest talker in the class was a woman, but there were also five women who never spoke at all, only one of whom was Japanese. I decided to try something different.

16   I broke the class into small groups to discuss the issues raised in the readings and to analyze their own conversational transcripts. I devised three ways of dividing the students into groups: one by the degree program they were in, one by gender, and one by conversational style, as closely as I could guess it. This meant that when the class was grouped according to conversational style, I put Asian students together, fast talkers together, and quiet students together. The class split into groups six times during the semester, so they met in each grouping twice. I told students to regard the groups as examples of interactional data and to note the different ways they participated in different groups. Toward the end of the term, I gave them a questionnaire asking about their class and group participation.

17   I could see plainly from my observation of the groups at work that women who never opened their mouths in class were talking away in the small groups. In fact, the Japanese woman commented that she found it particularly hard to contribute to the all-woman group she was in because "I was overwhelmed by how talkative the female students were in the female-only group." This is particularly revealing because it highlights that the same person who can be "oppressed" into silence in one context can become the talkative "oppressor" in another. No one's conversational style is absolute; everyone's style changes in response to the context and others' styles.

18   Some of the students (seven) said that they preferred the same-gender groups; others preferred the same-style groups. In answer

to the question "Would you have liked to speak in class more than you did?" six of the seven who said Yes were women; the one man was Japanese. Most startlingly, this response did not come only from quiet women; it came from women who had indicated they had spoken in class never, rarely, sometimes, and often. Of the 11 students who said the amount they had spoken was fine, 7 were men. Of the four women who checked "fine," two added qualifications indicating it wasn't completely fine: One wrote in "maybe more," and one wrote, "I have an urge to participate but often feel I should have something more interesting/relevant/wonderful/intelligent to say!!"

I counted my experiment a success. Everyone in the class 19 found the small groups interesting, and no one indicated he or she would have preferred that the class not break into groups. Perhaps most instructive, however, was the fact that the experience of breaking into groups, and of talking about participation in class, raised everyone's awareness about classroom participation. After we had talked about it, some of the quietest women in the class made a few voluntary contributions, though sometimes I had to insure their participation by interrupting the students who were exuberantly speaking out.

Americans are often proud that they discount the signifi- 20 cance of cultural differences: "We are all individuals," many people boast. Ignoring such issues as gender and ethnicity becomes a source of pride: "I treat everyone the same." But treating people the same is not equal treatment if they are not the same.

The classroom is a different environment for those who feel 21 comfortable putting themselves forward in a group than it is for those who find the prospect of doing so chastening, or even terrifying. When a professor asks, "Are there any questions?," students who can formulate statements the fastest have the greatest opportunity to respond. Those who need significant time to do so have not really been given a chance at all, since by the time they are ready to speak, someone else has the floor.

In a class where some students speak out without raising hands, 22 those who feel they must raise their hands and wait to be recognized do not have equal opportunity to speak. Telling them to feel free to jump in will not make them feel free; one's sense of timing, of one's rights and obligations in a classroom, are automatic, learned over years of interaction. They may be changed over time, with motivation and effort, but they cannot be changed on the spot. And everyone assumes his or her own way is best. When I asked my students how the class could be changed to make it easier for them to speak more, the most talkative woman said she would prefer it if no one had to raise hands, and a foreign student said he wished people would raise their hands and wait to be recognized.

23   My experience in this class has convinced me that small-group interaction should be part of any class that is not a small seminar. I also am convinced that having the students become observers of their own interaction is a crucial part of their education. Talking about ways of talking in class makes students aware that their ways of talking affect other students, that the motivations they impute to others may not truly reflect others' motives, and that the behaviors they assume to be self-evidently right are not universal norms.

24   The goal of complete equal opportunity in class may not be attainable, but realizing that one monolithic classroom-participation structure is not equal opportunity is itself a powerful motivation to find more-diverse methods to serve diverse students—and every classroom is diverse.

Content

1. In your experience, are boys (more often than girls) "expected to use language to seize center stage: by exhibiting their skill, displaying their knowledge, and challenging and resisting challenges" (¶ 3)? How does this translate into classroom performance (¶s 4, 7)? In your experience, is Walter Ong's claim true that "ritual opposition . . . is fundamental to the way most males approach almost any activity" (¶ 5)?

2. "Treating people the same is not equal treatment if they are not the same" (¶ 20). Explain how this idea applies in a classroom.

3. Does Tannen equate student talkativeness in class with an inquiring mind? With intelligent preparation? If so, is she justified in equating the two? Or does she base her equation exclusively on gender?

4. Does Tannen argue that the differences between men's and women's communication styles are biologically or culturally determined? Explain your answer.

Strategies/Structures

5. Tannen's article follows the format of physical science and social research: statement of the problem, review of the literature, identification of research methodology, explanation of the research procedure, interpretation of the research findings, and generalizations to other situations or recommendations for either further research or practical applications or both. Show where each stage occurs in this article.

Language

6. "No one's conversational style is absolute; everyone's style changes in response to the context and others' styles" (¶ 17). Explain, with reference to your own experience and other students' behavior in your classes—and out.

For Writing

7. If you go to a co-ed school, do some primary investigation to replicate Tannen's observation that "when young women sit next to [presumably she means *share the same classroom*, not necessarily *sit in immediate proximity to*] young men in classrooms, the males talk more" (¶ 2). Is this true in any or all of your classes? Typically, do men speak more than women in classes taught by men? Do women speak more or less than men in classes taught by women? Do the ages and life experiences of men and women influence the extent of their class participation? Generalize from your findings and interpret them with regard to Tannen's findings. Do you think the men and women students at your school are typical of students at all American colleges or only at colleges of the type that yours represents (private or public community college, four-year undergraduate school, research university)?

8. Do you agree with Tannen's conclusion that "small-group interaction should be part of any class that is not a small seminar" (¶ 23)? If so, why? If not, why not? What demands does this format place on the students? What does this format imply about the way we learn?

9. Write an essay about any of the Content questions. Base your essay on your own experience, and reinforce it with three interviews—one with a student of a different gender from yours, another with a student of a different racial background, another with a student from a different socio-economic class. (To control for teaching style and content, all the students should be enrolled in the same course at the same time.) To

what extent are your conclusions influenced by your informants' class and ethnicity, in comparison with their gender?

10.   Examine a class in which you wanted to talk more (or at all), but did not do so. Why were you more silent than you wanted to be? What in the class format—teacher's instructional style, other students' behavior, your own preparation or maturity—would have had to change in order for you to have been willing to talk more? Would you have gained more from the class if you'd been a more talkative (and hence, active) participant?

STEWART BRAND

> Brand—writer, consultant, gadfly, and futurist—founded *The Whole Earth Catalog* in the late 1960s, an award-winning compendium of book reviews, recommendations for tools, alternative energy sources, natural fibers, and personal testimonials such as, "Here are the tools" (a key word of Brand's) to make your life go better. And to make the world go better. That they're the same tools is our theory of civilization." Despite the book's counterculture orientation, Brand (born 1938) himself grew up in Rockford, Illinois, was educated at Phillips Exeter Academy and Stanford (B.S., 1960), and served in the Army, training to be a paratrooper, before a stint as a psychedelic member of Ken Kesey's Merry Pranksters. Today he lives on a houseboat in Sausalito, California; his office is in a crumbling fishing boat moored in a parking lot, flanked by two cargo containers that house his vast library.
>
> In recent years Brand, who remains independent-minded though no longer psychedelic, has edited the *Coevolution Quarterly*, a think-tank journal that publishes a mix of left, right, and mainstream opinions; founded the WELL, a teleconference system that has become "a seminal institution of cyberspace"; and also founded Global Business Network, an organization that helps businesses and industries anticipate the future with creative innovations. One of his early predictions, for instance, was that the first e-mail system in the country would be provided not by AT&T, which had been proceeding slowly, step-by-step to figure out the optimal system, but by the Internet, which was quickly up and running and then tinkered with through a process of trial-and-error. "Written on the Wind," first published in the

Library of Congress's magazine *Civilization*, "the cultural search engine," in November, 1988, addresses problems caused by rapid technological changes that make digital information "irretrievable almost as soon as it is stored."

Written on the Wind

T he promise has been made: "Digital information is forever. It 1 doesn't deteriorate and requires little in the way of material media." So said one of the chieftains of the emerging digital age, computer-chip maker Andy Grove, the head of the Intel Corporation. Another chieftain, Librarian of Congress James H. Billington, has set about digitizing the world's largest library so that its contents can become accessible by anyone, from anywhere, forever.

But a shadow has fallen. "It is only slightly facetious," wrote 2 RAND researcher Jeff Rothenberg in *Scientific American*, "to say that digital information lasts forever—or five years, whichever comes first."

Digitized media do have some attributes of immortality. 3 They possess great clarity, great universality, great reliability and great economy—digital storage is already so compact and cheap it is essentially free. Many people have found themselves surprised and embarrassed by the reemergence of perfectly preserved e-mail or online newsgroup comments they wrote nonchalantly years ago and forgot about.

Yet those same people discover that they cannot revisit their 4 own word-processor files or computerized financial records from ten years before. It turns out that what was so carefully stored was written with a now-obsolete application, in a now-obsolete operating system, on a long-vanished make of computer, using a now-antique storage medium (where do you find a drive for a 5 ¼-inch floppy disk?)

Fixing digital discontinuity sounds like exactly the kind of 5 problem that fast-moving computer technology should be able to solve. But fast-moving computer technology is the problem: By constantly accelerating its own capabilities (making faster, cheaper, sharper tools that make ever faster, cheaper, sharper tools), the technology is just as constantly self-obsolescing. The great creator becomes the great eraser.

6   Behind every hot new working computer is a trail of bodies of extinct computers, extinct storage media, extinct applications, extinct files. Science fiction writer Bruce Sterling refers to our time as "the Golden Age of dead media, most of them with the working lifespan of a pack of Twinkies." On the Internet, Sterling is amassing a roll call of their once-honored personal computer names: Altair, Amiga, Amstrad, Apples I, II and III, Apple Lisa, Apricot, Atari, AT&T, Commodore, CompuPro, Cromemco, Epson, Franklin, Grid, IBM PCjr, IBM XT, Kaypro, Morrow, NEC PC-8081, NorthStar, Osborne, Sinclair, Tandy, Wang, Xerox Star, Yamaha CX5M. Buried with them are whole clans of programming languages, operating systems, storage formats, and countless rotting applications in an infinite variety of mutually incompatible versions. Everything written on them was written on the wind, leaving not a trace.

7   Computer scientist Danny Hillis notes that we have good raw data from previous ages written on clay, on stone, on parchment and paper, but from the 1950s to the present, recorded information increasingly disappears into a digital gap. Historians will consider this a dark age. Science historians can read Galileo's technical correspondence from the 1590s but not Marvin Minsky's from the 1960s.

8   It's not just that file formats quickly become obsolete; the physical media themselves are short-lived. Magnetic media, such as disks and tape, lose their integrity in 5 to 10 years. Optically etched media, such as CD-ROMS, if used only once, last only 5 to 15 years before they degrade. And digital files do not degrade gracefully like analog audio tapes. When they fail, they fail utterly.

9   Beyond the evanescence of data formats and digital storage media lies a deeper problem. Computer systems of large scale are at the core of driving corporations, public institutions, and indeed whole sectors of the economy. Over time, these gargantuan systems become dauntingly complex and unknowable, as new features are added, old bugs are worked around with layers of "patches," generations of programmers add new programming tools and styles, and portions of the system are repurposed to take on novel functions. With both respect and loathing, computer professionals call these monsters "legacy systems." Teasing a new

function out of a legacy system is not done by command, but by conducting cautious alchemic experiments that, with luck, converge toward the desired outcome.

And the larger fear looms: We are in the process of building   10
one vast global computer, which could easily become The Legacy System from Hell that holds civilization hostage—the system doesn't really work; it can't be fixed; no one understands it; no one is in charge of it; it can't be lived without; and it gets worse every year.

Today's bleeding-edge technology is tomorrow's broken legacy   11
system. Commercial software is almost always written in enormous haste, at ever-accelerating market velocity; it can foresee an "upgrade path" to next year's version, but decades are outside its scope. And societies live by decades, civilizations by centuries.

Digital archivists thus join an ancient lineage of copyists   12
and translators. The process, now as always, can introduce copying errors and spurious "improvements," and can lose the equivalent of volumes of Aristotle. But the practice also builds the bridge between human language eras—from Greek to Latin, to English, to whatever's next.

Archivist Howard Besser points out that digital artifacts   13
are increasingly complex to revive. First there is the viewing problem—a book displays itself, but the contents of a CD-ROM are invisible until opened on something. Then there's the scrambling problem—the innumerable ways that files are compressed and, increasingly, encrypted. There are interrelationship problems—hypertext or Web-site links that were active in the original, now dead ends. And translation problems occur in the way different media behave—just as a photograph of a painting is not the same experience as the painting, looking through a screen is not the same as experiencing an immersion medium, watching a game is not the same as playing it.

Gradually a set of best practices is emerging for ensuring   14
digital continuity: Use the most common file formats, avoid compression where possible, keep a log of changes to a file, employ standard metadata, make multiple copies and so forth.

Another approach is through core standards, like the DNA   15
code in genes or written Chinese in Asia, readable through epochs while everything changes around and through them. The

platform-independent programming language called Java boasts the motto "Write Once, Run Anywhere." One of Java's creators, Bill Joy, asserts that the language "is so well specified that if you write a simple version of Java in Java, it becomes a Rosetta Stone. Aliens, or a sufficiently smart human, could eventually figure it out because it's an implementation of itself." We'll see.

16   Exercise is always the best preserver. Major religious works are impressively persistent because each age copies, analyzes and uses them. The books live and are kept contemporary by frequent use.

17   Since digital artifacts are quickly outnumbering all possible human users, Jaron Lanier recommends employing artificial intelligences to keep the artifacts exercised through centuries of forced contemporaneity. Still, even robot users might break continuity. Most reliable of all would be a two-path strategy: To keep a digital artifact perpetually accessible, record the current version of it on a physically permanent medium, such as silicon disks microetched by Norsam Technologies in New Mexico, then go ahead and let users, robot or human, migrate the artifact through generations of versions and platforms, pausing from time to time to record the new manifestation on a Norsam disk. One path is slow, periodic and conservative; the other, fast, constant and adaptive. When the chain of use is eventually broken, it leaves a permanent record of the chain until then, so the artifact can be revived to begin the chain anew.

18   How can we invest in a future we know is structurally incapable of keeping faith with its past? The digital industries must shift from being the main source of society's ever-shortening attention span to becoming a reliable guarantor of long-term perspective. We'll know that shift has happened when programmers begin to anticipate the Year 10,000 Problem, and assign five digits instead of four to year dates. "01998" they'll write, at first frivolously, then seriously.

Content

1. "Behind every hot new working computer is a trail of bodies of extinct computers, extinct storage media, extinct applications, extinct files. . . . Everything written on them was written on the wind, leaving

not a trace" (¶ 6). What does this trail of obsolescence from the past imply for the future?

2. Brand summarizes, "We are in the process of building one vast global computer, which could easily become The Legacy System from Hell that holds civilization hostage—the system doesn't really work; it can't be fixed; no one understands it; no one is in charge of it; it can't be lived without; and it gets worse every year" (¶ 10). Does the evidence Brand cites in the essay's opening (¶s 1–2), or the solutions he proposes at the end provide a reassuring solution to the problem? In your answer, draw on your own knowledge and experience to assess his evidence. What does Brand himself think ought to be done?

Strategies/Structures

3. Explain the paradox that Brand points out, "It is only slightly facetious . . . to say that digital information lasts forever—or five years, whichever comes first" (¶ 2).

4. Brand devotes twice as much space to stating the problem (¶s 1–13) as to identifying possible solutions (¶s 14–18). Does the proportioning of the space convey the message that the problems are of greater magnitude than the solutions?

5. In what ways (if any) does Brand establish his authority to write about this subject?

Language

6. Brand uses quite breezy language in discussing a problem of great seriousness. Find examples of his breezy language, and decide whether the language undercuts or reinforces his point.

7. Brand invents memorable paradoxical epigrams, "The great creator becomes the great eraser" (¶ 5). What's gained with an epigrammatic statement? What's lost?

For Writing

8. Elaborate on both halves of a paradox in the essay—or anywhere else—such as Brand's observations that "digitized media do have some attributes of immortality" while concurrently possessing the potential for great (self-) destruction.

9. Pick a current invention or discovery, such as cloning, genetic alteration, innovations in computer technology, and discuss its worst case/best case scenario.

STEPHEN JAY GOULD

Gould (born, 1941) graduated from Antioch in 1963, earned a
Ph.D. from Columbia in 1967, and since then has been a geology
professor at Harvard, where he teaches paleontology, biology,
and history of science. He provides exceptionally clear definitions, explanations, and arguments in his writings for students,
colleagues, and general readers of his columns in *Natural History*.
These have been collected in several volumes, including *Ever
Since Darwin* (1977); *Hen's Teeth and Horse's Toes* (1983); *Bully for
Brontosaurus* (1991), *Eight Little Piggies* (1993); and *Leonardo's
Mountain of Clams and the Diet of Worms* (1998). Gould's scientific
orientation favors the underdog, as is evident in *The Mismeasure
of Man* (1981). There he reinterprets two centuries of IQ testing
and other quantitative ways of determining intelligence to
show how flawed measurement procedures and wrong interpretations of information invariably favored educated white
Anglo-Saxon males and contributed to the oppression of everyone else. Gould has received numerous honors, including the
American Book Award in Science and a MacArthur Fellowship
(a "genius grant").

Gould's analysis of the qualities of great scientific essayists
(T. H. Huxley, J. B. S. Haldane, P. B. Medawar) applies equally
well to his own writings:

> All write about the simplest things and draw from them
> a universe of implications. . . . All maintain an unflinching
> commitment to rationality amid the soft attractions of an
> uncritical mysticism. . . . All demonstrate a deep commitment
> to the demystification of science by cutting through jargon;
> they show by example rather than exhortation that the most
> complex concepts can be rendered intelligible to everyone.

These qualities are apparent in "Evolution as Fact and
Theory," originally published in *Discover* (1981), a journal of
popular science. Gould uses the crucial definitions and distinctions between fact and theory as the basis for contrasting the
evolutionists' scientific position with the creationists' pseudo-
scientific position, which he argues against in most of the rest
of the essay. He contends—by means of another contrast—that
"'scientific creationism' is a self-contradictory, nonsense phrase
precisely because it cannot be falsified."

Evolution as Fact and Theory

K irtley Mather, who died last year at age 89, was a pillar of 1
both science and the Christian religion in America and one
of my dearest friends. The difference of half a century in our ages
evaporated before our common interests. The most curious thing
we shared was a battle we each fought at the same age. For
Kirtley had gone to Tennessee with Clarence Darrow to testify for
evolution at the Scopes trial of 1925. When I think that we are
enmeshed again in the same struggle for one of the best documented, most compelling and exciting concepts in all of science, I
don't know whether to laugh or cry.

According to idealized principles of scientific discourse, the 2
arousal of dormant issues should reflect fresh data that give
renewed life to abandoned notions. Those outside the current
debate may therefore be excused for suspecting that creationists
have come up with something new, or that evolutionists have
generated some serious internal trouble. But nothing has
changed; the creationists have not a single new fact or argument.
Darrow and Bryan were at least more entertaining than we lesser
antagonists today. The rise of creationism is politics, pure and
simple; it represents one issue (and by no means the major concern) of the resurgent evangelical right. Arguments that seemed
kooky just a decade ago have re-entered the mainstream.

Creationism Is Not Science

The basic attack of the creationists falls apart on two general 3
counts before we even reach the supposed factual details of their
complaints against evolution. First, they play upon a vernacular
misunderstanding of the word "theory" to convey the false impression that we evolutionists are covering up the rotten core of
our edifice. Second, they misuse a popular philosophy of science
to argue that they are behaving scientifically in attacking evolution. Yet the same philosophy demonstrates that their own belief
is not science, and that "scientific creationism" is therefore meaningless and self-contradictory, a superb example of what Orwell
called "newspeak."

4   In the American vernacular, "theory" often means "imperfect fact"—part of a hierarchy of confidence running downhill from fact to theory to hypothesis to guess. Thus the power of the creationist argument: evolution is "only" a theory, and intense debate now rages about many aspects of the theory. If evolution is less than a fact, and scientists can't even make up their minds about the theory, then what confidence can we have in it? Indeed, President Reagan echoed this argument before an evangelical group in Dallas when he said (in what I devoutly hope was campaign rhetoric): "Well, it is a theory. It is a scientific theory only, and it has in recent years been challenged in the world of science—that is, not believed in the scientific community to be as infallible as it once was."

5   Well, evolution *is* a theory. It is also a fact. And facts and theories are different things, not rungs in a hierarchy of increasing certainty. Facts are the world's data. Theories are structures of ideas that explain and interpret facts. Facts do not go away when scientists debate rival theories to explain them. Einstein's theory of gravitation replaced Newton's, but apples did not suspend themselves in mid-air pending the outcome. And human beings evolved from apelike ancestors whether they did so by Darwin's proposed mechanism or by some other, yet to be discovered.

6   Moreover, "fact" does not mean "absolute certainty." The final proofs of logic and mathematics flow deductively from stated premises and achieve certainty only because they are *not* about the empirical world. Evolutionists make no claim for perpetual truth, though creationists often do (and then attack us for a style of argument that they themselves favor). In science, "fact" can only mean "confirmed to such a degree that it would be perverse to withhold provisional assent." I suppose that apples might start to rise tomorrow, but the possibility does not merit equal time in physics classrooms.

7   Evolutionists have been clear about this distinction between fact and theory from the very beginning, if only because we have always acknowledged how far we are from completely understanding the mechanisms (theory) by which evolution (fact) occurred. Darwin continually emphasized the difference between his two great and separate accomplishments: establishing the fact of evolution, and proposing a theory—natural selection—to explain

the mechanism of evolution. He wrote in *The Descent of Man*: "I had two distinct objects in view; firstly, to show that species had not been separately created, and secondly, that natural selection had been the chief agent of change . . . Hence if I have erred in . . . having exaggerated its [natural selection's] power . . . I have at least, as I hope, done good service in aiding to overthrow the dogma of separate creations."

Thus Darwin acknowledged the provisional nature of nat- 8
ural selection while affirming the fact of evolution. The fruitful theoretical debate that Darwin initiated has never ceased. From the 1940s through the 1960s, Darwin's own theory of natural selection did achieve a temporary hegemony that it never enjoyed in his lifetime. But renewed debate characterizes our decade, and, while no biologist questions the importance of natural selection, many now doubt its ubiquity. In particular, many evolutionists argue that substantial amounts of genetic change may not be subject to natural selection and may spread through populations at random. Others are challenging Darwin's linking of natural selection with gradual, imperceptible change through all intermediary degrees; they are arguing that most evolutionary events may occur far more rapidly than Darwin envisioned.

Scientists regard debates on fundamental issues of theory as 9
a sign of intellectual health and a source of excitement. Science is—and how else can I say it?—most fun when it plays with interesting ideas, examines their implications, and recognizes that old information may be explained in surprisingly new ways. Evolutionary theory is now enjoying this uncommon vigor. Yet amidst all this turmoil no biologist has been led to doubt the fact that evolution occurred; we are debating *how* it happened. We are all trying to explain the same thing: the tree of evolutionary descent linking all organisms by ties of genealogy. Creationists pervert and caricature this debate by conveniently neglecting the common conviction that underlies it, and by falsely suggesting that we now doubt the very phenomenon we are struggling to understand.

Using another invalid argument, creationists claim that "the 10
dogma of separate creations," as Darwin characterized it a century ago, is a scientific theory meriting equal time with evolution in high school biology curricula. But a prevailing viewpoint among

philosophers of science belies this creationist argument. Philosopher Karl Popper has argued for decades that the primary criterion of science is the falsifiability of its theories. We can never prove absolutely, but we can falsify. A set of ideas that cannot, in principle, be falsified is not science.

11   The entire creationist argument involves little more than a rhetorical attempt to falsify evolution by presenting supposed contradictions among its supporters. Their brand of creationism, they claim, is "scientific" because it follows the Popperian model in trying to demolish evolution. Yet Popper's argument must apply in both directions. One does not become a scientist by the simple act of trying to falsify another scientific system; one has to present an alternative system that also meets Popper's criterion— it too must be falsifiable in principle.

12   "Scientific creationism" is a self-contradictory, nonsense phrase precisely because it cannot be falsified. I can envision observations and experiments that would disprove any evolutionary theory I know, but I cannot imagine what potential data could lead creationists to abandon their beliefs. Unbeatable systems are dogma, not science. Lest I seem harsh or rhetorical, I quote creationism's leading intellectual, Duane Gish, Ph.D., from his recent (1978) book *Evolution? The Fossils Say No!* "By creation we mean the bringing into being by a supernatural Creator of the basic kinds of plants and animals by the process of sudden, or fiat, creation. We do not know how the Creator created, what processes He used, *for He used processes which are not now operating anywhere in the natural universe* [Gish's italics]. This is why we refer to creation as special creation. We cannot discover by scientific investigations anything about the creative processes used by the Creator." Pray tell, Dr. Gish, in the light of your last sentence, what then is "scientific" creationism?

The Fact of Evolution

13   Our confidence that evolution occurred centers upon three general arguments. First, we have abundant, direct, observational evidence of evolution in action, from both the field and the laboratory. It ranges from countless experiments on change in nearly everything about fruit flies subjected to artificial selection in the laboratory to

the famous British moths that turned black when industrial soot darkened the trees upon which they rest. (The moths gain protection from sharp-sighted bird predators by blending into the background.) Creationists do not deny these observations; how could they? Creationists have tightened their act. They now argue that God only created "basic kinds," and allowed for limited evolutionary meandering within them. Thus toy poodles and Great Danes come from the dog kind and moths can change color, but nature cannot convert a dog to a cat or a monkey to a man.

The second and third arguments for evolution—the case for 14 major changes—do not involve direct observation of evolution in action. They rest upon inference, but are no less secure for that reason. Major evolutionary change requires too much time for direct observation on the scale of recorded human history. All historical sciences rest upon inference, and evolution is no different from geology, cosmology, or human history in this respect. In principle, we cannot observe processes that operated in the past. We must infer them from results that still survive: living and fossil organisms for evolution, documents and artifacts for human history, strata and topography for geology.

The second argument—that the imperfection of nature 15 reveals evolution—strikes many people as ironic, for they feel that evolution should be most elegantly displayed in the nearly perfect adaptation expressed by some organisms—the chamber of a gull's wing, or butterflies that cannot be seen in ground litter because they mimic leaves so precisely. But perfection could be imposed by a wise creator or evolved by natural selection. Perfection covers the tracks of past history. And past history—the evidence of descent—is our mark of evolution.

Evolution lies exposed in the *imperfections* that record a his- 16 tory of descent. Why should a rat run, a bat fly, a porpoise swim, and I type this essay with structures built of the same bones unless we all inherited them from a common ancestor? An engineer, starting from scratch, could design better limbs in each case. Why should all the large native mammals of Australia be marsupials, unless they descended from a common ancestor isolated on this island continent? Marsupials are not "better," or ideally suited for Australia; many have been wiped out by placental mammals imported by man from other continents. This principle of imperfection extends to all historical sciences. When we recognize the etymology of September, October, November, and December (seventh, eighth, ninth, and tenth, from the Latin), we know that two additional items (January and February) must have been added to an original calendar of ten months.

17   The third argument is more direct: transitions are often found in the fossil record. Preserved transitions are not common—and should not be, according to our understanding of evolution (see next section)—but they are not entirely wanting, as creationists often claim. The lower jaw of reptiles contains several bones, that of mammals only one. The non-mammalian jawbones are reduced, step by step, in mammalian ancestors until they become tiny nubbins located at the back of the jaw. The "hammer" and "anvil" bones of the mammalian ear are descendants of these nubbins. How could such a transition be accomplished? the creationists ask. Surely a bone is either entirely in the jaw or in the ear. Yet paleontologists have discovered two transitional lineages or therapsids (the so-called mammal-like reptiles) with a double jaw joint—one composed of the old quadrate and articular bones (soon to become the hammer and anvil), the other of the squamosal and dentary bones (as in modern mammals). For that matter, what better transitional form could we desire than the oldest human, *Australopithecus afarensis*, with its apelike palate, its human upright stance, and a cranial capacity larger than any ape's of the same body size but a full 1,000 cubic centimeters below ours? If God made each of the half dozen human species discovered in ancient rocks, why did he create in an unbroken temporal sequence of progressively more modern features—increasing cranial capacity, reduced face and teeth, larger body size? Did he create to mimic evolution and test our faith thereby?

An Example of Creationist Argument

18   Faced with these facts of evolution and the philosophical bankruptcy of their own position, creationists rely upon distortion and innuendo to buttress their rhetorical claim. If I should sound sharp or bitter, indeed I am—for I have become a major target of these practices.

19   I count myself among the evolutionists who argue for a jerky, or episodic, rather than a smoothly gradual, pace of change. In

1972 my colleague Niles Eldredge and I developed the theory of punctuated equilibrium. We argued that two outstanding facts of the fossil record—geologically "sudden" origin of new species and failure to change thereafter (stasis)—reflect the predictions of evolutionary theory, not the imperfections of the fossil record. In most theories, small isolated populations are the source of new species, and the process of speciation takes thousands or tens of thousands of years. This amount of time, so long when measured against our lives, is a geological microsecond. It represents much less than 1 percent of the average life span for a fossil invertebrate species—more than 10 million years. Large, widespread, and well-established species, on the other hand, are not expected to change very much. We believe that the inertia of large populations explains the stasis of most fossil species over millions of years.

We proposed the theory of punctuated equilibrium largely   20
to provide a different explanation for pervasive trends in the fossil record. Trends, we argued, cannot be attributed to gradual transformation within lineages, but must arise from the differential success of certain kinds of species. A trend, we argued, is more like climbing a flight of stairs (punctuations and stasis) than rolling up an inclined plane.

Since we proposed punctuated equilibria to explain trends,   21
it is infuriating to be quoted again and again by creationists—whether through design or stupidity, I do not know—as admitting that the fossil record includes no transitional forms. Transitional forms are generally lacking at the species level, but are abundant between larger groups. The evolution from reptiles to mammals, as mentioned earlier, is well documented. Yet a pamphlet entitled "Harvard Scientists Agree Evolution Is a Hoax" states: "The facts of punctuated equilibrium which Gould and Eldredge . . . are forcing Darwinists to swallow fit the picture that Bryan insisted on, and which God has revealed to us in the Bible."

Continuing the distortion, several creationists have equated   22
the theory of punctuated equilibrium with a caricature of the beliefs of Richard Goldschmidt, a great early geneticist. Goldschmidt argued, in a famous book published in 1940, that new groups can arise all at once through major mutations. He referred to these suddenly transformed creatures as "hopeful monsters." (I am attracted to some aspects of the non-caricatured version, but Goldschmidt's theory still has nothing to do with punctuated

equilibrium.) Creationist Luther Sunderland talks of the "punctuated equilibrium hopeful monster theory" and tells his hopeful
readers that "it amounts to tacit admission that anti-evolutionists
are correct in asserting there is no fossil evidence supporting the
theory that all life is connected to a common ancestor." Duane
Gish writes, "According to Goldschmidt, and now apparently
according to Gould, a reptile laid an egg from which the first bird,
feathers and all, was produced." Any evolutionist who believed
such nonsense would rightly be laughed off the intellectual stage;
yet the only theory that could ever envision such a scenario for
the evolution of birds is creationism—God acts in the egg.

Conclusion

23   I am both angry at and amused by the creationists; but mostly I am
deeply sad. Sad for many reasons. Sad because so many people
who respond to creationist appeals are troubled for the right
reason, but venting their anger at the wrong target. It is true that
scientists have often been dogmatic and elitist. It is true that we
have often allowed the white-coated, advertising image to represent us—"Scientists say that Brand X cures bunions ten times
faster than . . ." We have not fought it adequately because we
derive benefits from appearing as a new priesthood. It is also true
that faceless bureaucratic state power intrudes more and more
into our lives and removes choices that should belong to individuals and communities. I can understand that requiring that evolution be taught in schools might be seen as one more insult on all
these grounds. But the culprit is not, and cannot be, evolution or
any other fact of the natural world. Identify and fight your legitimate enemies by all means, but we are not among them.

24   I am sad because the practical result of this brouhaha will
not be expanded coverage to include creationism (that would also
make me sad), but the reduction or excision of evolution from
high school curricula. Evolution is one of the half dozen "great
ideas" developed by science. It speaks to the profound issues
of genealogy that fascinate all of us—the "roots" phenomenon
writ large. Where did we come from? Where did life arise? How
did it develop? How are organisms related? It forces us to think,
ponder, and wonder. Shall we deprive millions of this knowledge

and once again teach biology as a set of dull and unconnected facts, without the thread that weaves diverse material into a supple unity?

But most of all I am saddened by a trend I am just beginning to discern among my colleagues. I sense that some now wish to mute the healthy debate about theory that has brought new life to evolutionary biology. It provides grist for creationist mills, they say, even if only by distortion. Perhaps we should lie low and rally round the flag of strict Darwinism, at least for the moment— a kind of old-time religion on our part. 25

But we should borrow another metaphor and recognize that we too have to tread a straight and narrow path, surrounded by roads to perdition. For if we ever begin to suppress our search to understand nature, to quench our own intellectual excitement in a misguided effort to present a united front where it does not and should not exist, then we are truly lost. 26

Content

1. Identify Gould's two different definitions of "theory," one scientific, the other vernacular (common, everyday) (¶s 3–4, and elsewhere). Define what he means by a "fact" (¶s 5–7). Using these definitions, explain what he means by "Well, evolution *is* a theory. It is also a fact." What differentiation does Gould make between evolution as a fact and evolution as a theory (¶s 5–7 and throughout)?

2. What does Gould mean by insisting that any set of scientific ideas must be able to be falsified? Why does he identify creationism as an "unbeatable system" that cannot be falsified?

3. "Scientists regard debates on fundamental issues of theory as a sign of intellectual health and a source of excitement," says Gould (¶ 9). Why is this so? Why is evolutionary theory so much fun, in Gould's view? Why would creationist theories stifle debate and take the "fun" out of doing science (¶s 9–12)?

Strategies/Structures

4. How does Gould use definitions in constructing his argument against creationism?

5. Using Gould's definitions, derive Gould's rules for scientific debate. Does he follow his own rules in this essay?

Language

6. Gould says, "The rise of creationism is politics, pure and simple" (¶ 2). What does he mean by this? How does politics influence the language we use?

7. How does the language we use influence our beliefs about a particular subject? In reference to this essay, you could talk about *science* and *creationism*, but there are many other possibilities for discussion.

8. Gould says, "I am both angry at and amused by the creationists; but mostly I am deeply sad" (¶ 23). Does the language Gould uses in addressing the ideas of his opponents (both creationists and fellow strict Darwinist geologists who dispute his theories and would suppress them for different reasons [¶s 23–26]) reflect any or all of these attitudes? Does he treat his opponents with courtesy? With respect?

For Writing

9. Science, like any other body of knowledge, is ever-changing. Facts can be reassessed, reinterpreted; intellectual constructs can be reconfigured—suppose someone redrew the constellations to represent great works of art instead of mythological stories. New contexts can be provided to enable new ways to understand familiar information. Select a definition of a term central to medicine, psychology, sociology, or an empirically oriented science, that has undergone major changes (*race, homosexual, family,* are among the possible terms). Trace the history of this definition to highlight the changes in the word's meaning, and explore some of the implications of the old and new definitions.

10. Judging from Gould's practice in this essay, construct a set of rules for appropriate treatment of one's opponents in an argument. (You could use your answers to Language question 8 as a point of departure.) Under what, if any, circumstances are irony, sarcasm, invective, humor suitable in referring to ideas or people with whom you disagree?

VICKI HEARNE

Hearne's dual professions, writer and animal trainer, reinforce each other in unusual and enlightening ways. Hearne (born, 1946) earned a B.A. from the University of California, Riverside (1971) and studied poetry writing at Stanford on a Stegner Fellowship. She has published poetry, *Nervous Horses* (1980) and *In Absence of Horses*

(1984); a novel, *The White German Shepherd* (1988); and three non-fiction works, *Adam's Task: Calling Animals by Name* (1986), *Bandit: Dossier of a Dangerous Dog* (1991), and *Animal Happiness* (1994).

As in "What's Wrong with Animal Rights?" first published in *Harper's* in 1991, Hearne's nonfiction, poetry, and fiction provide subtle interpretations, sophisticated and wise, of the complex relationships between animals and humans. Her common sense and experience as a trainer of dogs and horses is buttressed by wide reading in philosophy, literature, and natural history. In the introduction to *Adam's Task*, she explains how her unique membership in two communities enabled her to write that book:

> If I had remained firmly within the worlds of discourse provided by the stable and the kennel, I would have been content, not because there is no philosophy in those worlds, but because there is such a rich and ever-changing web of philosophies when good trainers talk and write. . . .
>
> However, my temperament regularly led me away from the kennel and tack room to university libraries and cafeterias, laboratories and classrooms. The result was that for some years I uneasily inhabited at least two completely different worlds of discourse, each using a group of languages that were inter-translatable—dog trainers can talk to horse trainers, and philosophers can talk to linguists and psychologists, but dog trainers and philosophers can't make much sense of each other.

In bridging the gap between these different worlds, Hearne is able to see each from the point of view of the other. Her dual vision not only enables but mandates an implicit perspective of continual comparison and contrast. From this vantage point she questions the generalizations humans make about animals, and challenges what people take for granted in their stereotyping of animal behavior, even animal rights.

What's Wrong with Animal Rights?

Not all happy animals are alike. A Doberman going over a hurdle after a small wooden dumbbell is sleek, all arcs of harmonious power. A basset hound cheerfully performing the same exercise exhibits harmonies of a more lugubrious nature. There are chimpanzees who love precision the way musicians or fanatical housekeepers or accomplished hypochondriacs do; others for whom happiness is a matter of invention and variation—chimp vaudevillians. There is a rhinoceros whose happiness, as near as I can make out, is in needing to be trained every morning, all over again, or else he "forgets" his circus routine, and in this you find a clue to the slow, deep, quiet chuckle of his happiness and to the glory of the beast. Happiness for Secretariat is in his ebullient bound, that joyful length of stride. For the draft horse or the weight-pull dog, happiness is of a different shape, more awesome and less obviously intelligent. When the pulling horse is at its most intense, the animal goes into himself, allocating all of the educated power that organizes his desire to dwell in fierce and delicate intimacy with that power, leans into the harness, and MAKES THAT SUCKER *MOVE*.

2   If we are speaking of human beings and use the phrase "animal happiness," we tend to mean something like "creature comforts." The emblems of this are the golden retriever rolling in the grass, the horse with his nose deep in the oats, the kitty by the fire. Creature comforts are important to animals—"Grub first, then ethics" is a motto that would describe many a wise Labrador retriever, and I have a pit bull named Annie whose continual quest for the perfect pillow inspires her to awesome feats. But there is something more to animals, a capacity for satisfactions that come from work in the fullest sense—what is known in philosophy and in this country's Declaration of Independence as "happiness." This is a sense of personal achievement, like the satisfaction felt by a good wood-carver or a dancer or a poet or an accomplished dressage horse. It is a happiness that, like the artist's, must come from something within the animal, something trainers call "talent." Hence, it cannot be imposed on the animal. But it is also something that does not come *ex nihilo*. If it had not been a fairly ordinary thing, in one part of the world, to teach young children to play the pianoforte, it is doubtful that Mozart's music would exist.

3   Happiness is often misunderstood as a synonym for pleasure or as an antonym for suffering. But Aristotle associated happiness with ethics—codes of behavior that urge us toward the sensation of getting it right, a kind of work that yields the "click" of satisfaction upon solving a problem or surmounting an obstacle. In his *Ethics*, Aristotle wrote, "If happiness is activity in accordance with excellence, it is reasonable that it should be in accordance with

the highest excellence." Thomas Jefferson identified the capacity for happiness as one of the three fundamental rights on which all others are based: "life, liberty, and the pursuit of happiness."

I bring up this idea of happiness as a form of work because 4 I am an animal trainer, and work is the foundation of the happiness a trainer and an animal discover together. I bring up these words also because they cannot be found in the lexicon of the animal-rights movement. This absence accounts for the uneasiness toward the movement of most people, who sense that rights advocates have a point but take it too far when they liberate snails or charge that goldfish at the county fair are suffering. But the problem with the animal-rights advocates is not that they take it too far, it's that they've got it all wrong.

Animal rights are built upon a misconceived premise that rights 5 were created to prevent us from unnecessary suffering. You can't find an animal-rights book, video, pamphlet, or rock concert in which someone doesn't mention the Great Sentence, written by Jeremy Bentham in 1789. Arguing in favor of such rights, Bentham wrote: "The question is not, Can they *reason?* nor, can they *talk?* but, can they suffer?"

The logic of the animal-rights movement places suffering at 6 the iconographic center of a skewed value system. The thinking of its proponents—given eerie expression in a virtually sado-pornographic sculpture of a tortured monkey that won a prize for its compassionate vision—has collapsed into a perverse conundrum. Today the loudest voices calling for—demanding—the destruction of animals are the humane organizations. This is an inevitable consequence of the apotheosis of the drive to relieve suffering: Death is the ultimate release. To compensate for their contradictions, the humane movement has demonized, in this century and the last, those who made animal happiness their business: veterinarians, trainers, and the like. We think of Louis Pasteur as the man whose work saved you and me and your dog and cat from rabies, but antivivisectionists of the time claimed that rabies increased in areas where there were Pasteur Institutes.

An anti-rabies public-relations campaign mounted in Eng- 7 land in the 1880s by the Royal Society for the Prevention of Cruelty to Animals and other organizations led to orders being issued to club any dog found not wearing a muzzle. England still has her cruel and unnecessary law that requires an animal to spend six months in quarantine before being allowed loose in the country. Most of the recent propaganda about pit bulls—the crazy claim that they "take hold with their front teeth while they chew away with their rear teeth" (which would imply, incorrectly, that they have double jaws)—can be traced to literature published by the Humane Society of the United States during the fall of 1987 and earlier. If your neighbors want your dog or horse impounded and destroyed because he is a nuisance—say the dog barks, or the horse attracts flies—it will be the local Humane Society to whom your neighbors turn for action.

8   In a way, everyone has the opportunity to know that the history of the humane movement is largely a history of miseries, arrests, prosecutions, and death. The Humane Society is the pound, the place with the decompression chamber or the lethal injections. You occasionally find worried letters about this in Ann Landers's column.

9   Animal-rights publications are illustrated largely with photographs of two kinds of animals—"Helpless Fluff" and "Agonized Fluff," the two conditions in which some people seem to prefer their animals, because any other version of an animal is too complicated for propaganda. In the introduction to his book *Animal Liberation*, Peter Singer says somewhat smugly that he and his wife have no animals and, in fact, don't much care for them. This is offered as evidence of his objectivity and ethical probity. But it strikes me as an odd, perhaps obscene, underpinning for an ethical project that encourages university and high school students to cherish their ignorance of, say, great bird dogs as proof of their devotion to animals.

10   I would like to leave these philosophers behind, for they are inept connoisseurs of suffering who might revere my Airedale for his capacity to scream when subjected to a blowtorch but not for his wit and courage, not for his natural good manners that are a gentle rebuke to ours. I want to celebrate the moment not long ago when, at his first dog show, my Airedale, Drummer, learned that there can be a public place where his work is respected. I want to celebrate his meticulousness, his happiness upon realizing at the dog show that no one would swoop down upon him and swamp him

with the goo-goo excesses known as the "teddy-bear complex" but that people actually got out of his way, gave him room to work. I want to say, "There can be a six-and-a-half-month-old puppy who can care about accuracy, who can be fastidious, and whose fastidiousness will be a foundation for courage later." I want to say, "Leave my puppy alone!"

I want to leave the philosophers behind, but I cannot, in part 11 because the philosophical problems that plague academicians of the animal-rights movement are illuminating. They wonder, do animals have rights or do they have interests? Or, if these rightists lead particularly unexamined lives, they dismiss that question as obvious (yes, of course, animals have rights, prima facie) and proceed to enumerate them, James Madison style. This leads to the issuance of bills of rights—the right to an environment, the right not to be used in medical experiments—and other forms of trivialization.

The calculus of suffering can be turned against the philoso- 12 phers of festering flesh, even in the case of food animals, or exotic animals who perform in movies and circuses. It is true that it hurts to be slaughtered by a man, but it doesn't hurt nearly as much as some of the cunningly cruel arrangements meted out by "Mother Nature." In Africa, 75 percent of the lions cubbed do not survive to the age of two. For those who make it to two, the average age at death is ten years. Asali, the movie and TV lioness, was still working at age twenty-one. There are fates worse than death, but twenty-one years of a close working relationship with Hubert Wells, Asali's trainer, is not one of them. Dorset sheep and polled Herefords would not exist at all were they not in a symbiotic relationship with human beings.

A human being living in the "wild"—somewhere, say, with- 13 out the benefits of medicine and advanced social organizations— would probably have a life expectancy of from thirty to thirty-five years. A human being living in "captivity"—in, say, a middle-class neighborhood of what the Centers for Disease Control call a Metropolitan Statistical Area—has a life expectancy of seventy or more years. For orangutans in the wild in Borneo and Malaysia, the life expectancy is thirty-five years; in captivity, fifty years. The wild is not a suffering-free zone or all that frolicsome a location.

The questions asked by animal-rights activists are flawed, 14 because they are built on the concept that the origin of rights is in the avoidance of suffering rather than in the pursuit of happiness.

The question that needs to be asked—and that will put us in closer proximity to the truth—is not, do they have rights? or, what are those rights? but rather, what is a right?

15   Rights originate in committed relationships and can be found, both intact and violated, wherever one finds such relationships—in social compacts, within families, between animals, and between people and nonhuman animals. This is as true when the nonhuman animals in question are lions or parakeets as when they are dogs. It is my Airedale whose excellencies have my attention at the moment, so it is with reference to him that I will consider the question, what is a right?

16   When I imagine situations in which it naturally arises that A defends or honors or respects B's rights, I imagine situations in which the relationship between A and B can be indicated with a possessive pronoun. I might say, "Leave her alone, she's my daughter" or, "That's what she wants, and she is my daughter. I think I am bound to honor her wants." Similarly, "Leave her alone, she's my mother." I am more tender of the happiness of my mother, my father, my child, than I am of other people's family members; more tender of my friends' happiness than your friends' happiness, unless you and I have a mutual friend.

17   Possession of a being by another has come into more and more disrepute, so that the common understanding of one person possessing another is slavery. But the important detail about the kind of possessive pronoun that I have in mind is reciprocity: If I have a friend, she has a friend. If I have a daughter, she has a mother. The possessive does not bind one of us while freeing the other; it cannot do that. Moreover, should the mother reject the daughter, the word that applies is "disown." The form of disowning that most often appears in the news is domestic violence. Parents abuse children; husbands batter wives.

18   Some cases of reciprocal possessives have built-in limitations, such as "my patient/my doctor" or "my student/my teacher" or "my agent/my client." Other possessive relations are extremely limited but still remarkably binding: "my neighbor" and "my country" and "my president."

19   The responsibilities and the ties signaled by reciprocal possession typically are hard to dissolve. It can be as difficult to give up an enemy as to give up a friend, and often the one becomes the

other, as though the logic of the possessive pronoun outlasts the forms it chanced to take at a given moment, as though we were stuck with one another. In these bindings, nearly inextricable, are found the origin of our rights. They imply a possessiveness but also recognize an acknowledgment by each side of the other's existence.

The idea of democracy is dependent on the citizens' having knowledge of the government; that is, realizing that the government exists and knowing how to claim rights against it. I know this much because I get mail from the government and see its "representatives" running about in uniforms. Whether I actually have any rights in relationship to the government is less clear, but the idea that I do is symbolized by the right to vote. I obey the government, and, in theory, it obeys me, by counting my ballot, reading the *Miranda* warning to me, agreeing to be bound by the Constitution. My friend obeys me as I obey her; the government "obeys" me to some extent, and, to a different extent, I obey it.

What kind of thing can my Airedale, Drummer, have knowledge of? He can know that I exist and through that knowledge can claim his happiness, with varying degrees of success, both with me and against me. Drummer can also know about larger human or dog communities than the one that consists only of him and me. There is my household—the other dogs, the cats, my husband. I have had enough dogs on campuses to know that he can learn that Yale exists as a neighborhood or village. My older dog, Annie, not only knows that Yale exists but can tell Yalies from townies, as I learned while teaching there during labor troubles.

Dogs can have elaborate conceptions of human social structures, and even of something like their rights and responsibilities within them, but these conceptions are never elaborate enough to construct a rights relationship between a dog and the state, or a dog and the Humane Society. Both of these are concepts that depend on writing and memoranda, officers in uniform, plaques and seals of authority. All of these are literary constructs, and all of them are beyond a dog's ken, which is why the mail carrier who doesn't also happen to be a dog's friend is forever an intruder— this is why dogs bark at mailmen.

It is clear enough that natural rights relations can arise between people and animals. Drummer, for example, can insist, "Hey, let's go outside and do something!" if I have been at my computer several days on end. He can both refuse to accept various of my suggestions and tell me when he fears for his life—such as the time when the huge, white flapping flag appeared out of nowhere, as it seemed to him, on the town green one evening when we were working. I can (and do) say to him either, "Oh, you don't have to worry about that" or "Uh oh, you're right, Drum, that guy looks dangerous." Just as the government and I—two different species of organism—have developed improvised ways of communicating, such as the vote, Drummer and I have worked out a number of ways to make our expressions known. Largely through obedience, I have taught him a fair amount about how to get responses from me. Obedience is reciprocal; you cannot get responses from a dog to whom you do not respond accurately. I have enfranchised him in a relationship to me by educating him, creating the conditions by which he can achieve a certain happiness specific to a dog, maybe even specific to an Airedale, inasmuch as this same relationship has allowed me to plumb the happiness of being a trainer and writing this article.

24   Instructions in this happiness are given terms that are alien to a culture in which liver treats, fluffy windup toys, and miniature sweaters are confused with respect and work. Jack Knox, a sheepdog trainer originally from Scotland, will shake his crook at a novice handler who makes a promiscuous move to praise a dog, and will call out in his Scottish accent, "Eh! Eh! Get back, get BACK! Ye'll no be abusin' the dogs like that in my clinic." America is a nation of abused animals, Knox says, because we are always swooping at them with praise, "no gi'ing them their freedom." I am reminded of Rainer Maria Rilke's account in which the Prodigal Son leaves—has to leave—because everyone loves him, even the dogs love him, and he has no path to the delicate and fierce truth of himself. Unconditional praise and love, in Rilke's story, disenfranchise us, distract us from what truly excites our interest.

25   In the minds of some trainers and handlers, praise is dishonesty. Paradoxically, it is a kind of contempt for animals that masquerades as a reverence for helplessness and suffering. The idea of freedom means that you do not, at least not while Jack Knox is nearby, helpfully guide your dog through the motions of, say, herding over and over—what one trainer calls "explainy-wainy."

This is rote learning. It works tolerably well on some handlers, because people have vast unconscious minds and can store complex pre-programmed behaviors. Dogs, on the other hand, have almost no unconscious minds, so they can learn only by thinking. Many children are like this until educated out of it.

If I tell my Airedale to sit and stay on the town green, and 26 someone comes up and burbles, "What a pretty thing you are," he may break his stay to go for a caress. I pull him back and correct him for breaking. Now he holds his stay because I have blocked his way to movement but not because I have punished him. (A correction blocks one path as it opens another for desire to work; punishment blocks desire and opens nothing.) He holds his stay now, and—because the stay opens this possibility of work, new to a heedless young dog—he watches. If the person goes on talking, and isn't going to gush with praise, I may heel Drummer out of his stay and give him an "Okay" to make friends. Sometimes something about the person makes Drummer feel that reserve is in order. He responds to an insincere approach by sitting still, going down into himself, and thinking, "This person has no business pawing me. I'll sit very still, and he will go away." If the person doesn't take the hint from Drummer, I'll give the pup a little backup by saying, "Please don't pet him, he's working," even though he was not under any command.

The pup reads this, and there is a flicker of working trust 27 now stirring in the dog. Is the pup grateful? When the stranger leaves, does he lick my hand, full of submissive blandishments? This one doesn't. This one says nothing at all, and I say nothing much to him. This is a working trust we are developing, not a mutual-congratulation society. My backup is praise enough for him; the use he makes of my support is praise enough for me.

Listening to a dog is often praise enough. Suppose it is just 28 after dark and we are outside. Suddenly there is a shout from the house. The pup and I both look toward the shout and then toward each other: "What do you think?" I don't so much as cock my head, because Drummer is growing up, and I want to know what he thinks. He takes a few steps toward the house, and I follow. He listens again and comprehends that it's just Holly, who at fourteen is much given to alarming cries and shouts. He shrugs at me and goes about his business. I say nothing. To praise him

for this performance would make about as much sense as prais-
ing a human being for the same thing. Thus:

> A. *What's that?*
> B. *I don't know. [Listens] Oh, it's just Holly.*
> C. *What a goooooood human being!*
> B. *Huh?*

29   This is one small moment in a series of like moments that will
culminate in an Airedale who on Friday will have the discrimination and confidence required to take down a man who is attacking
me with a knife and on Saturday clown and play with the children
at the annual Orange Empire Dog Club Christmas party.

30   People who claim to speak for animal rights are increasingly
devoted to the idea that the very keeping of a dog or a horse or
a gerbil or a lion is in and of itself an offense. The more loudly they
speak, the less likely they are to be in a rights relation to any given
animal, because they are spending so much time in airplanes or
transmitting fax announcements of the latest Sylvester Stallone
anti-fur rally. In a 1988 *Harper's* forum, for example, Ingrid
Newkirk, the national director of People for the Ethical Treatment
of Animals, urged that domestic pets be spayed and neutered and
ultimately phased out. She prefers, it appears, wolves—and
wolves someplace else—to Airedales and, by a logic whose interior structure is both emotionally and intellectually forever closed
to Drummer, claims thereby to be speaking for "animal rights."

31   She is wrong. I am the only one who can own up to my
Airedale's inalienable rights. Whether or not I do it perfectly at
any given moment is no more refutation of this point than
whether I am perfectly my husband's mate at any given moment
refutes the fact of marriage. Only people who know Drummer,
and whom he can know, are capable of this relationship. PETA
and the Humane Society and the ASPCA and the Congress and
NOW—as institutions—do have the power to affect my ability to
grant rights to Drummer but are otherwise incapable of creating
conditions or laws or rights that would increase his happiness.
Only Drummer's owner has the power to obey him—to obey
who he is and what he is capable of—deeply enough to grant him
his rights and open up the possibility of happiness.

Content

1. Compare Hearne's definition of "animal happiness" (¶s 1–3) with the view of "animal happiness" she attributes to the animal rights movement.

2. "Animal rights," says Hearne, "are built upon a misconceived premise that rights were created to prevent us from unnecessary suffering" (¶ 5) "rather than in the pursuit of happiness" (¶ 14). Why does she say that premise is "misconceived"? What is the proper premise for ensuring animal rights?

3. What, in Hearne's view, are the right animal rights? Why does she take issue with the conventional animal rights advocate's view that "possession of one being by another" is wrong (¶ 17 and following ¶s)?

4. Compare and contrast Hearne's conception of a "symbiotic relationship" between animals and humans with the "cunningly cruel arrangements meted out by 'Mother Nature'" (¶ 12). Which is preferable, and why?

Strategies/Structures

5. Hearne uses numerous examples of cooperation between animals and their trainers or owners. Identify several of these and show how each reinforces her definition of "animal rights."

6. "Animal-rights publications," says Hearne, "are illustrated largely with photographs of two kinds of animals—'Helpless Fluff' and 'Agonized Fluff.'" Why does she interpret these illustrations as oversimplified "propaganda" (¶ 9)? What sorts of illustrations would be satisfactory to Hearne?

Language

7. What aspects of Hearne's language tell her readers of her deep love and respect for animals? How can she convey her strong feeling without lapsing into the sentimentality of the "Helpless Fluff" and "Agonized Fluff" views she attributes to animal rights publications (¶ 9)?

8. Hearne's seemingly straightforward language is punctuated with contemptuous references to animal-rights advocates: "inept connoisseurs of suffering" (¶ 9), "the philosophers of festering flesh" (¶ 12) who confuse "liver treats, fluffy windup toys, and miniature sweaters . . . with respect and work" (¶ 24). To what extent does this loaded language reinforce or diminish Hearne's argument? To what extent does your answer to this question depend on whether or not you agree with Hearne?

For Writing

9. "Rights," explains Hearne, "originate in committed relationships and can be found, both intact and violated, wherever one finds such relationships—in social compacts, within families, and between people and nonhuman animals" (¶ 15). Identify such a "right" that originates in a committed relationship between two individuals or groups, for instance as the Declaration of Independence asserts, "the right to life, liberty, and the pursuit of happiness." Explain the right for an audience who is likely to have taken that right for granted, and show how the mutual commitment of the parties involved reinforces that right. What could violate it? (Check with your instructor before choosing a topic; there may be some subjects with which he or she is overly familiar and would prefer not to receive papers on.)

10. "Today the loudest voices calling for—demanding—the destruction of animals are the humane organizations," says Hearne (¶ 6). How does she account for this paradox? Does she approve of this? Do you? Write a paper arguing for or against Hearne's view. One half of the paper should be directed to an audience of conventional animal-rights advocates; another should be directed to an audience favorable to Hearne's position.

═══════════════════════════════════════

JENNY SPINNER

An essayist and poet, Spinner (born, 1970) attended the University of Illinois and Oxford University (England), earned a B.A. at Millikin University (1992), an M.F.A. in nonfiction writing at Pennsylvania State University (1995), and an M.A. at the University of Connecticut (1999), where she is currently at work on a Ph.D. in English. Her columns, often about her sister and her family in Illinois, have appeared in the *Washington Post,* the *Hartford Courant,* and elsewhere.

Spinner grew up in Decatur, Illinois, a sprawling factory town on the Central Illinois prairie. In much of her writing, Spinner returns to this setting and to the large extended family of her childhood days. The most frequently appearing "character" in her personal essays—besides herself—is her twin sister Jackie. "I use the word *character* on purpose," Spinner explains. "In many of my essays, Jackie is a true wit. Of course she's charming and funny in reality, but she's extraordinarily charming and funny in my essays. She's there to make the reader laugh, to make me look good, and in a technical sense, to act as a transition between two paragraphs.

"It is when I write seriously about her, when I try to describe our unique relationship as twins, adopted twins for that matter, that I most struggle. I was twenty-eight when I began writing "In Search of Our Past." I had been writing since I was 18. It took me ten years to find the courage to write the story of our beginning. Our relationship is so powerful, and so powerfully imbedded in who I am, that I was almost afraid to touch it, as if touching it would either cheapen it or prove entirely inadequate.

"I had to remind myself, as I remind my students, that 'I am not the page.' In other words, my writing is a construction of myself, of my sister, of our relationship. I am not writing a life; I am writing *about* a life (and in writing about a life, creating a new life, in print). To that end, I cannot possibly write about our life in a single essay, or even in a book of essays. The initial drafts of "In Search of Our Past" include too much detail, too many stories, too many angles on our relationship. . . . I'd lost track of my readers—who didn't need them—and of my focus for this essay: to write about our adoption.

When revising "In Search of Our Past," as is the case each time I write about my sister, I had to forgive myself: for not being able to write perfectly about what means most to me. In the process, I also felt relieved. After all, my readers have access only to that which I give them. I, the writer and chief engineer, remain in control of construction. My writing about my sister, and about myself, represents many choices. I choose to include some details, leave behind others. I choose to make my sister savvy and myself a bit awkward. These choices are grounded in reality, in what is true, but they remain creations. I create."

❄ *In Search of Our Past*

W hen we were young, my twin sister Jackie and I shared 1 everything. Although our childhood years were not the last we shared, they were the least divided. We had the same Baby Alives dolls that burbled slime which Grandpa Spinner once heroically ate; same Buster Browns, brown, narrow, fitted with arch supports for flat feet; same cotton dresses that barely touched the knees; same Trixie Belden books bought for us to share. And share we did: the dresser, its drawers; bathroom towels; gum sometimes; earrings, make-up, the car during high school; perfectionism, ambition and eating disorders after that. But what really mattered is that we shared the door to our bedroom, the way in, the way out, the lock that could be opened with a toothpick: one door, one way, one lock. There is little dignity in running to a room mid-tantrum, sobbing, slamming a door so hard that the second-floor windows rattle, only to turn around and find someone sitting in the middle of her bed watching you unfold.

2   It seems fitting that we shared so much of our lives together in our strawberry pink room with its strawberry walls, strawberry carpet, strawberry gingham bedspreads and curtains. What came before the pink was colorless, blank, *tabula rasa* in its purest sense, and we shared that blankness, too. Unlike our brother Tim, twenty months younger and biological child of our parents, we had no roots before birth. The first few weeks following that birth hinged on tiny, gathered bits of information. Adopted at twenty-three days old, we came into the world free of any heritage other than the one we chose for ourselves.

3   It was something we always knew: adoption. One of my earliest memories is of the two of us begging my parents to "tell the story." "Don't you ever get tired of hearing it?" my mother asked, amused. "No." No, even though there was not much to it, or to the answers we sought: A poor young woman and her husband could not afford two infants. They loved them, yes, enough to give them up—because that is what you do, when you love something more than yourself. And so, after repeated tellings, the myth of our birth evolved, out of one "lady," whom we carefully never called mother and one man who soon disappeared from the stories we told ourselves.

4   For my parents, the story actually began two years before my sister and I were born. In June 1968, three years after they were married, my mother lay in bed trying not to bleed. She was three months pregnant with their first child. Trying hard to save the baby, to go twenty-four hours without spotting, she stayed in bed for several days. On the black-and-white Zenith at the edge of the bed, she watched as Sirhan B. Sirhan shot Bobby Kennedy two thousand miles away in a Los Angeles hotel. Kennedy did

not survive; neither did my parents' baby. For a long time, my sister and I celebrated quietly the death of this child. Beneath a blanket tent on one of our beds, we whispered our understanding: Had the baby lived, we would not have—at least not in the lives we knew.

In 1969, after four years of trying to conceive, my parents contacted Lutheran Child and Family Services—a private adoption agency affiliated with the Lutheran Church Missouri Synod. At that time, my mother's oldest sister already had three children; my father's oldest brother, two. My parents so desperately wanted to contribute a baby to the family that when their adoption counselor asked if they were willing to adopt multiple birth babies, they agreed. So rare was this possibility that the question was more formality than reality.

That reality soon reordered itself, however, when my mother received a telephone call from their counselor on July 28, 1970. Would she and my father be interested in adopting twin girls born on the fifteenth? This phone call is the closest thing my sister and I have to a conception. It is the moment in which the idea of us was first presented to our parents, and it is the moment we call birth. Details about the days before are scattered and incomplete. According to information given to my parents by the adoption agency, I had been living in a foster home in the Chicago area since July 24. Not released until July 31, my sister (four pounds at birth compared to my plumper five) was still in the hospital when my mother received the counselor's phone call.

Thinking about these early days creates questions for which there are few answers. We do know on July 15, 1970, at 2:08 and 2:10 P.M. we were delivered by cesarean in the former Chicago Masonic Medical Center (now Illinois Masonic Medical Center). Cesarean is important because it indicates a trace of permanence, a visible scar. On our birthday each year, we imagined her, "the lady," running her fingers across that scar, feeling the hard skin, wondering. Because of the scar, she can't forget. The hospital is important, too, because it means a place exists, means in some building we were there, all three of us. One year, during a visit to Chicago relatives, our parents drove us by the Medical Center. Intimidated by the hospital's reality, we didn't ask to go inside. Behind closed eyes, I imagined pale green walls and gray filing cabinets hiding manila folders. In those folders were names—and a past. A few years later I ventured inside, just to see, but I wasn't allowed on the maternity ward. A nurse told me visitors might infect new mothers and babies. I paced the main lobby for an hour trying to find something that "she" saw, too. When my parents, waiting in the car, came in to find me, my mother tried to cheer me by buying me a pink baby shirt that she would have bought herself had I been hers at that hospital. Back in the car, I hid my face from her good intentions and swallowed sobs.

8   When I was twelve, I went searching for names and didn't find them. I did discover several pages of biographical data which the adoption agency had given to my parents and which my parents chose not to share with us—perhaps because we never asked, careful not to hurt their feelings by reminding them that we were not biologically theirs. In the bottom drawer of a filing cabinet, behind tax records, insurance papers and department store bills, I found a folder marked in my dad's neat block-letter hand: "GIRLS ADOPTION." I sat on his office floor for several minutes, unable to open the folder, the weight of my past leaning hard against my chest. When I finally peered inside, a twenty-seven-year-old man and a twenty-three-year-old woman stepped out to greet me, brushing the dust from their clothes—or trying to pull it back around them. She was tiny with dark brown hair and blue-green eyes. He was tall, had blond hair and blue eyes. These physical details were important. Ever since we were old enough to realize what we were doing, my sister and I had been searching crowds for the woman who gave birth to us. At the World's Fair in Tennessee we thought we saw her, but she disappeared before we could be sure.

9   When we were younger, a number of people told us we looked like our adoptive mother, and we did. We shared her straight brown hair, cut boyishly short like hers, parted in the middle, her brown eyes and fair skin. Our father and brother, with their dark blond hair and green eyes, were their own perfect match. When required to fill out heredity worksheets during what became the dreaded genetics unit in grade- and high-school science classes, we came close, pretending our parents' and grandparents' blood was really ours, at least by association. But the widows' peaks never matched; neither did the blood. In the end,

those nights we spent in our pink room filling out our biological family trees were unhappy ones, and we wondered why it never occurred to our teachers that not everyone lived by science.

I memorized other details in the file, adding them to the pictures in my head and measuring myself. A talented cartoonist and fiction writer, the woman graduated from college and planned to attend graduate school. The man was a college graduate, manager of a bank, dabbled in photography and art. They both swam and played tennis. The tomboy in me who loved taking pictures and writing beamed—until I read the next lines. Although they were college sweethearts and intended to marry, the man changed his mind after learning about the woman's pregnancy. "He didn't reject her but tried to help," the black ink scrawled onto my heart. "Mother felt best thing to do was give up for adoption." I realized then that my biological parents were not married, that what changed the man's mind was my sister and me. Moreover, the vision of them sharing a life together was a myth, even though my mother always referred to him as the lady's husband. Probably she gave birth, they parted and went on with their lives, trying not to remind themselves of what they had done. Probably. Nothing is sure. It was a lot to swallow at twelve, especially for someone surrounded in school and at home by a conservative religious doctrine that demanded men and women have sex only after marriage, that chastised people who ran from pregnancies. Until I was old enough to establish my own rules, make mistakes, understand, then forgive, I lived with the burden of sin. At the very least, I knew we were a mistake.

Near the bottom of the papers I found a physical description of Jackie and me at birth: petite feminine build, fair complexions, brown hair with blond highlights, dark blue eyes. When I shared my findings with my sister, we wondered if that description was all the woman knew. How soon did they take us away? Did she ask to hold us? Did she cry? We wondered, of course, if she now wondered, too. But most of our questions were not grounded in a dramatic fairy tale of two happy people ready to apologize and explain once discovered by their progeny. We simply wanted to color in a black hole that swallowed the beginning of our lives. "Dear Lady," I wrote to her when I was thirteen, "Some day my sister and I will open our adoption records and find out your name. We won't try to contact you. We just want a name. We're not looking for a mother because we have one. We're looking for some answers to questions we've had for a long time, questions that might remain unanswered forever." Every year I wrote to her a version of that letter, always addressed "Dear Lady." I never put the letter in an envelope, and every year it asked fewer questions and told more about me and my sister. I wasn't bragging as much as insisting: that we turned out okay, that she would be proud.

12   Although the darkness surrounding our birth bothered us, my sister and I never opened our adoption records, even after we turned twenty-one and were old enough to do so. The desire for name finally lost its pull. Mostly we didn't want to hurt our parents. The hole, after all, had nothing to do with them, and we had no intention of creating a new one—in their hearts. A few years ago, I ran into a childhood friend in a bar in my hometown. She had recently been hired by Lutheran Child and Family Services, and, she told me excitedly, she'd read our file. She knew our original names. Leaning close, smiling, she asked, "Do you want to know anything else?" I set my glass on the table and told her I needed a minute to think. I walked to the back of the bar, found a pay phone and called my sister. At first I thought she couldn't hear me over the juke box. Neither of us said anything for a long time. Finally I understood her silence as "no," told our friend "no" and left. Our past stayed behind in the bar, washed down by glass after glass of ordinary beer.

13   From the time we began attending elementary school and our classmates learned of our adoption—how, I don't remember—we knew we were different. One morning in third grade, I stood in front of a long mirror in the girls' bathroom alongside Karen, both of us examining our faces.

14   "Do you ever wonder if you look like her?" she asked.

15   "Who?" I replied, avoiding her eyes, and my own.

16   "Your mother."

17   "I do look like my mother."

18   "Really? Have you seen a picture?"

19   "No."

20   "Then how do you know?"

21   "Because I see her every day." I knew what she was asking but I was determined not to let her make me feel different than

she, the tall, skinny girl with long brown flapping braids who was a miniature version of her mother.

"I mean your real mother, not Mrs. Spinner," she said, turn- 22 ing away from the mirror.

"She is my real mother." 23

"It's not the same," she said, walking away and tossing her 24 braids.

Although I hated Karen then, I knew she was right. But my 25 sister and I were good at pretending.

Our brother Tim was not always as skilled. In angry moods, 26 he reminded us that we did not belong as much as he did. We, too, were good at throwing an occasional "You love him better because he's yours" tantrum. Usually, however, we kept such comparisons inside. In trips to the grocery store or K Mart, Tim pushed ahead of us, pointing out boxes of cold cereal and stuffed bears he wanted. Jackie and I hung back, reluctant to ask for too much, afraid the expense would force my parents to give us back. We were eleven before we understood adoption well enough to know they couldn't return us. "Don't ask for anything," I whispered to my sister beneath a row of blonde Barbies. "Timmy can afford to, but not us."

One afternoon, we kneeled in front of the couch in our base- 27 ment, tallying how much we had cost our parents since they brought us home. "Did you pay anything to get us?" my sister asked, nervously eyeing the lengthening expense column. "A little," my father said, buried in his own stack of bills and unaware of why she asked. In actuality, they paid $1,000 to the adoption agency and about $300 in lawyer's fees. The thought of any money at all, however, even "a little," was a shock to my sister and me who viewed the transaction as one of love—poor parents handing over their babies to richer ones. Money turned love into business. It made us bought.

"All things considered," I asked my father when I was older, 28 "do you think your investment has paid off?"

"Of course," he laughed. It wasn't always that easy. Yet it 29 was. The adoption story we lived was nothing like the dramas that entertained television audiences in the late 1980s, especially following the Baby M and Baby Jessica cases. For people who know nothing about it, adoption is fascinating, embarrassing or sad; for people who do, it just is. No woman ever demanded us back. We never considered going back. Our parents loved us completely, loved us as much as our brother. We also had a wonderful relationship with both sets of grandparents with whom we spent a great deal of time and considered best friends as we grew older. Only once did I feel the awkwardness of being an adopted child in my family. I had just returned home from the first three weeks of my freshman year at college—they were actually my only three weeks as I withdrew, homesick and disenchanted, a failure. I'd always made good grades and given my family reasons to be proud. Now, in the dark of my grandmother's living room, I tried to explain what went wrong. Reaching out from her chair to touch my hand, she told me, "We don't know certain things about you girls that could explain a lot. There could be ugly things in your past." Her explanation startled me. Later I realized she was right, not about why I left college, but in some sense still right. My sister and I didn't know anything beyond what we created for ourselves.

30   What we *had* created was each other. Eventually I learned there would be gaps even in what we constructed, times when I would be left alone to make sense of the absence that thrust us into this world. Until that time, the only world I knew contained my sister and what we held together—and I could not imagine any experience outside that bond. What lay outside was nothing we could name, touch, hold onto. Nothing would belong only to me, or to her, until we moved away from one another and began to create our own lives.

31   Those lives remain a curious mix of fervent attachment and the desire to be individuals. We are both writers, she a journalist, I, an essayist. We both run, physically and emotionally, until exhausted. She injures herself, and hundreds of miles away, I feel her pain. I cry, and she calls to ask what's wrong. We fight tortured fights. We make up like lovers, whispering over and over, "Don't leave me," "I won't," until we are convinced that we will be okay, that no one, that nothing, can destroy us. Together, separately we live, stepping carefully from our shared past, from that dry well falling deep into the dark.

Content

1. As young girls, Spinner and her sister, twins adopted as infants, spent considerable time speculating on their heritage. What couldn't they take for granted, or even know, that children living with their birth parents know and accept? Why, when Spinner finally has the chance to learn her birth parents' names and other information about them (¶ 12), does she reject the opportunity?

2. Why did Spinner write this essay? What is its thesis? Is it implied or stated explicitly?

3. This essay could be interpreted from the perspective of contrasts: insiders/outsiders; people with an identifiable past/people without; people with twin siblings/people without; adoptive siblings/birth siblings living in the same family. Explain how these divisions govern what Spinner tells us about these relationships, and what she implies.

Strategies/Structures

4. Show through an analysis of "In Search of Our Past" the implicit and explicit comparisons between the lives of children living with their birth parents and of adoptive children.

5. What does Spinner choose to tell us about her adoptive parents? What sorts of information does she omit? Why?

Language

6. What's the meaning of Spinner's concluding paradox, "Together, separately we [Jenny and her twin sister] live, stepping carefully from our shared past, from that dry well falling deep into the dark" (¶ 19)? Is the essay's ending optimistic, pessimistic, realistic?

For Writing

7. What problems exist for school children who are asked to write family histories when they don't know those histories? Or when the family stories are difficult to understand or full of problems? How can teachers adjust their assignments to be sensitive to issues of individual and family heritages? Construct such an assignment, and explain why you've written it in the way you have. Elicit responses to it from your fellow students before showing it to your instructor.

8. Write an essay that explores the relations between outsiders and a particular insider group such as a family; a group united by race, religion, ethnicity, class, or immigrant status; a gang; a club, a residence-hall group, a sorority or fraternity; or people of particular geographic area whether urban, suburban, or rural, in a particular state or country. See essays by Davidson (6–17), Tan (17–25), Wiesel (53–60), Cofer (179–86), Rodriguez (398–405), among others. Consider your audience to be outsiders to the group you are discussing.

Additional Topics for Writing
Comparison and Contrast

(For strategies for writing comparison and contrast, see 535.)

1. Write an essay, full of examples, that compares and contrasts any of the following pairs:

    a. Two people with a number of relevant characteristics in common (two of your teachers, roommates, friends, relatives playing the same role—i.e., two of your sisters or brothers, two of your grandparents, a father or mother and a stepparent)
    b. Two cities or regions of the country you know well, or two neighborhoods you have lived in
    c. Two comparable historical figures with similar positions, such as two presidents, two senators, two generals, two explorers, or others
    d. Two religions or two sects or churches within the same religion
    e. Two utopian communities (real or imaginary)
    f. Two explanations or interpretations of the same scientific, economic, religious, psychological, or political phenomenon (for instance, creationism versus Darwinism; Freudian versus Skinnerian theory of behavior)
    g. The cuisine of two different countries or two or more parts of a country (Greek versus French cooking; Szechuan, Cantonese, and Peking Chinese food)

2. Write a balanced essay involving a comparison and contrast of one of the subjects below that justifies your preference for one over the other. Write for a reader who is likely to debate your choice.

    a. American-made versus foreign-made cars (specify the country and the manufacturer)
    b. The styles of two performers—musicians, actors or actresses, dancers, athletes participating in the same sport, comedians
    c. The work of two writers, painters, theater or film directors; or two (or three) works by the same writer or painter
    d. Two political parties, campaigns, or machines, past or present
    e. Two colleges or universities (or programs or sports teams within them) that you know well
    f. Two styles of friendship, courtship, marriage, or family (both may be contemporary, or you may compare and contrast past and present styles)

    g. Two academic majors, professions, or careers

    h. Life in the mainstream or on the margin (specify of which group, community, or society)

3. Write an essay, for an audience of fellow students, comparing the reality with the ideal of one of the following :

    a. Dating styles

    b. Your current job and the most satisfying job you could have

    c. Your current accomplishment in a particular area (sports, a performing art, a skill, or a level of knowledge) with what you hope to attain

    d. Friendship

    e. Parenthood

    f. Your present dwelling and your dream house

    g. The way you currently spend your leisure time and the way you'd like to spend it

    h. The present state of affairs versus the future prospects of some issue of social significance, such as world population, ecology, the control of nuclear arms, the treatment of hijackers and other international terrorists

Part IV

Arguing Directly and Indirectly

13 Appealing to Reason: Deductive and Inductive Arguments

When you write persuasively you're trying to move your readers to either belief or action or both. You can do this through appealing to their reasons, their emotions, or their sense of ethics, as you know if you've ever tried to prove a point on an exam or change an attitude in a letter to the editor. The next section discusses appeals to emotion and ethics; here we'll concentrate on argumentation.

An argument, as we're using the term here, does not mean a knockdown confrontation over an issue: "Philadelphia is the most wonderful place in the world to live!" "No, it's not. Social snobbery has ruined the City of Brotherly Love." Nor is an argument hard-sell brainwashing that admits of no alternatives: "America—love it or leave it!" When you write an argument, however, as a reasonable writer you'll present a reasonable proposition that states what you believe ("In the twenty-first century, the United States will continue to remain the best country in the world for freedom, democracy, and the opportunity to succeed.") You'll need to offer logic, evidence, and perhaps emotional appeals, to try to convince your readers of the merits of what you say. Sometimes, but not always, you'll also argue that they should adopt a particular course of action. ("Consequently, the United States should establish an 'open door' immigration policy to enable the less fortunate to enjoy these benefits, too." Or, "Consequently, the United States should severely restrict immigration, to prevent overcrowding and enable every citizen to enjoy these hard-won benefits.")

Unless you're writing an indirect argument that makes its point through satire, irony, an imagined character whose actions or life story illustrate a point (see Jonathan Swift, "A Modest Proposal," [650–60]), or some other oblique means, you'll probably want to identify the issue at hand and justify its significance early in the essay: "Mandatory drug-testing is essential for public officials with access to classified information." If it's a touchy subject, you may wish at this point to demonstrate good will toward readers likely to disagree with you by showing the basis for your common concern: "Most people would agree that it's important to protect children and adolescents from harmful influences." You could follow this by acknowledging the merits of their valid points: "And it's also true that drug abuse is currently a national crisis, and deserves immediate remedy." You'll need to follow this with an explanation of why, nevertheless, your position is better than theirs: "But mandatory drug testing for everyone would be a violation of their civil liberties, incredibly costly, and subject to abuse through misuse of the data."

There are a number of suitable ways to organize the body of your argument. If your audience is inclined to agree with much of what you say, you might want to put your strongest point first and provide the most evidence for that, before proceeding to the lesser points, arranged in order of descending importance:

1. Mandatory drug testing for everyone is unconstitutional.
   (three paragraphs)
2. Mandatory drug testing would be extremely costly, an expense grossly disproportionate to the results.
   (two paragraphs)
3. The results of mandatory drug testing would be easy to abuse—to falsify, to misreport, to misinterpret.
   (one paragraph)

4. Consequently, mandatory drug testing for everyone would
   cause more problems than it would solve.
   (conclusion—one paragraph)

For an antagonistic audience you could do the reverse, beginning
with the points easiest to accept or agree with and concluding
with the most difficult. Or you could work from the most familiar
to the least familiar parts.

No matter what organizational pattern you choose, you'll
need to provide supporting evidence—through specific examples,
facts and figures, the opinions of experts, case histories, narratives, analogies, considerations of cause and effect. Any or all of
these techniques can be employed in either *inductive* or *deductive*
reasoning. Chances are that most of your arguments will proceed
by induction. You might use an individual example intended as
representative of the whole, as Scott Russell Sanders does in
anatomizing his father's alcoholism to illustrate the alcoholic's
characteristic behavior (451–56).

Or you might use a larger number of examples and apply
inductive reasoning to prove a general proposition. Research scientists and detectives work this way, as do some social commentators
and political theorists. Robert Reich identifies the characteristics of
"The Global Elite" (624–36) and uses them both to counteract the
myths that the United States is a benevolent, egalitarian society and
to argue against the separatism—moral and economic secession—
that upper-income Americans currently practice to dissociate
themselves from responsibilities toward the rest of society.

An essay of deductive reasoning proceeds from a general
proposition to a specific conclusion. The model for a deductive
argument is the syllogism, a three-part sequence that begins with a
major premise, is followed by a minor premise, and leads to a conclusion. Aristotle's classic example of this basic logical pattern is

Major premise: All men are mortal.
Minor premise: Socrates is a man.
Conclusion: Therefore, Socrates is mortal.

Sometimes an essay will identify all parts of the syllogism; sometimes one or more parts will be implied. In "The Declaration of
Independence" (591–96), Thomas Jefferson and his coauthors
explore the consequences of the explicitly stated propositions
that "all men are created equal" and that, as a consequence, their

"unalienable Rights" cannot be denied. In "Letter from Birmingham Jail" (596–616), Martin Luther King, Jr., argues for the proposition that "one has not only a legal but a moral responsibility to disobey unjust laws" and uses a vast range of resources to demonstrate his point. He uses Biblical and historical examples to explain the situation in Birmingham; illustrations from his own life and from the lives of his own children and other victims of racial segregation; and more generalized incidents of brutal treatment of "unarmed, nonviolent Negroes." Lani Guinier designs her deductive argument, "The Tyranny of the Majority" (616–24), to illustrate the thesis that the rules of fair play "should reward those who win, but they must be acceptable to those who lose"; as an acceptable alternative to a "zero-sum game" ("I win; you lose"), she substitutes "the principle of taking turns." To make her point, Guinier draws on examples from constitutional law, American history, and analogies in playing sports and games.

Amy Jo Keifer in "The Death of a Farm" (636–39) implies a number of fundamental principles, which could be parts of syllogisms. Which of these, identified below, themselves incorporate still other principles?

  a. a family heritage has a right to be preserved
  b. hard work should be rewarded
  c. land is a scared trust, to be held and treated with respect
  d. those who love the land have a right to live on it—and to make a living from it
  e. a heritage of family possession should take precedence over a land developer's right to make money
  f. a farm, if run with appropriate intelligence and effort, should enable farmers to be self-sustaining
  g. something is fundamentally wrong with a society that will let small farmers down in hard times
  h. something is fundamentally wrong with a society that favors big developers over small farmers

No matter what your argumentative strategy, you will want to avoid *logical fallacies*, errors of reasoning that can lead you to the wrong conclusion. The most common logical fallacies to be aware of are the following:

  • *Arguing from analogy:* Comparing only similarities between things, concepts, or situations while overlooking significant differences that might weaken the argument. "Having a standing army is just like having a loaded gun in the house. If it's around, people will want to use it."

- *Argumentation ad hominem* (from Latin, "argument to the man"): Attacking a person's ideas or opinions by discrediting him or her as a person. "Napoleon was too short to be a distinguished general." "She was seen at the Kit Kat Lounge one night last week; she can't possibly be a good mother."

- *Argument from doubtful or unidentified authority:* Treating an unqualified, unreliable, or unidentified source as an expert on the subject at hand. "They say you can't get pregnant the first time." " 'History is bunk!' said Henry Ford."

- *Begging the question:* Regarding as true from the start what you set out to prove; asserting that what is true is true. "Rapists and murderers awaiting trial shouldn't be let out on bail" assumes that the suspects have already been proven guilty, which is the point of the impending trial.

- *Arguing in a circle:* Demonstrating a premise by a conclusion and a conclusion by a premise. "People should give 10 percent of their income to charity because that is the right thing to do. Giving 10 percent of one's income to charity is the right thing to do because it is expected."

- *Either/or reasoning:* Restricting the complex aspects of a difficult problem or issue to only one of two possible solutions. "You're not getting any younger. Marry me or you'll end up single forever."

- *Hasty generalization:* Erroneously applying information or knowledge of one or a limited number of representative instances to an entire, much larger category. "Poor people on welfare cheat. Why, just yesterday I saw a Cadillac parked in front of the tenement at 9th and Main."

- *Non sequitur* (from the Latin, "it does not follow"): Asserting as a conclusion something that doesn't follow from the first premise or premises. "The Senator must be in cahoots with that shyster developer, Landphill. After all, they were college fraternity brothers."

- *Oversimplification:* Providing simplistic answers to complex problems. "Ban handguns and stop murderous assaults in public schools."

- *Post hoc ergo propter hoc* (from Latin, "after this, therefore because of this"): Confusing a cause with an effect and vice versa. "Bicyclists are terribly unsafe riders. They're always getting into accidents with cars." Or confusing causality with proximity: just because two events occur in sequence doesn't necessarily mean that the first caused the second. Does war cause famine, or is famine sometimes the cause of war?

After you've written a logical argument, have someone who disagrees with you read it critically to look for loopholes. Your critic's guidelines could be the same questions you might ask yourself while writing the paper, as indicated in the process strategies below. If you can satisfy yourself and a critic, you can take on the world. Or is that a logical fallacy?

STRATEGIES FOR WRITING— APPEALING TO REASON: DEDUCTIVE AND INDUCTIVE ARGUMENTS

1. Do I want to convince my audience of the truth of a particular matter? Do I want essentially to raise their consciousness of an issue? Do I want to promote a belief or refute a theory? Or do I want to move my readers to action? If action, what kind? To change their minds, attitudes, or behavior? To right a wrong, or alter a situation?
2. At the outset, do I expect my audience to agree with my ideas? To be neutral about the issues at hand? Or to be opposed to my views? Can I build into my essay responses to my readers' anticipated reactions, such as rebuttals to their possible objections? Do I know enough about my subject to be able to do this?
3. What is my strongest (and presumably most controversial) point, and where should I put it? At the beginning, if my audience agrees with my views? At the end, after a gradual build-up, for an antagonistic audience? How much development (and consequent emphasis) should each point have? Will a deductive or inductive format best express my thesis?
4. What will be my best sources of evidence? My own experience? The experiences of people I know? Common sense or common knowledge? Opinion from experts in a relevant field? Scientific evidence? Historic records? Economic, anthropological, or statistical data?
5. What tone will best reinforce my evidence? Will my audience also find this tone appealing? Convincing? Would an appropriate tone be sincere? Straightforward? Objective? Reassuring? Confident? Placating? What language can I use to most appropriately convey this tone?

THOMAS JEFFERSON

Politician, philosopher, architect, inventor, and writer, Jefferson (1743–1826) was born near Charlottesville, Virginia, and was educated at the College of William and Mary. He served as a delegate to the Continental Congress in 1775, as Governor of the Commonwealth of Virginia, and as third President of the United States. With help from Benjamin Franklin and John Adams, he wrote *The Declaration of Independence* in mid-June 1776, and after further revision by the Continental Congress in Philadelphia, it was signed on July 4. Frequently called "an expression of the American mind," Jefferson's Declaration is based on his acceptance of democracy as the ideal form of government, a belief also evidenced in his refusal to sign the Constitution until the Bill of Rights was added. Jefferson died at Monticello, his home in Charlottesville, on July 4, 1826, the fiftieth anniversary of the signing of the Declaration.

The Declaration is based on a deductive argument, with the fundamental premises stated in the first sentence of the second paragraph, "We hold these truths to be self-evident. . . ." The rest of the argument follows logically—patriots among the Colonists who read this might say inevitably—from the premises of this emphatic, plainspoken document. What evidence is there in the Declaration that the British might react to it as a hot-headed manifesto, perhaps even a declaration of war? Can a cluster of colonies simply secede by fiat?

The Declaration of Independence

When in the course of human events, it becomes necessary for one people to dissolve the political bands which have connected them with another, and to assume among the Powers of the earth, the separate and equal station to which the Laws of Nature and of Nature's God entitle them, a decent respect to the opinions of mankind requires that they should declare the causes which impel them to the separation. 1

We hold these truths to be self-evident, that all men are created equal, that they are endowed by their Creator with certain unalienable Rights, that among these are Life, Liberty and the pursuit of Happiness. That to secure these rights, Governments are 2

instituted among Men deriving their just powers from the consent
of the governed. That whenever any Form of Government becomes destructive of these ends, it is the Right of People to alter or
to abolish it, and to institute new Government, laying its foundation on such principles and organizing its powers in such form, as
to them shall seem most likely to effect their Safety and Happiness.
Prudence, indeed, will dictate that Governments long established
should not be changed for light and transient causes; and accordingly all experience hath shown, that mankind are more disposed
to suffer, while evils are sufferable, than to right themselves by
abolishing the forms to which they are accustomed. But when a
long train of abuses and usurpations pursuing invariably the same
Object evinces a design to reduce them under absolute Despotism,
it is their right, it is their duty, to throw off such government, and
to provide new Guards for their future security. Such has been the
patient sufferance of these Colonies; and such is now the necessity
which constrains them to alter their former Systems of Government. The history of the present King of Great Britain is a history
of repeated injuries and usurpations, all having in direct object the
establishment of an absolute Tyranny over these States. To prove
this, let Facts be submitted to a candid world.

3   He has refused his Assent to Laws, the most wholesome and
necessary for the public good.

4   He had forbidden his Governors to pass Laws of immediate
and pressing importance, unless suspended in their operation till
his Assent should be obtained; and when so suspended, he has
utterly neglected to attend them.

5   He has refused to pass other Laws for the accommodation
of large districts of people, unless those people would relinquish
the right of Representation in the Legislature, a right inestimable
to them and formidable to tyrants only.

6   He has called together legislative bodies at places unusual,
uncomfortable, and distant from the depository of their Public
Records, for the sole purpose of fatiguing them into compliance
with his measures.

7   He has dissolved Representative Houses repeatedly, for
opposing with manly firmness his invasions on the rights of
the people.

8   He has refused for a long time, after such dissolutions,
to cause others to be elected; whereby the Legislative Powers,

incapable of Annihilation, have returned to the People at large for their exercise; the State remaining in the mean time exposed to all the dangers of invasion from without, and convulsions within.

He has endeavoured to prevent the population of these 9 States; for that purpose obstructing the Laws of Naturalization of Foreigners; refusing to pass others to encourage their migration hither, and raising the conditions of new Appropriations of Lands.

He has obstructed the Administration of Justice, by refusing 10 his Assent to Laws for establishing Judiciary Powers.

He has made Judges dependent on his Will alone, for the ten- 11 ure of their offices, and the amount and payment of their salaries.

He has erected a multitude of New Offices, and sent hither 12 swarms of Officers to harass our People, and eat out their substance.

He has kept among us, in time of peace, Standing Armies 13 without the Consent of our Legislature.

He has affected to render the Military independent of and 14 superior to the Civil Power.

He has combined with others to subject us to jurisdictions 15 foreign to our constitution, and unacknowledged by our laws; giving his Assent to their acts of pretended Legislation:

For quartering large bodies of armed troops among us: 16

For protecting them, by a mock Trial, from Punishment for 17 any Murders which they should commit on the Inhabitants of these States:

For cutting off our Trade with all parts of the world: 18

For imposing Taxes on us without our Consent: 19

For depriving us in many cases, of the benefits of Trial 20 by Jury:

For transporting us beyond Seas to be tried for pretended 21 offenses:

For abolishing the free System of English Laws in a Neigh- 22 bouring Province, establishing therein an Arbitrary government, and enlarging its boundaries so as to render it at once an example and fit instrument for introducing the same absolute rule into these Colonies:

For taking away our Charters, abolishing our most valuable 23 Laws, and altering fundamentally the Forms of our Governments:

For suspending our own Legislatures, and declaring them- 24 selves invested with Power to legislate for us in all cases whatsoever.

25   He has abdicated Government here, by declaring us out of his Protection and waging War against us.

26   He has plundered our seas, ravaged our Coasts, burnt our towns and destroyed the Lives of our people.

27   He is at this time transporting large Armies of foreign Mercenaries to compleat works of death, desolation and tyranny, already begun with circumstances of Cruelty & perfidy scarcely paralleled in the most barbarous ages, and totally unworthy the Head of a civilized nation.

28   He has constrained our fellow Citizens taken Captive on the high Seas to bear Arms against their Country, to become the executioners of their friends and Brethren, or to fall themselves by their Hands.

29   He has excited domestic insurrections amongst us, and has endeavoured to bring on the inhabitants of our frontiers, the merciless Indian Savages, whose known rule of warfare, is an undistinguished destruction of all ages, sexes and conditions.

30   In every stage of these Oppressions We Have Petitioned for Redress in the most humble terms: Our repeated petitions have been answered only be repeated injury. A Prince, whose character is thus marked by every act which may define a Tyrant, is unfit to be the ruler of a free People.

31   Not have We been wanting in attention to our British brethren. We have warned them from time to time of attempts by their legislature to extend an unwarrantable jurisdiction over us. We have reminded them of the circumstances of our emigration and settlement here. We have appealed to their native justice and magnanimity and we have conjured them by the ties of our common kindred to disavow these usurpations, which would inevitably interrupt our connections and correspondence. They too have been deaf to the voice of justice and of consanguinity. We must, therefore acquiesce in the necessity, which denounces our Separation, and hold them, as we hold the rest of mankind, Enemies in War, in Peace Friends.

32   We, therefore, the Representatives of the United States of America, in General Congress, Assembled, appealing to the Supreme Judge of the world for the rectitude of our intentions, do, in the Name, and by Authority of the good People of these Colonies, solemnly publish and declare, That these United Colonies are, and

of Right ought to be Free and Independent States; that they are Absolved from all Allegiance to the British Crown and that all political connection between them and the State of Great Britain, is and ought to be totally dissolved; and that as Free and Independent States, they have full power to levy War, conclude Peace, contract Alliances, establish Commerce, and to do all other Acts and Things which Independent States may of right do. And for the support of this Declaration, with a firm reliance on the protection of Divine Providence, we mutually pledge to each other our lives, our Fortunes and our sacred Honor.

Content

1. What are "the Laws of Nature and of Nature's God" to which Jefferson refers in paragraph 1? Why doesn't he specify what they are? Is a brief allusion to them in the first paragraph sufficient support for the fundamental premise of the second paragraph?

2. What is Jefferson's fundamental premise (¶ 2)? Does he ever prove it? Does he need to?

3. In paragraphs 3–31 the Declaration states a series of the American colonists' grievances against the British King, George III. What are some of these grievances? Can they be grouped into categories related to the "unalienable rights" Jefferson has specified at the outset, the rights to "Life, Liberty and the pursuit of Happiness"?

4. From the nature of the grievances Jefferson identifies, what ideal of government does he have in mind? Can such a government exist among colonial peoples, or only in an independent nation?

5. Is the conclusion (¶ 32) the inevitable consequence of the reasoning that precedes it? Are there any feasible alternatives?

Strategies/Structures

6. Why has Jefferson listed the grievances in the order in which they appear?

7. Is *The Declaration of Independence* written primarily for an audience of the British King and his advisors? Who else would be likely to be vitally involved?

8. Could the American colonists have expected the British simply to agree with what they said? Or is *The Declaration of Independence* in effect a declaration of war?

Language

9. What is the tone of this document? How would Jefferson have expected this tone to have affected King George III and associates? How might the same tone have affected the American patriots of 1776?

10. Look up in a good college dictionary the meanings of any problematic words, such as station (¶ 1), unalienable (¶ 2), despotism (¶ 2), usurpations (¶ 2), abdicated (¶ 25), perfidy (¶ 27), redress (¶ 30), magnanimity (¶ 31), rectitude (¶ 32).

For Writing

11. Write an essay in which you discuss the extent to which the federal government of the United States exhibits the ideals of government that Jefferson promoted in *The Declaration of Independence*.

12. Write your own "declaration of independence," in which you justify setting yourself (or yourself as a member of a particular social, occupational, economic, ethnic, or cultural group) free from an oppressor or oppressive group.

13. Is colonialism ever justified? In an essay on this issue, supplement your knowledge of history with *The Declaration of Independence*, Zitkala-Sa's excerpts from *The School Days of an Indian Girl* (273–83), Lim's "Pomegranates and English Education" (388–98), and King's "Letter from Birmingham Jail" (596–616). Bear in mind that each was written from the viewpoint of considerable sympathy with oppressed people.

MARTIN LUTHER KING, JR.

"Letter from Birmingham Jail," a literary and humanitarian masterpiece, reveals why Martin Luther King, Jr. was the most influential leader of the American civil rights movement in the 1950s and 1960s, and, why, with Mahatma Gandhi, he was one of this century's most influential advocates for human rights. King was born in Atlanta in 1929, the son of a well-known Baptist clergyman, educated at Morehouse College, and ordained in his father's denomination.

A forceful and charismatic leader, Dr. King became at twenty-six a national spokesperson for the civil rights movement when in 1955 he led a successful boycott of the segregated bus system of Montgomery, Alabama. Dr. King became president of the Southern Christian Leadership Conference and led the sit-ins and demonstrations—including the 1964 march on Washington, D.C., which climaxed with his famous "I Have a Dream" speech—that helped to ensure passage of the 1964 Civil Rights Act and the Voting Rights Act of 1965. He received the Nobel Peace Prize in 1964. Toward the end of his life, cut short by assassination in 1968, Dr. King was increasingly concerned with improving the rights and the lives of the nation's poor, irrespective of race, and with ending the war in Vietnam. His birthday became a national holiday in 1986.

In 1963 King wrote the letter reprinted below while imprisoned for "parading without a permit." Though ostensibly replying to eight clergymen—Protestant, Catholic, and Jewish—who feared violence in the Birmingham desegregation demonstrations, King actually intended his letter for the worldwide audience his civil rights activities commanded. Warning that America had more to fear from passive moderates ("the appalling silence of good people") than from extremists, King defended his policy of "nonviolent direct action" and explained why he was compelled to disobey "unjust laws"—supporting his argument with references to Protestant, Catholic, and Jewish examples ("Was not Jesus an extremist for love. . . ."), as well as to the painful examples of segregation in his own life.

Letter from Birmingham Jail[1]

April 16, 1963

My Dear Fellow Clergymen:

While confined here in the Birmingham city jail, I came   1
across your recent statement calling my present activities "unwise and untimely." Seldom do I pause to answer criticism of my work and ideas. If I sought to answer all the criticisms that cross my

---

[1] AUTHOR'S NOTE: This response to a published statement by eight fellow clergymen from Alabama (Bishop C. C. J. Carpenter, Bishop Joseph A. Durick, Rabbi Hilton L. Grafman, Bishop Paul Hardin, Bishop Holan B. Harmon, the Reverend George M. Murray, the Reverend Edward V. Ramage and the Reverend Earl Stallings) was composed under somewhat constricting circumstances. Begun on the margins of the newspaper in which the statement appeared while I was in jail, the letter was continued on scraps of writing paper supplied by a friendly Negro trusty, and concluded on a pad my attorneys were eventually permitted to leave me. Although the text remains in substance unaltered, I have indulged in the author's prerogative of polishing it for publication.

desk, my secretaries would have little time for anything other than such correspondence in the course of the day, and I would have no time for constructive work. But since I feel that you are men of genuine good will and that your criticisms are sincerely set forth, I want to try to answer your statement in what I hope will be patient and reasonable terms.

2   I think I should indicate why I am here in Birmingham, since you have been influenced by the view which argues against "outsiders coming in." I have the honor of serving as president of the Southern Christian Leadership Conference, an organization operating in every southern state, with headquarters in Atlanta, Georgia. We have some eighty-five affiliated organizations across the South, and one of them is the Alabama Christian Movement for Human Rights. Frequently we share staff, educational and financial resources with our affiliates. Several months ago the affiliate here in Birmingham asked us to be on call to engage in a nonviolent direct-action program if such were deemed necessary. We readily consented, and when the hour came we lived up to our promise. So I, along with several members of my staff, am here because I was invited here. I am here because I have organizational ties here.

3   But more basically, I am in Birmingham because injustice is here. Just as the prophets of the eighth century B.C. left their villages and carried their "thus saith the Lord" far beyond the boundaries of their home towns, and, just as the Apostle Paul left his village of Tarsus and carried the gospel of Jesus Christ to the far corners of the Greco-Roman world, so am I compelled to carry the gospel of freedom beyond my own home town. Like Paul, I must constantly respond to the Macedonian call for aid.

4   Moreover, I am cognizant of the interrelatedness of all communities and states. I cannot sit idly by in Atlanta and not be concerned about what happens in Birmingham. Injustice anywhere is a threat to justice everywhere. We are caught in an inescapable network of mutuality, tied in a single garment of destiny. Whatever affects one directly, affects all indirectly. Never again can we afford to live with the narrow, provincial "outside agitator" idea. Anyone who lives inside the United States can never be considered an outsider anywhere within its bounds.

5   You deplore the demonstrations taking place in Birmingham. But your statement, I am sorry to say, fails to express a similar

concern for the conditions that brought about the demonstrations. I am sure that none of you would want to rest content with the superficial kind of social analysis that deals merely with effects and does not grapple with underlying causes. It is unfortunate that demonstrations are taking place in Birmingham, but it is even more unfortunate that the city's white power structure left the Negro community with no alternative.

In any nonviolent campaign there are four basic steps: 6 collection of the facts to determine whether injustices exist; negotiation; self-purification; and direct action. We have gone through all these steps in Birmingham. There can be no gainsaying the fact that racial injustice engulfs this community. Birmingham is probably the most thoroughly segregated city in the United States. An ugly record of brutality is widely known. Negroes have experienced grossly unjust treatment in the courts. There have been more unsolved bombings of Negro homes and churches in Birmingham than in any other city in the nation. These are the hard brutal facts of the case. On the basis of these conditions, Negro leaders sought to negotiate with the city fathers. But the latter consistently refused to engage in good-faith negotiation.

Then, last September, came the opportunity to talk with 7 leaders of Birmingham's economic community. In the course of the negotiations, certain promises were made by the merchants— for example, to remove the stores' humiliating racial signs. On the basis of these promises, the Reverend Fred Shuttlesworth and the leaders of the Alabama Christian Movement for Human Rights agreed to a moratorium on all demonstrations. As the weeks and months went by, we realized that we were the victims of a broken promise. A few signs, briefly removed, returned; the others remained.

As in so many past experiences, our hopes had been blasted, 8 and the shadow of deep disappointment settled upon us. We had no alternative except to prepare for direct action, whereby we would present our very bodies as a means of laying our case before the conscience of the local and the national community. Mindful of the difficulties involved, we decided to undertake a process of self-purification. We began a series of workshops on nonviolence, and we repeatedly asked ourselves: "Are you able to accept blows without retaliating?" "Are you able to endure the ordeal of jail?" We decided to schedule our direct-action program for the Easter season, realizing that except for Christmas, this is the main shopping period of the year. Knowing that a strong economic-withdrawal program would be the by-product of direct action, we felt that this would be the best time to bring pressure to bear on the merchants for the needed change.

9   Then it occurred to us that Birmingham's mayoralty election was coming up in March, and we speedily decided to postpone action until after election day. When we discovered that the Commissioner of Public Safety, Eugene "Bull" Connor, had piled up enough votes to be in the run-off, we decided again to postpone action until the day after the run-off so that the demonstrations could not be used to cloud the issues. Like many others, we waited to see Mr. Connor defeated, and to this end we endured postponement after postponement. Having aided in this community need, we felt that our direct-action program could be delayed no longer.

10   You may well ask: "Why direct action? Why sit-ins, marches and so forth? Isn't negotiation a better path?" You are quite right in calling for negotiation. Indeed this is the very purpose of direct action. Nonviolent direct action seeks to create such a crisis and foster such a tension that a community which has constantly refused to negotiate is forced to confront the issue. It seeks so to dramatize the issue that it can no longer be ignored. My citing the creation of tension as part of the work of the nonviolent-resister may sound rather shocking. But I must confess that I am not afraid of the word "tension." I have earnestly opposed violent tension, but there is a type of nonviolent tension which is necessary for growth. Just as Socrates felt that it was necessary to create a tension in the mind so that individuals could rise from the bondage of myths and half-truths to the unfettered realm of creative analysis and objective appraisal, so must we see the need for nonviolent gadflies to create the kind of tension in society that will help men rise from the dark depths of prejudice and racism to the majestic heights of understanding and brotherhood.

11   The purpose of our direct-action program is to create a situation so crisis-packed that it will inevitably open the door to negotiation. I therefore concur with you in your call for negotiation. Too long has our beloved Southland been bogged down in a tragic effort to live in monologue rather than dialogue.

One of the basic points in your statement is that the action   12
that I and my associates have taken in Birmingham is untimely.
Some have asked: "Why didn't you give the new city administration time to act?" The only answer that I can give to this query is
that the new Birmingham administration must be prodded about
as much as the outgoing one, before it will act. We are sadly mistaken if we feel that the election of Albert Boutwell as mayor will
bring the millennium to Birmingham. While Mr. Boutwell is a
much more gentle person than Mr. Connor, they are both segrega-
tionists, dedicated to maintenance of the status quo. I have hope
that Mr. Boutwell will be reasonable enough to see the futility of
massive resistance to desegregation. But he will not see this without pressure from devotees of civil rights. My friends, I must say
to you that we have not made a single gain in civil rights without
determined legal and nonviolent pressure. Lamentably, it is an
historical fact that privileged groups seldom give up their privileges voluntarily. Individuals may see the moral light and voluntarily give up their unjust posture; but, as Reinhold Niebuhr has
reminded us, groups tend to be more immoral than individuals.

We know through painful experience that freedom is never   13
voluntarily given by the oppressor; it must be demanded by the
oppressed. Frankly, I have yet to engage in a direct-action campaign that was "well-timed" in the view of those who have not
suffered unduly from the disease of segregation. For years now I
have heard the word "Wait!" It rings in the ear of every Negro
with piercing familiarity. This "Wait" has almost always meant
"Never." We must come to see, with one of our distinguished
jurists, that "justice too long delayed is justice denied."

We have waited for more than 340 years for our constitu-   14
tional and Godgiven rights. The nations of Asia and Africa are
moving with jetlike speed toward gaining political independence,
but we still creep at horse-and-buggy pace toward gaining a cup of
coffee at a lunch counter. Perhaps it is easy for those who have
never felt the stinging darts of segregation to say, "Wait." But when
you have seen vicious mobs lynch your mothers and fathers at will
and drown your sisters and brothers at whim; when you have seen
hate-filled policemen curse, kick and even kill your black brothers
and sisters; when you see the vast majority of your twenty million
Negro brothers smothering in an airtight cage of poverty in the

midst of an affluent society; when you suddenly find your tongue twisted and your speech stammering as you seek to explain to your six-year-old daughter why she can't go to the public amusement park that has just been advertised on television, and see tears welling up in her eyes when she is told that Funtown is closed to colored children, and see ominous clouds of inferiority beginning to form in her little mental sky, and see her beginning to distort her personality by developing an unconscious bitterness toward white people; when you have to concoct an answer for a five-year-old son who is asking: "Daddy, why do white people treat colored people so mean?"; when you take a cross-country drive and find it necessary to sleep night after night in the uncomfortable corners of your automobile because no motel will accept you; when you are humiliated day in and day out by nagging signs reading "white" and "colored"; when your first name becomes "nigger," your middle name becomes "boy" (however old you are) and your last name becomes "John," and your wife and mother are never given the respected title "Mrs."; when you are harried by day and haunted by night by the fact that you are a Negro, living constantly at tiptoe stance, never quite knowing what to expect next, and are plagued with inner fears and outer resentments; when you are forever fighting a degenerating sense of "nobodiness"—then you will understand why we find it difficult to wait. There comes a time when the cup of endurance runs over, and men are no longer willing to be plunged into the abyss of despair. I hope, sirs, you can understand our legitimate and unavoidable impatience.

15   You express a great deal of anxiety over our willingness to break laws. This is certainly a legitimate concern. Since we so diligently urge people to obey the Supreme Court's decision of 1954 outlawing segregation in the public schools, at first glance it may seem rather paradoxical for us consciously to break laws. One may well ask: "How can you advocate breaking some laws and obeying others?" The answer lies in the fact that there are two types of laws: just and unjust. I would be the first to advocate obeying just laws. One has not only a legal but a moral responsibility to obey just laws. Conversely, one has a moral responsibility to disobey unjust laws. I would agree with St. Augustine that "an unjust law is no law at all."

16   Now, what is the difference between the two? How does one determine whether a law is just or unjust? A just law is a man-made

code that squares with the moral law or the law of God. An unjust law is a code that is out of harmony with the moral law. To put it in the terms of St. Thomas Aquinas: An unjust law is a human law that is not rooted in eternal law and natural law. Any law that uplifts human personality is just. Any law that degrades human personality is unjust. All segregation statutes are unjust because segregation distorts the soul and damages the personality. It gives the segregator a false sense of superiority and the segregated a false sense of inferiority. Segregation, to use the terminology of the Jewish philosopher Martin Buber, substitutes an "I-it" relationship for an "I-thou" relationship and ends up relegating persons to the status of things. Hence segregation is not only politically, economically and sociologically unsound, it is morally wrong and sinful. Paul Tillich has said that sin is separation. Is not segregation an existential expression of man's tragic separation, his awful estrangement, his terrible sinfulness? Thus it is that I can urge men to obey the 1954 decision of the Supreme Court, for it is morally right; and I can urge them to disobey segregation ordinances, for they are morally wrong.

Let us consider a more concrete example of just and unjust 17 laws. An unjust law is a code that a numerical or power majority group compels a minority group to obey but does not make binding on itself. This is *difference* made legal. By the same token, a just law is a code that a majority compels a minority to follow and that it is willing to follow itself. This is *sameness* made legal.

Let me give another explanation. A law is unjust if it is in- 18 flicted on a minority that, as a result of being denied the right to vote, had no part in enacting or devising the law. Who can say that the legislature of Alabama which set up that state's segregation laws was democratically elected? Throughout Alabama all sorts of devious methods are used to prevent Negroes from becoming registered voters, and there are some counties in which even though Negroes constitute a majority of the population, not a single Negro is registered. Can any law enacted under such circumstances be considered democratically structured?

Sometimes a law is just on its face and unjust in its applica- 19 tion. For instance, I have been arrested on a charge of parading without a permit. Now, there is nothing wrong in having an ordinance which requires a permit for a parade. But such an ordinance becomes unjust when it is used to maintain segregation and to deny citizens the First-Amendment privilege of peaceful assembly and protest.

20   I hope you are able to see the distinction I am trying to point out. In no sense do I advocate evading or defying the law, as would the rabid segregationist. That would lead to anarchy. One who breaks an unjust law must do so openly, lovingly, and with a willingness to accept the penalty. I submit that an individual who breaks a law that conscience tells him is unjust, and who willingly accepts the penalty of imprisonment in order to arouse the conscience of the community over its injustice, is in reality expressing the highest respect for the law.

21   Of course, there is nothing new about this kind of civil disobedience. It was evidenced sublimely in the refusal of Shadrach, Meshach and Abednego to obey the laws of Nebuchadnezzar, on the ground that a higher moral law was at stake. It was practiced superbly by the early Christians, who were willing to face hungry lions and the excruciating pain of chopping blocks rather than submit to certain unjust laws of the Roman Empire. To a degree, academic freedom is a reality today because Socrates practiced civil disobedience. In our own nation, the Boston Tea Party represented a massive act of civil disobedience.

22   We should never forget that everything Adolf Hitler did in Germany was "legal" and everything the Hungarian freedom fighters did in Hungary was "illegal." It was "illegal" to aid and comfort a Jew in Hitler's Germany. Even so, I am sure that, had I lived in Germany at the time, I would have aided and comforted my Jewish brothers. If today I lived in a Communist country where certain principles dear to the Christian faith are suppressed, I would openly advocate disobeying that country's anti-religious laws.

23   I must make two honest confessions to you, my Christian and Jewish brothers. First, I must confess that over the past few years I have been gravely disappointed with the white moderate. I have almost reached the regrettable conclusion that the Negro's great stumbling block in his stride toward freedom is not the White Citizen's Counciler or the Ku Klux Klanner, but the white moderate, who is more devoted to "order" than to justice; who prefers a negative peace which is the absence of tension to a positive peace which is the presence of justice; who constantly says:

"I agree with you in the goal you seek, but I cannot agree with your methods of direct action"; who paternalistically believes he can set the timetable for another man's freedom; who lives by a mythical concept of time and who constantly advises the Negro to wait for a "more convenient season." Shallow understanding from people of good will is more frustrating than absolute misunderstanding from people of ill will. Lukewarm acceptance is much more bewildering than outright rejection.

I had hoped that the white moderate would understand that law and order exist for the purpose of establishing justice and that when they fail in this purpose they become the dangerously structured dams that block the flow of social progress. I had hoped that the white moderate would understand that the present tension in the South is a necessary phase of the transition from an obnoxious negative peace, in which the Negro passively accepted his unjust plight, to a substantive and positive peace, in which all men will respect the dignity and worth of human personality. Actually, we who engage in non-violent direct action are not the creators of tension. We merely bring to the surface the hidden tension that is already alive. We bring it out in the open, where it can be seen and dealt with. Like a boil that can never be cured so long as it is covered up but must be opened with all its ugliness to the natural medicines of air and light, injustice must be exposed, with all the tension its exposure creates, to the light of human conscience and the air of national opinion before it can be cured.

In your statement you assert that our actions, even though peaceful, must be condemned because they precipitate violence. But is this a logical assertion? Isn't this like condemning a robbed man because his possession of money precipitated the evil act of robbery? Isn't this like condemning Socrates because his unswerving commitment to truth and his philosophical inquiries precipitated the act by the misguided populace in which they made him drink hemlock? Isn't this like condemning Jesus because his unique God-consciousness and never-ceasing devotion to God's will precipitated the evil act of crucifixion? We must come to see that, as the federal courts have consistently affirmed, it is wrong to urge an individual to cease his efforts to gain his basic constitutional rights because the quest may precipitate violence. Society must protect the robbed and punish the robber.

26   I had also hoped that the white moderate would reject the myth concerning time in relation to the struggle for freedom. I have just received a letter from a white brother in Texas. He writes: "All Christians know that the colored people will receive equal rights eventually, but it is possible that you are in too great a religious hurry. It has taken Christianity almost two thousand years to accomplish what it has. The teachings of Christ take time to come to earth." Such an attitude stems from a tragic misconception of time, from the strangely irrational notion that there is something in the very flow of time that will inevitably cure all ills. Actually, time itself is neutral; it can be used either destructively or constructively. More and more I feel that the people of ill will have used time much more effectively than have the people of good will. We will have to repent in this generation not merely for the hateful words and actions of the bad people but for the appalling silence of the good people. Human progress never rolls in on wheels of inevitability; it comes through the tireless efforts of men willing to be coworkers with God, and without this hard work, time itself becomes an ally of the forces of social stagnation. We must use time creatively, in the knowledge that the time is always ripe to do right. Now is the time to make real the promise of democracy and transform our pending national elegy into a creative psalm of brotherhood. Now is the time to lift our national policy from the quicksand of racial injustice to the solid rock of human dignity.

27   You speak of our activity in Birmingham as extreme. At first I was rather disappointed that fellow clergymen would see my nonviolent efforts as those of an extremist. I began thinking about the fact that I stand in the middle of two opposing forces in the Negro community. One is a force of complacency, made up in part of Negroes who, as a result of long years of oppression, are so drained of self-respect and a sense of "somebodiness" that they have adjusted to segregation; and in part of a few middle-class Negroes who, because of a degree of academic and economic security and because in some ways they profit by segregation, have become insensitive to the problems of the masses. The other force is one of bitterness and hatred, and it comes perilously close to advocating violence. It is expressed in the various black nationalist groups that are springing up across the nation, the largest and best-known being Elijah Muhammad's Muslim movement. Nourished

by the Negro's frustration over the continued existence of racial discrimination, this movement is made up of people who have lost faith in America, who have absolutely repudiated Christianity, and who have concluded that the white man is an incorrigible "devil."

I have tried to stand between these two forces, saying that   28
we need emulate neither the "do-nothingism" of the complacent nor the hatred and despair of the black nationalist. For there is the more excellent way of love and nonviolent protest. I am grateful to God that, through the influence of the Negro church, the way of nonviolence became an integral part of our struggle.

If this philosophy had not emerged, by now many streets of   29
the South would, I am convinced, be flowing with blood. And I am further convinced that if our white brothers dismiss as "rabble-rousers" and "outside agitators" those of us who employ nonviolent direct action, and if they refuse to support our non-violent efforts, millions of Negroes will, out of frustration and despair, seek solace and security in black-nationalist ideologies—a development that would inevitably lead to a frightening racial nightmare.

Oppressed people cannot remain oppressed forever. The   30
yearning for freedom eventually manifests itself, and that is what has happened to the American Negro. Something within has reminded him of his birthright of freedom, and something without has reminded him that it can be gained. Consciously or unconsciously, he has been caught up by the *Zeitgeist*, and with his black brothers of Africa and his brown and yellow brothers of Asia, South America and the Caribbean, the United States Negro is moving with a sense of great urgency toward the promised land of racial justice. If one recognizes this vital urge that has engulfed the Negro community, one should readily understand why public demonstrations are taking place. The Negro has many pent-up resentments and latent frustrations, and he must release them. So let him march; let him make prayer pilgrimages to the city hall; let him go on freedom rides—and try to understand why he must do so. If his repressed emotions are not released in nonviolent ways, they will seek expression through violence; this is not a threat but a fact of history. So I have not said to my people: "Get rid of your discontent." Rather, I have tried to say that this normal and healthy discontent can be channeled into the creative outlet of nonviolent direct action. And now this approach is being termed extremist.

31   But though I was initially disappointed at being categorized as an extremist, as I continued to think about the matter I gradually gained a measure of satisfaction from the label. Was not Jesus an extremist for love: "Love your enemies, bless them that curse you, do good to them that hate you, and pray for them which despitefully use you, and persecute you." Was not Amos an extremist for justice: "Let justice roll down like waters and righteousness like an ever-flowing stream." Was not Paul an extremist for the Christian gospel: "I bear in my body the marks of the Lord Jesus." Was not Martin Luther an extremist: "Here I stand; I cannot do otherwise, so help me God." And John Bunyan: "I will stay in jail to the end of my days before I make a butchery of my conscience." And Abraham Lincoln: "This nation cannot survive half slave and half free." And Thomas Jefferson: "We hold these truths to be self-evident, that all men are created equal. . . ." So the question is not whether we will be extremists, but what kind of extremists we will be. Will we be extremists for hate or for love? Will we be extremists for the preservation of injustice or for the extension of justice? In that dramatic scene on Calvary's hill three men were crucified. We must never forget that all three were crucified for the same crime—the crime of extremism. Two were extremists for immorality, and thus fell below their environment. The other, Jesus Christ, was an extremist for love, truth and goodness, and thereby rose above his environment. Perhaps the South, the nation and the world are in dire need of creative extremists.

32   I had hoped that the white moderate would see this need. Perhaps I was too optimistic; perhaps I expected too much. I suppose I should have realized that few members of the oppressor race can understand the deep groans and passionate yearnings of the oppressed race, and still fewer have the vision to see that injustice must be rooted out by strong, persistent and determined action. I am thankful, however, that some of our white brothers in the South have grasped the meaning of this social revolution and committed themselves to it. They are still all too few in quantity, but they are big in quality. Some—such as Ralph McGill, Lillian Smith, Harry Golden, James McBride Dabbs, Ann Braden and Sarah Patton Boyle—have written about our struggle in eloquent and prophetic terms. Others have marched with us down nameless streets of the South. They have languished in filthy,

roach-infested jails, suffering the abuse and brutality of policemen who view them as "dirty nigger-lovers." Unlike so many of their moderate brothers and sisters, they have recognized the urgency of the moment and sensed the need for powerful "action" antidotes to combat the disease of segregation.

Let me take note of my other major disappointment. I have been so greatly disappointed with the white church and its leadership. Of course, there are some notable exceptions. I am not unmindful of the fact that each of you has taken some significant stands on this issue. I commend you, Reverend Stallings, for your Christian stand on this past Sunday, in welcoming Negroes to your worship service on a nonsegregated basis. I commend the Catholic leaders of this state for integrating Spring Hill College several years ago. 33

But despite these notable exceptions, I must honestly reiterate that I have been disappointed with the church. I do not say this as one of those negative critics who can always find something wrong with the church. I say this as a minister of the gospel, who loves the church; who was nurtured in its bosom; who has been sustained by its spiritual blessings and who will remain true to it as long as the cord of life shall lengthen. 34

When I was suddenly catapulted into the leadership of the bus protest in Montgomery, Alabama, a few years ago, I felt we would be supported by the white church. I felt that the white ministers, priests and rabbis of the South would be among our strongest allies. Instead, some have been outright opponents, refusing to understand the freedom movement and misrepresenting its leaders; all too many others have been more cautious than courageous and have remained silent behind the anesthetizing security of stained-glass windows. 35

In spite of my shattered dreams, I came to Birmingham with the hope that the white religious leadership of this community would see the justice of our cause and, with deep moral concern, would serve as the channel through which our just grievances could reach the power structure. I had hoped that each of you would understand. But again I have been disappointed. 36

I have heard numerous southern religious leaders admonish their worshipers to comply with a desegregation decision because it is the law, but I have longed to hear white ministers 37 declare: "Follow this decree because integration is morally right and because the Negro is your brother." In the midst of blatant injustices inflicted upon the Negro, I have watched white churchmen stand on the sideline and mouth pious irrelevancies and sanctimonious trivialities. In the midst of a mighty struggle to rid our nation of racial and economic injustice, I have heard many ministers say: "Those are social issues, with which the gospel has no real concern." And I have watched many churches commit themselves to completely other-worldly religion which makes a strange, un-Biblical distinction between body and soul, between the sacred and the secular.

38   I have traveled the length and breadth of Alabama, Mississippi and all the other southern states. On sweltering summer days and crisp autumn mornings I have looked at the South's beautiful churches with their lofty spires pointing heavenward. I have beheld the impressive outlines of her massive religious-education buildings. Over and over I have found myself asking: "What kind of people worship here? Who is their God? Where were their voices when the lips of Governor Barnett dripped with words of interposition and nullification? Where were they when Governor Wallace gave a clarion call for defiance and hatred? Where were their voices of support when bruised and weary Negro men and women decided to rise from the dark dungeons of complacency to the bright hills of creative protest?"

39   Yes, these questions are still in my mind. In deep disappointment I have wept over the laxity of the church. But be assured that my tears have been tears of love. There can be no deep disappointment where there is not deep love. Yes, I love the church. How could I do otherwise? I am in the rather unique position of being the son, the grandson and the great-grandson of preachers. Yes, I see the church as the body of Christ. But, oh! How we have blemished and scarred that body through social neglect and through fear of being nonconformists.

40   There was a time when the church was very powerful—in the time when the early Christians rejoiced at being deemed worthy to suffer for what they believed. In those days the church was not merely a thermometer that recorded the ideas and principles of popular opinion; it was a thermostat that transformed the mores of society. Whenever the early Christians entered a town,

the people in power became disturbed and immediately sought to convict the Christians for being "disturbers of the peace" and "outside agitators." But the Christians pressed on, in the conviction that they were "a colony of heaven," called to obey God rather than man. Small in number, they were big in commitment. They were too God-intoxicated to be "astronomically intimidated." By their effort and example they brought an end to such ancient evils as infanticide and gladiatorial contests.

Things are different now. So often the contemporary church 41 is a weak, ineffectual voice with an uncertain sound. So often it is an archdefender of the status quo. Far from being disturbed by the presence of the church, the power structure of the average community is consoled by the church's silent—and often even vocal—sanction of things as they are.

But the judgment of God is upon the church as never before. 42 If today's church does not recapture the sacrificial spirit of the early church, it will lose its authenticity, forfeit the loyalty of millions, and be dismissed as an irrelevant social club with no meaning for the twentieth century. Every day I meet young people whose disappointment with the church has turned into outright disgust.

Perhaps I have once again been too optimistic. Is organized 43 religion too inextricably bound to the status quo to save our nation and the world? Perhaps I must turn my faith to the inner spiritual church, the church within the church, as the true *ekklesia* and the hope of the world. But again I am thankful to God that some noble souls from the ranks of organized religion have broken loose from the paralyzing chains of conformity and joined us as active partners in the struggle for freedom. They have left their secure congregations and walked the streets of Albany, Georgia, with us. They have gone down the highways of the South on tortuous rides for freedom. Yes, they have gone to jail with us. Some have been dismissed from their churches, have lost the support of their bishops and fellow ministers. But they have acted in the faith that right defeated is stronger than evil triumphant. Their witness has been the spiritual salt that has preserved the true meaning of the gospel in these troubled times. They have carved a tunnel of hope through the dark mountain of disappointment.

I hope the church as a whole will meet the challenge of this 44 decisive hour. But even if the church does not come to the aid of justice, I have no despair about the future. I have no fear about the outcome of our struggle in Birmingham, even if our motives are at present misunderstood. We will reach the goal of freedom in Birmingham and all over the nation, because the goal of America is freedom. Abused and scorned though we may be, our destiny is tied up with America's destiny. Before the pilgrims landed at Plymouth, we were here. Before the pen of Jefferson etched the majestic words of the Declaration of Independence across the pages of history, we were here. For more than two centuries our forebears labored in this country without wages; they made cotton king; they built the homes of their masters while suffering gross injustice and shameful humiliation—and yet out of a bottomless vitality they continued to thrive and develop. If the inexpressible cruelties of slavery could not stop us, the opposition we now face will surely fail. We will win our freedom because the sacred heritage of our nation and the eternal will of God are embodied in our echoing demands.

45   Before closing I feel impelled to mention one other point in your statement that has troubled me profoundly. You warmly commended the Birmingham police force for keeping "order" and "preventing violence." I doubt that you would have so warmly commended the police force if you had seen its dogs sinking their teeth into unarmed, nonviolent Negroes. I doubt that you would so quickly commend the policemen if you were to observe their ugly and inhumane treatment of Negroes here in the city jail; if you were to watch them push and curse old Negro women and young Negro girls; if you were to see them slap and kick old Negro men and young boys; if you were to observe them as they did on two occasions, refuse to give us food because we wanted to sing our grace together. I cannot join you in your praise of the Birmingham police department.

46   It is true that the police have exercised a degree of discipline in handling the demonstrators. In this sense they have conducted themselves rather "nonviolently" in public. But for what purpose? To preserve the evil system of segregation. Over the past few years I have consistently preached that nonviolence demands that the means we use must be as pure as the ends we seek. I have tried to make clear that it is wrong to use immoral means to attain moral

ends. But now I must affirm that it is just as wrong, or perhaps even more so, to use moral means to preserve immoral ends. Perhaps Mr. Connor and his policemen have been rather nonviolent in public, as was Chief Pritchett in Albany, Georgia, but they have used the moral means of nonviolence to maintain the immoral end of racial injustice. As T. S. Eliot has said: "The last temptation is the greatest treason: To do the right deed for the wrong reason."

I wish you had commended the Negro sit-inners and demon- 47 strators of Birmingham for their sublime courage, their willingness to suffer and their amazing discipline in the midst of great provocation. One day the South will recognize its real heroes. They will be the James Merediths, with the noble sense of purpose that enables them to face jeering and hostile mobs, and with the agonizing loneliness that characterizes the life of the pioneer. They will be old, oppressed, battered Negro women, symbolized in a seventy-two-year-old woman in Montgomery, Alabama, who rose up with a sense of dignity and with her people decided not to ride segregated buses, and who responded with ungrammatical profundity to one who inquired about her weariness: "My feet is tired, but my soul is at rest." They will be the young high school and college students, the young ministers of the gospel and a host of their elders, courageously and nonviolently sitting in at lunch counters and willingly going to jail for conscience' sake. One day the South will know that when these disinherited children of God sat down at lunch counters, they were in reality standing up for what is best in the American dream and for the most sacred values in our Judaeo-Christian heritage, thereby bringing our nation back to those great wells of democracy which were dug deep by the founding fathers in their formulation of the Constitution and the Declaration of Independence.

Never before have I written so long a letter. I'm afraid it is 48 much too long to take your precious time. I can assure you that it would have been much shorter if I had been writing from a comfortable desk, but what else can one do when he is alone in a narrow jail cell, other than write long letters, think long thoughts and pray long prayers?

If I have said anything in this letter that overstates the truth 49 and indicates an unreasonable impatience, I beg you to forgive me. If I have said anything that understates the truth and indicates my having a patience that allows me to settle for anything less than brotherhood, I beg God to forgive me.

50   I hope this letter finds you strong in faith. I also hope that circumstances will soon make it possible for me to meet each of you, not as an integrationist or a civil-rights leader but as a fellow clergyman and a Christian brother. Let us all hope that the dark clouds of racial prejudice will soon pass away and the deep fog of misunderstanding will be lifted from our fear-drenched communities, and in some not too distant tomorrow the radiant stars of love and brotherhood will shine over our great nation with all their scintillating beauty.

> Yours for the cause of Peace and Brotherhood,
> *Martin Luther King, Jr.*

Content

1. In paragraph 4 King makes several assertions on which he bases the rest of his argument. What are they? Does he ever prove them, or does he assume that readers will take them for granted?

2. In paragraph 5 King asserts that Birmingham's "white power structure left the Negro community with no alternative" but to commit civil disobedience. Does he ever prove this? Does he need to? Is it a debatable statement?

3. What, according to King, are the "four basic steps" in "any nonviolent campaign" (¶ 6)? What is the goal of "nonviolent direct action" (¶ 10)? What is the constructive, "nonviolent tension" (¶ 10) King favors?

4. Why has King been disappointed by white moderates (¶s 23–32)? By the white church (¶ 33–44)? What does he want white moderates to do? What does he claim that the church should do?

5. How does King deal with the argument that civil rights activists are too impatient, that they should go slow because "It has taken Christianity almost two thousand years to accomplish what it has" (¶ 26)? How does he refute the argument that he is an extremist (¶ 27)?

Strategies/Structures

6. How does King establish, in the salutation and first paragraph, his reasons for writing? The setting in which he writes? His intended audience? A sensitive, reasonable tone?

7. King's letter ostensibly replies to that of the eight clergymen. Find passages in which he addresses them, and analyze the voice he uses. In what relation to the clergymen does King see himself? He also has a secondary audience; who are its members? Locate passages that seem especially directed to this second audience. In what relation to this audience does King see himself?

8. Why does King cite the theologians Aquinas (a Catholic), Buber (a Jew), and Tillich (a Protestant) in paragraph 16? What similarities link the three?

9. After defending his actions against the criticisms of the clergymen, King takes the offensive in paragraphs 23–44. How does he signal this change?

10. Which parts of King's letter appeal chiefly to reason? To emotion? How are the two types of appeals interrelated?

11. King uses large numbers of rhetorical questions throughout this essay (see ¶s 18, 25, 31, 38, 39). Why? With what effects?

Language

12. How does King define a "just law" (¶s 16, 17)? An "unjust law" (¶s 16, 17)? Why are these definitions crucial to the argument that follows?

13. Consult your dictionary, if necessary, for the meanings of the following words or others you do not understand: cognizant (¶ 4), gainsaying (¶ 6), moratorium (¶ 7), gadflies (¶ 10), harried (¶ 14), degenerating (¶ 14), abyss (¶ 14), incorrigible (¶ 27), *Zeitgeist* (¶ 30), scintillating (¶ 50).

For Writing

14. Under what circumstances, if any, is breaking the law justifiable? If you use Dr. King's definition of just and unjust law (¶s 15–20), or make any distinction, say, between moral law and civil law, be sure to explain what you mean. You may, if you wish, use examples with which you are personally familiar. Or you may elaborate on some of the examples King uses (¶ 22) or on examples from King's own civil-rights activities, such as the boycotts in the early 1950s of the legally segregated Montgomery bus system (¶ 35).

15. If you are a member of a church, or attend a church regularly, address members of the congregation on what, if any, commitment you think your church should make to the betterment of minorities, the poor, or other groups who do not attend that church. Does this commitment extend to civil disobedience?

16. Would you ever be willing to go to jail for a cause? What cause? Under what circumstances? If you knew that a prison record might bar you from some privileges in some states (such as practicing law or medicine), would you still be willing to take such a risk?

LANI GUINIER

Guinier, the daughter of black and Jewish parents in Queens, New York, was born (1950) into a complex heritage of concern for racial equality. Her father's scholarship to Harvard had been withdrawn in the 1930s when administrators realized that Harvard had already admitted its quota of black scholarship students—one—that year. Decades later Ewart Guinier chaired Harvard's Afro-American studies department. Guinier herself received a scholarship to Harvard-Radcliffe College (B.A., 1971) and received her law degree from Yale (1974), where she was a friend and classmate of Bill Clinton and Hillary Rodham. Implications of the Voting Rights Act of 1965, central to the civil rights movement, became the legal specialty that led Guinier to four years of service as an attorney in the Civil Rights Division of the Department of Justice during the Carter administration, followed by six years with the NAACP Legal Defense Fund.

In 1988 she became a professor at the University of Pennsylvania, doing research, as she had previously practiced litigation, on ways to remedy racial discrimination: "Inspired by James Madison, I explored ways to ensure that even a self-interested majority could work with, rather than 'tyrannize,' a minority. . . . I imagined a more consensual, deliberative, and participatory democracy for all voters." In 1993, when Clinton nominated Guinier for Assistant Attorney General for Civil Rights, her even-handed record of consensus-building was distorted by opponents ("Czarina of Czeparatism") and in the ensuing controversy the nomination was withdrawn. Guinier's new visibility, however, has given her a national audience, whom she has addressed in *Lift Every Voice: Turning a Civil Rights Setback into a Strong New Vision of Social Justice* (1998). In *The Tyranny of the Majority* (1994), from which the following essay is taken. She explains her philosophy: "My point is simple: 51 percent of the people should not always get 100 percent of the power [especially] if they use that power to exclude the 49 percent. In that case we do not have majority rule. We have majority tyranny."

The Tyranny of the Majority

I have always wanted to be a civil rights lawyer. This lifelong 1 ambition is based on a deep-seated commitment to democratic fair play—to playing by the rules as long as the rules are fair. When the rules seem unfair, I have worked to change them, not subvert them. When I was eight years old, I was a Brownie. I was especially proud of my uniform, which represented a commitment to good citizenship and good deeds. But one day, when my Brownie group staged a hatmaking contest, I realized that uniforms are only as honorable as the people who wear them. The contest was rigged. The winner was assisted by her milliner mother, who actually made the winning entry in full view of all the participants. At the time, I was too young to be able to change the rules, but I was old enough to resign, which I promptly did.

To me, fair play means that the rules encourage everyone 2 to play. They should reward those who win, but they must be acceptable to those who lose. The central theme of my academic writing is that not all rules lead to elemental fair play. Some even commonplace rules work against it.

The professional milliner competing with amateur Brownies 3 stands as an example of rules that are patently rigged or patently subverted. Yet, sometimes, even when rules are perfectly fair in form, they serve in practice to exclude particular groups from meaningful participation. When they do not encourage everyone to play, or when, over the long haul, they do not make the losers feel as good about the outcomes as the winners, they can seem as unfair as the milliner who makes the winning hat for her daughter.

Sometimes, too, we construct rules that force us to be divided 4 into winners and losers when we might have otherwise joined together. This idea was cogently expressed by my son, Nikolas, when he was four years old, far exceeding the thoughtfulness of his mother when she was an eight-year-old Brownie. While I was writing one of my law journal articles, Nikolas and I had a conversation about voting prompted by a *Sesame Street Magazine* exercise. The magazine pictured six children: four children had raised their hands because they wanted to play tag; two had their hands down because they wanted to play hide-and-seek. The magazine asked its readers to count the number of children whose hands were raised and then decide what game the children would play.

5   Nikolas quite realistically replied, "They will play both. First they will play tag. Then they will play hide-and-seek." Despite the magazine's "rules," he was right. To children, it is natural to take turns. The winner may get to play first or more often, but even the "loser" gets something. His was a positive-sum solution that many adult rule-makers ignore.

6   The traditional answer to the magazine's problem would have been a zero-sum solution: "The children—all the children—will play tag, and only tag." As a zero-sum solution, everything is seen in terms of "I win; you lose." The conventional answer relies on winner-take-all majority rule, in which the tag players, as the majority, win the right to decide for all the children what game to play. The hide-and-seek preference becomes irrelevant. The numerically more powerful majority choice simply subsumes minority preferences.

7   In the conventional case, the majority that rules gains all the power and the minority that loses gets none. For example, two years ago Brother Rice High School in Chicago held two senior proms. It was not planned that way. The prom committee at Brother Rice, a boys' Catholic school, expected just one prom when it hired a disc jockey, picked a rock band, and selected music for the prom by consulting student preferences. Each senior was asked to list his three favorite songs, and the band would play the songs that appeared most frequently on the lists.

8   Seems attractively democratic. But Brother Rice is predominantly white, and the prom committee was all white. That's how they got two proms. The black seniors at Brother Rice felt so shut out by the "democratic process" that they organized their own prom. As one black student put it: "For every vote we had, there were eight votes for what they wanted. . . . [W]ith us being in the minority we're always outvoted. It's as if we don't count."

Some embittered white seniors saw things differently. They 9
complained that the black students should have gone along with
the majority: "The majority makes a decision. That's the way it
works."

In a way, both groups were right. From the white students' 10
perspective, this was ordinary decisionmaking. To the black students, majority rule sent the message: "we don't count" is the
"way it works" for minorities. In a racially divided society, majority rule may be perceived as majority tyranny.

That is a large claim, and I do not rest my case for it solely 11
on the actions of the prom committee in one Chicago high school.
To expand the range of argument, I first consider the ideal of majority rule itself, particularly as reflected in the writings of James
Madison and other founding members of our Republic. These
early democrats explored the relationship between majority rule
and democracy. James Madison warned, "If a majority be united
by a common interest, the rights of the minority will be insecure."
The tyranny of the majority, according to Madison, requires safe-
guards to protect "one part of the society against the injustice of
the other part."

For Madison, majority tyranny represented the great danger 12
to our early constitutional democracy. Although the American
revolution was fought against the tyranny of the British monarch,
it soon became clear that there was another tyranny to be
avoided. The accumulations of all powers in the same hands,
Madison warned, "whether of one, a few, or many, and whether
hereditary, self-appointed, or elective, may justly be pronounced
the very definition of tyranny."

As another colonist suggested in papers published in 13
Philadelphia, "We have been so long habituated to a jealousy of
tyranny from monarchy and aristocracy, that we have yet to learn
the dangers of it from democracy." Despotism had to be opposed
"whether it came from Kings, Lords or the people."

The debate about majority tyranny reflected Madison's con- 14
cern that the majority may not represent the whole. In a homo-
geneous society, the interest of the majority would likely be that of
the minority also. But in a heterogeneous community, the majority
may not represent all competing interests. The majority is likely to
be self-interested and ignorant or indifferent to the concerns of the

minority. In such case, Madison observed, the assumption that the majority represents the minority is "altogether fictitious."

15   Yet even a self-interested majority can govern fairly if it cooperates with the minority. One reason for such cooperation is that the self-interested majority values the principle of reciprocity. The self-interested majority worries that the minority may attract defectors from the majority and become the next governing majority. The Golden Rule principle of reciprocity functions to check the tendency of a self-interested majority to act tyrannically.

16   So the argument for the majority principle connects it with the value of reciprocity: You cooperate when you lose in part because members of the current majority will cooperate when they lose. The conventional case for the fairness of majority rule is that it is not really the rule of a fixed group—The Majority— on all issues; instead it is the rule of shifting majorities, as the losers at one time or on one issue join with others and become part of the governing coalition at another time or on another issue. The result will be a fair system of mutually beneficial cooperation. I call a majority that rules but does not dominate a Madisonian Majority.

17   The problem of majority tyranny arises, however, when the self-interested majority does not need to worry about defections. When the majority is fixed and permanent, there are no checks on its ability to be overbearing. A majority that does not worry about defectors is a majority with total power.

18   In such a case, Madison's concern about majority tyranny arises. In a heterogeneous community, any faction with total power might subject "the minority to the caprice and arbitrary decisions of the majority, who instead of consulting the interest of the whole community collectively, attend sometimes to partial and local advantages."

19   "What remedy can be found in a republican Government, where the majority must ultimately decide," argued Madison, but to ensure "that no one common interest or passion will be likely to unite a majority of the whole number in an unjust pursuit." The answer was to disaggregate the majority to ensure checks and balances or fluid, rotating interests. The minority needed protection against an overbearing majority, so that "a common sentiment is less likely to be felt, and the requisite concert less likely to be formed, by a majority of the whole."

Political struggles would not be simply a contest between 20
rulers and people; the political struggles would be among the
people themselves. The work of government was not to transcend
different interests but to reconcile them. In an ideal democracy, the
people would rule, but the minorities would also be protected
against the power of majorities. Again, where the rules of decisionmaking protect the minority, the Madisonian Majority rules
without dominating.

But if a group is unfairly treated, for example, when it forms 21
a racial minority, *and* if the problems of unfairness are not cured
by conventional assumptions about majority rule, then what is to
be done? The answer is that we may need an *alternative* to winner-
take-all majoritarianism. In this book, a collection of my law review
articles, I describe the alternative, which, with Nikolas's help, I
now call the "principle of taking turns." In a racially divided society, this principle does better than simple majority rule if it
accommodates the values of self-government, fairness, delibera-
tion, compromise, and consensus that lie at the heart of the democratic ideal.

In my legal writing, I follow the caveat of James Madison 22
and other early American democrats. I explore decisionmaking
rules that might work in a multi-racial society to ensure that
majority rule does not become majority tyranny. I pursue voting
systems that might disaggregate The Majority so that it does not
exercise power unfairly or tyrannically. I aspire to a more cooperative political style of decisionmaking to enable all of the students
at Brother Rice to feel comfortable attending the same prom. In
looking to create Madisonian Majorities, I pursue a positive-sum,
taking-turns solution.

Structuring decisionmaking to allow the minority "a turn" 23
may be necessary to restore the reciprocity ideal when a fixed majority refuses to cooperate with the minority. If the fixed majority
loses its incentive to follow the Golden Rule principle of shifting
majorities, the minority never gets to take a turn. Giving the
minority a turn does not mean the minority gets to rule; what it
does mean is that the minority gets to influence decisionmaking
and the majority rules more legitimately.

Instead of automatically rewarding the preferences of the 24
monolithic majority, a taking-turns approach anticipates that the

majority rules, but is not overbearing. Because those with 51 percent of the votes are not assured 100 percent of the power, the majority cooperates with, or at least does not tyrannize, the minority.

25   The sports analogy of "I win; you lose" competition within a political hierarchy makes sense when only one team can win; Nikolas's intuition that it is often possible to take turns suggests an alternative approach. Take family decisionmaking, for example. It utilizes a taking-turns approach. When parents sit around the kitchen table deciding on a vacation destination or activities for a rainy day, often they do not simply rely on a show of hands, especially if that means that the older children always prevail or if affinity groups among the children (those who prefer movies to video games, or those who prefer baseball to playing cards) never get to play their activity of choice. Instead of allowing the majority simply to rule, the parents may propose that everyone take turns, going to the movies one night and playing video games the next. Or as Nikolas proposes, they might do both on a given night.

26   Taking turns attempts to build consensus while recognizing political or social differences, and it encourages everyone to play. The taking-turns approach gives those with the most support more turns, but it also legitimates the outcome from each individual's perspective, including those whose views are shared only by a minority.

27   In the end, I do not believe that democracy should encourage rule by the powerful—even a powerful majority. Instead, the idea of democracy promises a fair discussion among self-defined equals about how to achieve our common aspirations. To redeem that promise, we need to put the idea of taking turns and disaggregating the majority at the center of our conception of representation. Particularly as we move into the twenty-first century as a more highly diversified citizenry, it is essential that we consider the ways in which voting and representational systems succeed or fail at encouraging Madisonian Majorities.

28   To use Nikolas's terminology, "it is no fair" if a fixed, tyrannical majority excludes or alienates the minority. It is no fair if a fixed, tyrannical majority monopolizes all the power all the time. It is no fair if we engage in the periodic ritual of elections, but only the permanent majority gets to choose who is elected. Where we have tyranny by The Majority, we do not have genuine democracy.

Content

1. Throughout the essay, Guinier provides several definitions of "the tyranny of the majority" (see ¶s 12–21, for instance). Identify some of these definitions and the distinctions among them. Why won't a single definition suffice?

2. Guinier says one solution to majority tyranny is to "disaggregate the majority" (¶s 19, 22). What does she mean by this? Why does she see this as important in preventing the tyranny of the majority?

3. What does Guinier mean by the "'principle of taking turns'" (¶ 21)? How does this relate to her son's solution to the *Sesame Street Magazine* exercise (¶s 4–5)?

4. Has Guinier provided sufficient evidence to support her view that "'It is no fair' if a fixed, tyrannical majority excludes or alienates the minority" (¶ 28)? As you explain your answer, bear in mind that this essay is but a single chapter from an entire book; the writer can't cram every argument into one chapter.

Strategies/Structures

5. Many writings that attempt to explain complicated phenomena or to discuss difficult issues begin with down-to-earth examples, as Guinier's essay does (¶s 1–10). Why?

6. The standard advice for constructing arguments is to give the opposition a fair hearing in the course of presenting the side one favors. Does Guinier do this? Can you think of any instances in which "the tyranny of the majority" might be both good and necessary?

Language

7. Although it forms a chapter in a book, "The Tyranny of the Majority" could be read as an essay composed essentially of definitions. Why is this so, and why are definitions so important in discussing majority rule?

8. Given the prominence of definitions in "The Tyranny of the Majority," where do you suppose this chapter appeared in the book of the same name? Why do you think so?

For Writing

9. Elaborate on Guinier's view that "taking turns attempts to build consensus while recognizing political or social differences, and it encourages everyone to play" (¶ 26). Extend her application to some aspect

of politics, education, social welfare, or other area of public policy that affects a sizable population; and argue for or against her position. Even if you oppose her view, you'll need to take her arguments into account.
10. Use Guinier's argument to provide a reading of Martin Luther King, Jr.'s "Letter from Birmingham Jail" (596–616), Jonathan Swift's "A Modest Proposal" (650–60), or some other essay with social or humanitarian concerns.

ROBERT REICH

Reich (born, 1946), earned a B.A. at Dartmouth College (1968) and a J.D. degree from Yale Law School (1973), was a Rhodes scholar at Oxford, and since 1981 has been a professor at Harvard's John F. Kennedy School of Government. Active in politics since his student days, Reich has served as summer intern for Senator Robert Kennedy; coordinator of Eugene McCarthy's 1968 presidential campaign; and as economic advisor to presidential candidates Walter Mondale and Michael Dukakis. He was U. S. Secretary of Labor during Clinton's first term as president, 1993–96; *Locked in the Cabinet* (1997) discusses his experiences.

Many of Reich's books on economics have been intended for a general audience, including *Tales of a New America: The Anxious Liberal's Guide to the Future* (1988); and *The Work of Nations: Preparing Ourselves for 21st-Century Capitalism* (1991). *The Next American Frontier* (1983) provided a rationale for the Democratic party's economic policy, explaining that "government intervention sets the boundaries, decides what's going to be marketed, sets the rules of the game through procurement policies, tax credits, depreciation allowances, loans and loan guarantees." *Tales of a New America*, also popular with Democrats, defines four economic myths: "Mob at the Gate" labels foreigners as adversaries to American citizens; "The Triumphant Individual" reinforces the myth of the American Dream; "The Benevolent Community" claims that Americans act out of social responsibility to one another; and "The Rot at the Top" accuses the elite class of corruption and abuse of their power. "The Global Elite," first published in the *New York Times Magazine* (1991) provides factual information to counteract the myths of a benevolent, egalitarian society and implicitly argues for a more equitable—and democratic—distribution of our country's wealth.

The Global Elite

T he idea of "community" has always held a special attraction 1
for Americans. In a 1984 speech, President Ronald Reagan
celebrated America's "bedrock"—"its communities where neighbors help one another, where families bring up kids together,
where American values are born." Governor Mario M. Cuomo of
New York, with a very different political leaning, has been almost
as lyrical. "Community . . . is the reality on which our national life
has been founded," he said in 1987.

There is only one problem with this picture. Most Americans 2
no longer live in traditional communities. They live in suburban
subdivisions bordered by highways and sprinkled with shopping
malls, or in tony condominiums and residential clusters, or in
ramshackle apartment buildings and housing projects. Most of
them commute to work and socialize on some basis other than
geographic proximity. And most people pick up and move to a
different neighborhood every five years or so.

But Americans generally have one thing in common with 3
their neighbors: They have similar incomes. And that simple fact
lies at the heart of the new community. This means that their educational backgrounds are likely to be similar, that they pay
roughly the same in taxes, and that they indulge in the same consumer impulses. "Tell me someone's ZIP code," the founder of a
direct-mail company once bragged, "and I can predict what they
eat, drink, drive—even think."

Americans who own their homes usually share one political 4
cause with their neighbors: a near obsessive concern with maintaining or upgrading property values. And this common interest
is responsible for much of what has brought neighbors together in
recent years. Complete strangers, although they may live on the
same street or in the same condominium complex, suddenly feel
intense solidarity when it is rumored that low-income housing
will be constructed in their midst or that a poorer school district
will be consolidated with their own.

The renewed emphasis on "community" in American life 5
has justified and legitimized these economic enclaves. If generosity and solidarity end at the border of similarly valued properties, then the most fortunate can be virtuous citizens at little cost.

Since most people in one neighborhood or town are equally well off, there is no cause for a guilty conscience. If inhabitants of another area are poorer, let them look to one another. Why should *we* pay for *their* schools?

6   So the argument goes, without acknowledging that the critical assumption has already been made: "We" and "they" belong to fundamentally different communities. Through such reasoning, it has become possible to maintain a self-image of generosity toward, and solidarity with, one's "community" without bearing any responsibility to "them"—the other "community."

7   America's high earners—the fortunate top fifth—thus feel increasingly justified in paying only what is necessary to insure that everyone in their community is sufficiently well educated and has access to the public services they need to succeed.

8 Last year, the top fifth of working Americans took home more money than the other four-fifths put together—the highest portion in postwar history. These high earners will relinquish somewhat more of their income to the Federal Government this year than in 1990 as a result of last fall's tax changes, although considerably less than in the late 1970s, when the tax code was more progressive. But the continuing debate over whether the wealthy are paying their fair share of taxes obscures a larger issue, with more profound implications for America: The fortunate fifth is quietly seceding from the rest of the nation.

9   This is occurring gradually, without much awareness by members of the top group—or, for that matter, by anyone else. And the Government is speeding this process as Washington shifts responsibility for many public services to state and local governments.

10   The secession is taking several forms. In many cities and towns, the wealthy have in effect withdrawn their dollars from the support of public spaces and institutions shared by all and dedicated the savings to their own private services. As public parks and playgrounds deteriorate, there is a proliferation of private health clubs, golf clubs, tennis clubs, skating clubs, and every other type of recreational association in which costs are shared among members. Condominiums and the omnipresent residential communities dun their members to undertake work that financially strapped local governments can no longer afford

to do well—maintaining roads, mending sidewalks, pruning trees, repairing street lights, cleaning swimming pools, paying for lifeguards, and, notably, hiring security guards to protect life and property. (The number of private security guards in the United States now exceeds the number of public police officers.)

Of course, wealthier Americans have been withdrawing 11 into their own neighborhoods and clubs for generations. But the new secession is more dramatic because the highest earners now inhabit a different economy from other Americans. The new elite is linked by jet, modem, fax, satellite, and fiber-optic cable to the great commercial and recreational centers of the world, but it is not particularly connected to the rest of the nation.

That is because the work this group does is becoming less 12 tied to the activities of other Americans. Most of their jobs consist of analyzing and manipulating symbols—words, numbers, or visual images. Among the most prominent of these "symbolic analysts" are management consultants, lawyers, software and design engineers, research scientists, corporate executives, financial advisors, strategic planners, advertising executives, television and movie producers, and other workers whose job titles include terms like "strategy," "planning," "consultant," "policy," "resources," or "engineer."

These workers typically spend long hours in meetings or on 13 the telephone and even longer hours in planes or hotels—advising, making presentations, giving briefings, and making deals. Periodically, they issue reports, plans, designs, drafts, briefs, blueprints, analyses, memorandums, layouts, renderings, scripts, or projections. In contrast with people whose jobs tend to be tedious and repetitive, symbolic analysts find their work varied and intellectually challenging. In fact, the work is often enjoyable.

These symbolic analysts are in ever greater demand in a world 14 market that places an increasing value on identifying and solving problems. Requests for their software designs, financial advice, or engineering blueprints come from all parts of the globe. This largely explains why most (but by no means all) symbolic analysts have become wealthier, even as the ever-growing worldwide supply of unskilled labor continues to depress the wages of other Americans.

Successful Americans have not completely disengaged themselves 15 from the lives of their less fortunate compatriots. Some devote substantial resources and energies to helping the rest of society, not through their tax payments, but through voluntary efforts. "Generosity is a reflection of what one does with his or her resources—and not what he or she advocates the government do with everyone's money," Ronald Reagan said in 1984.

16   The argument is fair enough. Government is not the only device for redistributing wealth. In his speech accepting the Presidential nomination at the Republican National Convention in 1988, George Bush said that the real magnanimity of America was to be found in a "brilliant diversity" of private charities, "spread like stars, like a thousand points of light in a broad and peaceful sky."

17   No nation congratulates itself more enthusiastically on its charitable acts than America; none engages in a greater number of charity balls, bake sales, benefit auctions, and border-to-border hand holdings for good causes. Much of this is sincerely motivated and admirable.

18   But close examination reveals that many of these acts of benevolence do not help the needy. Particularly suspect is the private givings of those in the top income-tax bracket. Studies have revealed that their largess does not flow mainly to social services for the poor—to better schools, health clinics, or recreational centers. Instead, most voluntary contributions of wealthy Americans go to the places and institutions that entertain, inspire, cure, or educate wealthy Americans—art museums, opera houses, theaters, orchestras, ballet companies, private hospitals, and elite universities.

19   And even these charitable contributions are relatively skimpy. Last year, American households with incomes of less than $10,000 gave an average of 5.5 percent of their earnings to charity or to a religious organization; those making more than $100,000 a year gave only 2.9 percent. After the 1986 tax-code overhaul reduced the benefits of charitable giving, the very rich became even stingier. According to Internal Revenue Service data, taxpayers earning $500,000 or more slashed their average donations to $16,062 in 1988 from $47,432 in 1980.

20   Corporate philanthropy is following the same general pattern. In recent years, the largest American corporations have been sounding the alarm about the nation's fast deteriorating primary and secondary schools. Few are more eloquent and impassioned about the need for better schools than American executives. "How well we educate all of our children will determine our competitiveness globally, and our economic health domestically, and our

communities' character and vitality," said a report of The Business Roundtable, a New York–based association of top executives.

Accordingly, there are numerous "partnerships" between 21 corporations and public schools: scholarships for poor children qualified to attend college, and programs in which businesses adopt individual schools by making conspicuous donations of computers, books, and, on occasion, even money. That such activities are loudly touted by public relations staffs should not detract from the good they do.

Despite the hoopla, business donations to education and 22 charitable causes actually tapered off markedly in the 1980s, even as the economy boomed. In the 1970s, corporate giving to education jumped an average of 15 percent a year. In 1990, however, giving was only 5 percent over that in 1989; and in 1989 it was 3 percent over 1988. Moreover, most of this money goes to colleges and universities—in particular, to the alma maters of symbolic analysts, who expect their children and grandchildren to follow in their footsteps. Only 1.5 percent of corporate giving in the late 1980s was to public primary and secondary schools.

Notably, these contributions have been smaller than the 23 amounts corporations are receiving from states and communities in the form of subsidies or tax breaks. Companies are quietly procuring such deals by threatening to move their operations— and jobs—to places around the world with a more congenial tax climate. The paradoxical result has been even less corporate revenue to spend on schools and other community services than before. The executives of General Motors, for example, who have been among the loudest to proclaim the need for better schools, have also been among the most relentless in pursuing local tax abatements and in challenging their tax assessments. G.M.'s successful efforts to reduce its taxes in North Tarrytown, N.Y., where the company has had a factory since 1914, cut local revenues by $1 million in 1990, part of a larger shortfall that forced the town to lay off scores of teachers.

The secession of the fortunate fifth has been apparent in how and 24 where they have chosen to work and live. In effect, most of America's large urban centers have splintered into two separate cities. One is composed of those whose symbolic and analytic services are linked to the world economy. The other consists of local service workers—custodians, security guards, taxi drivers, clerical aides, parking attendants, salespeople, restaurant employees—whose jobs are dependent on the symbolic analysts. Few blue-collar manufacturing workers remain in American cities. Between 1953 and 1984, for example, New York City lost 600,000 factory jobs; in the same interval, it added about 700,000 jobs for symbolic analysts and service workers.

25   The separation of symbolic analysts from local service workers within cities has been reinforced in several ways. Most large cities now possess two school systems—a private one for the children of the top-earning group and a public one for the children of service workers, the remaining blue-collar workers, and the unemployed. Symbolic analysts spend considerable time and energy insuring that their children gain entrance to good private schools, and then small fortunes keeping them there—dollars that under a more progressive tax code might finance better public education.

26   People with high incomes live, shop, and work within areas of cities that, if not beautiful, are at least esthetically tolerable and reasonably safe; precincts not meeting these minimum standards of charm and security have been left to the less fortunate.

27   Here again, symbolic analysts have pooled their resources to the exclusive benefit of themselves. Public funds have been spent in earnest on downtown "revitalization" projects, entailing the construction of clusters of post-modern office buildings (complete with fiber-optic cables, private branch exchanges, satellite dishes, and other communications equipment linking them to the rest of the world), multilevel parking garages, hotels with glass enclosed atriums, upscale shopping plazas and galleries, theaters, convention centers, and luxury condominiums.

28   Ideally, these complexes are entirely self-contained, with air-conditioned walkways linking residences, businesses, and recreational space. The lucky resident is able to shop, work, and attend the theater without risking direct contact with the outside world—that is, the other city.

29   When not living in urban enclaves, symbolic analysts are increasingly congregating in suburbs and exurbs where corporate headquarters have been relocated, research parks have been created, and where bucolic universities have spawned entrepreneurial ventures. Among the most desirable of such locations are

Princeton, N.J.; northern Westchester and Putnam Counties in New York; Palo Alto, Calif.; Austin, Tex.; Bethesda, Md.; and Raleigh-Durham, N.C.

Engineers and strategists of American auto companies, for 30 example, do not live in Flint or Saginaw, Mich., where the blue-collar workers reside; they cluster in their own towns of Troy, Warren, and Auburn Hills. Likewise, the vast majority of financial specialists, lawyers, and executives working for the insurance companies of Hartford would never consider living there; after all, Hartford is the nation's fourth-poorest city. Instead, they flock to Windsor, Middlebury, West Hartford, and other towns that are among the wealthiest in the country.

This trend, too, has been growing for decades. But technol- 31 ogy has accelerated it. Today's symbolic analysts linked directly to the rest of the globe can choose to live and work in the most pastoral of settings.

The secession has been encouraged by the Federal Govern- 32 ment. For the last decade, Washington has in effect shifted re-sponsibility for many public services to local governments. At their peak, Federal grants made up 25 percent of state and local spending in the late 1970s. Today, the Federal share has dwindled to 17 percent. Direct aid to local governments, in the form of programs introduced in the Johnson and Nixon Administrations, has been the hardest hit by budget cuts. In the 1980s, Federal dollars for clean water, job training and transfers, low-income housing, sewage treatment, and garbage disposal shrank by some $50 billion a year, and Washington's share of spending on local transit declined by 50 percent. (The Bush Administration has pro-posed that states and localities take on even more of the costs of building and maintaining roads, and wants to cut Federal aid for mass transit.) In 1990, New York City received only 9.6 percent of all its revenue from the Federal Government, compared with 16 percent in 1981.

States have quickly transferred many of these new expenses 33 to fiscally strapped cities and towns, with a result that by the start of the 1990s, localities were bearing more than half the costs of water and sewage, roads, parks, welfare, and public schools. In New York State, the local communities' share has risen to about 75 percent of these costs.

34   Cities and towns with affluent inhabitants can bear these burdens relatively easily. Poorer ones, faced with the twin problem of lower incomes and greater demand for social services, have had far more difficulty. And as the gap between the richest and poorest communities has widened, the shift in responsibility for public services to cities and towns has functioned as another means of relieving wealthier Americans of the cost of aiding less fortunate citizens.

35   The result has been a growing inequality in basic social and community services. While the city tax rate in Philadelphia, for example, is about triple that of communities around it, the suburbs enjoy far better schools, hospitals, recreation, and police protection. Eighty-five percent of the richest families in the greater Philadelphia area live outside the city limits, and 80 percent of the region's poorest live inside. The quality of a city's infrastructure—roads, bridges, sewage, water treatment—is likewise related to the average income of its inhabitants.

36   The growing inequality in government services has been most apparent in the public schools. The Federal Government's share of the costs of primary and secondary education has dwindled to about 6 percent. The bulk of the cost is divided about equally between the states and local school districts. States with a higher concentration of wealthy residents can afford to spend more on their schools than other states. In 1989, the average public-school teacher in Arkansas, for example, received $21,700; in Connecticut, $37,300.

37   Even among adjoining suburban towns in the same state the differences can be quite large. Consider three Boston-area communities located within minutes of one another. All are predominantly white, and most residents within each town earn about the same as their neighbors. But the disparity of incomes between towns is substantial.

38   Belmont, northwest of Boston, is inhabited mainly by symbolic analysts and their families. In 1988, the average teacher in its public schools earned $36,100. Only 3 percent of Belmont's eighteen-year-olds dropped out of high school, and more than 80 percent of graduating seniors chose to go on to a four-year college.

39   Just east of Belmont is Somerville, most of whose residents are low-wage service workers. In 1988, the average Somerville

teacher earned $29,400. A third of the town's eighteen-year-olds did not finish high school, and fewer than a third planned to attend college.

Chelsea, across the Mystic River from Somerville, is the poorest of the three towns. Most of its inhabitants are unskilled, and many are unemployed or only employed part time. The average teacher in Chelsea, facing tougher educational challenges than his or her counterparts in Belmont, earned $26,200 in 1988, almost a third less than the average teacher in the more affluent town just a few miles away. More than half of Chelsea's eighteen-year-olds did not graduate from high school, and only 10 percent planned to attend college.

Similar disparities can be found all over the nation. Students at Highland Park High School in a wealthy suburb of Dallas, for example, enjoy a campus with a planetarium, indoor swimming pool, closed-circuit television studio and state-of-the-art science laboratory. Highland Park spends about $6,000 a year to educate each student. This is almost twice that spent per pupil by the towns of Wilmer and Hutchins in southern Dallas County. According to Texas education officials, the richest school district in the state spends $19,300 a year per pupil; its poorest, $2,100 a year.

The courts have become involved in trying to repair such imbalances, but the issues are not open to easy judicial remedy.

The four-fifths of Americans left in the wake of the secession of the fortunate fifth include many poor blacks, but racial exclusion is neither the primary motive for the separation not a necessary consequence. Lower-income whites are similarly excluded, and high-income black symbolic analysts are often welcomed. The segregation is economic rather than racial, although economically motivated separation often results in *de facto* racial segregation. Where courts have found a pattern of racially motivated segregation, it usually has involved lower-income white communities bordering on lower-income black neighborhoods.

In states where courts have ordered equalized state spending in school districts, the vast differences in a town's property values—and thus local tax revenues—continue to result in substantial inequities. Where courts or state governments have tried to impose limits on what affluent communities can pay their teachers, not a few parents in upscale towns have simply removed their children from the public schools and applied the money they might otherwise have willingly paid in higher taxes to private school tuitions instead. And, of course, even if statewide expenditures were better equalized, poorer states would continue to be at a substantial disadvantage.

45   In all these ways, the gap between America's symbolic analysts and everyone else is widening into a chasm. Their secession from the rest of the population raises fundamental questions about the future of American society. In the new global economy—in which money, technologies, and corporations cross borders effortlessly—a citizen's standard of living depends more and more on skills and insights, and on the infrastructure needed to link these abilities to the rest of the world. But the most skilled and insightful Americans, who are already positioned to thrive in the world market, are now able to slip the bonds of national allegiance, and by so doing disengage themselves from their less-favored fellows. The stark political challenge in the decades ahead will be to reaffirm that, even though America is no longer a separate and distinct economy, it is still a society whose members have abiding obligations to one another.

Content

1. Does Reich prove convincingly that "the fortunate fifth [those Americans with the highest income] is quietly seceding from the rest of the nation" (¶ 8)? To what extent does your receptivity to his argument depend on whether or not you consider yourself or your family a member of the "fortunate fifth"?

2. Who are "symbolic analysts" (¶s 12–14, 25–31)? Does Reich demonstrate that these persons comprise a significant portion of the "fortunate fifth"? Why does he identify their job titles (¶ 12), activities (¶ 13), lifestyles (¶s 25–28), and places of work and residence (¶s 28–30) in long lists? In what ways does he expect his readers to interpret these lists?

3. Reich illustrates many of the points of his argument with reference to the public schools in rich and poor districts (¶s 36–44, for example). Why does he focus on schools?

4. If Reich has convinced you of his premise (see question 1 above), has he also convinced you of his conclusion that "the most skilled and insightful Americans . . . are now able to slip the bonds of national allegiance, and by so doing disengage themselves from their less-favored fellows. The stark political challenge . . . will be to reaffirm that . . . [America] is still a

society whose members have abiding obligations to one another" (¶ 45)? If he has convinced you, what does he want you to do as a consequence? If he hasn't convinced you, why hasn't he?

Strategies/Structures

5. The specific statistical information and other figures in Reich's 1991 article change annually, if not more often. Is their alteration within the next decade likely to affect either Reich's argument or your receptivity to it? Since numbers are always in flux, why use them in an argument?

6. Reich says that corporations threaten to move to a "more congenial tax climate" unless they get substantial tax breaks from the communities in which they're located. But what they return to the communities in philanthropic contributions is much less than they receive: "G.M.'s successful efforts to reduce its taxes in North Tarrytown, N.Y., where the company has had a factory since 1914, cut local revenues by $1 million in 1990, part of a larger shortfall that forced the town to lay off scores of teachers" (¶ 23). What is the point of including this and comparable information? What response from readers is Reich looking for?

7. Reich's sentences are fairly long, but his paragraphs are short, usually from one to three sentences. (The longest paragraph, ¶ 32, has eight sentences.) This is because the article was originally published in a newspaper, the *New York Times Magazine*; newspapers provide paragraph breaks not to indicate where the material logically breaks or changes course but to rest readers' eyes as they roam the page. What is the effect, if any, of such a large number of short paragraphs in a serious article?

8. Which side does Reich favor? At what point in the argument does he expect his readers to realize this?

Language

9. Does Reich's division of workers into "symbolic and analytic services" and "local service workers" cover most people in cities? Where do "blue-collar manufacturing workers" live (see ¶ 24)? Are such labels necessary or helpful in constructing the argument Reich makes?

For Writing

10. Argue, as Reich does but using your own examples (and some of his factual information, among other sources) that, as Reich concludes, "even though America is no longer a separate and distinct economy, it is still a society whose members have abiding obligations to one another" (¶ 45).

One way to address the subject is to consider the implications of a particular public policy issue (such as school vouchers, school busing, property taxation, equalization of school funding across rich and poor districts, gated residential communities with private security guards). See, for example, Martin Luther King, Jr.'s, "Letter from Birmingham Jail" (596–616), and the essays by Kozol, Coontz, and Nocton identified in the next question.

11. Is it socially desirable for the upper fifth in income to "secede," however quietly, "from the rest of the nation," as Reich asserts in paragraph 8? Shouldn't everyone have the right to live where they want to? Should people be required to live in the same geographical area where they work? If you wish, supplement your argument with reference to the essays by Jonathan Kozol, "The Human Cost of an Illiterate Society," 283–94; Stephanie Coontz, "A Nation of Welfare Families," 294–301; and "Matt Nocton, "Harvest of Gold, Harvest of Shame," 675–83.

AMY JO KEIFER

Keifer was born in 1972, and grew up on her family's farm in Bangor, Pennsylvania. She wrote "The Death of a Farm" in 1991 at American University, Washington, D.C., in a freshman composition course, "Writing About Contemporary Issues." Her instructor required all his students to submit a piece of writing to either the *Washington Post* or the *New York Times*, and promised an A for the semester to anyone whose work got published. However, he originally gave Keifer an F on the paper; at three pages it was too short, he said, for an op-ed (opposite the editorial page) piece.

Keifer trusted her own judgment, a good lesson for the readers of *The Essay Connection*. Although the *Times* receives hundreds of op-ed submissions each month, mostly by experienced writers and professionals in various fields, Keifer submitted her paper to the *Times* exactly as she had written it. It was published as an op-ed article on June 30, 1991, and the following semester the instructor changed her grade to an A. In 1993 Keifer graduated from American University with a B.A. in International Relations, and a strong interest in multicultural education and in the agricultural aspects of international trade.

"The Death of a Farm" was read by many people in the United States Department of Agriculture, and landed Keifer a summer internship on the *Express-Times* (Easton, Pennsylvania). Keifer's essay indeed proves that her personal experience has given her an expert's understanding of her subject. "It was easy to write," she says, "because it's a subject I know a lot about, although it was hard to get the tone right because I am so emotionally involved with the subject. My younger sister doesn't like the essay because she doesn't want to think that the farm is dying. My parents like the essay, however, because it represents our strong attachment to the land." She continues, "We are near the Delaware Water Gap, and the land is beautiful at all seasons, especially in the fall. The farm's status today is as it was eight years ago. My younger brother will keep the family farm going, but he will have to work at a full-time job elsewhere in order to do so."

❄ *The Death of a Farm*

I am a farmer's daughter. I am also a 4-H member, breeder and   1
showman of sheep and showman of cattle. My family's farm is dying and I have watched it, and my family, suffer.

Our eastern Pennsylvania farm is a mere 60 acres. The green   2
rolling hills and forested land are worth a minimum of $300,000 to developers, but no longer provide my family with the means to survive. It's a condition called asset rich and cash poor, and it's a hard way of life.

My grandfather bought our farm when he and my grand-   3
mother were first married. He raised dairy cattle and harvested the land full time for more than 20 years. When he died, my father took over and changed the farm to beef cattle, horses and pigs, and kept the crops. But it wasn't enough to provide for a young family, so he took on a full-time job, too.

I can remember, when I was young, sitting on the fence with   4
my sister and picking out a name for each calf. My sister's favorite cow was named Flower, and so we named her calves Buttercup, Daisy, Rose and Violet. Flower was the leader of a herd of more than 20. The only cattle left on our farm now are my younger sister's and brother's 4-H projects.

5   I can remember a huge tractor-trailer backed into the loading chute of our barn on days when more than 200 pigs had to be taken to market. That was before the prices went down and my father let the barn go empty rather than take on more debt.

6   I can remember my father riding on the tractor, larger than life, baling hay or planting corn. When prices started dropping, we began to rent some land to other farmers, so they could harvest from it. But prices have dropped so low this year there are no takers. The land will go unused; the tractor and the equipment have long since been sold off.

7   I don't remember the horses. I've seen a few pictures in which my father, slim and dark, is holding his newborn daughter on horseback amid a small herd. And I've heard stories of his delivering hay to farms all over the state, but I can't ever remember his loading up a truck to do it.

8   Piece by piece, our farm has deteriorated. We started breeding sheep and now have about 25 head, but they yield little revenue. My mother, who works as a registered nurse, once said something that will remain with me forever: "Your father works full-time to support the farm. I work full-time to support the family."

9   I've seen movies like "The River" and "Places in the Heart." They tell the real struggle. But people can leave a movie theater, and there's a happy ending for them. There aren't many happy endings in a real farmer's life. I was reared hearing that hard work paid off, while seeing that it didn't. My younger brother would like to take over the farm some day, but I'm not sure it will hold on much longer. Its final breath is near.

Content

1. Keifer's family history is embedded in the story of the family farm. Explain how they are interrelated.

2. What's the point of Keifer's mother's observation, "Your father works full-time to support the farm. I work full-time to support the family" (¶ 8)?

3. Why is Keifer telling this story? To whom is she telling it? Is she trying to influence any individual action? Public policy? Is this a cautionary tale, a warning? Why would an urban newspaper, the *New York Times*, print this story?

Strategies/Structures

4. Why is it important for Keifer to state her credentials at the very outset of the essay?

5. Is it appropriate for Keifer to tip her hand in the second sentence ("My family's farm is dying and I have watched it, and my family, suffer" [¶ 1])? Or would the essay be more effective if she waited until the end, to make this the inevitable conclusion to the series of steps of the progressive deterioration of the farm which in fact she presents as the essay proceeds?

6. Keifer provides a series of snapshots of the farm and farm life. Identify some and show how they reinforce her case.

Language

7. What is the effect of beginning paragraphs 4, 5, and 6 with "I can remember"? And then of varying this pattern with "I don't remember the horses"?

8. In what ways does Keifer's simple, unadorned language convince us that she's "been there"? How does that language put her readers there as well?

For Writing

9. Keifer says, "I was reared hearing that hard work paid off, while seeing that it didn't" (¶ 9). Tell a story whose thesis contradicts conventional wisdom, as Keifer's does. Since your readers will probably be prepared, initially, to accept the conventional view, you'll have to use signals throughout (incidents, natural symbols, connotative language) that point in the opposite direction.

10. Write an essay to protest "the death of . . ." a subject close to your heart, though not necessarily close to your reader's heart or conscience. (This might be an endangered species; a vanishing way of life; a lost art or profession; a major change in the way people do things—for instance, have e-mail and the telephone meant the death of personal letters? Or of even face-to-face conversations? Avoid sentimentality.

Additional Topics for Writing
Appealing to Reason:
Deductive and Inductive Arguments

(For strategies for appealing to reason, see 590.)

1. Write a logical, clearly reasoned, well-supported argument appropriate in organization, language, and tone to the subject and appealing to your designated audience. Be sure you have in mind a particular reader or group of readers whom you know (or suspect) are likely to be receptive or hostile to your position, or uncommitted people whose opinion you're trying to influence.

   a. A college education is (or is not) worth the effort and expense.
   b. Smoking, drinking, or using "recreational" drugs is (is not) worth the risks.
   c. Economic prosperity is (is not) more important to our country than conservation and preservation of our country's resources.
   d. The Social Security system should (should not) be preserved at all costs.
   e. Everyone should (should not) be entitled to comprehensive medical care (supply one: from the cradle to the grave; in early childhood; while a student; in old age).
   f. Drunk drivers should (should not) be jailed, even for a first offense.
   g. Auto safety belts should (should not) be mandatory.
   h. Companies manufacturing products that may affect consumers' health or safety (such as food, drugs, liquor, automobiles, pesticides) should (should not) have consumer representatives on their boards of directors.
   i. The civil rights, women's liberation, gay liberation, or some comparable movement has (has not) accomplished major and long-lasting benefits for the group it represents.
   j. Intercollegiate athletic teams that are big business should (should not) hire their players; intercollegiate athletes should (should not) have professional status.
   k. Strong labor unions should (should not) be preserved at all costs.
   l. The costs of America's manned space program are worth (far exceed) the benefits.
   m. The federal government should (should not) take over the nation's health care system.
   n. The postal service should (should not) be privatized.

2. Write a letter to your campus, city, or area newspaper in which you take a stand on an issue, defending or attacking it. You could write on one of the topics in Additional Topics 1 above, or differ with a recent column or editorial. Send in your letter (keep a copy for yourself) and see if it is published. If so, what kind of response did it attract?

3. Write to your state or federal legislator urging the passage or defeat of a particular piece of legislation currently being considered. (You will probably find at least one side of the issue being reported in the newspapers or a newsmagazine.) An extra: If you receive a reply, analyze it to see whether it addresses the specific points you raise. In what fashion? Does it sound like an individual response or a form letter?

14 Appealing to Emotion and Ethics

The essence of an emotional appeal is passion. You write from passion, and you expect your readers to respond with equal fervor. "I have a dream." "The only thing we have to fear is fear itself." "We have nothing to offer but blood, toil, tears, and sweat." "The West wasn't won with a loaded gun!" "We shall overcome." You'll be making your case in specific, concrete, memorable ways that you expect to have an unusually powerful impact on your readers. So your writing will probably be more colorful than it might be in less emotional circumstances, with a high proportion of vivid examples, narratives, anecdotes, character sketches, analogies ("Will Bosnia or Rwanda or X be another Vietnam?"), and figures of speech, including metaphors ("a knee-jerk liberal"), and similes ("The Southern Senator had a face like an old Virginia ham and a personality to match").

You can't incite your readers, either to agree with you or to take action on behalf of the cause you favor, by simply bleeding all over the page. The process of writing and rewriting and revising again (see Chapter 4) will act to cool your red-hot emotion and will enable you to modulate in subsequent drafts what you might have written the first time just to get out of your system. "Hell, no! We won't go!" As the essays in this section and elsewhere reveal, writers who appeal most effectively to their readers' emotions themselves exercise considerable control over the organization and examples they use to make their points.

They also keep particularly tight rein over their own emotions, as revealed in the tone and connotations of their language, crucial in an emotional appeal. Tone, the prevailing mood of the essay, like a tone of voice conveys your attitude toward your subject and toward the evidence you present in support of your point. It is clear from the tone of all the essays in this chapter—indeed, all the essays in the entire *Essay Connection*—that the authors care deeply about their subjects. Amy Jo Keifer's tone in "The Death of a Farm" (636–39) might almost be objective, but the technique she uses throughout, comparing the invariably better past, almost a golden era, with the deteriorating conditions for farmers in the present, evokes considerable emotion in the reader: "Your father works full time to support the farm," says Keifer's mother. "I work full time to support the family." Matt Nocton's "Harvest of Gold, Harvest of Shame" (675–83) is a useful companion piece to Keifer's (see also Ntozake Shange's "What Is It We Really Harvestin' Here?" (240–49). Like Keifer, Nocton reports in a relatively objective tone on his personal experience with an aspect of farming—in this case, the harvesting of tobacco by a business that employs migrant and contract laborers, racial and ethnic minorities overseen by white bosses. Keeping himself out of the essay, he does not say in the essay that as a teenager, after two days on the job he was promoted to "bentkeeper" over the heads of minority employees with far more experience. Nevertheless, Nocton's concern for the workers and anger over their exploitation is apparent in the way he recounts the harvesting process, detail by detail, dirty, dusty, hot, and humiliating: each worker "must tie [a burlap sack] around his waist as a source of protection against the dirt and rocks that he will be dragging himself through for the next eight hours." The essays by Keifer and Nocton illustrate that these days, in nonfiction, anyway, unless it's satire, readers generally prefer understatement to overkill. To establish a climate that encourages readers to sympathize emotionally, you as a writer can present telling facts and allow the readers to interpret them, rather than continually nudging the audience with verbal reminders to see the subject your way.

Another technique for convincing readers to share your perspective is to put them in your shoes, as Terry Tempest Williams does in "The Clan of One-Breasted Women" (660–70). We see through her clear-eyed perspective, as a young child and again as the adult writing the essay, "this flash of light in the night in the desert . . . this image (that) had so permeated my being that I could not venture south without seeing it again, on the horizon, illuminating buttes and mesas." Thirty-five years after the fact, her father quietly corroborates this image of nuclear detonation that his daughter had for her whole life thought of as a "recurring dream," "You did see it." Now we see it too, as the family "saw it, clearly, this golden-stemmed cloud, the mushroom. The sky seemed to vibrate with an eerie pink glow." Within a few minutes, "a light ash was raining," as the fallout causes the cancers whose existence Williams writes to protest, and to prevent in the future.

If you are appealing to your readers' emotions through irony, the tone of your words, their music, is likely to be at variance with their overt message—and to intentionally undermine it. Thus the narrator of Swift's "A Modest Proposal" (650–60) can, with an impassive face, advocate that year-old children of the poor Irish peasants be sold for "a most delicious, nourishing, and wholesome food, whether stewed, roasted, baked, or broiled"; and, in an additional inhumane observation, "I make no doubt that it will equally serve in a fricassee or a ragout."

The connotations, overtones of the language, are equally significant in emotional appeals, as they subtly (or not so subtly) reinforce the overt, literal meanings of the words. Lincoln deliberately uses biblical language ("Fourscore" instead of "eighty"), biblical phrasing, biblical cadences to reinforce the solemnity of the occasion—dedication of the graveyard at Gettysburg. This language also underscores the seriousness of the Civil War, then in progress, and its profound consequences. In contrast to the majesty of Lincoln's language, Swift's narrator depersonalizes human beings, always calling the children *it,* with an impersonal connotation, and never employing the humanizing terms of *he, she,* or *baby.* The *it* emphasizes the animalistic connotations of the narrator's references to a newborn as "a child just dropped from its dam," further dehumanizing both mother and child.

Language, tone, and message often combine to present an *ethical appeal*—a way of impressing your readers that you as the author (and perhaps as a character in your own essay) are a knowledgeable person of good moral character, good will, and good sense. Consequently, you are a person of integrity, and to be believed as a credible, reasonable advocate of the position you take in your essay. In "None of This is Fair" (398–405), Richard Rodriguez explains that as a Mexican-American he benefited considerably from Affirmative Action programs to gain financial aid in college and to get highly competitive job offers afterward. Having thus established his fitness to discuss the subject, Rodriguez agrees with the critics of Affirmative Action, that "none of this is fair." His actions reinforce his words. Not only does he decide to reject all the job offers obtained by his "unfair" means; he turns his attention, at the conclusion, to the "seriously disadvantaged," irrespective of color, the poor on whom he wishes us all to focus our best efforts.

Because they usually make their point indirectly, fables, parables, and other stories with subtle moral points are often used to appeal to readers' emotions and ethical sense. The photographs of winsome (never repulsive, never ugly!) waifs often grace fund raising advertisements for famine relief, amplified by biographies of their pitiful lives; only our contributions can save them. One of the dangers in using such poster-child appeals is the possibility that you'll include too many emotional signals or ultraheavy emotional language and thereby write a paper that repels your readers by either excessive sentimentality or overkill. Lynda Barry's "The Sanctuary of School" (670–75) uses at the beginning techniques similar to the famine relief ads to present a dramatic and moving picture of herself (and her brother) as young children: "In an overcrowded and unhappy home, it's incredibly easy for any child to slip away. The high levels of frustration, depression, and anger in my house made my brother and me invisible. We were children with the sound turned off." The beginning of the essay reflects the emotional level of Barry's panic as a young child after her parents "had been fighting all night." Realizing she was "lost," she headed for "the sanctuary of school," with its host of reassuring teachers, janitor, and secretary. As the school day unfolded, so did the predictable opportunity "to sit at my desk, with my crayons and pencils and books and classmates all around me, and for the next six hours I was going to enjoy a thoroughly secure, warm, and stable world." The tone shifts gradually to reflect the calmness of the "world that I absolutely relied on," and the essay ends with an emphatic, unsentimental plea for our country to pledge allegiance to its schoolchildren. How readily we accept these arguments depends, in part, on the values, beliefs, and other experiences we bring to our reading of the work at hand. The more emotionally engaged we are at the outset, the easier it will be for such writers to enlist us in their cause.

Although ethical appeals usually tap our most profound moral values, they can be made in humorous ways, as in Judy Brady's "I Want a Wife" (506–10), which argues, implicitly, that given all the work they do—housekeeping, cleaning, cooking, childrearing, hostessing, nurturing—everyone, wives included, wants a "wife."

Appeals to emotion and ethics are often intertwined. Such appeals are everywhere, for example, in the connotations of descriptions and definitions. Furthermore, if your readers like and trust you, they're more likely to believe what you say and to be moved to agree with your point of view. The evidence in a scientific report, however strong in itself, is buttressed by the credibility of the researcher. The sense of realism, the truth of a narrative, is enhanced by the credibility of the narrator. We believe Lincoln and Barry and Nocton; and we trust the spirit of satirist Swift, even if we believe he is are exaggerating, if not downright inventing, the substance of his narrative. Hearts compel agreement where minds hesitate. Don't hesitate to make ethical use of this understanding.

STRATEGIES FOR WRITING— APPEALING TO EMOTION AND ETHICS

1. Do I want to appeal primarily to my readers' emotions (and which emotions) or to their ethical sense of how people ought to behave? (Remember that in either case the appeals are intertwined with reason—see Chapter 13.)

2. To what kinds of readers am I making these appeals? What ethical or other personal qualities should I as an author exhibit? How can I lead my readers to believe that I am a person of sound character and good judgment?

3. What evidence can I choose to reinforce my appeals and my authorial image? Examples from my own life? The experiences of others? References to literature or scientific research? What order of arrangement

would be most convincing? From the least emotionally moving or involving to the most? Or vice versa?

4. How can I interpret my evidence to move my readers to accept it? Should I explain very elaborately, or should I let the examples speak for themselves? If you decide on the latter, try out your essay on someone unfamiliar with the examples to see if they are in fact self-evident.

5. Do I want my audience to react with sympathy? Pity? Anger? Fear? Horror? To accomplish this, should I use much emotional language? Should my appeal be overt, direct? Or would indirection, understatement, be more effective? Would irony, saying the opposite of what I really mean (as Swift does), be more appropriate than a direct approach? Could I make my point more effectively with a fable, parable, comic tale, or invented persona than with a straightforward analysis and overt commentary?

ABRAHAM LINCOLN

> For a discussion of the biographical, political, historical, and literary aspects of this speech see Gilbert Highet's "The Gettysburg Address" (691–98).

The Gettysburg Address

1   F our score and seven years ago our fathers brought forth on this continent, a new nation, conceived in liberty, and dedicated to the proposition that all men are created equal.

2   Now we are engaged in a great civil war, testing whether that nation, or any nation so conceived and so dedicated, can long endure. We are met on a great battlefield of that war. We have come to dedicate a portion of that field, as a final resting place for those who here gave their lives that the nation might live. It is altogether fitting and proper that we should do this.

3   But, in a larger sense, we cannot dedicate—we cannot consecrate—we cannot hallow—this ground. The brave men, living and dead, who struggled here, have consecrated it, far above our poor power to add or detract. The world will little note, nor long remember what we say here, but it can never forget what they did here. It is for us the living, rather, to be dedicated here to the unfinished work which they who fought here have thus far so nobly advanced. It is rather for us to be here dedicated to the great task remaining before us—that from these honored dead we take increased devotion—that we here highly resolve that these dead shall not have died in vain—that this nation, under God, shall have a new birth of freedom—and that the government of the people, by the people, for the people, shall not perish from the earth.

Content

1. What principles of the founding of the United States does Lincoln emphasize in the first sentence? Why are these so important to the occasion of his address? To the theme of this address?

2. What does Lincoln imply and assert is the relation of life and death? Birth and rebirth?

Strategies/Structures

3. Why would Lincoln, knowing that his audience expected longer orations, deliberately have decided to make his speech so short?

4. Lincoln's speech commemorated a solemn occasion: the dedication of a major battlefield of the ongoing Civil War. Wouldn't such a short speech have undermined the significance of the event?

Language

5. Identify the language and metaphors of birth that Lincoln uses throughout this address. For what purpose? With what effect?

6. Why did Lincoln use biblical language and phrasing conspicuously at the beginning and end of the address, such as "four score and seven years ago" instead of the more common "eighty-seven"?

7. Lincoln uses many *antitheses*—oppositions, contrasts. Identify some and show how they reinforce the meaning.

8. Another important rhetorical device is the *tricolon*, "the division of an idea into three harmonious parts, usually of increasing power,"—for example, "government of the people, by the people, for the people. . . ." Find others and show why they are so memorable.

For Writing

9. Write a short, dignified speech for a solemn occasion, real or imaginary. Let the majesty of your language and the conspicuous rhetorical patterns of your sentences and paragraphs (through such devices as antithesis and parallelism) reinforce your point.

10. Rewrite the "Gettysburg Address" as it might have been spoken by a more recent president or other politician, using language, paragraphing, and sentence structures characteristic of the speaker and the times. One such speech, a parody, is William Safire's "Carter's Gettysburg Address," which begins: "Exactly two hundred and one years, five months and one day ago, our forefathers—and our foremothers, too, as my wife, the First Lady, reminds me—our highly competent Founding Persons brought forth on this land mass a new nation, or entity, dreamed up in liberty and dedicated to the comprehensive program of insuring that all of us are created with the same basic human rights."

JONATHAN SWIFT

Swift, author of *Gulliver's Travels* (1726) and other satiric essays, poems, and tracts, was well acquainted with irony. Born in Dublin in 1667, the son of impoverished English Anglicans, he obtained a degree from Trinity College, Dublin, in 1685 only by "special grace." When Cromwell invaded Ireland, Swift, along with many Anglo-Irish, was forced to flee to England, was eventually ordained as an Anglican priest, and rose prominently in London literary and political circles until 1713. Although he had hoped for a church appointment in England, his desertion of the Whig Party for the Tories was ironically rewarded with an appointment as dean of St. Patrick's (Anglican) Cathedral in Dublin, which he regarded as virtual exile. Nevertheless, despite his religious differences with the Irish people, Swift became a beloved leader in the Irish resistance to English oppression, motivated less by partisan emotions than by his own "savage indignation" against injustice. He died in 1745.

Swift wrote "A Modest Proposal" in the summer of 1729, after three years of drought and crop failure had forced over 35,000 peasants to leave their homes and wander the countryside looking for work, food, and shelter for their starving families, ignored by the insensitive absentee landowners. The "Proposal" carries the English landowners' treatment of the Irish to its logical—but repugnant—extreme: if they are going to devour any hope the Irish have of living decently, why don't they literally eat the Irish children? The persona Swift creates is logical, consistent, seemingly rational—and utterly inhumane, an advocate of infanticide and cannibalism. Yet nowhere in the "Proposal" does the satirist condemn the speaker; he relies on the readers' sense of morality for that. This tactic can be dangerous, for a reader who misses the irony may take the "Proposal" at face value. But Swift's intended readers, English (landlords included) as well as Irish who could act to alleviate the people's suffering, understood very well what he meant. The victims themselves, largely illiterate, would probably have been unaware of this forceful plea on their behalf.

A Modest Proposal

1   I t is a melancholy object to those who walk through this great town or travel in the country, when they see the streets, the roads, and cabin doors, crowded with beggars of the female sex,

followed by three, four, or six children, all in rags and importuning every passenger for an alms. These mothers, instead of being able to work for their honest livelihood, are forced to employ all their time in strolling to beg sustenance for their helpless infants: who as they grow up either turn thieves for want of work, or leave their dear native country to fight for the pretender in Spain, or sell themselves to the Barbadoes.

I think it is agreed by all parties that this prodigious number 2 of children in the arms, or on the backs, or at the heels of their mothers, and frequently of their fathers, is in the present deplorable state of the kingdom a very great additional grievance; and, therefore, whoever could find out a fair, cheap, and easy method of making these children sound, useful members of the commonwealth, would deserve so well of the public as to have his statue set up for a preserver of the nation.

But my intention is very far from being confined to provide 3 only for the children of professed beggars; it is of a much greater extent, and shall take in the whole number of infants at a certain age who are born of parents in effect as little able to support them as those who demand our charity in the streets.

As to my own part, having turned my thoughts for many 4 years upon this important subject, and maturely weighed the several schemes of our projectors, I have always found them grossly mistaken in their computation. It is true, a child just dropped from its dam may be supported by her milk for a solar year, with little other nourishment; at most not above the value of two shillings, which the mother may certainly get, or the value in scraps, by her lawful occupation of begging; and it is exactly at one year old that I propose to provide for them in such a manner as instead of being a charge upon their parents or the parish, or wanting food and raiment for the rest of their lives, they shall on the contrary contribute to the feeding, and partly to the clothing, of many thousands.

There is likewise another great advantage in my scheme, 5 that it will prevent those voluntary abortions, and that horrid practice of women murdering their bastard children, alas! too frequent among us! sacrificing the poor innocent babes I doubt more to avoid the expense than the shame, which would move tears and pity in the most savage and inhuman breast.

The number of souls in this kingdom being usually reckoned 6 one million and half, of these I calculate there may be about two hundred thousand couple whose wives are breeders; from which number I subtract thirty thousand couple who are able to maintain their own children (although I apprehend there cannot be so many, under the present distress of the kingdom); but this being granted, there will remain an hundred and seventy thousand breeders. I again subtract fifty thousand for those women who miscarry, or whose children die by accident or disease within the year. There only remain an hundred and twenty thousand children of poor parents annually born. The question therefore is, how this number shall be reared and provided for? which, as I have already said, under the present situation of affairs, is utterly impossible by all the methods hitherto proposed. For we can neither employ them in handicraft or agriculture; we neither build houses (I mean in the country) nor cultivate land; they can very seldom pick up a livelihood by stealing, till they arrive at six years old, except where they are of towardly parts; although I confess they learn the rudiments much earlier; during which time they can, however, be properly looked upon only as probationers; as I have been informed by a principal gentleman in the country of Cavan, who protested to me that he never knew above one or two instances under the age of six, even in a part of the kingdom so renowned for the quickest proficiency in that art.

7   I am assured by our merchants, that a boy or a girl before twelve years old is no saleable commodity; and even when they come to this age they will not yield above three pounds, or three pounds and a half a crown at most on the Exchange; which cannot turn to account either to the parents or kingdom, the charge of nutriment and rags having been at least four times that value.

8   I shall now therefore humbly propose my own thoughts, which I hope will not be liable to the least objection.

9   I have been assured by a very knowing American of my acquaintance in London, that a young healthy child well nursed is at a year old the most delicious, nourishing, and wholesome food, whether stewed, roasted, baked, or broiled; and I make no doubt that it will equally serve in a fricassee or a ragout.

10   I do therefore humbly offer it to public consideration that of the hundred and twenty thousand children already computed, twenty thousand may be reserved for breed, whereof only one fourth part to be males; which is more than we allow to sheep,

black cattle, or swine; and my reason is, that these children are seldom the fruits of marriage, a circumstance not much regarded by our savages; therefore, one male will be sufficient to serve four females. That the remaining hundred thousand may, at a year old, be offered in sale to the persons of quality and fortune through the kingdom; always advising the mother to let them suck plentifully in the last month, so as to render them plump and fat for a good table. A child will make two dishes at an entertainment for friends; and when the family dines alone, the fore or hind quarter will make a reasonable dish, and seasoned with a little pepper or salt will be very good boiled on the fourth day, especially in winter.

11   I have reckoned upon a medium that a child just born will weigh twelve pounds, and in a solar year, if tolerably nursed, will increase to twenty-eight pounds.

12   I grant this food will be somewhat dear, and therefore very proper for landlords, who, as they have already devoured most of the parents, seem to have the best title to the children.

13   Infant's flesh will be in season throughout the year, but more plentiful in March, and a little before and after: for we are told by a grave author, an eminent French physician, that fish being a prolific diet, there are more children born in Roman Catholic countries about nine months after Lent than at any other season; therefore, reckoning a year after Lent, the markets will be more glutted than usual, because the number of popish infants is at least three to one in this kingdom: and therefore it will have one other collateral advantage, by lessening the number of papists among us.

14   I have already computed the charge of nursing a beggar's child (in which list I reckon all cottagers, laborers, and four-fifths of the farmers) to be about two shillings per annum, rags included; and I believe no gentleman would repine to give ten shillings for the carcass of a good fat child, which, as I have said, will make four dishes of excellent nutritive meat, when he has only some particular friend or his own family to dine with him. Thus the squire will learn to be a good landlord, and grow popular among the tenants; the mother will have eight shillings net profit, and be fit for work till she produces another child.

15   Those who are more thrifty (as I must confess the times require) may flay the carcass; the skin of which artificially dressed

will make admirable gloves for ladies, and summer boots for fine gentlemen.

16   As to our city of Dublin, shambles may be appointed for this purpose in the most convenient parts of it, and butchers we may be assured will not be wanting: although I rather recommend buying the children alive, and dressing them hot from the knife as we do roasting pigs.

17   A very worthy person, a true lover of his country, and whose virtues I highly esteem, was lately pleased in discoursing on this matter to offer a refinement upon my scheme. He said that many gentlemen of this kingdom, having of late destroyed their deer, he conceived that the want of venison might be well supplied by the bodies of young lads and maidens, not exceeding fourteen years of age nor under twelve; so great a number of both sexes in every country being now ready to starve for want of work and service; and these to be disposed of by their parents, if alive, or otherwise by their nearest relations. But with due deference to so excellent a friend and so deserving a patriot, I cannot be altogether in his sentiments; for as to the males, my American acquaintance assured me from frequent experience that their flesh was generally tough and lean, like that of our schoolboys by continual exercise, and their taste disagreeable; and to fatten them would not answer the charge. Then as to the females, it would, I think, with humble submission be a loss to the public, because they soon would become breeders themselves: and besides, it is not improbable that some scrupulous people might be apt to censure such a practice (although indeed very unjustly), as a little bordering upon cruelty; which, I confess, has always been with me the strongest objection against any project, how well soever intended.

18   But in order to justify my friend, he confessed that this expedient was put into his head by the famous Psalmanazar, a native of the island Formosa, who came from thence to London about twenty years ago: and in conversation told my friend, that in his country when any young person happened to be put to death, the executioner sold the carcass to persons of quality as a prime dainty; and that in his time the body of a plump girl of fifteen, who was crucified for an attempt to poison the emperor, was sold to his imperial majesty's prime minister of state, and other great mandarins of the court, in joints from the gibbet, at four hundred

crowns. Neither indeed can I deny, that if the same use were made of several plump young girls in this town, who without one single groat to their fortunes cannot stir abroad without a chair, and appear at the playhouse and assemblies in foreign fineries which they never will pay for, the kingdom would not be the worse.

Some persons of a desponding spirit are in great concern 19 about that vast number of poor people, who are aged, diseased, or maimed, and I have been desired to employ my thoughts what course may be taken to ease the nation of so grievous an encumbrance. But I am not in the least pain upon that matter, because it is very well known that they are every day dying and rotting by cold and famine, and filth and vermin, as fast as can be reasonably expected. And as to the young laborers, they are now in as hopeful a condition: they cannot get work, and consequently pine away for want of nourishment, to a degree that if at any time they are accidentally hired to common labor, they have not strength to perform it; and thus the country and themselves are happily delivered from the evils to come.

I have too long digressed, and therefore shall return to my 20 subject. I think the advantages by the proposal which I have made are obvious and many, as well as of the highest importance.

For first, as I have already observed, it would greatly lessen 21 the number of papists, with whom we are yearly overrun, being the principal breeders of the nation as well as our most dangerous enemies; and who stay at home on purpose to deliver the kingdom to the Pretender, hoping to take their advantage by the absence of so many good Protestants, who have chosen rather to leave their country than stay at home and pay tithes against their conscience to an Episcopal curate.

Secondly, The poor tenants will have something valuable of 22 their own, which by law may be made liable to distress and help to pay their landlord's rent, their corn and cattle being already seized, and money a thing unknown.

Thirdly, Whereas the maintenance of a hundred thousand 23 children from two years old and upward, cannot be computed at less than ten shillings a piece per annum, the nation's stock will be thereby increased fifty thousand pounds per annum, beside the profit of a new dish introduced to the tables of all gentlemen of fortune in the kingdom who have any refinement in taste. And the money will circulate among ourselves, the goods being entirely of our own growth and manufacture.

24   Fourthly, The constant breeders beside the gain of eight shillings sterling per annum by the sale of their children, will be rid of the charge of maintaining them after the first year.

25   Fifthly, This food would likewise bring great custom to taverns, where the vintners will certainly be so prudent as to procure the best receipts for dressing it to perfection, and consequently have their houses frequented by all the fine gentlemen, who justly value themselves upon their knowledge in good eating; and a skillful cook who understands how to oblige his guests, will contrive to make it as expensive as they please.

26   Sixthly, This would be a great inducement to marriage, which all wise nations have either encouraged by rewards or enforced by laws and penalties. It would increase the care and tenderness of mothers toward their children, when they were sure of a settlement for life to the poor babes, provided in some sort by the public, to their annual profit instead of expense. We should see an honest emulation among the married women, which of them would bring the fattest child to the market. Men would become as fond of their wives during the time of their pregnancy as they are now of their mares in foal, their cows in calf, their sows when they are ready to farrow; nor offer to beat or kick them (as is too frequent a practice) for fear of a miscarriage.

27   Many other advantages might be enumerated. For instance, the addition of some thousand carcasses in our exportation of barreled beef, the propagation of swine's flesh, and improvement in the art of making good bacon, so much wanted among us by the great destruction of pigs, too frequent at our table; which are no way comparable in taste or magnificence to a well-grown, fat, yearling child, which roasted whole will make a considerable figure at a lord mayor's feast or any other public entertainment. But this and many others I omit, being studious of brevity.

28   Supposing that one thousand families in this city would be constant customers for infants' flesh, besides others who might have it at merry-meetings, particularly at weddings and christenings, I compute that Dublin would take off annually about twenty thousand carcasses; and the rest of the kingdom (where probably they will be sold somewhat cheaper) the remaining eighty thousand.

I can think of no one objection that will possibly be raised 29
against this proposal, unless it should be urged that the number
of people will be thereby much lessened in the kingdom. This I
freely own, and it was indeed one principal design in offering
it to the world. I desire the reader will observe, that I calculate my
remedy for this one individual kingdom of Ireland and for no
other that ever was, is, or I think ever can be upon earth. Therefore let no man talk to me of other expedients; of taxing our
absentees at five shillings a pound: of using neither clothes nor
household furniture except what is of our own growth and manufacture: of utterly rejecting the materials and instruments that
promote foreign luxury: of curing the expensiveness of pride,
vanity, idleness, and gaming in our women: of introducing a vein
of parsimony, prudence, and temperance: of learning to love our
country, in the want of which we differ even from Laplanders and
the inhabitants of Topinamboo: of quitting our animosities and
factions, nor acting any longer like the Jews, who were murdering one another at the very moment their city was taken: of being
a little cautious not to sell our country and conscience for nothing:
of teaching landlords to have at least one degree of mercy toward
their tenants; lastly, of putting a spirit of honesty, industry, and
skill into our shopkeepers; who, if a resolution could now be
taken to buy only our native goods, would immediately unite to
cheat and exact upon us in the price, the measure, and the goodness, nor could ever yet be brought to make one fair proposal of
just dealing, though often and earnestly invited to it.

Therefore I repeat, let no man talk to me of these and the like 30
expedients, till he has at least some glimpse of hope that there
will be ever some hearty and sincere attempts to put them in
practice.

But as to myself, having been wearied out for many years 31
with offering vain, idle, visionary thoughts, and at length utterly
despairing of success, I fortunately fell upon this proposal; which,
as it is wholly new, so it has something solid and real, of no expense and little trouble, full in our own power, and whereby we
can incur no danger in disobliging England. For this kind of commodity will not bear exportation, the flesh being of too tender a
consistence to admit a long continuance in salt, although perhaps
I could name a country which would be glad to eat up our whole
nation without it.

32   After all, I am not so violently bent upon my own opinion as to reject any offer proposed by wise men, which shall be found equally innocent, cheap, easy, and effectual. But before something of that kind shall be advanced in contradiction to my scheme, and offering a better, I desire the author or authors will be pleased maturely to consider two points. First, as things now stand, how they will be able to find food and raiment for a hundred thousand useless mouths and backs. And secondly, there being a round million of creatures in human figure throughout this kingdom, whose subsistence put into a common stock would leave them in debt two millions of pounds sterling, adding those who are beggars by profession to the bulk of farmers, cottagers, and laborers, with the wives and children who are beggars in effect; I desire those politicians who dislike my overture, and may perhaps be so bold as to attempt an answer, that they will first ask the parents of these mortals, whether they would not at this day think it a great happiness to have been sold for food at a year old in the manner I prescribe, and thereby have avoided such a perpetual scene of misfortunes as they have since gone through by the oppression of landlords, the impossibility of paying rent without money or trade, the want of common sustenance, with neither house nor clothes to cover them from the inclemencies of the weather, and the most inevitable prospect of entailing the like or greater miseries upon their breed for ever.

33   I profess, in the sincerity of my heart, that I have not the least personal interest in endeavoring to promote this necessary work, having no other motive than the public good of my country, by advancing our trade, providing for infants, relieving the poor, and giving some pleasure to the rich. I have no children by which I can propose to get a single penny; the youngest being nine years old, and my wife past child-bearing.

Content

1. What is the overt thesis of Swift's essay? What is its implied (and real) thesis? In what ways do these theses differ?

2. What are the primary aims and values of the narrator of the essay? Identify the economic advantages of his proposal that he offers in paragraphs 9–16. How do the narrator's alleged aims and values differ from the aims and values of Swift as the essay's author?

3. What do the advantages that the narrator offers for his proposal (¶ 21–26) reveal about the social and economic conditions of Ireland when Swift was writing?

4. Why is it a "very knowing *American*" who has assured the narrator of the suitability of year-old infants for food (¶ 9)?

5. Swift as the author of the essay expects his readers to respond to the narrator's cold economic arguments on a humane, moral level. What might such an appropriate response be?

Strategies/Structures

6. What persona (a created character) does the speaker of Swift's essay have? How are readers to know that this character is not Swift himself?

7. Why does the narrator use so many mathematical computations throughout? How do they reinforce his economic argument? How do they enhance the image of his cold-bloodedness?

8. Why did Swift choose to present his argument indirectly rather than overtly? What advantages does this indirect, consistently ironic technique provide? What disadvantages does it have (for instance, do you think Swift's readers are likely to believe he really advocated eating babies)?

Language

9. What is the prevailing tone of the essay? How does it undermine what the narrator says? How does the tone reinforce Swift's implied meaning?

10. Why does Swift say "a child just dropped from its dam" (¶ 4) instead of "just born from his mother"? What other language reinforces the animalistic associations (see, for instance, "breeders" in ¶ 17)?

11. In paragraph 21 Swift refers to Roman Catholics by the common term "papists." What clues does the context provide as to whether this usage is complimentary or derogatory? How does this emphasize the sense of a split between the English Anglican landowners and the Irish Catholic tenants that prevails throughout the essay?

For Writing

12. Write a modest proposal of your own. Pick some problem that you think needs to be solved, and propose, for a critical audience, a radical solution—perhaps a dramatic way to bring about world peace, preserve endangered species, dispose of chemical or nuclear waste, or use genetic engineering.

13. Write an essay in which a created character, a narrative persona, speaks ironically (as Swift's narrator does) about your subject. The character's values should be at variance with the values you and your audience share. For instance, if you want to propose stiff penalties for drunk driving, your narrator could be a firm advocate of drinking, and of driving without restraint, and could be shown driving unsafely while under the influence of alcohol, indifferent to the dangers.

TERRY TEMPEST WILLIAMS

A fifth-generation Utah Mormon, Williams (born, 1955) earned a bachelor's and a master's degree in environmental education from the University of Utah. Her writings reflect her intense commitment, intellectual and spiritual, to family and to place, particularly the natural environment. *The Book of Mormon,* she explains, "taught me the power of story because [it] is one story after another. It has taught me the power of a homeland, that place matters to a people, that each individual is entitled to [his or her] own personal vision."

Williams's best known work is *Refuge: An Unnatural History of Family and Place* (1991), in which "The Clan of One-Breasted Women" is the epilogue; others include *Desert Quartet: An Erotic Landscape* (1995) and *An Unspoken Hunger: Stories from the Field* (1994). *Refuge* began in 1983 when Williams's mother was dying of ovarian cancer, and for respite from the hospital Williams drove to a favorite bird refuge, only to find it being flooded by the Great Salt Lake. "I realized devastation knows no boundaries. The landscape of my childhood and the landscape of my family—the two things I had always regarded as bedrock—were now subject to change," says Williams. The "family moving through illness together" and "being with the birds . . . allowed me to discover the story that was there." Using "memory as a tool for reflection," Williams proceeded to uncover many layers in the process of writing the book. The process she describes is characteristic of many nonfiction writers: "The actual living of it, the recording of it in my journals, then letting the whole story steep like a hot cup of tea." Then writing down the exact details "in a nonperfunctory way . . . the lake levels, the dates of [her] mother's illness, literally

. . . an outline of time." "Then I had to go back," says Williams, and say, "What are the ideas here? What is the essence here? What are the universalities? And what is my place within this story? Where is my narrative apart from my mother's and grandmother's stories?" That these stories coalesce and intertwine is apparent in the following narrative.

The Clan of One-Breasted Women

Epilogue

I belong to a Clan of One-Breasted Women. My mother, my grandmothers, and six aunts have all had mastectomies. Seven are dead. The two who survive have just completed rounds of chemotherapy and radiation.

I've had my own problems: two biopsies for breast cancer and a small tumor between my ribs diagnosed as a "borderline malignancy."

This is my family history.

Most statistics tell us breast cancer is genetic, hereditary, with rising percentages attached to fatty diets, childlessness, or becoming pregnant after thirty. What they don't say is living in Utah may be the greatest hazard of all.

We are a Mormon family with roots in Utah since 1847. The "word of wisdom" in my family aligned us with good foods—no coffee, no tea, tobacco, or alcohol. For the most part, our women were finished having their babies by the time they were thirty. And only one faced breast cancer prior to 1960. Traditionally, as a group of people, Mormons have a low rate of cancer.

Is our family a cultural anomaly? The truth is, we didn't think about it. Those who did, usually the men, simply said, "bad genes." The women's attitude was stoic. Cancer was part of life. On February 16, 1971, the eve of my mother's surgery, I accidentally picked up the telephone and overheard her ask my grandmother what she could expect.

"Diane, it is one of the most spiritual experiences you will ever encounter."

8   I quietly put down the receiver.

9   Two days later, my father took my brothers and me to the hospital to visit her. She met us in the lobby in a wheelchair. No bandages were visible. I'll never forget her radiance, the way she held herself in a purple velvet robe, and how she gathered us around her.

10   "Children, I am fine. I want you to know I felt the arms of God around me."

11   We believed her. My father cried. Our mother, his wife, was thirty-eight years old.

12   A little over a year after Mother's death, Dad and I were having dinner together. He had just returned from St. George, where the Tempest Company was completing the gas lines that would service southern Utah. He spoke of his love for the country, the sandstoned landscape, bare-boned and beautiful. He had just finished hiking the Kolob trail in Zion National Park. We got caught up in reminiscing, recalling with fondness our walk up Angel's Landing on his fiftieth birthday and the years our family had vacationed there.

13   Over dessert, I shared a recurring dream of mine. I told my father that for years, as long as I could remember, I saw this flash of light in the night in the desert—that this image had so permeated my being that I could not venture south without seeing it again, on the horizon, illuminating buttes and mesas.

14   "You did see it," he said.

15   "Saw what?"

16   "The bomb. The cloud. We were driving home from Riverside, California. You were sitting on Diane's lap. She was pregnant. In fact, I remember the day, September 7, 1957. We had just gotten out of the Service. We were driving north, past Las Vegas. It was an hour or so before dawn, when this explosion went off. We not only heard it, but felt it. I thought the oil tanker in front of us had blown up. We pulled over and suddenly, rising from the desert floor, we saw it, clearly, this golden-stemmed cloud, the mushroom. The sky seemed to vibrate with an eerie pink glow. Within a few minutes, a light ash was raining on the car."

17   I stared at my father.

18   "I thought you knew that," he said. "It was a common occurrence in the fifties."

It was at this moment that I realized the deceit I had been 19
living under. Children growing up in the American Southwest,
drinking contaminated milk from contaminated cows, even from
the contaminated breasts of their mothers, my mother—members,
years later, of the Clan of One-Breasted Women.

It is a well-known story in the Desert West, "The Day We 20
Bombed Utah," or more accurately, the years we bombed Utah:
above ground atomic testing in Nevada took place from January
27, 1951 through July 11, 1962. Not only were the winds blowing
north covering "low-use segments of the population" with fallout
and leaving sheep dead in their tracks, but the climate was right.
The United States of the 1950s was red, white, and blue. The
Korean War was raging. McCarthyism was rampant. Ike was it,
and the cold war was hot. If you were against nuclear testing, you
were for a communist regime.

Much has been written about this "American nuclear trag- 21
edy." Public health was secondary to national security. The Atomic
Energy Commissioner, Thomas Murray, said, "Gentlemen, we
must not let anything interfere with this series of tests, nothing."

Again and again, the American public was told by its gov- 22
ernment, in spite of burns, blisters, and nausea, "It has been found
that the tests may be conducted with adequate assurance of safety
under conditions prevailing at the bombing reservations."
Assuaging public fears was simply a matter of public relations.
"Your best action," an Atomic Energy Commission booklet read,
"is not to be worried about fallout." A news release typical of the
times stated, "We find no basis for concluding that harm to any
individual has resulted from radioactive fallout."

On August 30, 1979, during Jimmy Carter's presidency, a 23
suit was filed, *Irene Allen* v. *The United States of America*. Mrs.
Allen's case was the first on an alphabetical list of twenty-four test
cases, representative of nearly twelve hundred plaintiffs seeking
compensation from the United States government for cancers
caused by nuclear testing in Nevada.

Irene Allen lived in Hurricane, Utah. She was the mother of 24
five children and had been widowed twice. Her first husband,
with their two oldest boys, had watched the tests from the roof of
the local high school. He died of leukemia in 1956. Her second
husband died of pancreatic cancer in 1978.

25   In a town meeting conducted by Utah Senator Orrin Hatch, shortly before the suit was filed, Mrs. Allen said, "I am not blaming the government, I want you to know that, Senator Hatch. But I thought if my testimony could help in any way so this wouldn't happen again to any of the generations coming up after us . . . I am happy to be here this day to bear testimony of this."

26   God-fearing people. This is just one story in an anthology of thousands.

27   On May 10, 1984, Judge Bruce S. Jenkins handed down his opinion. Ten of the plaintiffs were awarded damages. It was the first time a federal court had determined that nuclear tests had been the cause of cancers. For the remaining fourteen test cases, the proof of causation was not sufficient. In spite of the split decision, it was considered a landmark ruling. It was not to remain so for long.

28   In April 1987, the Tenth Circuit Court of Appeals overturned Judge Jenkins's ruling on the ground that the United States was protected from suit by the legal doctrine of sovereign immunity, a centuries-old idea from England in the days of absolute monarchs.

29   In January 1988, the Supreme Court refused to review the Appeals Court decision. To our court system it does not matter whether the United States government was irresponsible, whether it lied to its citizens, or even that citizens died from the fallout of nuclear testing. What matters is that our government is immune: "The King can do no wrong."

30   In Mormon culture, authority is respected, obedience is revered, and independent thinking is not. I was taught as a young girl not to "make waves" or "rock the boat."

31   "Just let it go," Mother would say. "You know how you feel, that's what counts."

32   For many years, I have done just that—listened, observed, and quietly formed my own opinions, in a culture that rarely asks questions because it has all the answers. But one by one, I have watched the women in my family die common, heroic deaths. We sat in waiting rooms hoping for good news, but always receiving the bad. I cared for them, bathed their scarred bodies, and kept their secrets. I watched beautiful women become bald as Cytoxan, cisplatin, and Adriamycin were injected into their veins. I held their foreheads as they vomited green-black bile, and I shot them with morphine when the pain became inhuman. In the end, I

witnessed their last peaceful breaths, becoming a midwife to the rebirth of their souls.

The price of obedience has become too high.   33

The fear and inability to question authority that ultimately   34
killed rural communities in Utah during atmospheric testing of atomic weapons is the same fear I saw in my mother's body. Sheep. Dead sheep. The evidence is buried.

I cannot prove that my mother, Diane Dixon Tempest, or   35
my grandmothers, Lettie Romney Dixon and Kathryn Blackett Tempest, along with my aunts developed cancer from nuclear fallout in Utah. But I can't prove they didn't.

My father's memory was correct. The September blast we   36
drove through in 1957 was part of Operation Plumbbob, one of the most intensive series of bomb tests to be initiated. The flash of light in the night in the desert, which I had always thought was a dream, developed into a family nightmare. It took fourteen years, from 1957 to 1971, for cancer to manifest in my mother—the same time, Howard L. Andrews, an authority in radioactive fallout at the National Institutes of Health, says radiation cancer requires to become evident. The more I learn about what it means to be a "downwinder," the more questions I drown in.

What I do know, however, is that as a Mormon woman of   37
the fifth generation of Latter-day Saints, I must question everything, even if it means losing my faith, even if it means becoming a member of a border tribe among my own people. Tolerating blind obedience in the name of patriotism or religion ultimately takes our lives.

When the Atomic Energy Commission described the coun-   38
try north of the Nevada Test Site as "virtually uninhabited desert terrain," my family and the birds at Great Salt Lake were some of the "virtual uninhabitants."

One night, I dreamed women from all over the world circled a   39
blazing fire in the desert. They spoke of change, how they hold the moon in their bellies and wax and wane with its phases. They mocked the presumption of even-tempered beings and made promises that they would never fear the witch inside themselves. The women danced wildly as sparks broke away from the flames and entered the night sky as stars.

40   And they sang a song given to them by Shoshone grandmothers:

Ah ne nah, nah	Consider the rabbits
nin nah nah—	How gently they walk on the earth—
ah ne nah, nah	Consider the rabbits
nin nah nah—	How gently they walk on the earth—
Nyaga mutzi	We remember them
oh ne nay—	We can walk gently also—
Nyaga mutzi	We remember them
oh ne nay—	We can walk gently also—

The women danced and drummed and sang for weeks, preparing
themselves for what was to come. They would reclaim the desert
for the sake of their children, for the sake of the land.

41   A few miles downwind from the fire circle, bombs were
being tested. Rabbits felt the tremors. Their soft leather pads on
paws and feet recognized the shaking sands, while the roots of
mesquite and sage were smoldering. Rocks were hot from the
inside out and dust devils hummed unnaturally. And each time
there was another nuclear test, ravens watched the desert heave.
Stretch marks appeared. The land was losing its muscle.

42   The women couldn't bear it any longer. They were mothers.
They had suffered labor pains but always under the promise of
birth. The red hot pains beneath the desert promised death only,
as each bomb became a stillborn. A contract had been made and
broken between human beings and the land. A new contract was
being drawn by the women, who understood the fate of the earth
as their own.

43   Under the cover of darkness, ten women slipped under a
barbed-wire fence and entered the contaminated country. They
were trespassing. They walked toward the town of Mercury, in
moonlight, taking their cues from coyote, kit fox, antelope squirrel, and quail. They moved quietly and deliberately through the
maze of Joshua trees. When a hint of daylight appeared they
rested, drinking tea and sharing their rations of food. The women
closed their eyes. The time had come to protest with the heart,
that to deny one's genealogy with the earth was to commit treason against one's soul.

At dawn, the women draped themselves in mylar, wrapping 44
long streamers of silver plastic around their arms to blow in the
breeze. They wore clear masks, that became the faces of humanity.
And when they arrived at the edge of Mercury, they carried all the
butterflies of a summer day in their wombs. They paused to allow
their courage to settle.

The town that forbids pregnant women and children to enter 45
because of radiation risks was asleep. The women moved through
the streets as winged messengers, twirling around each other in
slow motion, peeking inside homes and watching the easy sleep of
men and women. They were astonished by such stillness and
periodically would utter a shrill note or low cry just to verify life.

The residents finally awoke to these strange apparitions. 46
Some simply stared. Others called authorities, and in time, the
women were apprehended by wary soldiers dressed in desert
fatigues. They were taken to a white, square building on the other
edge of Mercury. When asked who they were and why they were
there, the women replied, "We are mothers and we have come to
reclaim the desert for our children."

The soldiers arrested them. As the ten women were blind- 47
folded and handcuffed, they began singing:

> *You can't forbid us everything*
> *You can't forbid us to think—*
> *You can't forbid our tears to flow*
> *And you can't stop the songs that we sing.*

The women continued to sing louder and louder, until they heard
the voices of their sisters moving across the mesa:

> *Ah ne nah, nah*
> *nin nah nah—*
> *Ah ne nah, nah*
> *nin nah nah—*
> *Nyaga mutzi*
> *oh ne nay—*
> *Nyaga mutzi*
> *oh ne nay—*

"Call for reinforcements," one soldier said.

48   "We have," interrupted one woman, "we have—and you have no idea of our numbers."

49   I crossed the line at the Nevada Test Site and was arrested with nine other Utahns for trespassing on military lands. They are still conducting nuclear tests in the desert. Ours was an act of civil disobedience. But as I walked toward the town of Mercury, it was more than a gesture of peace. It was a gesture on behalf of the Clan of One-Breasted Women.

50   As one officer cinched the handcuffs around my wrists, another frisked my body. She found a pen and a pad of paper tucked inside my left boot.

51   "And these?" she asked sternly.

52   "Weapons," I replied.

53   Our eyes met. I smiled. She pulled the leg of my trousers back over my boot.

54   "Step forward, please," she said as she took my arm.

55   We were booked under an afternoon sun and bused to Tonopah, Nevada. It was a two-hour ride. This was familiar country. The Joshua trees standing their ground had been named by my ancestors, who believed they looked like prophets pointing west to the Promised Land. These were the same trees that bloomed each spring, flowers appearing like white flames in the Mojave. And I recalled a full moon in May, when Mother and I had walked among them, flushing out mourning doves and owls.

56   The bus stopped short of town. We were released.

57   The officials thought it was a cruel joke to leave us stranded in the desert with no way to get home. What they didn't realize was that we were home, soul-centered and strong, women who recognized the sweet smell of sage as fuel for our spirits.

Content

1. Identify and explain the polarities that Williams illustrates in this essay: natural versus man-made; health versus breast cancer; man's domination versus woman's submission; moral righteousness (including civil disobedience) versus legalities.

2. Since Williams's sentiments are clearly predisposed to favor women on these issues, how does—or can—she expect men to be sympathetic readers of her essay?

3. In what ways do the women of this Clan exhibit strength, even while their bodies are vulnerable to breast cancer?

4. How does Williams link breast cancer to the natural wildlife in the Utah desert (see, for instance, ¶s 34 and 38)?

Strategies/Structures

5. Why does Williams begin with a medical history of the adult women in her family (¶s 1–2)? She says, "This is my family history" (¶ 3); why does she focus on breast cancer and on no other aspect of her family's lives and deaths?

6. Why has Williams included the episode of the "women from all over the world" drumming, and dancing and singing "a song given to them by Shoshone grandmothers" (¶s 39–48)?

7. Williams says she "dreamed" the protest episode, yet her account seems so realistic readers are likely to believe it really happened: "Rabbits felt the tremors" from the nuclear bomb testing. "Their soft leather pads on paws and feet recognized the shaking sands" (¶ 41). What other devices of verisimilitude (apparent truth) does Williams use? Do they harmonize with the more mythic elements of her story? Does it matter whether we believe the dream or not?

Language

8. Williams invents a metaphorical label for herself and her female ancestors, the "Clan of One-Breasted Women." In what ways and for what purposes does she use this label? What are some of the differences between using the label and simply saying "my female ancestors"?

9. Since this essay is, in part, a protest against the nuclear testing that took her mother's life, why does Williams quote her grandmother, also stricken with breast cancer, telling her mother "'Diane, [the mastectomy] is one of the most spiritual experiences you will ever encounter'" (¶ 7). Why does she show her mother's "radiance" after the operation (¶ 9)?

For Writing

10. Write an essay in which you link a natural phenomenon to an unnatural one. Show (or imply) how the two are related. Are they mutually beneficial? Or does one phenomenon thrive at the expense of the other? Is that desirable?

11. Is breast cancer exclusively, even primarily, a women's issue? Explain, using evidence from this essay and from other sources, as well. Or

pick some other social issue with political implications for a particular group—children, for example—and argue the case for an audience of general readers, men and women alike.

=====

LYNDA BARRY

Lynda Barry (born, 1956), daughter of a Filipino mother and an American father, grew up in an interracial neighborhood in Seattle. She told an interviewer, "Anybody who was coming from the Philippines would stay with us or with one of our [numerous] relatives. There was always a lot of commotion in the house, mostly in the kitchen. We didn't have a set dinner or lunch or breakfast time; when we wanted to eat there was always food on the stove. . . . At the time it was a little frustrating for me, because I looked to all the world like a regular little white American kid, but at home we were eating real different food and there was sometimes octopus in the refrigerator and stuff that was scary looking to my friends. . . . We ate with our hands, and when you say that, people think that you're also squatting on the floor . . . but it wasn't like that. There's a whole etiquette to the way that you eat with your hands, just like you hold a fork. And it was lively and unusual, an atmosphere where I . . . could pretty much do whatever I wanted to do."

As "The Sanctuary of School" indicates, "drawing came to mean everything" to the little girl who grew up to be a cartoonist. Nevertheless, when she began Evergreen State College she "wanted to be a fine artist," she says. "Cartoons to me were really base." Then she realized that her drawings could make her friends laugh, and shortly after she graduated, in 1978, she created "Ernie Pook's Comeek," a wry, witty, and feminist strip now syndicated in over sixty newspapers in the United States, Canada, Russia, and Hungary. Barry has compiled her eighth comic collection, *It's So Magic* (1994); has written her second novel, *Cruddy* (1998); and is doing commentaries for National Public Radio's *Morning Edition*. Her first novel, *The Good Times Are Killing Me,* was published in 1988. Like many satirists, Barry cares deeply about her subjects, as illustrated in her compassionate plea for social justice for children that permeates "The Sanctuary of School," first published in the *New York Times* Education Section, January 5, 1992.

The Sanctuary of School

I was 7 years old the first time I snuck out of the house in the dark. It was winter and my parents had been fighting all night. They were short on money and long on relatives who kept "temporarily" moving into our house because they had nowhere else to go. 1

My brother and I were used to giving up our bedroom. We slept on the couch, something we actually liked because it put us that much closer to the light of our lives, our television. 2

At night when everyone was asleep, we lay on our pillows watching it with the sound off. We watched Steve Allen's mouth moving. We watched Johnny Carson's mouth moving. We watched movies filled with gangsters shooting machine guns into packed rooms, dying solders hurling a last grenade and beautiful women crying at windows. Then the sign-off finally came and we tried to sleep. 3

The morning I snuck out, I woke up filled with a panic about needing to get to school. The sun wasn't quite up yet but my anxiety was so fierce that I just got dressed, walked quietly across the kitchen and let myself out the back door. 4

It was quiet outside. Stars were still out. Nothing moved and no one was in the street. It was as if someone had turned the sound off on the world. 5

I walked the alley, breaking thin ice over the puddles with my shoes. I didn't know why I was walking to school in the dark. I didn't think about it. All I knew was a feeling of panic, like the panic that strikes kids when they realize they are lost. 6

That feeling eased the moment I turned the corner and saw the dark outline of my school at the top of the hill. My school was made up of about 15 nondescript portable classrooms set down on a fenced concrete lot in a rundown Seattle neighborhood, but it had the most beautiful view of the Cascade Mountains. You could see them from anywhere on the playfield and you could see them from the windows of my classroom—Room 2. 7

I walked over to the monkey bars and hooked my arms around the cold metal. I stood for a long time just looking across 8

Rainier Valley. The sky was beginning to whiten and I could hear a few birds.

9   In a perfect world my absence at home would not have gone unnoticed. I would have had two parents in a panic to locate me, instead of two parents in a panic to locate an answer to the hard question of survival during a deep financial and emotional crisis.

10   But in an overcrowded and unhappy home, it's incredibly easy for any child to slip away. The high levels of frustration, depression and anger in my house made my brother and me invisible. We were children with the sound turned off. And for us, as for the steadily increasing number of neglected children in this country, the only place where we could count on being noticed was at school.

11   "Hey there, young lady. Did you forget to go home last night?" It was Mr. Gunderson, our janitor, whom we all loved. He was nice and he was funny and he was old with white hair, thick glasses and an unbelievable number of keys. I could hear them jingling as he walked across the playfield. I felt incredibly happy to see him.

12   He let me push his wheeled garbage can between the different portables as he unlocked each room. He let me turn on the lights and raise the window shades and I saw my school slowly come to life. I saw Mrs. Holman, our school secretary, walk into the office without her orange lipstick on yet. She waved.

13   I saw the fifth-grade teacher, Mr. Cunningham, walking under the breezeway eating a hard roll. He waved.

14   And I saw my teacher, Mrs. Claire LeSane, walking toward us in a red coat and calling my name in a very happy and surprised way, and suddenly my throat got tight and my eyes stung and I ran toward her crying. It was something that surprised us both.

15   It's only thinking about it now, 28 years later, that I realize I was crying from relief. I was with my teacher, and in a while I was going to sit at my desk, with my crayons and pencils and books and classmates all around me, and for the next six hours I was going to enjoy a thoroughly secure, warm and stable world. It was a world I absolutely relied on. Without it, I don't know where I would have gone that morning.

Mrs. LeSane asked me what was wrong and when I said   16
"Nothing," she seemingly left it at that. But she asked me if I
would carry her purse for her, an honor above all honors, and she
asked if I wanted to come into Room 2 early and paint.

She believed in the natural healing power of painting and drawing   17
for troubled children. In the back of her room there was always a
drawing table and an easel with plenty of supplies, and sometimes
during the day she would come up to you for what seemed like no
good reason and quietly ask if you wanted to go to the back table
and "make some pictures for Mrs. LeSane." We all had a chance at
it—to sit apart from the class for a while to paint, draw and silently
work out impossible problems on 11 × 17 sheets of newsprint.

Drawing came to mean everything to me. At the back table   18
in Room 2, I learned to build myself a life preserver that I could
carry into my home.

We all know that a good education system saves lives, but   19
the people of this country are still told that cutting the budget for
public schools is necessary, that poor salaries for teachers are all
we can manage and that art, music and all creative activities must
be the first to go when times are lean.

Before- and after-school programs are cut and we are told that   20
public schools are not made for baby-sitting children. If parents are
neglectful temporarily or permanently, for whatever reason, it's
certainly sad, but their unlucky children must fend for themselves.
Or slip through the cracks. Or wander in a dark night alone.

We are told in a thousand ways that not only are public   21
schools not important, but that the children who attend them, the
children who need them most, are not important either. We leave
them to learn from the blind eye of a television, or to the mercy of
"a thousand points of light" that can be as far away as stars.

I was lucky. I had Mrs. LeSane. I had Mr. Gunderson. I had   22
an abundance of art supplies. And I had a particular brand of
neglect in my home that allowed me to slip away and get to them.
But what about the rest of the kids who weren't as lucky? What
happened to them?

By the time the bell rang that morning I had finished my   23
drawing and Mrs. LeSane pinned it up on the special bulletin

board she reserved for drawings from the back table. It was the same picture I always drew—a sun in the corner of a blue sky over a nice house with flowers all around it.

24   Mrs. LeSane asked us to please stand, face the flag, place our right hands over our hearts and say the Pledge of Allegiance. Children across the country do it faithfully. I wonder now when the country will face its children and say a pledge right back.

Content

1. What is the point of calling school a "sanctuary" (in the title)? How does Barry reinforce this image throughout the essay? Identify some of the life-saving features of Barry's second grade. Is Barry's view likely to convince even those readers whose elementary school experiences were quite different from hers, for instance, readers who regarded school as a form of prison or punishment?

2. Barry tells a personal story to make a general point about the values and economic priorities of the entire country. What is her point? Is it appropriate to make such a sweeping generalization on the basis of a single incident from one person's experience?

Strategies/Structures

3. How does Barry manage to tell an extremely painful and moving tale without lapsing into either sentimentality (emotion disproportionate to the subject) or self-pity?

4. Barry compresses her family history into a single sentence: "[My parents] were short on money and long on relatives who kept 'temporarily' moving into our house because they had nowhere else to go" (¶ 1). What is the effect of reading the rest of the essay through the lens of this statement? What additional dimensions does the essay's opening sentence add: "I was 7 years old the first time I snuck out of the house in the dark" (¶ 1)?

5. By analogy with the sentence quoted in question 4 above, are readers to believe that Barry compresses her childhood into this story of a single morning in second grade? Why or why not?

6. Barry explains, "[Mrs. LeSane] asked me if I would carry her purse for her, an honor above all honors, and she asked if I wanted to come into Room 2 early and paint" (¶ 16). She expects her readers to interpret this and the entire piece from two perspectives: that of the seven-year-old child who experienced "the sanctuary of school," and their own viewpoint as adults. Is this expectation justified? What does Barry do to reinforce this dual perspective? (See Language question 7 below.)

Language

7. If Barry's conversational language occasionally sounds childlike, "I snuck out of the house" (¶ 1), "[Mr. Gunderson] was nice and he was funny and he was old with white hair . . ." (¶ 11), what features of her vocabulary, sentence structure, and point of view remind us that "The Sanctuary of School" is written by an adult and for adult readers?

8. "The Sanctuary of School" is full of natural symbols. Among these are watching TV with the sound off (¶ 3)—echoed in "We were children with the sound turned off" (¶ 10); "walking to school in the dark" (¶ 6) and watching the sun rise over the "beautiful view of the Cascade Mountains" (¶ 7); seeing her teacher (is it a happy accident or Barry's invention that she was named "Claire LeSane"?) "calling my name in a very happy and surprised way" (¶ 14); saying the Pledge of Allegiance (¶ 24). Explain the literal and symbolic meanings of these and others in the essay.

For Writing

9. Tell a story of your own experience—as a child, teenager, or adult—that throughout implies a social or political message. Although your message may be familiar to your audience, as Barry's is, the story itself should render the experience in a new and meaningful way. Select details to reinforce your point, but don't preach.

10. Write an essay that employs several natural symbols (see Language question 8, above) or an elaboration of a single natural symbol to make a point about which you can generalize (see Ruffin, "Mama's Smoke" [148–58] and Swanson, "The Turning Point" [249–52]).

MATT NOCTON

Nocton (born, 1975) has spent most of his life in the vicinity of his hometown, Simsbury, Connecticut, except for a year's sojourn in California—a cross-country trek that stimulated some of his best writing. An English major at the University of Connecticut (B.A., expected 2000), he explained "Why I Write" in the short paper, whose essence is quoted here:

> I write to dispel lies. I write because I seek the truth. Writing for me is a source of discovery. I write because I feel a sense of freedom and adventure in writing. To me writing is a

place that I can return to again and again where the scenery of my life is always new and exciting. I write because I am always in the process of changing, and writing is a way to take a snapshot of who I am today. I want to rediscover myself and remind myself of who I was. I like to discover where I am going and where I am coming from. I write because I find it relaxing and it takes my mind off the dreadful events in the world today. I write to prove that I exist.

I write because I can express myself in ways I find impossible with spoken words. I write to prove a fact or sway an opinion. Through writing, I find that I can put things in perspective and see things differently, more clearly. I write to express my ideas or feelings. I write to emulate the styles of writers I admire. I write to delve into places that I have never been, and to explore new places within myself. I also write for others. I write to apologize and I write to forgive. I write to greet people and I write to amuse. I write to sustain my mind with the exercise and nourishment that it needs to stay healthy.

Being a quiet person, one thing I most enjoy about writing is the ability to avoid interruptions that occur in conversation. Arguing with words on paper can be an excellent method for waging war while eluding enemy fire, at least temporarily.

Nocton himself worked harvesting tobacco in Connecticut; the tobacco fields are adjacent to the state's largest airport, Bradley International Airport. "Harvest of Gold, Harvest of Shame" is the seventh revision Nocton submitted, every draft reinforcing the gulf between the bosses and the workers in the tobacco fields and sheds, every draft increasing his own awareness of the workers' exploited and powerless condition.

Harvest of Gold, Harvest of Shame

1   Simsbury is a small affluent town located in the heart of the Connecticut River Valley. It is not a particularly exciting place and its high school students refer to it as "Simsboring." But in fact there is something unique about this quiet town. Simsbury is home to Culbro Tobacco Company's Farm No. 2. The Culbro Tobacco Company prides itself on growing the finest shade tobacco in the world. Its leaves are used to wrap expensive cigars.

Culbro employs three kinds of people: migrant workers, 2
most of whom are from Jamaica and live on the farm headquarters, inner-city people, most of whom are Hispanic and are bussed
from Hartford to Simsbury at 6:15 in the morning; and finally, a
few local white residents. The latter are typically the men who
oversee all of the other employees. Each supervisor is referred to
as the "boss man" by the less fortunate workers. When a boss man
speaks to one of his subordinates, the usual response comes either
in the form of Spanglish, which most of the Hispanics speak, or
Patoi, which is what the Jamaicans speak.

Working in tobacco fields is demanding and repetitious and 3
the pay is minimum wage. In a typical day, a field worker is
bussed to the field where he will be working with his group of
roughly fifty to two hundred workers. When he gets off the bus he
will find a pick-up truck parked nearby full of burlap and twine.
He must tie this burlap around his waist as a source of protection
against the dirt and rocks that he will be dragging himself through
for the next eight hours. He will then find another pick-up truck
containing wooden stakes with numbers on them. There he will
find the stake with his number and stick it into the ground before
the row of tobacco plants where he is about to work. A recorder or
"bentkeeper" (so called because the distance between two tobacco
posts is called a bent) stands under the blazing sun and monitors
all the workers. He does this by looking at the numbers of each
stake in each row. He flips through the pages on his clipboard until
he finds the corresponding employee number. Then he checks the
number of poles in the row and adds the number of "bents" in the
row to a particular worker's sum total. He does this for fifty to two
hundred laborers. At times when the rows are very short it is difficult to add all of the numbers fast enough to keep up with the
pace of the pickers. The pickers who complete the most bents earn
the most money. The bentkeeper is the only one authorized to
carry the clipboard and add the bent numbers. Every so often the
unshaven field boss man with the coarse black mustache and cowboy hat calls the bentkeeper. "Hey, who was working in this row?
Twelve six-four-five is still staked in here. Who was working next
to twelve six-four-five?" The bentkeeper nervously hands over his
clipboard and the boss man takes off his sunglasses and draws on
his cigarette while he examines it.

4   "What the hell is this!?! This is an eight bent row! You've been adding nine! It changed from nine to eight way the hell back there! Look at the goddamn post! Goddamn are you blind or can't you read!?! Go fix it!" He shoves the clipboard into the bent-keeper's stomach and jumps in his truck. The truck kicks up dirt and a cloud of dust as it speeds down the rocky dirt road. It comes to an abrupt halt about one hundred yards down. As the bentkeeper tries to figure out where the bents changed from nine to eight and from which numbers he must deduct points, he hears the boss man in the distance. "Hey eleven two-nine-two! Were you working next to twelve six-four-five?! You're bruising the leaves! Look at this? See this? This is from your row! We can't use these! You're going too fast. Stop bruising the goddamn leaves or I'm going to dock ten bents from your total!"

5   The humiliated bentkeeper tries not to listen as he attempts to correct his blunder while keeping pace with the pickers at the same time. A tough looking Hispanic kid breaks his concentration. "Hey bentkeeper! How many I got?" He holds up his stake so the bentkeeper can see the number.

6   The bentkeeper flips through the pages, "Uhhmm . . . sixty-eight."

7   "What!? I got more than that!"

8   "No, you've got sixty-eight."

9   "Ahh man this is bullshit. How'd you get that job anyway?" The complaining worker walks over to the water truck to get a drink.

10   In the middle of two towering tobacco plants under the white netting eleven two-nine-two mumbles slowly in a deep raspy voice with smoke in his breath "Duh boss mon is crazy mon." He finishes his row and approaches the bentkeeper. "Hey mon, eleven two-nine-two, how many I got now?"

11   The bentkeeper replies "Yeah I know your number Stanley, you have one-hundred and fifteen."

12   Stanley's smile reveals a gold front tooth with a black clover on it, "Ohkay mon, yuh shades uh looking fat mon. All shades uh fat in my book mon."

13   After field, "asparagus 1032," is finished, the nets are dropped and the boss man selects two unlucky souls to spray the

field. They reluctantly don cumbersome yellow suits that resemble something NASA designed for the planned mission to Mars. The only obvious difference is that the sprayers wear back packs of insecticides rather than oxygen.

Beneath the foggy mask of his suit, David's pockmarked 14 hairy face contorts into a nasty expression as he argues with his partner. Everyone hated David. He talked in the belligerent tongue of a junkyard dog. He was likened to a Neanderthal, though an allusion to something more ancient would probably suit him better. In the middle of the argument David blurts out, "I was in prison you know. . . .you know why I was there? . . . I killed a cop. . . . strangled him. . . . I'm on parole now." The significance of his comment seemed to bear no relation to the argument and his partner ignored it. He wasn't afraid of David.

All of the leaves from "asparagus 1032" are transported to 15 the shed on a trailer pulled by a big blue Ford tractor. The shed operations are run by a short stocky Hispanic man who wears a blue Hawaiian tee shirt with buttons and flowers. Working in the shed is better than working in the field. Many women work in the shed. There, by means of a giant sewing machine, they monotonously sew tobacco leaves to a stick called a "lath." Every time a worker finishes fifty laths she gets credit for one bundle. That is recorded by the bundlekeeper who patrols the shed monitoring daily progress. When a sewer calls out "bundle!" the bundlekeeper acknowledges "bundle!" and he hurries over to the end of the shed and hoists the heavy bundle from the bundle stockpile onto his shoulder. He then carries it to the idle sewer and he drops the bundle of fifty laths on top of her sewing machine. He then withdraws his hole puncher and he punches a hole in her card. Every time he punches a sewer's card he punches the master card which he wears around his neck. The master card shows how many bundles the shed completes on a daily basis. The bundlekeeper is the only one authorized to carry the hole puncher and the master card. Every so often a "boss man" will summon the bundlekeeper over and yank the master card from the bundlekeeper's neck to examine it. Then the boss man marches up and down the shed to exercise his authority. Then he stops in a thick cloud of dust to bark his favorite motivational speech "you not gonna get paid if you don't speed up!" The sewers ignore him and try to keep up with their mindless sewing machines. Those who complete the most bundles make the most money.

16   Every time a lath is completed it is racked. Then a man who has precariously positioned himself on the bottom level of rafters in the shed reaches down to the rack and picks it up. He then passes it to his partner above him on the next level who passes it up to the man above him and so on until the lath reaches the highest level that is available for another row of lath. Each lath is suspended between two rafters in the barn. They are carefully packed about a foot and a half apart across the width of the shed on every level of rafters and along the length of the barn. It normally takes about three days or a million and a half tobacco leaves to fill a shed.

17   On the dry dusty floor of the shed, the sweaty bundlekeeper looks up and admires the beautiful ceiling as it is painted with enormous green leaves with a splotch of a red shirt on one level and a yellow shirt above it and black arms with extended hands reaching to one another. For a moment he is gazing at the ceiling of the Sistine Chapel in Rome. He can imagine he is actually witnessing Michelangelo paint his masterpiece. For a moment the two men with extended hands remind the bundlekeeper of God in the heavens reaching to Adam. His imagination is suddenly snapped by a falling lath misplaced by an imperfect human being hanging from the rafters. The bundlekeeper ducks and after a loud 'thump!' he thanks God for his green hard hat.

18   As the clock rolls onto ten o'clock the boss man calls out "Coffee! Last lath!" The sewers finish sewing their last fifty leaves and the squeaky machines fall silent. The silence is invaded by the chatter of relieved sewers who have temporarily escaped the heat and dust in the shed to drink their coffee outside under the shade of a nearby tree or the side of the barn. The men in the rafters descend to retrieve their coolers to snack on bread and beer for a leisurely ten minutes.

19   Work resumes promptly at ten after ten with the boss man's "back to work!" The dissipating dust is replenished by a fresh cloud churned from the feet of a tired troop heading back to the barn. Next to the crack in the shed where a ray of sunlight illuminates floating dust particles, an old machine resumes its

monotonous humming and clicking as a carefree Jamaican man whistles while feeding it leaves.

    The boss man steps outside his dark shed for a breath of fresh 20 air and a chance to blow his nose and spit the gritty sand from his mouth. Then he sees the next load of green leaves preceding a light brown dust cloud in field "Ketchen 918" with the new hybrid seed. Those leaves cannot be mixed. He grows red in the face because the next shed has not yet been prepared for those leaves. He stomps over to his dust colored pickup truck to call base. After talking to the base coordinator he realizes that he will have to divide his crew into two sections with one half in one shed and another in the other shed. Now the bundlekeeper will have to run back and forth between the two sheds because of the field boss man's mistake. The stressed-out shed boss man invents another motivational speech "Hey, dees is not a carnival! dees is not the beach!" By lunch time the boss man has resumed his composure. He sneaks a peek at his watch and yells "last lath! break time! last lath!"

    The shed workers rush to the water truck outside to wash 21 their hands before lunch. They sit in the weeds against the shady side of the shed and eat their lunches. The bundlekeeper and the shed boss eat in the pickup truck and listen to the Spanish radio. Out in the field the boss man calls "lunch time! Finish your rows!" The dirty and smelly pickers crawl out from underneath the nets and remove the tape from their fingers and try to wash the sticky tape, tobacco juices, and dirt from their finger tips. Then they head to the bus to find their coolers of beer and candy bars. They eat and drink for half an hour. Stanley puffs his harsh "Craven A" cigarette between mouthfuls of ham and cheese and tries not to think about tobacco.

    The bentkeeper and the field boss eat in the dusty pickup 22 and the field boss lights his Marlboro and explains: "You know, when I yell at you it's nothing personal. I have to yell at you because it's my job. Man I know how it is, I was in your shoes once." The bentkeeper nods in agreement. His mind is on his lunch. It appears inedible. After growing tired of drinks and sandwiches that became warm and soggy in the hot sun for the past month, he has devised an unreliable system to solve that problem. Instead of just packing his lunch in ice, he actually freezes his entire lunch overnight. Unfortunately, when he opened his cooler on this hot day he discovered his peanut butter and jelly to be hard as a brick. Likewise his Boku juice boxes were still frozen solid.

23   As he sits there listening to his boss's rambling, he places his sandwich on the dash and he peels away the walls of his juice box and gnaws on it as if it were some kind of primitive popsicle. No matter how he prepares his lunch he can never seem to achieve a proper balance between hot and cold. When the sun is high and it's time to eat, he discovers either a frozen block of bread and jam or a soggy something suffering heat stroke.

24   At half past the hour Stanley strikes his stake into the dirt with a swift robotic motion. He sucks deeply on his cigarette and marches down to the end of the row. Large veins puff out of his forearm like the veins on the bottom green leaf that he snaps from the lower stalk of a thriving tobacco plant. Three more hours to go.

25   At the shed yet another blue tractor arrives with its precious load of fresh leaves. The shed boss man orders two rafter men down to disperse the containers of tobacco among the sewers. The bundlekeeper manages to help with the heavy containers between bundle runs. He is thoroughly exhausted and his eyes are bloodshot from the irritating smoke and dust in the shed. Although three hours remain every shed laborer is anticipating the boss man's "last lath! Get on the bus!"

26   At three-thirty in the hot afternoon three buses and two Chevy pick-up trucks carry exhausted tobacco workers back to farm headquarters where the workers can rest before returning to work early tomorrow in the cool morning hours.

Content

1.   Nocton identifies a variety of tasks the tobacco farm workers perform. What similarities are there among the jobs? What differences? Are readers to assume that all jobs are "demanding and repetitive and the pay is minimum wage" (¶ 3)? What's the difference between the tobacco harvesting process and the harvesting activities that Shange describes (240–49)?

2.   Which workers are Hispanics and Jamaicans? Are any white Americans? Who performs which tasks?

3.   Nocton evidently doesn't expect his readers to know much about the work of harvesting tobacco. What does he expect them to learn from reading his essay? What does he expect them to do?

4. Is Nocton himself a worker in the scene he describes? If so, can you ascertain what his job is? What are your clues? In what ways, if any, does the effectiveness of his argument depend on the authority of his personal experience?

Strategies/Structures

5. Where does Nocton use dialogue? With what effects?
6. What is the point of comparing the ceiling of the shed with Michelangelo's painting on the Sistine Chapel ceiling (¶ 17)?

Language

7. Nocton's language is slow and repetitive. How does the style fit the subject?
8. Why does Nocton call the shed boss's speeches "motivational" (¶s 15, 20)? Are there other ironies present in this account?

For Writing

9. Have you ever thought about how any crop that provides common raw materials—wheat, sugar, potatoes, rice, coffee, cotton—is grown and harvested? Have you or your relatives ever worked in such harvests? Find out about the production of one of these crops and compare it with the tobacco harvest that Nocton describes. On the basis of your investigation, formulate some principles of how agricultural workers should be treated and what their compensation and protection should be.
10. Have you or any family members ever had a menial, minimum-wage job, or do you currently hold such a job? What elements, if any, does it have in common with the jobs Nocton describes? (See also the jobs described in Soto's "Black Hair" (510–20). Are there any significant differences? Write a satiric paper about a day on the job, intended to serve as a critique and to imply a plan for better working conditions or employee benefits.

Additional Topics for Writing
Appealing to Emotion and Ethics

(For strategies for appealing to emotional ethics, see 646.)

Write an essay that attempts to persuade one of the following audiences through a combination of appeals to reason, emotion, and ethics.

1. To someone you'd like for a friend, fiancé(e), or spouse: Love me.
2. To an athlete, or to an athletic coach: Play according to the rules, even when the referee (umpire, or other judge) isn't looking.
3. To a prospective employer: I'm the best person for the job. Hire me.
4. To a police officer: I shouldn't receive this traffic ticket. Or, to a judge or jury: I am innocent of the crime of which I'm accused.
5. To the voters: Vote for me (or for a candidate of my choice).
6. To admissions officers of a particular college, university, or of a program within that institution (such as medical or law school, graduate program, or a division with a special undergraduate degree): Let me in.
7. To the prospective buyer of something you want to sell or service you can perform: Buy this.
8. To an audience prejudiced against a particular group or simply to a majority audience: X is beautiful. (X may be black, yellow, Hispanic, female, a member of a particular national or religious group . . .)
9. To an antagonist on any issue: As Joan Didion says, *"Listen to me, see it my way, change your mind."*
10. To people engaging in behavior that threatens their lives or their health: Stop doing X (or stop doing X to excess)—smoking, drinking, overeating, undereating, or using drugs. Or: Start doing X— exercising regularly, using bike helmets or seatbelts, planning for the future by getting—an education, a stable job, an investment plan, a retirement plan . . .
11. Pick a work of fiction or nonfiction whose content intrigues you and whose style you admire and write a brief parody (probably involving considerable exaggeration) of it to show your understanding of the content and your appreciation of the style.
12. Write a satire to argue implicity for a point, as Swift does in "A Modest Proposal" (650–60). Use whatever techniques seem appropriate, such as creating a character who does the talking for you; setting a scene (such as of pathos or misery) that helps make your point; using a tone involving understatement, irony, or exaggeration. Be sure to supply enough clues to enable your readers to understand what you really mean.

15 | Critical Argument: Biographical, Historical, Political, Literary

There are as many ways of reading and writing as there are readers and writers. There's no way we can read and write with total objectivity, for each of us brings to a text private as well as public associations, derived from our culture, our beliefs and values, and our personal experience. Our reading and writing about families, for instance, is inevitably affected by the family we grew up in (and its changes over time) (see Spinner and Sanders) and by the family we're currently part of or hope to have. It is also affected by our firsthand knowledge of other people's families; our cultural sense of what a family ought to be, gleaned, perhaps, from the Bible, the newspapers, and TV programs as diverse as *Friends* and *X-Files*; and our reading about families, ranging from psychology textbooks to novels to *King Lear*. So when we read Eudora Welty's account of how her family influenced her as a writer or Scott Russell Sanders's description of his father under the destructive influence of alcohol, or Linda Hogan's nostalgic re-creation of her Native American heritage, our response resonates with our own experiences. So it does when we read the opening lines of Tolstoy's *Anna Karenina*, "Happy families are all alike. Every unhappy family is unhappy in its own way." The meaning of any work of literature, fiction or nonfiction, resides both in the words on the page and in our interpretations—what we emphasize and endow with significance, what captures our hearts as well as our minds.

All writing is, to an extent, creative, for all writers of fiction and nonfiction alike, even makers of lists as in telephone books, seek to impose *order* and *structure* on materials, thoughts that might otherwise appear random or haphazard. Although the order that results may seem natural, even inevitable, it is not inherent in the material (the telephone book doesn't necessarily *have* to proceed from A to Z); it is an artifact of the writer's imagination, an intellectual construct. We have seen throughout *The Essay Connection* what some of these structures are, such as various patterns for comparison and contrast or for argumentation. A *story* says E. M. Forster, is a narrative of events in a time sequence ("The king died, and then the queen died."), as distinguished from a *plot*, which reflects causes and their effects and consequences ("The king died, and then the queen died of grief."). Unlike a story, which can merely be recounted, a plot can be explained and interpreted. Indeed, even the same plot can have a variety of interpretations. In real life, for instance, everybody's love story is individual, despite its common elements. Likewise, the plot of planting, cultivating, and harvesting crops can be interpreted variously, as the essays by Ntozake Shange ("What Is It We Really Harvestin' Here?" 240–49), Amy Jo Keifer ("The Death of a Farm" 636–39), and Matt Nocton ("Harvest of Gold, Harvest of Shame" 675–83) reveal. This is apparent in imaginative literature, as we see in the ancient and contemporary Chinese *Cinderellas* included here (699–701), in Anne Sexton's poetic version (713–18), and in Ning Yu's essay, "The Nurturing Woman Rewarded: A Study of Two Chinese Cinderellas" (705–13), dealing with Freudian, Marxist, and cross-cultural interpretations of the Cinderella story. It is also apparent in the varied reactions to Arthur Miller's *Death of a Salesman*, the subject of the next chapter.

All writers are concerned with *form;* any piece of writing, fiction or nonfiction, has to start somewhere, proceed for a while, and end somewhere else, whether it's a list, a ballad ("He was her man, but he done her wrong"), an argument, or a tale, tall or short. One major aspect of form is *emphasis,* as Gilbert Highet's analysis of "The Gettysburg Address" (691–98) makes clear. Writing with a computer makes us aware of how many times we *add, delete,* and *move* material, within sentences, paragraphs, entire works. Thus emphasis can derive from position; what comes first or last in any unit gets more emphasis than what's stuck in the middle. If a writer develops some points or characters more extensively than others, they will get the most emphasis from sheer bulk, but presumably from diversity and complexity as well. While longer units, on the whole, are more emphatic than shorter ones, epigrams and occasional one-sentence paragraphs can drive their point home with rapier efficiency: "Hypocrisy is the homage that vice pays to virtue."

Each genre and sub-genre usually has enough typical features of form to enable readers to distinguish it from other major types of writings. We recognize a *poem* by its short, metrical lines which are sometimes rhymed; and an *epic poem* by its long length and heroic subjects, in contrast to lyrics and songs, which are much shorter and not necessarily heroic. Anne Sexton's "Cinderella" (713–18) looks like a poem, though it is in free verse, irregular meter, and not rhymed. Sexton sets the rags-to-riches Cinderella story in a framework of similar stories, fairy tales all: "From toilets to riches," "From diapers to Dior./That story." We recognize a *play* by its format—an abundance of dialogue and division into acts and scenes. Though most of us understand a *novel* to be an extended fictional prose narrative representing a character or characters either in a static or developing state (the *plot* or *theme*), it can encompass a wide variety of forms, ranging from letters to stream-of-consciousness. Likewise, we recognize a *research article in the social or physical sciences* by its conventional pattern that (usually) begins with an abstract, a statement of the problem, followed (in some instances) by a review of the relevant professional research on the topic. It then proceeds to a step-by-step description of the research design and the methodology; a statement of research results; an analysis of the results; and a conclusion, sometimes augmented with suggestions for further research.

We read, as we write, according to what we understand to be the conventions of the genre, but even these conventions are susceptible to infinite variations. Yet as cultural anthropologist Clifford Geertz has observed in "Blurred Genres," the opening chapter of *Local Knowledge,* 1989, "there has been an enormous amount of genre mixing in intellectual life and recent years" as enormous changes occur in "the way we think about the way we think." Among the results are historical or philosophical inquiries blended with literary criticism (see Ning Yu's "The Nurturing Woman Rewarded: A Study of Two Chinese Cinderellas" [705–13]), scientific discussions resembling familiar essays (as in Lewis Thomas's work), and "nonfiction novels" such as Truman Capote's *In Cold Blood*. Indeed, a great many belletristic essays employ many of the techniques of fiction: development of character(s); use of dialogue; setting of scenes; presentation of social, cultural, intellectual, or other contexts through details of the characters' clothing, behavior, lifestyle, and so on—as, for instance, Joan Didion's "Marrying Absurd" (330–35). These techniques are conspicuous in full-length *autobiography* and *personal essays* with an autobiographical emphasis, including "Under the Influence" (441–56) by Scott Russell Sanders, and Nancy Mairs's "On Being a Cripple" (456–71).

As readers and writers, we decide how to interpret what we read according to both the conventions of the form and our assumptions about whether we are reading fiction or nonfiction. Indeed, given the blurring of genres and the many characteristics that fiction and literary (or creative or belletristic) nonfiction share, our response to a particular personal writing, for instance, may not necessarily depend on its structural or stylistic features but on whether we believe it is true. If we believe a work to be, essentially, true, derived from facts that are verifiable independently of the text, we will read it as an autobiography. If, on the other hand, we believe the work to be drawn largely from the author's imagination, we will read and respond to it as fiction. Thus, we read Richard Wright's "The Power of Books" (425–35) from *Black Boy*, an angry, searing account of Wright's own life of deprivation and prejudice, as true. But we read Wright's equally angry, searing account of Bigger Thomas's life of deprivation and prejudice in *Native Son* as fiction, because although the events *could* have happened, we believe we are reading a work of fiction. Yet Wright has selected, shaped, and structured the materials in both works; he has presented characters, dialogue, scenes, motives in both. And both convey a "felt truth" reflective of emotional and psychological reality.

When we read and when we write critical analyses, we are also concerned with *style*, "as organic to the person doing the writing" says editor William Zinsser, as is one's hair. "Trying to add style is like adding a toupee." *Tone, voice,* and *choice of words* reflect the writer's character and personality, as well as his or her attitude toward the subject. In *A Way Out* Robert Frost addresses this matter of personal resonance:

> A dramatic necessity goes deep into the nature of the sentence. Sentences are not different enough to hold the attention unless they are dramatic. No ingenuity of varying structure will do. All that can save them is the speaking tone of voice somehow entangled in the words and fastened to the page for the ear of the imagination. That is all that can save poetry from sing-song, all that can save prose from itself. (272–73)

Although *voice* is hard to pin down, it emerges as a sense of authority, honesty, and truth when the writing is fresh, individual—not suppressed by clichés or subdued by formulaic thinking. The *tone* of a writing conveys its mood or emotional temper. Though this may vary considerably even within a single work, an essay may have a dominant tone—objective, pleading, argumentative, playful, for instance, or a combination of compatible tones, like adjacent shades of the rainbow, optimistic and cheerful, or serious and sad, the prevailing tone of Lincoln's "Gettysburg Address" (642–49). Voice, tone, sentence structure, and vocabulary combine to signal a work's degree of formality or informality. Although there is no necessary connection between formality of vocabulary and sentence complexity (including parallel and repeated structures—"of the people, by the people, for the people") or length, informal writing seems simpler in both—as if the author were conversing with the reader. Do you feel as if Mike Rose ("I Just Wanna Be Average"), Nancy Mairs ("On Being a Cripple"), and the student writers are talking directly to you? Formal writing, on the other hand, may sound impersonal, as it does in scientific and other types of academic writing (see Stephen Jay Gould's "Evolution as Fact and Theory," 550–60). Or it may appear stylized, with its vocabulary a mixture of native and borrowed words, simple and elevated, contemporary and archaic, as Gilbert Highet notes in his own formal analysis of Lincoln's "Gettysburg Address."

Whether you are analyzing fiction or nonfiction of any sort, the following considerations may be helpful (see also the suggestions for reading essays, 1–3):

1. What is the genre (novel, play, story, poem, essay) of this writing? What is its subgenre or form (historical novel, romance, western . . .)?
2. In what ways does the author follow the conventions of the forms he or she is writing in? In what ways does the work depart from these? With what effects?
3. Why is the author writing this work? How can I tell?
4. For what audience(s) is the author writing? In what ways has the author accommodated this audience, through simplicity or complexity of language, supplying background information, anticipating objections to the expressed point of view? Or is the author essentially indifferent to the audience?
5. What is the author's approach to the subject—theoretical and abstract? Concrete and specific? Or some mixture? Is the language plain and simple? Figurative? Engaging? Does it suit the work's subject and tone?
6. Most important of all, what is my reaction to this work? Why do I like or dislike it, or does it simply leave me cold? Will I remember it? Recommend it to others? Reread it? Why?

GILBERT HIGHET

Highet took "all literature for his province." As Anthon Professor of Latin Language and Literature at Columbia University, where he taught from 1938 until retirement in 1972 (with time out for military service during World War II), he wrote and edited critical works on poetry, satire, literary history, criticism, classicism, and "the joy of teaching and learning." He wrote "the English language with affectionate ease," from a personal, enthusiastic, anecdotal perspective that charmed general readers and antagonized literary scholars who objected to his popular treatment of canonical works—as the erudite often do when laypeople are invited into their exclusive circle. Born in Glasgow, Scotland, in 1906, Highet emigrated to the United States in 1937, after an education at Glasgow and Oxford, from which he later received honorary degrees, as well. Among his most popular works are *The Classical Tradition: Greek and Roman Influences on Western Literature* (1949), *The Art of Teaching* (1950); and *The Anatomy of Satire* (1962). His last book, *The Immortal Profession: The Joy of Teaching and Learning*, was published two years before his death in 1978.

With the same understated eloquence and ease that Lincoln used in "The Gettysburg Address" (648–49), Highet places the speech and the speaker in their biographical, historical, literary, and political contexts. Highet's knowledge of his subject is equaled by his love of Lincoln and profound respect for his work, indeed a work of art as well as oratory.

The Gettysburg Address

F *ourscore and seven years ago . . .* 1
These five words stand at the entrance to the best-known 2
monument of American prose, one of the finest utterances in the entire language and surely one of the greatest speeches in all history. Greatness is like granite: it is molded in fire, and it lasts for many centuries.

Fourscore and seven years ago. . . . It is strange to think that 3
President Lincoln was looking back to the 4th of July 1776, and

that he and his speech are now further removed from us than he himself was from George Washington and the Declaration of Independence. Fourscore and seven years before the Gettysburg Address, a small group of patriots signed the Declaration. Fourscore and seven years after the Gettysburg Address, it was the year 1950,[1] and that date is already receding rapidly into our troubled, adventurous, and valiant past.

4   Inadequately prepared and at first scarcely realized in its full importance, the dedication of the graveyard at Gettysburg was one of the supreme moments of American history. The battle itself had been a turning point of the war. On the 4th of July 1863, General Meade repelled Lee's invasion of Pennsylvania. Although he did not follow up his victory, he had broken one of the most formidable aggressive enterprises of the Confederate armies. Losses were heavy on both sides. Thousands of dead were left on the field, and thousands of wounded died in the hot days following the battle. At first, their burial was more or less haphazard; but thoughtful men gradually came to feel that an adequate burying place and memorial were required. These were established by an interstate commission that autumn, and the finest speaker in the North was invited to dedicate them. This was the scholar and statesman Edward Everett of Harvard. He made a good speech— which is still extant: not at all academic, it is full of close strategic analysis and deep historical understanding.

5   Lincoln was not invited to speak, at first. Although people knew him as an effective debater, they were not sure whether he was capable of making a serious speech on such a solemn occasion. But one of the impressive things about Lincoln's career is that he constantly strove to *grow.* He was anxious to appear on that occasion and to say something worthy of it. (Also, it has been suggested, he was anxious to remove the impression that he did not know how to behave properly—an impression which had been strengthened by a shocking story about his clowning on the battlefield of Antietam the previous year.) Therefore when he was invited he took considerable care with his speech. He drafted

---

[1] In November 1950 the Chinese had just entered the war in Korea.

rather more than half of it in the White House before leaving, finished it in the hotel at Gettysburg the night before the ceremony (not in the train, as sometimes reported), and wrote out a fair copy the next morning.

There are many accounts of the day itself, 19 November 1863. There are many descriptions of Lincoln, all showing the same curious blend of grandeur and awkwardness, or lack of dignity, or—it would be best to call it humility. In the procession he rode horseback: a tall lean man in a high plug hat, straddling a short horse, with his feet too near the ground. He arrived before the chief speaker, and had to wait patiently for half an hour or more. His own speech came right at the end of a long and exhausting ceremony, lasted less than three minutes, and made little impression on the audience. In part this was because they were tired, in part because (as eye-witnesses said) he ended almost before they knew he had begun, and in part because he did not speak the Address, but read it, very slowly, in a thin high voice, with a marked Kentucky accent, pronouncing "to" as "toe" and dropping his final R's.

Some people of course were alert enough to be impressed. Everett congratulated him at once. But most of the newspapers paid little attention to the speech, and some sneered at it. The *Patriot and Union* of Harrisburg wrote, "We pass over the silly remarks of the President; for the credit of the nation we are willing . . . that they shall be no more repeated or thought of"; and the London *Times* said, "The ceremony was rendered ludicrous by some of the sallies of that poor President Lincoln," calling his remarks "dull and commonplace." The first commendation of the Address came in a single sentence of the Chicago *Tribune*, and the first discriminating and detailed praise of it appeared in the Springfield *Republican*, the Providence *Journal*, and the Philadelphia *Bulletin*. However, three weeks after the ceremony and then again the following spring, the editor of *Harper's Weekly* published a sincere and thorough eulogy of the Address, and soon it was attaining recognition as a masterpiece.

At the time, Lincoln could not care much about the reception of his words. He was exhausted and ill. In the train back to Washington, he lay down with a wet towel on his head. He had caught smallpox. At that moment he was incubating it, and he was stricken down soon after he reentered the White House. Fortunately it was a mild attack, and it evoked one of his best jokes: he told his visitors, "At last I have something I can give to everybody."

9   He had more than that to give to everybody. He was a unique person, far greater than most people realize until they read his life with care. The wisdom of his policy, the sources of his statesmanship—these were things too complex to be discussed in a brief essay. But we can say something about the Gettysburg Address as a work of art.

10   A work of art. Yes: for Lincoln was a literary artist, trained both by others and by himself. The textbooks he used as a boy were full of difficult exercises and skillful devices in formal rhetoric, stressing the qualities he practiced in his own speaking: antithesis, parallelism, and verbal harmony. Then he read and reread many admirable models of thought and expression: the King James Bible, the essays of Bacon, the best plays of Shakespeare. His favorites were *Hamlet, Lear, Macbeth, Richard III,* and *Henry VIII,* which he had read dozens of times. He loved reading aloud, too, and spent hours reading poetry to his friends. (He told his partner Herndon that he preferred getting the sense of any document by reading it aloud.) Therefore his serious speeches are important parts of the long and noble classical tradition of oratory which begins in Greece, runs through Rome to the modern world, and is still capable (if we do not neglect it) of producing masterpieces.

11   The first proof of this is that the Gettysburg Address is full of quotations—or rather of adaptations—which give it strength. It is partly religious, partly (in the highest sense) political: therefore it is interwoven with memories of the Bible and memories of American history. The first and last words are Biblical cadences. Normally Lincoln did not say "fourscore" when he meant eighty; but on this solemn occasion he recalled the important dates in the Bible—such as the age of Abram when his first son was born to him, and he was "fourscore and six years old."[2] Similarly he did not say there was a chance that democracy might die out: he

------

[2] Genesis 16:16; and Exodus 7:7.

recalled the somber phrasing of the Book of Job—where Bildad speaks of the destruction of one who shall vanish without a trace, and says that "his branch shall be cut off: his remembrance shall perish from the earth."[3] Then again, the famous description of our State as "government of the people, by the people, for the people" was adumbrated by Daniel Webster in 1830 (he spoke of "the people's government, made for the people, made by the people, and answerable to the people") and then elaborated in 1854 by the abolitionist Theodore Parker (as "government of all the people, by all the people, for all the people"). There is good reason to think that Lincoln took the important phrase "under God" (which he interpolated at the last moment) from Weems, the biographer of Washington; and we know that it had been used at least once by Washington himself.

Analyzing the address further, we find that it is based on a highly 12 imaginative theme, or group of themes. The subject is—how can we put it, so as not to disfigure it?—the subject is the kinship of life and death, that mysterious linkage which we see sometimes as the physical succession of birth and death in our world, sometimes as the contrast, which is perhaps a unity, between death and immortality. The first sentence is concerned with birth:

> Our *fathers brought forth* a *new* nation, *conceived* in liberty.

The final phrase but one expresses the hope that

> this nation, under God, shall have a *new birth* of freedom.

And the last phrase of all speaks of continuing life as the triumph over death. Again and again throughout the speech, this mystical contrast and kinship reappear: "those who *gave their lives* that that nation might *live*," "the brave men *living* and *dead*," and so in the central assertion that the dead have already consecrated their own burial place, while "it is for us, the *living*, rather to be dedicated . . . to the great task remaining." The Gettysburg Address is a prose poem; it belongs to the same world as the great elegies, and the adagios of Beethoven.

---

[3] Job 18:16–17; Jeremiah 10:11; Micah 7:2

13   Its structure, however, is that of a skillfully contrived speech. The oratorical pattern is perfectly clear. Lincoln describes the occasion, dedicates the ground, and then draws a larger conclusion by calling on his hearers to dedicate themselves to the preservation of the Union. But within that, we can trace his constant use of at least two important rhetorical devices.

14   The first of these two is *antithesis:* opposition, contrast. The speech is full of it. Listen:

> The world will little *note*
>   nor long *remember*   what *we say* here
> but   it can never *forget*   what *they did* here.

And so in nearly every sentence: "brave men, *living* and *dead*"; "to *add* or *detract*." There is the antithesis of the Founding Fathers and the men of Lincoln's own time:

> Our *fathers brought forth* a new nation . . .
> now *we* are testing whether that nation . . . can *long endure.*

And there is the more terrible antithesis of those who have already died and those who still live to do their duty. Now, antithesis is the figure of contrast and conflict. Lincoln was speaking in the midst of a great civil war.

15   The other important pattern is different. It is technically called *tricolon*—the division of an idea into three harmonious parts, usually of increasing power. The most famous phrase of the Address is a tricolon:

> government of the people
>   by the people
> and   for the people.

The most solemn sentence is a tricolon:

> we cannot dedicate
> we cannot consecrate
> we cannot hallow this ground.

And above all, the last sentence (which has sometimes been criticized as too complex) is essentially two parallel phrases, with a tricolon growing out of the second and then producing another tricolon: a trunk, three branches, and a cluster of flowers. Lincoln says that it is for his hearers to be dedicated to the great task remaining before them. Then he goes on,

> that from these honored dead

—apparently he means "in such a way that from these honored dead"—

> we take increased devotion to that cause.

Next, he restates this more briefly:

> that we here highly resolve . . .

And now the actual resolution follows, in three parts of growing intensity:

> that these dead shall not have died in vain
> that this nation, under God, shall have a new birth
> of freedom

and that (one more tricolon)

> government of the people
>   by the people
> and   for the people
> shall not perish from the earth.

Now the tricolon is the figure which, through division, emphasizes basic harmony and unity. Lincoln used antithesis because he was speaking to people at war. He used the tricolon because he was hoping, planning, praying for peace.

No one thinks that when he was drafting the Gettysburg Address, 16 Lincoln deliberately looked up these quotations and consciously chose these particular patterns of thought. No, he chose the theme. From its development and from the emotional tone of the entire occasion, all the rest followed, or grew—by that marvelous process of choice and rejection which is essential to artistic creation. It does not spoil such a work of art to analyze it as closely as we have done; it is altogether fitting and proper that we should do this: for it helps us to penetrate more deeply into the rich meaning of the Gettysburg Address, and it allows us the very rare privilege of watching the workings of a great man's mind.

Sources

W. E. Barton. *Lincoln at Gettysburg*. Bobbs-Merrill. 1930.
R. P. Basler. "Abraham Lincoln's Rhetoric." *American Literature:* 11:1939–40, 167–82.
L. E. Robinson. *Abraham Lincoln as a Man of Letters*. Chicago, 1918.

There are no study questions on Highet's "The Gettysburg Address." See questions following Lincoln's "The Gettysburg Address" (648).

Four Cinderellas: Political Texts, Political Contexts

Each telling and retelling of a familiar tale incorporates something of the teller's culture and values, as does each critical interpretation. The ninth and twentieth century Chinese Cinderella tales printed here have some obvious points of similarity. Each tells of a poor, hardworking girl exploited by her wicked stepmother and stepsister(s), who is transformed into a beautiful woman through association with the supernatural, for whom she unselfishly performs good deeds. Uniquely fitted to (and identifiable by) a special slipper, she is the object of a quest by the royal ruler, who finds her and marries her. Yet each tale may be read very differently. Ning Yu's essay interprets the "nurturing woman" motif in the context of two very different Chinese cultures, imperial (ninth century) and Communist (twentieth century, even though the story is a translation of the Walt Disney version of a seventeenth century French version), and finds significant differences in the tales. Sexton's poem, "Cinderella," offers a twentieth-century American feminist interpretation.

TUAN CH'ÊNG-SHIH (ninth century)

The Chinese "Cinderella"

A mong the people of the south there is a tradition that before 1
the Ch'in and Han dynasties there was a cave-master called
Wu. The aborigines called the place the Wu cave. He married two
wives. One wife died. She had a daughter called Yeh-hsien, who
from childhood was intelligent and good at making pottery on
the wheel. Her father loved her. After some years the father died,
and she was ill-treated by her step-mother, who always made her
collect firewood in dangerous places and draw water from deep
pools. She once got a fish about two inches long, with red fins and
golden eyes. She put it into a bowl of water. It grew bigger every
day, and after she had changed the bowl several times she could
find no bowl big enough for it, so she threw it into the back pond.
Whatever food was left over from meals she put into the water to
feed it. When she came to the pond, the fish always exposed its
head and pillowed it on the bank; but when anyone else came, it
did not come out. The step-mother knew about this, but when she
watched for it, it did not once appear. So she tricked the girl, saying, "Haven't you worked hard! I am going to give you a new
dress." She then made the girl change out of her tattered clothing.
Afterwards she sent her to get water from another spring and
reckoning that it was several hundred leagues, the step-mother at
her leisure put on her daughter's clothes, hid a sharp blade up
her sleeve, and went out to the pond. She called to the fish. The
fish at once put its head out, and she chopped it off and killed it.
The fish was now more than ten feet long. She served it up and it
tasted twice as good as an ordinary fish. She hid the bones under
the dung-hill. Next day, when the girl came to the pond, no fish
appeared. She howled with grief in the open countryside, and
suddenly there appeared a man with his hair loose over his
shoulders and coarse clothes. He came down from the sky. He

consoled her, saying, "Don't howl! Your step-mother has killed the fish and its bones are under the dung. You go back, take the fish's bones and hide them in your room. Whatever you want, you only have to pray to them for it. It is bound to be granted." The girl followed his advice, and was able to provide herself with gold, pearls, dresses and food whenever she wanted them.

2   When the time came for the cave-festival, the step-mother went, leaving the girl to keep watch over the fruit-trees in the garden. She waited till the step-mother was some way off, and then went herself, wearing a cloak of stuff spun from kingfisher feathers and shoes of gold. Her step-sister recognized her and said to the step-mother, "That's very like my sister." The step-mother suspected the same thing. The girl was aware of this and went away in such a hurry that she lost one shoe. It was picked up by one of the people of the cave. When the step-mother got home, she found the girl asleep, with her arms round one of the trees in the garden, and thought no more about it.

3   This cave was near to an island in the sea. On this island was a kingdom called T'o-han. Its soldiers had subdued twenty or thirty other islands and it had a coast-line of several thousand leagues. The cave-man sold the shoe in T'o-han, and the ruler of T'o-han got it. He told those about him to put it on; but it was an inch too small for even the one among them that had the smallest foot. He ordered all the women in his kingdom to try it on; but there was not one that it fitted. It was light as down and made no noise even when treading on stone. The king of T'o-han thought the cave-man had got it unlawfully. He put him in prison and tortured him, but did not end by finding out where it had come from. So he threw it down at the wayside. Then they went everywhere[1] through all the people's houses and arrested them. If there was a woman's shoe, they arrested them and told the king of T'o-han. He thought it strange, searched the inner-rooms and found Yeh-hsien. He made her put on the shoe, and it was true.

4   Yeh-hsien then came forward, wearing her cloak spun from halcyon feathers and her shoes. She was as beautiful as a heavenly

---

[1] Something here seems to have gone slightly wrong with the text. [WALEY]

being. She now began to render service to the king, and he took the fish-bones and Yeh-hsien, and brought them back to his country.

The step-mother and step-sister were shortly afterwards 5 struck by flying stones, and died. The cave people were sorry for them and buried them in a stone-pit, which was called the Tomb of the Distressed Women. The men of the cave made mating-offerings there; any girl they prayed for there, they got. The king of T'o-han, when he got back to his kingdom made Yeh-hsien his chief wife. The first year the king was very greedy and by his prayers to the fish-bones got treasures and jade without limit. Next year, there was no response, so the king buried the fish-bones on the sea-shore. He covered them with a hundred bushels of pearls and bordered them with gold. Later there was a mutiny of some soldiers who had been conscripted and their general opened (the hiding place) in order to make better provision for his army. One night they (the bones) were washed away by the tide.

This story was told me by Li Shih-yüan, who has been in the 6 service of my family a long while. He was himself originally a man from the caves of Yung-chou and remembers many strange things of the South.

The Dust Girl

There are over a thousand variants of the familiar tale of "Cinderella." Ning Yu (for biography, see 405–18) read an anony-mous Chinese Communist translation of Walt Disney's 1949 inter-pretation to his young son, and in 1990 translated it into English for *The Essay Connection*. The Disney version has a venerable ancestry, being adapted from Charles Perrault's 1697 French translation of an even older tale. New versions are continually being written, including this one.

O nce upon a time there was a little girl whose father married 1 again after her mother's death. The stepmother had two daughters of her own, and all three of them were evil-hearted: they would bully the little girl and backbite her before her father whenever they had a chance.

2   Before long, the little girl's father followed his first wife, and the girl cried till her eyes swelled like two red peaches for she was now a poor, friendless little thing.

3   No sooner did they come home from the father's funeral than the stepmother started yelling at the poor little girl, banging the table with her fists. "How dare you think you are good enough to live in the same house with us? Go and live in the kitchen by yourself!" The elder stepsister said, "You don't deserve these good clothes either. Take them off and put on those rags and wooden shoes." The second stepsister said, "If you want to eat, you'll have to do all the chores in the house."

4   From then on, the little girl had to sleep in the kitchen, dress in rags, and wear wooden shoes. What is more, she had to get up before daybreak to fetch water from the well, start the fire, cook all the meals, wash up things and clean the whole house. The work made her very dusty and they began to call her Dust Girl.

5   The stepmother and her daughters were lazybones who loved nothing but to eat and drink and seek pleasure in parties. The two sisters would spend hours upon hours before the mirror and for good clothes they would fight each other fiercely, scratching faces and tearing hair, smashing bowls and plates, and making a mess of the house. Driven crazy by her own daughters, the stepmother would vent her anger on Dust Girl by making her mend the torn clothes and clean up the broken pieces on the floor.

6   Though Dust Girl toiled very hard in the house every day, she was given for food the leftovers from her stepmother's table. However, she was such a kind-hearted girl that she would always save something from her meager ration to offer to a poor old beggar woman.

7   One day the king gave a ball, which would last for three days, and invited all the girls in the kingdom, from whom the prince would choose a wife.

8   When Dust Girl's two stepsisters heard of the ball they were beside themselves with ecstasy and anticipation, and started another fight for the best costumes in the family wardrobe. Extremely angry at them, their mother yelled, "Fight! Fight! How can you expect to appear at such a grand ball with disheveled hair and torn faces?"

Upon hearing this, the two sisters let go of each other, and ⁹
ordered Dust Girl rudely, "Hurry up! put a lace on my new dress!"
"Be quick! shine up my dancing slippers." "Move on! Fetch me a
bowl of water to wash my face with." "Come! Come! Dress my
hair in the latest fashion."

After hours of bustle and hustle, the sisters left with their ¹⁰
mother in a carriage for the palace, but before the horses started,
the two sisters turned around and asked Dust Girl, "What do you
think? We are going to the royal palace to attend the ball while
you only deserve to watch the stove at home!"

Dust Girl sat lonely in the kitchen for a long while, staring ¹¹
into the flames. How she longed to attend that ball too! But suddenly she heard someone knocking at the door. "Who could that
be?" she asked herself. As the girl opened the door, who should
come in but the old beggar.

"Grandmother! come on in. It's so cold out there. Come and ¹²
warm yourself by the stove. I still have two pieces of bread and
let's share them for supper."

As soon as the old woman sat down, she began to ask Dust ¹³
Girl, "All the girls in the country are invited to the royal ball
tonight. Why didn't you go?"

"My two stepsisters have gone and they wanted me to stay ¹⁴
and take care of the stove. How can I go in these wooden shoes
and dusty rags, anyway?"

"But don't you want to go?" ¹⁵

"Sure. I'd love to. It'd be a great treat for me if I could simply ¹⁶
watch the people dance."

"If so, let me help you." As the old woman spoke, she ¹⁷
pointed at Dust Girl with her walking stick and the poor girl's rags
turned into a silvery satin evening dress, and her wooden shoes
into a pair of crystal slippers.

"I won't let you go to the palace on foot either," said the old ¹⁸
woman, picking up a pumpkin and rolling it out of the door. The
pumpkin at once turned into a gold carriage; she pointed her
walking stick toward the corner of the kitchen and eight mice ran
out of the hole in the wall to become eight beautiful horses; she
then pointed her stick to the sleeping cat, and the cat woke up to
be a handsome coachman. "All right, my child," said the old

woman. "Now you may go to the palace. But, remember, you must come back before midnight, for at that moment all these things will return to their original shapes."

19   In the palace, Dust Girl outshone all the other girls who came to the ball from all over the country. Though terribly jealous of her success, her two stepsisters never dreamed that the most beautiful girl at the ball was none but Dust Girl.

20   But the prince came to Dust Girl, bowed, shook her hand, and asked to dance with her. Dust Girl had the most wonderful time in her life that night, but she did not forget the old woman's advice and bid the prince good-by shortly before midnight. When she got home in her gold carriage, it had just struck twelve. The pumpkin was back on the table, the mice in their hole, the cat to her sleep, and Dust Girl herself was back in her old rags and wooden shoes again. Soon her stepmother and stepsisters were back and they ordered Dust Girl to help them undress saying, "Oh, you are ugly! especially after we saw those beautiful goddess-like ladies in the palace."

21   The next evening, Dust Girl went to the palace again; and again she returned home before midnight. The third was the last evening of the ball, and the prince danced with Dust Girl all night. Dust Girl was so happy that she forgot the old woman's warning till the clock struck the first stroke of twelve. She then suddenly remembered her warning, tore herself away from the prince, and rushed out of the palace. The prince tried to run after her but was only fast enough to find a crystal slipper that she lost in her hurry.

22   However, the prince had made up his mind; the girl in the crystal slippers should be his wife. But how could he find that girl again? The king's men were sent with the slipper to check every house in the kingdom—to look for the girl whose foot fit the slipper exactly. Whoever that girl might have been, she was to become the prince's wife.

23   The king's men had tried almost every house in the country when they finally came to the house where Dust Girl and her stepmother and stepsisters lived. The two sisters shouted at each other in fighting to be first to try on the crystal slipper, but their shouts turned into wails when they found out that neither one of them could cram her foot into the slipper.

Disappointed, the king's men asked whether there was any 24 other girl in the house.

The stepmother answered, "There is only one more ugly 25 servant girl. But she is so dusty that she is not fit to be seen by gentlemen like you. What is more, she never had any crystal slippers and she never went to the palace."

"But the king's order is to have every girl in the country try 26 on this slipper," said the king's men.

Reluctantly the stepmother called out Dust Girl. But behold! 27 how perfectly the slipper fit Dust Girl's foot—neither tight nor loose!

As Dust Girl was taken into the palace, the stepmother's 28 and the stepsisters' mouths became lopsided because of jealousy.

NING YU

(For biographical information, see page 405.) Ning Yu explains how he wrote this essay: "A writer once said, 'It is hard to decide what should be put on paper, but it is even harder to decide what should be left in the inkwell.' Yet every writer has to make such hard decisions. I knew my audience for this comparative study of the two Chinese versions of Cinderella would be American college students who didn't know much about Chinese culture, especially the Maoist ideology. So I knew I had to supply brief background knowledge. But how brief is too little, and how brief is just enough? I had to find out by writing.

"The early Chinese version is not so difficult to present because the historical events about Ch'in Shi Huang's effort to preserve his dynasty are generally regarded as facts, and there is nothing subtle about the story. However, my interpretation of the second piece had to be very sensitive because I do not want my readers to misunderstand the translator-editor of the tale as an unscrupulous hack who twisted the original out of shape to please the party. Might he be smuggling Western humanism ('love is classless,' for example) into China? Or, on the contrary, might he be an unconscious victim of the 'Big Brother's propaganda' who changed the Western tale because his politically-influenced taste demanded it? To clarify the point, I felt I had to expound the effects of 'Big Brother's propaganda' first, citing long passages from Orwell's *1984*.

"When I finished the first draft the paper was off-balance; I had spent five pages on the early Chinese version and ten on the later one. By defending the translator I had also digressed from the intended focus of the essay, the common elements in the two tales. So I eliminated the defense and took the risk of having the translator's role misunderstood. While I gained the sharpened focus of a shapely essay, I still wonder whether it is justifiable to sacrifice one element in the interests of a clear and balanced essay. Taking such a risk is painful. But taking any risk is also exciting."

❄ The Nurturing Woman Rewarded: A Study of Two Chinese Cinderellas

1   The Victorian collector Joseph Jacobs might be inaccurate but he was by no means exaggerating when he said that the Cinderella story he was printing was "an English version of an Italian adaptation of a Spanish translation of a Latin version of a Hebrew translation of an Arabic translation of an Indian original." According to Jane Yolen, a noted American author and critic of children's books, "over five hundred variants [of Cinderella] have been located by folklorists in Europe alone" (23) and the earliest datable literary source is a ninth-century Chinese tale.

2   Perhaps it is because of the great variety of versions that critics such as Jack Zipes (160–182) and Madonna Kolbenschlag (53–58) are not satisfied with Bruno Bettelheim's famous and insightful psychological study of Cinderella as a model case of "sibling rivalry and Oedipal conflicts"; one is compelled by the cross-cultural development of the tale to elevate the study of Cinderella beyond Bettelheim's personal and psychological level. It is the purpose of this essay to examine the ninth-century and the twentieth-century Chinese versions of the story against their respective ideological backgrounds, and to point out some common features of the two Chinese versions that are chronologically so remote and textually so different.

In the early Chinese version of the story, there are many 3
elements to which the orthodox Freudian approach, which Bettelheim used so well to analyze the Grimm, Basile, and Perrault
versions, is not sufficient for a thorough and convincing interpretation. Sibling rivalry, for example, is hardly an issue; the single
sentence that Yeh-hsien's stepsister utters during her extremely
brief appearance in the tale does not reveal any hostility between
the two girls. On the contrary, that the stepsister referred to Yeh-
hsien as "my sister" seems to imply that the relationship between
the two girls is much friendlier than the one between the stepmother and the stepdaughter. Neither is it convincing to say that
Yeh-hsien projected hatred on her stepmother because she herself
hated the stepmother as the competitor for the father's love, for
while the father was alive, though he had already remarried, he
loved Yeh-hsien. This is a significant difference between the early
Chinese version and the Western variants of the tale; the girl began
to suffer only after the father's death.

On the other hand, if we study the early tale against the 4
Chinese cultural and historical background, using some psycho-
analytic technique on the auxiliary level, we may come closer to
the real message of that specific version.

Though the early Chinese version of "Cinderella" was writ- 5
ten in the ninth century, the events in the story "happened" before
the Ch'in and Han dynasties (B.C. 306–221, and B.C. 206–A.D. 220).
Ch'in dynasty was the first dynasty in Chinese history when
China became a united kingdom under a central power, and Ch'in
Shi Huang (Ch'in the First Emperor) was known for his conquests
of the other contemporary super-power states and his uniting
China into a central kingdom. After he united China, one of the
first things that Ch'in Shi Huang did was to put hundreds of girls
from the noble families of those states into his harem, reportedly
to reproduce over a hundred sons (no one has taken the trouble
to count the daughters). The idea behind that was the more sons
he had, the longer his dynasty, the rule of his family over China,
could be preserved.

Now the king of T'o-han in the early Chinese version had 6
just done something very similar. He had a strong kingdom whose
"soldiers had subdued twenty or thirty other islands and it had a
coastline of several thousand leagues," a coastline as long as that

of China. As the ruler of a super power, the king of T'o-han may very well have been concerned with the continuation of the rule of his family. That's why, probably, he had quite a number of royal concubines. Then why did he make Yeh-hsien, the ninth-century Chinese Cinderella, his "chief wife"? What was so special about Yeh-hsien that she was made the head of those royal baby-makers?

7   To answer those questions one must first study the real tension between the girl and the stepmother, which is, as I noted earlier, neither the Oedipal complex of the girl nor the sibling rivalry between her and her stepsisters and stepmother. It is, I believe, the fact that the girl is a nurturing figure while the stepmother is a destroyer of life; the girl fed the fish but the stepmother killed it.

8   The nurturing power of Yeh-hsien, as demonstrated in the raising of the fish, is extraordinary; with no special feed—"whatever food was left over from meals she put in the water to feed it"—she made the fish grow from "two inches" to "ten feet" in a very short period of time. The manner in which the girl kept the fish is analogous to the way a mother conceives, delivers, and rears a child. When the fish was of fetal size—two inches—it was kept in a bowl, the shape of which makes it reasonable for one to associate it with the womb. Then, as the fish grew, the bowls became larger and larger; this parallels the swelling belly of a pregnant woman. Finally, when the fish became so big that no bowl was big enough to contain it, it was thrown into the pond, a new and open world compared with bowls, a process similar to the birth of a child—a new life being transferred from the mother's body to the open world. Yet the fish was to be nurtured by the girl; the way it "pillowed" its head on the bank when the girl fed it is exactly the way a baby leans its head on its mother's arm while feeding at its mother's breasts.

9   The mother-child relationship between the fish and the girl is further indicated by the fish's instinctive knowledge and trust of Yeh-hsien's nurturing power, just as a baby knows its mother by instinct. What is more revealing, the fish wouldn't trust anyone but the girl: "When she came to the pond, the fish always exposed its head and pillowed it on the bank; but when anyone else came, it did not come out."

10   The stepmother is such an "anyone else." When she came to the pond and "watched for" the fish, "it did not once appear." She

knew that the girl had an unusual power and the fish might have received some of this power from the girl because she had nurtured it. The stepmother's killing, serving, and eating the fish reveal a strong desire in her to transplant the girl's unusual nurturing power to herself. But to say the stepmother lacked the nurturing power that Yeh-hsien enjoyed does not mean that the stepmother was sterile. She had her own daughter. However, to be able to have a daughter is no womanly virtue in ancient China, unless the daughter possessed the strong nurturing power that Yeh-hsien did.

Then, why do I suggest that, being able to "bear" and rear a 11 fish, Yeh-hsien is supposed to be more nurturing than the stepmother who had borne and raised a real daughter? The reason is this. The Chinese word for fish is *yu*, which is homonymic with another Chinese word, *yu*, meaning "abundance." Therefore, the fish is regarded in Chinese culture as an auspicious thing. That's why up to this day, fish is still necessarily the first course for a family banquet in the Chinese New Year's Eve; it presages a prosperous new year for the family. In some areas in China, where fish is not available to lower and middle class families, a wooden fish is served before any other dishes—to be looked at, and to transmit the auspicious atmosphere to the other courses, as that propitious moment will transmit its blessing to the many days of the new year.

However, for the Chinese family to be truly prosperous, the 12 abundance in wealth alone is not enough; it must be accompanied by the abundance in offspring. That's why many Chinese New Year pictures have in them a fat boy straddling the back of a carp, a theme that presages both the abundance in wealth and the abundance in male offspring in the family. So in the Chinese culture, as a good omen for the future, the fish and the boy are inseparable. In this sense Yeh-hsien is not simply nurturing, but the mystic mother-child relationship between her and the fish also symbolizes her great potential of bringing an abundance of male offspring into her future husband's family. It is small wonder then that she was finally "rewarded" for the virtue of being nurturing, the highest position that a Chinese woman could expect then—to be the chief baby producer of a king. In contrast, the stepmother who had only one daughter was certainly not nurturing enough, and her killing the fish alienated her further from the category of virtuous women.

13   The twentieth-century Chinese version is a mixed rendering of the European Grimm version and the North American Walt Disney version. The translator was obviously unaware of the existence of the early Chinese Cinderella when he introduced the story from the West to China. In the new Chinese version there are more details identical with or similar to those in the Grimm and the Walt Disney versions than those in the old Chinese version: the presence of the fairy godmother, the girl's ill treatment before her father's death, the crystal slipper rather than the embroidered slipper, the three-day bride-finding ball, the pumpkin carriage, the mice horses, and the cat coachman, etc. But, of course, there are many things in that version which are unique to the drastically changed Chinese ideology after 1949.

14   The Chinese Communist Party has claimed that the 1949 Revolution is a proletarian revolution successfully carried out with the help of the ally of the proletariat—the poor and lower-middle-class Chinese peasants—and under the leadership of the Party, which is both the son and the leader of the proletariat and the peasants. It goes without saying that after 1949 the predominant ideology is that of the proletarian revolution. The propaganda function of literature is so emphasized by the Party that it is no exaggeration to say that since 1949 every poem, every story, every play and every novel must reflect and enhance the various aspects of that ideology. The twentieth-century Chinese translation of Cinderella is no exception.

15   The depiction of Cinderella as an oppressed and exploited proletarian is in the main a twentieth-century Chinese invention. The new Chinese version follows the trend started by the Walt Disney version to minimize the girl's upper-class background by omitting her life before her father's second marriage. Thus the girl is transformed into a member of the working class who has to sell her labor for her survival. "If you want to eat," says her second stepsister, "you'll have to do all the chores in the house." Her job was no longer the meaningless torture of picking lentils out of ash, but the real work of a housekeeper-cook-servant.

16   Consequently, the stepmother and her two daughters are no longer the selfish but forgivable friends of the Perrault version, nor the sadistic "sibling rivals" of the Grimm version, but Dust Girl's oppressors, exploiters, and class enemies. They have all the

characteristics of the parasitic leisure class. They are lazy, vain, and cruel. They never work to get what they consume, but spend hours before the mirror or in pleasure-seeking parties; they make a mess of the house fighting for the best dress but order Dust Girl to clean up the mess; they treat Dust Girl like dirt because they have the power in the house.

Yes, power is the essential issue in this version of the tale. It 17 is interesting to note that the way they treat Dust Girl changes drastically after her father's death. Though when he was still alive they had already been bullying and backbiting Dust Girl, it is after the father died and they seized the absolute power in the house that their maltreatment of the girl assumed the aspects of class oppression and class exploitation. Unlike their counterparts in the Western versions, they maltreated Dust Girl not for the "fun" of it, but to keep her from rebelling against them. The excuse they used to justify their behavior is the one that any advantaged class adopts to persuade the disadvantaged class—you are not good enough to be our equals; therefore, you don't deserve to live as we do.

Such a "Marxist" reading of the new Chinese version seems 18 to be endorsed by its ending. Unlike the Grimm version, which ends with the couple being married in the church; unlike the Walt Disney version which ends with the cute cliché that "Cinderella became the prince's bride, and lived happily ever after—and the little pet mice lived in the palace and were happy ever after, too"; the new Chinese version ends with Dust Girl going into the palace—the proletariat rising to power. Of course, the story is nevertheless a fairy tale, and the theme is still a poor girl marrying a prince, but the omitting of the wedding scene deemphasizes the marriage theme and makes it possible for one to read for the underlying power struggle.

Though the fairy godmother is obviously transplanted from 19 the Grimm version and the Disney version, the new Chinese version has made a significant change in her. Here she is an old beggar, rather than the spirit of the dead mother, or just some goddess who takes pity on the poor girl. On the surface level of the story, the change may seem trivial, but in fact, the change in status of the fairy godmother has changed the relationship between her and the girl, which parallels that between the party and the proletariat. As I noted earlier, the Party claims itself to be both the son and the leader of the Chinese proletariat and the poor peasants: as the son, it must be nurtured and supported by the people; as the leader, the word in Chinese having a connotation very similar to the German word *führer*, it has absolute power over the people. In order to get to the promised land free from exploitation or oppression, the proletariat must first nurture and then obey the Party, and this is exactly what happens between the beggar-grandmother and Dust Girl.

20   The old woman revealed herself as an omnipotent goddess only after the girl had treated her kindly for some extended period of time. Before that, the girl nurtured the old woman out of her own "meager ration." Afterward, the girl strictly followed the old woman's order; the minute she began to forget her warnings, she was stripped of the magic power borrowed from the godmother/Big-Brother figure. However, the girl withstood the trial and proved her loyalty to the Party to be sound, and as a reward, she went into the center of political power.

21   The ideologies reflected in the two Chinese versions are very different—the main concern of one is the preservation of an imperial dynasty, while that of the other is how the proletariat seizes power under the leadership of the Party. But one thing is common to both—they both reflect an underlying power struggle, the conscientious strife either to seize or to maintain power. Without nurturing virtue, a woman is no good whether in the time "before Ch'in and Han dynasties" or after the Communist Revolution. That is why the Chinese translator added that essential virtue to the Western variants that he worked on. The ideology reflected in the new story is very different from the one reflected in the old story.

22   The two young female protagonists in the two Chinese versions are also as different as possible. But because they both act in fictive worlds of power struggles, they are doomed to have something in common too. In order for them to be rewarded, they must have a nurturing power, whether to nurture male offspring or to nurture a class comrade or leader. That is probably why the episode in the new Chinese version in which the girl not only *fed* the beggar, but also fed her with *leftovers* from the meals is something the Grimm and Disney versions do not have but something

the old Chinese version has as its central issue. This nurturing power, the power to rear either a powerful party or powerful princes out of their own meager supplies, is the major virtue that is demanded of a Chinese woman who is to receive the highest reward possible—to have power over men and women alike, except, of course, the person or party who gave her the power in the first place.

Cinderella, on the whole, is a "virtue rewarded" story, but to say so to the hundreds of variants may sound like hasty generalization. However, to study the variants against their individual cultures and to examine what particular virtue "deserves" to be "rewarded" in that particular culture is sound research, because in this way only can the richness of the great variety of the tale be revealed to the reader. 23

Works Cited

Kolbenschlag, Madonna. *Kiss Sleeping Beauty Good-Bye: Breaking the Spell of Feminine Myths and Models.* New York: Doubleday, 1979.

Yolen, Jane. "America's 'Cinderella'." *Children's Literature in Education* 8 (1977) 22–29.

Zipes, Jack David. *Breaking the Magic Spell: Radical Theories of Folk and Fairy Tales.* Austin, Texas: U of Texas P, 1979.

ANNE SEXTON

Sexton was born in 1928 in Newton, Massachusetts, grew up in Wellesley, and dropped out after a year at Garland Junior College to marry in 1948. Throughout the 1950s she adopted the socially sanctioned life pattern expected of women of the time—rearing two daughters and, stunningly attractive, working occasionally as a fashion model. But her inner life was "troubled and chaotic," according to her best friend, poet Maxine Kumin; she was intermittently hospitalized, seeking "sanctuary" from "voices that urged her to die." Her psychiatrist encouraged her to study poetry writing, which she did, with Robert Lowell and John Clellon Holmes, and in 1960 she published her first book, *To Bedlam and Part Way Back*. Her third book, *Live or Die*, won the Pulitzer Prize in 1966 and astonishing fame for this poet who had great difficulty making the transformation from housewife to serious writer. Indeed, in 1971 she published *Transformations*, adapting familiar fairy tales about women such as Cinderella, Snow White, and Briar Rose, beautiful dolls and objects and prizes of male conquest, into social criticism of the lives and expectations of contemporary women.

Sexton, reared as a Roman Catholic, continued to write what became known as "confessional poetry," focusing with a combination of pathos, sardonic humor, and disillusioned worldliness on "self-abasement, sin, sexual transgression, and bodily disgust." She published *The Book of Folly* in 1972 and *Death Notebooks* in 1974. But stature as a distinguished and controversial artist whose topics included menstruation, abortion, masturbation, incest, adultery, and drug addiction further incited her troubled spirit. Divorced at her insistence in her forties, dependent on alcohol, and despondent, she committed suicide in 1975. *The Awful Rowing Toward God* and *Mercy Street* were published posthumously; her work continues to be a vital force in American letters.

Cinderella

1   Y ou always read about it:
        the plumber with twelve children
    who wins the Irish Sweepstakes.
    From toilets to riches.
    That story.

2   Or the nursemaid,
    some luscious sweet from Denmark
    who captures the oldest son's heart.
    From diapers to Dior.
    That story.

3   Or a milkman who serves the wealthy,
    eggs, cream, butter, yogurt, milk,

the white truck like an ambulance
who goes into real estate
and makes a pile.
From homogenized to martinis at lunch.

Or the charwoman   4
who is on the bus when it cracks up
and collects enough from the insurance.
From mops to Bonwit Teller.
That story.

Once   5
the wife of a rich man was on her deathbed
and she said to her daughter Cinderella:
Be devout. Be good. Then I will smile
down from heaven in the seam of a cloud.
The man took another wife who had
two daughters, pretty enough
but with hearts like blackjacks.
Cinderella was their maid.
She slept on the sooty hearth each night
and walked around looking like Al Jolson.
Her father brought presents home from town,
jewels and gowns for the other women
but the twig of a tree for Cinderella.
She planted that twig on her mother's grave
and it grew to a tree where a white dove sat.
Whenever she wished for anything the dove
would drop it like an egg upon the ground.
The bird is important, my dears, so heed him.

Next came the ball, as you all know.   6
It was a marriage market.
The prince was looking for a wife.
All but Cinderella were preparing
and gussying up for the big event.
Cinderella begged to go too.
Her stepmother threw a dish of lentils
into the cinders and said: Pick them

up in an hour and you shall go.
The white dove brought all his friends;
all the warm wings of the fatherland came,
and picked up the lentils in a jiffy.
No, Cinderella, said the stepmother,
you have no clothes and cannot dance.
That's the way with stepmothers.

7   Cinderella went to the tree at the grave
and cried forth like a gospel singer:
Mama! Mama! My turtledove,
send me to the prince's ball!
The bird dropped down a golden dress
and delicate little gold slippers.
Rather a large package for a simple bird.
So she went. Which is no surprise.
Her stepmother and sisters didn't
recognize her without her cinder face
and the prince took her hand on the spot
and danced with no other the whole day.

8   As nightfall came she thought she'd better
get home. The prince walked her home
and she disappeared into the pigeon house
and although the prince took an axe and broke
it open she was gone. Back to her cinders.
These events repeated themselves for three days.
However on the third day the prince
covered the palace steps with cobbler's wax
and Cinderella's gold shoe stuck upon it.

9   Now he would find whom the shoe fit
and find his strange dancing girl for keeps.
He went to their house and the two sisters
were delighted because they had lovely feet.
The eldest went into a room to try the slipper on
but her big toe got in the way so she simply
sliced it off and put on the slipper.
The prince rode away with her until the white dove

told him to look at the blood pouring forth.
That is the way with amputations.
They don't just heal up like a wish.
The other sister cut off her heel
but the blood told as blood will.
The prince was getting tired.
He began to feel like a shoe salesman.
But he gave it one last try.
This time Cinderella fit into the shoe
like a love letter into its envelope.

At the wedding ceremony   10
the two sisters came to curry favor
and the white dove pecked their eyes out.
Two hollow spots were left
like soup spoons.

Cinderella and the prince   11
lived, they say, happily ever after,
like two dolls in a museum case
never bothered by diapers or dust,
never arguing over the timing of an egg,
never telling the same story twice,
never getting a middle-aged spread,
their darling smiles pasted on for eternity.

Regular Bobbsey Twins.   12
That story.

For Writing

1. Pick a historical document, either published (such as the Declaration
of Independence) or unpublished. An unpublished document might be a
photograph or letter your family may own that concerns an event that has
passed into history, such as an invention—the atomic bomb, personal
computers, a particular car; the Great Depression or other period of unemployment; or a war—the Civil War, World War I or II, the Korean War,
the Vietnam War; or a major sporting or literary event; or the outcome of
an election. Flesh out the meaning of the event through consulting family

members involved in the document (either as its producers or subjects) and appropriate reference works and Web sites, on or offline. Then, write a paper explaining what you've come to understand about the event, using the document as the focal point of your discussion. (See Gilbert Highet's essay on the "Declaration of Independence" for a very detailed model of this type of interpretation.)

2.   Write your own version of a fairy tale or some other familiar tale, such as a fable or a Br'er Rabbit or Dr. Seuss story or Maxine Hong Kingston's "On Discovery" either for adults or children. Then write an analysis comparing your version with the earlier one. What changes—of subject, character, emphasis, or style—did you make, and why?

3.   Translate a favorite poem or short story from a language with which you have a comfortable reading knowledge into English, or vice versa. What changes have you felt it necessary to make between the original and the translation? Have you made these in the interests of fidelity to the original meaning? Original language? The artistry of the translation? Cultural differences? Or according to some other criteria?

4.   Write a poem or short story inspired by a favorite poem or short story, but not intentionally duplicating it. What changes of subject, character, emphasis, or style have you made, and why?

5.   With a classmate or small group, find a photograph, cartoon, advertisement, or painting that tells a story. Does it have the same meanings to everyone who sees it? Using this as the source for your writing, tell the story of the picture. This can be either a brand new story, serious or comical, or a reinterpretation of a story you already know, whether a folk or fairy tale, TV commercial, or serious work of fiction.

16 Death of a Salesman: *Responses to An American Classic*

In combination with "Building and Writing" (82–88), the excerpt from Arthur Miller's autobiography, *Timebends,* the five readings that follow focus on the genesis, history, reception, and critical reactions to *Death of a Salesman* over a fifty-year period. That this play continues to speak to audiences today, as it did to theatergoers over a half-century ago, demonstrates that it taps into America's deepest values, aspirations, and sense of family, and of work. If you have read or seen the *Death of a Salesman,* the pieces that follow will make particular sense—singly or in combination—as biography, history, reviews, and criticism from the perspectives of cultural history and of feminism. If you haven't seen the play, these commentaries written from biographical, historical, and critical perspectives should encourage you to watch a videotape or a live production of the play, or both.

As the following readings indicate, *Death of a Salesman* was recognized as a masterpiece of theater from its first appearance on Broadway in 1949. Brooks Atkinson's opening night review establishes the grounds for the next half-century of commentary: "By common consent, this is one of the finest dramas in the whole range of the American theater"—in part because Miller "is writing as an American with an affectionate understanding of American family people and their family problems." In reviewing a play the audience is unfamiliar with, it's necessary to provide—as Atkinson does—information about the *themes* ("the life and death of a traveling salesman," Willy Loman) and *plot* (how and for what did he live? Why did he die?), and to *characterize the major characters* and *delineate their relationships* ("worn-out" Willy, crawling home to die; living in a "world of illusion" like his son, the popular Biff; sustained by Linda, his "warmly devoted" wife). Without giving away the play's secrets or its ending, the reviewer also has to offer sufficient *evaluation of the play and its acting* to enable readers to decide whether or not to see the play themselves. Thus Atkinson concludes that Arthur Miller has told Willy's story with "compassion" and "decent respect for Willy's dignity as a man," that Lee J. Cobb, who played Willy, "fills the play with so much solid humanity" that although a business failure, in "terms of life he is a hero." Atkinson's judgment, like Ben Brantley's comparable judgment fifty years later ("Attention Must Be Paid, Again"), makes us want to rush out and buy tickets—"When people hurt as Willy does, it is inhuman to look away." Because Brantley, writing in 1999, can assume that his readers know the play, he has space to *sketch in other characters* (Happy, the younger son as vulnerable as his father; Charley, "Willy's gruff, argumentative and ultimately beneficent next-door neighbor"), to *describe the staging and sets* ("rooms of the Lomans' house as moving platforms that shift into and out of focus, just as Willy himself is unable to remain fixed in an immediate reality"); and to *assess its long-term significance.*

John Lahr's "Making Willy Loman" presents an engaging history of *Death of a Salesman* to show how it was written ("Where does the alchemy of a great play begin?") and received ("Why is *Death of a Salesman* such a great play?") This was published in the *New Yorker* January 25, 1999, shortly after the fiftieth-anniversary production of *Death of a Salesman* opened on Broadway (which Brantley reviewed). The evidence that Lahr produces from Miller's writer's notebook, his 1987 autobiography, *Timebends,* interviews, biographical evidence, examinations of various drafts of the play, and quotations from directors and critics, encourages thoughtful contemplation of this most moving, thought-provoking play: " 'It is a combination of guilt (of failure), hate, and love—all in conflict that [Willy] resolves by 'accomplishing' a [$]20,000 death'" through committing suicide, explains Miller. Lahr expands, "In death, Willy is worth more than in life. His suicide is the ultimate expression of his confusion of success with love and also his belief in winning at all costs"—motifs of American tragedy worth seeing on stage at all costs.

Brenda Murphy's "Willy Loman: Icon of Business Culture" complements Lahr's essay by offering an historical review of the American business community's uncomfortable reaction to *Death of a Salesman*, particularly its central character, a defeated traveling salesman. The "American way of life is identified with the salesman," whom Willy represents, says Murphy, and because "he has failed in business . . . the wages of sin is death." Murphy shows how the business world tried to dissociate itself from Willy, interpreting the play as an "individualized tragedy": "'It does not follow'" said a writer in *Women's Wear Daily*, "'that all salesmen necessarily are discarded to the ashcan after thirty-five years of service for one firm, that they crack mentally and that they dash themselves to pieces on a mad and suicidal ride to the hereafter.'" Business executives supported a rebuttal to be shown with the 1950 film adaptation of the play, using quotations from New York's City College Business School professors who "blithely explained that Willy Loman was entirely atypical . . . [That] nowadays selling was a fine profession with limitless spiritual compensations as well as financial ones." Notes Murphy dryly, the professors "all sounded like Willy Loman with a diploma. Only when Miller threatened to sue did Columbia withdraw the short film." Presenting evidence from a half-century of business publications, Murphy concludes that "To read these . . . is to discover a mindset that simultaneously loathes Willy Loman and identifies with him. The writers want to put as much distance between themselves and what Willy stands for—failure and death—but they can't help embracing him like a brother."

In contrast to the business perspective on *Death of a Salesman*, which Murphy presents but does not share, is Valerie M. Smith's feminist reaction to the play, "Death of a Salesman's Wife." Smith's critical analysis shows the destructive consequences of the sexism of Willy Loman and his two sons, Biff and Happy. In struggling to live up to "outmoded conceptions of masculinity" Willy "destroys himself through his inability to change"; Biff and Happy "nearly destroy themselves in their attempt to live up to his expectations"; and Linda, trying desperately to "smooth things over, conciliate, act the part of the submissive wife," contributes to the destruction of all the family members, including herself. The five pieces in this chapter represent only a fraction of the many ways it is possible to respond to a rich, and enriching, work of literature—a work that reaches through time, culture, class, and gender to resonate in our hearts.

JOHN LAHR

Lahr was born in 1941 into a theatrical family, the son of Bert Lahr, the comic actor best known for his role as the Cowardly Lion in *The Wizard of Oz*. Educated at Yale (B.A.) and Oxford (M.A.), Lahr has devoted his career to the theater, writing inspired work for and about the stage that conveys the flavors of the live perform-ance. He served as literary advisor to two distinguished theaters, the Tyrone Guthrie in Minneapolis (1968) and the Lincoln Center Theater in New York (1969–71). He has written numerous movie scripts, including *Sticky My Fingers, Fleet My Feet*, a 1971 Academy Award nominee, and co-produced the 1987 film *Prick Up Your Ears*, based on his 1978 biography of Joe Orton, with the same title. His stage adaptations include *Accidental Death of an Anarchist, The Manchurian Candidate*, and *The Bluebird of Unhappiness: A Woody Allen Revue*. He has published two novels and fifteen books on the theater, including *Notes on a Cowardly Lion* (1969), a biography of his father. Lahr's award-winning *Dame Edna Everage and the Rise of Western Civilization: Backstage with Barry Humphries* (1992) is a pseudo-biography of this fictive character and an analysis of Humphries' performances as England's favorite drag queen, who "has taken us on that giddy journey only a great clown can make with the public—to the frontiers of the marvellous."

In his role as *New Yorker* drama critic (since 1992), Lahr—whose own father, "a friendly absence," sometimes forgot his child's name—explained how Arthur Miller created the play that focuses on another father, absent but well-meaning. In "Making Willy Loman," Lahr explores Arthur Miller's sixty-six-page writer's notebook on *Death of a Salesman*, which the playwright kept during the genesis and creation of the play. Lahr supple-ments the notebook with excerpts from Miller's autobiography, *Timebends* (see 82–88), his own interpretation of the play and Miller's life, historical information about the theater of the time, and quotations from the play itself.

Making Willy Loman

1   In his notebook for "Death of a Salesman"—a sixty-six-page document chronicling the play's creation, which is kept with his papers at the University of Texas at Austin—he wrote, "He

who understands everything about his subject cannot write it. I write as much to discover as to explain." After that first day of inspiration, it took Miller six weeks to call forth the second act and to make Willy remember enough "so he would kill himself." The form of the play—where past and present coalesce in a lyrical dramatic arc—was one that Miller felt he'd been "searching for since the beginning of my writing life." "Death of a Salesman" seems to spill out of Willy's panic-stricken, protean imagination, and not out of a playwright's detached viewpoint. "The play is written from the sidewalk instead of from a skyscraper," Miller says of its first-person urgency. But, ironically, it was from the deck of a skyscraper that Miller contemplated beginning his drama, in a kind of Shakespearean foreshadowing of Willy's suicidal delirium. The notebook's first entry reads:

> Scene 1—Atop Empire State. 2 guards "Who will die today? It's that kind of day . . . fog, and poor visibility. They like to jump into a cloud. Who will it be today?"

As Miller navigated his way through the rush of characters and plot ideas, the notebook acted as ballast. "In every scene remember his size, ugliness," Miller reminds himself about Loman on its second page. "Remember his own attitude. Remember *pity*." He analyzes his characters' motives. "Willy wants his sons to destroy his failure," he writes, and on a later page, "Willy resents Linda's unbroken, patient forgiveness (knowing there must be great hidden hatred for him in her heart)." In Miller's notebook, characters emerge sound and fully formed. For instance, of Willy's idealized elder son, Biff, who is a lost soul fallen from his high-school glory and full of hate for his father, he writes, "Biff is travelled, oppressed by guilt of failure, of not making money although a kind of indolence pleases him: an easygoing way of life. . . . Truthfully, Biff is not really bright enough to make a businessman. *Wants everything too fast.*" Miller also talks to himself about the emotional stakes and the trajectory of scenes:

> Have it happen that Willy's life is in Biff's hands— aside from Biff succeeding. There is Willy's guilt to Biff re: The Woman. But is that retrievable? There is Biff's disdain for Willy's character, his false aims, his pretense and these Biff cannot finally give up or alter. Discover the link between Biff's work views and his anti-work feelings.

3   Although the notebook begins with a series of choppy asides and outlines, it soon becomes an expansive, exact handwritten log of Miller's contact with his inner voices. For instance, it reveals the development of Charley, Loman's benevolent next-door neighbor, whose laconic evenhandedness was, in Miller's eyes, partly a projection of his own father. Charley speaks poignantly to Biff at Willy's graveside ("Nobody dast blame this man"); what appears in the last scene as a taut and memorable nine-line speech, a kind of eulogy, was mined from words (here indicated in italics) that were part of a much longer improvisation in the notebook:

> A salesman doesn't build anything, *he don't put a bolt to a nut* or a seed in the ground. A man who doesn't build anything must be liked. He must be cheerful on bad days. Even calamities mustn't break through. Cause one thing, he has got to be liked. *He don't tell you the law or give you medicine.* So there's no rock bottom to your life. All you know is that on good days or bad, you gotta come in cheerful. No calamity must be permitted to break through, Cause one thing, always, you're a man who's gotta be believed. You're way out there *riding on a smile and a shoeshine. And when they start not smilin' back,* the sky falls in. *And then you get a couple of spots on your hat, and you're finished. Cause there's no rock bottom to your life.*

4   Here, as in all his notes for the play, Miller's passion and his flow are apparent in the surprising absence of cross-outs; the pages exude a startling alertness. He is listening not just to the voices of his characters but to the charmed country silence around him, which seems to define his creative state of grace:

> Roxbury—At night the insects softly thumping the screens like a blind man pushing with his fingers in the dark. . . . The crickets, frogs, whippoorwills altogether, a scream from the breast of the earth when everyone is gone. The evening sky, faded gray, like the sea pressing up against the windows, or an opaque gray screen. (Through which someone is looking in at me?) . . .

5   Where does the alchemy of a great play begin? The seeds of "Death of a Salesman" were planted decades before Miller stepped into his

cabin. "Selling was in the air through my boyhood," says Miller, whose father, Isidore, was the salesman-turned-owner of the Miltex Coat and Suit Company, which was a thriving enough business to provide the family with a spacious apartment on 110th Street in Harlem, a country bungalow, and a limousine and driver. "The whole idea of selling successfully was very important." Just as Miller was entering his teens, however, his father's business was wiped out by the Depression. Isidore's response was silence and sleep ("My father had trouble staying awake"); his son's response was anger. "I had never raised my voice against my father, nor did he against me, then or ever," wrote Miller, who had to postpone going to college for two years—until 1934—because "nobody was in possession of the fare." "As I knew perfectly well, it was not he who angered me, only his failure to cope with his fortune's collapse," Miller went on in his autobiography. "Thus I had two fathers, the real one and the metaphoric, and the latter I resented because he did not know how to win out over the general collapse."

"Death of a Salesman" is a lightning rod both for a father's 6 bewilderment ("What's the secret?" Willy asks various characters) and for a son's fury at parental powerlessness ("You fake! You phoney little fake!" Biff tells Willy when they finally square off, in Act II). After the play's success, Miller's mother, Augusta, found an early manuscript called "In Memoriam," a forgotten autobiographical fragment that Miller had written when he was about seventeen. The piece, which was published in these pages in 1995, is about a Miltex salesman called Schoenzeit, who had once asked Miller for subway fare when Miller was helping him carry samples to an uptown buyer. The real Schoenzeit killed himself the next day by throwing himself in front of the El train; the character's "dejected soul"—a case of exhaustion masquerading as gaiety—is the first sighting of what would become Willy Loman. "His emotions were displayed at the wrong times always, and he knew when to laugh," Miller wrote. In 1952, Miller, rummaging through his papers, found a 1937 notebook in which he had made embryonic sketches of Willy, Biff, and Willy's second son, Happy. "It was the same family," he says of the twenty pages of realistic dialogue. "But I was unable in that straightforward, realistic form to contain what I thought of as the man's poetry—that is, the zigzag shots of his mind." He adds, "I just blotted it out."

7   Every masterpiece is a story of accident and accomplishment. Of all the historical and personal forces that fed the making of "Death of a Salesman," none was more important than a moment in 1947 when Miller's uncle Manny Newman accosted him in the lobby of the Colonial Theatre in Boston after a matinée of "All My Sons." "People regarded him as a kind of strange, completely untruthful personality," Miller says of Newman, a salesman and a notorious fabulist, who within the year would commit suicide. "I thought of him as a kind of wonderful inventor. There was something in him which was terribly moving, because his suffering was right on his skin, you see. He was the ultimate climber up the ladder who was constantly being stepped on by those climbing past him. My empathy for him was immense. I mean, how could he possibly have succeeded? There was no way." According to Miller, Newman was "cute and ugly, a bantam with a lisp. Very charming." He and his family, including two sons, Abby and Buddy, lived modestly in Brooklyn. "It was a house without irony, trembling with resolutions and shouts of victories that had not yet taken place but surely would tomorrow," Miller recalled in "Timebends." Newman was fiercely, wackily competitive; even when Miller was a child, in the few hours he spent in Newman's presence his uncle drew him into some kind of imaginary contest "which never stopped in his mind." Miller, who was somewhat ungainly as a boy, was often compared unfavorably with his cousins, and whenever he visited them, he said, "I always had to expect some kind of insinuation of my entire life's probable failure."

8   When Newman approached Miller after that matinée, he had not seen his nephew for more than a decade. He had tears in his eyes, but, instead of complimenting the playwright, he told Miller, "Buddy is doing very well." Miller says now, "He had simply picked up the conversation from fifteen years before. That element of competitiveness—his son competing with me—was so alive in his head that there was no gate to keep it from his mouth. He was living in two places at the same time." Miller continues, "So everything is in the present. For him to say 'Buddy is doing very well'—there are no boundaries. It's all now. It's all now. And that to me was wonderful."

9   At the time, Miller was absorbed in the tryout of "All My Sons" and had "not the slightest interest in writing about a salesman." Until "All My Sons," Miller's plays had not been naturalistic

in style; he had "resolved to write a play that could be put on," and had "put two years into 'All My Sons' to be sure that I believed every page of it." But Miller found naturalism, with its chronological exposition, "not sensuous enough" as a style; he began to imagine a kind of play where, as in Greek drama, issues were confronted head on, and where the transitions between scenes were pointed rather than disguised. The success of "All My Sons" emboldened him. "I could now move into unknown territory," Miller says. "And that unknown territory was basically that we're thinking on several planes at the same time. I wanted to find a way to try to make everything happen at once." In his introduction to the fiftieth-anniversary edition of "Death of a Salesman," Miller writes, "The play had to move forward not by following a narrow discreet line, but as a phalanx." He continues, "There was no model I could adapt for this play, no past history for the kind of work I felt it could become." The notebook for the play shows Miller formulating a philosophy for the kind of Cubist stage pictures that would become his new style:

> Life is formless—its interconnections are cancelled by lapses of time, by events occurring in separate places, by the hiatus of memory. We live in the world made by man and the past. Art suggests or makes the interconnection palpable. Form is the tension of these interconnections: man with man, man with the past and present environment. The drama at its best is a mass experience of this tension.

At first, the Manny Newman encounter inspired in Miller 10 only the intimation of a new, slashing sense of dramatic form. The play's structure is embedded in the structure of Loman's turbulent mind, which, Miller says, destroys the boundaries between then and now. As a result, "there are no flashbacks, strictly speaking, in 'Death of a Salesman,'" he says. "It's always moving forward." In this way, Miller jettisoned what he calls "the daylight continuity" of naturalism for the more fluid dark logic of dreams. "In a dream you don't have transitional material," Miller says. "The dream starts where it starts to mean something." He continues, "I wanted to start every scene at the last possible instant, no matter where that instant happened to be." He picked up a copy of his play and read me its first beats: " 'Willy?' 'It's all right. I came back.' 'Why? What happened? Did something happen, Willy?' 'No, nothing happened.'" He added, "We're into the thing in three lines." His new structure jump-started both the scenes and the stage language, whose intensity Miller called "emergency speech"—an "unashamedly open" idiom that replaced "the crabbed dramatic hints and pretexts of the natural." Willy dies without a secret; the play's structure, with its crosscutting between heightened moments, encouraged the idea of revelation. The audience response that Miller wanted to incite, he said, "was not 'What happens next and why?' so much as 'Oh, God, of course.'"

11   When, early in 1948, Miller visited his cousin Abby Newman to talk about the blighted life of his late father, Miller himself had just such an epiphany. Newman told Miller, "He wanted a business for us. So we could all work together. A business for the boys." Miller, who repeated Newman's words in the play, wrote in his autobiography, "This conventional, mundane wish was a shot of electricity that switched all the random iron filings in my mind in one direction. A hopelessly distracted Manny was transformed into a man with a purpose: he had been trying to make a gift that would crown all those striving years; all those lies he told, all his imaginings and crazy exaggerations, even the almost military discipline he had laid on his boys, were in this instant given form and point. I suddenly understood him with my very blood."

12   Willy Loman is a salesman, but we're never told what product he lugs around in his two large sample cases. Once, a theatregoer buttonholded Miller and put the question to him: "What's he selling? You never say what he's selling." Miller quipped, "Well, himself. That's who's in the valise." Miller adds, "You sell yourself. You sell the goods. You become the commodity." Willy's house echoes with exhortations to his two floundering sons about the presentation of self ("The man who creates personal interest is the man who gets ahead. Be liked and you will never want") and the imperialism of self ("Lick the world. You guys together could absolutely lick the civilized world"). In his notebook Miller writes, "Willy longs to take off, be great," and "Willy wants his boys prepared for any life. 'Nobody will laugh at them—take advantage. They'll be big men.' It's the big men who command respect." In Willy's frenzied and exhausted attempt to claim himself, Miller had stumbled onto a metaphor for a postwar society's eagerness

to pursue its self-interest after years of postponed life. In Willy's desperate appetite for success and in the brutal dicta offered by his rich brother Ben ("Never fight fair with a stranger, boy. You'll never get out of the jungle that way)" "Death of a Salesman" caught the spirit of self-aggrandizement being fed by what Miller calls "the biggest boom in the history of the world." Americans had struggled through the Depression, then fought a world war to keep the nation's democratic dream alive; that dream was, broadly speaking, a dream of self-realization. America, with its ideal of freedom, challenged its citizens to see how far they could go in a lifetime—"to end up big," as Willy says. (In the play, Ben, whom Willy looks to for answers—the notebook points to him as "the visible evidence of what the boys can do and be. Superior family"—is literally the predatory imperialist who at seventeen walked into the African jungle and emerged four years later as a millionaire.) Miller was not the first to dramatize the barbarity of American individualism; but, in a shift that signalled the changing cultural mood, he was the first to stage this spiritual battle of attrition as a journey to the interior of the American psyche. "In a certain sense, Willy is all the voices," Miller said later. In fact, "The Inside of His Head" was Miller's first title for the play; he also briefly toyed with the idea of having the proscenium designed in the shape of a head and having the action take place inside it.

In the economic upheavals of the thirties, social realism reflected the country's moods; plays held a mirror up to the external world, not an internal one. But in the postwar boom Tennessee Williams's "The Glass Menagerie" (1945) and "A Streetcar Named Desire" (1947), written in what Williams called his "personal lyricism," suddenly found an audience and struck a deep new chord in American life. The plays were subjective, poetic, symbolic; they made a myth of the self, not of social remedies. Indeed, the name "Willy Loman" was not intended by Miller as a sort of socioeconomic indicator ("low man"). Miller took it from a chilling moment in Fritz Lang's film "The Testament of Dr. Mabuse" (1933) when, after a long and terrifying stakeout, a disgraced detective who thinks he can redeem himself by exposing a gang of forgers is pursued and duped by them. The chase ends with the detective on the phone to his former boss ("Lohmann? Help me, for God's sake! Lohmann!"); when we see him next, he is in an asylum, gowned

13

and frightened and shouting into an invisible phone ("Lohmann? Lohmann? Lohmann?"). "What the name really meant to me was a terrified man calling into the void for help that will never come," Miller said.

14   Willy Loman's particular terror goes to the core of American individualism, in which the reputable self and the issue of wealth are hopelessly tangled. "A man can't go out the way he came in," Willy says to Ben. "A man has got to add up to something." Willy, who, at sixty, has no job, no money, no loyalty from his boys, is sensationally lacking in assets and in their social corollary—a sense of blessing. "He envies those who are blessed; he feels unblessed, but he's striving for it," Miller says. Although Willy's wife, Linda, famously says of him that "attention must be paid," he feels invisible to the world. "I'm not noticed," he says. Later, Linda confides to the boys, "For five weeks he's been on straight commission, like a beginner, an unknown!" As Miller puts it now, "The whole idea of people failing with us is that they can no longer be loved. You haven't created a persona which people will pay for, see, experience, or come close to. It's almost like death. You have a deathly touch. People who succeed are loved because they exude some magical formula for fending off destruction, fending off death." He continues, "It's the most brutal way of looking at life that one can imagine, because it discards anyone who does not measure up. It wants to destroy them. It's been going on since the Puritan times. You are beyond the blessing of God. You're beyond the reach of God. That God rewards those who deserve it. It's a moral condemnation that goes on. You don't want to be near this failure."

15   "Death of a Salesman" was the first play to dramatize this punishing—and particularly American—interplay of panic and achievement. Before "Salesman," Eugene O'Neill's "The Iceman Cometh" (1946) raised the issue in the eerie calm of Harry Hope's bar, whose sodden habitués have retreated from competitiveness into a perverse contentment; as one of the characters says, "No one here has to worry about where they're going next, because there is no farther they can go." But in Willy Loman, Miller was able to bring both the desperation and the aspiration of American life together in one character.

16   Willy is afflicted by the notion of winning—what Brecht called "the black addiction of the brain." He cheats at cards; he

encourages his boys to seek every advantage. Victory haunts him and his feckless sons. In a scene from the notebook, Biff and Happy tell Willy of their plan to go into business. "Step on it, boys, there ain't a minute to lose," Willy tells them, but their souls are strangled by their father's heroic dreams, which hang over them like some sort of spiritual kudzu. In another notebook entry, Biff rounds fiercely on Willy: "I don't care if you live or die. You think I'm mad at you because of the Woman, don't you? I am, but I'm madder because you botched up my life, because I can't tear you out of my heart, because I keep trying to make good, be something for you, to succeed for you."

In dramatizing the fantasy of competition. Miller's play was the first to dissect cultural envy in action—that process of invidious comparison which drives society forward but also drives it crazy. "You lose your life to it!" Miller says of the envy that feeds Willy's restlessness. "It's the ultimate outer-directional emotion. In other words, I am doing this not because it's flowing from me but because it's flowing against him." He goes on, "You're living in a mirror. It's a life of reflections. Emptiness. Emptiness. Emptiness. Hard to go to sleep at night. And hard to wake up." In his mind, Willy is competing with his brother Ben; with Dave Singleman, a successful old salesman who could make a living "without ever leaving his room" and died a placid, accomplished death on a train to Boston; with his neighbor Charley, who owns his own business; and with Charley's successful lawyer son, Bernard. "Where's Willy in all this?" Miller asks. "He's competed himself to death. He's not existing anymore, or hardly."

In his notebook Miller wrote, "It is the combination of guilt (of failure), hate, and love—all in conflict that he resolves by 'accomplishing' a 20,000 dollar death." In death, Willy is worth more than in life. His suicide is the ultimate expression of his confusion of success with love and also of his belief in winning at all costs. As a father, he overlooked Biff's small childhood acts of larceny—taking sand from a building site, stealing basketballs, getting the answers for tests from the nerdy, studious Bernard—and Biff has continued his habit into adulthood, out of a combination of envy and revenge. A notebook citation reads, "It is necessary to (1) reveal to Willy that Biff stole to queer himself, and did it to hurt Willy," and "(2) And that he did it because of the Woman and all the disillusionment it implied." In the final version of the play, Biff, admitting in passing

17

18

that he spent three months in a Kansas City jail for lifting a suit, tells Willy, "I stole myself out of every good job since high school!" At first, Miller saw the twenty thousand dollars of insurance money as cash to put Biff on the straight and narrow. "'My boy's a thief—with 20,000 he'd stop it,'" he wrote in the notebook. Instead, Willy's suicide—the final show of force and fraud, in keeping with his demented competitive fantasies—is pitched on a more grandiose and perverse note. In an early draft of the terrific penultimate scene, where Biff exposes Willy and calls it quits with him and his dream, there is this exchange:

> BIFF (*to him*): What the hell do you want from me?
> What do you want from me?
> WILLY: —Greatness—
> BIFF: —No—

19   In Miller's final draft, Willy, who will not accept his son's confession of thievery, takes Biff's greatness as a given as he visualizes his own suicide. "Can you imagine that magnificence with twenty thousand dollars in his pocket?" he says to Ben. He adds, "Imagine? When the mail comes he'll be ahead of Bernard again." When he goes to his death, Willy, in his mind, is on a football field with Biff, and full of vindictive triumph ("When you hit, hit low and hit hard, because it's important, boy"). "He dies sending his son through the goalposts," Miller says. "He dies moving." Miller pauses. "I think now that Kazan had it right from the beginning. He said, 'It's a love story.'"

BROOKS ATKINSON

After majoring in English at Harvard (B.A., 1917), Atkinson (1894–1984) followed his father's calling as a reporter on the *Boston Evening Transcript,* taking several months' leave in 1918 to serve in the Army. In 1922 he joined the staff of the *New York Times,* where he worked until 1965, first as a book reviewer until he became a full-time drama critic in 1925, with time out during World War II to serve as a *Times* correspondent in China and in Moscow. He won the Pulitzer Prize in journalism for a series of articles on postwar Russia arguing that the Soviet Union's "fundamentally reactionary" spirit led it to "instinctively think in terms of force in international affairs."

Atkinson was a model critic, known—and uniformly loved— for being fair and judicious. He never read out-of-town reviews before attending a New York performance, and he discouraged personal relationships with actors and directors, whose careers depended on his judgment. His high standards combined a vast knowledge of theater—plays, stagecraft, acting—with common sense, compassion, and the ability to compress a play's several acts into a thousand words with eloquent precision. He said he judged every play he saw by one overriding criterion: Did it provide enjoyment for the audience? At his death, Arthur Miller praised Atkinson as the only critic who ever "presided over Broadway." A *Times* colleague characterized him as "the conscience of the theater"—an accolade befitting his review of the opening performance of *Death of a Salesman* that appeared in the *New York Times* on February 17, 1949. As Atkinson says, "This is one of the finest dramas in the whole range of the American theatre. Humane in its point of view, it has stature and insight, awareness of life, respect for people and knowledge of American manners and of modern folkways. From the technical point of view, it is virtuoso theatre. It brings the whole theatre alive."

Arthur Miller's Tragedy of an Ordinary Man

E ven the people who have had nothing to do with the pro- 1 duction of Arthur Miller's "Death of a Salesman" take a kind of platonic pride in it. What Mr. Miller has achieved somehow seems to belong to everybody. For he is writing as an American with an affectionate understanding of American family people and their family problems; and everybody recognizes in his tragic play things that they know are poignantly true. Although Mr. Miller is the author, he does not dissociate himself from his simple story of an ordinary family. He participates by recording it with compassion.

Discarded in his old age from the only world he knows, Willy 2 Loman, the worn-out salesman, crawls into his grave where he thinks he is worth more to his family than he would be if he were still tinkering around the house. But Mr. Miller does not blame Willy, his sons, his boss or the system, and he draws no moral conclusions. In the space of one somber evening in the theatre he has caught the life and death of a traveling salesman and told it tenderly with a decent respect for Willy's dignity as a man.

Virtuoso Theatre

3   In "All My Sons" two seasons ago Mr. Miller was arguing a moral point: like an efficient craftsman, he constructed his drama to reach a conclusion. That was a first-rate piece of work by an author of high convictions. But without being precious or self-conscious, "Death of a Salesman" is a creative work of art in which the form is so completely blended with the theme that you are scarcely aware of the writing. You accept it as a whole—play, acting, directing and scene designing fused into a unit of expression.

4   From the technical point of view Mr. Miller has accomplished some remarkable things in this drama. Without moving scenery, he has covered the past and present of Willy's itinerant career in Brooklyn, New York and Boston, recorded the separate careers of his two sons and the neighbors, touched on the problems and personality of Willy's boss and introduced some imagery from Willy's separate dream-world.

5   At one time, this would have been highly daring and experimental in the theatre. We once had a jargon for things like these—"expressionistic," "constructivist," "centrifugal." But "Death of a Salesman" belongs in none of the categories. It is a fresh creation in a style of its own. Mr. Miller has mastered his material and turned it directly into the grievous life of an affable man.

6   Strictly speaking there is a moral basis for the catastrophe in the last act. Willy has always believed in something that is unsound. He has assumed that success comes to those who are "well-liked," as he puts it. He does not seem to be much concerned about the quality of the product he is selling. His customers buy, he thinks, because they like him—because he is hale and hearty and a good man with jokes.

7   Out of sheer physical exuberance he rears his son, Biff, in the same tradition. Biff is popular, too. Willy indulgently overlooks Biff's easy going cheating in school and petty pilfering from the contractor next door. So long as Biff plays good football, wins games,

gets his name in the newspapers and makes friends Willy thinks that he will succeed in life and carry on the jovial Loman tradition.

But these are the most unsubstantial things in a life. Although Biff is well liked, he is flunked out of school because he is not interested in studying. Although he is as good hearted as his father, he never gets over his habit of stealing, which finally lands him in jail. Willy has staked his whole happiness on Biff's success, but Biff is a failure. 8

Formula for Failure

And the unsubstantial quality of his own success catches up with Willy in his old age. The formula of personal popularity no longer works. The competition of chain stores has eliminated the personal element. Willy's friends are old or dead. Willy is old himself. He no longer has the physical gusto for slapping people on the back and breaking down resistance with good fellowship. He cannot stand the nervous strain of driving his car. Willy has lost his usefulness to the business world because he has founded a career on things that are ephemeral. He and Biff are good fellows and good animals—strong, full of fun and carefree. But they live in a world of golden illusion and they founder on reality in the end. 9

Not that Mr. Miller is holding them up as bad examples. On the contrary he knows that they are good men—especially Willy, who has never had a mean thought in his life. Out of sheer good nature he has gone cheerfully down a dead end street, always devoted to his family and carelessly sure of himself. Although his two boys do not understand him, they love him. His wife not only loves him but understands him thoroughly. Mr. Miller is not writing about ideas but about human beings, whom he is sufficiently modest to be able to value properly. And the tragedy of "Death of a Salesman" is almost unbearable in the last act because Mr. Miller has drawn the portrait of a good man who represents the homely, decent, kindly virtues of a middle-class society. 10

Respect for People

By common consent, this is one of the finest dramas in the whole range of the American theatre. Humane in its point of view, it has stature and insight, awareness of life, respect for people and 11 knowledge of American manners and of modern folkways. From the technical point of view, it is virtuoso theatre. It brings the whole theatre alive. Although Elia Kazan has done some memorable jobs of direction in the past few years, he has never equaled the selfless but vibrant expression of this epic drama which has force, clarity, rhythm and order in the performing. Without being fastidious, the performance has taste. Jo Mielziner's skeletonized setting is a brilliant design, tragic in mood, but also selfless and practical. Alex North has composed a stirring interpretive score which, like the direction and scenery, has the grace to melt unobtrusively into the work as a whole.

12   The acting is superb, particularly in Mildred Dunnock's warmly devoted portrait of the wife and Arthur Kennedy's turbulent, anxious playing of Biff. Although the part of the bewildered salesman is fully developed in Mr. Miller's writing, Lee J. Cobb brings a touch of human grandeur to the acting. He keeps it on the high plane of tragic acting—larger than the specific life it is describing. Willy is not a great man, but his tragedy is great, partly because of the power and range of Mr. Cobb's acting. When Willy's life collapses, a whole world crashes because Mr. Cobb fills the play with so much solid humanity. In terms of the business world Willy is insignificant. But in terms of life he is a hero. Like Mr. Miller, Mr. Cobb knows what Willy is worth, and so do all of us.

BEN BRANTLEY

Benjamin D. Brantley, a lifelong newspaperman, was born in North Carolina in 1954; he earned a B.A. in English from Swarthmore College in 1975. He served as an editorial assistant at *The Village Voice* (1975), a summer intern at *The Winston-Salem Sentinel* (1976), and then worked from 1978 to 1985 for *Women's Wear Daily*, as reporter, editor, and Paris bureau chief and European editor. From 1987 to 1992 he was a staff writer at *Vanity Fair* before beginning moving to *Elle* (1988–93), as a film critic. In 1993 he joined the *New York Times* as a drama critic, succeeding Vincent Canby as chief theater critic in 1996. Like all notable reviewers, Brantley shares Canby's joy of coming "upon something that you like so much that you can't bear the idea it won't be seen and you can't wait to write the first word. You're excited and on fire for something. It's great fun to write those reviews."

Because *Death of a Salesman* is so familiar to theatergoers after 50 years, Brantley doesn't need to sketch the plot, but he does need to make comparisons between earlier productions (which readers may remember) and the current one. He concentrates here on two conspicuous features of the 1999 production, the acting and the "powerhouse staging," in which the rooms in the Loman's house are "moving platforms that shift into and out of focus," matching Willy's unstable view of his world. When Brantley examines the acting, he focuses on the ways that the acting, insightful and powerful, reinforces the play's major motifs, the "tragic, conflicted familial love story, between husband and wife, between father and sons." He attempts to recreate the performance, comparing Brian Dennehy's Willy with Dustin Hoffman's 1984 version, and bringing the review's readers right into the theater: "What this actor goes for is close to an everyman quality, with a grand emotional expansiveness that matches his monumental physique. Yet these emotions ring so unerringly true that Mr. Dennehy seems to kidnap you by force, trapping you inside Willy's psyche." When Brantley concludes his review with "I could hear people around me not just sniffling but sobbing," his readers share both the emotion and the desire to see the play again, and again.

Attention Must Be Paid, Again

H is right hand, so sturdy and thick-fingered, keeps flying pitifully to his forehead, to what he assumes is the source of all that pain. He presses at his temples, he pulls at his cheek, so hard that you're surprised that his face remains intact. You get the sense that Willy Loman would crush his own skull to destroy the images inside. The most frightening thing of all is that you understand exactly what he's feeling.   1

In the harrowing revival of Arthur Miller's "Death of a Salesman" that opened last night at the Eugene O'Neill Theater, 50 years to the day after it made its epochal Broadway debut, you walk right into the mind of its decimated hero, played with majestic, unnerving transparency by Brian Dennehy.   2

3   Robert Falls's powerhouse staging, first seen at the Goodman Theater in Chicago last fall, never looks down on Mr. Miller's deluded Brooklyn dreamer or looks ennoblingly up to him as a martyr to a success-driven country. Instead, it demands that you experience Willy's suffering without sociological distance, that you surrender to the sense of one man's pain and of the toll it takes on everyone around him.

4   Mr. Miller, who had originally titled the play "The Inside of His Head," has said he thought of having it occur in a set that would indeed be in the shape of a man's head. Although Mr. Falls and his expert production team are mercifully less literal, that is effectively the landscape they create here.

5   The Brooklyn home to which Willy Loman returns from an aborted road trip at the play's beginning is no stable sanctuary. The designer Mark Wendland has conceived the rooms of the Lomans' house as moving platforms that shift into and out of focus, just as Willy himself is unable to remain fixed in an immediate reality; the lines between the play's harsh present and Willy's reimagining of the past have seldom seemed so fluid. Michael Philippi's lighting floods the stage with a darkness that is always threatening to consume, the image of the tidal pull of depression itself.

6   In the opening scene the audience's eyes are seared by the headlights of Willy's car. Mr. Dennehy first appears, fabled salesman's cases in hand, as a sinister silhouette. A jagged, fragmented jazz score, by Richard Woodbury, slices the air. When Willy's wife, Linda, played by the sublime Elizabeth Franz, materializes in her bathrobe on a raised platform, her voice spectrally amplified as she calls his name, she seems a phantom whom her husband can't quite summon into full being. "It's all right," Willy says wearily. "I've come back." The lines, Willy's first, have seldom registered so clearly as lies.

7   There is admittedly a flavor of melodrama in this insistent air of urgency, but it doesn't feel disproportionate. When Linda admonishes the couple's grown sons, Biff (Kevin Anderson) and Happy (Ted Koch), saying that Willy is "a human being, and a terrible thing is happening to him," it is not mere hyperbole.

8   Linda goes on to conclude the sentence with the famous words "so attention must be paid." That line has traditionally been held up as a social signpost, a cry to heed the plight of an

aging, insignificant man seduced and abandoned by a capitalist system that promised unattainable glory. Yet as Ms. Franz delivers the words with a rage that seems shaped by both horrified compassion and selfish fears, they are at once more particular and universal: when people hurt as Willie does, it is inhuman to look away.

Scholarly analyses of "Salesman" have most often focused 9 on its political consciousness (surely you remember discussing "tragedy and the common man" in high school) or its expressionistic form. The play certainly provides ample fodder, including those now clunky-seeming "j'accuse" declarations aimed at the corporate dream machine, for both kinds of dissection.

But these aspects of the drama are secondary to what gives 10 "Salesman" its staying power and has allowed it to grip audiences as far from the United States as Beijing: its almost operatic emotional sweep in examining one unhappy family and the desperate, mortally wounded father at its center.

For Mr. Falls and his fiercely engaged cast are, above all, 11 committed to the work's tragic, conflicted familial love story, between husband and wife, between father and sons. The play's most remarkable aspect is that even as it conjures Willy's grimly distorted worldview, it lets us see clearly his effect on those around him. In this staging, those people express, in highly personalized portraits, the genuine pity and terror given more abstract voice by the choruses of Greek tragedy.

"I live in fear," says Linda at one point. Ms. Franz's astonishing portrayal shatters that character's traditional passivity to create a searing image of a woman fighting for her life, for that is what Willy is to Linda. She also emerges as the only realist in the family, even as she does everything she can to bolster Willy's sagging illusions.

Watch how Ms. Franz's face changes from taut, smiling reassurance to a fearful exhaustion the moment Mr. Dennehy looks away from her. The continuing, tremulous nodding of her head registers as a direct consequence of having worked too hard and too long to be a reassuring wife. When she speaks to her neglectful sons in their father's absence, it is with a fury that scorches. If need be, she will sacrifice her children for her husband, to whom she clearly remains, on some level, sexually bonded.

14   The second and equally important love story in "Salesman" is that of a father and his elder son. And the ambivalent, tentative dance of courtship and rejection enacted by Mr. Anderson's Biff, who has returned home after a long, self-imposed exile, and Mr. Dennehy's Willy is heartbreaking.

15   In his deeply affecting performance, Mr. Anderson tempers the adolescent rage of a man who has never overcome a father's betrayal with a more profound sense of conflict: the only way to win Willy's approval is to give in to his fantasies, and that way lies self-destruction. The cocky, callous Happy, sharply drawn by Mr. Koch, doesn't bear the burden of such consciousness, and you can already sense that one not so distant day he is going to wake up as lonely and frightened as his father.

16   The rest of the supporting cast is fine, especially Howard Witt as Charley, Willy's gruff, argumentative and ultimately beneficent next-door neighbor. A scene set in the more successful Charley's business office offers the evening's most jolting shock of recognition. Mr. Dennehy, his face inches from Mr. Witt's, stares hard, as though in prelude to a fistfight. What he says, after a long pause, is: "Charley, you're the only friend I got. Isn't that a remarkable thing?"

17   Mr. Dennehy's performance will probably be the most debated aspect of this production. It is not in the idiosyncratic, finely detailed vein so memorably provided by Dustin Hoffman in 1984. What this actor goes for is close to an everyman quality, with a grand emotional expansiveness that matches his monumental physique. Yet these emotions ring so unerringly true that Mr. Dennehy seems to kidnap you by force, trapping you inside Willy's psyche.

18   The rhythms of his performance are exactly those of the play itself, in which every scene moves from artificially inflated optimism into free-falling despair. Mr. Dennehy's eyes go bleak and fearful even as that broad salesman's smile splits his face. He continually brings his finger to his lower lip, like a fretful child, as though suddenly forced to remember what he had been trying so very hard to forget.

19   It is also jarring, and utterly appropriate, to see such a large man physically pushed around by the other, smaller men in the play. And I will always be haunted by the image of Mr. Dennehy's

infantile fragility when he shields his face with his hands, palms outward, before an angry, confrontational Mr. Anderson.

In art, greatness and perfection seldom keep close company, 20 and the flaws of "Salesman" are apparent here: the contrived, detective-story like exposition of why Biff resents Willy; the unfortunate moments of speechifying, especially in the final requiem scene, and the iconic presence of the fantasy figure of Willy's older brother, Ben (Allen Hamilton, who looks a bit too much like Colonel Sanders here) as the American Dream incarnate.

Watching "Salesman" in this production, you acknowledge 21 the flaws, but only fleetingly. In willing himself into the imagination of a small-time, big-thinking loser, Mr. Miller generated an immense natural force of empathy that, oddly, he never equaled in his more autobiographical works, like "After the Fall."

I could hear people around me not just sniffling but sob- 22 bing. I feel sure that audiences for "Salesman" will be doing the same thing 50 years from now.

BRENDA MURPHY

Murphy (born, 1950) earned a Ph.D. at Brown in 1975 and taught for fourteen years at St. Lawrence University before she became professor of English at the University of Connecticut, where she has taught since 1989. Her most recent books include *Congressional Theatre: Dramatizing McCarthyism on Stage, Film, and Television* (1999); *Miller: "Death of a Salesman"* (1995); *Understanding Death of a Salesman: A Student Casebook to Issues, Sources, and Historical Documents* (with Susan C. W. Abbotson, 1999); and *The Cambridge Companion to American Women Playwrights* (1999).

Murphy tells her readers, "When a special issue of the *Michigan Quarterly Review* was being dedicated to Arthur Miller on the occasion of the fiftieth anniversary of *Death of a Salesman*'s premiere, I was asked to write an essay explaining the importance of the play to American culture at large, rather than address a critical article to students of drama or literature. In order to discover this broader significance, I knew I had to find out what Willy meant to people in business, people who lived with the image of Willy Loman and experienced its cultural resonance as an everyday occurrence, regardless of their knowledge of the play. Having studied Arthur Miller's plays for many years, I have large files of articles and clippings gleaned from research in many libraries and archives. These were helpful, but this project required a wider net. Aided by many new electronic indexes and the ever-enlarging Internet, my investigation took me into unfamiliar but fascinating areas of research, where I was able to uncover references to Willy Loman not only in mainstream magazines like *Newsweek, Mother Jones, National Review,* and *U.S. News and World Report,* but in the real registers of the business culture, like *Automotive News* and *Business Insurance.* It was an interesting and unexpectedly revealing look into another American subculture."

Willy Loman: Icon of Business Culture

1   Willy Loman and his failure and death have a status as defining cultural phenomena, both inside and outside America's borders, that began to be established in the first year of the play's life. In February 1950, as the original production approached its first anniversary, a newspaper reporter marveled that *Salesman* had "already become a legend in many parts of the world," commenting that "why this play has approached the stature of an American legend in these distant lands defies analysis.[1] In a single year, Arthur Miller had received more than a thousand letters explaining the personal ways in which the play was related to their writers' lives. A number claimed to be the model for Willy, or suggested that Miller record their lives too, because they were so much like Willy's. A number of sermons, both spiritual and secular, had been preached on the text of the play, with ministers, rabbis, and priests explaining its exposure of the emptiness of Willy's dreams of material success, and sales managers using Willy as an object lesson of how not to be a salesman.

2   In the years immediately following the original production, Willy Loman entered the world's consciousness as the very image of the American traveling salesman, an identity with which the business world was far from comfortable. Writing in the garment

industry's own *Women's Wear Daily* shortly after the play's premiere, Thomas R. Dash articulated the conflict between identification with Willy and resistance to him that characterized the typical relationship that people in business were to have with the play. Noting that Willy's was an "individualized tragedy," and that "it does not follow that all salesmen necessarily are discarded to the ashcan after thirty-five years of service for one firm, that they crack mentally and that they dash themselves to pieces on a mad and suicidal ride to the hereafter," he nonetheless had to concede that, "if you have traveled the road and are honest with yourself, you may recognize certain traits of Willy's in your own behavior pattern, both professional and personal." Since the very art of salesmanship "is predicated upon a talent for fictionalizing and romanticizing," Dash suggested, "from the habits formed by this forgivable fantasy and hyperbolic praise of the product, certain illusions of grandeur inevitably creep into the mental fabric of the practitioner. Frequently, as in the case of Willy Loman, these habits percolate into the salesman's personal life." As for Willy's infidelities on the road, Dash wrote, "this writer does not propose to have the wrath of the whole craft descend upon him by making any generalizations . . . let each man probe his own conscience and answer 'True' or 'False.'"[2]

The most immediate and overwhelming response of the business world to the failure and death of Willy Loman was to try to erase it from the public's consciousness. When the first film adaptation of the play was done in 1950, the executives of Columbia Pictures, fearing a public reaction against the movie for its failure to uphold the values of American capitalism, made a short film which they planned to distribute to theaters along with the feature. The short was filmed at the Business School of the City College of New York, and consisted, according to Miller, of "interviews with professors who blithely explained that Willy Loman was entirely atypical, a throwback to the past when salesmen did indeed have some hard problems. But nowadays selling was a fine profession with limitless spiritual compensations as well as financial ones. In fact, they all sounded like Willy Loman with a diploma."[3] Only when Miller threatened to sue did Columbia withdraw the short film.

By the 1960s, businessmen were nearly desperate to divorce the salesman's identity from that of Willy Loman. Only one in seventeen college students was willing to try selling as a career in

1964.[4] Business executives blamed this largely on Arthur Miller. "To many novelists, playwrights, sociologists, college students, and many others," wrote Carl Reiser in *Fortune* magazine, the salesman "is aggressively forcing on people goods that they don't want. He is the drummer, with a dubious set of social values—Willy Loman in the Arthur Miller play."[5] In direct opposition to Willy's image, American business was trying to define a "new salesman" in the 1960s, "a man with a softer touch and greater breadth, a new kind of man to do a new—much more significant—kind of job."[6] Despite the best efforts of corporate America, however, Willy's image remained the public's clearest vision of the salesman. "To be sure," suggested *Newsweek* in 1964, "the old-style drummer is no longer in the mainstream. But he's still paddling around out there with his smile and shoeshine, his costume a bit more subdued and his supply of jokes, sad to relate, a bit low."[7] *Newsweek*'s article, "The New Breed of Salesman—Not Like Willy," was tellingly illustrated with the familiar Joseph Hirsch drawing of Willy with his sample cases, over the caption: "Willy Loman: An image lingers on."

5   When plans were announced for the CBS television production of *Salesman* in 1966, the Sales Executives Club of New York mobilized itself to prevent further erosion of the salesman's image. Complaining that "Willy Loman has been plaguing our 'selling as a career' efforts for years," the club suggested changes in the script "to improve the image of the salesman depicted in the drama." As had been tried with the Columbia picture, the sales executives suggested a prologue to the play, "alerting viewers that they were about to see the tragedy of a man who went into selling with the wrong ideas, a man who had been improperly trained by today's standards. The prologue would warn that Willy Loman would have been a failure 'in anything else he tackled.'" In case that wasn't enough, an epilogue could be added, called "The Life of the Salesman." The epilogue would indicate that, "with modern, customer-oriented selling methods, Willy Lomans are ghosts of the past." The Xerox Corporation, which sponsored the telecast, had a golden opportunity, the sales executives thought, "to enlighten the public about what a well-trained modern salesman really does, and dispel the idea that the rewards of a selling career are often disillusionment and death."[8] Arthur Miller, the writer of the newspaper report on this effort noted, "could not be reached for comment." It is not hard to imagine what his comment would have been.

In the year following the telecast, an industrial film pro- 6
ducer, David R. Hayes, made a film called "Second Chance," an
inspirational film for salesmen that featured football coach Vince
Lombardi in a narrative that allowed him to use his "break-'em
up football coaching technique on a fictionalized typical salesman." Hayes explained that the reason for scripting the film as a
play rather than an inspirational talk was that "we had to undo
for the art, science and business of selling . . . what Arthur Miller
had done in damage to the field in his stageplay, 'Death of a Salesman,' I decided to do it with Miller's own tools—that is, drama."[9]
Within two years, the trade film had been sold to 7,000 companies,
and had made the fortune of Hayes's industrial film company,
Take Ten, Inc. The introduction of dramatic conflict into trade
films wrought a major change in the industry, one of Willy Loman's
many influences on American business.

Throughout the 1970s, the effort to expunge the image of 7
Willy Loman from the public's view of the salesman continued
without much success, despite the continually improving material
circumstances of the typical salesman, and the greater security that
came from an ever-higher ratio of salary to commission throughout
the sales profession. Willy and the play had become an unconscious
part of the businessman's vision and vocabulary, as is evident from
the titles of articles in business publications. "The Salesman Isn't
Dead—He's Different" and "The New Breed of Salesman—Not
Like Willy" were succeeded by titles like "Deaths of a Salesman,"
"The Rebirth of a Salesman," and "The New Life of a Salesman."

With the worsening economy of the 1980s, the cultural reso- 8
nance of Willy Loman had a new meaning for the generation that
had not been born when the play was first produced. Speaking of
"underemployed 30-year-olds" who were being forced to "bring
their families home to live with bewildered and resentful parents,"
and middle-aged people "with kids and mortgages who have
been out of work for three months," Jeff Faux suggested in 1983
that "Willy Loman could again symbolize a widespread middle-
class tragedy—people trapped by expectations of status that no
longer fit the cruel realities of the labor market."[10] Meanwhile,
business executives were moving salesmen off salary and back
onto commission—just as Howard Wagner had done to Willy—
and calling it "Motivating Willy Loman."[11] As one executive put
it, "You really should get the carrot as big as possible without

making the guy die to reach it . . . Give him salary for the essentials, to help pay the rent and put food on the table, but not much else. Hell, he's supposed to be a salesman."[12]

9   By this time, Willy Loman had taken on a life of his own, with little or no reference to the play. Edward Spar, the president of a marketing statistics firm, used Willy's putative sales route as an example of sensible county-based marketing for the Association of Public Data Users in 1987. Noting that Willy's territory was simply a matter of convenience and logic, Spar commented that, "if that company existed in reality, Willy's territory wouldn't have changed."[13] Interestingly, the route that Spar gave to Willy was completely imaginary: "Up to Westchester, through Putnam—all the way to Albany, Route 23 over to Pittsfield in Berkshire County, then down to Hartford and back to New York." Although Willy does mention having seen a hammock in Albany, the only indications of his route in the play are his turning back from Yonkers on the night the play begins and his description of his route to the boys when he returns from his trip in the first daydream scene: Providence, where he met the Mayor, Waterbury, Boston, "a couple of other towns in Mass., and on to Portland and Bangor and straight home,"[14] a not very logical and rather improbable route. To Spar, however, Willy was not a character in a play, but the prototypical salesman with the "New England territory."

10   Evidence of the extent to which Willy and the American salesman have become identical to the culture at large is everywhere, in the most casual of references. A 1993 *Wall Street Journal* article on the certification, and thus professionalization, of salesmen is entitled, "Willy Loman Might Have Had a Better Self-Image."[15] One on the introduction of portable computers to the sales force is called "What Would Willy Loman Have Done with This?"[16] Neither has any reference to Miller's play. An article on the faltering U.S. balance of trade in *U.S. News and World Report,* called "The Yankee Trader: Death of a Salesman," makes no reference to the play, but carries the familiar Joseph Hirsch image of Willy with his sample cases as an icon on each page of the article.[17] An article opposing advertising for law firms is entitled "Willy Loman Joins the Bar: Death of a Profession?"[18] An article on Fred Friendly's efforts to use television to popularize the U.S. Constitution is called "TV's 'Willy Loman' of the Law."[19] And so on. There is no doubt that, at

the end of the twentieth century, Willy Loman, and the Joseph Hirsch image of him, have achieved the status of cultural icon.

The conflict between identification with and resistance to Willy is obvious for members of the sales profession. As Miller has so eloquently put it, "Willy Loman has broken a law without whose protection life is insupportable if not incomprehensible to him and to many others; it is the law which says that a failure in society and in business has no right to live."[20] Willy has failed in business, and the wages of his sin is death. Having experienced his own father's failure during the Depression, and its personal consequences, Miller knew this business creed intimately when he wrote *Salesman*. The extraordinary thing about the universality and endurance of Willy Loman as cultural icon, however, is that it is not necessary to have experienced Willy's sin and its wages at first hand in order to respond to Willy in the most primal way. This may be because Willy Loman has become the prime site for working out our deepest cultural conflicts and anxieties about the identity and fate of the salesman. And, being Americans, we are all salesmen in one way or another.

The extent to which the American way of life is identified with the salesman, and with Willy, becomes obvious from a cursory look at the numerous obituaries each year that are entitled "Death of a Salesman." This phrase has been used recently to sum up the lives of many successful businessmen, among them Commerce Secretary Ron Brown, who was lauded for his efforts to forge commercial links between the U.S. and China; record promoter Charlie Minor, who was shot by his former girlfriend, stripper Suzette McClure; and Victor Potemkin, known to a generation of New Yorkers for the TV commercials advertising his car dealerships. Less immediately evident is the connection between Willy Loman and counterculture guru and LSD promoter Timothy Leary, or Jerry Rubin, who, noted the *Hartford Courant*, "came to stand for hypocrisy" for the counterculture "when he committed the mortal sin—selling out." As the *Courant* pointed out, however, "Mr. Rubin was always a good salesman who knew how to market a message. Like many others of his generation, he realized that idealism alone doesn't put bread on the table."[21]

There is affection and even respect in identifying Willy Loman with men who are as successful in their fields as Ron

Brown and Victor Potemkin. Potemkin, whose death, according to *Automotive News*, was "mourned by the whole automotive community,"[22] might be said to embody Willy's dream of achieving business success and being "well-liked" at the same time. Most often, however, identification with Willy Loman is cultural shorthand for failure, no matter what the field of endeavor. A review of the movie *Cop Land* refers to the local sheriff played by Sylvester Stallone as "a failed American dreamer, a Willy Loman of the police world, a profoundly poignant figure."[23] Failed presidential candidate Phil Gramm is described as "a pathetic self-destroyer like traveling salesman Willy Loman."[24] Political pundit George Will describes President Bill Clinton as "a political Willy Loman" in his unsuccessful attempt to sell his Mideast foreign policy to the American people.[25]

14   While accepting the iconography of failure that is associated with Willy and his death, business writers often situate themselves in opposition to its implications about the American socioeconomic system. Willy Loman didn't have to die, these writers contend. If only he had had better sales training, or better job counseling, or a laptop computer, he would not have failed. The anxiety of having to master new technology, or at worst, of being replaced by it, is displaced by a hopeful rhetoric that suggests technology might be the salesman's salvation. The references to Willy Loman in these articles simultaneously evoke and attempt to dispel the typical salesman's anxiety about losing a job for failing to keep up with technology. "If Only Willy Loman Had Used a Laptop" explains the "competitive edge" that salespeople can get from "having access to product information at the point of sale."[26] Similarly optimistic portrayals of the necessity for updating the salesman's technology are presented in articles like *Business Week*'s "Rebirth of a Salesman: Willy Loman Goes Electronic" and *Advertising Age*'s "Willy Loman Never Had It So Good: New Technologies Enhance the Job of Selling." Upbeat reminders to the sales force that they need to keep up in order to compete have pervaded business journals since the early part of the century. What the evocation of Willy Loman provides is the subliminal suggestion of failure and its consequences should the reader disregard the writer's advice.

15   Willy Loman appears more substantially in another group of articles that purport to save his successors from his fate by addressing some of the issues that Miller addressed in the play,

but within the context of the business environment. "He had the wrong dreams," says Biff of Willy, "All, all wrong." Writing for *Industry Week,* Joseph McKenna asks, "Was Willy Loman in the Wrong Job?" In the article he suggests that the reason Willy Loman "never made a lot of money" was that he "should have been plying another trade—just as many of today's real-life salesmen should be."[27] He goes on to cite an industry consultant who estimates that 55% of those working as sales professionals "don't have the ability to sell" and another 25% are selling the wrong product. This can be remedied through the consultant's method of "job matching," "marrying the appropriate job to the appropriate person with the appropriate skills or correctable weaknesses or both." Similarly, an article on "Career Entrenchment" uses Willy as a case study of the tendency to remain in a job despite one's obvious unfitness for it and suggests ways out of this inappropriate career direction.[28] In "Taking a Lesson From Willy Loman: Brokers Must Move Beyond Sales to Satisfy Risk Manager Demands," readers of *Business Insurance* are advised to "break free of their sales roles" and "act as consultants and partners to risk managers" if they are to avoid Willy's fate.[29] In "The Death of Some Salesmen," Allen Myerson writes that "the old-style career salesman is dead," but that a new force of part-timers is replacing "the likes of Willy Loman," eschewing the old door-to-door methods and replacing them with home parties and demonstrations.

The subliminal message of these articles is clear. To be like   16
Willy is to be a failure. Therefore we will make the job of sales as different as we can from the job as Willy did it. These articles all define the modern, successful salesperson in opposition to a putative Willy Loman. Of course, this is a cultural, not a literary evocation. The fact that Miller's character did not sell door-to-door, nor did he sell insurance, matters little. The point is that he represents the conjunction of traditional sales methods and failure to sell—precisely the formula that the business advisors want to place in opposition to their own ideas. To escape Willy's fate, the salesperson need simply follow this good advice. As one advisor to life insurance salespeople writes in the hopefully entitled "Goodbye, Willy Loman": "as long as we continue to participate in solutions to society's insurance problems and are receptive to change, the challenges that lie before us will be easy to meet . . . if only Willy Loman had known what we do now."[30]

17   Sometimes the context is darker than this, however. *Death of a Salesman* and Willy Loman are also evoked in cultural commentary that is not selling a quick fix for the individual, but is pointing to significant economic changes and trends that create deep anxiety for some part of the populace. In these cases, *Salesman's* cultural iconography is a shorthand that reaches the reader's emotions before the analysis begins. In "Ageism and Advertising: It's Time the Ad Industry Got Past Its *Death of a Salesman* View of Employees Over 40," for example, Blake Brodie complains that executives in ad agencies are worried about being seen as surrounding themselves with "older staff," which is "death" in most ad agencies, making it rare to find a creative director who is over thirty-nine or an account executive over forty-five. Associating the anxiety of these relatively youthful executives over the possible loss of their jobs with Willy's predicament—"you can't eat the orange and throw the peel away. A man is not a piece of fruit!"— not only heightens the reader's emotional response but suggests that what might be viewed as an isolated difficulty in a particular "fast-track" yuppie career is part of a pervasive social problem— what the writer is calling "Ageism." Similarly, the mounting fear that one's chosen career could evaporate in the context of the rapidly developing technologies of the business world is expressed in serious articles like *The Economist's* "Death of a Salesman: Travel Agents," which analyzes the declining profits of travel agents as customers do more of their own travel reservations online, and *Maclean's* "Death of a Car Salesman," which delineates major changes in the tactics of car sales as a result of online buying and the increasing replacement of commissioned agents by salaried sales forces at large car dealerships. These articles are fundamentally optimistic. They endorse the changes in the ways of doing business as better uses of technology that will result in greater efficiency and productivity. But the reference to Willy Loman creates a subtext of anxiety that undermines the positive rhetoric. Older salespeople will not be able to keep up, it reminds the reader. People will lose their jobs. Smaller agencies will be swallowed up by bigger ones. Humanity is losing out to technology.

18   To read these publications is to discover a mindset that simultaneously loaths Willy Loman and identifies with him. The writers want to put as much distance as possible between themselves

and what Willy stands for—failure and death—but they can't help embracing him like a brother. After all, he has enacted their own deepest fears, and the experience has killed him. In Willy Loman, Arthur Miller has supplied to America's business culture—and as Calvin Coolidge reminded us, the business of America *is* business—the site where these deeply conflicted feelings can be engaged with some safety. Much as we try to deny it, Americans need Willy Loman. As long as our socio-economic system survives, Willy Loman will be right there with it, reminding us of our lyrical, fantastic dreams, and our darkest fears.

Notes

[1] Luke P. Carroll, "Birth of a Legend: First Year of 'Salesman,'" *New York Tribune* (5 February 1950), section 5, 1.

[2] Thomas R. Dash, "'Life' of a Salesman," *Women's Wear Daily* (24 February 1949), 51.

[3] *Timebends: A Life* (New York; Grove, 1987), 315.

[4] "The New Breed of Salesmen—Not Like Willy," *Newsweek* 64 (5 October 1964), 94.

[5] Carl Reiser, "The Salesman Isn't Dead—He's Different," *Fortune* 66 (November 1962), 124.

[6] Ibid.

[7] "The New Breed," 94.

[8] Val Adams, "Willy Loman Irks Fellow Salesmen," *New York Times* (27 March 1966).

[9] Morry Roth, "Un-Do 'Death of a Salesman'" *Variety* (16 April 1969), 7.

[10] "What Now, Willy Loman?" *Mother Jones* (8 November 1983), 52.

[11] John A. Byrne, "Motivating Willy Loman," *Forbes* 133 (30 January 1984), 91.

[12] Ibid.

[13] Martha Farnsworth Riche, "Willy Loman Rides Again," *American Demographics* 10 (March 1988), 8.

[14] Arthur Miller, *Death of a Salesman*, Acting Edition (New York: Dramatists Play Service, 1952), 21.

[15] April 1993, B1.

[16] *The Wall Street Journal* (26 November 1990), B1.

[17]"The Yankee Trader: *Death of a Salesman,*" *U.S. News and World Report* 98 (8 April 1985), 64–70.

[18]*ABA Journal* 76 (October 1988), 88–92.

[19]*The National Law Journal* 9 (6 October 1986), 6.

[20]*Arthur Miller's Collected Plays* (New York: Viking, 1957), 35.

[21]"Death of a Salesman," *Hartford Courant* (30 November 1994), A18.

[22]Jim Henry, "Death of a 'Salesman,'" *Automotive News* (12 June 1995), 3.

[23]Brian D. Johnson, "*Cop Land,*" *Maclean's* 110 (25 August 1997), 74.

[24]Francis X. Clines, "Downbeat Days for Salesman Gramm," *New York Times* (10 February 1996), 10.

[25]George F. Will, "A Political Willy Loman," *Newsweek* (2 March 1998), 92.

[26]Jonathan B. Levine and Zachary Schiller, "If Only Willy Loman Had Used a Laptop," *Business Week* (12 October 1987), 137.

[27]Joseph F. McKenna, "Was Willy Loman in the Wrong Job?" *Industry Week* 239 (17 September 1990), 11.

[28]Kerry D. Carson and Paula Phillips Carson, "Career Entrenchment: A Quiet March Toward Occupational Death?" *Academy of Management Executives* 11 (February 1997), 62–75.

[29]Sally Roberts, "Taking a Lesson from Willy Loman: Brokers Must Move Beyond Sales to Satisfy Risk Manager Demands," *Business Insurance* 30 (6 May 1996), 49.

[30]Alan Press, "Goodbye, Willy Loman," *Best's Review (Life-Health-Insurance)* 90 (September 1989), 70.

VALERIE M. SMITH

Smith (born, 1958) grew up in New Jersey and lived and traveled extensively throughout Europe and the Middle East before returning to college. She earned a B.A. in English from Wesleyan University (1992) and a M.A. from the University of Connecticut in 1994. She is currently completing a doctorate in English, writing a dissertation, "Crossroads," on twentieth-century American travel narratives.

She observes that to date very few feminist essays have been published on Miller's *Death of a Salesman,* probably because the

play's female characters appear to be more static and less interesting than the play's male characters. While doing research on
twentieth-century conceptions of masculinity for her dissertation,
she grew curious about issues of gender in *Death of a Salesman*.
The next step was to look closely at conceptions of femininity
during the late 1940s and early 1950s to see how they might be
read in the terms of the play. This research inspired her to consider the question that works as the essay's first sentence. The
rest of her essay explores that question from the perspective of
feminist/gender criticism.

❄ *Death of a Salesman's Wife*

T he central question this paper explores is whether Arthur 1
Miller's *Death of a Salesman* is a play that applauds sexual
stereotypes, challenges sexual stereotypes, or whether it is a play
that merely reflects the stereotypes of an era. The stage directions
for Act I, with the "small and fine" flute that provides a romanti-
cized view of nature juxtaposed with the "towering angular
shapes" and the "angry glow" of a hostile man-made world, let
us know that one of the play's central concerns will be to consider
the debate of nature versus culture. In relation to feminist/gender
criticism, this debate concerns the question of whether men and
women are shaped by biology or culture. Thus, within the first
seven sentences of stage direction the play's audience is invited
into a world of contrasts, change, and flux, a world of multiple possibilities, a world in which movement and change are inescapable.
But it appears to be a world of multiple complexities and possibilities for the play's masculine characters only; its female characters
remain fixed, one-dimensional, without the possibility of change.

The play's complexities, contrasts, and movement are illus- 2
trated in the characters of the Salesman, Willy Loman, and his two
sons, Biff and Happy, as they struggle with living up to outmoded
conceptions of masculinity, conceptions which in the end prove
destructive to all they touch. Alternative conceptions of masculinity are illustrated in the characters of Charley and his son Bernard,
the play's two most successful characters—Charley owns a thriving business, Bernard argues cases before the Supreme Court. Willy

derides the alternative models of masculinity—kindness, generosity, modesty, and hardwork—represented by Charley and his
bookish son Bernard. The masculine role models he clings to are
his vanishing father, a brother who "personifies the male world
of capitalism, imperialism, and the American myth of success"
(Balakian 118), and an eighty-four-year-old salesman who was
"remembered and loved and helped" in the days when there was
"respect, and comradeship, and gratitude" (Miller 773). Even
though Willy and his sons are failures, successful masculinity in
another form allows the play to end on a note of optimism—not all
men are doomed to failure; some can and do succeed by following
other conceptions of masculinity. Thus the play tells us that masculinity can be conceived of in a variety of complex and competing
forms, it can change and evolve according to social circumstances
if one allows it to do so. It is therefore not bound by nature.

3   But what about femininity? Is femininity determined by culture or nature? In the context of the play only one answer initially
appears possible. Since Linda Loman is the only main female
character, our access to multiple conceptions of femininity is constricted. The other women we meet are constructed solely as objects of sexual desire; it is their looks and their willingness to
participate in sexual acts, not the complexity of their characters,
that moves the action along. They are easily dismissed as "ruined"
women, potentially dangerous, virtually speechless, and good for
one thing only.

4   The play's main female character, although she has more
lines, remains one-dimensional as well. As Gayle Austin has
noted, "the wife and mother, Linda, is restricted before the play
begins by her description in the opening stage directions" (61).
Our initial introduction to Linda Loman in the play's Overture
contrasts sharply with our introduction to Willy. Willy, though
growing older and exhausted from his line of work, is described in
terms of actions: he enters, carries, hears, crosses, speaks. Linda
Loman, on the other hand, is described only in terms of her relationship to Willy: she wakens when she hears him arrive home,
she loves him, she admires him, "she has developed an iron
repression of her exceptions to Willy's behavior," she shares his
longings but "lacks the temperament to utter and follow [them]
to their end" (734). The rest of the paragraph, ostensibly devoted
to a description of Linda, describes Willy's character traits instead,

"his temper, his massive dreams and little cruelties . . . the turbulent longings within him." In the play women exist only in their relation to men. They are either the epitome of the enabler (sometimes referred to as the feminine ideal), "the foundation that has allowed the Loman men to build themselves up, if only in their dreams . . . the support that enables them to continue despite their failures. . . . the one element holding the facade of the family together" (75) as Kay Stanton has described Linda, or they are the "strudel" and "crumpets" that Linda despises and Happy chases—dangerously tempting but not wholesome. In either case, they remain constricted in their one-dimensional roles.

Thus, the message the play ostensibly delivers is that femininity has no complexity; one is either a good, downtrodden woman/wife like Linda or a whore/single-woman willing to sell her services for "two boxes of size nine sheers" (Miller 796). In any event, the conception of femininity remains solely relational, closed and fixed with no possibility for change or choice. This lack of choice is made clear in the above mentioned Overture in which Linda's "lack" clearly delimits her ability to act on her own "turbulent longings." Women can be and feel but they cannot act on their own behalf outside of their relations with men. The text of the play tells us that Linda's "turbulent longings" are not the same as Willy's. Whereas Willy wants fame and glory within the parameters of his vision of acceptable masculinity, Linda accepts the idea that "life is a casting off" (Miller 735)—that things change. She questions Willy's and Ben's desire to "conquer the world" (Miller 776), and believes that it's "enough to be happy right here, right now." We don't have a clue as to what Linda's "turbulent longings" might be, although we know they differ from Willy's, but we do know that she can neither "utter" nor "follow" them because of her "lack" (Miller 734). Which again brings us to the central question of whether women's roles are culturally or naturally determined within the terms of the play. Is Linda's "lack" biologically or culturally determined?

Does *Death of a Salesman* consider women's roles to be determined by natural forces or does it merely reflect the social constrictions facing women in the late 1940s? Brett Harvey tells us that "the fifties . . . really began in 1946, the year after the war ended" (226) and that "the postwar era represented a dramatic retreat from the trends of previous decades" (xiv). Up to this point women's roles and opportunities had been expanding since the twenties when women first won the vote and achieved more opportunities for college and work. Large numbers of women were drafted into the work force during the Second World War, working at jobs previously open only to men, earning men's wages for the first time, and living self-sufficient, independent lives at a time in which "the frigid sexual codes of previous times" had been replaced by "a more free-and-easy sexuality." Following the war, women's jobs were given back to returning veterans and women were expected to focus their lives around home and family—to lose the gains they'd won and retreat backwards a couple of decades.

7   The U.S. government, social scientists, and the media engaged in a "massive effort" to ensure this occurred. Harvey notes, "Increasingly, marriage and family were expected to be a woman's whole world. Her intelligence, energy, creativity, and sexuality all were funneled into the constricted sphere of family life" (xv–xvi) and that "this narrowing of women's sphere was reinforced by the lack of desirable options outside of marriage" (xvi)—options deliberately restricted in order to ensure compliance with the prescribed social "norm." Once again few professions were available to women and those that were generally paid poorly. Sexual experience outside marriage could result in a "loss of reputation—an essential commodity if marriage was to be your sole identity" (xvi). Women's options were severely and deliberately limited during this time in order to contain "potentially dangerous" political and social forces. As Elaine Taylor May explains, "containment aptly describes the way in which public policy, personal behavior, and even political values were focused on the home" (qtd. in Harvey xiv). Severe social constrictions were brought into play in order to ensure women's energy was refocused on their homes rather than on the social, political, and economic issues of the day.

8   During a time in which the potential for social upheaval and unrest was tremendous due to turbulent economic and political circumstances, a variety of forces, including the mass media, began extolling the virtues and rewards of femininity as well as the punishments for acting outside its boundaries. As Herman and Chomsky explain, such systems "amuse, entertain . . . inform . . . and inculcate individuals with the values, beliefs, and codes of

behavior that will integrate them into the institutional structures of the large society" (1). The rewards for conformity to the feminine ideal were supposed to be financial security, social approval and respect, and a loving and happy family. On the other hand, instability, social ostracism, and loneliness were the penalties (among others) for acting outside socially approved modes of femininity. While Linda Loman does indeed appear to receive social approval from her family (they sing her praises even while disrespecting her), her financial security is precarious throughout the play (until Willy kills himself to collect on his insurance), her family is anything but loving and happy, and in the end "there'll be nobody home" (Miller 808). Thus, though Linda appears to be the epitome of self-sacrificing femininity she receives few of its promised rewards, just as Willy, the epitome of a certain type of masculinity, receives none of its rewards.

The play's final message appears to be that conforming to outmoded gender roles is destructive in a variety of ways. Willy destroys himself through his inability to change. His children have nearly destroyed themselves in their attempt to live up to his expectations. His wife retains none of the promised rewards for maintaining her role; indeed, she has contributed to the destruction of both her husband and her children by constantly trying to smooth things over, conciliate, act the part of the submissive wife. Thus, the play's message is that society needs men *and* women capable of seizing new possibilities and engaging in fruitful change unless it is to self-destruct. Society needs multidimensional people like Biff Loman; people who are capable of struggling with identity (Biff moves from feeling lost to claiming "I know who I am" (Miller 807), people who are capable of overcoming the fear of attempting new modes of behavior (Biff picks up the flowers his mother has knocked to the floor). Finally, society needs people capable of understanding that sexual conquest and selling one's soul for the sake of status are not the only pathways to success.

Works Cited

Austin, Gayle. "The Exchange of Women and Male Homosocial Desire in Arthur Miller's *Death of a Salesman* and Lillian Hellman's *Another Part of the Forest*." *Feminist Rereadings of*

Modern American Drama. Ed. June Schlueter. Rutherford, N.J.: Fairleigh Dickinson UP, 1989. 59–66.

Balakian, Jan. "Beyond the Male Locker Room: *Death of a Salesman* from a Feminist Perspective." *Approaches to Teaching Miller's Death of a Salesman.* Ed. Matthew C. Roundané. New York: MLA, 1995. 115–24.

Harvey, Brett. *The Fifties: A Woman's Oral History.* New York: HarperPerennial, 1993.

Herman, Edward S., and Noam Chomsky. *Manufacturing Consent: The Political Economy of the Mass Media.* New York: Pantheon, 1998.

Miller, Arthur. *Death of a Salesman.* 1949. *The Heath Introduction to Drama.* Ed. Jordan Y. Miller. Lexington, MA: Heath, 1996. 733–808.

Stanton, Kay. "Women and the American Dream of *Death of a Salesman.*" *Feminist Rereadings of Modern American Drama.* Ed. June Schlueter. Rutherford, N.J.: Fairleigh Dickinson UP, 1989. 67–102.

For Writing

1. Write a critical analysis of a poem, short story, novel, play, film, TV program, advertisement, concert, art exhibit, or other work according to criteria that you—and perhaps your classmates—determine, or that your instructor specifies.

2. Working either individually or in a team, pick a work of literature, film, or TV that you enjoy, and find out what you can either about why and how it was written, or how it was received by reviewers or original audiences and more contemporary ones.

3. Write a review of the film or video version of a play or novel, comparing and evaluating the two versions according to whatever criteria you wish (see reviews of *Death of a Salesman* by Atkinson, 732–36, and Brantley, 736–41).

4. The stage and film versions of many plays are significantly different, though they tell the same story, as are adaptations of novels for stage, screen, or video. Likewise, *West Side Story* is a twentieth-century adaptation of Shakespeare's *Romeo and Juliet.* Translate a scene from a familiar story, play, or poem from its existing idiom or mode into another.

Glossary

abstract refers to qualities, ideas, or states of being that exist but that our senses cannot perceive. What we perceive are the concrete by-products of abstract ideas. No single object or action can be labeled *love*, but a warm embrace or a passionate kiss is a visible, concrete token of the abstraction we call "love." In "Notes of a Native Speaker," Eric Liu, though Asian, characterizes his cultural self as "white" (335–49). In many instances abstract words such as *beauty, hatred, stupidity,* or *kindness* are more clearly understood if illustrated with **concrete** examples (*see* **concrete** and **general/specific**).

allusion is a writer's reference to a person, place, thing, literary character, or quotation that the reader is expected to recognize. Because the reader supplies the meaning and the original context, such references are economical; writers don't have to explain them. By alluding to a young man as a *Romeo, Don Juan,* or *Casanova,* a writer can present the subject's amorous nature without needing to say more. To make sure that references will be understood, writers have to choose what their readers can reasonably be expected to recognize.

analogy is a comparison made between two things, qualities, or ideas that have certain similarities although the items themselves may be very different. For example, Scott Russell Sanders characterizes his alcoholic father, "Like a torture victim who refuses to squeal, he would never admit that he had touched a drop, not even in his last year when he seemed to be dissolving in alcohol before our very eyes" ("Under the Influence," 441–56). The emphasis is on the similarities between Mr. Sanders, drunk or sober, and the torture victim; dissimilarities would have weakened the analogy. **Metaphors** and **similes** are two figures of speech that are based on analogies, and such comparisons are often used in argumentation (*see* **figures of speech** *and* **argumentation**).

appeal to emotion is one of several ways writers can move their readers to accept what they say. As a means of persuasion, the writer's appeal to emotion allows words and examples to affect readers in ways that advertisements sometimes affect consumers. Mairs's powerful essay "On Being a Cripple" (456–71) engages readers' emotions as she describes what it is like to be crippled (not "differently abled"), both positive ("as a cripple, I swagger") and negative ("I don't like having MS. I hate it."). As momentary eyewitnesses, we are moved by the descriptions and convinced of her truthfulness. When a writer presents himself as a person of integrity, intelligence, and goodwill, he appeals to the readers' sense of ethics, as Martin Luther King, Jr., does in "Letter from Birmingham Jail" (596–616). Although one approach touches the heart and the other the mind, these appeals are not mutually exclusive and, indeed, are often intertwined. *See* Chapter 14 introduction (642–47).

argument, in a specialized literary sense, is a prose summary of the plot, main idea, or subject of a prose or poetic work.

argumentation is one of the four modes of discourse, as commonly identified (*see* **description, exposition,** *and* **narration**). It seeks to convince the reader of the truth or falseness of an idea. Writers sometimes accomplish this by appealing to readers' emotions, as Barry does in "The Sanctuary of School" (670–75) or by appealing to readers' ethics, as is the case in "None of This Is Fair" by Richard Rodriguez (398–405). Others, such as Stephen Jay Gould in "Evolution as Fact and Theory" (550–60), can argue for or against a volatile issue by appealing to the readers' sense of reason, though often in an argument these appeals are interrelated. An argument can be *overt,* when its real point is explicitly stated, or *implied,* when its point is made more obliquely. Common techniques of implied argument include using illustrative case (*see* Scott Russell Sanders, "Under the Influence" [441–56], satire (*see* Jonathan Swift, "A Modest Proposal" [650–60]), or an ironic tone (*see* Joan Didion, "Marrying Absurd" [330–35]). *See* Chapter 13 introduction (585–90).

audience consists of the readers of a given writing. Writers may write some pieces solely for themselves; others for their peers, teachers, or supervisors; others for people with special interest in and knowledge of the subject. Writers aware of some of the following dimensions can adapt the level of their language and the details of their presentation to different sorts of readers. What is the age range of the intended readers? The educational level? Their national, regional, or local background? Have they relevant biases, beliefs? How much do they know about the subject? Why should they be interested in it or in the writer's views? Gertrude Stein once observed, "I write for myself and strangers." By answering some of the questions above, the writer can try to convert strangers into friends or, at least, into willing participants in the ongoing dialogue between writer and readers.

cause and effect writing examines in detail the relationship between the *why* (cause) and *what* (effect) of an incident, phenomenon, or event. A writer could focus on the causes of a particular social, medical, or fictional occurrence (the Depression, psychotic depression in general, or Hamlet's depression in particular), or she might emphasize the effects of one or a combination of causes, such as the consequences of excessive indulgence in drugs, alcohol, or video games. In "I Just Wanna Be Average" (263–73) Mike Rose explains both the causes and effects of wanting to be average; one cause produces an effect that causes other effects, and so on. As the poet William Butler Yeats observed, "How can we know the dancer from the dance?"

classification groups items or concepts to emphasize their similarities, and then, through division, breaks down the larger category into its separate components or subgroups to show their distinguishing features, as Lewis Thomas does in "The Technology of Medicine" (375–81). The writer who classifies information first determines the overall features of the forest and then identifies the specific trees it contains.

cliché is a commonplace expression that reveals the writer's lack of imagination to use fresher, more vivid language. If a person finds himself *between a rock and a hard place,* he might decide to use a cliché, *come hell or high water,* in hopes that it will hit his reader *like a ton of bricks.* Such expressions, though, *fall on deaf ears* and roll off the reader *like water off a duck's back.* A cliché is *as dead as a mackerel;* its excessive familiarity dulls the reader's responses. Avoid clichés *like the plague.*

coherence indicates an orderly relationship among the parts in a whole essay or other literary work. Writing is coherent when the interconnections among clauses, sentences, and paragraphs are clearly and logically related to the main subject under discussion. The writer may establish and maintain coherence through the use of transitional words or phrases (however; likewise), a consistent point of view, an ordered chronological or spatial presentation of information, appropriate pronoun references for nouns, or strategic repetition of important words or sentence structures.

colloquial expressions (*see* **diction**)

colloquialism (*see* **diction**)

comparison and contrast aims to show the reader similarities and differences that exist between two or more things or ideas. Items that are alike (all apples) are compared, while those that are dissimilar are contrasted (cherries, kumquats, passion fruit). *See* Deborah Tannen, "Communication Styles" (536–44).

conclusion refers to sentences, paragraphs, or longer sections of an essay that bring the work to a logical or psychologically satisfying end. Although a conclusion may (**a**) summarize or restate the essay's main point, and thereby refresh the reader's memory, it may also end with (**b**) the most important point, or (**c**) a memorable example, anecdote, or quotation, or (**d**) identify the broader implications or ultimate development of the subject, or (**e**) offer a prediction. Stylistically, it's best to end with a bang, not a whimper; Lincoln's "Gettysburg Address" (648) concludes with the impressive ". . . and that government of the people, by the people, for the people, shall not perish from the earth." A vigorous conclusion grows organically from the material that precedes it and is not simply tacked on to get the essay over with.

concrete terms give readers something specific to see, hear, touch, smell, or feel, while abstract terms are more general and intangible. Writers employ concrete words to show their subject or characters in action, rather than merely to tell about them. Yet a concrete word does not have to be hard, like cement; anything directly perceived by the senses is considered concrete, including an ostrich plume, the sound of a harp, a smile, or a cone of cotton candy (*see* **abstract** *and* **general/specific**).

connotation and denotation refer to two levels of interpreting the meanings of words. Denotation is the literal, explicit "core" meaning—the "dictionary" definition. Connotation refers to additional meanings implied or suggested by the word, or associated with it, depending on the user's or reader's personal experience, attitudes, and cultural conditioning. For example, the word *athlete* denotes a skilled participant in a sport. But to a sports enthusiast, *athlete* is likely to connote not just the phenomenon of one's participation in sports, but positive physical and moral qualities, such as robust physical condition, well-coordinated movements, a wholesome character, a love of the outdoors, and a concern with fair play. Those disenchanted with sports might regard an *athlete* as a marketable commodity for unscrupulous businessmen, an overpaid exploiter of the public, a drug user, or someone who has developed every part of his anatomy but his brain—a "dumb jock."

contrast (*see* **comparison/contrast**)

deduction (*see* **induction/deduction**)

deductive (*see* **induction/deduction**)

definition explains the meaning of a word, identifying the essential properties of a thing or idea. Dictionaries furnish the various literal interpretations of individual words (*see* **connotation/denotation**), but a writer may provide extended or altered definitions, sometimes of essay length, to expand or supplement "core" meanings. "My Dog, Phydeaux" might be an extended personal definition of *dog*. Whether short or long, definitions may employ other strategies of exposition, such as classification ("Phydeaux, a collie"), comparison and contrast ("is better natured than Milo, my brother's basset . . ."), description ("and has an unusual star-shaped marking on his forehead"). *See* Chapter 11, introduction (477–82).

denotation (*see* **connotation/denotation**)

description is a mode of discourse (*see* **argumentation, exposition,** *and* **narration**) aimed at bringing something to life by telling how it looks, sounds, tastes, smells, feels, or acts. The writer tries to convey a sense impression, depict a mood, or both. Thus, the writer who conveys the heat of an August sidewalk; the sound, sight, and smell of the Atlantic breaking on the jagged coastline of Maine; or the bittersweetness of an abandoned love affair, enables readers to experience the situations. Description is a writer's spice; a little goes a long way. Except in extensively descriptive travel pieces, description is primarily used to enhance the other modes of discourse and is seldom an end in itself (*see* Cynthia Ozick's "A Drugstore Eden," 316–30).

diction is word choice. Hemingway was talking about diction when he explained that the reason he allegedly rewrote the last page of *A Farewell to Arms* thirty-nine times was because of problems in "getting the words right." Getting the words right means choosing, arranging, and using words appropriate to the purpose, audience, and sometimes the form of a particular piece of writing. Puns are fine in limericks and shaggy-dog stories ("I wouldn't send a knight out on a dog like this"), but they're out of place in technical reports and obituaries. Diction ranges on a continuum from highly formal (a *repast*) to informal writing and conversation (a *meal*) to slang (*eats*), as illustrated below.

formal English words and grammatical constructions used by educated native speakers of English in sermons, oratory, and in many serious books, scientific reports, and lectures. *See* Abraham Lincoln, "The Gettysburg Address" (648).

informal (conversational or colloquial) *English* the more relaxed but still standard usage in polite (but not stuffy) conversation or writing, as in much popular newspaper writing and in many of the essays in this book. In informal writing it's all right to use contractions ("I'll go to the wedding, but I won't wear tails") and some abbreviations, but not all ("As Angela attached the IV bottle to the holder, she wondered whether the patient had OD'd on carbohydrates"). OK is generally acceptable in conversation, but it's not OK in most formal or informal writing.

slang   highly informal (often figurative) word choice in speech or writing. It may be used by specialized groups (*pot, grass, uppers*) or more general speakers to add vividness and humor (often derogatory) to their language. Although some slang is old and sometimes even becomes respectable (*cab*), it often erupts quickly into the language and just as quickly disappears (*twenty-three skidoo*); it's better to avoid all slang than to use outmoded slang.

regionalisms   expressions used by people of a certain region of the country, often derived from the native languages of earlier settlers, such as *arroyo* for *deep ditch* used in the Southwest.

dialect   the spoken (and sometimes written) language of a group of people that reflects their social, educational, economic, and geographic status ("My mamma done tole me . . ."). Dialect may include regionalisms. In parts of the Northeast, *youse* is a dialect form of *you,* while its counterpart in the South is *y'all.* Even some educated Southerners say *ain't,* but they don't usually write it except to be humorous.

technical terms (jargon)   words used by those in a particular trade, occupation, business, or specialized activity. For example, medical personnel use *stat* (immediately) and *NPO* (nothing by mouth); surfers' vocabularies include *shooting the curl, hotdogging,* and *hang ten; hardware* has different meanings for carpenters and computer users.

division (*see* **classification**)
effect (*see* **cause/effect**)
emphasis makes the most important ideas, characters, themes, or other elements stand out. The principal ways of achieving emphasis are through the use of the following:

proportion   saying more about the major issues and less about the minor ones.
position   placing important material in the key spots, the beginning or ends of paragraphs or larger units. Arrangement in climactic order, with the main point of an argument or the funniest joke last, can be particularly effective.
repetition   of essential words, phrases, and ideas ("Ask not what your country can do for you; ask what you can do for your country.")
focus   pruning of verbal underbrush and unnecessary detail to accentuate the main features.

mechanical devices such as capitalization, underlining (italics), and exclamation points, conveying enthusiasm, excitement, and emphasis, as advertisers and new journalists well know. Tom Wolfe's title *Las Vegas (What?) Las Vegas (Can't Hear You! Too Noisy) Las Vegas!!!!* illustrates this practice, as well as the fact that nothing exceeds like excess.

essay refers to a composition, usually or primarily nonfiction, on a central theme or subject, usually brief and written in prose. As the contents of this book reveal, essays come in varied modes—among them descriptive, narrative, analytic, argumentative—and moods, ranging from humorous to grim, whimsical to bitterly satiric. Essays are sometimes categorized as *formal* or *informal*, depending on the author's content, style, and organization. Formal essays, written in formal language, tend to focus on a single significant idea supported with evidence carefully chosen and arranged, such as Robert Reich's "The Global Elite" (624–36). Informal essays sometimes have a less obvious structure than formal essays; the subject may seem less significant, even ordinary; the manner of presentation casual, personal, or humorous. Yet these distinctions blur. Although E. B. White's "Once More to the Lake" (171–79) discusses a personal experience in conversation and humorous language, its apparently trivial subject, the vacation of a boy and his father in the Maine woods, takes on universal, existential significance.

evidence is supporting information that explains or proves a point. General comments or personal opinions that are not substantiated with evidence leave the reader wanting some proof of accuracy. Writers establish credibility by backing general statements with examples, facts, and figures that make evident their knowledge of the subject. We believe what Joan Didion says about Las Vegas weddings in "Marrying Absurd" (330–35) because her specific examples show that she's been there and has understood the context.

example (*see* **illustration**)

exposition is a mode of discourse that, as its name indicates, exposes information, through explaining, defining, or interpreting its subject. Expository prose is to the realm of writing what the Ford automobile has been historically to the auto industry—useful, versatile, accessible to the average person, and heavy duty—for it is the mode of the most research reports, critical analyses, examination answers, case histories, reviews, and term papers. In exposition, writers employ a variety of techniques, such as definition, illustration, classification, comparison and contrast, analogy, and cause-and-effect reasoning. Exposition is not an exclusive mode; it is often blended with other modes (*see* **argumentation, description,** *and* **narration**) to provide a more complete or convincing discussion of a subject.

figures of speech are used by writers who want to make their subject unique or memorable through vivid language. Literal language often lacks the connotations of figurative language. Instead of merely conveying information ("The car was messy"), a writer might use a figure of speech to attract attention ("The car was a Dumpster on wheels"). Figures of speech enable the writer to play with words and with the reader's imagination. Some of the most frequently used figures of speech include the following:

metaphor   an implied comparison that equates two things or qualities. "No dictionary of synonyms for **drunk** would soften the anguish of watching our prince turn into a frog" (Scott Russell Sanders).

simile   a direct comparison; usually with the connecting word *like* or *as*. ". . . inside [the sawed board] there was this smell waiting, as of something freshly baked" (Scott Russell Sanders).

personification   humanization of inanimate or nonhuman objects or qualities, as in giving a car, a boat, or a plane a person's name.

hyperbole   an elaborate exaggeration, often intended to be humorous or ironic. "When I was younger I could remember anything, whether it had happened or not; but my faculties are decaying now, and soon I shall be so I cannot remember any but the things that never happened" (Mark Twain).

understatement   a deliberate downplaying of the seriousness of something. As with the *hyperbole,* the antithesis of understatement, this is often done for the sake of humor or irony. [My **Modest Proposal**] is "innocent, cheap, easy, effectual" (Jonathan Swift).

paradox   a contradiction that upon closer inspection is actually truthful. ("You never know what you've got until you lose it.")

rhetorical question   a question that demands no answer, asked for dramatic impact. In "Letter from Birmingham Jail" (596–616) Martin Luther King, Jr. asks, "Will we be extremists for hate or for love? Will we be extremists for the preservation of injustice or for the extension of justice?"

metonomy   the representation of an object, public office, or concept by something associated with it. ("Watergate brought down the White House, as Woodward and Bernstein explain in *All the President's Men.*")

dead metaphor   a word or phrase, originally a figure of speech, that through constant use is treated literally (the *arm* of a chair, the *leg* of a table, the *head* of a bed).

focus represents the writer's control and limitation of a subject to a specific aspect or set of features, determined in part by the subject under discussion (*what* the writer is writing about), the audience (to *whom* the writer is writing), and the purpose (*why* the writer is writing). Thus, instead of writing about food in general, someone writing for college students on limited budgets might focus on imaginative but economical meals.

general and specific are the ends of a continuum that designates the relative degree of abstractness or concreteness of a word. General terms identify the class (*house*); specific terms restrict the class by naming its members (a *Georgian mansion*, a *Dutch colonial*, a *brick ranch*). To clarify relationships, words may be arranged in a series from general to specific: writers, twentieth-century authors, Southern novelists, Eudora Welty (*see* **abstract** *and* **concrete**).

generalization (*see* **induction/deduction** *and* **logical fallacies**)

hyperbole (*see* **figures of speech**). See Judy Brady, "I Want a Wife" (506–10).

illustration refers to providing an example, sometimes of essay length, that clarifies a broad statement or concept for the reader. This technique takes the reader from a general to a specific level of interpretation (*see* **general/specific**). See Chapter 10, introduction (421–24).

induction and deduction refer to two different methods of arriving at a conclusion. Inductive reasoning relies on examining specific instances, examples, or facts in an effort to arrive at a general conclusion. If you were to sample several cakes—chocolate, walnut, mocha, and pineapple upside-down—you might reach the general conclusion that all cakes are sweet. Conversely, deductive reasoning involves examining general principles in order to arrive at a specific conclusion. If you believe that all cakes are sweet, you would expect the next cake you encounter, say, lemon chiffon, to be sweet. Yet both of these types of reasoning can lead to erroneous generalizations if the reasoner or writer has not examined all of the relevant aspects of the issue. For instance, not all cakes are sweet—consider the biscuit cake in strawberry shortcake. Likewise, even if a writer cited five separate instances in which members of a particular ethnic group displayed criminal behavior, it would be incorrect to conclude that all members of this group are criminal. Beware, therefore, of using absolute words such as *always, never, everyone, no one, only,* and *none. See* Chapter 13, introduction (585–90).

inductive (*see* **induction/deduction**)

introduction is the beginning of a written work that is likely to present the author's subject, focus (perhaps including the thesis), attitude toward it, and possibly the plan for organizing supporting materials. The length of the introduction is usually proportionate to the length of what follows; short essays may be introduced by a sentence or two; a book may require an entire introductory chapter. In any case, an introduction should be sufficiently forceful and interesting to let readers know what is to be discussed and entice them to continue reading. An effective introduction might do one or more of the following:

1. state the thesis or topic emphatically;
2. present a controversial or startling focus on the topic;
3. offer a witty or dramatic quotation, statement, metaphor, or analogy;
4. provide background information to help readers understand the subject, its history, or significance;
5. give a compelling anecdote or illustration from real life;
6. refer to an authority on the subject.

irony is a technique that enables the writer to say one thing while meaning another, often with critical intention. Three types of irony are frequently used by writers: *verbal, dramatic,* and *situational.* Verbal irony is expressed with tongue in cheek, often implying the opposite of what is overtly stated. The verbal ironist maintains tight control over tone, counting on the alert reader (or listener) to recognize the discrepancy between words and meaning, as does Jonathan Swift in "A Modest Proposal" (650–60), where deadpan advocacy of cannibalism is really a monstrous proposal. Dramatic irony, found in plays, novels, and other forms of fiction, allows readers to see the wisdom or folly of characters' actions in light of information they have—the ace up their sleeve—that the characters lack. For example, readers know Desdemona is innocent of cheating on her husband, Othello, but his ignorance of the truth and of the behavior of virtuous women leads him to murder her in a jealous rage. Situational irony, life's joke on life, entails opposition between what would ordinarily occur and what actually happens in a particular instance. In O. Henry's "The Gift of the Magi," the husband sells his watch to buy his wife combs for her hair, only to find out she has sold her hair to buy him a watch chain.

jargon (*see* **diction**)

logical fallacies are errors in reasoning and often occur in arguments. *See* Chapter 13, introduction (585–90).

metaphor (*see* **figures of speech**)

metonomy (*see* **figures of speech**)

modes of discourse are traditionally identified as narration, description, argumentation, and exposition. In writing they are often intermingled. The *narration* of Frederick Douglass's "Resurrection" (164–70), for instance, involves *description of characters* and settings, an explanation (*exposition*) of their motives, while the expression of its theme serves as an *argument*, direct and indirect. Through its characters, actions, and situations it argues powerfully against slavery.

narration is one of four modes of discourse (*see* **argumentation, description,** *and* **exposition**) that recounts an event or series of interrelated events. Jokes, fables, fairy tales, short stories, plays, novels, and other forms of literature are narrative if they tell a story. Although some narrations provide only the basic *who, what, when, where,* and *why* of an occurrence in an essentially chronological arrangement, as in a newspaper account of a murder, others contain such features as plot, conflict, suspense, characterization, and description to intensify readers' interest. Whether as pared down as a nursery rhyme ("Lizzie Borden took an axe/Gave her father forty whacks . . ."), of intermediate length such as Frederick Douglass's "Resurrection" (164–70), or as full blown as Melville's *Moby Dick,* the relaying of what happened to someone or something is a form of narration. *See* Chapter 5, introduction (159–63).

nonfiction is writing based on fact but shaped by the writer's interpretations, point of view, style, and other literary techniques. Nonfiction writings in essay or book form include interviews, portraits, biographies and autobiographies, travel writings, direct arguments, implied arguments in the form of narratives or satires, investigative reporting, reviews, literary criticism, sports articles, historical accounts, how-to instructions, and scientific and technical reports, among other types. These vary greatly in purpose (to inform, argue, entertain . . .), form, length (from a paragraph to multiple volumes), intended audience (from general readers to specialists), mood (somber to joyous, straightforward to parody), and techniques, including those of fiction—scene setting, characterization, dialogue, and so forth. *The Essay Connection* gives examples of most of these.

non sequitur a conclusion that does not follow logically from the premises. In humorous writing, the *non sequitur* conclusion is illogical, unexpected, and perhaps ridiculous: the resulting surprise startles readers into laughter—as when George Bernard Shaw's Eliza Dolittle says, upon devouring a chocolate, "I wouldn't have eaten it, but I'm too ladylike to take it out of my mouth."

objective refers to the writer's presentation of material in a personally detached, unemotional way that emphasizes the topic, rather than the author's attitudes or feelings about it as would be the case in a **subjective** presentation. Some process analyses, such as many computer instruction manuals, are written objectively. Many other process writings combine objective information with the author's personal, and somewhat subjective, views on how to do it (*see*

Chapter 6). The more heavily emotional the writing, the more subjective it is.

oxymoron a contradiction in terms, such as "study date" or "airline
food." Thus Judy Brady might consider a liberated housewife (see
"I Want a Wife," 506–10) an oxymoron.

paradox (*see* **figures of speech**)

paragraph has a number of functions. Newspaper paragraphs, which are
usually short and consist of a sentence or two, serve as punctuation—visual units to break up columns for ease of reading. A paragraph in most other prose is usually a single unified group of
sentences that explain or illustrate a central idea, whether expressed
overtly in a topic sentence, or merely implied. Paragraphs emphasize ideas; each new topic (or sometimes each important subtopic)
demands a new paragraph. Short (sometimes even one-sentence)
paragraphs can provide transitions from one major area of discussion to another, or indicate a change of speakers in dialogue.

parallelism is the arrangement of two or more equally important ideas in
similar grammatical form ("I came, I saw, I conquered"). Not only
is it an effective method of presenting more than one thought at a
time, it also makes reading more understandable and memorable
for the reader because of the almost rhythmic quality it produces.
Within a sentence parallel structure can exist between words that
are paired ("All work and no play made Jack a candidate for cardiac
arrest"), items in a series ("His world revolved around debits,
credits, cash flows, and profits"), phrases ("Reading books, preparing reports, and dictating interoffice memos—these were a few of
his favorite things"), and clauses ("Most people work only to live;
Jack lived only to work"). Parallelism can also be established between sentences in a paragraph and between paragraphs in a
longer composition, often through the repetition of key words and
phrases, as Lincoln does throughout the Gettysburg Address (648).

parallel structure (*see* **parallelism**)

paraphrase is putting someone else's ideas—usually the essential points
or illustrations—into your own words, for your own purposes. Although a summary condenses the original material, a paraphrase
is a restatement that may be short or as long as the original, even
longer. Students writing research papers frequently find that para-
phrasing information from their sources eliminates excessive
lengthy quotations, and may clarify the originals. Be sure to acknowledge the source of either quoted or paraphrased material to
avoid plagiarism.

parody exaggerates the subject matter, philosophy, characters, language,
style, or other features of a given author or particular work. Such

imitation calls attention to both versions; such scrutiny may show the original to be a masterpiece—or to be in need of improvement. Parody derives much of its humor from the double vision of the subject that writer and readers share, as in Ann Upperco Dolman's "Learning to Drive" (196–200).

person is a grammatical distinction made between the speaker (first person—*I, we*), the one spoken to (second person—*you*), and the one spoken about (third person—*he, she, it, they*). In an essay or fictional work the point of view is often identified by person. Eric Liu's "Notes of a Native Speaker" (335–49) is written in the first person, while Gilbert Highet's "The Gettysburg Address" (691–98) is a third-person work (*see* **point of view**).

persona, literally a "mask," is a fictitious mouthpiece or an alter ego character devised by a writer for the purpose of telling a story or making comments that may or may not reflect the author's feelings and attitudes. The persona may be a narrator, as in Swift's "A Modest Proposal" (650–60), whose ostensibly humanitarian perspective advocates cannibalism and regards the poor as objects to be exploited. Swift as author emphatically rejects these views. In such cases the persona functions as a disguise for the highly critical author.

personification (*see* **figures of speech**)

persuasion, like argumentation, seeks to convince the reader or listener of an idea's truth or falseness. A persuasive argument can not only convince, but also arouse, or even move a reader to action, as in Martin Luther King, Jr.'s "Letter from Birmingham Jail" (596–616). *See* **argumentation** *and* **appeal to emotion.** *Also see* Chapters 13 and 14.

plot is the cause-and-effect relationship between events that tell a story. Unlike narration, which is an ordering of events as they occur, a plot is a writer's plan for showing how the occurrence of these events actually brings about a certain effect. The plot lets the reader see how actions and events are integral parts of something much larger than themselves.

point of view refers to the position—physical, mental, numerical—a writer takes when presenting information (*point*), and his attitude toward the subject (*view*). A writer sometimes adopts a point of view described as "limited," which restricts the inclusion of thoughts other than the narrator's, as Scott Russell Sanders does in "Under the Influence" (441–56). Conversely, the "omniscient" point of view allows the writer to know, see, and tell everything, not only about himself, but about others as well, as Isaac Asimov does in "Those Crazy Ideas" (208–20).

prewriting is a writer's term for thinking about and planning what to say before the pen hits the legal pad. Reading, observing, reminiscing, and fantasizing can all be prewriting activities if they lead to writing something down. The most flexible stage in the writing process, prewriting enables writers to mentally formulate, compose, edit, and discard before they begin the physical act of putting words on paper. Peter Elbow discusses this in *Writing Without Teachers*.

process analysis is an expository explanation of how to do something or how something is done. Sometimes the writer provides directions that the reader can follow to achieve the desired results, as in Ntozake Shange's "What Is It We Really Harvestin' Here?" (240–49). Other discussions of a process explain how something was made or discovered (*see* Isaac Asimov, "Those Crazy Ideas" [208–20]), or how it works (*see* Tom and Ray Magliozzi's "Inside the Engine" [233–40]), or the narrative processes, or procedures of a field, discipline, or profession (*see* Thomas Kuhn, "The Route to Normal Science" [221–33]). There is often more than one good way to perform any processes, and the directions reflect the writer's preferences, philosophy, and experience. See Chapter 6.

purpose identifies the author's reasons for writing. The purposes of a writing are many and varied. One can write to *clarify an issue for oneself,* or to *obtain self-understanding* ("Why I Like to Eat"). One can write to *tell a story,* to *narrate* ("My 1000-Pound Weight Loss"), or to *analyze a process* ("How to Make Quadruple Chocolate Cake"). Writing can explain *cause and effect* ("Obesity and Heart Attacks: The Fatal Connection"); it can *describe* ("The Perfect Meal"), *define* ("Calories"), *divide and classify* ("Fast Food, Slow Food, and Food That Just Sits There"). Writing can *illustrate* through examples ("McDonald's as a Symbol of American Culture"), and it can *compare and contrast* people, things, or ideas. Writing can *argue, deductively* or *inductively* ("Processed Foods Are Packaged Problems"), sometimes appealing more to emotions than to reason ("Anorexia! Beware!"). Writing can also provide *entertainment,* sometimes through parody or satire.

revise to revise is to make changes in focus, accommodation of audience, structure or organization, emphasis, development, style, mechanics, and spelling in order to bring the written work closer to one's ideal. For most writers, revising is the essence of writing. Donald M. Murray discusses the revising process in "The Maker's Eye" (126–37); Chapter 4 also includes original drafts and revisions of writing by Mary Ruffin for "Mama's Smoke" (148–58).

rhetoric, the art of using language effectively to serve the writer's purpose, originally referred to speech-making. Rhetoric now encompasses composition; its expanded definition includes a host of dynamic relationships between writer (or speaker), text (or message), and readers (or hearers). The information in this book is divided into rhetorical modes, such as exposition, narration, description, and argumentation.

rhetorical question (*see* **figures of speech**)

satire is humorous, witty criticism of people's foolish, thoughtless, or evil behavior. The satirist ridicules some aspect of human nature—or life in general—that should be changed. Depending on the subject and the severity of the author's attack, a satire can be mildly abrasive or ironic, as in Joan Didion's "Marrying Absurd" (330–35), or viciously scathing, as is Swift in "A Modest Proposal" (650–60). Usually (although not always) the satirist seeks to bring about reform through criticism.

sentence, grammatically defined, is an independent clause containing a subject and verb, and may also include modifiers and related words. *Sentence structure* is another name for *syntax,* the arrangement of individual words in a sentence that shows their relationship to each other. Besides word choice (*diction*), writers pay special attention to the way their chosen words are arranged to form clauses, phrases, entire sentences. A *thesis sentence* (or *statement*) is the main idea in a written work that reflects the author's purpose. Some writings, notably parodies and satires, only imply a thesis; direct arguments frequently provide an explicitly stated thesis, usually near the beginning, and organize subsequent paragraphs around this central thought. A *topic sentence* clearly reflects the major idea and unifying thought of a given paragraph. When it is placed near the beginning of a paragraph, a topic sentence provides the basis for other sentences in the paragraph. When the topic sentence comes at the end of a paragraph or essay, it may function as the conclusion of a logical argument, or the climax of an escalating emotional progression.

simile (*see* **figures of speech**)

slang (*see* **diction**)

specific (*see* **general/specific**)

style, the manner in which a writer says what he wants to say, as the result of the author's *diction* (word choice) and *syntax* (sentence structure), *arrangement of ideas, emphasis,* and *focus.* It is also a reflection of the author's *voice* (personality). Although Ntozake Shange, "What Is It We Really Harvestin' Here? (240–49); Cynthia Ozick, "A Drugstore Eden" (316–30); Amy Jo Keifer, "The Death of a Farm" (636–39); and Matt Nocton, "Harvest of Gold, Harvest of Shame" (675–83) all describe farming, the writers' styles differ considerably.

subjective (*see* **objective**)

summary (*see* **paraphrase**)

symbol refers to a person, place, thing, idea, or action that represents something other than itself. In Maxine Hong Kingston's "On Discovery" (141–43), the man painfully transformed into a woman symbolizes the denigrated status of all Chinese women.

tone the author's attitude toward a subject being discussed can be serious (Coontz's "A Nation of Welfare Families" [294–301]), critical (Guinier's "The Tyranny of the Majority" [616–24]), or loving (Mary Ruffin's "Mama's Smoke" [148–58]) among many possibilities. Tone lets readers know how they are expected to react to what the writer is saying.

topic sentence (*see* **sentence**)

transition is the writer's ability to move the reader smoothly along the course of ideas. Abrupt changes in topics confuse the reader, but transitional words and phrases help tie ideas together. Stylistically, transition serves another purpose by adding fullness and body to otherwise short, choppy sentences and paragraphs. Writers use transition to show how ideas, things, and events are arranged chronologically (*first, next, after, finally*), spatially (*here, there, next to, behind*), comparatively (*like, just as, similar to*), causally (*thus, because, therefore*), and in opposition to each other (*unlike, but, contrary to*). Pronouns, connectives, repetition, and parallel sentence structure are other transitional vehicles that move the reader along.

understatement (*see* **figures of speech**)

voice refers to the extent to which the writer's personality is expressed in his or her work. In *personal voice,* the writer is on fairly intimate terms with the audience, referring to herself as "I" and the readers as "you." In *impersonal voice,* the writer may refer to himself as "one" or "we," or try to eliminate personal pronouns when possible. Formal writings, such as speeches, research papers, and sermons, are more likely to use an impersonal voice than are more informal writings, such as personal essays. In grammar, *voice* refers to the form of a verb: *active* ("I *mastered* the word processor") or *passive* ("The word processor *was mastered* by me").

Text Credits

NATALIE ANGIER Copyright © 1999 the New York Times Co. Reprinted by permission.

ISAAC ASIMOV "Those Crazy Ideas," copyright © 1959 by Mercury Press, from *Fact and Fancy* by Isaac Asimov. Used by permission of Doubleday, a division of Random House, Inc.

BROOKS ATKINSON Copyright © 1949 The New York Times Co. Reprinted by permission.

LYNDA BARRY "The Sanctuary of School," by Lynda Barry from the *New York Times*, January 5, 1992. Copyright © 1992 by Lynda Barry. Reprinted by permission of the author.

JUDY BRADY "I Want a Wife," by Judy Brady. Copyright © 1972 by Judy Brady. Reprinted by permission of the author.

STEWART BRAND "Written on the Wind," by Stewart Brand from *Civilization*, October/November 1998, pp. 70–72. Reprinted by permission of Civilization.

BILL BRANTLEY Copyright © 1999 The New York Times Co. Reprinted by permission.

JUDITH ORTIZ COFER Reprinted from *Prairie Schooner* by permission of the University of Nebraska Press. Copyright © 1989 by the University of Nebraska Press.

STEPHANIE COONTZ "A Nation of Welfare Families," excerpted from *The Way We Never Were* by Stephanie Coontz. Copyright © 1992 by Basic Books, a division of HarperCollins Publishers, Inc. Reprinted by permission of Basic Books, a member of Perseus Books, L.L.C.

CATHY N. DAVIDSON "From the Best Families,"excerpted from *36 Views of Mount Fuji* by Cathy N. Davidson. Copyright © 1993 by Cathy N. Davidson. Used by permission of Dutton Signet, a division of Penguin Putnam, Inc.

JOAN DIDION "Marrying Absurd" from *Slouching Toward Bethlehem* by Joan Didion. Copyright © 1968 and copyright renewed © 1996 by Joan Didion. Reprinted by permission of Farrar, Straus & Giroux, Inc.

Index of Authors

❋ *Student writings.*